1. *The A to Z of Buddhism*
2. *The A to Z of Catholicism* by William J. Collinge, 2001.
3. *The A to Z of Hinduism* by Bruce M. Sullivan, 2001.
4. *The A to Z of Islam* by Ludwig W. Adamec, 2002. *Out of Print. See No. 123.*
5. *The A to Z of Slavery and Abolition* by Martin A. Klein, 2002.
6. *Terrorism: Assassins to Zealots* by Sean Kendall Anderson and Stephen Sloan, 2003.
7. *The A to Z of the Korean War* by Paul M. Edwards, 2005.
8. *The A to Z of the Cold War* by Joseph Smith and Simon Davis, 2005.
9. *The A to Z of the Vietnam War* by Edwin E. Moise, 2005.
10. *The A to Z of Science Fiction Literature* by Brian Stableford, 2005.
11. *The A to Z of the Holocaust* by Jack R. Fischel, 2005.
12. *The A to Z of Washington, D.C.* by Robert Benedetto, Jane Donovan, and Kathleen DuVall, 2005.
13. *The A to Z of Taoism* by Julian F. Pas, 2006.
14. *The A to Z of the Renaissance* by Charles G. Nauert, 2006.
15. *The A to Z of Shinto* by Stuart D. B. Picken, 2006.
16. *The A to Z of Byzantium* by John H. Rosser, 2006.
17. *The A to Z of the Civil War* by Terry L. Jones, 2006.
18. *The A to Z of the Friends (Quakers)* by Margery Post Abbott, Mary Ellen Chijioke, Pink Dandelion, and John William Oliver Jr., 2006.
19. *The A to Z of Feminism* by Janet K. Boles and Diane Long Hoeveler, 2006.
20. *The A to Z of New Religious Movements* by George D. Chryssides, 2006.
21. *The A to Z of Multinational Peacekeeping* by Terry M. Mays, 2006.
22. *The A to Z of Lutheranism* by Günther Gassmann with Duane H. Larson and Mark W. Oldenburg, 2007.
23. *The A to Z of the French Revolution* by Paul R. Hanson, 2007.
24. *The A to Z of the Persian Gulf War 1990–1991* by Clayton R. Newell, 2007.
25. *The A to Z of Revolutionary America* by Terry M. Mays, 2007.
26. *The A to Z of the Olympic Movement* by Bill Mallon with Ian Buchanan, 2007.
27. *The A to Z of the Discovery and Exploration of Australia* by Alan Day, 2009.
28. *The A to Z of the United Nations* by Jacques Fomerand, 2009.
29. *The A to Z of the "Dirty Wars"* by David Kohut, Olga Vilella, and Beatrice Julian, 2009.
30. *The A to Z of the Vikings* by Katherine Holman, 2009.
31. *The A to Z from the Great War to the Great Depression* by Neil A. Wynn, 2009.
32. *The A to Z of the Crusades* by Corliss K. Slack, 2009.
33. *The A to Z of New Age Movements* by Michael York, 2009.
34. *The A to Z of Unitarian Universalism* by Mark W. Harris, 2009.
35. *The A to Z of the Kurds* by Michael M. Gunter, 2009.
36. *The A to Z of Utopianism* by James M. Morris and Andrea L. Kross, 2009.
37. *The A to Z of the Civil War and Reconstruction* by William L. Richter, 2009.
38. *The A to Z of Jainism* by Kristi L. Wiley, 2009.
39. *The A to Z of the Inuit* by Pamela K. Stern, 2009.
40. *The A to Z of Early North America* by Cameron B. Wesson, 2009.

41. *The A to Z of the Enlightenment* by Harvey Chisick, 2009.
42. *The A to Z Methodism* by Charles Yrigoyen Jr. and Susan E. Warrick, 2009.
43. *The A to Z of the Seventh-day Adventists* by Gary Land, 2009.
44. *The A to Z of Sufism* by John Renard, 2009.
45. *The A to Z of Sikhism* by William Hewat McLeod, 2009.
46. *The A to Z Fantasy Literature* by Brian Stableford, 2009.
47. *The A to Z of the Discovery and Exploration of the Pacific Islands* by Max Quanchi and John Robson, 2009.
48. *The A to Z of Australian and New Zealand Cinema* by Albert Moran and Errol Vieth, 2009.
49. *The A to Z of African-American Television* by Kathleen Fearn-Banks, 2009.
50. *The A to Z of American Radio Soap Operas* by Jim Cox, 2009.
51. *The A to Z of the Old South* by William L. Richter, 2009.
52. *The A to Z of the Discovery and Exploration of the Northwest Passage* by Alan Day, 2009.
53. *The A to Z of the Druzes* by Samy S. Swayd, 2009.
54. *The A to Z of the Welfare State* by Bent Greve, 2009.
55. *The A to Z of the War of 1812* by Robert Malcomson, 2009.
56. *The A to Z of Feminist Philosophy* by Catherine Villanueva Gardner, 2009.
57. *The A to Z of the Early American Republic* by Richard Buel Jr., 2009.
58. *The A to Z of the Russo-Japanese War* by Rotem Kowner, 2009.
59. *The A to Z of Anglicanism* by Colin Buchanan, 2009.
60. *The A to Z of Scandinavian Literature and Theater* by Jan Sjåvik, 2009.
61. *The A to Z of the Peoples of the Southeast Asian Massif* by Jean Michaud, 2009.
62. *The A to Z of Judaism* by Norman Solomon, 2009.
63. *The A to Z of the Berbers (Imazighen)* by Hsain Ilahiane, 2009.
64. *The A to Z of British Radio* by Seán Street, 2009.
65. *The A to Z of The Salvation Army* by Major John G. Merritt, 2009.
66. *The A to Z of the Arab-Israeli Conflict* by P. R. Kumaraswamy, 2009.
67. *The A to Z of the Jacksonian Era and Manifest Destiny* by Terry Corps, 2009.
68. *The A to Z of Socialism* by Peter Lamb and James C. Docherty, 2009.
69. *The A to Z of Marxism* by David Walker and Daniel Gray, 2009.
70. *The A to Z of the Bahá'í Faith* by Hugh C. Adamson, 2009.
71. *The A to Z of Postmodernist Literature and Theater* by Fran Mason, 2009.
72. *The A to Z of Australian Radio and Television* by Albert Moran and Chris Keating, 2009.
73. *The A to Z of the Lesbian Liberation Movement: Still the Rage* by JoAnne Myers, 2009.
74. *The A to Z of the United States–Mexican War* by Edward R. Moseley and Paul C. Clark, 2009.
75. *The A to Z of World War I* by Ian V. Hogg, 2009.
76. *The A to Z of World War II: The War Against Japan* by Ann Sharp Wells, 2009.
77. *The A to Z of Witchcraft* by Michael D. Bailey, 2009.
78. *The A to Z of British Intelligence* by Nigel West, 2009.
79. *The A to Z of United States Intelligence* by Michael A. Turner, 2009.
80. *The A to Z of the League of Nations* by Anique H. M. van Ginneken, 2009.
81. *The A to Z of Israeli Intelligence* by Ephraim Kahana, 2009.
82. *The A to Z of the European Union* by Joaquín Roy and Aimee Kanner, 2009.

83. *The A to Z of the Chinese Cultural Revolution* by Guo Jian, Yongyi Song, and Yuan Zhou, 2009.
84. *The A to Z of African American Cinema* by S. Torriano Berry and Venise T. Berry, 2009.
85. *The A to Z of Japanese Business* by Stuart D. B. Picken, 2009.
86. *The A to Z of the Reagan–Bush Era* by Richard S. Conley, 2009.
87. *The A to Z of Human Rights and Humanitarian Organizations* by Robert F. Gorman and Edward S. Mihalkanin, 2009.
88. *The A to Z of French Cinema* by Dayna Oscherwitz and MaryEllen Higgins, 2009.
89. *The A to Z of the Puritans* by Charles Pastoor and Galen K. Johnson, 2009.
90. *The A to Z of Nuclear, Biological and Chemical Warfare* by Benjamin C. Garrett and John Hart, 2009.
91. *The A to Z of the Green Movement* by Miranda Schreurs and Elim Papadakis, 2009.
92. *The A to Z of the Kennedy–Johnson Era* by Richard Dean Burns and Joseph M. Siracusa, 2009.
93. *The A to Z of Renaissance Art* by Lilian H. Zirpolo, 2009.
94. *The A to Z of the Broadway Musical* by William A. Everett and Paul R. Laird, 2009.
95. *The A to Z of the Northern Ireland Conflict* by Gordon Gillespie, 2009.
96. *The A to Z of the Fashion Industry* by Francesca Sterlacci and Joanne Arbuckle, 2009.
97. *The A to Z of American Theater: Modernism* by James Fisher and Felicia Hardison Londré, 2009.
98. *The A to Z of Civil Wars in Africa* by Guy Arnold, 2009.
99. *The A to Z of the Nixon–Ford Era* by Mitchell K. Hall, 2009.
100. *The A to Z of Horror Cinema* by Peter Hutchings, 2009.
101. *The A to Z of Westerns in Cinema* by Paul Varner, 2009.
102. *The A to Z of Zionism* by Rafael Medoff and Chaim I. Waxman, 2009.
103. *The A to Z of the Roosevelt–Truman Era* by Neil A. Wynn, 2009.
104. *The A to Z of Jehovah's Witnesses* by George D. Chryssides, 2009.
105. *The A to Z of Native American Movements* by Todd Leahy and Raymond Wilson, 2009.
106. *The A to Z of the Shakers* by Stephen J. Paterwic, 2009.
107. *The A to Z of the Coptic Church* by Gawdat Gabra, 2009.
108. *The A to Z of Architecture* by Allison Lee Palmer, 2009.
109. *The A to Z of Italian Cinema* by Gino Moliterno, 2009.
110. *The A to Z of Mormonism* by Davis Bitton and Thomas G. Alexander, 2009.
111. *The A to Z of African American Theater* by Anthony D. Hill with Douglas Q. Barnett, 2009.
112. *The A to Z of NATO and Other International Security Organizations* by Marco Rimanelli, 2009.
113. *The A to Z of the Eisenhower Era* by Burton I. Kaufman and Diane Kaufman, 2009.
114. *The A to Z of Sexspionage* by Nigel West, 2009.
115. *The A to Z of Environmentalism* by Peter Dauvergne, 2009.
116. *The A to Z of the Petroleum Industry* by M. S. Vassiliou, 2009.
117. *The A to Z of Journalism* by Ross Eaman, 2009.
118. *The A to Z of the Gilded Age* by T. Adams Upchurch, 2009.
119. *The A to Z of the Progressive Era* by Catherine Cocks, Peter C. Holloran, and Alan Lessoff, 2009.

120. *The A to Z of Middle Eastern Intelligence* by Ephraim Kahana and Muhammad Suwaed, 2009.
121. *The A to Z of the Baptists* William H. Brackney, 2009.
122. *The A to Z of Homosexuality* by Brent L. Pickett, 2009.
123. *The A to Z of Islam, Second Edition* by Ludwig W. Adamec, 2009.
124. *The A to Z of Buddhism* by Carl Olson, 2009.
125. *The A to Z of United States–Russian/Soviet Relations* by Norman E. Saul, 2010.
126. *The A to Z of United States–Africa Relations* by Robert Anthony Waters Jr., 2010.
127. *The A to Z of United States–China Relations* by Robert Sutter, 2010.
128. *The A to Z of U.S. Diplomacy since the Cold War* by Tom Lansford, 2010.
129. *The A to Z of United States–Japan Relations* by John Van Sant, Peter Mauch, and Yoneyuki Sugita, 2010.
130. *The A to Z of United States–Latin American Relations* by Joseph Smith, 2010.
131. *The A to Z of United States–Middle East Relations* by Peter L. Hahn, 2010.
132. *The A to Z of United States–Southeast Asia Relations* by Donald E. Weatherbee, 2010.
133. *The A to Z of U.S. Diplomacy from the Civil War to World War I* by Kenneth J. Blume, 2010.
134. *The A to Z of International Law* by Boleslaw A. Boczek, 2010.
135. *The A to Z of the Gypsies (Romanies)* by Donald Kenrick, 2010.
136. *The A to Z of the Tamils* by Vijaya Ramaswamy, 2010.
137. *The A to Z of Women in Sub-Saharan Africa* by Kathleen Sheldon, 2010.
138. *The A to Z of Ancient and Medieval Nubia* by Richard A. Lobban Jr., 2010.
139. *The A to Z of Ancient Israel* by Niels Peter Lemche, 2010.
140. *The A to Z of Ancient Mesoamerica* by Joel W. Palka, 2010.
141. *The A to Z of Ancient Southeast Asia* by John N. Miksic, 2010.
142. *The A to Z of the Hittites* by Charles Burney, 2010.
143. *The A to Z of Medieval Russia* by Lawrence N. Langer, 2010.
144. *The A to Z of the Napoleonic Era* by George F. Nafziger, 2010.
145. *The A to Z of Ancient Egypt* by Morris L. Bierbrier, 2010.
146. *The A to Z of Ancient India* by Kumkum Roy, 2010.
147. *The A to Z of Ancient South America* by Martin Giesso, 2010.
148. *The A to Z of Medieval China* by Victor Cunrui Xiong, 2010.
149. *The A to Z of Medieval India* by Iqtidar Alam Khan, 2010.
150. *The A to Z of Mesopotamia* by Gwendolyn Leick, 2010.
151. *The A to Z of the Mongol World Empire* by Paul D. Buell, 2010.
152. *The A to Z of the Ottoman Empire* by Selcuk Aksin Somel, 2010.
153. *The A to Z of Pre-Colonial Africa* by Robert O. Collins, 2010.
154. *The A to Z of Aesthetics* by Dabney Townsend, 2010.
155. *The A to Z of Descartes and Cartesian Philosophy* by Roger Ariew, Dennis Des Chene, Douglas M. Jesseph, Tad M. Schmaltz, and Theo Verbeek, 2010.
156. *The A to Z of Heidegger's Philosophy* by Alfred Denker, 2010.
157. *The A to Z of Kierkegaard's Philosophy* by Julia Watkin, 2010.
158. *The A to Z of Ancient Greek Philosophy* by Anthony Preus, 2010.
159. *The A to Z of Bertrand Russell's Philosophy* by Rosalind Carey and John Ongley, 2010.
160. *The A to Z of Epistemology* by Ralph Baergen, 2010.
161. *The A to Z of Ethics* by Harry J. Gensler and Earl W. Spurgin, 2010.

162. *The A to Z of Existentialism* by Stephen Michelman, 2010.
163. *The A to Z of Hegelian Philosophy* by John W. Burbidge, 2010.
164. *The A to Z of the Holiness Movement* by William Kostlevy, 2010.
165. *The A to Z of Hume's Philosophy* by Kenneth R. Merrill, 2010.
166. *The A to Z of Husserl's Philosophy* by John J. Drummond, 2010.
167. *The A to Z of Kant and Kantianism* by Helmut Holzhey and Vilem Mudroch, 2010.
168. *The A to Z of Leibniz's Philosophy* by Stuart Brown and N. J. Fox, 2010.
169. *The A to Z of Logic* by Harry J. Gensler, 2010.
170. *The A to Z of Medieval Philosophy and Theology* by Stephen F. Brown and Juan Carlos Flores, 2010.
171. *The A to Z of Nietzscheanism* by Carol Diethe, 2010.
172. *The A to Z of the Non-Aligned Movement and Third World* by Guy Arnold, 2010.
173. *The A to Z of Shamanism* by Graham Harvey and Robert J. Wallis, 2010.
174. *The A to Z of Organized Labor* by James C. Docherty, 2010.
175. *The A to Z of the Orthodox Church* by Michael Prokurat, Michael D. Peterson, and Alexander Golitzin, 2010.
176. *The A to Z of Prophets in Islam and Judaism* by Scott B. Noegel and Brannon M. Wheeler, 2010.
177. *The A to Z of Schopenhauer's Philosophy* by David E. Cartwright, 2010.
178. *The A to Z of Wittgenstein's Philosophy* by Duncan Richter, 2010.
179. *The A to Z of Hong Kong Cinema* by Lisa Odham Stokes, 2010.
180. *The A to Z of Japanese Traditional Theatre* by Samuel L. Leiter, 2010.
181. *The A to Z of Lesbian Literature* by Meredith Miller, 2010.
182. *The A to Z of Chinese Theater* by Tan Ye, 2010.
183. *The A to Z of German Cinema* by Robert C. Reimer and Carol J. Reimer, 2010.
184. *The A to Z of German Theater* by William Grange, 2010.
185. *The A to Z of Irish Cinema* by Roderick Flynn and Patrick Brereton, 2010.
186. *The A to Z of Modern Chinese Literature* by Li-hua Ying, 2010.
187. *The A to Z of Modern Japanese Literature and Theater* by J. Scott Miller, 2010.
188. *The A to Z of Old-Time Radio* by Robert C. Reinehr and Jon D. Swartz, 2010.
189. *The A to Z of Polish Cinema* by Marek Haltof, 2010.
190. *The A to Z of Postwar German Literature* by William Grange, 2010.
191. *The A to Z of Russian and Soviet Cinema* by Peter Rollberg, 2010.
192. *The A to Z of Russian Theater* by Laurence Senelick, 2010.
193. *The A to Z of Sacred Music* by Joseph P. Swain, 2010.
194. *The A to Z of Animation and Cartoons* by Nichola Dobson, 2010.
195. *The A to Z of Afghan Wars, Revolutions, and Insurgencies* by Ludwig W. Adamec, 2010.
196. *The A to Z of Ancient Egyptian Warfare* by Robert G. Morkot, 2010.
197. *The A to Z of the British and Irish Civil Wars 1637–1660* by Martyn Bennett, 2010.
198. *The A to Z of the Chinese Civil War* by Edwin Pak-wah Leung, 2010.
199. *The A to Z of Ancient Greek Warfare* by Iain Spence, 2010.
200. *The A to Z of the Anglo–Boer War* by Fransjohan Pretorius, 2010.
201. *The A to Z of the Crimean War* by Guy Arnold, 2010.
202. *The A to Z of the Zulu Wars* by John Laband, 2010.
203. *The A to Z of the Wars of the French Revolution* by Steven T. Ross, 2010.
204. *The A to Z of the Hong Kong SAR and the Macao SAR* by Ming K. Chan and Shiuhing Lo, 2010.

205. *The A to Z of Australia* by James C. Docherty, 2010.
206. *The A to Z of Burma (Myanmar)* by Donald M. Seekins, 2010.
207. *The A to Z of the Gulf Arab States* by Malcolm C. Peck, 2010.
208. *The A to Z of India* by Surjit Mansingh, 2010.
209. *The A to Z of Iran* by John H. Lorentz, 2010.
210. *The A to Z of Israel* by Bernard Reich and David H. Goldberg, 2010.
211. *The A to Z of Laos* by Martin Stuart-Fox, 2010.
212. *The A to Z of Malaysia* by Ooi Keat Gin, 2010.
213. *The A to Z of Modern China (1800–1949)* by James Z. Gao, 2010.
214. *The A to Z of the Philippines* by Artemio R. Guillermo and May Kyi Win, 2010.
215. *The A to Z of Taiwan (Republic of China)* by John F. Copper, 2010.
216. *The A to Z of the People's Republic of China* by Lawrence R. Sullivan, 2010.
217. *The A to Z of Vietnam* by Bruce M. Lockhart and William J. Duiker, 2010.
218. *The A to Z of Bosnia and Herzegovina* by Ante Cuvalo, 2010.
219. *The A to Z of Modern Greece* by Dimitris Keridis, 2010.
220. *The A to Z of Austria* by Paula Sutter Fichtner, 2010.
221. *The A to Z of Belarus* by Vitali Silitski and Jan Zaprudnik, 2010.
222. *The A to Z of Belgium* by Robert Stallaerts, 2010.
223. *The A to Z of Bulgaria* by Raymond Detrez, 2010.
224. *The A to Z of Contemporary Germany* by Derek Lewis with Ulrike Zitzlsperger, 2010.
225. *The A to Z of the Contemporary United Kingdom* by Kenneth J. Panton and Keith A. Cowlard, 2010.
226. *The A to Z of Denmark* by Alastair H. Thomas, 2010.
227. *The A to Z of France* by Gino Raymond, 2010.
228. *The A to Z of Georgia* by Alexander Mikaberidze, 2010.
229. *The A to Z of Iceland* by Gudmundur Halfdanarson, 2010.
230. *The A to Z of Latvia* by Andrejs Plakans, 2010.
231. *The A to Z of Modern Italy* by Mark F. Gilbert and K. Robert Nilsson, 2010.
232. *The A to Z of Moldova* by Andrei Brezianu and Vlad Spânu, 2010.
233. *The A to Z of the Netherlands* by Joop W. Koopmans and Arend H. Huussen Jr., 2010.
234. *The A to Z of Norway* by Jan Sjåvik, 2010.
235. *The A to Z of the Republic of Macedonia* by Dimitar Bechev, 2010.
236. *The A to Z of Slovakia* by Stanislav J. Kirschbaum, 2010.
237. *The A to Z of Slovenia* by Leopoldina Plut-Pregelj and Carole Rogel, 2010.
238. *The A to Z of Spain* by Angel Smith, 2010.
239. *The A to Z of Sweden* by Irene Scobbie, 2010.
240. *The A to Z of Turkey* by Metin Heper and Nur Bilge Criss, 2010.
241. *The A to Z of Ukraine* by Zenon E. Kohut, Bohdan Y. Nebesio, and Myroslav Yurkevich, 2010.
242. *The A to Z of Mexico* by Marvin Alisky, 2010.
243. *The A to Z of U.S. Diplomacy from World War I through World War II* by Martin Folly and Niall Palmer, 2010.
244. *The A to Z of Spanish Cinema* by Alberto Mira, 2010.
245. *The A to Z of the Reformation and Counter-Reformation* by Michael Mullett, 2010.

The A to Z of Afghan Wars, Revolutions, and Insurgencies

Ludwig W. Adamec

The A to Z Guide Series, No. 195

THE SCARECROW PRESS, INC.
Lanham • Toronto • Plymouth, UK
2010

Published by Scarecrow Press, Inc.
A wholly owned subsidiary of
The Rowman & Littlefield Publishing Group, Inc.
4501 Forbes Boulevard, Suite 200, Lanham, Maryland 20706
http://www.scarecrowpress.com

Estover Road, Plymouth PL6 7PY, United Kingdom

Copyright © 2005 by Ludwig W. Adamec

Quotations from Crown Copyright documents in Oriental and India Office Collections of the British Library appear by permission of the Controller of Her Majesty's Stationary Office.

This book is a paperback version of the *Historical Dictionary of Afghan Wars, Revolutions, and Insurgencies: Second Edition.*

All rights reserved. No part of this book may be reproduced in any form or by any electronic or mechanical means, including information storage and retrieval systems, without written permission from the publisher, except by a reviewer who may quote passages in a review.

British Library Cataloguing in Publication Information Available

Library of Congress Cataloging-in-Publication Data

The hardback version of this book was cataloged by the Library of Congress as follows:
Adamec, Ludwig W.
  Historical dictionary of Afghan wars, revolutions, and insurgencies / Ludwig W. Adamec.—2nd ed.
    p. cm. — (Historical dictionaries of war, revolution, and civil unrest ; no. 30)
  Rev. ed. of: Dictionary of Afghan wars, revolutions, and insurgencies. 1996.
  Includes bibliographical references.
  1. Afghanistan—History—Dictionaries. 2. Afghanistan—History, Military—Dictionaries. I. Adamec, Ludwig W. Dictionary of Afghan wars, revolutions, and insurgencies. II. Title. III. Series.
  DS356.A26 2005
  958.1'003—dc22   2005014338

ISBN 978-0-8108-7624-8 (pbk. : alk. paper)

⊖™ The paper used in this publication meets the minimum requirements of American National Standard for Information Sciences—Permanence of Paper for Printed Library Materials, ANSI/NISO Z39.48-1992.
Printed in the United States of America

To Rahella

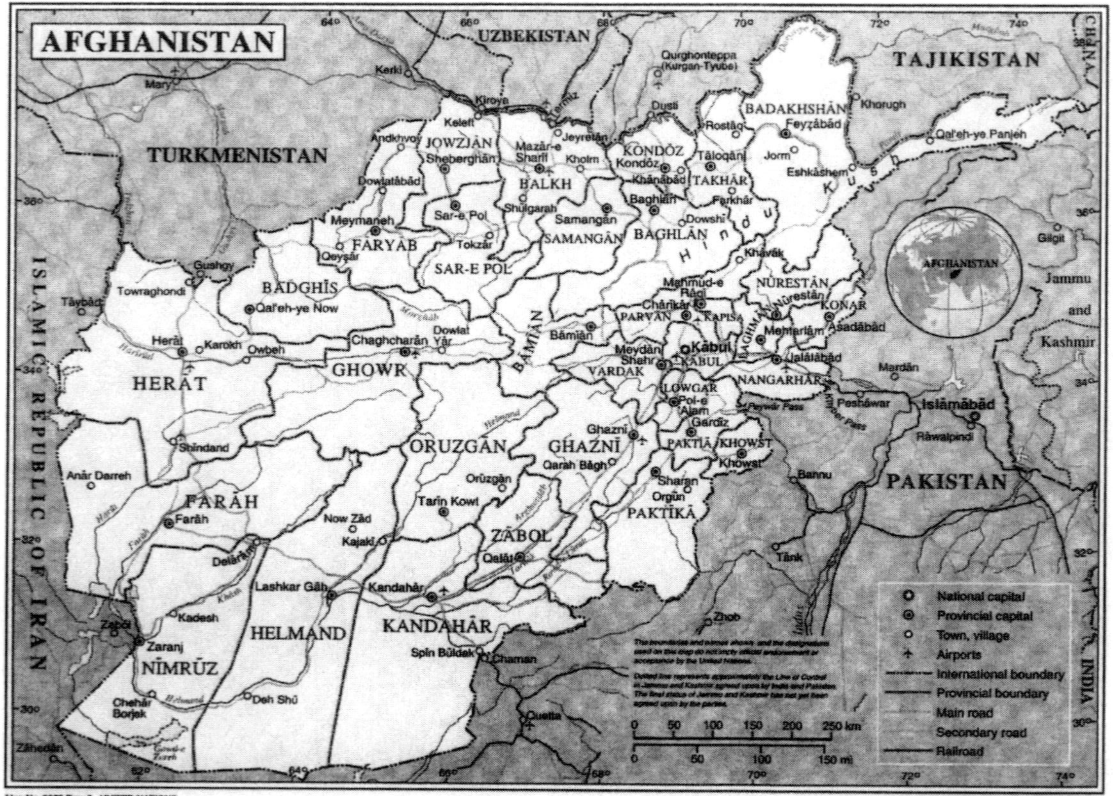

Map No. 3958 Rev. 3 UNITED NATIONS
January 2004

Department of Peacekeeping Operations
Cartographic Section

CONTENTS

List of Illustrations	ix
Editor's Foreword *Jon Woronoff*	xi
Acknowledgments	xiii
Reader's Note	xv
Acronyms and Abbreviations	xvii
Chronology	xxi
Introduction	1
THE DICTIONARY	31
Appendixes	343
Appendix 1: Soviet Report on Intervention, 1979	343
Appendix 2: Soviet–Afghan Treaty of Friendship	345
Appendix 3: Status of Soviet Forces Protocol	349
Appendix 4: Cease-Fire Protocol	352
Appendix 5: American Declaration of War	354
Appendix 6: Military Technical Agreement	357
Appendix 7: English–Afghan Military Terms	362
Bibliography	365
About the Author	403

ILLUSTRATIONS

Maps

1	Afghanistan Topography	30
2	Afghanistan Administrative Divisions	40
3	Kabul	184
4	Routes of Soviet Invasion	296

Plans

1	Action of Ahmad Khel		47
2	Action at Chaharasia		88
3	Plan of the Cantonment		121
4	First Afghan War		123
5	Fortress of Ghazni		146
6	Sketch of Herat City		165
7	General Sale Defeats Akbar Khan		179
8	Kandahar		190
9	Sketch Plan of Helmand	*facing*	210
10	Paiwar Kotal		242
11	Sherpur Cantonment		289

Plates

1	Amir Yaqub Signs Treaty of Gandomak		136
2	British Defeat at Maiwand	*facing*	211
3	Execution of the Kotwal	*facing*	268
4	Execution of a Ghazi	*facing*	269
5	Bala Hisar	*facing*	278
6	General Ross Crosses Loghur River	*following*	278
7	Evacuation of Wounded	*following*	278

List of Illustrations

8	Fort of Mullah Abdul Guffoor	*following*	278
9	Guns over the Khojak Pass	*following*	278
10	Ghazis Fire from Sangar	*facing*	279
11	Soviet "Stalin Organ"	*facing*	296
12	Burning Soviet Helicopter	*following*	296
13	Mujahed Aiming a Stinger Missile	*following*	296
14	Kabul Tank Force	*following*	296
15	Mujahedin Anti-Aircraft Unit	*following*	296
16	Mujahedin on a Mission	*following*	296
17	Destroyed Soviet Tank	*following*	296
18	Parade of Kabul Forces	*facing*	297
19	British Air Raid, 1919		310
20	Chinook Helicopter Lifts Humvee	*facing*	328
21	Marine Fast Ropes from Helicopter	*following*	328
22	U.S. Army Soldier in Defensive Position	*following*	328
23	Marines on Patrol in Khost Province	*following*	328
24	Marines on Patrol in Sarobi	*following*	328
25	Member of Special Forces Mans Machine Gun	*following*	328
26	Afghan National Army Recruits Receive Equipment	*following*	328
27	Afghan Security Forces Training	*facing*	329

EDITOR'S FOREWORD

It seems that the Afghans have been at war for ever. There were countless raids and skirmishes, and sometimes far larger operations, among the various tribal and ethnic groups in what became modern Afghanistan. But this just honed their skills for full-scale warfare against some of the major powers of the day, including a long list of neighboring kingdoms, then three Anglo-Afghan wars against the British Empire, and unrelenting warfare against the then Soviet Union. Time and again, the Afghans won against the foreign foe, only to fall out among themselves as when the Taliban came to power. This latest intervention, which we are still witnessing, was directed by the world's superpower, the United States, but even it was not able to overthrow the Taliban alone. Admittedly, there is cautious reason to hope that this may be the last war, but it would be rash to bet on it already. It is this long experience of warfare which justified the first edition of the *Historical Dictionary of Afghan Wars, Revolutions, and Insurgencies*. And it is the American phase which explains the need for a second edition. But this latest phase is very hard to understand without the historical background, reaching back centuries, which shows the extraordinary martial characteristics of the Afghans, who have not hesitated to take on all comers and then one another. Their history is replete with wars (including civil wars), revolutions and insurgencies, and this can most clearly and easily be traced in the chronology. An overall view can be sought in the introduction. The dictionary fills in many of the details, with entries on the more important wars and battles, outstanding leaders (on all sides), and crucial aspects of weaponry, tactics, and logistics. The lay of the land, often decisive in determining who came out on top, is described in other entries, while yet others explain the society, culture, and religion. The bibliography lists numerous sources for further information, some of them absorbing reading in their own right.

This second edition, like the first, was written by Ludwig W.

Adamec, one of the leading authorities on the region and the country and its warfare, past and present. He knows Afghanistan from personal travel and experience as well as more scholarly study. After serving briefly as head of Afghanistan Services of the Voice of America, he has spent most of his career as a professor of Near and Middle Eastern studies. He presently teaches at the University of Arizona. Dr. Adamec has written extensively on the topics of concern here, including books and articles on martial and diplomatic history, foreign affairs, and a who's who. He is already familiar to many of our readers thanks to three editions of the *Historical Dictionary of Afghanistan* and a *Historical Dictionary of Islam* (also an *A to Z of Islam*). Given the difficulty of making sense of the latest Afghan war, there are many who will undoubtedly be pleased to learn about this sequel.

Jon Woronoff
Series Editor

ACKNOWLEDGMENTS

It is my pleasant duty to express my thanks to various institutions and individuals who have provided sources necessary for completion of this project. Much of the historical information about the three Anglo-Afghan wars was gleaned from the archives of the Oriental and India Office Collection of the British Library in London, England. Official accounts of Afghan wars, maps, and illustrations from Crown copyright documents appear with permission of the Controller of Her Majesty's Stationery Office. Illustrations from the *Illustrated London News*, the *Penny Illustrated Newspaper*, the *Penny Pictorial News*, and the *Graphic* were acquired from the Newspaper Library of the British Library.

My thanks also go to Alain Marigo, a noted French cartographer, who provided maps of Kabul and Afghanistan. Mr. Marigo and the Centre de Recherches et d'Etudes Documentaires sur l'Afghanistan (CEREDAF) in Paris, France, provided a number of photos of the mujahedin war against the Soviet/Kabul forces. Several of the photo journalists whose works are presented in this publication died during the last years of the war or are still missing. Plate 11 is by Shah Bazgar (d. 1989); Plate 13 by S. Thiollier (d. 1990); Plate 15 by Edouard De Pazzi; Plate 16 by Thierry Niquet. One photo was provided by MAHAZ (Plate 12); others are from *Afghanistan Today*, Plate 14 and 18; and one is from Jam'iat, Plate 17. Plate 5 is by John Burke (1839) from the India Office Records. I also want to thank Etienne Gille, Vera Marigo, and all their colleagues of CEREDAF, whose *Les Nouvelles d'Afghanistan* has been an important source for my research. Illustrations depicting American combat activities were taken from Department of Defense files on the Internet.

This volume was produced as a camera-ready copy. To the extent that it conforms to a professional typesetting job, I am indebted to suggestions of the editorial staff of Scarecrow Press.

READER'S NOTE

Alphabetization and Spelling. Names beginning with "Abdul" (A. *'abd-al*, meaning servant or slave), followed by one of the names of Allah (God), as, for example, Abdul Rahman (Servant of the Merciful) or Abdul Karim (Servant of the Bountiful), form a unit and should not be taken as first and last names. Abdul Rahman (pronounced and often written Abdul Rahman) will therefore be found under "A" not "R." Compounds with Allah, such as Habibullah (Habib Allah) or Amanullah (Aman Allah), will be found in alphabetical order under its compound version. If the name Muhammad is followed only by one other name, like Muhammad Isma'il or Muhammad Nadir, the name will be found under "M." Titles, like general, shah (king), or khan (chief) are not counted in the alphabetization.

This volume describes major wars as well as revolts, skirmishes, and smaller armed actions. To maintain the narration in dictionary format, a major war was described in several entries and under subheadings discussing the objectives, causes, costs, lessons, and various aspects of a particular war. Cross-references in bold type refer the reader to related topics.

Statistics. Population statistics are estimates for the prewar (1979) period, unless otherwise indicated. No complete census has been taken in Afghanistan, and estimates of the Afghan population may serve only for comparison. The numbers of casualties, body counts, and so forth in armed conflicts are only approximations and often exaggerated according to the bias of the source. British official accounts often did not list casualties from causes other than enemy fire. Most of our sources on the Anglo-Afghan wars are British, and even official accounts vary as to the number of casualties.

Illustrations. A number of photographs are included in this work, but the greater part of illustrations consists of drawings from British illustrated newspapers. They are the artist's conception of events and individuals and therefore are not exact reproductions. Some stereotyping can be discerned in depicting the Afghans, Indian soldiers, and European officers. Photos depicting American military action are taken from Department of Defense files on the Internet. It has been necessary to reduce and adapt the maps, plans, and plates to fit the format of this publication. This was often accomplished at a loss in quality and legibility, but it was felt that the illustrations would enhance the usefulness of this book and the author hopes that his readers will agree.

ACRONYMS AND ABBREVIATIONS

A.	Arabic
ADA	Air Defense Artillery
A.D.C.	Aide-de-Camp
AGSA	Afghan Security Service
A.I.G.	Afghan Interim Government
AN	Antonov Soviet Aircraft
ANA	Afghan National Army
APC	Armored Personnel Carrier
AR	*The Life of Abdur Rahman*
Bde.	Brigade
BM	Ballistic Missile
Bn(s).	Battalion(s)
Brig.	Brigade
CENTCOM	United States Central Command
CENTO	Central Treaty Organization
CEREDAF	Centre de Recherches et d'Etudes Documentaires sur l'Afghanistan
Coy.	Company
DACOM	Deutsch-Afghanische Company
D.	Dari, the Farsi of Afghanistan
Div.	Division
DRA	Democratic Republic of Afghanistan
Fd. Coy.	Field Company
GAZ	*Historical and Political Gazetteer of Afghanistan*, by Adamec, vols. 1–6
GHQ	General Headquarters
G.S.O.	General Staff Organization
Harakat	Harakat-i Inqilab-i Islami of Muhammadi
HBAA	*Handbook of the Afghan Army*
Hizb (H)	Hizb-i Islami of Hekmatyar

Hizb (K)	Hizb-i Islami of Khales
HQ	Headquarters
IFV	Infantry Fighting Vehicle
IL	Ilyushin Soviet Aircraft
ILN	*Illustrated London News*
IOR	India Office Records
IRA	Islamic Republic of Afghanistan
ISAF	International Security Assistance Force
ISI	Inter-Services Intelligence
Ittihad	Ittihad-i Islami Barayi Azadi-yi Afghanistan of Sayyaf
Jabha	Jabha-yi Milli Najat-i Afghanistan of Mujaddidi
Jam'iat	Jam'iat-i Islami of Rabbani
KAM	Workers' Intelligence Service
KHAD	State Intelligence Service
LCSFA	Limited Contingent of Soviet Forces in Afghanistan
LWA	Ludwig W. Adamec
MI	Soviet Aircraft
MIG	Soviet Fighter Aircraft
MR	Military Report
MRD	Motorized Rifle Division
MRL	Multiple Rocket Launcher
NCO	Noncommissioned Officers
NGO	Non-Governmental Organization
NIFA	National Islamic Front of Afghanistan
NWFP	North-West Frontier Province of India, now Pakistan
OA (1,2,3)	Official Account (of First, Second, or Third Anglo-Afghan War)
Obs.	Obsolete
P.	Pashtu
PDPA	People's Democratic Party of Afghanistan
PFM	"Butterfly" Mine
PIN	*Penny Illustrated Newspaper*
PP Col.	Parliamentary Papers Collection
PRT	Provincial Reconstruction Team

P&S	Political and Secret
Regts.	Regiments
RFA	Artillery
RGA	Artillery
SAM	Surface-to-Air Missile
S&M	Sappers and Miners
Spetsnaz	Special Operations Forces
Sqn.	Squadron (Sqdn.)
SU	(Sukhoi) Fencer Bombers
TU	(Tupelov) Badger Bombers
WAD	State Intelligence Service

CHRONOLOGY

1747 Ahmad Shah crowned, begins 26-year rule during which he united Afghan tribes under the Sadozai dynasty.

1748 Durranis move against Lahore. In November Ahmad Shah begins third invasion of India.

1757 January: Khutba read in name of Ahmad Shah at Delhi, India, and coins are struck in his name, making him suzerain ruler of India.

1761 Afghans defeat Maratha confederacy at Battle of Panipat, marking greatest extent of Ahmad Shah's empire, which included Kashmir, the Panjab, and parts of Baluchistan.

1769-1770 Ahmad Shah moves into Khorasan.

1772 16-17 October: Ahmad Shah dies at Toba Maruf.

1773 Timur Shah begins 20-year rule. Moves capital from Kandahar to Kabul. Campaigns in Sind and Bukhara.

1793 Zaman Shah begins six-year rule.

1798 Britain, fearing Afghan invasions of India, initiates policy of containment, enlisting Persia to keep Afghanistan in check.

1800 Shah Mahmud deposes Shah Shuja, rules for three years.

1803 Shah Shuja deposes Shah Mahmud.

1805 Persian attempt to take Herat fails.

1807 At Tilsit, Alexander II and Napoleon plan joint Russian-French invasion of India through Persia.

1809 British envoy Mountstuart Elphinstone and Shah Shuja sign defensive alliance in first official contact between Afghanistan and a European power. Shah Mahmud defeats Shah Shuja at Gandomak and rules until blinding of Fateh Khan, his Barakzai wazir, causes Barakzai revolt and Shah Mahmud's downfall in 1817.

1816 Persian attempt to capture Herat fails.

1818 Civil war results in division of Afghanistan into virtually independent states until 1835. Ranjit Singh seizes Peshawar.

1819 Singh conquers Kashmir.

1826 Dost Muhammad, ruler of Ghazni, takes Kabul.

1833 Persians besiege Herat.

1834 Dost Muhammad defeats Shah Shuja and captures Kandahar.

1835 Dost Muhammad begins his first rule of Afghanistan.

1837 Lord Auckland appointed governor-general. Akbar Khan, son of Dost Muhammad, defeats Sikhs at Jamrud. **August:** Eldred Pottinger arrives at Herat. **20 September:** Alexander Burnes arrives in Kabul on a diplomatic mission for British. **23 November:** Commencement of second siege of Herat. **19 December:** Ivan Vitkewich (Vickovich), emissary from Russia, arrives in Kabul.

1838 26 April: Burnes leaves Kabul. **26 June:** Tripartite Treaty signed by Ranjit Singh, the British East India Company, and Shah Shuja to restore the latter to the Afghan throne. **9 September:** Siege of Herat raised. **1 October:** British break relations with Dost Muhammad and declare war.

1839 First Anglo-Afghan War: 14 January: "Army of the Indus" enters Sind. **21 January:** Shah Shuja's contingent at Shikapur. **20**

February: Cotton reaches Shikapur. **26 March:** Cotton reaches Quetta. **6 April:** John Keane assumes command. **25 April:** Sir John Keane's force arrives at Kandahar. **22 July:** Afghan Ghazis attack. **23 July:** British capture Ghazni. **2 August:** Amir Dost Muhammad flees. **7 August:** Kabul occupied by the Army of the Indus. **3 September:** Prince Timur arrives at Kabul. **18 September:** Part of British-Indian army leaves Kabul. **15 October:** Bengal troops begin return march to India. **18 October:** Bombay troops begin return march to India.

1840 August: Dost Muhammad escapes from Bukhara. **7-17 May:** Anderson moves against Ghilzais. **June:** British disaster at Bajgah. **August:** Dost Muhammad escapes from Bukhara. **30 August:** Attack on Bajgah. **September:** Rising in Afghan Turkestan. **14 September:** Dennis reinforces Bamian. **18 September:** Defeat of Uzbeks near Bamian. **3 October:** Sale attacks Julga. **11 October:** Dost Muhammad reaches Ghorband. Withdrawal of Bamian detachment. **2 November:** Action at Parwan Darra. Surrender of Amir Dost Muhammad. **12 November:** Dost Muhammad leaves for India.

1841 3 January: Farrington's action near Kandahar. Todd's mission leaves Herat. **7 April:** Action near Qalat-i Ghilzai. **May:** Wymer's action at Asiya-i Ilmi. **3 July:** Action at the Helmand. **5 August:** Chamber's expedition against the Ghilzai. **17 August:** Action at Girishk. **September:** Expedition to Tarin and Derawat. Capture of Akram Khan. **October:** Nott returns to Kandahar. **9 October:** Attack on Monteith's camp at Butkhak. **12 October:** Affair at Khurd-Kabul. March to Gandomak. **2 November:** Assassination of Burnes. Shelton arrives at the Bala Hisar. **3 November:** Arrival of the 37th Native Infantry at Kabul. Macnaghten writes to recall Sale's force and the troops returning to India. Abandonment of Mackenzie's post. **4 November:** Fort containing Commissariat stores abandoned. **6 November:** Capture of Muhammad Sharif's fort. Action by Anderson's Horse. **7 November:** Return of Akbar Khan to Bamian. **9 November:** Shelton returns to cantonments. **10 November:** Affair of Rikab Bashi's fort. News of Kabul outbreak reaches Sale. **11 November:** March to Jalalabad commenced. **12 November:** Rearguard action. Arrival at Jalalabad. **13 November:** Fighting begins at Bimaru Hills. **15 November:** Arrival of Pottinger after Charikar defeat. **16 November:** First action at Jalalabad. **18 November:** Macnaghten recommends holding out. **23 November:** Second fight on the Bemaru Hills. **25 November:** Macnaghten interviews the chiefs. **November:** Massacre at Ghazni and capitulation. **6 December:** Abandonment of Muhammad Sharif's fort. **8 December:** Macnaghten consults Elphinstone on question of retreat. Discussion of treaty. Return to Kandahar of Maclaren's brigade. **13 December:** Evacuation of Bala Hisar. **22 December:** Orders issued for the evacuation of Ghazni, Kandahar, and Jalalabad. **23 December:** Assassination of Macnaghten. **December:** Mutiny of Janbaz at Kandahar.

1842 Treaty of Capitulation ratified. **4 January:** First brigade of the Relief Force crosses the Sutlej. **6 January:** Retreat from Kabul commences. **7 January:** Skinner proceed to Akbar with truce flag. **8 January:** Sale receives letter from Pottinger. Kabul force marches to Tezin. **9 January:** Orders received at Jalalabad for evacuation. **12 January:** Action at Argandab. The end of Kabul force. **13 January:** British last stand at Jagdalak. Arrival of Brydon at Jalalabad. **26 January:** Sale convenes council of war. **10 February:** Governor general issues order to relief force. **13 February:** Earthquake at Jalalabad. **19 February:** British disaster at Ali Masjid. **21 February:** Order for evacuation reaches Kabul. **23 February:** Evacuation of Ali Masjid. **7 March:** Action near Kandahar. **10 March:** Attack on Kandahar. **25 March:** Wymer's action near Kandahar. **28 March:** England defeated at Haikalzai. **31 March:** Pollock reaches Jamrud. **7 April:** Battle at Jalalabad. General Pollock forces the Khaibar Pass. **25 April:** Shah Shuja assassinated at Kabul. **30 April:** Passage of the Khojak. **May:** Pollock at Jalalabad. Relief of Kalat-i Ghilzai. Akbar Khan captures Bala Hisar. **29 May:** Action near Kandahar. **June:** Operations in Shinwari valley. **June-October:** Fateh Jang becomes Amir. **7 August:** Evacuation of Kandahar. **20 August:** Pollock sets out from Jalalabad. Action near Gandomak. **28 August:** Cavalry action near Mukur. **30 August:** Battle at Karabagh. **5 September:** British reenter Ghazni. **8 September:** Action in Jagdalak Pass. **12 September:** Action at Sayyidabad. **13 September:** Action at Tezin. **15 September:** Pollock arrives at Kabul. **19 September:** Nott arrives at Kabul. **29 September:** Action at Istalif. **12 October:** British force leaves Kabul. **14 October:** Action at Haft Kotal. **End of First Anglo-Afghan War. 17 December:** British forces arrive at Firuzpur. **December:** Dost Muhammad returns to Kabul and rules for 21 years.

1855 Treaty of Peshawar reopens diplomatic relations between Britain and Afghanistan.

1856 October: Persians capture and hold Herat for a few months.

1857 January: Anglo-Afghan treaty signed in Peshawar. Provides subsidy for Dost Muhammad.

1863 Dost Muhammad takes Herat and dies. Shir Ali ascends Afghan throne. During next two years Shir Ali puts down revolts by half brothers, Azam and Afzal, and his brother, Muhammad Amin. Abdur Rahman and his uncle, Azam, attack Kabul, liberate Afzal, Abdur Rahman's father.

1866 Afzal becomes Amir. Shir Ali flees to Kandahar.

1867 Amir Afzal dies.

1868 Azam becomes amir.

1869 Shir Ali defeats Azam. Abdul Rahman goes into exile in Russia. British recognize Shir Ali as amir but refuse to recognize his son, Abdullah Jan, as successor. **March:** Ambala Conference held between Amir Shir Ali and Lord Mayo, viceroy of India.

1872 In Granville-Gorchakoff Agreement Russia assures Britain that Afghanistan is outside Russia's sphere of influence. British commission marks Sistan boundary.

1873 Abdullah Jan named heir to Afghan throne. Shir Ali's oldest son, Yakub Khan, revolts, flees to Herat. Russia takes Khiva.

1874 Yakub Khan imprisoned in Kabul.

1876 British occupy Quetta.

1878 22 July: Russian mission under General Stolietoff arrives in Kabul. **Second Anglo-Afghan War: 21 September:** General Faiz Muhammad, commander of Ali Masjid, denies the British envoy, General Sir Neville Chamberlain, passage into Afghanistan. Amir Shir Ali is given an ultimatum to apologize for this "insult" and to meet certain conditions lest he be treated as an enemy. Lord Lytton denounces alliance with Amir Dost Muhammad. **November:** Colonel Grodekoff arrives in Herat from Samarkand. **21 November:** Sir Samuel Brown attacks the fort of Ali Masjid, General Frederick Roberts crosses the frontier at Thal, and an advance guard of General Donald Steward marches from Quetta against

Kandahar. **22 November:** Fort Ali Masjid is captured. **2 December:** General Roberts defeats an Afghan force at the Paiwar Kotal. **20 December:** General Sam Brown occupies Jalalabad. **23 December:** Amir Shir Ali leaves Kabul and appoints his son Yaqub Khan governor of Kabul.

1879 2-30 January: General Roberts moves into the Khost Valley. **12 January:** General Donald Steward occupies Kandahar and takes Qalat-i Ghilzai on January 21. **21 February:** Amir Shir Ali dies at Mazar-i Sharif, Yaqub Khan proclaimed king. **2 April:** General Charles Gough defeats the Khugianis at Fathabad. **26 May:** Treaty of Gandomak signed by Sir Louis Cavagnari and Amir Yaqub Khan. **24 July:** Cavagnari arrives at Kabul to assume post of British envoy to amir. **3 September:** Cavagnari and his staff are killed. **11 September:** Brigadier General Massey occupies the Shuturgardan Pass with the advance guard of General Robert's force. **6 October:** General Roberts's Army of Retribution wins battle of Charasia. **12 October:** General Roberts occupies Kabul. **14-19 October:** Afghan forces unsuccessfully attack British troops at Ali Khel and Shuturgardan. **16 October:** Explosion of the ammunition depot at Bala Hisar. **28 October:** Amir Yaqub abdicates, British take over the government of Kabul. **10 December:** General Macpherson defeats Kohistani force at Karez Mir. **11 December:** General Massey fails in attack on Muhammad Jan and his forces advancing from Ghazni. **12 December:** MacPherson's brigade under Colonel Money fails in attack on Takht-i Shah. **13 December:** General Baker drives Afghans from Takht-i Shah. **14 December:** General Thomas Baker driven from Asmai hills with losses. General Roberts abandons Bala Hisar and Kabul city and stations his forces at Sherpur. **15-22 December:** Muhammad Jan cuts Roberts's communications and lays siege to Sherpur. **23 December:** Muhammad Jan's forces are defeated and Roberts returns to Bala Hisar the next day.

1880 1 April: Sir Donald Stewart begins his march from Kandahar to Kabul. **19 April:** Battle at Ahmad Khel. **21 April:** Stewart defeats Afghan forces at Ghazni. **2 May:** Stewart arrives at Kabul. ca. **15 June:** Sardar Ayub Khan moves from Herat against Kandahar. **10 July:** A brigade under General Burrows moves against Ayub. **22 July:** Britain recognizes Sardar Abdul Rahman as Amir of Kabul and its Dependencies. **27 July:** General G. R. S. Burrows is totally defeated in Battle of Maiwand, and the remnant of his brigade forced to seek safety in Kandahar. **6 August:** Ayub Khan invests Kandahar. **8 August:** General Roberts begins march from

Kabul to Kandahar. **11 August:** General Steward withdraws from Kabul and Amir Abdul Rahman moves in. **16 August:** Sortie of the British garrison of Kandahar is repulsed with great losses. **31 August:** Sir Roberts arrives at Kandahar. **1 September:** Sir Roberts defeats Ayub Khan at Baba Wali Kotal. **9 September:** British troops return to India from the Paiwar Kotal and the Kurram Valley and begin withdrawal from Jalalabad.

1881 **21 April:** British troops withdraw from Kandahar. **End of Second Anglo-Afghan War.**

1882 Muslim agent appointed to represent British in Kabul.

1883 Russia occupies Tejend Oasis. Britain annexes Quetta district. Abdul Rahman occupies Shignan and Roshan. Britain grants Abdul Rahman subsidy of 12 lakhs (1,200,000 rupees).

1884 Britain and Russia open negotiations on northern boundary of Afghanistan. Sir Peter Lumsden leads British mission to Herat. British again start building Quetta railroad. Russians occupy Pul-I-Khatun.

1885 Russians occupy Zulfikar and Akrobat and take Panjdeh.

1886 British construct Bolan railway to Quetta. **October:** British boundary mission returns to India by way of Kabul.

1887 Russia occupies Karki. Britain and Russia make final settlement and demarcation of Afghan-Russian frontier. Ayub Khan escapes from Persia, but rebellion in Afghanistan fails; he surrenders at Mashhad and is exiled to India.

1888 **January:** British extend Quetta Railway to Kila Abdullah. **July:** Ishaq Khan, son of Azam, revolts in Turkestan, retreats to Samarkand.

1891 Abdul Rahman introduces oath of allegiance on the Koran among his councillors.

1892 Uprising of Hazaras suppressed.

1893 **12 November:** Afghanistan and Britain sign Durand Agreement that sets eastern and southern boundaries. British increase Amir Abdul

Rahman's subsidy by six lakhs and permit Afghanistan to import munitions. British occupy New Chaman as railway terminus.

1895 Abdul Rahman abolishes slavery in Afghanistan. Abdul Rahman accepts oaths of allegiance from whole state of Afghanistan and adopts title of *Zia ul- Millat wa ud-Din*. Sardar Nasrullah, second son of Abdul Rahman, visits England. Russia and Britain agree on Wakhan border.

1896 Kafiristan brought under Afghan control by Amir Abdul Rahman; renamed Nuristan.

1900 Russia presses for direct Afghan-Russian relations along northern Afghan border in memorandum of February 6 to Britain.

1901 1 October: Abdul Rahman dies. **3 October:** Habibullah proclaimed amir, rules 18 years.

1902 British envoy, Sir Henry Dobbs, supervises re-erection of boundary pillars on Afghan-Russian border during 1902 and 1903.

1903 A. H. McMahon leads British mission in demarcating Sistan boundary. Habibia College, first secular high school, opened in Kabul. British begin construction of Quetta-Nushki railroad.

1905 British agreements of 1880 and 1893 with Abdul Rahman confirmed by treaty with Amir Habibullah.

1906 Shah of Iran rejects McMahon arbitration award.

1907 January: Amir Habibullah visits India. **31 August:** Britain and Russia sign convention concerning spheres of influence in Afghanistan, Persia, and Tibet.

1909 Plot on Amir Habibullah's life fails.

1910 First telephone line in Afghanistan built between Kabul and Jalalabad.

1911 Mahmud Tarzi begins publishing the newspaper *Seraj al- Akhbar*.

Chronology xxix

1914 General Muhammad Nadir Khan named commander-in-chief of the Afghan Army. Habibullah declares Afghanistan's neutrality in World War I.

1915 September: Hentig-Niedermayer mission from Germany arrives in Kabul and remains nine months.

1918 Kabul Museum opened.

1919 20 February: Amir Habibullah assassinated in Laghman. Nasrullah Khan named amir in Jalalabad. **25 February:** Amanullah proclaimed amir in Kabul. **28 February:** Nasrullah arrested. **3 March:** Amanullah suggests new Anglo-Afghan agreement to viceroy of India. **13 April:** Amanullah proclaims Afghanistan independent. **1 May:** Saleh Muhammad Khan, the commander-in-chief, moves to the Indian border with two companies of infantry and two guns, for the ostensible purpose of inspecting the border. **Third Anglo-Afghan War: 3 May:** An escort of British Khaibar Rifles accompanying a caravan is stopped in the disputed area between Landi Khana and Torkham. **4 May:** Afghan uniformed troops occupy Bagh and begin to cut the water supply to Landi Kotal. A **fatwa** proclaimed jihad. **7 May:** Afghan forces at Bagh strengthened, and Nadir Khan moves to Khost. **8 May:** Peshawar uprising suppressed. **9 May:** First Battle of Bagh, British forces stopped. **11 May:** Second Battle of Bagh. **12 May:** On the Chitral front, Afghan troops occupy Arnawai. **13 May:** British occupy Dakka. **21 May:** General Nadir Khan crosses Indo-Afghan boundary, marches on Thal. Decision made to evacuate the militia posts on the Waziristan front. **May 24:** Kabul bombed by Royal Air Force. **27 May:** Battle of Spin Buldak. **28 May:** Wali Muhammad Khan arrives at Tashkent on way to Moscow and Europe as Amanullah's envoy. **1 June:** General Dyer occupies Thal. **2 June:** Armistice. **8 August:** Preliminary Anglo-Afghan treaty signed at Rawalpindi peace conference. **End of Third Anglo-Afghan War. September:** Soviet envoy arrives at Kabul. **10 October:** Muhammad Wali Khan arrives in Moscow.

1920 17 April: Mussoorie Conference opens. Mahmud Tarzi represents Afghanistan and Henry Dobbs, Britain. **18 July:** Mussoorie Conference ends.

1921 Amir of Bukhara seeks asylum in Afghanistan. **20 January:** Kabul conference between Afghanistan and Britain opens. **28 February:** Treaty of friendship signed by Afghanistan and the Soviet Union. **1 March:** Treaty of friendship signed by Afghanistan and Turkey. **30 May:** Fundamental law of government of Afghanistan goes into force. **3 June:** Treaty of friendship signed by Afghanistan and Italy. **22 June:** Treaty of friendship signed by Afghanistan and Persia. **2 December:** Kabul Conference ends. Britain recognizes Afghanistan as independent in internal and external relations. Diplomatic relations established between the two states.

1922 28 April: Treaty establishes diplomatic and commercial relations between France and Afghanistan. **9 September:** Agreement gives France rights to conduct archaeological excavations in Afghanistan.

1923 January: Istiqlal Lycée founded. **10 April:** First Constitution adopted. **5 June:** British-Afghan trade convention signed. **September:** French legation opened in Afghanistan. **October:** Criminal code adopted. **November:** Statute governing marriage issued. **December:** Statute on civil servants confirmed. **December:** German legation opens in Afghanistan.

1924 January: Amani (Najat) high school founded. First hospital for women and children opened in Kabul. **March:** Uprising of tribes in Khost.

1925 January: Khost rebellion defeated.

1926 Afghani introduced as new monetary unit. Ten afghanis equal 11 Kabuli ropea. **3 March:** Treaty of friendship signed by Afghanistan and Germany. **7 June:** Amanullah adopts title of king. **15 August:** Soviet Union agrees to cede Urta Tagai Islands in Amu River to Afghanistan. **31 August:** Treaty of neutrality and mutual nonaggression signed by Afghanistan and Soviet Union.

1927 *Anis* founded as fortnightly, later major national daily newspaper. **27 November:** Treaty of neutrality and mutual nonaggression signed by Afghanistan and Persia. **December:** King Amanullah visits India, Egypt, and Europe.

1928 25 May: Treaty of friendship and collaboration signed by Afghanistan and Turkey. **July:** King Amanullah returns to Afghanistan. **July-September:** Amanullah introduces reforms in dress. **November:**

Uprising of Shinwari near Jalalabad. **December:** Habibullah Kalakani leads uprising in Kohistan.

1929 14 January: Amanullah renounces the throne. His brother, Enayatullah, abdicates after three days. **18 January:** Habibullah Kalakani proclaimed amir. **14 October:** Kabul seized by Nadir Khan's troops. **17 October:** Nadir Khan proclaimed king. **3 November:** Habibullah Kalakani caught and shot.

1930 May: Nadir Shah confirms validity of 1921 and 1923 Anglo-Afghan agreements and other international treaties. **20 September:** Nadir Shah confirms statute governing elections of members of National Assembly.

1931 24 June: New treaty of neutrality and mutual nonaggression signed by Afghanistan and Soviet Union. **July:** Nadir Shah opens National Assembly session. Literary Society founded. **31 October:** New constitution confirmed by Nadir Shah.

1932 Medical school founded; other schools closed by Habibullah Kalakani reopened. **24 August:** Statute setting up new administrative divisions issued. Five major and four minor provinces formed. **October:** Uprising begins in Khost. **8 November:** Ghulam Nabi executed on charge of complicity in Dari Khel Ghilzai revolt.

1933 Road over Shibar Pass to north completed. **6 June:** Muhammad Aziz, Afghan minister to Germany, assassinated in Berlin. **8 November:** Nadir Shah assassinated. His son, Muhammad Zahir, becomes king, and brother of Nadir Shah, Muhammad Hashim, prime minister.

1934 16 February: Zahir Shah orders general election for National Assembly. **21 August:** United States formally recognizes Afghanistan. **25 September:** Afghanistan joins League of Nations.

1935 April-May: W.H. Hornibrook accredited as nonresident American minister to Kabul. **May:** Turkey arbitrates Afghanistan's boundary dispute with Persia. **8 June:** National Assembly session opened by Zahir Shah. **September:** Mohmand uprising.

1936 March: Treaty on commerce and noninterference signed by Afghanistan and Soviet Union. **26 March:** Treaty of friendship signed by Afghanistan and United States.

1937 Lufthansa starts weekly service between Berlin and Kabul: first regular air link between Afghanistan and Europe. Turkish military mission arrives at Kabul. **7 July:** Treaty of Saadabad signed by Afghanistan, Iran, Iraq, and Turkey.

1938 May: Afghan Air Force expanded by purchase of planes from Italy and Britain. Officers sent to Britain, Soviet Union, and Italy for training. Arms bought from Britain and Czechoslovakia.

1939 3 September: Beginning of World War II and Afghan armed forces mobilized as precautionary measure.

1940 12 January: All men over 17 obliged to do national service. Special taxes imposed to pay for arms, build radio station. Radio Kabul gets 20 kilowatt medium wave transmitter. **29 July:** Trade agreement between Afghanistan and Soviet Union signed. **17 August:** Zahir Shah declares Afghanistan's neutrality in World War II in statement to National Assembly.

1941 28 July: Afghanistan reaffirms its neutrality in World War II. **19 October:** Afghanistan agrees to expel German and Italian residents at demand of Britain and the Soviet Union.

1942 27 April: Cornelius van Engert, consul-general in Beirut, named resident U.S. minister to Afghanistan. **5 November:** Afghanistan reaffirms neutrality in World War II.

1943 16 May: Afghan consulate opened in New York. **5 June:** Abdul Husain Aziz, first Afghan minister to United States, presents credentials. **28 December:** Saadabad pact reported automatically renewed after five years.

1944 5 March: Treaty of friendship signed by Afghanistan and China.

1946 Kabul University established by combining already existing faculties, such as medicine and law. **22 January:** King Zahir orders election of deputies for session of National Assembly to meet April 21. **9 May:** Muhammad Hashem Khan resigns as prime minister, citing poor health as reason. Mahmud Khan, minister of defense, asked to form new government. **13 June:** Boundary treaty signed with Soviet Union. Soviet Union gets Kushka River water rights. **9 November:** United Nations General Assembly approves entry of Afghanistan. **19 November:** Abdul Husain Aziz, Afghanistan's first representative to United Nations, takes seat.

1947 24 April: Afghan delegation arrives in Tashkent to start demarcation of Afghan-Soviet border. **13 June:** Afghanistan sends note to British and Indian governments saying that inhabitants of region between Afghan-Indian border and Indus River are Afghans and must decide themselves whether to join Afghanistan, Pakistan, or India or become independent. **3 July:** Britain replies it holds to treaty of 1921 by which boundary was recognized by both nations and asks Afghanistan to abstain from any act of intervention on northwest frontier at time of transfer of powers to Indian government. **10 July:** Afghanistan reiterates views on Pashtuns in second note to Britain. **26 July:** Prime Minister Mahmud arrives in London. **3 August:** Prime Minister Mahmud arrives in New York City. **18 September:** Iran says diversion of Helmand waters in Afghanistan causes crop failures in Sistan. **30 September:** Afghanistan casts only vote against admitting Pakistan to United Nations on grounds that Pashtuns have not had fair plebiscite.

1948 1 April: Muhammad Naim named Afghan ambassador to United States. **23 April:** Sir Giles Squire named British ambassador to Afghanistan. **6 May:** Faiz Muhammad named Afghan ambassador to Britain. **5 June:** United States legation elevated to status of embassy. Ely E. Palmer presents credentials as first U.S. ambassador. **16 June:** Pakistan arrests Abdul Ghaffar Khan and other Khuda-i Khetmatgar leaders. Afghanistan begins press and radio campaign for independent Pashtunistan. Agreement signed fixing revised boundary.

1949 24 March: Foreign ministry says statement of Pakistani governor general that tribal territory is integral part of Pakistan is contrary to pledges of Jinnah in 1948. **2 April:** Chargé d'affaires in Karachi recalled after Pakistani bombing in Waziristan. **20 April:** Louis G. Dreyfus named U.S. ambassador to Afghanistan. **4 June:** Afghanistan restricts movement of vehicles along border with Pakistan. **12 June:** Pakistani plane bombs Moghalgai (inside Afghan territory), killing 23. **20 June:** Alfred Gardener named British ambassador to Afghanistan. **30 June:** Afghan National Assembly opens seventh session, known as "Liberal Assembly." **11 July:** Pakistani foreign minister says Pakistan will discuss economic cooperation with Afghanistan but rejects Afghanistan's claims to tribal territory. **26 July:** Afghan National Assembly repudiates treaties with Britain regarding tribal territory.

1950 4 January: Treaty of peace and friendship signed by Afghanistan and India. **13 January:** Afghanistan recognizes People's Republic of China (PRC). **8 March:** Zahir Shah begins visit to Europe. **26 May:** Recall of Pakistan embassy staff member for violating Afghan laws, requested by Afghanistan. **18 July:** Four-year trade agreement signed by Afghanistan and Soviet Union. **14 October:** New cabinet announced by Prime Minister Shah Mahmud. **October:** Emigration of Afghan Jews to Israel authorized by Afghan government.

1951 9 February: Agreement for technical assistance under Point Four program signed by Afghanistan and United States. **19 March:** George R. Merrell appointed U.S. ambassador to Afghanistan. **25 April:** Prime Minister Shah Mahmud arrives in United States. **28 May:** United Nations assists in drilling exploratory oil wells in north.

1952 15 January: United States suspends economic and technical aid to Afghanistan until bilateral agreement under Mutual Security Act signed. **23 September:** Soviet note expressing concern over activities of UN technical assistance experts in areas near Afghan-Soviet border rejected by Afghan government.

1953 8 January: United States extends loan of $1.5 million for emergency purchase of wheat and flour from it. **18 March:** Sultan Muhammad named foreign minister to succeed Ali Muhammad who remains deputy prime minister. **6 September:** Shah Mahmud resigns as prime minister, citing poor health. Zahir Shah asks cousin, Muhammad Daud, present defense and interior minister, to form new cabinet. **20 September:** Prime Minister Muhammad Daud announces cabinet members. **26 October:** Muhammad Hashim, prime minister from 1929 to 1946, dies. **November:** U. S. Export-Import Bank makes loan of $18.5 million for development of Helmand Valley. **30 December:** Prime Minister Daud describes proposed U.S. military aid to Pakistan as a "grave danger to security and peace of Afghanistan."

1954 27 January: Soviet Union makes loan of $3.5 million for construction of two grain mills and two silos. Soviet technicians to help carry out projects. **17 September:** Foreign Minister Naim arrives in Karachi to

Chronology   xxxv

continue talks begun in Kabul on improving relations between Afghanistan and Pakistan. **7 November:** Foreign Minister Naim says Pashtunistan issue is not question of territorial adjustment but of giving Pashtuns an opportunity to express their wishes.

1955 14 January: Former Prime Minister Shah Mahmud meets Pakistan prime minister. **19 January:** Afghanistan and the PRC establish diplomatic relations at embassy level. **25 January:** Legislation strengthening armed forces approved by upper house of parliament. **2 March:** Fine arts college opened under A. G. Breshna. **29 March:** Prime Minister Daud warns Pakistan of "grave consequences" if Pashtun areas of the Northwest-Frontier Province are included in unified West Pakistan. **30 March:** Demonstrators march on Pakistani embassy and ambassador's residence in Kabul. **31 March:** Demonstrators march on Pakistani consulate in Kandahar. **1 April:** Demonstrators march on Pakistani consulate in Jalalabad. Afghan consulate in Peshawar attacked. **12 April:** Pakistan rejects Afghan replies to its protests, evacuates families of diplomats and nationals, closes Jalalabad consulate. **18 April:** Foreign Minister Naim goes to Bandung Conference. **29 April:** Gamal Abdul Nasser, prime minister of Egypt, visits Afghanistan. Afghanistan says it is willing to apologize, pay compensation for damage, and make amends for the insult to Pakistani flag if similar amends are made for the insult to its flag. **1 May:** Pakistan demands closing of all Afghan consulates in Pakistan, says it will close its consulates in Afghanistan. **4 May:** Afghanistan mobilizes troops. **13 May:** Afghanistan and Pakistan accept Saudi Arabian offer of mediation. **21 June:** Five-year agreement signed with Soviet Union allowing goods of each nation free transit across territory of other. **28 June:** Saudi Arabian mediator announces his proposals have been rejected. **5 July:** Thin Kuo Yu, PRC ambassador to Afghanistan, presents credentials. **14 July:** Afghanistan tells Pakistan it will be held responsible for any loss or damage to goods held up in transit to Kabul or Quetta. Afghanistan becomes member of International Monetary Fund (IMF) and World Bank. **28 July:** State of emergency ended; Afghan army demobilized. **14 August:** Postal agreement signed by Afghanistan and Soviet Union. **9 September:** Foreign Minister Naim and Pakistan ambassador negotiate agreement to stop hostile propaganda. **13 September:** Pakistan flag raised over Pakistani embassy in Kabul. **15 September:** Afghan flag raised over consulate in Peshawar. **11 October:** Afghan leaders request meeting with Pakistani leaders on condition one-unit act can be postponed. Pakistan says postponement impossible. **17 October:** Afghanistan recalls ambassador from Karachi. **18 October:** Pakistan recalls ambassador from Kabul. **8 November:** Afghanistan protests further restrictions by Pakistan on transit of goods to Afghanistan. **20 November:** During five-day session, Loya Jirga gives its approval to resolutions calling for plebiscite to decide future of Pashtun area disputed with Pakistan, recommending government find means to reestablish balance of power upset by Pakistan's decision to accept arms from the United States, and refusing to recognize Pashtunistan as part of Pakistan. **6 December:** Defense Minister Muhammad Arif resigns. **15-18 December:** Soviet Prime Minister Bulganin and Soviet Communist Party Secretary Nikita Khrushchev make official visit to Kabul. **16 December:** Soviet Union backs Afghanistan in Pashtunistan dispute. **18 December:** Three agreements signed by Afghanistan and Soviet Union: a loan of $100 million; a protocol extending 1931 treaty of neutrality and nonaggression; and a statement of foreign policy matters. Foreign Minister Naim says agreements do not weaken Afghan determination to remain neutral.

1956 8 January: Afghan consul in Quetta recalled at request of Pakistan. Pakistan military attaché requested to leave Afghanistan. **24 January:** Soviet economic delegation begins talks with Afghan government on use of $100 million loan. **30 January:** Soviet Union presents Ilyushin 14 to Zahir Shah. **18 February:** Technical cooperation agreement signed by Afghanistan and the United States for 1956. **1 March:** Technical assistance agreement signed by Afghanistan and the Soviet Union for building of hydroelectric plants, highway through Hindu Kush, air fields, motor repair shop, and reservoirs. **6 March:** SEATO powers declare region up to Durand Line is Pakistani territory and within treaty area. **21 March:** Afghanistan formally protests SEATO decision to uphold Durand Line as Afghan-Pakistani border. **26 March:** United States International Cooperation Administration announces grant of $997,000 to Teachers College of Columbia University to set up English language program for Afghan secondary schools and train English teachers. **31 March:** Gift of 15 buses and equipment for 100-bed hospital to Kabul municipality from Soviet Union arrives. **4-18 April:** Afghan military mission visits Czechoslovakia. **7 May:** Regular air service available to Europe through Karachi, after air agreement signed by Afghanistan and Pakistan. **27 June:** Agreement for $14 million to develop Afghan civil aviation signed by Afghanistan and United States. **26 July:** Soviet Union agrees to carry out Nangarhar irrigation project. **7-11 August:** Pakistan President Iskander Mirza visits Kabul. **25 August:** Prime Minister Daud announces military arms agreements with Czechoslovakia and Soviet Union. **12 September:**

Pan American Airlines to supervise pilot and ground crew training of Ariana Afghan Airlines. A $2.5 million contract to be part of $14 million program announced earlier which also includes $5.5 million for Kandahar airport. **24 September:** Air service to Iran inaugurated. **27 September:** First installment of arms from Soviet Union and Czechoslovakia arrives. **17-30 October:** Prime Minister Daud visits Soviet Union. **28 October:** Afghan Air Force receives 11 jet planes from Soviet Union. **24 November:** Prime Minister Daud discusses Pashtunistan question with Pakistani leaders during visit to Karachi.

1957 8 January: Trade protocol signed with Soviet Union. **19-23 January:** Chou En-lai, PRC prime minister, visits Afghanistan. **27 January:** M.C. Gillett named British ambassador to Afghanistan. **10 February:** Radio Moscow inaugurates Pashtu program. **8-11 June:** Pakistani Prime Minister Suhrawardy visits Kabul. Afghanistan and Pakistan agree to restore diplomatic relations. **30 June:** United States makes loan of $5,750,000 for Helmand Valley Authority and $2,860,000 for building roads and training personnel. **17-31 July:** Communiqué says Soviet Union will aid Afghanistan in prospecting for oil, that a special commission to regulate boundary questions will be created, and that an agreement was reached regarding use of waterways crossing the two countries. **28 July:** Trade agreement signed by Afghanistan and PRC. **31 August:** Foreign Minister Naim says Afghanistan to receive about $25 million in military assistance under arms agreement signed with Soviet Union in 1956. **22 October:** Prime Minister Daud begins visit to People's Republic of China. **21 December:** Andrei Gromyko, Soviet foreign minister, meets Afghan mission in Moscow to negotiate new frontier agreement.

1958 8 January: Soviet Union agrees to survey oil deposits in Afghanistan. **18 January:** Treaty regulating Afghan-Soviet border signed by Afghanistan and Soviet Union. **1-6 February:** Zahir Shah visits Pakistan. **11-27 February:** Zahir Shah arrives in India for two-week visit. **26 June:** Cultural agreement signed by Afghanistan and United States. Protocol on utilization of Amu Darya signed by Afghanistan and Soviet Union. **30 June:** Prime Minister Daud begins U.S. visit. United States agrees to help Afghanistan improve highway from Spin Boldak to Kabul and makes $7,708,000 grant to Pakistan to improve its transport lines with Afghanistan. **17 July:** Agreement on transport of goods by road signed by Afghanistan and Pakistan. **1-5 October:** Marshal Klementi Voroshilov, president of the Supreme Soviet of the Soviet Union, visits Afghanistan.

1959 1-6 January: Foreign Minister Naim visits the USSR. **12 January:** United States agrees to ship 50,000 tons of wheat to Afghanistan. **20 January:** Henry A. Byroade named U.S. ambassador to Afghanistan. **5-13 February:** Prime Minister Daud visits India. **9 March:** Prime Minister Daud calls Baghdad Pact aggravation of international tension. **23 April:** Afghanistan and Soviet Union sign protocol on exchange of goods. **18-22 May:** Prime Minister Daud visits USSR. **28 May:** Afghanistan and Soviet Union sign agreement on building of 750 km Kandahar-Herat-Kushka Highway. **15 July:** Afghan military mission visits Turkey and United Arab Republic. **23 August:** Soviet Union agrees to provide assistance to complete Nangarhar irrigation project. **5 September:** Foreign Minister Naim begins visit to PRC. **14 September:** Indian Prime Minister Jawaharlal Nehru visits Afghanistan. Afghan women appear without veils at dinner for Nehru. Henceforth veil is no longer obligatory. **1 December:** Afghanistan and Soviet Union to begin joint survey of Amu Daria for construction of dam to provide electricity and water for irrigation. **9 December:** U.S. President Eisenhower spends six hours in Kabul. Assures Afghanistan of continued economic support. **21 December:** Police and army units suppress rioting in Kandahar.

1960 19 January: Afghanistan and Soviet Union sign agreement for construction of irrigation and power project on Kabul River. **2-5 March:** Soviet Prime Minister Nikita Khrushchev visits Kabul. Inspects Soviet aid projects, signs cultural cooperation agreement, assures Afghanistan support on Pashtun question. **6 March:** Pakistan calls Soviet support of Afghanistan on Pashtun question interference in Pakistan's internal affairs. **7 March:** Prime Minister Daud says Pakistan is putting out propaganda against reforms in Afghanistan such as the emancipation of women. Says Afghan monarchy has decided to give Afghans complete freedom to choose form of government and to organize political parties. **3 April:** Construction work begins on Kandahar-Herat-Kushka Highway. **26 April:** Former King Amanullah dies in Switzerland. **13 May:** Prime Minister Daud meets Soviet Prime Minister Khrushchev while in Moscow for medical treatment. **15 July:** Soviet prospecting team announces discovery of petroleum and natural gas deposits in northern Afghanistan. **18 August:** Darunta Canal opened. Built with Soviet assistance. **21-26 August:** Chen Yi, PRC foreign minister, visits Afghanistan. **26 August:** Treaty of friendship and nonaggression signed by Afghanistan and People's Republic of China. Commercial and payments agreement re-newed. **3 December:** Agreements on trade and transit signed with Iran during visit of Iranian prime minister to Kabul.

Chronology

1961 5 April: Prime Minister Daud confers with Soviet Prime Minister Khrushchev in Moscow on return from Rome where Daud underwent a spinal operation. *Pravda* article says Pashtun situation is not a matter of indifference to Soviet Union. **19 May:** Afghanistan denies Pakistani reports that Afghan soldiers are taking part in border fighting. **6 June:** Prime Minister Daud says Pakistan has savagely bombarded Afghan populations with aid of arms furnished by United States and has confined more than 1,200 leaders of Pashtunistan in Peshawar in past five days. Denies that Afghanistan has pushed Pashtun tribes to revolt. **15 June:** Pakistan protests acts of provocation and aggression in note to Afghan government. **22 June:** Pakistan says nomads will no longer be allowed to enter Pakistan without valid passports, visas, and international health certificates. **23 June:** Pakistan says friendlier atmosphere should exist between Afghanistan and Pakistan before any summit meeting held. **26 June:** Prime Minister Daud confers with British Foreign Secretary Lord Home and is received by Queen Elizabeth during visit to London. **28 June:** Foreign Minister Naim tells news conference that Pashtun self-determination is only problem in Afghan-Pakistani relations that requires negotiation. **23 July:** Muhammad Hashem Maiwandwal, ambassador to the United States, expresses his government's grave concern over Pakistan's use of American arms against Pashtun tribes during meeting with President John F. Kennedy. **23 August:** Pakistan announces it is closing Afghan consulates and trade offices in Pakistan and is considering prohibiting transit facilities given to Afghanistan. **30 August:** In reply to Pakistani note of August 23, Afghanistan says it considers decision to close consulates an inimical act and threatens to break diplomatic relations. Prime Minister Daud leaves for Belgrade Conference of Nonaligned Nations. **3 September:** Afghanistan seals border. Transfer of merchandise suspended between Afghanistan and Pakistan. **6 September:** Afghanistan breaks diplomatic relations with Pakistan. **12 September:** Islamic Congress of Jerusalem appeals to Afghanistan and Pakistan to resolve their differences. **18 September:** Pakistan accepts Iranian offer of mediation in dispute. **19 September:** Saudi Arabia agrees to look after Pakistani interest in Afghanistan. **21 September:** United Arab Republic agrees to look after Afghan interest in Pakistan. **27 September:** Foreign Minister Naim says Afghanistan will not allow its transit trade to pass through Pakistan unless its trade offices and consulates in Pakistan are reopened. **29 September:** Pakistani President Ayub Khan rejects possibility of reopening Afghan consulates and trade offices, says they were used for subversive activities. **11 October:** Soviet delegation arrives in Kabul for 11-day visit. **16 October:** Afghan-Soviet technical and economic cooperation agreement signed. **19 November:** Supplementary transit agreement, providing expansion of facilities for Afghan foreign trade, signed with Soviet Union.

1962 23 January: Four-year agreement signed with Soviet Union to develop Afghan meteorological services. **24 January:** John M. Steeves named U.S. ambassador to Afghanistan. **29 January:** Afghanistan opens border with Pakistan for eight weeks to allow entry of U.S. aid goods. **14 April:** Prime Minister Daud announces Second Five-Year Plan. Calls for spending Afs. 31.3 billion for economic development. **20 April:** Five-year transit agreement signed by Iran and Afghanistan. **6 May:** Pul-i Khumri power station opened. Built with Soviet assistance. **1 July:** Pakistan accepts Shah of Iran's offer to mediate its dispute with Afghanistan. **12 July:** Afghanistan accepts Shah of Iran's offer to mediate its dispute with Pakistan. **27-31 July:** Formal talks held in Kabul between Shah of Iran and Zahir Shah and in Rawalpindi between the Shah and President Ayub Khan in effort to settle Afghan-Pakistani dispute. **6 August:** During meeting in Quetta, Pakistani President Ayub Khan suggests a confederation of Afghanistan, Iran, and Pakistan. **6-15 August:** Zahir Shah makes visit to Soviet Union.

1963 12 February: United States decides to ship all its foreign aid goods to Afghanistan via Iran because of the continuing dispute between Afghanistan and Pakistan. **25 February:** Trade and assistance agreement signed by Afghanistan and Soviet Union. **10 March:** Resignation of Prime Minister Daud announced. **14 March:** King Zahir Shah asks Muhammad Yusuf, former minister of mines and industries, to form new government. **18 April:** At press conference Prime Minister Yusuf says introducing democracy and improving economic conditions are major aims of the government. He estimates that the United States has furnished about $252 million and the Soviet Union an equivalent amount plus arms. **26 April:** U. S. grants loan of $2,635,000 for purchase of a DC-6 and two convairs for Ariana Afghan Airlines. Purchase will bring Ariana's fleet to nine planes. **29 April:** Cultural cooperation agreement signed by Afghanistan and Soviet Union. **11-15 May:** Indian President Sarvepalli Radhakrishnan visits Afghanistan. **25 May:** Afghan and Pakistani representatives begin meetings in Tehran to resolve dispute over Pashtunistan. **28 May:** Shah of Iran announces that Afghanistan and Pakistan have agreed to reestablish diplomatic and commercial relations. **29 May:** Joint Afghan-Pakistani communiqué confirms reestablishment of relations. **20 July:** Afghan consulates reopened in Peshawar and Quetta. Communication reestablished on Afghan-Pakistani border. **25 July:** First trucks cross Afghan-Pakistani border in 22 months. Ariana Afghan Airlines resumes flights halted at same time. **12 August:** Afghanistan and Pakistan exchange ambassadors. **15 August:** Shah of Iran says confederation of Afghanistan, Iran, and Pakistan is good idea but cites many obstacles. **2-19 September:** Zahir Shah and Queen Homaira visit United States. **6 September:** Afghanistan and Soviet Union sign agreement for construction of atomic reactor in Afghanistan and training of specialists in peaceful use of atomic energy. **12-17 October:** Soviet President Leonid Brezhnev visits Afghanistan; lays cornerstone for new polytechnic institute in Kabul. **16 October:** Agreement signed with Soviet Union for technical assistance in extraction and exploitation of natural gas in northern Afghanistan. **2 December:** Border treaty signed by Afghanistan and PRC.

1964 29 February: Consultative Constitutional Commission, headed by Abdul Zahir, begins sessions which last through May 14. **31 May:** Zahir Shah opens new Aliabad campus of Kabul University, built with U. S. assistance. **29 June-14 July:** Afghan military delegation visits Soviet Union. **1 July:** During one-day stay in Kabul, Pakistani President Ayub Khan discusses ways to improve Afghan-Pakistani relations with King Zahir Shah and Prime Minister Yusuf. **4-5 July:** Anastas Mikoyan, deputy prime minister of Soviet Union, visits Kabul. **13 July:** Soviet Union makes loan of $25.2 million for Pul-i Khumri—Mazar-i Sharif—Shiberghan Highway. **27 July:** Cabinet approves new constitution. It allows freedom of speech and press and formation of political parties, calls for two-house parliament and independent judiciary, and bars members of royal family from serving as prime minister, cabinet member, chief justice, or parliament members. King appoints prime minister and commands armed forces. **3 September:** Zahir Shah and Soviet Deputy Prime Minister Alexei Kosygin open Kabul-Doshi Highway over Salang Pass, built with Soviet assistance. **6 September:** Delegation returns from demarcating 90 km border with People's Republic of China. **9-19 September:** Loya Jirga debates and approves constitution after adding that members of royal family cannot become members of political parties nor renounce their titles to participate in politics. **1 October:** Zahir Shah endorses new constitution. National Assembly dissolved. Transitional government to govern for a year. **27 October:** Soviet Union agrees to loan $6.2 million to build polytechnic institute in Kabul. **29 October-12 November:** Zahir Shah, accompanied by Queen Homaira, makes first visit to People's Republic of China by any Afghan head of state.

1965 1 January: Founding of the PDPA. **12 January:** United States agrees to loan $7.7 million for construction of 121 km Herat-Islam Kala Highway. **18 January:** Soviet Union agrees to loan Afghanistan $11.1 million over three years for import of consumer goods. **15 February:** Protocol on exchange of goods and prices for 1965 signed by Afghanistan and Soviet Union. **11 March:** Zahir Shah and Soviet Prime Minister Dimitri Polyansky open Nangarhar irrigation and power project, built with Soviet assistance. **22-25 March:** Chen Yi, PRC deputy prime minister and foreign minister, confers with Zahir Shah and Prime Minister Yusuf during a three-day visit. Boundary protocol, cultural agreement, and economic and technical cooperation agreement signed. **21-30 April:** Prime Minister Yusuf makes official visit to Soviet Union. Gets assurance of Soviet help with Third Plan. **11 May:** New electoral law, providing for universal, direct vote by secret ballot for all Afghan men and women over 20, goes into effect. **23 May:** Ariana Airlines begins weekly flight to Tashkent, its first to Soviet Union. **5 June:** Mazar-i Sharif airport completed. Built with U.S. assistance. **22 June:** Jangalak smelts its first iron ore mined in Afghanistan. **7 July:** King Zahir Shah announces plan to rebuild old city of Kabul. **24 July:** Soviet Union agrees to build 97 km pipeline from Shiberghan gas fields to Soviet border and 88 km line from fields to fertilizer and power plants in Balkh Province. **28 July:** Soviet Union agrees to extend payment on loans to Afghanistan by 30 years and provide teachers for Polytechnic Institute. **3-14 August:** Zahir Shah and Queen Homaira visit USSR. Afghanistan and Soviet Union agree to extend treaty on neutrality and mutual nonaggression of 1931 for 10 years. **8 August:** First census of Kabul finds population of 435,203. **26 August-28 September:** Election of parliament members held. Over 1,000 run for 216 seats in Wolesi Jirga (House of the People) and 100 for 28 elective seats in Meshrano Jirga (House of Elders). All run as independents. **9 September:** New press law goes into effect allowing Afghan citizens freedom of expression while safeguarding the fundamental values of Islam and the principles embodied in the constitution. **12 October:** Dr. Abdul Zahir elected president of Wolesi Jirga. Zahir Shah names Abdul Hadi Dawai president of Meshrano Jirga. **13 October:** Zahir Shah's appointees to Meshrano Jirga announced. Prime Minister Yusuf presents report of interim government and offers resignation. King asks him to form new government. **19 October:** Wolesi Jirga decides proposed cabinet members should submit lists of property they hold before vote of confidence is taken. **24 October:** Prime Minister Yusuf's presentation of his cabinet to Wolesi Jirga postponed when spectators crowd into deputies' seats and refuse to leave. **25 October:** Wolesi Jirga decides 191-6 to hold vote of confidence in secret session.

Student demonstrations are dispersed by force by police and army; three persons are killed. Schools are closed and public meetings banned. Wolesi Jirga approves Prime Minister Yusuf's cabinet. Vote reported to be 198 in favor and 15 abstaining. **27 October:** King Zahir Shah receives cabinet. **29 October:** In wake of demonstrations, Prime Minister Yusuf resigns, giving poor health as reason. King Zahir Shah asks Muhammad Hashem Maiwandwal to form cabinet. **6 November:** Ministry of Interior announces three people died during demonstrations on October 25. **27 November:** Kabul University senate refuses to accept student demands for a lower passing grade and postponement of exams. **13 December:** Kabul University's college of science closed because of continued disturbances. **14 December:** Ministry of Interior forbids public gatherings after two days of demonstrations.

1966 1-2 January: President Ayub Khan of Pakistan makes stop in Kabul on way to Tashkent talks. **2 March:** New Kabul University constitution approved by cabinet. **4-9 April:** Liu Shao-Chi, PRC president, makes official visit to Kabul. **11 April:** *Khalq*, a Pashtu and Dari newspaper published by Nur Muhammad Taraki, puts out first issue. **13 April:** Wolesi Jirga begins consideration of political parties draft law. **4 May:** After debate on *Khalq*, Meshrano Jirga passes resolution saying any publication against values of Islam should be halted. **22 May:** Wolesi Jirgah passes resolution, asking government to take action against *Khalq* for not following values of constitution. **23 May:** Government bans distribution of *Khalq* under Art. 48 of the press law. **19 July:** Wolesi Jirga approves political parties draft law. **20 August:** Supreme judiciary committee set up as foundation of future supreme court. **20 September:** Abdul Rahman Pazhwak, Afghan representative to the United Nations, elected president of the UN General Assembly.

1967 25 March-9 April: Prime Minister Maiwandwal visits United States. **10 May:** Protocol on export of natural gas signed by Afghanistan and Soviet Union. **30 May-2 June:** Nikolai Podgorny, chairman of the Presidium of the Supreme Soviet, visits Afghanistan. **20 August:** Direct telephone link between Kabul and Herat completed. **11 October:** Prime Minister Maiwandwal resigns because of poor health. King Zahir Shah names Abdullah Yaftali acting prime minister. **15 October:** Zahir Shah inaugurates supreme court. **1 November:** Zahir Shah asks Nur Ahmad Etemadi to form new government. **15 November:** Prime Minister Etemadi gets vote of confidence 173 to 7 with 6 abstentions after three-day debate. Etemadi pledges to work against bribery and corruption.

1968 **31 January:** Soviet Prime Minister Kosygin stops in Kabul to discuss economic questions. **22 April:** Shiberghan gas pipelines officially opened. **13 June:** King Muhammad Zahir ends a 10- day visit to the USSR. **23 August:** The country celebrates the 50th anniversary of its independence.

1969 **25 May:** U.S. Secretary of State William Rogers pays a brief visit to Kabul for talks with government leaders. **22 June:** Afghan government ordered closing of all primary and secondary schools in Kabul, after a wave of student unrest and a student boycott of Kabul University. **17 July:** Soviet military delegation begins a visit. **25 December:** Soviet military delegation led by Defense Minister Andrei Grechko arrives for an official visit.

1970 **21 January:** The USSR signs a protocol for the export of 2.5 billion cubic meters of Afghan natural gas in 1970. **26 January:** Defense Minister Khan Mohammed begins an official visit to the United States. **20 September:** King Muhammad Zahir leaves for a state visit to Czechoslovakia. **20 October:** King Muhammad Zahir arrives in Moscow for an "unofficial friendly" visit.

1971 **17 May:** It was announced that the government of Prime Minister Nur Ahmad Etemadi has resigned. King Zahir Shah accepts the resignation and requests him to stay in office until a new government can be formed. **8 June:** Former ambassador to Italy, Abdul Zahir, is asked to form a new cabinet. **26 July:** The National Assembly gives Abdul Zahir a vote of confidence after a 17-day debate, and he takes office along with his cabinet. **August:** Afghanistan suffers the worst drought in its recorded history.

1972 **3 January:** The USSR signs an agreement for expanding natural gas refining and collection centers in the north. **11 January:** Pakistan President Zulfikar Ali Bhutto arrives in Kabul for official talks. **3 April:** Indian Foreign Affairs Minister Swaran Singh leaves after a three-day visit and talks on economic aid and cooperation. **16 May:** Kabul Radio broadcasts a demand for Pashtunistan's independence from Pakistan. **21 July:** U. S. special envoy John Connally tells the government that the United States cannot make any further commitment of aid. **25 August:** A natural gas discovery at Jarquduq is estimated to be the second largest in the country. **5 December:** Muhammad Zahir Shah accepts the resignation of Prime Minister Abdul Zahir who agrees to remain in office until a new prime minister can be appointed. **9 December:** Musa Shafiq is appointed to form a new government. **11 December:** A new cabinet is announced with Muhammad Musa Shafiq prime minister and foreign affairs minister.

1973 17 January: It is announced that diplomatic relations will be established with the German Democratic Republic. **13 March:** Iranian Prime Minister Amir Abbas Hoveyda and Prime Minister Muhammad Musa Shafiq of Afghanistan sign a formal settlement of the Helmand River dispute. **21 April:** A royal decree is issued setting general parliamentary election dates. **11 May:** The border with Pakistan is ordered closed for two weeks for "administrative reasons." **8 July:** Zahir Shah arrives in Italy for a vacation. **17 July:** Sardar Muhammad Daud deposes his cousin, the king, and proclaims a republic. **18 July:** Muhammad Daud proclaimed president and defense minister. **19 July:** The Soviet Union and India extend diplomatic recognition to the new government. **27 July:** President Daud abrogates the Constitution of 1964 and dissolves Parliament. **2 August:** New cabinet announced with Muhammad Daud holding the portfolios of prime minister, defense, and foreign affairs. **24 August:** Deposed King, Muhammad Zahir, announces his abdication. **23 September:** It is announced that a plot to overthrow the government was discovered and a number of senior army officers arrested. Pakistan is accused of supporting the group. **30 October:** Indian Foreign Minister Swaran Singh arrives for an official visit.

1974 5 April: It is reported that a new trade and payments agreement between Afghanistan and the Soviet Union was concluded after a visit to Moscow by Minister of Trade Muhammad Khan Jalallar. **7 July:** A trade protocol is signed with India. **19 July:** Soviet assistance in the development of the Jarquduq natural gas field and in oil exploration is reported. **24 July:** Iran and Afghanistan sign a protocol for cooperation in a large-scale development program in the "joint region of the Helmand River." **1 November:** U.S. Secretary of State Henry Kissinger arrives and meets with Premier Muhammad Daud.

1975 26 February: The government issues a statement protesting the U.S. decision to lift the arms ban on Pakistan. **13 March:** President Muhammad Daud concludes an official visit to India. **1 May:** The government announces the nationalization of all banks and banking affairs. **11 July:** Deputy Foreign Minister Wahid Abdallah flies to Saudi Arabia to attend the Islamic Foreign Ministers Conference. **28 July:** Afghan security forces capture a "terrorist" group in Panjshir that was allegedly armed by Pakistan. **17 October:** Iran signs an agreement to provide aid and technical assistance to construct a railroad system and Kabul airport and build a meat processing plant. **21 November:** New cabinet is appointed. **2 December:** Afghanistan denies Pakistani charges that it has mobilized troops along its border with Pakistan.

1976 2 January: An agreement is concluded with the Soviet Union for the development of the Jarquduq gas fields and the provision of gas production and processing facilities. **7 June:** Pakistani President Zulfikar Ali Bhutto begins a visit to Afghanistan. **8 June:** Pakistani President Bhutto meets with President Muhammad Daud. **4 July:** Indian Premier Indira Gandhi arrives in Kabul for a three-day visit. **8 August:** U.S. Secretary of State Henry Kissinger meets with President Daud in Kabul. **9 December:** According to reports, more than 50 people have been arrested and accused of a plot to overthrow the government.

1977 30 January: President Muhammad Daud convenes the Loya Jirga to approve the draft of a new constitution. **14 February:** The new constitution is approved by the Loya Jirga. **15 February:** Muhammad Daud is sworn in and the Loya Jirga is dissolved. **24 February:** President Daud promulgates a new constitution. **26 February:** Daud disbands the cabinet and central revolutionary committee. **13 March:** The Afghan government announces formation of a new cabinet. **23 March:** A Soviet trade delegation begins a trip to Afghanistan to hold talks on bilateral trade. **29 March:** An agreement is reached in Kabul to resume air links between Pakistan and Afghanistan. **22 June:** Pakistani Premier Zulfikar Ali Bhutto arrives in Kabul for talks with President Daud. **5 July:** General Zia-ul-Haq deposes Zulfikar Ali Bhutto. **29 July:** Afghanistan and the USSR concludes a six-year consumer goods agreement in Kabul. **20-24 August:** President Daud pays official visit to Islamabad. **11 October:** Pakistani Chief Martial Law Administrator Muhammad Zia-ul-Haq meets with President Daud at the presidential palace. **16 November:** Minister of Planning Ali Ahmad Khurram is assassinated in Kabul.

1978 19 February: Sayyid Abdulillah is appointed vice president. **21 February:** President Muhammad Daud leaves Kabul for Belgrade on an official visit to Yugoslavia. **24 February:** A trial of 25 people accused of plotting to assassinate President Daud begins in Kabul. **4 March:** President Daud meets with Indian Premier Morarji Desai in New Delhi. **17 April:** Mir Akbar Khaibar, one of the founders of the PDPA, is assassinated in Kabul. **20 April:** Thousands turn Khaibar's funeral into an antigovernment demonstration. **26 April:** President Daud has PDPA leaders arrested. **27 April: Communist Coup.** Members of the PDPA gain power in a coup led by insurgents in the armed forces. The military Revolutionary Council forms a new government. **29 April:** The government radio reports that Defense Minister Ghulam Haidar Rasuli, Interior Minister Abdul Qadir Nuristani, and Vice President Sayyid Abdulillah have been killed in the coup along with President Daud and his brother Muhammad Naim. **30 April:** A "Revolutionary Council" is proclaimed. Nur Muhammad Taraki is named president and premier of the Democratic Republic of Afghanistan. The Revolutionary Council selects the following leading ministers:

Babrak Karmal	Deputy Prime Minister
Hafizullah Amin	Deputy Prime Minister and Foreign Minister
Muhd. Aslam Watanjar	Deputy Prime Minister and Communications
Abdul Qadir	National Defense
Shah Wali	Health
Nur Ahmad Nur	Interior
Dastagir Panjshiri	Education
Sultan Ali Keshtmand	Planning
Sulaiman Layeq	Radio, Television
Saleh Muhd. Zirai	Agriculture
Abdul Karim Misaq	Finance
M. Hasan Bareq-Shafi'i	Information, Culture
Abdul Hakim Shara'i	Justice, Attorney General
Anahita Ratebzad	Social Affairs
Abdul Quddus Ghorbandi	Commerce
Muhd. Ismail Danesh	Mines, Industries
Muhammad Rafi'i	Public Works
Muhd. Mansur Hashimi	Water & Power
Mahmud Suma	Higher Education
Nizamuddin Tahzib	Tribal Affairs

1 May: Shah Muhammad Dost and Abdul Hadi Mokamel are named deputy ministers of foreign affairs. **6 May:** Premier Taraki says Afghanistan is "nonaligned and independent." **18 May:** Foreign Minister Hafizullah Amin leaves Kabul for Havana for a meeting of nonaligned countries. **May-June:** First mujahedin camp set up in Pakistan. **June:** Parchamis purged. **5 July:** Kabul Radio says that Interior Minister Nur Ahmad Nur has been named ambassador to Washington and that Vice President and Deputy Premier Babrak Karmal has been named ambassador to Czechoslovakia. **17 August:** The central committee of the Peoples Democratic Party decides that President of the Revolutionary Council Nur Muhammad Taraki will assume the duties of minister of defense. **18 August:** Kabul Radio announces that a plot to overthrow the government has been foiled and Defense Minister Abdul Qadir has been arrested for his role in the plot. **23 August:** The politburo of the PDPA orders the arrest of Planning Minister Sultan Ali Keshtmand and Public Works Minister Muhammad Rafi'i for their parts in the conspiracy. **9 September:** Pakistani Chief Martial Law Administrator Muhammad Zia-ul-Haq meets with Chairman of the Revolutionary Council Taraki at Paghman, near Kabul. **17 September:** The government announces it is breaking diplomatic relations with South Korea. **19 September:** Indian External Affairs Minister Anal Bihari Vajpayee meets with Taraki in Kabul. **22 September:** Taraki dismisses six ambassadors who had been appointed in July. All were members of the Parcham section of the PDPA. **19 October:** Afghanistan adopts a red flag as its new national emblem. **3 December:** President Nur Muhammad Taraki arrives in Moscow for talks with Soviet leaders. **5 December:** Afghanistan and the Soviet Union signs a 20-year treaty of friendship and cooperation in Moscow.

1979 16 January: Shah of Iran flees, Ruhullah Khomeyni takes over. **28 January:** Guerrillas fight government troops in the eastern provinces bordering Pakistan. **2 February:** It is reported that Afghan dissidents are undergoing guerrilla training at a Pakistan military base north of Peshawar. **14 February:** U.S. ambassador to Afghanistan Adolph Dubs is taken hostage by terrorists in Kabul. Afghan forces rush the building in which he is held, and he is slain. The United States protests the use of force by the Afghan government to free the ambassador. **19 February:** Foreign Minister Hafizullah Amin rejects a U.S. protest over the incident leading to the slaying of the U.S. ambassador as "completely baseless." **22 February:** President Jimmy Carter orders American aid to Afghanistan reduced. **10-20 March:** Revolt and uprising in Herat with the participation of the military garrison. Thousands are said to have been killed in recapture of town by government troops. **23 March:** A U.S. spokesman says Washington expects that the "principle of noninterference" in Afghanistan will be respected by all parties in the area, "including the Soviet Union." **27 March:** Foreign Minister Hafizullah Amin is named prime minister. **1 April:** The new Afghan government is announced. Hafizullah Amin, premier and foreign affairs; Shah Wali, deputy prime minister. **2 April:** Washington denies Soviet charges that America is arming Afghan guerrillas. **8 April:** Soviet Vice Minister of Defense Aleksey Yepishev meets with President Nur Muhammad Taraki in Kabul. **30 April:** Taraki says Pakistani President Muhammad Zia-ul-Haq was "involved" in attacks on border positions in eastern Afghanistan. **13 June:** Afghanistan accuses Pakistan of involvement in a rebellion against the Afghan government. **23 June:** Kabul Radio reports that antigovernment demonstrators (Hazaras) in Kabul had been "annihilated and arrested" during the day. **June:** Soviet special forces occupy Bagram air force base. **28 July:** The cabinet is reshuffled: Hafizullah Amin, prime minister and vice president of the Revolutionary Council; Shah Wali deputy prime minister and foreign minister. **5 August:** Heavy fighting breaks out in Kabul between loyal troops and a rebellious army unit at the Bala Hissar Fort. The rebellion is crushed and a curfew imposed on the city. **19 August:** Premier Hafizullah Amin says there are "no more than 1,600 Soviet advisers" in Afghanistan. **14 September:** Hafizullah Amin deposes Nur Muhammad Taraki. **15 September:** Radio Kabul reports that Interior Minister Aslam Watanjar and Frontier Affairs Minister Sherjan Mazduryar have been removed from their posts. It is reported that gunfire and explosions had occurred in Kabul following the announcement of the cabinet dismissals. **16 September:** Radio Kabul reports that President Taraki has asked to be relieved of his government positions because of "bad health and nervous weakness." Premier Amin assumes the additional post of president. Other appointments include: Faqir Muhd. Faqir, Interior, and Sahibjan Sahra'i, Frontier Affairs. **23 September:** President Amin says that former President Taraki is "alive but definitely sick." **8 October:** Kabul announces that President Amin has commuted death sentences of former Defense Minister Abdul Qadir and former Planning Minister Sultan Ali Keshtmand to 15 years imprisonment. Rebel tribesmen say they have cut the road leading from Kabul to Gardez during fighting with government troops. **9 October:** Radio Kabul announces that Taraki has died. President Amin publishes a list of 12,000 killed by Taraki regime. **14 October:** Heavy fighting takes place at Rishkhur barracks southwest of Kabul. **16 October:** It is reported that the government has crushed an army mutiny near Kabul. Soviet forces take command of Shindand air force base. **9 November:** It is reported that several ambush attacks have been launched on government troops near Kabul, killing 200 persons. **21 December:** U.S. officials say that the Soviet Union has moved three army divisions to the border with Afghanistan and has sent about 1,500 combat soldiers to an air base near Kabul. **26 December:** A U.S. government spokesman says that in the past 24 hours there has been "a large-scale Soviet airlift" to Kabul, raising Soviet military involvement in Afghanistan to "a new threshold." **27 December:** President Hafizullah Amin is overthrown with the assistance of Soviet forces and assassinated. Former Deputy Premier Babrak Karmal assumes the post of president. It is reported that Soviet troops have taken part in the fighting in Kabul. **28 December:** President Karmal says the Soviet Union has agreed to supply Afghanistan "urgent political, moral and economic aid, including military aid." U.S. President Jimmy Carter calls the Soviet military intervention "a grave threat to the peace" and a "blatant violation of accepted rules of international behavior." A cabinet is formed as follows: Babrak Karmal, prime minister, chairman, Revolutionary Council, and secretary general, Central Committee; Asadullah Sarwari, deputy prime minister; Sultan Ali Keshtmand, deputy prime minister and minister of planning; Muhammad Rafi'i, national defense; Sayyid Muhdammad Gulabzoi, interior; and Shah Muhammad Dost, foreign minister.

1980 January: The Jimmy Carter administration requests about $30 million in covert aid to the Afghan guerrillas. United States begins covertly channeling Soviet-made weapons including Kalashnikov AK-47 automatic rifles to the rebels in Pakistan. **1 January:** Afghanistan says it has invited Soviet troops into the country "in view of the present aggressive actions of the enemies of Afghanistan." **2 January:** Karmal addresses government leaders near Kabul and calls on the Afghan people to "come together and support our glorious revolution." **5 January:** The UN Security Council opens a debate on Afghanistan. **7 January:** The Soviet Union vetoes a UN resolution that called for the immediate withdrawal of "all foreign troops in Afghanistan." The vote is 13 to two in favor of the resolution. **9 January:** The Security Council votes 12 to two with one abstention for a resolution to move the issue of Afghanistan to the General Assembly. **14 January:** The General Assembly votes 104 to 18 with 18 abstentions for a resolution that "strongly deplored" the "recent armed intervention" in Afghanistan and called for the "total withdrawal of foreign troops" from the country. **23 January:** President Carter announces sanctions against the Soviet Union, including a grain embargo. **27 January:** A conference of Islamic Foreign Ministers opens in Islamabad to consider the situation in Afghanistan. **29 January:** The conference adopts a resolution that condemns "the Soviet military aggression against the Afghan people." **13 February:** Egyptian Defense Minister Kamal Hasan 'Ali says that Egypt is providing assistance to

Afghan rebels and is "training some of them." **14 February:** The UN Human Rights Commission votes 27 to eight with six abstentions to condemn the Soviet intervention in Afghanistan as "an aggression against human rights." **15 February:** The *New York Times* cites "White House officials" as saying the United States had begun an operation to supply light infantry weapons to Afghan insurgent groups. **19 February:** Foreign ministers of the European Economic Community (EEC) propose that Afghanistan be declared a neutral country under international guarantees if the Soviet Union withdraws its troops. **22 February:** Soviet President Leonid Brezhnev says that the Soviet Union will withdraw its troops from Afghanistan "as soon as all forms of outside interference" were "fully terminated." Demonstrations and rioting against the government and the Soviet Union take place in Kabul. **25 February:** Shops remain closed in Kabul. **26 February:** It is reported that mass arrests have been made in Kabul during the day. **28 February:** Almost all shopkeepers open for business in Kabul. It is reported that striking civil servants have returned to work. **3 March:** The Hizb-i Islami of Gulbuddin Hekmatyar, one of six Afghan insurgent groups negotiating an alliance, says it has withdrawn from the alliance. **7 March:** Soviet soldiers appear on the streets of Kabul. Soviet fighter planes and helicopter gun ships fly over the city. **10 March:** Justice Minister Abdurrashid Arian says that 42 associates of former President Hafizullah Amin are being held for trial. **13 March:** Foreign Minister Shah Muhammad Dost arrives in Moscow on a "friendly visit." **April:** Status of Soviet Armed Forces Agreement signed. **18 May:** Indian Foreign Secretary R.D. Satha meets with President Babrak Karmal in Kabul. **22 May:** A conference of Islamic foreign ministers, meeting in Islamabad, adopts a resolution that demands the "immediate, total and unconditional withdrawal of all Soviet troops from Afghanistan" and decides to establish a committee that will open "appropriate consultations" to seek a solution to the crisis in Afghanistan. **24 May:** Demonstrators protesting the Soviet presence in Afghanistan march in Kabul. **8 June:** Radio Kabul announces that 10 supporters and aides of slain former President Hafizullah Amin have been executed. **14 June:** Kabul news service reports that former Communications Minister Muhammad Zarif, former Frontier Affairs Minister Sahibjan Sahra'i, and former Planning Minister Muhammad Siddiq Alemyar have been executed. **July.** Sixty countries boycott the Moscow Olympics in protest over the invasion of Afghanistan. **2 July:** The Soviet Communist Party newspaper *Pravda* says that for a political settlement of the situation in Afghanistan to take place, armed incursions by the "mercenaries of the imperialist and reactionary forces from the territory of neighboring states" must first be ended. **16**

August: Radio Kabul reports that Justice Minister Abdurrashid Arian has been named to the additional post of deputy prime minister. **14 September:** Frontier Affairs Minister Faiz Muhammad is killed earlier in the week while trying to enlist the support of Afghan tribes. **October:** The CIA provides some SAM-7 portable surface-to-air missiles to Ahmad Shah Mas'ud. **15 October-5 November:** President Karmal and other high officials leave Kabul on a visit to the Soviet Union. **13 November:** President Karmal says that those who are not working for the good of the party will be expelled "even if they had been heroes in the past." **20 November:** The UN General Assembly votes by 111 to 22 with 12 abstentions for a resolution that calls for the "unconditional" pullout of "foreign troops" from Afghanistan. **21 November:** Foreign Affairs Minister Shah Muhammad Dost says the UN resolution is "a flagrant interference in Afghanistan's internal affairs." **25 December:** Egyptian President Anwar al-Sadat says that he has "sent weapons" and would "send more weapons" to Afghan insurgents. **27 December:** Deposed King Muhammad Zahir says in exile that he prays to God "to aid the Afghan people in its heroic struggle and its legitimate war for independence."

1981 20 January: Ronald Reagan becomes president. Pakistan government declares that henceforth it will recognize only six Pakistan-based resistance organizations. **18 February:** President Babrak Karmal arrives in Moscow for talks with Soviet leaders. **9 March:** U.S. President Ronald Reagan says that if Afghan "freedom fighters" who are fighting Soviet forces ask for weapons, it will be something "to be considered." **7 April:** Saudi Arabia announces it is severing diplomatic relations with "the current illegal regime" in Afghanistan. **9 May:** Pakistani officials estimate the number of Afghan refugees in Pakistan at two million. **11 May:** Sultan Ali Keshtmand becomes prime minister. **11 June:** President of the Revolutionary Council Babrak Karmal turns the post of prime minister over to Sultan Ali Keshtmand and removes Abdul Rashid Arian as deputy prime minister. **13 June:** The Revolutionary Council elects as its vice presidents Nur Ahmad Nur and Abdul Rashid Arian. **12 July:** Member of the national committee of the National Fatherland Front Gen. Fateh Muhammad is killed by rebels. **22 July:** Diplomatic sources in Kabul report heavy fighting between the rebels and Soviet forces in Paghman, 16 miles from the capital. **6 August:** Foreign Minister Shah Muhammad Dost meets with UN Representative Javier Perez de Cuellar. **12 August:** Radio Kabul announces changes in the land distribution program that lift restrictions on acreage held by religious and tribal leaders. **22 August:** Five Afghan resistance groups form an alliance and create a 50-member

Chronology   liii

advisory council. **9 September:** Foreign Minister Dost meets with Prime Minister Indira Gandhi in New Delhi. **22 September:** Egyptian President Anwar al-Sadat says in a U.S. television interview that the United States has been buying old Soviet-made arms from Egypt and sending them to rebels fighting Soviet forces in Afghanistan. U.S. officials have no comment. **18 November:** By a vote of 116 to 23 with 12 abstentions the UN General Assembly votes for the third time that the Soviet Union must withdraw its troops from Afghanistan. **15 December:** President Karmal begins a visit to Moscow.

1982 6 January: In Washington, military analysts say Soviet troops in Afghanistan have grown to 110,000-120,000. **20 February:** The Afghan government rejects the appointment of Archer K. Blood, designated U.S. chargé d'affaires to Kabul. In response, the U.S. State Department imposes travel restrictions on Afghan diplomats in Washington. **10 March:** President Reagan proclaims March 21 "Afghanistan Day." **8 June:** Soviet and Afghan troops regain control of the key Panjshir Valley in a major offensive against mujahedin forces. **16-25 June:** The first UN-sponsored direct talks between Afghanistan and Pakistan begin in Geneva. **2 August:** The Afghan government amends the conscription law, lengthening the term of service. **30 October:** An explosion in the Salang Tunnel north of Kabul kills more than 1,000 people, including 700 Soviet troops. **November:** The UN General Assembly approves a resolution demanding "the immediate withdrawal of foreign troops from Afghanistan" by a vote of 114 to 21 with 13 abstentions. **December:** It is reported that the CIA was ordered to provide the Afghan insurgents with bazookas, mortars, grenade launchers, mines, and recoilless rifles.

1983 19 January: UN Deputy Secretary General Diego Cordovez begins a peace mission to Geneva, Tehran, Islamabad, and Kabul to resolve the Afghan crisis. **16 February:** The UN Human Rights Commission votes 29 to seven with five abstentions for an immediate Soviet withdrawal from Afghanistan. **15 June:** The foreign ministers of Afghanistan and Pakistan arrive in Geneva for a third series of talks on the withdrawal of foreign troops. **24 June:** UN-sponsored talks on Soviet troop withdrawal end in Geneva without progress. **23 November:** The UN General Assembly calls for the immediate withdrawal of Soviet troops by a vote of 116 to 20 with 16 abstentions. **27 December:** The Afghan government says it will request the departure of 105,000 Soviet troops if it receives international guarantees that all opposition would end.

1984 24 January: President Karmal has replaced his three top military advisers. Chief of Staff Gen. Baba Jan is replaced by Lt. Gen. Nazar Muhammad; Deputy Defense Minister Maj. Gen. Khalilullah by Maj. Gen. Muhammad Nabi Azami; and Chief of Operations Gen. Nuristani by Maj. Gen. Ghulam Qadir Miakhel. **11 April:** The Kabul government orders the expulsion of Third Secretary Richard S. Vandiver of the U.S. embassy in Kabul on charges of espionage. The United States denies the charge. **14 May:** The National Olympic Committee announces that Afghanistan will boycott the Summer Olympics in Los Angeles. **17 May:** U.S. Vice President George Bush visits the Khaiber Pass, where he condemns the Soviet invasion and expresses support for the Afghan resistance. **26 July:** The U.S. House of Representatives appropriations committee approves $50 million in covert aid to Afghan, according to intelligence sources. **27 August:** The foreign ministers of Afghanistan and Pakistan meet separately in Geneva with a UN intermediary in talks on a political settlement to the Afghan war. **30 August:** The third round of talks between Afghanistan and Pakistan adjourns in Geneva with no sign of progress. **4 November:** Nine people are executed for the bomb explosion at Kabul airport. **3 December:** Radio Kabul reports that President Karmal has appointed Army Chief of Staff Brig. Gen. Nazar Muhammad to replace Lt. Gen. Abdul Qadir as defense minister.

1985 18 January: The United States announces it will increase its aid to Afghan mujahedin in 1985 to approximately $280 million. Saudi Arabia, Israel, and China are also reportedly assisting the rebels. **26 January:** The Afghan mujahedin leader, Khan Gul, is sentenced to death in Paktia Province. **29 January:** Zabiullah, a leader of the Jam'iat-i Islami, is killed when his jeep hits a mine. **3 March:** According to reports from Iran, four Shi'a mujahedin groups have merged: the Sazman-i Nasr, the Pasdaran, Guards, the Islamic Movement of Afghanistan, and the United Front of the Islamic Revolution. **11 March:** Mikhail Gorbachev becomes general secretary of the Soviet Union. **23 April:** President Karmal opens a grand tribal assembly (Loya Jirga) in Kabul in an effort to gain popular support in the government's war against the mujahedin. **10 May:** Leaders of three of the main mujahedin groups in Peshawar denounce the attempt by Abd al-Rasul Sayyaf to appoint himself for another term as head of the seven-member Alliance of Afghan Mujahedin. **17 June:** U.S. and Soviet officials meet in Washington to discuss the war in Afghanistan. **20 June:** UN-sponsored "proximity talks" begin in Geneva between Afghan and Pakistan governments regarding the war in Afghanistan. **30 August:** UN mediator Diego Cordovez says progress had been made on three of four points in the UN plan for ending the Afghan war. The two sides remain divided on the question of withdrawing Soviet troops. **23 October:** Afghan authorities order all males of up to 40 years of age to enlist for three years of military service. Afghan Foreign Minister Shah Muhammad Dost says Afghanistan could not reach agreement on the withdrawal of Soviet troops unless Pakistan enters direct negotiations. **13 November:** By a vote of 122 to 19 with 12 abstentions, the UN General Assembly adopts a Pakistani resolution calling for the immediate withdrawal of Soviet troops from Afghanistan. **6 December:** Radio Kabul announces that Ghulam Faruq Yaqubi has been named director of the KHAD, Afghanistan's secret police. **13 December:** The State Department notifies the UN that the United States is ready to act as guarantor of a peace settlement in Afghanistan that would involve a Soviet troops withdrawal and an end to U.S. aid to the mujahedin. **19 December:** In Geneva, Afghanistan and Pakistan suspend their latest round of peace talks to study new UN proposals for a timetable for Soviet withdrawal. **31 December:** The Afghan government presents an informal timetable for the withdrawal of Soviet troops as part of an overall accord, during UN-sponsored Geneva talks December 16 to 19, according to the State Department.

1986 11 January: President Babrak Karmal rejects the U.S. offer to serve as guarantor of a peace settlement. **4 February:** Guerrilla activity near Kandahar has reportedly declined in recent days after former rebel leader Asmatullah Achakzai Muslim and his militia decided to back the Kabul government. **20 February:** The Revolutionary Council Presidium appoints a 74-member commission to draft a constitution. **17 March:** The Foreign Ministry rejects a UN report on human rights violations in Afghanistan as "a collection of groundless slanders and accusations." **20 March:** Pakistan lodges a "strong protest" over Afghan attacks on a border post and refugee camp in Khurram Agency that killed six people on March 16 and 18. **2 April:** The United States reportedly agrees to supply hundreds of Stinger missiles to Afghan mujahedin. **4 May:** Babrak Karmal resigns as secretary general of the PDPA because of "ill health," according to Kabul Radio. He is replaced by Najibullah, former head of KHAD, the secret police. Babrak retains the post of chairman of the Revolutionary Council and a seat in the seven-member politburo. **5 May:** The seventh round of peace talks between the foreign ministers of Afghanistan and Pakistan opens at UN headquarters in Geneva. **15 May:** Najibullah announces a collective leadership including himself as party leader, Babrak as head of the Revolutionary Council Presidium, and Prime Minister Sultan Ali Keshtmand. **16 June:** President Ronald Reagan meets with Afghan mujahedin in Washington and promises an "unshakable commitment" to their cause. **17 June:** Mujahedin leaders Gulbuddin Hekmatyar and Rasul Sayyaf criticize the four other Peshawar leaders for the Washington visit. **21 July:** It was reported that hundreds of idealistic Arab men had joined the Afghan resistance. **28 July:** Soviet leader Mikhail Gorbachev announced the withdrawal of six Soviet regiments by the end of the year. **8 August:** UN-sponsored negotiations between Afghanistan and Pakistan are suspended because of the issue of timing of Soviet troop withdrawal. **5 November:** The UN General Assembly passed its eight annual resolution calling on the Soviet Union to withdraw from Afghanistan. **20 November:** Babrak Karmal resigns as president of the Revolutionary Council and chairmanship of the Presidium. **12 December:** Mujahedin have begun using U.S. Stinger missiles. **23 December:** Najibullah is elected president by the Revolutionary Council Presidium.

1987 1 January: President Najibullah offers a six-month "cease-fire and peace plan." **3 January:** Mujahedin groups reject peace plan as a trap. **18 February:** Prime Minister Sultan Ali Keshtmand arrives in Moscow for talks. **23 February:** Pakistan's Foreign Minister Yaqub Khan meets with Soviet Foreign Minister Shevardnadze in Moscow to discuss Afghanistan. **26 February:** The tenth round of negotiations aimed at ending the war in Afghanistan opens in Geneva. **4 March:** Mujahedin stage rocket attacks into Soviet territory from Imam Sahib in Kunduz Province. **20 July:** Afghan leader Najibullah meets with Soviet leader Mikhail Gorbachev. **11 August:** Felix Ermacora, the UN special human rights investigator, is allowed to visit three Afghan prisons and interview political prisoners. **September:** Najibullah elected president in a special session of the Revolutionary Council. **10 October:** Najibullah authorizes the purchase of weapons from mujahedin who put down their arms. **13 October:** Yunus Khales, leader of the Hizb-i Islami, denies reports that his commanders have sold Stinger missiles to Iranian Pasdaran. **18 October:** Maulawi Yunus Khales is elected spokesman of the seven-party mujahedin alliance. **24 October:** Shi'a groups headquartered in Iran announce a new coalition of mujahedin groups in Iran. **10 November:** Kabul Radio announces that the Revolutionary Council Presidium endorses a decree providing for the formation and registration of political parties. **24 November:** Lt. Gen. Muhammad Nabi Azimi, first deputy of defense, is reported to have committed suicide after an offensive he led ended in failure. **29 November:** A Loya Jirga has been called to approve a new constitution. **30 November:** The Loya Jirga confirms Najibullah as president under the new "Islamized" constitution. **6 December:** Mujahedin leader Yunus Khales says the seven-party alliance will not accept communist participation in any future Afghan government. **10 December:** UN envoy Diego Cordovez is reported to have opened negotiations between exiled King Muhammad Zahir and mujahedin leaders regarding formation of a transitional coalition government.

1988 .6 January: In an interview with Afghan News Agency, Shevardnadze says the Soviet Union hopes to be out of Afghanistan by the end of 1988 regardless of the type of rule established there. He, however, links troop withdrawal to the cessation of U.S. aid to the mujahedin. **12 January:** Pakistani President Zia-ul-Haq and Prime Minister Muhammad Khan Junejo say in separate interviews that members of the pro-Moscow govern-ment must be allowed to participate in any future government as a condition for the withdrawal of Soviet troops from the country. **17 January:** Mujahedin leader Yunus Khales rejects statements by Pakistani leaders that the mujahedin would have to "coexist with remnants of a communist regime." **20 January:** At a press conference Najibullah states that his government will be committed to nonalignment, following the withdrawal of Soviet forces, and that Kabul is willing to accept aid from any country willing to give it. **22 January:** In Jalalabad at least 17 people are killed when two bombs explode at the public funeral of Khan Abd al-Ghaffar Khan, who died on January 20. **8 February:** Soviet leader Mikhail Gorbachev says Soviet troops will begin pulling out of Afghanistan on May 15 if a settlement can be reached by mid-March. **11 February:** Sayyid Bahauddin Majruh, head of the Afghan Information Office in Peshawar, is assassinated in Peshawar city. **23 February:** The mujahedin alliance announces the formation of an interim government. **4 March:** The Reagan administration says it will not halt aid to the mujahedin until Moscow stops its supply to the Afghan government. **14 March:** Gulbudin Hekmatyar is reported appointed spokesman of the mujahedin alliance. **23 March:** Nikolai Egorchev (?) is reported to have replaced Pavel Mojayev as Soviet ambassador to Afghanistan after Mojayev suffers a heart attack. **26 March:** The Reagan administration is reported ending its supply of Stinger missiles to the mujahedin in anticipation of a Geneva settlement. **29 March:** President Najibullah promises opposition groups 54 of the 229 lower house seats and 18 out of 62 in the senate if they will participate in the coming parliamentary elections. **30 March:** The mujahedin reject President Najibullah's offer to form a coalition government. **1 April:** Geneva Conference ends, accord is signed. **3 April:** The Kabul government creates Sar-i Pol Province and appoints Gharib Husain as governor.

The new province is part of the Hazarajat. **14 April:** Afghanistan, Pakistan, the Soviet Union, and the United States sign the Geneva accords. Under the agreement the Soviet Union will withdraw its troops within nine months. The United States and the Soviet Union will be the guarantors of the agreement, which also provides for the return of Afghan refugees and a halt to military aid by both sides. **21 April:** President Najibullah says that 1.55 million voted in the Afghan elections. **25 April:** A UN "implementation assistance group," headed by Finnish Maj. Gen. Rauli Helminen, arrives in Islamabad to monitor the Geneva accords. **28 April:** President Najibullah says that Soviet military advisers will remain after the Soviet troop withdrawal. **11 May:** The United Nations appoints Sadruddin Agha Khan as coordinator for relief and resettlement in Afghanistan. **15 May:** The Soviet Union begins withdrawing troops from Afghanistan. **25 May:** The Soviet Union announces the following casualties in the Afghan war: 13,310 dead, 35,478 wounded, and 311 missing. **26 May:** Muhammad Hasan Sharq is appointed prime minister, replacing Sultan Ali Keshtmand who becomes secretary of the PDPA central committee. **31 May:** A State Department official says U.S. aid to the mujahedin will continue because the Soviet Union plans to leave $1 billion worth of equipment in Afghanistan. **7 June:** President Najibullah addresses the UN General Assembly, complaining that Pakistan continues to violate the Geneva accords. **9 June:** President Najibullah says, according to the Bakhtar news agency, that 243,900 soldiers and civilians have died in 10 years of war. **15 June:** Pir Sayyid Ahmad Gailani, head of the National Islamic Front, becomes spokesman of the seven-member mujahedin alliance. **16 June:** President Najibullah announces the formation of a new government:

Muhammad Hasan Sharq	Prime Minister
Abdul Wakil	Foreign Affairs
Sayyid Muhammad Gulabzoi	Interior
Ghulam Faruq Yaqubi	State Security
Hamidullah Tarzi	Finance
Muhammad Bashir Baghlani	Justice
Shah Muhammad Dost	UN Representative
Muhd. Aslam Watanjar	Communications
Muhd. Khan Jalallar	Commerce
Abdul Ghafur	Returnees Affairs
Sulaiman Layeq	Tribal Affairs
Sultan Husain	Planning
Muhd. Asef Zaher	Rural Development

Muhammad Ghofran	Agric. & Land Reform
Abdul Fatah Najm	Public Health
Ghulam Rasul	Education
Nur Ahmad Barits	Higher Education
Muhd. Ishaq Kawa	Mines, Industries
Muhammad Aziz	Transportation
Nazar Muhammad	Construction
Pacha Gul Wafadar	Civil Aviation
Dost Muhd. Fazl	Light Industries and Foodstuffs
Raz Muhammad Paktin	Water and Power

Without Portfolio: Nematullah Pazhwak, Fazl Haq Khaliqyar, Sarjang Khan Jaji. **18 July:** Sebghatullah Mujaddidi's National Front for the Liberation of Afghanistan joins Sayyid Ahmad Gailani's National Islamic Front of Afghanistan in expressing support for UN envoy Diego Cordovez's peace plan to establish a neutral government. **27 July:** The Kabul government announces the permission for formation of a new party, the Union of God's Helpers (Ittehadia-ye Ansarullah). **1 August:** The Constitution Council is set up to examine the constitutionality of laws and compliance of treaties and laws. **8 August:** Soviet troops begin withdrawing from Kabul. **17 August:** Lt. Gen. Shahnawaz Tanai is appointed defense minister and Maj. Gen. Muhammad Asef Delawar is appointed chief of the Armed Forces General Staff. **13 October:** Yuli Vorontsov, Soviet first deputy foreign minister, is appointed ambassador to Kabul. **17 October:** Burhanuddin Rabbani, head of the Jam'iat-i Islami, becomes spokesman of the seven-member mujahedin alliance. **19 November:** Soviet military command in Afghanistan warns if guerrillas escalate war, they will jeopardize the withdrawal of Soviet troops. **3 December:** Alliance leaders, headed by Burhanuddin Rabbani, meet in Ta'if, Saudi Arabia, for talks with Soviet Deputy Minister Vorontsov. **25 December:** Soviet Deputy Yuri Vorontsov meets with ex-King Muhammad Zahir in Rome (at the request of Moscow).

1989 2 January: Sebghatullah Mujaddidi succeeds Rabbani as spokesman of the alliance. **13 January:** Soviet Foreign Minister Edward Shevardnadze arrives in Kabul. **18 January:** Sebghatullah Mujaddidi returns from Iran where he unsuccessfully tries to invite the Shi'a mujahedin groups to join an interim government. **25 January:** The United States decides to close its embassy. **27 January:** Britain, France, Japan, and Italy announce their decision to withdraw their diplomats from Kabul.

28 January: Soviet Defense Minister Dimitri Yazov ends two days of talks with President Najibullah. He says Moscow will "not abandon its friends." **30 January:** The United States formally closes its embassy. **2 February:** President Najibullah denounces the closing of Western embassies as "psychological war." In Peshawar some 500 Afghans demonstrate for the return of ex-King Muhammad Zahir. **7 February:** A mujahedin commander says that the "Pakistanis are pushing us now to do an all-out attack on Jalalabad," but the mujahedin want to wait to prevent a bloodbath. **13 February:** President George Bush signs a National Security Directive pledging continued financial and military support. **14 February:** The last Soviet soldier leaves Kabul airport. **15 February:** The United States rejects a Soviet call for an end to arms shipments to Afghanistan. **18 February:** The government declares a nationwide state of emergency. President Najibullah appoints new cabinet members. Muhammad Nabi Muhammadi becomes spokesman of the mujahedin alliance. **20 February:** Prime Minister Sharq resigns. **21 February:** Sultan Ali Keshtmand is appointed chairman of the executive committee of the council of ministers. **23 February:** Mujahedin leaders elect Abdul Rasul Sayyaf as acting prime minister and Sebghatullah Mujaddidi as acting president of the interim government. The portfolios are distributed as follows:

Muhd. Nabi Muhammadi	Defense
Muhd. Shah Fazli (Harakat)	Scientific Research
Maulawi Islamuddin (Harakat)	Agriculture
Gulbuddin Hekmatyar (Hizb)	Foreign Affairs
Ali Ansari (Hizb-H)	Frontier Affairs
Qazi Najibullah (Hizb-H)	Justice
Yunus Khalis (Hizb-K)	Interior
Haji Din Muhd. (Hizb-K)	National Security
Maulawi Abdul Razzaq (H-K)	Religious Affairs
Burhanuddin Rabbani (Jam)	Reconstruction
Najibullah Lafra'i (Jam)	Islamic Guidance
Ishan Jan (Jam)	Mining, Industries
Ahmad Shah (Ittihad)	Communications
Sayyid Nadir Khurram (Jabha)	Health

Pir Sayyid Gailani challenges the legitimacy of the government. **5 March:** The mujahedin launch an offensive against Jalalabad. **16 March:** Afghan Army Chief of Staff Lt. Gen. Asef Delawar is reported in Jalalabad supervising its defense. **20 March:** Mujahedin attempt to capture

Jalalabad fails. **24 March:** An 85-truck government convoy breaks through to Jalalabad. **27 March:** President Najibullah offers mujahedin commanders autonomy if they end the war. A council of 35 commanders rejects the offer. **6 April:** U.S. Secretary of State James Baker recommends Peter Tomsen as special envoy to the mujahedin with the rank of ambassador. **12 April:** The mujahedin cabinet begin a three-day session in Afghan territory. **24 April:** Afghan Foreign Minister Abdul Wakil accuses Pakistan of aggression. **6 May:** Valentin I. Varennikov, Soviet deputy minister of defense, ends a four-day visit to Kabul. **9 May:** Sayyid Ahmad Gailani challenges the legitimacy of the interim government. **16 May:** KHAD chief Abdul Rahman is said to have defected to Yunis Khalis mujahedin group. **17 May:** Government troops reopen Jalalabad-Kabul road. **21 May:** President Najibullah invites mujahedin leaders and commanders to take part in the Loya Jirga. **24 May:** President Najibullah offers regional autonomy to mujahedin commanders if they agree to stop fighting. A convoy of Soviet-made tanks and artillery arrives in Kabul. **24 June:** President Najibullah appoints Mahmud Baryalai as first deputy prime minister. **5 July:** Government troops recapture Tor Kham. **19 July:** Units of Burhanuddin Rabbani and Muhd. Nabi Muhammadi are fighting over turf in Helmand Province. **24 July:** Defense Minister Shahnawaz Tanai is said to be under house arrest. **26 July:** Najmuddin Kawiani, head of foreign relations committee of the national assembly and politburo member, reports secret peace talks with the "opposition." **29 July:** Nur Ahmad Nur is appointed ambassador and permanent representative to the United Nations. **1 August:** Defense Minister Tanai is reported to be implicated in coup attempt. **11 August:** Abdul Rasul Sayyaf, prime minister, rejects Gulbuddin Hekmatyar's suggestion that the rebels should take control by backing an army coup. **14 August:** Government spokesman Muhammad Nabi Amani says 183 civilians were killed in Kabul by rockets in one week. **25 August:** Jam'iat-i Islami Commander Ahmad Shah Mas'ud accuses Hizb-i-Islami of collusion with Kabul government. **29 August:** Fighters of Sayyaf and Muhammadi battle over control of a bridge in Helmand Province that produces lucrative tax and toll revenues. **30 August:** Gulbuddin Hekmatyar's Hizb-i Islami withdraws from the mujahedin alliance. **17 October:** Boris Nikolayevich Pastukhov, Soviet ambassador, presents his credentials. **7 November:** Lt. Gen. Ali Akbar is killed in fighting in Kandahar. **14 November:** Mujahedin launch a three-pronged attack on Jalalabad that is repulsed. **21 November:** President Najibullah extends the state of emergency for another six months. **30 November:** Mujahedin leaders Burhanuddin Rabbani and Gulbuddin Hekmatyar announce a cease-fire and exchange of prisoners and captured land. **2 December:** The Kabul government arrests 127 people suspected of plotting a coup. Brig. Gen. Ghulam Haidar is killed in fighting at Jalalabad. **21 December:** Jam'iat executes four members of Hizb, including Sayyid Jamal, who had ambushed Jam'iat commanders. **31 December:** President Najibullah calls for PDPA to change its name.

1990 24 January: President Najibullah says that he will step down if his government is defeated in UN-supervised elections. **2 February:** Some 10,000 refugees demonstrate in favor of the return of Zahir Shah in Quetta. **5 March:** Trials begin of some 124 Afghans arrested in December and charged with plotting a coup. **6 March:** Defense Minister Shahnawaz Tanai launches a coup against President Najibullah. **7 March:** Gulbuddin Hekmatyar says his forces are supporting the Tanai coup. **9 March:** Government troops recapture the Bagram air base. Other mujahedin groups refuse to support the Tanai coup. **6 April:** Two generals and 11 other people are killed at a ceremony when a mujahedin group that promised to surrender opens fire on government troops. Fazl Haq Khaliqyar, governor of Herat, is wounded. **14 April:** The Kabul government accuses the United Nations of failing to monitor alleged violations of the Geneva accords. **21 May:** Prime Minister Khaliqyar presents his new cabinet. **28 May:** Kabul government convenes a Loya Jirga in preparation for amending the constitution. **16 June:** Nine Shi'a mujahedin parties unite in the Hizb-i Wahdat, Party of Unity. **22 June:** Conference of mujahedin commanders in Paktia Province. **27 June:** Opening of the second party congress that reelects Dr. Najibullah and changes the name of the party to "Homeland Party" (Hizb-i Watan). **30 June:** Meeting of former prominent government officials at the invitation of President Mujaddidi. Members invited include:

Muhammad Yusuf, prime minister
Abdul Samad Hamed, minister
Rawan Farhadi, minister and diplomat
Sabbahuddin Kushkaki, minister and writer
Abdul Hakim Tabibi, minister and diplomat
Nangyalai Tarzi, diplomat
Humayun Asefi, diplomat
Agha Jan Barakzai
Sayyid Ishaq Gailani, mujahedin leader
Sayyid Makhdum Rahin, poet and writer

Abdul Ahad Karzai, member of parliament
Abdul Hai Tokhi (Tukhay)
Abdur Rahman Ulfat, adviser
Ihsanullah Mayar
Sayyid Asadullah Nuktadan
Abdul Aziz Firogh
Abdul Qadir Nurzai
Wali Ahmad Sherzai
Enayatullah Iblagh
Ishaq Akhlaqi
Muhammad Akram, scholar and diplomat
Muhammad Anwar Sherzai
Siddiq Rashid Saljuqi
Muhammad Gulab Nangarhari, minister and poet
Muhammad Hashim Mujaddidi, educator and senator
Muhammad Yahya Nauruz, general

Members of the Shi'a Wahdat alliance of mujahedin groups also participated. **29 July-25 August:** Najibullah visits the Soviet Union; Abdul Rahim Hatef is acting president. **11 September:** Najibullah decrees legalization of political parties. **5 October:** Tirin Kot, administrative center of Oruzgan Province, captured by mujahedin forces. **15 October:** Mas'ud, the Jam'iat commander, visits Islamabad where he meets the Pakistani head of state and Gulbuddin Hekmatyar. **25 October:** The U.S. Congress reduces its aid to the Afghan resistance. **19 November:** President Najibullah arrives in Switzerland for discussions with Afghan personalities.

1991 31 March: Khost captured by mujahedin forces headed by Commander Haqani, prisoners taken included seven generals (including Col. Gen. Muhammad Zahir Solamal, deputy minister of defense; Maj. Gen. Ghulam Mustafa, chief of political affairs of the armed force; Maj. Gen. Muhammad Qasim, commander of artillery, special guards; Major Muhammad Azam, an air force commander; Lt. Gen. Shirin, commander of the Khost militia units). **2 April:** Kabul government declares a "Day of Mourning." **10 April:** Vice President Sultan Ali Keshtmand is dismissed. **16 April:** President Najibullah offers a new amnesty to all Afghans living abroad who return to Afghanistan. **20 April:** Explosion at Jamilurrahman's Asadabad (Wahhabi) headquarters in Kunar Province results in some 500 killed and 700 wounded. **26 April:** Representatives of the Pakistani military intelligence service (ISI) meet in Geneva with representatives of the Kabul government. **21 May:** Javier Perez de Cuéllar, United Nations secretary general, issues a five-point proposal for a political settlement in Afghanistan. **27-28 May:** Soviet-Pakistan talks in Moscow about Afghanistan. **20 June:** Babrak Karmal returns to Afghanistan from exile in the Soviet Union. **22 July:** Mas'ud takes Ishkashem and shortly thereafter the Wakhan Corridor. **13 September:** USSR and United States agree to end delivery of weapons to the Afghan combatants as of January 1, 1992. **4 November:** Former King Zahir is slightly wounded in an assassination attempt. **5 December:** UN agrees on solution for transfer of government. **15 December:** Soviet Union stops arms deliveries to Afghanistan.

1992 1 January: Moscow ends assistance to Afghanistan. **14 January:** Najibullah annuls Decree 14, depriving the royal family of its property. **6 February:** Gens. Dostum, Shah Nasir Naderi, and Momen rebel against Najibullah government. **15 March:** Mujahedin seize Samangan Province. **18 March:** President Najibullah agrees to resign as soon as interim government is installed. **29 March:** Wahdat party takes Sar-i Pol. **8 April:** Gen. Dostum takes over Mazar-i Sharif. **12 April:** Masud takes control of Salang Tunnel. **15 April:** Dostum militia takes Kabul airport. **16 April:** Najibullah takes refuge in UN compound. Ghazni and Gardez taken by the resistance. **18 April:** Kunduz and Jalalabad fall to the resistance. Rahim Hatef nominated as interim president. **21 April:** Pul-i Alam in Logar taken by Hizb-i Islami. **22 April:** Gardez taken by Jalaluddin Haqani. **24 April:** Resistance leaders set up interim Islamic council of 51 members. Sebghatullah Mujaddidi assumes provisional control. Jalalabad taken by mujahedin. **25 April:** Resistance enters Kabul, partisans of Mas'ud and Hekmatyar fight. **26 April:** Mas'ud takes presidential palace and takes barracks from Hizb-i Islami. Shi'a Harakat-i Islami takes missile base of Darulaman. **28 April:** Mujaddidi arrives in Kabul, proclaims Islamic State of Afghanistan, and announces general amnesty. **29 April:** Hizb-i Islami fighters ejected from interior ministry. Mas'ud arrives in Kabul. **3 May:** Egypt recognizes Islamic State of Afghanistan. Hekmatyar threatens to attack if Dostum does not leave Kabul. **6 May:** First session of the Jehad Council under the presidency of Prof. Rabbani. **10 May:** Sayyid Ahmad Gailani arrives at Kabul. **21 May:** Mas'ud and Hekmatyar conclude cease-fire. Yunus Khales arrives at Kabul. **30 May:** Dostum and Hekmatyar fight for control of Karte Nau district. **19 June:** Dostum militia and Mas'ud's forces clash. **28 June:** Mujaddidi surrenders presidency to Rabbani. **4 July:** Violent artillery combat between forces of Dostum and

Hekmatyar. **2 August:** Khales resigns from Jehad Council. **27 August:** Cease-fire concluded between Rabbani and Hekmatyar. **5 September:** Uzbek militia quits Kabul. **17 September:** Agreement of Paghman between Rabbani and Hekmatyar, designation of an assembly for choosing the successor of Rabbani. **27 October:** Leadership Council, headed by President Rabbani, elected to extend Rabbani's term by two months. **12 December:** Interim President Rabbani announced that he would hold his post beyond his term until a successor is chosen. **30 December:** The Resolution and Settlement Council voted to keep Rabbani in power. Five of the nine mujahedin factions refused to participate.

1993 2 January: Rabbani steps down as head of the Jami'at Party. **3 February:** UN suspends its aid shipments by way of south and eastern Afghanistan. **6 February:** General Dostum is nominated deputy minister of defense. **11 February:** The imam of al-Azhar University calls on the mujahedin to stop fighting and direct their efforts to areas where Muslims are still oppressed. **16 February:** Shooting in Kabul stopped for the first time since January 19. **7 March:** The Islamabad Accord between Afghan parties (except Khales and Dostum) nominates Rabbani president for 18 months and Hekmatyar prime minister. A defense council of all parties is to be in charge of the ministry of defense; all heavy weapons are to be removed from the capital; a council to be elected in eight months, and presidential and legislative elections to be held in mid-1995. The Organization of the Islamic Conference, the Afghan parties, and Pakistan should supervise the cease-fire. **8 March:** Hizb-i Islami and Wahdat fire 70 missiles on Kabul. **11 March:** The leaders assemble at Mecca to fix the details of the prerogatives of the prime minister, the control of the defense council, and the power of the Uzbek militia. The accord is countersigned by King Fahd. **19-20 March:** Reunion at Jalalabad fails to achieve agreement. **22 March:** Fighting between Wahdat and Ittihad continues in Kabul. **23 March:** Hizb-i Islami captures Naghlu dam from Harakat-e Inqilab-i-Islami. Pakistani militia seize Stinger missiles from Mulla Abdul Salam (Mulla Roketi), and the mulla takes 27 hostages in reprisal. **28 March:** General Fauzi, a spokesman of Dostum, declares that there will be no peace without representation of Dostum in the Kabul government. **1 April:** Jam'iat and Hizb form a committee to resolve their problems. **2 April:** Jam'iat and Wahdat agree to release prisoners and restore quiet. **7 April:** Afghan defense minister claims that Hekmatyar and Sayyaf supply weapons to Tajik Islamists. **9 April:** First break in the cease-fire between Jam'iat and Wahdat. **15 April:** The governors of Herat and Khorasan, Iran, sign an accord of cooperation against the drug traffic. **9-10 May:**

Heavy fighting between forces of Ittihad and Wahdat in Kabul. **11 May:** Kabul Museum burns. **12 May:** Bombardment of Kabul resumed. **13 May:** Mas'ud gains help of Dostum against Hizb-i Islami forces. **19 May:** Rabbani and Hekmatyar agree to a cease-fire. **20 May:** Mas'ud resigns as defense minister. **6 June:** Hekmatyar presides at the first meeting of his government at Charasiab. **17 June:** Government meets in Paghman. **21 June:** Council of ministers meets in Darulaman. **23-28 June:** Fighting between Wahdat and Mas'ud forces. **3 July:** President Rabbani receives General Dostum. **12 July:** Dostum and Hekmatyar meet and agree to a cease-fire. **26 July:** Mas'ud's forces take Bagram air base from Ittihad. **31 August:** Cease-fire between Ittihad and Wahdat. **14 September:** Hizb-i Islami bombards eastern Kabul. **15 September:** The Afghan Communist Party is said to have had a meeting in Microrayon and elected Mahmud Baryalai to head the party. **19 October:** Kabul-Jalalabad Highway is reopened for traffic. **24 October:** Afghanistan and Tajikistan sign an agreement to export natural gas to Tajikistan. **2 November:** A Russian plane bombards Badakhshan. **9 November:** Ms. Robin Raphel, American undersecretary of state for South Asia, visits Kabul regarding economic and humanitarian aid. She meets Rabbani, Hekmatyar, Mas'ud, and Dostum. **21 November:** Islamist ideologue Hasan Al-Turabi visits Kabul. **3 December:** Telephone connection with Kabul restored. **23 December:** Gen. Dostum regains Sher Khan Bandar without a fight.

1994 1 January: Forces of Dostum and Hekmatyar attack Kabul forces. **5 January:** Rabbani forces take Kabul airport. General Momen killed in helicopter accident. **6 January:** Fighting around Bala Hisar and Microrayon. Mujaddidi supports Dostum-Hekmatyar alliance. **10 January:** Pul-i Khishti mosque destroyed. **2 April:** M. Mestiri, UN emissary, arrives in Kabul and meets with Rabbani, Mas'ud, and Hekmatyar. **4 April:** Mas'ud's forces attack Pul-i Khumri, held by Dostum and Isma'ili forces. **6 April:** Mestiri leaves Kabul without obtaining a cease-fire between the belligerents. **19 April:** Rabbani announces his intention to extend his mandate until December 1994, because his adversaries did not respect the accords of Jalalabad. **24 April:** Mulla Salam, also called Mulla Roketi, holds two Chinese engineers and 10 Pakistanis and demands that Pakistan free his brother and return the three Stingers captured from him. **27 April:** According to the International Red Cross, the civil war in Kabul has resulted in 2,500 deaths, 17,000 wounded, and 632,000 refugees from Kabul since January 1, 1994. At least 20,000 houses were destroyed. **1 May:** Offensive of Hekmatyar forces against Kabul is stopped. **9 May:**

Kabul air force bombards Mazar and Pul-i Khumri. **13-14 May:** Dostum bombards the 10th Division at Qargha near Kabul. **17-18 May:** Sayyaf takes Maidan Shahr from Hekmatyar forces. **21-22 May:** General Dostum indicates having used six Stinger missiles to down two of Rabbani's aircraft. Dostum's head of the air force, Gen. Jalil, claims to have 32 operational planes, more than 22,000 bombs, and 100 pilots. **28 May:** Conflict within Wahdat between supporters of Muhammad Akbari and Abdul Ali Mazari. **3 June:** Dostum and Isma'il Khan forces clash in Shindand. Dostum bombs Herat. **8 June:** Rabbani proposes that his successor be chosen by a Loya Jirga. **10 June:** Fighting resumes in Kabul. **15 June:** Rabbani extends his "mandate," which was to expire in June, for another six months. **19 June:** Isma'il Khan escapes an assassination attempt. **25 June:** Harakat recaptures control of Darulaman palace from Hizb-i Islami. **26 June:** Rabbani's forces expel Dostum's forces from the Bala Hisar and Maranjan hill. **8 July:** The parties of Gailani, Hekmatyar, Mujaddidi, Muhammadi, Muhseni, Mazari, and Dostum form a commission to negotiate with Rabbani and Sayyaf. **14 July:** Pakistani minister of foreign affairs threatens to close the offices of Sayyaf's party if Mulla Roketi does not liberate his hostages. They are freed on July 21. **20 July:** Official opening of the Herat assembly in the presence of 700 participants. **24 July:** Rabbani arrives at Herat, but does not participate in the assembly. **August:** Mulla Muhammad Omar founds Taliban movement. **7 August:** Rabbani receives Muhammadi, Muhseni, and Gailani at Kabul. **8 September:** Hizb-i Islami takes control of Khenjan north of the Salang Pass. **12 September:** Fighting breaks out between Wahdat and Harakat for control of Darulaman. Akbari defects from Wahdat. **25 September:** Iranian intermediaries help in establishing a cease-fire between the Shi'a parties. **2 October:** Pakistan holds goods destined for Afghanistan in Karachi. **11 October:** According to the International Red Cross, 1,100 people were killed and 23,000 wounded in Kabul in September. **2 November:** A Pakistani convoy of goods destined for Turkmenistan is stopped by commanders between Spin Boldak and Kandahar. Taliban clash with commanders. **5 November:** The Taliban free the route to Kandahar; the commander of the Muslim group is hanged. **7 November:** A spokesman of Rabbani accuses Uzbekistan of interference in Afghan internal affairs for having delivered 30 Russian tanks to Dostum. **8 November:** Visit to Kabul by a UN delegation for the first time in seven months. **13 November:** Having repelled the commanders Lalay (Mahaz) and Sarkateb (Hizb-i-Hekmatyar), the Taliban take control of Kandahar. **17 November:** The Pakistani minister of the interior announces that

Pakistan will start to repair the route from Kandahar to Herat. Kabul calls this an invasion of Afghanistan. **25 November:** Taliban take control of Helmand Province. **5 December:** Arrival at Kabul of the first aid convoy in six months, 32 trucks for Rabbani and 32 for his opponents. **6 December:** Return to Pakistan of the convoy from Turkmenistan. **13 December:** Arrival of a UN aid convoy in Kunduz, the first in two years. **20 December:** Dostum arrives in Islamabad. **28 December:** Mestiri arrives in Islamabad to restart his peace effort.

1995 1 January: Some 3,000 Pakistani Taliban leave for Afghanistan. M. Mestiri arrives in Kabul during an unofficial cease-fire. Yunus Khales returns to Jalalabad after an absence of 19 years. **4 January:** Mestiri opens a new UN office in Jalalabad and meets with Hekmatyar. The American ambassador to Pakistan meets Rabbani at Kabul. **22 January:** The access roads to Kabul are again closed by the Hizb of Hekmatyar. **24 January:** The Taliban take Ghazni. **30 January:** Dostum's forces capture Kunduz. **10 February:** Taliban capture Maidan Shahr. Mestiri announces a power transfer for February 20, at which Rabbani is to transfer power to a committee of 20 persons. **11 February:** The Taliban claim capture of Pul-i Alam and control of the entire Logar Province. **14 February:** Hekmatyar withdraws his forces from the Kabul area to Sarobi, abandoning his heavy weapons. **15 February:** The Taliban occupy Pul-i Charkhi and expel the Hizb-i Islami from Khost. **16 February:** Rabbani's forces retake Kunduz. **17 February:** Kabul airport reopens after being closed for more than a year. **19 February:** The Taliban take Sharan, center of Paktika, and Gardez, center of Paktia. **20 February:** Jam'iat forces fight Wahdat. Mestiri admits failure of his plan for transfer of power in Kabul. **25 February:** The Taliban threaten to attack Kabul if Rabbani does not lay down his arms. **5 March:** Mazari declares his readiness to recognize the Kabul government if the Hazara get 25% representation. **6 March:** Jam'iat forces attack the positions of Wahdat at Kabul. **7 March:** Mazari threatens to use SCUD missiles if Rabbani's forces will not stop their attacks. **9 March:** Wahdat surrenders its position south of Kabul to the Taliban. **10 March:** Nabi Muhammadi deserts Rabbani for the Taliban. Sayyaf sells his arms depot at the Pakistani border to a Trimangal tribal chief. **11 March:** Kabul forces capture all the territory held by Wahdat, including the SCUD base at Darulaman and Kabul Museum. **13 March:** Mazari and a number of Wahdat leaders are killed while in Taliban captivity. **14 March:** The Taliban claim conquest of Nimruz Province. **19 March:** Mas'ud's forces take Charasiab from the Taliban. **1 April:**

Mujaddidi replaces Hekmatyar as head of the four-party opponents of Rabbani. **4 April:** Taliban attack the Shindand air base and Herat. Also fight Jam'iat forces in Maidan Shahr. **7 April:** Iran prohibits commercial transit to Afghanistan. **12 April:** Jam'iat emissary Abdul Rahman meets Dostum in Tashkent. **13 April:** Taliban demand that foreign states not reopen their embassies in Kabul. **19 April:** The Taliban block the delivery of fuel to Kabul. Hizb and Taliban establish contacts. **27 April:** The Taliban free 300 captives of Dostum's forces. **28 April:** Taliban defeated in the Farah area. **9 May:** The Pakistani ambassador returns to Kabul. Forces of Isma'il Khan take Farah. **15 May:** Forces of Rabbani capture Zaranj from the Taliban. **24 May:** Continuation of stalled negotiation between representatives of Dostum and Rabbani. Questions raised are opening of the Salang route and lifting of the fatwa proclaiming holy war against Dostum. **20 June:** Jam'iat forces take control of Bamian from the Shi'a Wahdat. **29 June:** Sardar Abdul Wali, son-in-law of ex-King Zahir Shah, arrives in Islamabad at invitation of Pakistan government. **20 August:** Abdul Wali returns to Rome. **26 August:** Taliban take Girishk. **31 August:** Taliban take Delaram. **2 September:** Taliban take Shindand. **5 September:** Taliban take Herat and Islam Qala. Ismail Khan flees to Iran. **6 September:** Kabuli crowds attack Pakistan embassy, one is killed and 20 persons wounded, including the ambassador. **7 September:** Taliban take Ghor Province. **15 September:** Explosion in Herat by enemies of Taliban. **10 November:** UNICEF suspends educational assistance to Taliban-controlled areas because of the closing of girls' schools.

1996 3 April: About 1,000 members of the *ulama* choose Taliban Mulla Muhammad Omar as Amir al-Mu'minin. **24 May:** Hekmatyar concludes an anti-Taliban treaty with Rabbani. Hekmatyar rejoins Kabul government as prime minister; upon arrival in Kabul orders all cinemas closed and forbids music to be broadcast on Kabul Radio and Television. He advises women to observe Islamic code of dress and orders government officials to perform their noon prayers in their places of work. **1 June:** Taliban take Chaghcharan, capital of Ghor Province. **18 June:** Taliban take a government base at Nimruz. **6 July:** Prime Minister Hekmatyar forms new cabinet: Wahidullah Sabawun (of Hizb) Defense; Abdul Hadi Arghandiwal (of Hizb) Finance; Muhammad Yunus Qanuni (of Jam'iat) Interior; Ahmad Shah Ahmadzai (of Ittihad) Education; Qayamullah Kashaf (of Ittihad) Information and Culture; Sayyid Ali Javid (Harakat of Muhsini), Planning; Sayyid Husain Anwari (of Harakat) Work and Social Affairs; Maulawi Samiullah Najibi (of Kunar Jama'at Tauhid) Martyrs and

Disabled; Sayyid Husain Alami (of Akbari Wahdat) Commerce; and Qutbuddin Helal (faction not known) deputy prime minister. **10 July:** Norbert Holl, a German diplomat, is nominated as special representative of the UN for Afghanistan. **17 July:** Sayyid Gailani announces creation of a new alliance, including Mujaddidi, Dostum, Khalili (Wahdat), Muhammad Nabi, and the Jalalabad Shura, headed by Haji Qadir. **27 July:** Norbert Holl arrives at Kabul. **11 September:** Taliban capture Jalalabad from Shura and prepare for attack on Sarobi. **12 September:** Taliban capture Laghman Province and its capital, Mehterlam. **22 September:** Taliban capture Kunar Province. **25 September:** Taliban capture Sarobi. **27 September:** Taliban capture Kabul, torture and execute ex-President Najibullah and his brother Shapur Ahmadzai. They also kill General Jaffar and M. Tokhi who shared UN shelter with Najibullah. Taliban announce establishment of an Islamic state. Taliban take Bagram and Charikar. **28 September:** Sebghatullah Mujaddidi announces his support for the Taliban. Taliban close girls' schools, ban women from working in public. Women must wear the chatri (burqa) and be accompanied in public by a close male relative. **29 September:** Taliban take Jabal-us-Siraj. M. Holl, special UN envoy for Afghanistan, arrives in Kabul. **3 October:** Men ordered to wear turbans and grow fist-length beards. **10 October:** A defensive alliance is concluded between General Dostum, Ahmad Shah Mas'ud, and Abdul Karim Khalili. **12 October:** Forces of Mas'ud retake Jabal-us-Siraj. **13 October:** Mas'ud retakes Charikar. **15 October:** Mas'ud forces retake Bagram. **25 October:** Taliban claim to have captured Qala-i Nau in Badghis Province. **27 October:** Forces of Dostum retake Badghis Province. **31 October:** Troops of Ismail Khan flown from Iran to Maimana to fight Taliban forces. **5 November:** General Tanai, minister of defense under the Najibullah regime, gives his support to the Taliban. **24 November:** Taliban take Kalakan village. **27 November:** Taliban take Istalif. **1 December:** Babrak Karmal dies.

1997 4 January: Mulla Omar orders the people to pray for rain or snow. **6 January:** The medical faculty of Jalalabad University opens without female students. **6 January:** Forces of General Dostum attack Taliban troops in Badghis. **7 January:** An American delegation meets with Mulla Hasan, vice president of the Taliban council, to discuss the elimination of drug trafficking and the termination of international terrorism. **12 January:** The afghani has fallen to 28,200 for one dollar. **16 January:** Taliban take Bagram and Charikar. **17 January:** Taliban move into Kapisa Province, take Mahmud Raqi. **2 February:** Taliban delegation visits the United States. **15 February:** Government officials and military are not permitted to smoke. **27 February:** Taliban government forbids the possession of foreign magazines and books. Kabul University opens without female students. **20 March:** General Abdul Malik captures Badghis, Faryab, and Sar-i-Pol Provinces, surrenders 700 prisoners and Ismail Khan to the Taliban. Taliban prohibit New Year (nauruz) celebrations. **March:** Taliban government declines to extradite Osama bin Laden. The Taliban take Kunduz. **13 May:** Afghan opposition forms new government in Mazar-i Sharif. **19 May:** General Abdul Malik revolts, forces General Dostum to flee to Turkish exile. **24 May:** Taliban enter Mazar-i Sharif with the support of Abdul Malik. **25 May:** Pakistan recognizes the Taliban government. **26 May:** Saudi Arabia recognizes the Taliban government. **28 May:** Taliban want to disarm Abdul Malik's forces, he turns against them and, with the help of the shi'a hizb-i wahdat, defeats Taliban who suffer hundreds killed. **2 July:** The Taliban take Khanabad. **4 July:** General Malik closes the Pakistan consulate in Mazar-i Sharif. **11 August:** The principal leaders of the opposition, including Masud, Abdul Malik, Rabbani, and Khalili, meet at the Salang Pass for strategy discussions. **14 August:** United States decides to temporarily close the Afghan embassy in Washington to avoid recognizing the Taliban government. **21 August:** Abdul Rahim Ghafurzai, newly elected prime minister of the Northern Alliance, is killed in Bamian in an airplane accident. **5 September:** Abdullah Abdullah, deputy foreign minister of the Rabbani government, represents Afghanistan at the UN General Assembly. **9 September:** The Taliban take Mazar-i Sharif. General Malik is expelled with the support of the Pashtun hizb-i Islami. **12 September:** The Taliban are expelled from Mazar-i Sharif. **4 October:** The opposition takes Mazar-i Sharif from the Taliban. **14 October:** General Dostum returns to Mazar-i Sharif, forces Abdul Malik to flee. **19 October:** Sick women are removed from Wazir Akbar Khan and Karte Se hospitals. Women are to be kept in a separate hospital. **26 October:** The Taliban change the name of Afghanistan to The Islamic Emirate (Amirat) of Afghanistan. **November:** General Malik flees into exile. **16 November:** General Dostum reveals mass graves of 2,000 Taliban. **16 December:** A UN spokesman confirms that hundreds of Taliban were massacred in September and their bodies thrown into well pits.

1998 6 January: President Rabbani visits Iran, Pakistan, and Tajikistan to gain support for a regional conference on Afghanistan. The Taliban are accused of having massacred 600 civilians in Fariab Province. **4 February:** Earthquake in northeastern Afghanistan kills 4,000 and renders

15,000 homeless. **23 February:** Creation in Peshawar of the "World Front of Jihad against Jews and Crusaders." Osama bin Laden is one of the founders. **26 February:** Three men accused of sodomy were put against a wall in Kandahar, which was toppled over them. One man who survived was freed. Mulla Muhammad Omar, head of the Taliban, and a large number of spectators attended the event. **5 March:** The Taliban government adopted the lunar calendar as the official means of reckoning time. **7 April:** Osama bin Laden participates at public prayers in Kandahar on the occasion of the Feast of Sacrifice. **23 April:** American diplomats arrive in Kabul for discussion about the increase in poppy cultivation. **24 May:** The Taliban government punishes 490 men for cutting their beards and 110 women for being insufficiently veiled. **25 May:** The department for "Enjoining the Good and Forbidding Evil" is elevated to the rank of ministry. **27 May:** In a press conference in Khost, Osama bin Laden calls for a new jihad against the American forces stationed in Saudi Arabia. **29 May:** Mulla Omar cancels the amnesty granted to former communists. **16 June:** The Taliban orders all girls schools in private homes closed. **8 July:** The Taliban order all television sets destroyed and testing of individuals on their knowledge of Islam. **9 July:** Taliban forbid conversions of Afghan Muslims to another religion. **7 August:** Car bombs destroy U.S. embassies in Kenya and Tanzania. The attacks are blamed on Osama bin Laden. **9 August:** A force of 5,000 Taliban captures Mazar-i Sharif. Iran accuses the Taliban of having assassinated 10 Iranian diplomats and one journalist. **18 August:** Madeleine Albright, American foreign secretary, demands that the Taliban deliver Osama bin Laden, form a broad-based government, and improve the human rights condition in Afghanistan as a precondition to recognition by the United States. **20 August:** The United States fires cruise missiles on camps of Bin Laden and groups held responsible for attacks on American embassies in Kenya and Tanzania. **13 September:** Taliban capture Bamian. **22 September:** Saudi Arabia recalls it chargé d'affaires at Kabul. **27 September:** Mulla Omar announces that any believer who cannot recite correctly the five prayers will be punished. **14 October:** Lakhdar Bahimi holds talks with Mulla Muhammad Omar. **22 October:** The Taliban government orders Hindus to wear yellow distinguishing marks on their clothing. **4 November:** The United States offers $5 million for the capture of Osama bin Laden. **13 November:** Muhammad Akbari, a chief of the shi'a Hizb-i Wahdat, surrenders to the Taliban. **23 December:** Taliban government changes the name of Pashtunistan Square to Ahmad Shah Baba Square.

1999 2 February: U.S. Deputy Secretary of State Strobe Talbott meets with Taliban in Islamabad, demands surrender of Osama bin Laden. Taliban reject demand. **19 February:** The Taliban order the destruction of all heroin laboratories. **21 April:** Hizb-i Wahdat captures Bamian. **26 April:** Afghan Shi'ites celebrate their traditional Ashura ceremonies at Kabul. But public celebrations are prohibited. **30 April:** Ex-King Muhammad Zahir proposes formation of a Loya Jirga to restore peace in Afghanistan. **25 June:** Ex-king Zahir convenes a meeting of personalities in Rome to explore ways to solve the Afghan crisis. **6 July:** President Clinton orders commercial and financial sanctions against Afghanistan because of its support for Osama bin Laden. **14 July:** Abdul Ahad Karzai, chief of the Popalzai tribe, is assassinated in Quetta with two other persons. **5 August:** Ex-King Zahir firmly condemns the involvement of foreign forces in Afghanistan. **8 August:** Former President Mujaddidi leaves Pakistan after protesting Pakistani interference in Afghan affairs. **15 August:** At the call of Muhammad Omar, some 5,000 Afghan and Pakistani madrasa students have entered Afghanistan. **18 August:** The governments of Pakistan and Afghanistan sign an agreement for cooperation in the field of post and communications. **9 September:** Taliban spokesman Mulla Mutawakkil says that war is the only solution for the conflict in Afghanistan. **19 September:** According to a United Nations study, poppy cultivation increased from 64,000 to 91,000 hectares in 1999 and the opium production increased from 2,100 to 4,600 tons. **15 September:** The opposition announces formation of a new council, headed by Rabbani and including Sayyaf (vice president), Karimi (secretary), Massoud, Haji Qadir, Qurban Ali Erfani, Sabaoun, Nurullah Emad, and Abdullah Wardak. **12 October:** Military coup in Pakistan overthrows government of Prime Minister Nawaz Sharif and General Pervez Musharraf takes over. **15 October:** UN Security Council votes economic sanctions against the Taliban, effective 14 November, if they do not surrender Osama bin Laden. It also prohibited international flights of Afghan aircrafts and imposed a freeze on Taliban financial resources. **19 October:** A high American official met with Taliban representatives to warn them of consequences if they did not conform to the UN demands. **27 October:** Mulla Mutawakkil was named minister of foreign affairs, replacing Mulla Hasan Akhund. **14 November:** UN sanctions on Afghanistan begin. **17 November:** The Taliban government decrees Chechnya separatism is an Islamic cause. **21 November:** The Taliban accept the reopening of the Iranian consulate in Herat. **22 November:** At the initiative of Ex-king Zahir Shah, 55 Afghan personalities assembled in Rome to prepare holding a Loya Jirga. **28 November:** The Taliban government announces the formation of hundreds of Islamic councils to supervise judicial and administrative affairs in the provinces. **11 December:** General Malik, coming from the United States, rejoined Massoud's forces and General Dostum entered Afghanistan from Turkey. **14 December:** U.S. government let it be known that it will make the Taliban responsible for attacks organized by Bin Laden. **19 December:** UN Security Council adopts a resolution to broaden its sanctions if the Taliban do not hand over bin Laden, close alleged terrorist camps, and halt "illegal drug activities." **21 December:** The Taliban and Turkmenistan governments signed a contract for providing electricity for Faryab, Shiberghan, and Mazar-i Sharif.

2000 7 January: Mulla Omar accuses the United States of hostility to Islam and Muslims. **16 January:** Moscow accuses the Taliban of supplying weapons and men to Chechnya. The government of Chechnya opens an embassy at Kabul. **27 January:** The American news agency CNN and Al-Jazira are authorized to open information offices in Kabul. **27 February:** According to the International Drug Enforcement Agency, 75 percent of world production of opium is produced in Afghanistan. **6 March:** The Taliban destroy 355 kg of heroin and 4,350 kg of hashish in Kandahar Province. **20 March:** The Taliban prohibit the celebration of the new year at Kabul. **27 March:** Ismail Khan, the former governor of Herat, escapes from a prison in Kandahar. **31 March:** Generals Abdul Malik and Dostum form a common front against the Taliban. **9 April:** Pakistan demands the closure of terrorist training camps in Afghanistan and the extradition of Pakistanis responsible for religious attacks in Karachi. **15 April:** The Taliban government permits Shi'ite Muharram celebrations. **19 April:** Iran and Afghanistan resume postal relations via Herat, which had been interrupted for eight years. **17 May:** A delegation representing the ex-king visited the United States to promote the creation of a Loya Jirga for the formation of an Afghan government. The delegation was headed by Sultan Mahmud Ghazi and included Hamid Karzai, Ishaq Naderi, Runa Yusuf Mansuri, and Zalmai Rasul. **24 June:** Leaders of the Pakistani Jama'at-i Islami visiting Afghanistan urged the Taliban government not to extradite Osama bin Laden. **28 July:** Mulla Omar forbids the cultivation of the poppy in Afghanistan. **4 September:** Ismail Khan recruits soldiers from Iranian refugee camps. **7 October:** Commander Mas'ud meets Dostum and Ismail Khan in Meshhed to open a new front against the Taliban. **6 November:** Mulla Muhammad decrees that men without beards are not permitted to find work. According to a report, the Afghan foreign ministry demands the return of the Koh-i Noor from

Britain. **18 November:** The Taliban government refuses to extradite 23 Pakistanis accused of confessional killings. **1 December:** A resolution of the European Parliament demands that the European Union break all relations with the Taliban government. **18 December:** The UN decides to evacuate all its expatriate personnel. **19 December:** The UN Security Council imposes new sanctions on the Taliban government.

2001 **2 January:** Mulla Muhammad Omar decrees that conversions from Islam to Christianity are to be punishable by death. **4 January:** Abdul Sattar, Pakistan's minister of foreign affairs, says that Pakistan will comply with the UN sanction on Afghanistan. **6 January:** Rabbani promises to end the veil requirement after the fall of the Taliban. **8 January:** UN sanctions come into force in the absence of Taliban cooperation. **2 February:** The United Nations publishes a list of 54 Taliban dignitaries whose accounts are frozen. **7 February:** The Pakistani minister of interior, Muinuddin Haidar, visits Kabul to demand the extradition of some 60 Pakistanis wanted for criminal activities in Pakistan. **13 February:** The United States ordered the Taliban offices in New York closed. **26 February:** Mulla Omar orders the destruction of all statues. **1 March:** Taliban government begins destruction of the grand Buddha statues. **5 March:** In a broadcast of Radio Sharia, Mulla Omar justifies the destruction of "idols." **20 March:** Taliban prohibit *nauruz* (new year) celebrations. **28 March:** The religious police in Kabul orders the wearing of white turbans for primary students and black ones for secondary students. **31 March:** Seventy-five men were punished for cutting their beards. **3-7 April:** On his first visit to Europe, Mas'ud meets with the French minister of foreign affaires, the president of the European Parliament, and other dignitaries. He wants assistance against the Taliban government and pressure on the Pakistan government to stop its interference in Afghanistan. **10 April:** Pakistani religious parties hold a conference in which friendly messages of Osama bin Laden and Mulla Omar of Afghanistan are read. **16 April:** Mulla Rabbani, head of the Taliban council of ministers, dies of cancer in Pakistan. **1 May:** In its annual report on terrorism, the State Department accuses Pakistan of providing military support to the Taliban. **5 May:** Taliban issue a ruling to ban foreigners from drinking alcohol, eating pork, listening to loud music, and being in contact with members of the opposite sex. **17 May:** Ismail Khan returns to Afghanistan from Iran to head a western front against the Taliban. **18 May:** The Islamic ministry of Enjoining the Good and Forbidding Evil closes a hospital financed by Italy, because male and female nurses were eating together. **21 May:** A decree of Mulla Omar demands that Hindus wear a yellow mark on their clothing and homes and prohibits them from wearing a turban. **23 May:** An unmarried couple accused of sexual relations receives 100 lashes each. **24 May:** The Taliban government orders Afghan Hindus to wear a yellow sign on their dress and their women to wear the Afghan burqa. **29 May:** The Taliban burn thousands of photos of women. **31 May:** The Taliban prohibit foreign women from driving. **3 June:** The Taliban government approves a budget of $81 million and expenditures of $82.5 million, of which $43 million are placed at the disposal of Mulla Omar, $1 million for the religious police force (amr bi'l ma'ruf), $343,000 for public works, $200,000 for the ministry of refugees, $14 million for religious primary education, and $1.14 million for secondary education. **4 June:** The Taliban prepare a code which forces foreigners in Afghanistan to obey Islamic rules, prohibiting adultery, conducting missionary activities, playing music, watching television, eating pork or drinking alcohol, and wearing immoral clothing. **20 June:** U.S. Senate resolution condemns Taliban policies of discrimination of minorities and women. **21 June:** Pervez Musharraf, Pakistani chief executive, adopts the title "president." **26 June:** The Taliban government appoints Mulla Muhammad Taher minister of planning, Mulla Sa'duddin Sa'id minister of public works, and Ahmatullah Matih minister of agriculture. **27 June:** As a result of international criticism, the Taliban government revokes its compulsion for Hindus to wear yellow distinguishing marks. **29 June:** The American government warns the Taliban government about any possible attack by Osama bin Laden. It claims to have proof of Pakistani support for the Taliban. **2 July:** U.S. ambassador to Pakistan, Wendy Chamberlain, and Undersecretary of State Richard Armitage meet with the Taliban ambassador at Islamabad to threaten reprisals if bin Laden attacks any American interests. **4 July:** The Taliban recall their representatives in Saudi Arabia and the United Arab Emirates. **12 July:** The Taliban prohibit the use of the Internet, except for its high council in Kandahar. All state employees are ordered to wear black its 24 employees, accusing them of missionary activities. **7 August:** Dostum resumes his attacks on Taliban forces. **13 August:** Commander Abdul Haq demands the formation of a national union government in Afghanistan. **7 September:** In a sermon the Taliban minister of justice tells Afghans not to associate with foreigners and that Islam prohibits friendship with infidels. **9 September:** Ahmad Shah Masud is killed in a suicide attack by two Arabs posing as journalists. **11 September:** A terrorist attack destroys the World Trade Center. Masud dies and General Muhammad Fahim succeeds as commander of the

Northern Alliance forces. **13 September:** The United States mobilizes forces for action against the Taliban. President Musharref supports American military action from Pakistani territory. **17 September:** A Pakistani government delegation at Kandahar demands the surrender of Osama bin Laden within three days. Mulla Omar refuses. **18 September:** President George W. Bush declares that the United States want Bin Laden "dead or alive." **20 September:** An assembly of mullas asked Mulla Muhammad Omar to "invite" Osama bin Laden to leave Afghanistan. **22 September:** The United Arab Emirates break relations with the Taliban government. **24 September:** The U.S. government freezes the accounts of individuals and organizations accused of supporting terrorism. Pakistan withdraws its diplomatic personnel from Afghanistan. **25 September:** Saudi Arabia ends diplomatic relations with Afghanistan. **28 September:** A United Front delegation, headed by Yunus Qanuni, meets with Zahir Shah in Rome. Rabbani says that he sees no role for the ex-king. **29 September:** The United States announces that special American and British forces were operating in Afghanistan since mid-September. **1 October:** Zahir Shah and the United Front reach an accord for constituting a Loya Jirga of 120 members, nominated by both parties. **6 October:** Zahir Shah calls for UN participation in forming a new government. **7 October:** First attack by American and British aircraft on Taliban and al-Qaeda military bases at Kabul, Kandahar, Kunduz, Farah, Mazar, and Jalalabad. **10 October:** The American government announces control of Afghan airspace. **15 October:** Abdullah Abdullah, foreign minister of the Rabbani government, declares that the Alliance forces would not enter Kabul until an interim government is established. **24 October:** Pir Sayyid Ahmad Gailani convenes a meeting of tribal chiefs in Peshawar. **26 October:** Commander Abdul Haq is executed by the Taliban when trying to raise a force of Pashtuns against the Taliban. **2 November:** Hamid Karzai fights Taliban forces in the north of Kandahar. **6 November:** The United Front publishes a list of 60 representatives for a Loya Jirga, most of them from their own party. **9 November:** Hundreds of prisoners were massacred after they attempted a revolt. Forces of Generals Dostum and Muhaqiq take Mazar-i Sharif. **12 November:** Ismail Khans forces take Herat. The United States demands that the United Front forces not enter Kabul. **13 November:** Jami'at forces enter Kabul. **14 November:** United Front forces take Ghazni and most of western Afghanistan. Forces of Haji Qadir and Hazrat Ali take Jalalabad. **15 November:** General Dostum's forces take Taluqan. Northern Alliance troops enter Kabul, Abdullah Abdullah declares that there is no need for international forces. Northern Alliance takes Jalalabad. **16 November:** Britain deploys 100 at Bagram airport. **17 November:** Ex-president Rabbani arrives in Kabul. Forces of Isma'il Khan take Farah Province. Iran opens embassy at Kabul. **18 November:** Afghan television begins transmission, featuring also two female announcers. **21 November:** Pakistan orders the closing of Taliban consulates. **25 November:** Northern Alliance captures Kunduz, the last Taliban base in northern Afghanistan. **27 November–5 December:** An Afghan delegation, consisting of members of the Rome, Peshawar, and Cyprus representatives, meets under UN auspices in Bonn to agree on an interim government. Hamid Karzai is nominated as interim leader. The accord stipulates: creation of a 21-member commission to organize a Loya Jirga; establishment of an interim administration; formation of an international force for the maintenance of peace in Kabul; drafting of the ex-king to preside at the Loya Jirga; establishment of a commission to draft a constitution in 2003. **9 December:** Kandahar comes under Kabul control. **13 December:** Karzai arrives in Kabul. **20 December:** First international peacekeepers begin work in Kabul. **22 December:** Afghan Interim Government formed:

Hamid Karzai	Prime Minister
Yunus Qanuni	Interior
Abdullah Abdullah	Foreign Affairs
Muhammad Qasem Fahim	Defense
Sima Samar	Women's Affairs
Hedayat Amin Arsala	Finance
Abdul Qader	Urban Development
Suhaila Seddiq	Public Health
Abdur Rahman	Air Transport and Tourism
Muhammad Muhaqeq	Planning
Shaker Kargar	Water and Electricity
Sayyid Mustafa Kasemi	Commerce
Muhammad Alem Razm	Mines and Industries
Aref Nurzai	Small Industries
Makhdum Rahin	Information and Culture
Abdul Rahim	Communications
Mir Wais Sadeq	Labor and Social Affairs
Muhammad Hanif Balkhi	Pilgrimage
Abdullah Wardak	Martyrs and Disabled
Ghulam Muhammad Yailaqi	Education
Sharif Fayez	Higher Education
Abdul Khaliq Fazal	Public Works

Chronology   lxxix

Abdul Malik Anwar	Rural Development
Muhammad Amin Farhang	Reconstruction
Sultan Hamid Sultan	Transport
Enayatullah Nazeri	Return of Refugees
Sayyid Husain Anwari	Agriculture
Mangal Husain	Irrigation
Abdul Rahim Karimi	Justice
Amanullah Zadran	Border Affairs

Government begins its tenure. The peacekeeping International Security Assistance Force (ISAF) is formed under a United Nations mandate to help Afghan forces secure Kabul. **24 December:** General Dostum is nominated deputy minister of defense.

2002 11 January: The first contingent of Taliban/al-Qaida prisoners arrives at the American base at Guantánamo (Cuba). **17 January:** American Secretary of State Colin Powell arrives in Kabul, promises longterm American assistance. **21 January:** An international conference in Tokyo agrees to provide $4.5 billion for the reconstruction of Afghanistan. **24 January:** First publication of UNESCO-financed *Kabul Weekly*. **25 January:** A 21-member commission, headed by Ismail Qasimyar, is charged with selecting members for a Loya Jirga to be convened in June. **27 January:** The Interim Government adopts the national banner of the 1964 constitution. **10 February:** The offices of Hekmatyar in Meshed are closed by the Iran government. Germany and the Netherlands have formally taken control of ISAF for six months. **14 February:** Abdul Rahman, minister of transportation, is killed, purportedly by members of the Northern Alliance. **26 February:** Gulbuddin Hekmatyar has left Iran. **8 April:** General Fahim survived an attack during a trip to Jalalabad to meet with tribal chiefs and local commanders. **18 April:** Ex-King Muhammad Zahir returns to Afghanistan. **22 April:** Muhammad Nabi Muhammadi dies. **26 April:** Ex-president Rabbani offers his loyalty to the Loya Jirga. **28 April:** Ahmad Shah Masud is proclaimed "National Hero." **29 April:** General Fahim is proclaimed marshal. **20 May:** The Interim Government decrees formation of a voluntary national army. **23 May:** The UN Security Council extends the mandate of the international peace force for six months. **27 May:** The ex-king expresses his willingness to serve as head of state, if the Loya Jirga demands. **11 June:** The Loya Jirga, composed of 1,598 delegates (including 190 women) begins its deliberations. **13 June:** Hamid Karzai is elected head of the provisional government. **20 June:** New Transitional Government chosen which leaves

General Fahim minister of defense and Dr. Abdullah Abdullah foreign minister. Yunus Qanuni, the third of the Panjshiri leaders, was moved from interior to education as well as special adviser on national security.

Hamid Karzai	President
Muhammad Qasim Fahim	Vice President
Abdul Karim Khalili	Vice President
Hedayat Amin Arsala	Vice President
Ne'matullah Shahrani	Vice President
Muhammad Fahim	Defense
Abdul Rahim Wardak	Deputy
Abdullah Abdullah	Foreign Affairs
Rahim Sherzoi	Deputy (Polit. Affs.)
Ashraf Ghani	Finance
Taj Muhd. Wardak	Interior
Muhammad Muhaqeq	Planning
Muhammad Masum Stanakzai	Communications
Muhammad Arif Nurzai	Borders and Tribal Affairs
Enayatullah Nazeri	Refugee Affairs
Juma M. Muhammadi	Mines and Industries
Muhammad Alam Razm	Light Industries and Foodstuffs
Suhaila Siddiq	Public Health
Sayyid Mustafa Kazemi	Commerce
Sayyid Husain Anwari	Agriculture and Livestock
Abdul Rahim Karimi	Justice
Sayyid Makhdum Rahin	Information and Culture
Muhammad Amin Farhang	Reconstruction
Muhammad Amin Naziryar	Hajj and Endowments
Muhammad Yusuf Pashtun	Urban Development
Abdullah Ali	Public Works
Nur Muhammad Qarqin	Labor and Social Affairs
Ahmad Shakar Kargar	Water and Power
Ahmad Yusuf Nuristani	Irrigation and Environment
Abdullah Wardak	Martyrs and Disabled
Muhammad Sharif Fayez	Higher Education
Muhammad Mirwais Sadeq	Civil Aviation and Tourism
Sayyid Muhammad Ali Jawid	Transportation
Muhammad Yunus Qanuni	Education
Muhammad Hanif Atmar	Rural Development

Mahbuba Huquqmal — Women's Affairs
Sima Samar — Human Rights Commission
Fazl Hadi Shinwari — Chief Justice

Taj Muhammad Wardak became minister of interior, and Ashraf Ghani Ahmadzai became minister of finance. **20 June:** Turkey succeeds Great Britain to head the International Security Force for Afghanistan (ISFA). **22 June:** The Transitional Government is established with 29 members. **25 June:** Sima Samar loses the ministry of women's affairs, but is nominated president of the human rights commission. **30 June:** Queen Humaira is buried in Kabul. **July 6:** Vice President Haji Abdul Qadir and minister of public works is assassinated in Jalalabad. **13 August:** The Iranian President Muhammad Khatami makes an official visit to Kabul, the first by an Iranian chief of state in 40 years. **14 August:** A ceremony is held in Kabul on the formation by France of the second battalion of the Afghan army. It was attended by Mr. Brahimi, representative of the UN Secretary General. **3 September:** The French Minister of Foreign Affairs Dominique de Villepin makes official visit to Kabul. Assures Afghanistan of continued support. **4 September:** Hekmatyar proclaims jihad against American forces. **5 September:** Karzai escapes an assassination attempt in Kandahar. **13 September:** President Bush announces a major road-construction project, supported by a $180 million donation from the U.S., Saudi Arabia, and Japan. **22 September:** American General McNeil organizes a meeting at Herat of Ismail Khan and Gul Agha Sherzai to prevent clashes between their forces. Afghan government nominated Nangyalai Tarzi as ambassador to Pakistan. **25 September:** Ariana Afghan airlines resumes weekly flights from Kabul to Frankfurt with a stop at Istanbul. **7 October:** Afghan government introduces new currency, exchanging one new afghani for one thousand old ones. **23 October:** General Fahim makes an official visit to London. According to a UN report Afghanistan is again the major producer of opium in the world. **26 October:** The ex-king returns to Afghanistan. **3 November:** Curfew in existence since 1978 in Kabul is ended. The ex-king inaugurates the constitutional drafting commission, headed by Ne'matullah Shahrani. Human Rights Watch claims that Isma'il Khan has created a mini state in Herat in which civil rights are not respected. **11–12 November:** Students, most of them Pashtuns, protest the inadequate conditions at Kabul University. Police open fire, one student killed (four according to some sources), 10 wounded. **27 November:** The UN Security Council unanimously renews the ISFA mandate for one year. **December:** A message, purported to be from Mulla Muhammad Omar, calls on the

Afghans to wage holy war against the United States. **12 December:** The supreme court, headed by Fazl Hadi Shinwari, prohibits cable television at Jalalabad. **21 December:** Seven German soldiers of ISAF were killed in Kabul in an ambush. **23 December:** India donates a second Airbus 300-B4 to Afghanistan. **27 December:** Turkmenistan, Afghanistan, and Pakistan sign an accord for construction of a gas duct to export Turkmen gas to the Indian Ocean. The 1,500 kilometer pipeline is estimated to cost two billion dollars for which financing has, as yet, not been assured.

2003 January: Ismail Khan, governor of Herat, prohibits male teachers in girls' school. **4 January:** About 400 Pashtun chiefs arrive in Kabul to protest the arrest of an Achakzai chief by American forces. **7 January:** The American army has completed the formation of 400 recruits for the new Afghan army. **21 January:** The supreme court prohibits cable television in Afghanistan. **28 January:** General Ali Ahmad Jalali replaces Taj Muhammad Wardak as minister of interior. **30 January:** A Black Hawk crashes near the Bagram airbase, killing six of its occupants. Since October 2001 the United States has lost 25 men in combat and 22 to other causes. **10 February:** Germany and Netherlands replace Turkey in command of the International Security Force for Afghanistan (ISFA). **17 February:** Mulla Muhammad Omar calls for Afghans to join in holy war against Washington. **22 February:** Gulbuddin Hekmatyar calls on the people of Iraq to resist the American invasion. **24 February:** The Afghan minister of mines and industries, Juma M. Muhammadi and three of his colleagues die when a chartered plane crashes into the ocean off the coast of Karachi. **26 February:** The UN Agency for Narcotics Control announced that Afghanistan has been the primary producer of opium in 2002, producing about 3,400 tons. **15 March:** Afghan finance minister presents the budget for the year beginning March 21, amounting to $500 million. President Hamid Karzai initiates the first two battalions of the Afghan National Army. Each battalion counts 1,900 men. **17 March:** Donors conference pledges two billion dollars to help rebuild Afghanistan. **20 March:** Major American operation, called "Valiant Strike," of combined air and ground forces moves against Islamist forces in the mountains of Sami Ghar, east of Kandahar. **21 March:** Eighteen Afghans imprisoned at the American base of Guantánamo, Cuba, are freed and returned to Afghanistan. **31 March:** Mulla Omar, head of the Taliban government, calls for jihad against the American forces in Afghanistan and their supporters. **17 April:** Romanian coalition forces discover a vast arms cache, including 3,000 107-mm rockets, a large amount of munitions, and 30 antitank mines. **22 April:** President Karzai meets Pakistan president Perez Musharraf in Islamabad. **April:** American Special Forces discover some 90 tons explosives and 130 tons light ammunition in caves near Maimana. **21 May:** American guards of the embassy have mistakenly shot four Afghan soldiers who were loading weapons near the embassy. They mistook them for rebels. **24 May:** Some 200 persons protest the killing of four Afghan soldiers in front of the American embassy. **2 June:** Ismail Khan, governor of Herat, transfers $20 million of customs duties to the Kabul government. **3-6 June:** President Karzai visits Great Britain and meets Tony Blair and Queen Elizabeth II. **7 June:** Bomb hits ISAF convoy and kills six soldiers, four of them Germans, and wounds 16 other German soldiers. A public consultation process on drafting a constitution is launched. **24 June:** According to a Reuter's report Mulla Muhammad Omar has formed a 8-man resistance council composed of the following persons: Mulla Dadullah, former commander of Kunduz; Akhtar Muhammad Osmani, former chief of the Kandahar air base; Akhtar Muhammad Mansur, ex-minister of defense; Mulla Obaidullah, former chief of Kandahar security; Hafiz Abdul Majid; Mulla Abdurrazaq Nafiz, former chief of northern areas; Mulla Baradar, ex-governor of Herat and Nimruz; and Mulla Muhammad Rasul. **26-27 June:** President Karzai visits Switzerland. **2 July:** Gulbuddin Hekmatyar calls on Afghans to expel all foreigners from Afghanistan. **8 July:** USAID has granted the Afghan ministry of higher education $553,500 for a feasibility study on opening an American university at Kabul, similar to those in Lebanon and Egypt. **16 July:** President Karzai issues a decree for electing a Loya Jirga. Delegates are to include 500 members, of whom 450 are elected and 50 appointed by Karzai. **23 July:** First operation of 1,000 soldiers of the newly created Afghan army in the Zormat Valley, near Gardez. **1 August:** Members of the Northern Alliance, including General Muhammad Qasim Fahim, Vice President Abdul Karim Khalili, Foreign Minister Abdullah Abdullah, Education Minister Yunus Qanuni, and Mujahedin Leader Abdul Rasul Sayyaf to form a political party. **6 August:** The German airline company Lufthansa begins the first of weekly flights from Düsseldorf to Kabul. **9 August:** Sultan Mahmud Ghazi, a cousin of Zaher Shah, forms a political party called Movement of National Unity. The ex-king returns to Afghanistan after a visit to France. **11 August:** NATO succeeds ISAF in Kabul under the command of General Goetz Gliemeroth. **13 August:** General Baz Muhammad Ahmadi becomes military commander of Herat, leaving Ismail Khan only governor of the province. **15 August:** President Bush nominated Zalmai Khalilzad to be American ambassador to Kabul. **8 September:** The Afghan council of ministers has adopted a law authorizing the formation of parties. **20 September:** Abdul Rahim Wardak, a Pashtun, replaces Bismillah Khan, a Tajik, as deputy minister of defense. **3 November:** New draft constitution presented to former King Muhammad Zahir Shah. Draft was written during 11 months by a 35-member commission. **7 September:** The American Secretary of Defense, Donald Rumsfeld, met President Karzai in Kabul and promised a considerable increase in American aid. **30 September:** Afghanistan becomes the 169th country to sign the nuclear non-proliferation treaty. **8 November:** Local elections in all 32 provinces choose representatives to select a new 500-member Loya Jirga. President George Bush asked for $87 billion from Congress for Iraq and Afghanistan, 11 billion of which will be for the American military effort and $800 million for reconstruction aid to Afghanistan. **27 November:** Mrs. Clinton, in a visit to Kabul, promises that her country will continue to support Afghanistan. **1 December:** A Provincial Reconstruction Team (PRT) is established in Herat. Other PRT have been set up in Bamian, Kunduz, Mazar-i Sharif, Gardez, Kandahar, and Parwan. The teams have both military and civilian personnel. **14 December:** A 502-member Loya Jirga convenes in Kabul to debate and ratify the constitution.

2004 4 January: After three weeks of heated debates, the Loya Jirga agrees on establishing an Islamic state, a presidential system of government, a two-house parliament, recognition of local languages in the areas of majority, lifetime title of the king as "Father of the Nation." Men and women to have equal rights. **6 January:** NATO-led ISAF extends its mandate beyond Kabul and takes command of seven civil-military reconstruction teams set up in the provinces. **7 January:** A UN provincial reconstruction team (PRT) under German command has been established in Kunduz, northern Afghanistan. **11 January:** It was estimated that 3,000 soldiers of the new Afghan army have deserted since its founding in May 2002. Afghan soldiers are paid $70 a month once they are integrated into the army, officers are paid about $200. **18 January:** General Abdul Rashid Dostum declared that he would join the government if President Hamid Karzai appointed him minister of defense, chief of staff, or put him in charge of a military force of 20,000 men. Kari said "if Dostum demands a higher post, it is a legitimate demand and we will examine it." **22 January:** Muhammad Muhaqeq announces his candidacy for the position of president. **26 January:** In a ceremony in Kabul, headed by President Karzai and the former king, the new constitution is officially promulgated. **28 January:** Ali Ahmad Jalali, minister of interior, announces the creation of a 33rd province, Deh Kundi, created from the northern part of Urozgan Province. Masuda Jalal announced her intention to rum for the presidency, the first woman in Afghan history. **6 February:** Donald Rumsfeld, American secretary of defense, urges NATO to further engage in Afghanistan so that military operations could be transferred to the Alliance. **17 February:** A delegation of the European Union visits Kabul. **19 February:** Inauguration of a Provincial Reconstruction Team in Asadabad, capital of Kunar Province. **4 March:** NATO announces the establishment of a Provincial Reconstruction Team (PRT) in Ghazni; it is the 11th of its type in Afghanistan. **10 March:** A British 100-man Special Forces team has arrived at Kabul to participate in operations against al-Qa ida. **12 March:** An American PRT is established in Herat. **19 March:** An Antonov AN-124 Condor heavy-transport aircraft arrived at Kabul airport with donations of weapons, weapons systems components, and ammunition for the Afghan National Army (ANA). This is the fifth donation by Romania of Soviet weapons to Afghanistan. Afghanistan still uses primarily Soviet equipment which was originally supplied to the Kabul government from 1978 to 1990. **21 March:** Fighting erupted in Herat between forces loyal to Ismail Khan, governor of Herat, and General Abdul Zahir Nayebzadeh, who professed loyalty to the Kabul government. Ismail Khan's son, Mirwais Sadeq, who held the post of civil aviation and tourism minister in the Karzai government, is killed. **22 March:** The Kabul government dispatched a 600-strong force to Herat to maintain order and protect civilians. Negotiations lead to a cease-fire and a return to calm in the city. **31 March:** An international conference of 56 donor countries meets in Bonn to approve $8.2 billion in aid of which $4.4 billion is for the year 2004. **1 April:** A reinforcement of 2,000 U.S. Marines arrives from the Persian Gulf to reinforce the American forces in Afghanistan. **2 April:** NATO Council approves a plan for the enlargement of the ISAF mandate. **5 April:** Members of Jumbesh-i Milli of General Abdul Rashid Dostum held a conference in Mazar-i Sharif, attended by nearly 2,000 persons, that was to prepare their members for enrolling in the election rolls. Like other mujahedin groups, the Junbesh is developing into a political party. **7 April:** Forces of General Dostum take Maimana, capital of Fariab Province from government forces, retreat after three days. **13 April:** President Karzai orders the Panjshir area to become a province. **21 April:** The American Ambassador Zalmai Khalilzad announced in Kabul the end of American support for the militias who helped in the war against the Taliban government. **25 April:** The United Nations suspends its activities in Kandahar and environs after attacks on its members. **27 April:** Several thousand soldiers and, for the first time, women of the police corps parade in Kabul to mark the 20th anniversary of the mujahedin victory over the Soviet occupation. **30 April:** The Afghan minister of interior announces formation of a special police force for the protection of historical sites.

Chronology

April: Dai Kundi made into a province. **3 May:** The government approves the creation of a 2,000-strong Afghan National Guard. **26 May:** President Karzai enacts law permitting presidential and parliamentary elections. **20 August:** About 10.6 million Afghans are registered to vote. **7 September:** Thirty days of presidential campaigning begins. **11 September:** President Karzai dismisses Ismail Khan from his position as governor of Herat, appoints him as minister of water and power. **17 September:** UN Security Council extends ISAF's mandate until October 2005. **9 October:** Presidential elections with participation of some eight million Afghans begins. **24 October:** Hamid Karzai secures a simple majority of more than four million votes. **7 December:** Karzai sworn in for a five-year term as president of Afghanistan. **23 December:** Karzai presents new cabinet:

Gen Abdurrahim Wardak	National Defense
Ali Ahmad Jalali	Interior
Dr. Abdullah Abdullah	Foreign Affairs
Dr. Anwar-ul Haq Ahadi	Finance
Hedayat Amin Arsala	Commerce
Dr. Zalmai Rasul	Adviser
Nur Muhammad Qarqin	Education
Dr Muhammad Amin Farhang	Economy
Dr Enayatullah Qasemi	Transport
Eng. Amirzai Sangin	Communications
Eng. Mir Muhammad Sidiq	Mines and Industries
Gen Muhammad Ismael Khan	Water and Power
Dr Suhrab Ali Safari	Public Works
Engineer Yusuf Pashtun	Urban Development
Obaidullah Ramin	Agriculture and Food
Muhammad Sarwar Danish	Justice
Dr. Amir Shah Hasanyar	Higher Education
Dr. Sayyid Makhdum Rahin	Information and Culture
Dr. Sayed Muhammad Amin Fatemi	Public Health
Prof. Nematullah Shahrani	Haj and Islamic Affairs
Muhammad Karim Brahuye	Borders Affairs
Dr. Masuda Jalal	Womens Affairs
Sayyid Ekramuddin Agha	Social and Labor Affairs
Muhammad Azam Dadfar	Refugees
Sidiqa Balkhi	Martyrs and Disabled
Muhammad Hanif Atmar	Rural Development
Engineer Habibullah Qaderi	Anti-Narcotics

2005 31 January: The Afghan secret service announces a program to purchase Stinger missiles still in the hands of warlords. **6 February:** Ayatollah Muhammad Asef Muhsini announced his retirement from politics at a session of the Harrakat-i Islami. **9-10 February:** NATO ministers of defense announce the enlargement of their forces for maintaining the peace in Afghanistan. **15 February:** President Karzai appoints Habiba Sorabi governor of Bamian. She is the first woman appointed governor of a province in Afghan history. U.S. Senator John McCain visited Afghanistan and called for "joint military permanent bases" in Afghanistan. **1 March:** President Karzai nominates Abdul Rashid Dostum as his adviser for military affairs. **5 April:** American Ambassador Zalmai Khalilzad has been nominated to head the American embassy in Baghdad. **3 May:** President Karzai convenes a meeting of about 1,000 representatives to discuss the question of the continued presence of foreign troops in Afghanistan. The assembly agreed: "We need the assistance of the United States, NATO troops and international coalition forces until we have our own security forces and reach the point that we no longer need that assistance." But the decision on the long-term presence of foreign troops or permanent bases in Afghanistan was to be left for the elected parliament. No status of forces agreement exists between Afghanistan and the United States. The meeting also called for an end to unilateral American combat operations. **9 May:** *Newsweek* reports, and subsequently retracts, that U.S. interrogators at Guantánamo Bay desecrated the Muslim holy book, the Koran. **10 May:** Violent demonstrations started in Jalalabad which subsequently spread over 12 provinces. The Pakistan consulate, foreign aid agencies, UN buildings, and diplomatic missions were attacked. About 14 persons were killed and 120 wounded. Demonstrators took to the streets in the Gaza Strip, Pakistan, and Indonesia. **15 May:** *Newsweek* apologized for "errors in a story" alleging that interrogators at the U.S. detention center in Guantánamo Bay desecrated the Koran. *Newsweek* Editor Mark Whitaker said: "We regret that we got any part of our story wrong, and extend our sympathies to victims of the violence and to the U.S. soldiers caught in its midst." **23 May:** On the occasion of his visit to the United States, President Hamid Karzai signed an agreement with President George W. Bush which states "U.S. military forces operating in Afghanistan will continue to have access to Bagram Air Base and its facilities, and facilities at other locations as may be mutually determined and that the U.S. and coalition forces are to continue to have the freedom of action required to conduct appropriate military operation based on consultations and pre-approved procedures." The agreement, called by Karzai a "Memorandum of Understanding" and by President Bush a "Strategic Partnership," does not specify the duration of foreign troops in Afghanistan.

INTRODUCTION

Afghanistan is the creation of a martial race who revolted against Persian domination of its mountain fastness and destroyed Safavid rule (1501–1732) at the **Battle of Gulnabad** in 1722. The Afghans occupied much of Persia, but were not able to maintain themselves on the Iranian plateau and eventually were forced to yield to **Nadir Shah Afshar** (r. 1736–1747), founder of the short-lived Afsharid dynasty (1736–1795). Appreciating the martial value and intractable nature of the Afghan tribes and the geographical barriers preventing easy passage to the riches of India, Nadir Shah enlisted Afghan tribes to his colors rather than trying to destroy them. Nadir invaded India, humbled the Moghul emperor, and sacked Delhi, his capital; in the end the erratic military genius fell prey to a plot by his own officers.

The leaderless Persian army was in a state of disarray, which permitted Ahmad Khan, the barely 23-year-old chief of the **Sadozai** clan of the Abdali tribe, to step into the power vacuum. He proclaimed Afghan independence from Persia and was elected king, assuming the title "**Ahmad Shah Durrani**" (r. 1747–1773). His Abdali clansmen henceforth became known as the **Durrani** tribe. He captured a convoy with revenue from India valued at 20,000,000 rupees (about $2,500,000), which enabled him to consolidate his power and win the support of the most powerful tribes.

Rather than becoming an absolute monarch in the Persian tradition, Ahmad Shah established a system of military feudalism that succeeded in welding the Afghan tribes into a highly efficient force. He confirmed the Durrani chiefs in possession of the **Kandahar** area with the sole obligation of providing a requisite number of troops (*see* DURRANI, LAND TENURE). The Durrani chiefs were given the highest offices in the young state, and his own clan, the Sadozai, were elevated to the status of a royal clan. Ahmad Shah adopted a council of nine influential Afghan chiefs who shared in the responsibility of decisions but left all real authority with the young king.

Discussing the character of the Afghan king, a British historian stated:

The country, now termed Afghanistan, had merely consisted of a congeries of petty states, ruled by tyrannical Chiefs, who were frequently at war with one another. Later, it became provinces of great empires which were ruled by foreign conquerors and their descendants. Later again, it was a dismembered country, with its provinces held by three neighboring states. Now, for the first independent state, ruled by a monarch whose high descent and warlike qualities made him peculiarly acceptable to his aristocratic and virile Chiefs, as well as to his warlike subjects in general. (Sykes, I, 367)

Ahmad Shah succeeded as the founder of modern Afghanistan because he proved himself as a military genius. He quickly captured **Kabul**, **Ghazni**, and Peshawar and, in December 1747, embarked on the first of eight invasions of India (*see* AHMAD SHAH). The territorial conquests generated booty and revenues that assured him the loyalty of the unruly chiefs. He added Kashmir, Sind, and the Western **Panjab** to his domain and founded an empire that extended from eastern Persia to northern India and from the **Amu Daria** to the Indian Ocean. He began the unification of the Afghan heartland with an army of 12,000 men, and by the time he invaded the Panjab in January 1748, he commanded a force of 30,000 tribesmen, including **Qizilbash**, **Hazaras**, Khorasanians, and others who flocked to his colors. A setback at the **Battle of Manupur** (March 11, 1748), where the Afghans met an imperial army of 60,000 men, was avenged with the capture of Lahore. Ahmad Shah outflanked the defensive perimeter of the city by crossing the Indus River at midnight with a force of 10,000 horsemen and attacking the camp of Hayatullah Khan, the Moghul governor of this strategic city. Ahmad Shah agreed to make peace and accepted the Indus River as his eastern border. A year later (1749), following his third invasion of India, Ahmad Shah turned west to capture the province of **Herat** and advanced into **Khorasan**. In 1757 the Afghan king occupied Delhi, which resulted in indiscriminate slaughter and plunder when a group of Ahmad Shah's soldiers was attacked by a mob. *Khutba* (Friday sermon) was read in the name of Ahmad Shah, making him the de facto head of the Empire of Delhi. He did not remain but bestowed the sultanate of Hindustan upon Alamgir II.

He destroyed an enemy army near Sirhind, estimated at 80,000 men, and defeated the powerful **Maratha** confederation at the **Battle of Panipat** (January 14, 1761). The booty was said to have included 22,000 men and women, 50,000 horses, 500 elephants, 200,000 oxen, several thousand camels, artillery, and an enormous amount of jewelry and cash; but geopolitical factors militated against an Afghan conquest of northern

India. Afghan territorial possessions had reached their largest extent, and Ahmad Shah's lines of communication to India were overextended. Therefore, he had to resort to indirect rule, appointing governors over the newly acquired provinces. But as soon as the victorious army returned to Afghanistan, the newly conquered areas were in revolt.

A new socioreligious nation, the **Sikhs**, emerged in the Panjab and, in spite of suffering fearful massacres, was able to deprive the Afghans of their dream of replacing the Moghul Empire of India. Barely 70 years later the **British East India Company**, which had obtained a charter for exploration and commerce of Bengal in 1600, had become the dominant power in India. In the pursuit of never-ending acquisitions of territory and the search for the "scientific frontier" to close the Afghan "gateway to India," the stage was set for three Anglo-Afghan wars.

The wars of Ahmad Shah Durrani served two major objectives: liberation of the Afghan heartland and consolidation of the newly created state. The martial energies generated in the unification of the country inevitably found their release in the search for a new frontier and booty. The multitude of tribal and ethnic groups were able to set aside their mutual suspicions and join in the common enterprise.

Ahmad Shah carefully prepared his Indian campaigns: he would invite a provincial governor to submit, promising rewards or high office, thus winning his alliance against his previous master. Some, like Ali Muhammad Khan, governor of Sirhind, chose to withdraw as the easier solution to the dilemma of choosing sides; others, to their regret, left the decision to the battlefield. If met by opposition, Ahmad Shah ordered the immediate execution of any natives prowling in the vicinity of his camp to secure the secrecy of his movements. He counted on speed to take the enemy by surprise, attacking in the early hours of the morning. He permitted an irregular rabble to engage the enemy and then attacked, trying to encircle the enemy or push him against some geographical barrier —a river or mountain—and order his right and left wings to attack. Initially, he still lacked artillery and a regular army, and the tribes fought under their own chiefs. But size required organization, and Ahmad Shah appointed his most trusted *sardar* (chief) with the position of commander in chief (*sipah salar* or *sardar-i sardaran*) to be responsible for the organization, equipment, and training of troops and for the planning and conduct of campaigns. Heavy guns were captured, and eventually the Afghans learned the art of casting cannons from a mixture of brass and copper. At the Battle of Panipat, Ahmad Shah employed a cannon, almost 15 feet in length with a bore of about 9 inches, capable of launching balls of about 40 pounds.

Gradually, a regular army (*askar-i munazzam*) was established, supported by the much larger, irregular tribal levies (*askar-i ghair munazzam* or *khawanin sawaran*). Three-fourths of the army were cavalry men, armed with matchlocks and swords or spears—only a few had more modern firearms. Shields, daggers, axes, and various small weapons were used in close combat. Eventually, Ahmad Shah's arsenal of heavy guns increased, cannons were drawn by horses or camels, sometimes by elephants. The elephant was the "tank" of traditional warfare—used in battle to break the lines of the enemy or to carry the heavy artillery. Although useful in India, the pachyderm was difficult to "fuel" in the deserts and mountains of Afghanistan. The irregular tribal army was composed of tribesmen who joined for a particular campaign, or of levies from various tribes, whose chiefs were to provide tribal cavalry corresponding to the size of their fiefs. Some tribal forces were maintained for the protection of the frontiers or collection of revenues. (*See* AHMAD SHAH, MILITARY ADMINISTRATION.) Toward the end of his rule Ahmad Shah's army was estimated at 120,000, 40,000 of whom constituted the regular army. But only a small part of the army was employed in individual battles. Camp followers greatly increased these numbers, which gave rise to hyperbolic accounts by native historians of cataclysmic battles involving hundreds of thousands of troops.

Ahmad Shah's death marked the end of foreign conquests. His son **Timur Shah** (r. 1773–1793) was more scholarly inclined and lacked the military genius of his father. He moved the Afghan capital to Kabul, away from the center of Durrani power to a location that was strategically better suited for control of the eastern provinces. He established a bodyguard of some 12,000 clansmen of his Ishaqzai tribe, which he augmented with a division of 12,000 *qizilbash* troops. Thus, he was able to limit the power of the feudal forces and their powerful chiefs. A campaign into Sind in 1779, although victorious, could not prevent the eventual loss of this province, and a campaign into the north reaffirmed Afghan control of the northern provinces but left **Balkh** virtually independent. Revolts in Khorasan and Peshawar were only barely suppressed. **Zaman Shah** (r. 1793–1800), one of 23 recognized sons of Timur, succeeded to power, but was embroiled in internecine warfare with his brothers and was finally blinded and forced into exile in India. The Panjab was definitely lost to **Ranjit Singh**, king of the new Sikh nation. Civil war between Timur's sons led to the demise of the Sadozai branch of the Durranis and the emergence of the Barakzai/**Muhammadzai** branch under Amir **Dost Muhammad Khan** (r. 1826–1838 and 1842–1863).

In the 19th century, European rivalry for commerce and empire quickly extended to the Middle East. In 1798 the Napoleonic invasion of Egypt temporarily established a French foothold in this strategic area, which **Britain** feared as an important step in a move against India. Russia moved into Central Asia, and by the end of the 19th century the czar's influence extended to the Amu Daria. The British East India Company became an ally of Ranjit Singh and thus extended its influence to the borders of Afghanistan.

In 1826 Dost Muhammad, first of the Muhammadzai rulers, ascended the throne. He wanted an alliance with India and hoped to regain Peshawar, which had been lost to the emerging Sikh nation under Ranjit Singh. **Lord Auckland**, the British governor general of India, chose an alliance with the Sikh ruler instead and decided to restore **Shah Shuja** to the Afghan throne. The presence of a purported Russian agent at Kabul (*see* VITKEVICH) and Dost Muhammad's hostility to the Sikh ruler were the reasons for India's declaration of war (*see* SIMLA MANIFESTO). A tripartite treaty was signed in July 1838 between Shah Shuja, Ranjit Singh, and Lord Auckland, and the **"Army of the Indus"** invaded Afghanistan. The invaders met with little resistance, Shah Shuja was restored to the Kabul throne, and Dost Muhammad was forced into Indian exile. But it was soon apparent that the Sadozai ruler needed protection to keep himself in power, and the British army became a force of occupation. The families of British officers came to Kabul, and thousands of Indian camp followers engaged in the lucrative business of importing from India the necessities of colonial life. But all was not well. The occupation was costly, and retrenchments demanded a reduction in subsidies (or bribes) to tribal chiefs, which had the effect of turning them against the invaders. On November 2, 1841, Kabul rose in rebellion, and a mob stormed the British mission and killed all its members, including **Alexander Burnes**, its head. **Muhammad Akbar**, a son of Dost Muhammad, together with a number of chiefs, now rallied his forces and increasingly threatened the occupiers. The British were forced to negotiate a retreat, which very few of the 16,000 troops and camp followers survived. (*See* CAPITULATION, TREATY OF; DEATH MARCH.) Britain felt it necessary to have its martial reputation restored and in 1842 sent in General **George Pollock**, who wreaked vengeance on Kabul, laying torch to the covered bazaar and permitting plunder that destroyed much of the city. (*See* FIRST ANGLO-AFGHAN WAR.) The British forces left, and Amir Dost Muhammad returned in 1843 to rule Afghanistan until he died a natural death 20 years later. The "Signal Catastrophe" of the war inclined the British government to abandon its search for a "scientific" frontier and pursue a policy of "masterly inactivity," which was to leave Afghanistan to the Afghans. But a generation later the advocates of a "forward policy," to counter Russian moves in Central Asia, succeeded in being heard. Amir **Shir Ali** (r. 1863–1879), a son of Amir Dost Muhammad, had ascended the Afghan throne after eliminating a number of rivals. He gained British recognition in 1869 and was invited to meet Viceroy Lord Mayo in Ambala, India. (*See* AMBALA CONFERENCE.) Shir Ali was worried about Russian advances in Central Asia and wanted British guarantees from Russian aggression and recognition of his son, Abdullah Jan, as crown prince and his successor. But the viceroy was willing to give only presents of 600,000 rupees and a few pieces of artillery, and would not offer any guarantees from Russian attack. Disappointed, he was receptive when General **Constantin Kaufman**, the Russian governor general at Tashkent, made overtures, promising what Britain was not willing to give. Major-General **Stolietoff** arrived in Kabul on July 22, 1878, with the charge to draft a treaty of alliance with the Afghan ruler. Britain was now alarmed and sent General **Neville Chamberlain** to lead a military mission to Kabul. Arrangements had been made with the independent tribes on the frontier for the mission's escort of 1,000 troops, but when he reached the border, Chamberlain was prevented from entering Afghan territory. Britain chose this "insult" as a *casus belli* and dispatched an army under General **Sir Frederick Roberts**, which entered Kabul on July 24, 1879. Shir Ali fled north in the hope of receiving Russian support. No help was forthcoming and the amir died of natural causes in Mazar-i Sharif on February 21, 1879. (*See* SECOND ANGLO-AFGHAN WAR.)

Britain recognized Shir Ali's son **Yaqub Khan** as amir (Abdullah Jan, the crown prince, had preceded his father in death) and concluded with him the **Treaty of Gandomak** on May 26, 1879. **Louis Cavagnari** was established as British envoy at Kabul, and history repeated itself when after only six weeks in Kabul, mutinous troops whose pay was in arrears stormed the British mission and assassinated the envoy and his staff. Yaqub Khan resigned in October 1879, leaving the field to his brother, Muhammad Ayub, and his cousin Abdul Rahman Khan.

This ushered in a new era in Afghan history under Amir **Abdul Rahman** (r. 1880–1901) and a complete reorganization of the state, including the armed forces. Abdul Rahman, the oldest son of Amir Muhammad Afzal Khan (r. 1866–1867), had fought his uncle Amir Shir Ali in 1864 and was forced to flee to the court of the amir of Bukhara. He returned to Afghanistan in 1866 and defeated Amir Shir Ali, but rather than assume power himself, placed his father, Afzal Khan, on the Afghan throne. Forced into exile again, Abdul Rahman spent 11 years in Samarkand and Tashkent in the newly acquired Russian province of Turkestan. The "Iron Amir," as he came to be known to history, used his time well. He was able to acquaint himself with the relatively modern technology of the Russian army and, in discussions with General Kaufman, gained an insight into the Western imperialist mind, which saw its "manifest destiny" in the conquest of the Asian continent. Not overly burdened by tradition, he realized that the survival of Afghanistan depended on borrowing from the enemy the military technology that was superior to anything Afghanistan could muster. After the death of Amir Shir Ali in February 1879, Abdul Rahman Khan returned to Afghanistan. Kaufman had provided him with some 200 breech-loading rifles and some money; he borrowed 2,000 sovereigns from merchants to purchase horses and equipment and moved south. He issued a proclamation, saying, "I have not come to fight Afghans who are true believers, but to make **ghaza**" (war). But he did not expressly state that he was going to fight the British army of occupation (AR, 173).

The British government feared a repetition of the debacle of the **first Anglo-Afghan war**, and on March 14, 1880, the secretary of state for India sent a telegram to the viceroy, urging that it was

necessary to find, without delay, some Native authority to which we can restore Northern Afghanistan, without risk of immediate anarchy, on our evacuation of Kabul not later than next autumn, and, if possible, earlier. No prospect of finding in country any man strong enough for this purpose. I therefore advocate early public recognition of Abdur Rahman as legitimate heir of Dost Mahomed, and open deputation of Sirdars with British concurrence to offer him throne of Afghanistan, as sole means of saving country from anarchy.

Thereupon, the viceroy dispatched **Lepel Griffin**, the chief political officer at Kabul, to inquire as to the *sardar*'s (prince's) objectives. Negotiations culminated on July 22, 1880, in the grudging recognition of Abdul Rahman as "Amir of Kabul and its Dependencies," in spite of the fact that he had entered Afghanistan with the assistance of Russia. In an attempt at divide and rule, the London government intended to sever Herat and Kandahar from Kabul control, but the 35-year-old *sardar* had set his aim at the reunification of Afghanistan. The return of Abdul Rahman Khan had encouraged resistance elsewhere, while he was consolidating his power in northern Afghanistan, *ghazis* began to attack British bases in the south. Sir Percy Sykes tells the story of one battle at **Ahmad Khel** on April 19, 1880:

The Afghan cavalry charged, and at first, on the left flank, threw back the 19th Bengal Lancers, who had to charge uphill to meet them. Meanwhile the Afghan footmen pressed on with such fanatical valour, that neither the guns firing nor the heavy fire of the infantry seemed able to stop their rush. The situation became critical. However the arrival of further troops at the front and the steady fire of the guns and infantry, which moved down the *Ghazis* by hundreds, finally broke their charge. (Sykes, 131)

A British officer remarked, "I saw only two Afghans ask for mercy, and one cannot help admiring their reckless bravery" (Sykes, 132).

The British position at Kandahar was "unsatisfactory." Lieutenant General **J. M. Primrose** faced a serious problem of logistics—his long lines of communication came under increasing attack, and **Ayub Khan**, son of Amir Shir Ali and a contender to the Afghan throne, was said to be preparing for an attack on the city. Primrose sent Brigardier General **G. R. S. Burrows** with a brigade of some 2,500 men to strengthen the forces of the British-appointed governor, most of whose soldiers deserted to the army of Ayub Khan. The ensuing **Battle of Maiwand** resulted in the annihilation of the 66th British-Indian regiment. Kandahar came under siege, and the British garrison, some 3,000 strong, withdrew into the walled city, expelling the Afghan population of about 15,000.

The viceroy was alarmed. He sent a telegram to the secretary of state, reporting that

> General Burrows has been seriously defeated by Ayub Khan. Primrose has vacated cantonments at Kandahar and retired to citadel. We are pushing forward reinforcements already on their way, as quickly as possible, and sending large additional reinforcements from India. It may be necessary to anticipate despatch of troops from England intended for this season's reliefs. (PP, L/P&S/20/MEMO/2)

It was left to General Sir Frederick Roberts to avenge the defeat at Maiwand and to come to the relief of the Kandahar garrison.

Abdul Rahman quickly consolidated his power and set out to eliminate his rivals: on August 11 he occupied Kabul, and on September 22, 1881, he defeated Ayub Khan at Kandahar and then proceeded to take Herat.

The two Anglo-Afghan wars led the British-Indian general staff to reassess the lessons learned from its confrontation with the Afghans. In the secret *Handbook of Kandahar Province, 1933*, officers were told:

Introduction

Never surrender, when in a tight corner as it will merely lead to a degrading and barbarous death. A vigorous offensive at the right moment is the best policy; it may snatch victory from an apparently hopeless situation. Never relax precautions, the Afghans and the tribesmen will invariably punish a tactical error or lack of precautions. Do not allow Afghans to enter small military posts; they are very observant, and will soon spot the weak points in the defence. History provides numerous examples of the price paid for lack of alertness and for taking insufficient precautions, such as failures to piquet heights; neglect to adopt perimeter camps, and faulty siting camps; movements up and down *nalas* [dry riverbeds], instead of along spurs; columns being overtaken by darkness, before protective measures could be adopted; employment of detachments too weak for their tasks.
Never hesitate or remain inactive, or take purely defensive measures —they stimulate the Afghans in a remarkable manner. Be prepared for Afghan rushes—they are most notable for the fury with which they start, as for the rapidity with which they die away.
Afghans will hold a position with the utmost determination until their front is penetrated or their flank is turned—then they suddenly retire in the utmost disorder. Do unto the Afghans as they do unto you. Never make terms with the Afghans, unless they can be compelled to observe these terms.
Don't pay bribes to conceal weakness and pay cash on delivery only and never in advance. Punishment must be stern and drastic—inflict the heaviest possible casualties, followed by destruction of villages and the confiscation of livestock, grain, fodder, and fuel. The Afghans thoroughly appreciate and respect the enemy who can and does punish and then makes friends again.

A somewhat racist assessment of the "Afghan character" describes Afghans as a blend of "virtue and vice":

> They are hardy, brave, proud, simple in their mode of living, frank, prepared to die in accordance with their code of honour yet faithless and treacherous; generous to a degree yet devoured by greed for money; capable of great endurance and of feats of energy but constitutionally lazy.
>
> They are capable of strong personal attachments but never forget a wrong. Hospitality is part of their creed. A host will defend a guest at the risk of his life, but he may have little scruples against revealing his guest's future movements to others.

The pure Afghan tribes [meaning **Pashtuns**], no matter what their internal jealousies may be, will resist outside interference as strenuously now and in the future, as they have done in the past.

The Soviet expeditionary army had to learn these lessons a hundred years later.

Afghan irregular tribal forces (*lashkars*) were generally more effective than Afghan regulars. They excelled in guerrilla warfare, showing considerable bravery and determination. During the first Anglo-Afghan war the ranks of tribal forces were quickly increased with the addition of an unpaid reserve, called *alijaris*, forming a formidable force of about 100,000 men. Of these the Durrani, **Ghilzai**, and transborder Afghans were the most intrepid fighters. They were rapidly assembled by the sound of drums that quickly covered the entire tribal belt, including the Afghans on the British side of the border. In response to a call for holy war (**jihad**), an Afghan ruler could fire the martial spirit of the tribes and induce them to temporarily resolve their feuds and vendettas. Tribal pride and competition with others made them perform heroic deeds. The major weakness of tribal *lashkars* was that they preferred to fight close to home and carried provisions for a limited number of days, after which time they had to return to their homes. The British were at times able to snatch victory from defeat, when the Afghans dispersed to carry their plunder back to their areas and were cut off by a relatively small force.

Before the advent of aerial warfare the deserts and mountains of Afghanistan were a formidable barrier to an invader. Registan, the "Land of Sand," and a waterless desert on the southern border of Afghanistan with India (now **Pakistan**), and the difficult mountain passes to the east were the graveyards of many an Englishman. British troops were able to occupy the major cities on the periphery of the mountainous core, and Kabul, Ghazni, Kandahar, and Herat could be occupied while the Afghans retreated into the mountains. Problems of logistics would quickly emerge; the lines of supply would be cut, small forces of the invader would be destroyed, and with success the attacks would become increasingly brazen. Eventually, the British occupiers had to decide to take a stand and fight to the end—as in the first Afghan war; or treat with the most prominent of the Afghan *sardars* to ensure a dignified withdrawal to India. Britain chose the latter alternative.

Abdul Rahman concluded an agreement with the British government, by which Britain guaranteed him protection from unprovoked Russian aggression, provided he permitted Britain to conduct his foreign relations. He obtained a subsidy in money and materiel to strengthen the defenses of his country. Abdul Rahman considered this treaty an alliance between equals, and, having protected his northern borders, he kept the British at arm's length, never allowing them to gain any influence in the country under the aegis of their common defense. He formulated a "buffer-state policy," which aimed at playing off Afghanistan's imperialist neighbors against each other. This policy served Afghanistan well until the end of World War II, when changed conditions required new approaches in the conduct of Afghan foreign policy. Afghanistan's northern and eastern boundaries were demarcated during the amir's tenure, including the Durand Line (1893), which he accepted under "duress" in the **Durand Agreement**.

The Iron Amir used whatever taxes he could raise and the subsidy from the British-Indian government to purchase weapons from India. He also set up workshops to manufacture ammunition and small arms. The military reforms under Amir Dost Muhammad and Amir Shir Ali were not continued because of the chaos following their rule, and Amir Abdul Rahman had to start from the beginning. His major objectives were to unify the country and ward off foreign aggressors. The Iron Amir declared to a council of elders:

> The forces I am going to raise are intended only for the protection of Afghanistan in the event of a foreign invasion. You know your country is situated like a village between the two governments of the infidels, each of which is ambitious to invade and take Afghanistan. You must, therefore, be prepared for a time of emergency so as to safeguard yourself from invasion. If you fail to provide for such an event, you will then have to contend with the fate of your brethren in India, who, you know well, have no power over their wives. You will then all become women yourselves, with no influence over your families. (Kakar, 96)

Abdul Rahman set about creating an army that was initially officered by persons of little status, but eventually he also recruited the sons of notables (*khanzada*), and eventually Durranis of his own Muhammadzai clan who constituted a privileged elite. Within 10 years he had organized an army of some 60,000 and by the end of his reign his army probably amounted to 100,000 men, no fewer than a hundred years later. With the exception of most Hazara and Qizilbash, **Shi'a** minorities, all ethnic communities were represented in the army, and the Ghilzai, although traditional rivals of the Durranis, formed the largest component (Kakar, 97). Amir Abdul Rahman organized his regular army according to the British model into infantry (*piyada*), cavalry (*sawara*), and artillery (*topkhana*) branches. Royal bodyguards were enlisted that included, in addition to sections of the Durranis of Kandahar, the sons of notables of the non-Pushtun community. The irregular army consisted of the feudal cavalry (*sawara-i kushada* or *sawara-i khudaspa*), raised from feudal *khans* in lieu of payment of revenues. Tribes and ethnic groups were levied at a certain ratio for temporary service, whereas soldiering in the regular army was a lifetime profession.

With the defeat of his rival Ayub Khan at Kandahar (*see* KANDA-HAR, BATTLE OF) and the capture of Herat, Abdul Rahman had reunited Afghanistan under his resolute rule and was recognized by Britain as "Amir of Afghanistan and its Dependencies." This ended wars with Afghanistan's neighbors, except for the Panjdeh Incident of 1885, in which Russia was able to annex the Panjdeh oasis (*see* PANJDEH INCIDENT). The Iron Amir now turned to the task of eliminating the last pockets of autonomous rule. In a very vicious and protracted war, he pacified the Hazarajat (*see* HAZARA WARS), and in 1895–1896 he turned against **Kafiristan**, an area which Islam had not yet penetrated and converted the Kafirs, whose country became henceforth known as Nuristan, from *nur*, light, meaning the country enlightened by the spark of Islam. *See* KAFIR WAR.

Abdul Rahman was keenly aware of his predecessors' policies. He felt that during their administration "nearly every mullah and *khan* (chief) considered himself independent, and they gave themselves the airs of princes and prophets." He wanted to be the unchallenged master of his realm and considered the Ghilzai a threat. In his biography, *The Life of Abdur Rahman* (compiled by Sultan Mahomed Khan), he states:

> The Ghilzais had very influential chiefs, with a considerable number of fighting men. These khans or chiefs, as well as their armies, were very cruel and harsh to the subjects, their cruelties, their unlimited authority, their excessive taxation, their robberies and plunderings, their attacks on the caravans, their constant warfare with each other, the wholesale slaughter of humanity in general, were well known to the people. . . . It was natural, therefore, that I, who was the least likely person in the world to allow such misbehaviour under my very eyes, should be hated by them, and that every possible attempt would be made to upset my rule. (AR, I, 250)

Therefore, the amir stopped all the government allowances to Ghilzai chiefs and clergy (**ulama**) with the result that the Ghilzais staged a major uprising in 1886–1887 that was suppressed only with great difficulty. (*See* ABDUL KARIM; GHILZAI.)

Introduction

By the time Amir Abdul Rahman died, he had created a strong, centralized state with borders recognized by his neighbors and an army that freed the ruler from dependence on the tribes. The government passed into the hands of his first son, Habibullah, without any challenge or major domestic or foreign wars during his reign.

Amir **Habibullah** (r. 1901–1919) ordered a general amnesty and permitted many to return from foreign exile. His outstanding achievements were in the fields of education and diplomacy. He set up the beginnings of a modern system of education, employing members of the clergy (ulama) in the elementary levels and Afghan and foreign teachers in Habibia College, a high school patterned in part on the British Indian system. He also permitted publication of a modern newspaper, the *Siraj al-Akhbar*, edited by Sardar Mahmud Tarzi, which became quickly an important organ expressing Afghan nationalist sentiments and solidarity with the Islamic world.

The British government was not satisfied with some of the provisions of the agreements concluded with Amir Abdul Rahman, and therefore wanted to force certain changes before it recognized the new amir. London maintained that the agreements were with the *person* of the amir, not the state of Afghanistan, and therefore the agreements had to be renegotiated with his successor. In spite of severe pressures, Habibullah did not yield. In December 1904 he finally agreed to meet in Kabul with **Louis W. Dane**, foreign secretary of the government of India. The result was a complete victory for Habibullah when Britain was forced to renew the agreements concluded with Amir Abdul Rahman in the form of a treaty (March 1905), which recognized Habibullah's title, "Independent King of the State of Afghanistan and Its Dependencies." (*See* ANGLO-AFGHAN TREATY OF 1905.)

A crisis in relations with British India occurred when Habibullah learned that Afghanistan's neighbors had concluded the **Anglo-Russian Convention of 1907**. This agreement divided Afghanistan (and Iran) into spheres of influence with provisions for "equality of commercial opportunity" in Afghanistan for Russian and British traders and the appointment of commercial agents in Kabul. The amir was invited to ratify the agreement, but he refused and the convention was never implemented.

The outbreak of World War I posed another crisis in foreign relations: in spite of warnings not to do so from the viceroy of India, Amir Habibullah received a German-Ottoman mission at Kabul. He met with members of the **Hentig-Niedermayer expedition** and initialed the draft of a secret treaty of friendship and military assistance with Germany to provide for the eventuality of an Allied defeat. Germany could not deliver, and Britain promised a handsome reward for Afghan neutrality; therefore, a realistic appraisal of the situation prompted the Afghan ruler to stay out of the war. But Britain showed itself miserly and, once the crisis was over, wanted to continue its exclusive control of Afghanistan. The "war party" at his court felt that the amir had failed to take advantage of a unique opportunity of winning independence from Britain and his enemies conspired to depose him. He was assassinated on February 20, 1919, while he was on a hunting trip at Kala Gosh in **Laghman**.

Sardar Amanullah, eldest son of Habibullah, ascended the throne in February 1919 after a short palace coup against his uncle Nasrullah Khan. King **Amanullah** (r. 1919–1929) decided to win his country's independence, if necessary by means of war. He made it known that he wanted to base his relations with Britain on a new foundation. On March 3, 1919, he wrote to Lord Chelmsford, the viceroy of India, that the "usurpers" (Sardar Nasrullah) had abdicated and the "free Government of Afghanistan" was prepared to conclude such treaties "as may be useful to our government and yours."

On the occasion of a royal *darbar* (audience) on April 13, 1919, Amanullah showed himself more belligerent, announcing to an assembly of dignitaries:

> I have declared myself and my country entirely free, autonomous and independent both internally and externally. My country will hereafter be as independent a state as the other states and powers of the world are. No foreign power will be allowed to have a hair's breadth of right to interfere internally and externally with the affairs of Afghanistan, and if any ever does I am ready to cut its throat with this sword. (Adamec, 1974, 47)

He turned to the British agent and said, "Oh Safir, have you understood what I have said?" The British agent replied, "Yes, I have." The government of India was at a loss to decide whether it should accept this fait accompli. Having declared the previous agreements concluded with the "person" of the amir, India could not deny the need for a new treaty with King Amanullah. Therefore, the viceroy merely thanked Amanullah for the information that he was acknowledged as amir "by the populace of Kabul and its surroundings" and used the mourning for Amir Habibullah's assassination as an excuse for not discussing any new agreements.

Amanullah was ready for action. On March 11 he announced to the Afghan envoy in India that "the Government of Afghanistan hopes by the grace of God, within a short time, to have itself counted as one of the most well-known and honorable Governments in the world." On May 1, 1919, he sent Saleh Muhammad, the commander in chief, to Dakka, **Muhammad Nadir** (the subsequent king) moved to **Khost**, and **Abdul Quddus**, the prime minister, proceeded to Kandahar. Two days later Afghan pickets stopped a group of Khaibar Rifles escorting a caravan from moving into disputed territory between Landi Khana and Torkham. The British tribal militia withdrew. A *farman* (royal decree) by King Amanullah advised the frontier tribes that Hindus and Muslims in India were in revolt and that Saleh had advanced to the border for the protection of Afghanistan.

The first hostile action began on May 4, when Afghan troops occupied **Bagh**, a hamlet on the British side of the border, and cut the water supply to Landi Kotal. On May 5 the Indian government decided to stop demobilization of all combatant forces in India and recalled all British officers of the Indian army. In Peshawar the situation deteriorated rapidly. A force of some 8,000 holy warriors had gathered, ready to march on the cantonment, and it was only with great difficulty that the British commissioner, Sir George Roos-Keppel, had the walled city surrounded and cut the supplies of water, electricity, and food. A British messenger demanding the surrender of the Afghan postmaster in Peshawar was the only casualty. (*See* THIRD ANGLO-AFGHAN WAR.)

As so often in the past, the Indian government felt that war was the only way to save face, but London feared that an attack on one of the few remaining independent Muslim states would have serious repercussions elsewhere. It requested information as to what kind of armistice the Afghans wanted. Although there was no widespread rebellion in India, the situation was nevertheless serious. Pashtun soldiers of the British Khaibar Rifles deserted in large numbers, and tribes on the North-West Frontier prepared for jihad. London eventually authorized an invasion of Afghanistan and occupation of **Jalalabad**, but warned India "you will not have forgotten [the] lessons of history, that we have not so much to fear from [the] Afghan regular Army as from the irregular tribesmen and their constant attacks on our isolated camps and lines of communications" (Adamec, 1967, 116). In the meantime the Indian government considered such far-fetched measures as approaching the sultan/caliph of the defeated Ottoman Empire to prohibit jihad and "disowning those by whom it may be proclaimed."

While the frontier at Dakka became stabilized, Nadir Khan invaded Waziristan and advanced toward Thal, and Roos-Keppel, chief commissioner of the North-West Frontier, warned that all the Khurram border tribes seemed likely to rise "unless we have success against Nadir Khan shortly." John Maffey, the chief political officer with the field force, worried that an invasion of Afghanistan might leave no one to settle with, and he was greatly relieved when he heard that King Amanullah was ready to negotiate. He felt that "our peace terms can then be presented as an ultimatum" and added, "This time we shall have got the Afghan really cold, I hope." But caution prevailed. In view of the uncertainties of war, its repercussions in the Islamic world, and the possibility of widespread revolt by the Frontier Afghans, Denys Bray, foreign secretary to the government of India, favored peace. He recalled that the Indian government considered releasing Afghanistan from British tutelage as a reward for Amir Habibullah's neutrality in World War I.

The war had not led to any great territorial conquests: the British captured Dakka in the east and Spin Boldak in the south, but the British defenses on the Waziristan and Zhob frontier had collapsed and the situation in the Afghan tribal belt was critical. After aerial bombings of Jalalabad and Kabul, the Indian government agreed to make peace. A cease-fire was declared on June 3, and an Afghan delegation arrived in Rawalpindi on July 25 to begin peace negotiations, which resulted in a British declaration that the treaty and an appended letter "leave Afghanistan officially free and independent in its internal and external affairs" (Ibid., 183). (*See* ANGLO-AFGHAN TREATY OF 1919; 1921; MUSSOORIE CONFERENCE.)

As a result of the short war that won Afghanistan's independence from British tutelage, King Amanullah became a national hero. Relations with Britain eventually normalized, and Afghanistan established relations with the major states in the world.

King Amanullah was a reformer. He believed that his was an "era of the pen, not the sword," and he embarked on a series of social reforms that were to modernize Afghanistan and started the process toward the emancipation of women. He opened his country to foreign influences, permitting the establishment of embassies in Kabul, and sent students in large numbers abroad. Politically, he followed the policy of Amir Abdul Rahman by playing off his powerful neighbors against each other while inviting German experts in large numbers to help in the task of developing the country. He saw himself as the "Democratic King," drafting a modern constitution, greatly expanding the Afghan system of education, and building a new capital at Darulaman (Dar al-Aman), including a monumental parliamentary building. In the 10 years of his rule, he was able to create a cadre of "Young Afghans," who became his major supporters. His modernist tendencies were reinforced after a journey to European capitals in 1927–28 and meetings with Reza Shah of Iran and Mustafa Atatürk of Turkey. But reaction to his social reforms, such as permission for women to discard the veil and participate in the public life of the country, was growing. A tribal revolt, the **Khost Rebellion** in 1924–1925, was suppressed only with great difficulty; a general revolt in 1928–1929 led to the ouster of the Reformer King and the establishment of **Habibullah Kalakani**, the "Son of a Water Carrier" (*Bacha-i Saqqau*) on the Afghan throne for a violent seven-months rule.

Two factors prevented Kalakani from consolidating his rule: he was a Tajik and not a member of the dominant Pashtun majority; and he had a reputation as a bandit. He found some $1,800,000 when he captured the **Arg** (royal palace), which enabled him to win the temporary adherence of the major tribes. But they soon defected and joined Nadir Khan, one of King Amanullah's generals in the third Anglo-Afghan war, who defeated the dwindling forces of Habibullah Kalakani, and ascended the Afghan throne on October 15, 1929.

Muhammad Nadir Shah (r. 1929–1933) and his son **Zahir Shah** (r. 1933–1973) were, like King Amanullah, of the royal Muhammadzai clan of the Durranis and therefore acceptable to the Pashtun tribes. Nadir Shah began the process of consolidation during his short reign, a task that was greatly accelerated during the reign of his successor. The new monarchs did not have to fight any foreign wars. They devoted themselves to the task of greatly expanding the system of education and creating a modern army that was able to reduce the once formidable power of the tribes.

The Afghan **army** was organized according to the Western model into *qaul-i urdu* (corps), *firqa* (division), *ghund* (brigade), *kandak* (battalion), toli (company), and *baluk* (platoon, troop). To this was added the *shahi-firqa* (guards division). (*See* ARMY, AFGHAN.) Cavalry, artillery, pioneer, and signal divisions were set up as well as a fledgling air force, reorganized from King Amanullah's reign. In addition to the regular army, irregular tribal forces were levied. Initially, the army also performed police functions; small units were stationed in provincial centers with large garrisons in the major towns.

After Nadir Shah was assassinated in November 1933, a council of his brothers served as advisers to the young king. Muhammad Hashim became prime minister (1929–1946), followed by Shah Mahmud (1946–1953), after whom the position was held by Zahir Shah's cousin **Muhammad Daud** (1953–1963). The gradual modernization of the Afghan army was greatly accelerated under Muhammad Daud, and the Soviet Union became the principal supplier of weapons and military technology to Afghanistan. Already during the reign of King Amanullah, the **Soviet Union** provided some pilots and technical support for the creation of an Afghan air force (*see* AIR FORCE, AFGHAN). The Soviet Union had a concession for air service from Kabul to Moscow, which was, however, not renewed by Amanullah's successors. But the times seemed to have changed in the 1950s, and Soviet assistance again became necessary when it was not forthcoming from the West.

World War II resulted in the end of the colonial empires of Britain and France, and India became independent in 1947. In Kabul this was seen as the opportunity to reclaim territory Britain had annexed on Afghanistan's eastern and southern borders. The Afghan government demanded that the Pashtuns of the North-West Frontier Province of India be given the choice to vote for independence rather than merely for inclusion in India or the newly created state of Pakistan. This choice was not given, and Afghanistan's relations with Pakistan remained cool from the start and turned frequently hostile.

The beginning of the cold war further strained relations with Pakistan. The American government sought allies in its policy of containment of the Soviet Union and readily succeeded in 1955 to win Turkey, Iraq, Iran, and Pakistan in an alliance called the Baghdad Pact (later renamed Central Treaty Organization [CENTO]). Afghanistan was tacitly left in the Soviet sphere and the Indian subcontinent was to be defended at the **Khaibar Pass** rather than the Amu Daria, Afghanistan's northern border. A 1949 study for the U. S. Defense Department's Joint Chiefs of Staff said: "Afghanistan is of little or no strategic importance to the **United States**.... Its geographic location coupled with the realization by Afghan leaders of Soviet capabilities presages Soviet control of the country whenever the international situation so dictates" (Bradsher, 20).

Afghanistan was not to receive the promise of help in case of Russian aggression that Britain was willing to offer in the past; therefore, there was no alternative to coexisting with Afghanistan's powerful neighbor. Afghan policy was well summarized in 1932 by Sir Richard Maconachie, the British minister in Kabul:

> King Nadir Shah's foreign policy, as stated by himself and the Prime Minister, is one of quietism. Since the demands of internal reconstruction will absorb the whole resources of the Government for many years to come, such friendly relations as will insure against aggression from without are to be maintained with all foreign powers; there is to be no interference in areas beyond the Afghan frontiers, and Amanullah Khan's "irredentist" attitude towards Russian Turkestan on the one side, and India, on the other, is to be definitely abandoned.
> (Adamec, 1974, 201)

It was therefore natural that Afghanistan would drift into the neutralist camp of Asian and African countries led by Jawaharlal Nehru, Josef Broz Tito, Gamal Abdul Nasser, and others. Buffer-state politics seemed no longer possible, and the concept of peaceful coexistence and "positive neutrality" seemed the only possible course. Kabul observed the United States arming of Pakistan with considerable alarm, but efforts to obtain weapons from the West met with a cool response. Thus, like Egypt, the Afghan government turned to the Soviet Union for military assistance. A turning point occurred in December 1955, when Nikita Khrushchev and Nikolai Bulganin came to Kabul. The Russians supported Afghanistan in the "**Pashtunistan**" dispute and offered massive aid, which the United States was not willing to match. Among the projects financed was a network of roads, connecting to the Soviet Union, including the famous **Salang** tunnel and the air base at **Bagram**. Until the Marxist coup of 1978, the Soviet Union had provided $1,265 million in economic assistance compared to the United States's $532.87 million. Soviet military aid permitted 3,725 Afghan military personnel to go to the Soviet Union for training; only 20 Afghans were enrolled in American military institutions in 1978. In addition some 5,000 Afghan students received academic training, and some 1,600 obtained technical education in Soviet institutions. In 1955 President Daud convened a **Loya Jirga** to approve his acceptance of Soviet aid (Bradsher, 26ff.). Some observers noted that foreign students who attended Western educational institutions tended to become leftists, whereas those studying in Eastern bloc countries tended to become disenchanted with the Soviet system. But students in military academies were carefully segregated from civilian life, and it is not clear to what extent they were influenced by Soviet ideology. Western scholars were largely ignorant of developments in the Afghan armed forces. Unlike Afghan politicians, journalists, and members of the urban bureaucracy, military officers kept aloof of the social functions attended by foreigners and little of substance pertaining to the armed forces was published in Kabul. With the Soviet weapons arrived advisers and experts, who were in close daily contact with their counterparts in the Afghan services. No matter whether they were Marxists or not, it was not lost on the officers' corps that they had the capacity to stage a successful coup and make themselves masters of the country.

Afghanistan was one developing country where the United States did not try to outdo the Soviet Union in competitive assistance. Soviet aid was largely in low-interest loans as compared to outright American gifts, but it was nevertheless welcome to provide the means for Afghanistan's ambitious developmental projects. The Soviet Union and Afghanistan were natural trading partners. Afghanistan could offer one item of export that was much in demand in the Soviet Union—natural gas, which could not be sold elsewhere at the time. Furthermore, a barter trade in goods made it possible to import goods for which no hard currency was available. The massive foreign aid that also came from other European and Middle Eastern countries made it possible to establish the beginnings of a native small industry and to greatly expand Afghanistan's system of education. There is no question that there was considerable economic improvement and some prosperity, which, however, did not equally benefit all segments of society. With heightened expectations and the experiment with democracy after 1963, voices began to be heard in public that attacked the ancien régime and demanded the establishment of alternative political systems.

The expansion of the secular educational system in Afghanistan led to the emergence of an elite group of young Afghans who became the principal protagonists in a political dialogue between secular leftists and radical Islamists. The **People's Democratic Party of Afghanistan** (PDPA) was a Marxist party founded on January 1, 1965, by 27 original members who elected **Nur Muhammad Taraki** and **Babrak Karmal** as their leaders. They began a process of secret recruitment of followers in the army, the bureaucracy, and schools that was soon challenged by an Islamist reaction, headed by Sayyid Musa Tawana, Ghulam Muhammad Niazi, and **Burhanuddin Rabbani**, all professors at the school of theology at Kabul University who were disciples of Hasan al Banna, the founder of the Muslim Brotherhood in Egypt.

The conflict between the radical Left and Islamists seemed decided in favor of the former when, in July 1973, Muhammad Daud, a cousin of King Zaher, staged a palace coup and transformed Afghanistan into a republic. President Daud was a military man who had served as military governor in important provinces and as commander of the central forces and minister of defense, interior, and prime minister. He felt that he had the loyalty of the armed forces and was supported by Pashtun nationalists and modernist reformers who felt the development of the country would be best served by a strongman as the head of state. Babrak Karmal's wing of the PDPA, commonly called **Parcham**, supported the coup, and some of its members were appointed to government positions. Members of the Islamist opposition were jailed, or sought asylum abroad and the government took a decided turn to the left. At the same time the nucleus of an Islamist guerrilla force formed with support from Pakistan and staged limited operations into **Panjshir**, which did not seriously threaten the regime. President Daud eventually decided to disengage himself from

Introduction 21

the leftist embrace; he dismissed many of his leftist supporters, reestablished correct neighborly relations with Pakistan, and sought support from oil-rich states. His moves came too late: on April 27, 1978 (7 Saur 1357), in a rare move of unity, Parcham and **Khalq**, the two wings of the PDPA, staged a successful coup, which led to the establishment of the "Democratic Republic of Afghanistan" (DRA). This marked the end of continuous peace since the third Anglo-Afghan war, and the beginning of a civil war and a war of liberation when the Soviet Union intervened to support the faltering Marxist regime.

By the 1970s the Afghan government had a force of 90,000 to 100,000 men, about the same number it traditionally counted, but modernized and equipped with Soviet weapons and an air force of some 7,000 men. Corps headquarters existed in Kabul, home of the central forces; Kandahar, the second corps; and **Gardez**, the third corps, which served as regional headquarters. Into the 1980s the tactical organization of the Afghan army was as follows:

 11   Infantry divisions
 3–4 Mechanized brigades
 2   Mountain infantry brigades
 2–3 Commando brigades
 1   Paratroop brigade/regiment
 1   Artillery brigade
 Assorted combat support and service support regiments
 Equipment included:
 500–600 Light and medium tanks
 400–500 APC/IFV
 450 Artillery pieces, 100-mm or greater
 100 120-, 160-mm mortars
 50 BM-13, BM-16 MRLs (McMichael, 45)

The air force was organized into seven air regiments as follows:
 3 Fighter sqns. with MIG-21s
 3 Fighter-bomber sqns. with SU-7s and SU-22s
 4 Fighter-bomber sqns. with IL-28 light bombers
 2 Transport sqns. with AN-2s, AN-26sIL-14s
 3-4 Helo sqns. with Mi-4s, Mi-8s, and Mi-17s
 2 Independent helo sqns. with Mi-24s
 1 Training sqn.

Total aircraft amounted to 140–170 fighters and 45–60 helicopters (McMichael, 46).

In addition there was the **sarandoy**, a paramilitary police force of the ministry of interior, which operated in the provinces; combat units of **KHAD** (later WAD), the state security service (later ministry); a paramilitary border brigade; and the militias, recruited from tribes and ethnic minorities.

This considerable arsenal was further strengthened after 1980 with the Soviet intervention in Afghanistan. (*See* LIMITED CONTINGENT OF SOVIET FORCES IN AFGHANISTAN; SOVIET INTERVENTION/ INVASION.)

With the weapons at their disposal, the nascent resistance movement did not seem a serious threat to the Kabul government. The Kabul government had the backing of one of the superpowers, and in late December 1979, the Soviet intervention appeared to tilt the odds strongly in the regime's favor.

After about 60 years of peace in Afghanistan, a new, destructive civil war began soon after the Marxist coup, followed in 1980 by a war of liberation against the Soviet occupation, and again a civil war after the departure of Soviet forces. The victorious **mujahedin**, "holy warriors," as they called themselves, began a struggle for power that has not been resolved to this day. The mujahedin prevailed over the combined Soviet/Kabul forces for a number of reasons:

The nature of Afghan geography. The country's terrain, its mountains and deserts, offered a ready refuge from an invading army and staging areas for guerrilla attacks. The Soviet political leadership (members of the Soviet general staff now claim they were against the intervention) probably felt that with control of Afghanistan's airspace, its forces could overcome the disadvantages of the Afghan terrain. Unlike the Vietcong in Vietnam, the mujahedin did not have the protection of large forests, but they were able to move at night to cross open terrain and find shelter in rugged mountain terrain to avoid detection. Mujahedin groups usually operated in territory they knew well, which facilitated the movement of troops and supplies. McMichael points out "Most mountain valleys will not permit the movement of more than a division-sized formation. As the main valley narrows or as units move off into side-canyons, the command is split and there is no room for manoeuvre. Flanks are very difficult to secure; it is all but impossible to maintain contact with units to the left and right." The few roads make surprise impossible, and often there is only one vehicular approach, and once a unit has been blocked, it has nowhere to go until it is relieved (McMichael, 23). Helicopters and ground attack aircraft had to fly at low altitudes, and when the mujahedin acquired Blowpipe and Stinger shoulder-launched antiaircraft missiles, the Soviet command had to resort to less effective high-altitude bombing.

The availability of an abundance of manpower. The mujahedin had a considerable reservoir of manpower, some locally obtained and considerable numbers recruited from the refugee camps in Peshawar. About 3,500,000 Afghan refugees lived in camps in Pakistan, constituting a ready pool of recruits. In the latter part of the war, they were able to put 80,000 to 100,000 in the field, but not all those were active combatants at anyone time. This often exceeded the number of recruits available to the Kabul government. A common mujahedin complaint was that there were not enough weapons for the number of fighters available. Defections from the Afghan government forces replenished the ranks of the mujahedin with trained military personnel who often carried their weapons with them.

The existence of a safe haven in Pakistan. The mujahedin found a ready haven in Pakistan that permitted rotation of manpower, training, procurement of materiel, and political organization. In order to prevent a proliferation of parties and, no doubt, with an eye to control them, the Pakistan government required refugees to register with one of six, later seven, parties. The leaders were responsible for controlling their followers, providing logistical support, and acting as a coordinating council. These parties were loosely divided into two groups: the moderates headed by **Sayyid Ahmad Gailani, Muhammad Nabi Muhammadi,** and **Sebghatullah Mujaddidi**; and the radical Islamists of **Gulbuddin Hekmatyar,** Burhanuddin Rabbani, Muhammad **Yunus Khales,** and, somewhat later, **Abdul Rasul Sayyaf.** The leaders and their representatives were able to travel abroad to explain their cause and solicit materiel support. Journalists were taken into the field to witness guerrilla activities against Soviet and Kabul forces.

Recourse to Islam as a political ideology. Islam was a powerful ideology and rallying point of the mujahedin. They called their war a jihad (holy war) against an infidel invader, and their religion provided the enthusiasm and willingness to die for a sacred cause, with booty for the victor and instant Paradise for the fallen mujahed. Muslims are brothers and war between them is illegal; therefore, the enemy was accused of having strayed from Islam and become kafirs (unbelievers). Even the Kabul government of Taraki represented its campaign against its Islamist opponents (whom it called the *ikhwan al-shayatin,* the brotherhood of devils) as a jihad and had its council of clergy issue a **fatwa** (legal decision) to this effect, thus legitimizing the war against the rebels. But with the Soviet intervention the issue became clear: it was viewed by many Afghans and their supporters as a war of good versus evil, and the stigma of fighting on the wrong side was a powerful incentive to desert. As powerful an ideology as it was when faced with the Soviet enemy, Islam did not provide political unity, and from the beginning of the war, some leaders' aspirations to political power led to clashes between mujahedin organizations.

Tactical advantage of guerrilla warfare. Mujahedin enjoyed the tactical advantage of the classical guerrilla war, they held the initiative. Initially, they operated in small units against "targets of opportunity," outlying posts that were weakly defended. Their system of intelligence was excellent; they were usually well informed of Soviet and government troop movements and they were able to disperse quickly after hit-and-run attacks. The Soviet forces were not prepared for counterinsurgency, and were forced into defensive stronghold positions from where they conducted great sweeps but could count on few great victories that would be an indication of progress in the pacification of the country. Their tanks and heavy armor were of little use away from the few lines of communication. Originally employed to garrison strategic points, towns, and lines of communication, with the assumption that regime forces would bear the brunt of the combat, Soviet forces were inevitably drawn into search-and-destroy missions that did not produce the desired results. (*See* PANJSHIR, SOVIET OFFENSIVE.) The **"Limited Contingent of Soviet Forces in Afghanistan"** (LCSFA) entered Afghanistan to assist the people against "foreign aggressors," but its soldiers soon realized that the local population saw them as aggressors rather than liberators. While the mujahedin initially controlled little territory, they had the support of the majority of the people and eventually held much of the rural areas.

Confrontation with heterogeneous and unmotivated enemy. In his study of the LCSFA, entitled *Inside the Soviet Army in Afghanistan,* Alexander Alexiev highlights certain inherent weaknesses. He states that the army was divided into two distinct groups: the occupation forces and the counterinsurgency forces. About 80 percent of the total troops consisted of the former; they included most of the regular motorized rifle and tank units and performed primarily security and support duties. They were ethnically mixed, received relatively little training, and included undesirable elements. In spite of considerable efforts at political indoctrination, they were poorly motivated, riven by ethnic and sectarian conflicts, drug addicts, and corrupt. Discrimination, hazing, and beating of soldiers by their officers were rampant. The conscripted Soviet soldier wanted to survive his term without getting into harm's way.

Foreign military and diplomatic support was probably the most important factor in turning the tide in the war. During the early period of the war, the mujahedin obtained their weapons from defectors or captured them from their Soviet/Kabul enemy. When friendly states realized that the Afghans were willing to fight in the face of apparently overwhelming odds, they began to provide significant amounts of assistance. At first supplies of Soviet weapons from Egypt and China were clandestinely channeled to the mujahedin, but soon more sophisticated weapons arrived. In 1981 President Sa'dat declared at a press conference that the United States "told me, 'Please open your stores for us so that we can give the Afghanis the armaments they need to fight' and I gave them the armaments" (Bradsher, 223). In July 1984 the U.S. House of Representatives' Appropriation's Committee approved $50 million in clandestine aid to the Afghan mujahedin; and in April 1985 President Reagan signed a national security directive that provided for assistance "by all available means." U.S. support in 1987 reached $680 million and contributions by the European Community and Arab states increased this amount to more than $1 billion a year. Introduction of the **Stinger** missile ended Soviet aerial supremacy. On the diplomatic front, the American government announced the suspension of wheat exports to the USSR and called for a boycott of the 1980 Olympic Games in Moscow. The sanctions were supported by the majority of European states. The **United Nations** General Assembly in 1980 voted 104 to 18 with 18 abstentions for a resolution that "strongly deplored" the "recent armed intervention" in Afghanistan and demanded the "total withdrawal of foreign troops" from the country. This became a yearly event, and it was telling on the prestige and image of the Soviet Union. In the end, international isolation, the costs of the war, and growing casualties compelled the new Soviet leadership to withdraw its troops from Afghanistan.

In February 1989 Soviet troops completed their withdrawal from Afghanistan claiming losses of about 26,000 dead and many more wounded; Afghan losses according to the Kabul government amounted to some 243,900 soldiers and civilians killed. Some Western observers claim a toll of about one million casualties.

Soviet operational and strategic lessons of the war in Afghanistan, pertaining primarily to force structure and operational art, were summarized by one expert as follows:

> The importance of improved small unit capability for independent action;
> The importance of command of the air and neutralization of enemy air defense;
> The use of helicopters, airborne, and heliborne forces including special forces (not just **Spetsnaz**) for aerial and ground operations;
> Better training and logistics for unconventional wars;

The importance of morale and unit cohesion;
The need for better intelligence assessments;
The need to learn how to fight defensively;
Strategies for winning small wars: denial of cities to the enemy. (Blank, 1990)

The mujahedin captured Kabul on April 25, 1992, and the struggle for power between the mujahedin began. In late 1994 the major protagonists were Gulbuddin Hekmatyar's hizb-i Islami and Burhanuddin Rabbani's jam'iat-i Islami. A third force emerged in north-central Afghanistan, headed by the Junbish-i Milli-i Islami of **General Abdul Rashid Dostum**, and in November 1994 the **Taliban** began their spectacular conquest of most of Afghanistan.

The Taliban were able to take over much of the country with considerable support from **Pakistan** and from a veritable foreign legion of young Muslims: idealistic "freedom fighters," as President Ronald Reagan called them as long as they were fighting communists. The Afghan people were tired of anarchy and the domination of warlords and it was easy for the Taliban to take control of the Pashtun areas. It was more difficult for them to conquer the rest of the country, where the village-bred, monolingual tribesmen were seen as an alien occupation. Especially in the cities they had a disastrous impact with their radical enforcement of medieval punishments, stoning for adulterers, mutilation for theft, and strange executions for sodomy. The prohibition of music, games, girl's schools, mixing of sexes, and the banishment of women to their homes were carried out with ruthless enthusiasm. A religious police of young men, cruising the streets of major cities, inflicted on-the-spot punishment on violators. Men had to grow long beards, and attendance at prayers was compulsory. While their impact in the rural areas was minimal, it was serious in the cities where a large portion of women pursued various occupations (some 40 percent of women in Kabul were teachers) and were often the only support for their families. The government enforced its interpretation of Islam to the neglect of the economy and matters of statecraft. Its foreign allies, **al-Qaeda** and Muslim youth, became a state within the state. The **Sunni** majority of Afghanistan is of the Hanafi school of Islam, which is the largest and more moderate school, but many of the foreigners espoused a Wahhabi (Hanbali) interpretation which was hostile to sufism, a mystical Islam prevalent in Afghanistan.

Some fearful slaughter ensued, largely targeting the Hazara, whom the Taliban termed infidels, and in retaliation they slaughtered the Taliban when they were forced to surrender to their Hazara and Uzbek enemies. For a short time the Taliban were able to conquer most of the country, but

Introduction 27

they did not have the manpower to occupy all areas of the north. This became evident when, as a result of American intervention, the **Northern Alliance** was able to muster thousands of fighters to make possible the rout of the Taliban and their allies.

It was only the American intervention in fall 2001 that ended the Taliban regime and dispersed its al-Qaeda supporters. In its war preparations the United States government made arrangements for access to facilities in areas bordering Afghanistan. In Uzbekistan America gained facilities in the Karshi-Khanabad area which permitted the deployment of about 1,888 individuals, including air support and logistics personnel, military police, and a Special Forces battalion. This was made possible by concluding a U.S.-Uzbek Strategic Partnership. Another U.S. airbase was established in Manas, Kyrgyzstan, in a bilateral military cooperation agreement. Pakistan permitted overflight of American aircraft and provided temporary bases in Baluchistan.

A coalition force of some 37 countries was assembled, which included countries like Britain, providing ground forces from the beginning, or others which granted overflight permission, humanitarian assistance, hospital facilities, or, in the case of Portugal, just two Centcom delegates. Some countries provided little more than sympathy, claiming that for domestic political reasons they could not broadcast their participation (*see* INTERNATIONAL COALITION AGAINST TERROR). The first attacks began on October 7, 2001. Bombers from as far away as Diego Garcia in the Indian Ocean and the United States, as well as aerial attacks from the Gulf and bases in neighboring countries, quickly destroyed Afghanistan's communications infrastructure and its small Afghan air force. By October 10, the United States had complete control of Afghan airspace and began to support the **Northern Alliance** and other local militias who captured **Mazar-i Sharif**, Herat, Jalalabad, and Kandahar in quick succession.

Operation Enduring Freedom was launched to destroy the al-Qaeda network in Afghanistan, capture its members, and, secondarily, replace the Taliban regime. A new model of warfare, the "Afghanistan Model" was created. It consisted of a combination of **Special Forces Teams**, precision-guided munitions, and an indigenous ally. It led to a minimum of American casualties and achieved the objective of destroying the enemy. But it created new problems: some $70 million were spent in the early days of the war to pay for local leaders and their troops, and lacking sufficient American troops on the ground, local leaders/warlords filled the political vacuum. The unity achieved under the repressive Taliban regime was again ended as the mujahedin carved out areas under their control. With the support of the Northern Alliance, Pashtun tribal units in the south and east, and **Muhammad Ibrahim Khan** in the west, the major cities were quickly occupied. General Abdul Rashid Dostum took Mazar-i Sharif, Ibrahim Khan reestablished himself as "amir" in Herat, the **Panjshiris** under **Muhammad Qasim Fahim** controlled the northeast and the capital, and Pashtun forces took control of Kandahar and Jalalabad. They ruled the country in defiance of the Kabul government established in December 2002.

Operation Anaconda and **Operation Valiant Strike** were essentially mop-up operations. The Taliban and al-Qaeda were defeated, but neither Mulla Muhammad Omar nor Osama bin Laden was captured and units of both, supported by forces under **Gulbuddin Hekmatyar**, have begun a low-level guerrilla campaign.

On December 5, 2001, the **Bonn Conference** chose an **Interim Government**, which was replaced by a **Transitional Government** on June 20, 2002. Presidential elections were held on October 9, 2004, and **Hamid Karzai** was elected with a simple majority of more than four million votes. A new **Afghan National Army** (ANA) is being created, which in January 2005 reached a strength of about 21,000 men, supported by a **North Atlantic Treaty Organization (NATO)** force of about 9,000 soldiers and a U.S. contingent of about 20,000 troops. This has permitted the Kabul government to gradually extend its control over the rest of the country. Muhammad Ibrahim Khan joined the government, and the powerful General Muhammad Qasim Fahim was replaced as minister of defense. **Provincial Reconstruction Teams** manned with coalition and NATO troops contribute to provide a measure of security in the major cities. By 2007 the Afghan army is scheduled to have a troop strength of 47,000, which will eventually be increased to 70,000 men supported by a small air force. The protection afforded by foreign allies should be a guarantee that the war lords will realize that rule over their fiefdoms will come to an end.

Disarmament, Demobilization, and Reintegration (DDR) of Afghan militia forces, which constituted the former Northern Alliance and tribal contingents, is carried out with coalition support. A budget of $167 million and eight regional offices were established to facilitate demobilization. Disarmed combatants receive between $100 and $200 and some grain to ease their transition to civilian life. Germany took over the task of reorganizing the national police. This should help to reduced banditry in rural areas.

Later in 2005 parliamentary elections will be held, political parties will become active, and the institutions of a democratic government, including an independent judiciary to check the power of the executive and legislative branches, will exist. Questions that remain to be answered are:

Will the judicial branch follow a liberal interpretation of the law? Will the legislative branch result in the representation of all the people, or lead to the resurrection of the warlords as political leaders? Will there be a willingness to compromise, or will ethnic and sectarian leaders form irreconcilable blocs? Much depends also on an enlightened executive branch. Afghans want to be masters of their own destiny and an Afghan government will one day thank the coalition troops for their assistance and ask them to leave. It can only be hoped that the coalition's intervention will be a "mission well accomplished."

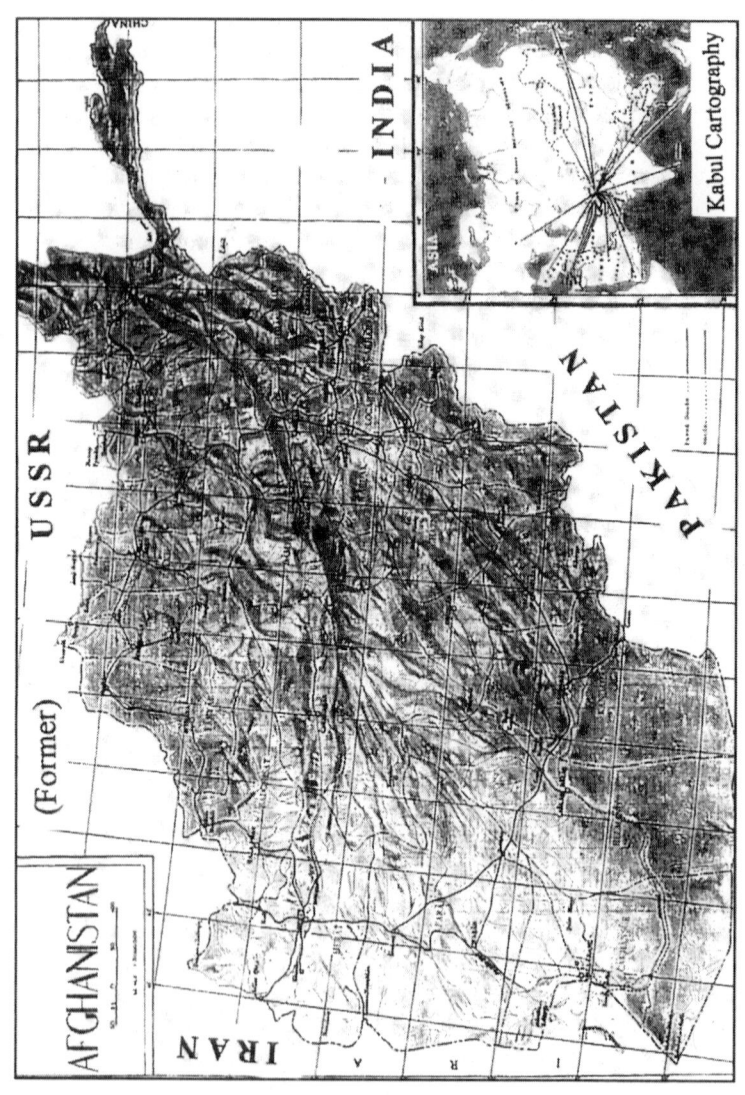

Map 1. Afghanistan Topography

THE DICTIONARY

- A -

A.B.C. Abbreviation for atomic, biological, and chemical agents used as weapons or weapons warheads. Several authors claim that the **Soviet** forces in Afghanistan used rockets with "toxic smoke and harassing agents" during the **Herat uprising** in March 1979 and later sporadically elsewhere. Blood, blister, and nerve agents as well as napalm was said to have been delivered by aircraft, rockets, artillery, and other means. The primary motive behind the use of chemical weapons may have been to use the battlefield as a testing ground (McMichael).

ABD AL–. *See* **ABDUL.**

ABDUL AZIZ KHAN, KANDAK MISHAR. He was a son of Ghulam Haidar Charkhi. In the **third Anglo-Afghan** war he was employed at the Asmar front, commanding Afghan troops in Arandu on October 1919, and refused British demands to move back across the Afghan border, as required by the cease-fire agreement, saying that he had not received any orders to do so from King **Amanullah**. He was promoted to Ghund Mishar in June 1920.

ABDUL HAQ (ABD AL-HAQQ). A **mujahedin** commander affiliated with the **Hizb-i Islami** (Islamic Party) of **Yunus Khales** who had been active in the **Kabul** area. He is an **Ahmadzai Pashtun**, born about 1958 in Hisarak near **Jalalabad**, and as a student was affiliated with the **Muslim Youth Organization** (jawanan-i musulman) which opposed the reformist regime of President **Muhammad Daud**. He was imprisoned in 1975 and freed in 1978 after the **Saur Revolt**. Based in the Shiwaki area, south of Kabul, he was responsible for organizing guerrilla attacks on government posts within Kabul. In 1987 he suffered a crippling injury to his foot that limited his active participation in raids. After the fall of the Marxist regime in April 1992, he was appointed chief of police and security as well as commander of the gendarmerie but resigned from his posts at the beginning of the civil war between the mujahedin groups. He and his brother, **Abdul Qadir**, who became acting governor of Jalalabad, remained neutral between the **Taliban** and **Jam'iat** forces and engaged in commerce with **Pakistan** and the Gulf area. On September 11 the Taliban captured Jalalabad and forced Abdul Haq and other members of the **shura** to flee the country. He lived in Peshawar from 1996 to 1999, when he was forced to leave and settled in Dubai where he became a prosperous businessman. His wife and daughter were assassinated in Peshawar. On October 21, 2001, Abdul Haq entered Afghanistan intending to recruit tribesmen to fight the Taliban government. He was said to be accompanied by two Americans and provided with a considerable amount of money. He was captured (rumored to have been betrayed by **Inter-Services Intelligence** officers) and brutally interrogated before being shot. His mission was said to have been supported by James Ritchie and his brother Joseph from Chicago, American millionaires, and Robert C. McFarlane, former presidential national security adviser.

ABDUL KARIM. A **Ghilzai mulla** of the Andar section who was the son of **Din Muhammad**, the famous mulla Mashk-i Alam (Din Muhammad). **Amir Abdul Rahman** gave him the title *Khan-i-Ulum* (Chief of [religious] Sciences), but he became disaffected when the **amir** ended the virtual autonomy enjoyed by the Ghilzai tribes and imposed taxes on hitherto exempt lands. He was one of the leaders of the Ghilzai Rebellion of 1886–1887, and called for a **jihad** against the amir. The rebellion was suppressed with great difficulty. It was the last of three uprisings of this tribe in the 19th century.

ABDULLAH, DR. ABDULLAH. Son of a **Panjshiri Tajik** father and a **Pashtun** mother. A friend of **Ahmad Shah Mas'ud**, he joined **Jamiat-i Islami** in the 1980s and became the major spokesman of the **Northern Alliance** and acting foreign minister. Upon the capture of **Kabul** from the **Taliban** in December 2001, Abdullah became foreign minister of the **Interim Government**, the **Transitional Government**, and maintained his position in the new government of **President Hamid Karzai**. An eloquent person, he is a medical doctor and speaks fluent English and French.

ABDUL MALIK, GENERAL (1962–). Son of Shamsuddin, he was born in the village of **Faizabad** of Shirin Tagab district in **Fariab** Province. He is the brother of Pahlawan who was assassinated in the summer of 1996. After finishing high school in Maimana, he went to **Mazar-i Sharif** where he graduated from the Teachers Training College (Dar al-Muallemin). During the time of President Najibullah, he was in charge of military logistics and recruitment. Together with General **Abdul Rashid Dostum** and Pahlawan he formed the Junbesh-i Milli-yi Islami and became head of foreign relations for Junbesh. Subsequently he was head of political affairs under General Dostum and governor of Fariab Province. In May 1997 Abdul Malik revolted against Dostum, permitting the **Taliban** to enter Mazar on May 24, and surrendered **Ismail Khan** to them. When the Taliban attempted to disarm his forces, Abdul Malik and the **Shi'a Hizb-i Wahdat** defeated the Taliban, decimating their army in northern Afghanistan. In September the Taliban recaptured Mazar and Abdul Malik was forced to flee into exile. He returned to **Kabul** after the fall of the Taliban government and founded a party, called Hizb-i Azadi-yi Afghanistan (Afghan Freedom Party) in anticipation of the general elections.

ABDUL QADIR, GENERAL. A **Parchami** member of the **Peoples Democratic Party of Afghanistan (PDPA)**. Commander of the Air Defense Forces in 1973, when he supported **Muhammad Daud** in his coup against **Muhammad Zahir Shah**. He actively participated in the **Saur Revolt** and was head of the Revolutionary Council until a civilian government was formed under **Nur Muhammad Taraki**. He became minister of defense for three months in May 1978, but in August he was sentenced to death (commuted to 15 years) for plotting against the **Khalqi** regime. Freed when **Babrak Karmal** came to power, he was restored to his party positions and served again as minister of defense (September 1982–1985). In November 1985 he resigned from the Politburo for "reasons of health" and in November 1986 was appointed ambassador to Warsaw. Recalled two years later and elected a lowly member of Parliament, he is said to have moved to Bulgaria in 1989 and sought asylum in Europe after the fall of the Marxist regime. Born in 1944 of a **Tajik** family in **Herat** Province, he went to military school and attended pilot training and staff college in the Soviet Union.

ABDUL QADIR, HAJI. Vice president, two-term governor of **Nangarhar**, and minister of public works in President **Hamid Karzai**'s **Transitional Government**. A powerful **Ahmadzai Pashtun** leader and ally of the **Northern Alliance**, he was, after Karzai, the most important Pashtun in the government dominated by the **Panjshir**is. During the war against the Marxist regime, Abdul Qadir was a member of the **Hizb-i Islami** of Yunus **Khales**. He walked out of the Bonn meeting, protesting the lack of Pastun representation in the **Interim Government**. He cooperated with American forces in the campaign against **al-Qaeda** and **Taliban** groups and took part in the **Tora Bora** campaign. He is a brother of **Abdul Haq** who was killed trying to rally Pashtun support against the Taliban regime. Abdul Qadir was killed in **Kabul** in early July 2002 by unknown assassins. He was the second Afghan minister killed since the fall of the Taliban regime.

ABDUL QUDDUS. A nephew of Amir **Dost Muhammad** and general who shared Amir **Abdul Rahman's** exile in Bukhara and Samarkand. On their return, he assisted the amir in extending his power over Afghanistan. He captured **Herat** from **Ayub Khan, Muhammad**, son of **Amir Shir Ali**, in 1881 with a small force of 400 cavalry and 400 infantry soldiers and two mountain guns, and in 1890–93 he pacified the **Hazarajat** (*see* HAZARA WARS). Amir **Habibullah** gave him the title *Itimad-ud-Daula* (Confidence of the State) and appointed him prime minister. He was confirmed in this position by King **Amanullah**. In the **third Anglo-Afghan war** Abdul Quddus commanded the **Kandahar** front. A British officer characterized him as "a Tory of the most crusted type in politics, and an apostle of Afghanistan for the Afghans." His descendants, who were prominent in education and government, adopted his title, "Etemadi," as their family name.

ABDUL RAHIM. He was born about 1886, the son of Abdul Qadir. He was a Safi from Kuh Daman, north of **Kabul**, who, from the age of 16, served in various military units and rose from the ranks to become general. At the outbreak of the civil war in 1928 he espoused the cause of **Habibullah Kalakani**. He captured Maimana and **Herat** for Habibullah and became governor of Herat. Because Abdul Rahim had a powerful base in Herat, the Afghan king was unable to remove him from his post until 1934. In June 1935 he was appointed minister of public works and subsequently served as deputy prime minister from 1938 to 1940. He was imprisoned from 1946 to 1948 on suspicion of plotting against the government of Prime Minister Muhammad Hashim. Abdul Rahim is the maternal uncle and father-in-law of Khalilullah Khalili, the poet laureate.

ABDUL RAHIM KHAN, GENERAL SARDAR. Known as "Jarnel-i Lang." He was employed in **Kabul** with household troops in 1917. In 1918 he was in charge of **Jalalabad** military district, and subsequently governor. In command of Afghan troops at Dakka, where he was forced to give way to British forces in the **third Anglo-Afghan war**.

ABDUL RAHMAN, AMIR (ABDUR RAHMAN, r. 1880–1901). Amir of Afghanistan, the oldest son of Amir Muhammad Afzal Khan, who assumed the **Kabul** throne at the end of the **second Anglo-Afghan war**. He fought his uncle Amir **Shir Ali** in 1864 and was forced to flee to the court of the amir of Bukhara. Returning to Afghanistan in 1866, he defeated Amir Shir Ali and recognized his father, Afzal Khan, as the new king. Three years later Amir Shir Ali regained the throne, and Abdul Rahman was forced into exile, spending some 10 years in Bukhara, Tashkent, and Samarkand. After the death of Amir Shir Ali in February 1879, Abdul Rahman Khan returned to Afghanistan. On his way south he gathered a large army. The British occupation force feared a repetition of the debacle of the **first Anglo-Afghan war** and, on July 22, 1880, grudgingly recognized Abdul Rahman as "Amir of Kabul and its Dependencies," in spite of the fact that he had come with Russian support. In September 1881 the **amir** took possession of **Kandahar**, defeating the forces of **Ayub Khan**. With the capture of **Herat**, Abdul Rahman was the undisputed ruler of Afghanistan.

Abdul Rahman concluded an agreement with the British government, in which **Britain** guaranteed him protection from unprovoked Russian aggression, provided he permit Britain to conduct his foreign relations. He obtained a subsidy in money and materiel to strengthen the defenses of his country. Abdul Rahman considered this treaty an alliance between equals, and, having protected his northern borders, he kept the British at arm's length, never allowing them to gain any influence in the country under the aegis of their common defense. He formulated a "buffer-state policy," which aimed at playing off Afghanistan's imperialist neighbors against each other. This policy served Afghanistan well until the end of World War II, when changed conditions required new approaches in the conduct of Afghan **foreign policy**. Afghanistan's northern and eastern boundaries were demarcated during the amir's tenure, including the Durand Line (1893), which he accepted under "duress" in the **Durand Agreement**.

ABDUL RAHMAN, CAMPAIGNS. The future Afghan king learned his trade as a military commander at an early age. His father, Muhammad Afzal Khan, was governor of **Balkh** and appointed Abdul Rahman, who was then about 13 years old, sub governor of Tashqurghan (now called Khulm), a flourishing town and district in Afghan Turkestan. He became a pupil of General Shir Muhammad Khan, a Scot formerly named **William Campbell**, who was captured at the Battle of Kandahar and converted to Islam. Abdul Rahman Khan succeeded him as commander of the army of Balkh. He defeated the **Uzbek** chiefs of Qataghan and **Badakhshan** and forced them to renew their loyalty to **Kabul**. He helped to place his father on the Kabul throne in 1866 and supported his uncle, Muhammad Azim, in his accession in 1867. He was the most obstinate rival of Amir **Shir Ali** Khan, defeating the amir's superior forces in encounters at Sayyidabad (1866), **Qalat** (1867), and the **Panjshir** Pass (1867), but was eventually forced into exile.

To capture a fortified position, Abdul Rahman first tried diplomacy, appealing to the defenders to avoid the bloodshed of fellow Muslims and promising leniency. Lured into a trap, when the spiritual leader of the Mirs of Qataghan invited him to dinner, he took his host prisoner and, dividing his force of some 1,600 *sowars* (cavalry) and two guns into small units, defeated an enemy of 10,000. When he returned from exile, the troops that had assembled to prevent his crossing into Afghanistan melted away. He proclaimed, "I inform you that I have come to release the country of Faiza from the hands of the English. If I succeed in doing so peacefully, well and good, otherwise we shall have to fight" (AR, 174). As he moved slowly south, his forces continued to grow, and **Sir Lepel Griffin**, the political officer with the British expeditionary forces at Kabul, initiated negotiations that led to Abdul Rahman's recognition as "Amir of Kabul." A final challenge to his power was **Ayub Khan**'s capture of **Kandahar** in August 1881, when Abdul Rahman took to the field and decisively defeated his rival. Having eliminated most of his major rivals, Amir Abdul Rahman proceeded to quell local revolts. He defeated Sayyid Mahmud of **Kunar** in 1881 and took direct control of Maimana in 1883. The **Shinwari** revolt was suppressed in 1883, and the **Ghilzai** Rebellion was crushed in 1886–1887. The Iron Amir's last rival, his cousin Ishaq Khan, was defeated at the **Battle of Ghaznigak** in 1888. Government control of the **Hazarajat** was achieved by 1893 after a long series of wars (*see* HAZARA WARS), and **Kafiristan** was the last area integrated into the state of Afghanistan (*see* KAFIR WAR). When Amir **Habibullah** succeeded to the throne in 1901, the entire country was pacified.

ABDUL RAZZAQ, MULLA. Minister of interior in the **Taliban** government and member of the Kabul **Shura**. He was governor of **Herat** and commander of the forces that captured **Kabul**. He was said to have taken ex-President **Najibullah** from the UN compound and ordered his execution. Captured in the Mazar uprising, he managed later to escape. Abdul Razzak is a **Durrani Popalzai** from **Kandahar** who served as a **mujahid** in the **Hizb-i Islami** of **Yunus Khalis**.

ABDUL WAHED, GENERAL. Major military commander of **Burhanuddin Rabbani**'s party after the fall of the Marxist regime in 1992. He defected with **Abdul Rashid Dostum** from the **Kabul** regime and thus contributed to the downfall of the **Najibullah** government. He was a member of the **Parcham** faction of the **Peoples Democratic Party of Afghanistan** (PDPA) and chief of the General Staff of the Armed Forces, January 1980–January 1984. For a short time he was a caretaker at the ministry of national defense. He was elected an alternate member of the PDPA central committee.

ABDUL WALI. Commander-in-chief of the Central Forces until 1973, he was imprisoned as a result of the coup by his cousin **Muhammad Daud** in 1973. He was born in 1924, the son of Marshal Shah Wali (and a cousin of ex-King Zahir), and educated in France and England where he attended Sandhurst as well as the Command and General Staff College at Camberley. He is married to Princess Bilqis, daughter of the former King **Muhammad Zahir**, and lived in Italy since 1976, where he acted as a spokesman for the former king. In August 1995 he went to **Pakistan** where he was received by large crowds. He talked with high-ranking Pakistani officials and conferred with leading Afghans. After the fall of the **Taliban** government, the **sardar** returned to Afghanistan and was involved in promoting a **Loya Jirga** for the formation of a new government.

ADMINISTRATIVE DIVISIONS. Since the time **Timur Shah** (r. 1773–1793) made it his capital, **Kabul** was the center of the kingdom, and princes ruled more or less autonomously in the provinces. Major provinces headed by princes included **Kandahar**, **Herat**, Afghan Turkestan, and Qataghan and **Badakhshan**. Amir **Abdul Rahman** centralized government, and **Muhammad Nadir Shah** divided the country into seven provinces.

As a result of the Constitution of 1964, Afghanistan was divided into 26 provinces (*wilayat*), each with a provincial center (*markaz*) that is graded according to importance into first, second, or third grade; Kabul, **Ghazni**, **Gardez**, **Jalalabad**, **Mazar-i Sharif**, Herat, and Kandahar are first-grade administrative centers. They were headed by a governor (*wali*), as the executive officer, responsible to the Ministry of Interior in Kabul. In addition, each province had representatives of various departments at the administrative center who reported directly to Kabul. There were also a number of sub provinces (*loy woluswali*), which have since been absorbed into provinces. Each province is subdivided into districts (*woluswali*), with an administrator called *woluswal*, who is responsible to his supervising governor and may himself be in charge of one or more subdistricts (*alaqadari*). The administrator of a subdistrict (*alaqadar*) resides in a major village and is responsible to all his supervising administrators. Districts are divided into four grades, depending on population. In the 1970s the 27 provinces were divided into six sub-provinces, 175 districts, and 118 subdistricts. Villages and rural subdivisions (*qarya*) are headed by a village headman (*qaryadar*, *malik*, or *arbab*) who acts as a link between the rural population and the district chief. Cities are divided into wards, or *nahiya*.

In the late 1970s the Afghan government estimated the Afghan population at 15.5 million. Since the defeat of the Marxist government in April 1992, the central government ceased to exist and the Afghan countryside came under the control of local commanders and warlords, while the capital was under siege. The Jam'iat of Professor

The Dictionary 39

Province	Area	Population	Wols.	Alaq	Center
Badakhashan	48,174	715,000	5	7	Faizabad
Badghis	21,854	301,000	4	1	Qala-i Nau
Baghlan	17,165	745,000	5	4	Baghlan
Balkh	11,833	869,000	7	3	Mazar-i Sharif
Bamian	17,411	356,000	4	2	Bamian
Farah	58,834	338,000	8	2	Farah
Fariab	22,274	782,000	7	5	Maimana
Ghazni	32,797	931,000	10	12	Ghazni
Ghor	38,658	485,000	5	1	Chaghcharan
Helmand	61,816	745,000	8	4	Lashkargah
Herat	50,245	1,182,000	11	1	Herat
Jozjan	25,548	441,000	5	6	Shiberghan
Kabul	4,583	3,314,000	8	4	Kabul
Kandahar	49,430	886,000	11	4	Kandahar
Kapisa	5,358	360,000			Mahmud Raqi
Khost		300,000			Khost/ Matun
Kunarha	3,742	321,000			Asadabad
Kunduz	7,926	820,000	5	1	Kunduz
Laghman	7,227	373,000	4	1	Mehterlam
Logar	4,409	292,000	3	3	Pul-i Alam
Maidan/Wardak	9,699	413,000	4	4	Kota-i Ashro
Nangarhar	18,636	1,089,000	17	14	Jalalabad
Nimruz	41,347	149,000	3	1	Zaranj
Nuristan	1,404	112,000			Kamdesh
Oruzgan	28,756	627,000	8		Tarinkot
Paktia	17,772	415,000	11	21	Gardez
Paktika	3,860	352,000			Sharan
Parwan	5,911	726,000			Charikar
Kapisa	5,358	336,000			Mahmud Raqi
Samangan	16,640	378,000	3	2	Aibak
Sar-i Pul		468,000			Sar-i Pul
Takhat	12,325	750,0000	6	5	Taluqan
Zabul	17,298	258,000	5	3	Qalat

The above population figures are only for comparison. The real numbers are certainly higher, which is apparent from the fact that more than 10 million voters registered during the presidential elections of October 2004. Areas are given in square kilometers. New provinces were established to permit a measure of tribal or ethnic autonomy, primarily for Hazaras, Nuristanis, Panjshiris, and one Pashtun community.

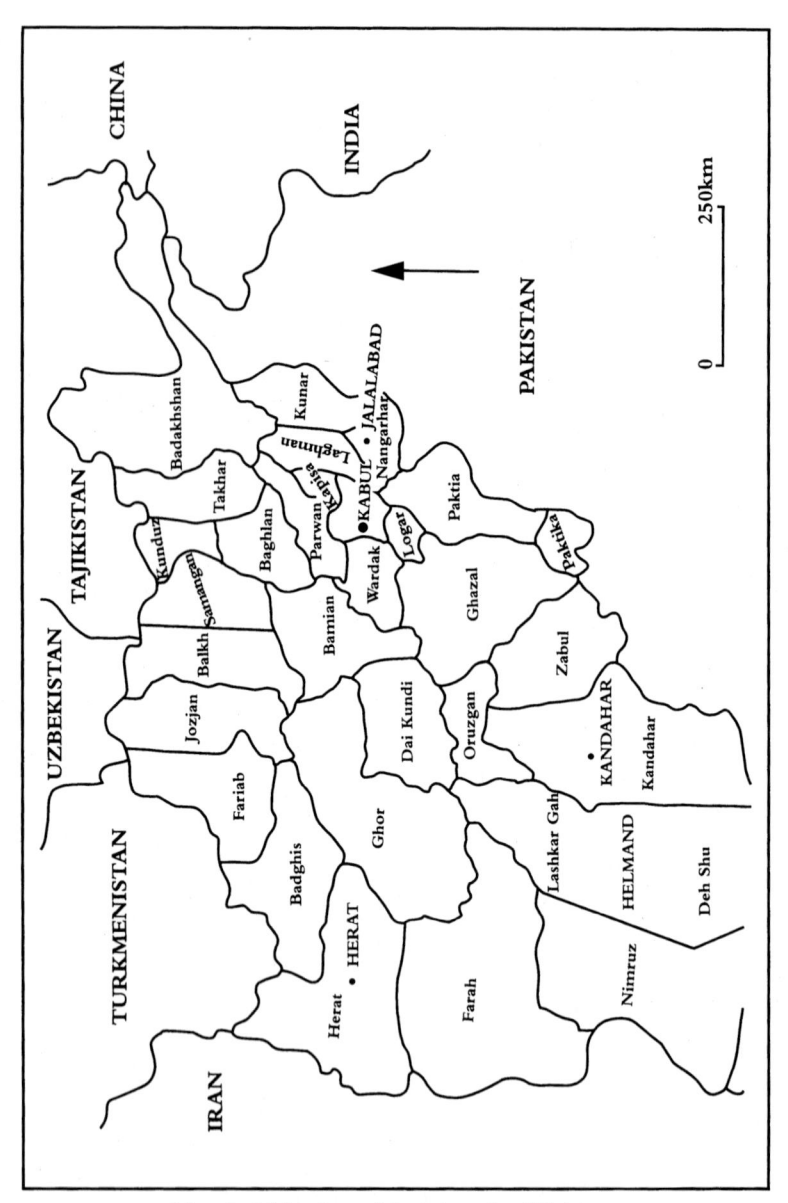

Map 2. Afghanistan Administrative Divisions

Burhanuddin Rabbani controlled Kabul and large portions of northeastern Afghanistan, **General Abdul Rashid Dostum** controlled the north-central provinces, the **Taliban** controlled the western and southern area, and various parties or coalitions controlled the area between Kabul and the **Pakistan** border. After the fall of the Taliban, the **Hamid Karzai** government raised the areas of **Nuristan** (out of **Kunar**), **Panjshir** (out of northern **Parwan**, April 12, 2004), and Dai Kundi (not listed on the above table, out of northern **Oruzgan**, March 28, 2004) to the level of provinces. Sar-i Pul became a province during the **Najibullah** regime. Finally, **Khost**, a district of southern **Paktia**, also became a province, making a total of 34 provinces.

AFGANTSY (Sing. *Afganets*). Soviet veterans of the Afghan war (1980–1989) who were mostly conscripts in a war that did not enjoy popular support. According to a recent study, about 750,000 served in troop units in Afghanistan from 1979 to 1989. Casualties included about 15,000 dead (later revised to 26,000), 50,000 wounded — of whom about 11,500 remained invalids — 330 missing in action, and 18 defectors (Galeotti). The number of dead was later given as about 26,000, including 2,990 officers (Grau, 2002). They felt neglected and that their needs were ignored. About a quarter of the veterans are organized in the "*afganets* movement" with the support of a Council of Soldiers' Mothers and Widows. *Afgantsy* in the highest military posts during 1979–1991 included Marshal S. L. Sokolov, "Hero of the Soviet Union," defense minister, 1984–1987, and first deputy minister, until 1985, a candidate member of the Politburo; Marshal D. Akhromeev, chief of general staff, 1984–1988, responsible for planning combat operations in Afghanistan and later adviser to Gorbachev; General Lobov, chief of general staff and commander-in-chief of the Warsaw Pact, 1991; Col. Gen. P. S. Grachev, first deputy minister, 1991, awarded "Hero of the Soviet Union"; Gen. V. Varennikov, commander of ground forces, 1989–1991, responsible for coordinating withdrawal from Afghanistan; and Gen. Yu. P. Maximov, commander of strategic rocket forces and deputy minister of defense, 1985–1989 (Galeotti, Colton). General **Boris Gromov** commanded the 40th Army and later became the commander of all Russian ground troops. Some observers see the *Afgantsy* as a "new force" of conservative nationalists who may have an impact on the future political life of Russia. *See also* LIMITED CONTINGENT OF SOVIET FORCES IN AFGHANISTAN.

AFGHAN FOREIGN RELATIONS. *See* **FOREIGN RELATIONS.**

AFGHANIS/ARABS. Radical Islamists popularly called Afghanis, mostly of Arab nationality but also from other Muslim countries, who gained fighting experience in the war in Afghanistan and returned to their countries with the intention of toppling their governments and establishing an "Islamic State." They are said to include some 5,000 Saudis; 3,000 Yemenis; 2,000 Egyptians; 2,800 Algerians; 400 Tunisians; 370 Iraqis; 200 Libyans; some Jordanians, as well as citizens of other Muslim countries. They are a serious threat to the military regime in Algeria, have started terrorist activities in Egypt, and are fighting as volunteers in regional wars from Bosnia to Kashmir and in the Philippines. Between 1987 and 1993 as many as 3,340 registered Arabs left **Pakistan**, but some 2,800 were still in Afghanistan and in the **North-West Frontier Province** of **Pakistan**. They were a veritable Foreign Legion, praised in the West as "idealistic young men" and "freedom fighters" when they fought the communist regime. They were missionaries, propagating a radical interpretation of Islam, and were supported in preference to secular or moderate groups fighting the communist government.

Most of the Afghanis fought in the ranks of **Gulbuddin Hekmatyar, Abdul Rasul Sayyaf**, and **Jamilurrahman**. **Osama Bin Laden**, a wealthy Saudi citizen, financed a number of Islamist groups and set up his own **al-Qaeda** organization. With the establishment of the **Taliban** regime, thousands of Afghanis and new recruits from borderland **madrasa**s entered the country for training and military action in Kashmir, Bosnia, Chechnya, and elsewhere. As a result of the 2001 attacks on the World Trade Center in New York and the Pentagon, the American government intervened and destroyed the al-Qaeda bases and their Taliban supporters. The allies of yesteryear became the enemies of today.

AFGHAN MILLAT (Afghan Nation). Popular name of the Afghan Social Democratic Party (ASDP—Da Afghanistan Tolanpal Woluswak Gund) and the title of its weekly newspaper, first published on April 5, 1966, by **Ghulam Muhammad Farhad** with his brother Qudratullah Haddad and Habibullah Rafi'i as editors. Because of its political activism the newspaper was frequently closed. It continued to be published at irregular intervals in Pakistan.

The ASDP was established during a meeting of the 62-member founding congress on March 8, 1966, at the residence of **Qiamuddin Khadem**. Ghulam Muhammad Farhad (one-time mayor of **Kabul**) was elected chairman and held the position until his death in 1984. During his tenure Afghan Millat, the popular name of the party, was more nationalist than socialist. It advocated the restoration of "Greater Afghanistan," including the territory of the **North-West Frontier Province** and Baluchistan, which now constitute the western provinces of Pakistan. Because of its irredentist policy, the party contributed to the friction existing between Afghanistan and **Pakistan**. The party did not support **Muhammad Daud**, even though it agreed with him on the "**Pashtunistan**" question and on the attempt to make **Pashtu** the national language. In October 1979 the **Hafizullah Amin** government accused the party of attempting a coup and arrested a number of its members in Kabul.

In the late 1960s Feda Muhammad Feda'i seceded and formed his own party, called Millat, and after the death of Ghulam Muhammad Farhad in 1984, Dr. Muhammad Amin Wakman, who resides in the **United States**, was elected chairman of Afghan Millat at a congress in Peshawar on March 8–9, 1990. It was attended by 390 (out of 500) delegates, who also elected a 29-member supreme council and chose Stana Gul Sherzad as its secretary general. Shams al-Huda Shams from Kunar Province and a number of his supporters did not participate in the election.

The party opposed the **Shahnawaz Tanai-Gulbuddin Hekmatyar** alliances against the **Najibullah** regime and called on its members and sympathizers to continue the struggle to capture political power. The party now emphasizes social democratic policies and, although largely Pashtun in membership, tries to broaden its base to become a national party. The ASDP had a small **mujahedin** force in the field, which was severely mauled by Hekmatyar's forces. The Pakistan government did not give Afghan Millat official recognition and material support because of its irredentism. A number of its activists were assassinated by unknown gunmen in Pakistan, including Dr. Ceded Shigawal, Zakir Khan, and, in September 1991, Taj Muhammad Khan.

On July 27, 1995, the party convened its fourth congress in Peshawar and elected Dr. **Anwar-ul-Haq Ahadi** as its new president, Abdul Hamid Yaqin Yusufzai as vice president, Stana Gul Sherzad as secretary general, and a supreme council of 35 members. The congress also adopted a new platform which emphasizes the independence, territorial integrity, and national sovereignty of Afghanistan and advocates national unity, democracy, Islam, progress, and social justice.

AFGHAN NATIONAL ARMY. *See* **ARMY, AFGHAN.**

AFGHAN SECURITY SERVICES. After the **Saur Revolt**, the **Nur Muhammad Taraki** government established a security service, named AGSA (Da Afghanistan da Gatay da Satanay Edara, Afghanistan Security Service Department), which was headed by Asadullah Sarwari from May 1978 until August 1979. After his accession to power, **Hafizullah Amin** renamed the service KAM (Da Kargarano Amniyati Mu'asasa, Workers Security Institution). Within a week of their assumption of power on December 27, 1979, the **Parchami** regime purged the security service of **Khalq** supporters and renamed it KHAD (Khedamat-i Ettela'at-i Daulati, State Information Service). It was headed by Dr. **Najibullah** before he succeeded to the position of general secretary of the **People's Democratic Party of Afghanistan** in 1986 and president of Afghanistan. Najibullah upgraded KHAD to ministerial status; hence its acronym WAD (Wizarat-i Ettela'at-i Daulati, Ministry of State Security). WAD was subsequently headed by General Ghulam Faruq Yaqubi. The organization is said to have controlled from 15,000 to 30,000 operatives, organized on the KGB model, with its own military units, including a national guard. Its task appeared to be similar to that of the KGB: Detecting and eradicating domestic political opposition; Subverting armed resistance; Penetrating opposition groups abroad; Providing military intelligence to the armed forces. It is said to have been set up with the assistance of Soviet and East German intelligence officers.

Yaqubi did not survive the downfall of the Marxist regime. Former Afghan prisoners have accused WAD and its predecessors of torture, intimidation, and murder. **Burhanuddin Rabbani** started his own security service, which was also popularly called KHAD.

AFGHAN TRANSITIONAL GOVERNMENT. *See* **TRANSITIONAL GOVERNMENT.**

AFRIDI. A **Pashtu**-speaking tribe that is located in the area of the **Khaibar Pass,** just beyond the Afghan border. Herodotus, the Greek historian, mentions the "Aprytae," a member of the tribe of Osman who called himself "God's Creature" (*afrideh-ye khoda*). Some Afghan scholars consider him the eponymic ancestor of the Afridis. For centuries, the Afridis saw themselves as the "guardians" of the gate to India, and invaders since ancient times have found it preferable to pay for passage rather than fight their way through the Khaibar. At times, Afridis entered the services of Afghan rulers, primarily as bodyguards and tribal militia. In conflicts between Afghanistan and British India, they supported the Afghans, although they could not resist the temptation to loot the Afghan arsenal when the British bombed **Jalalabad** in 1919. In the 1960s the Afridis were said to be able to muster an armed force of 50,000 men. A British officer described them as "wiry, shaven-headed, full-bearded, Pashtu-speaking hillmen of uncertain origin" (Ridgway). During the 1980s the **Kabul** government attempted to enlist Afridis into a militia to attack the supply lines of the **mujahedin,** and the Afridis accepted their pay but did not perform their assigned functions.

At the end of the **third Anglo-Afghan war,** Sir Hamilton Grant, chief commissioner of the North-West Frontier, complained to the viceroy of India that "the constant raiding by Afridi gangs into the Peshawar District is sorely discrediting our administration. It is astounding that such a state of affairs should be possible with the number of troops we have got in the Peshawar Valley and shows how very difficult it would be to make any military operation of transfrontier area really successful." He added that only subjugation of the Afridis would help, but this would be "a most formidable and undesirable undertaking" (G.C.).

AHADI, ANWAR AL-HAQ (ANWARULHAQ AHADY). Minister of finance in new government of President **Hamid Karzai.** He was governor of the Afghan Central Bank in the government, established after the fall of the **Taliban** regime. During his tenure at the central bank he successfully issued a new currency at the rate of one new afghani for 1,000 old ones. Ahadi draws on his experience as a banker in the **United States,** but then assumed a position as professor of political science at Providence College in Providence, Rhode Island. He was active in the resistance against the Marxist regime and was elected in July 1995 president of the Afghan Social Democratic

Party (**Afghan Millat**). A **Pashtun**, he was born on April 6, 1950, in the town of Jagdalak, in **Kabul** Province. He was educated at Kabul University and the American University of Beirut, where he graduated with B.A. (1974), and M.A. (1977) degrees. He continued his studies in the United States and obtained the M.B.A. and Ph.D. degrees from Northwestern University.

AHMAD KHEL, BATTLE OF. A battle on April 19, 1880, between the Bengal regiments, commanded by General **Sir Donald Steward**, and an army of 15,000 **Ghilzais**, some **Durranis**, and a force of some 4,000 ill-equipped **ghazis** in which the Afghan forces were eventually defeated. Steward was on his way from **Kandahar** to **Kabul** to replace **General Frederick Roberts** when at Ahmad Khel, about 20 miles from **Ghazni**, he came on a strong force of ghazis. His forces included the Bengal division, consisting of two infantry brigades commanded by Brigadier Generals Hughes and Barter, and the cavalry brigade commanded by Brigadier General Palliser. There were also the horse and field artillery with a cavalry and infantry escort, as well as six squadrons of Indian cavalry, Bengal Lancers, the elite 60th Rifles, and Gurka and **Sikh** infantries. His two 40 pounders and two 6.3-inch howitzers took up a mile of the road, "each gun with twenty yoke of oxen trudging slowly along" (Heathcote, 1980). A horde of **Hazaras** moved behind the British force, plundering and wreaking vengeance on **Pashtun** villages. A larger force of several thousand hostile ghazis marched day by day parallel with the British flank.

Steward did not seek battle, but when he reached the vicinity of Ahmad Khel his road was flanked by a spur of the Gul Kuh Mountain, and the low pass he needed to cross, was suddenly teeming with tribesmen. To the beating of "tom-toms" and the incitement of **mullas**, some 3,000 ghazis (largely Ghilzais) swept down swords in hand heedless of the steady fire of the British; some companies did not have time to fix their bayonets, and the British forces were forced to fall back. Some wounded tribesmen "or shaming dead, cut desperately up at the troops as they passed." Eventually, the British line steadied and their superior firepower of Martini-Henry and Snider rifles and artillery carried the day. Steward reported Afghan losses at 800 compared to his losses of 17 dead and 120 wounded. (British estimate of the number of Afghan forces and statistics of casualties are, at best, approximations upon which authors disagree.

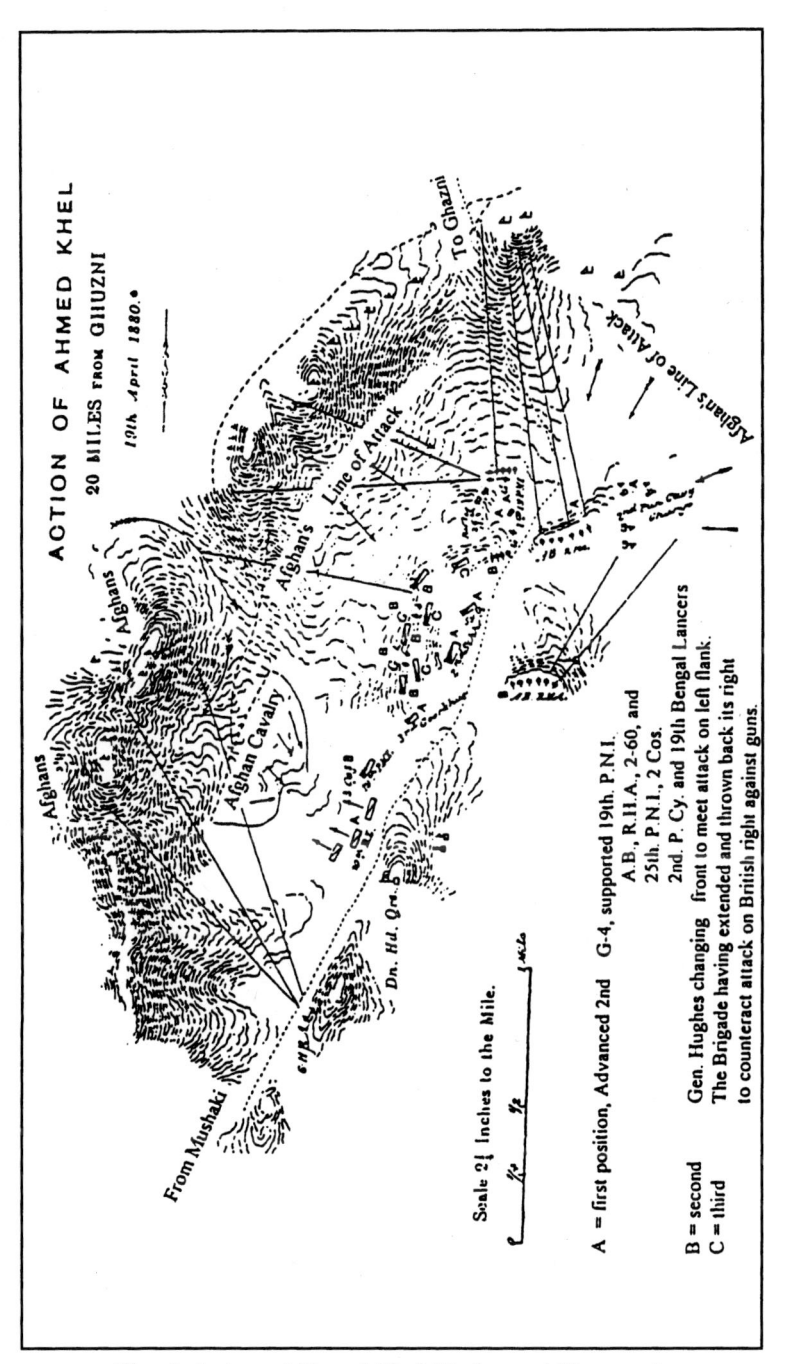

Plan 1. Action of Ahmad Khel (Forbes and Hensman)

According to Forbes [1892], one thousand dead bodies were counted, and the MR lists 3,000 Afghans killed and wounded. Most of the British wounded were injured by sword slashes and knife stabs during hand-to-hand combat.) One British officer wrote, "Anyone with the semblance of a heart under his khaki-jacket could not help feeling something akin to pity to see them advancing with their miserable weapons in the face of our guns and rifles, but their courage and their numbers made them formidable" (Heathcote, 1980). *See also* INTRODUCTION.

AHMAD SHAH, ABDALI DURRANI. King of Afghanistan, 1747-1773, and founder of the **Sadozai** dynasty of the Abdali (**Durrani**) tribe. He was born in 1722 in **Herat**, the son of Muhammad Zaman Khan, who was governor of Herat. After capturing **Kandahar, Nadir Shah Afshar** of Iran (r. 1736–1747) exiled Ahmad Khan to Mazandaran in northern Iran and subsequently appointed him governor of that province. When Nadir Shah Afshar died, Ahmad Khan was commander of an Afghan contingent of the Persian army at Kandahar. He was able to capture a caravan with booty from India, which assured his election as king (shah) of Afghanistan in October 1747 by an assembly of **Pashtun** chiefs. The Pashtun tribesmen rallied to his banner, and Ahmad Shah led them on eight campaigns into India in search of booty and territorial conquest. He added Kashmir, Sind, and the Western Panjab to his domain and founded an empire that extended from eastern Persia to northern India and from the **Amu Daria** to the Indian Ocean. Ahmad Shah appointed his son Timur as his successor and died a natural death two months later on April 14, 1773. He was buried in Kandahar, which became the capital of Afghanistan until **Timur Shah** (1773–1793) established his capital at **Kabul**. Sir Percy Sykes in his *History of Afghanistan* called Ahmad Shah "a monarch whose high descent and warlike qualities made him peculiarly acceptable to his aristocratic and virile Chiefs, as well as to his warlike subjects in general. In short, he possessed all the qualities that enabled him successfully to found the kingdom of Afghanistan" (I, 367).

AHMAD SHAH, MILITARY ADMINISTRATION. Ahmad Shah founded the first regular Afghan army. He appointed a deputy (the *sipah salar*), or commander in chief, who performed all the functions of minister of war, subject to the approval of the king. A quartermaster general (*suyursatchi bashi*) was in charge of the purchase and collection of supplies, and a director of arsenals (*qurchi bashi*) was in charge of munitions.

The army was divided into the regular army (*askar-i munazzam*) and irregular tribal levies (*askar-i ghair munazzam*); the regular army comprised one-third and the irregular forces two-thirds. The regular army was voluntary and a lifetime profession and consisted of cavalry, infantry, and artillery branches, most of them stationed at the capital. A regular soldier had to provide for his food and his horse out of his pay during his nine-months of active service, after which time he was on home leave for three months. Similar to the Ottoman system, the king depended on a bodyguard (*ghulam khana*) of foreigners for his protection, many of them **Qizilbash** who did not have any local ties.

Three-fourths of the army consisted of cavalry, armed with matchlocks and swords and some with carbines and spears. They also carried shields, daggers, and axes. The infantry carried primarily matchlocks and swords. Light artillery (*zamburak*) was used, carried on camels provided with swivels, which permitted firing without the need for unloading. Heavy artillery was carried primarily by elephants.

The formation of the army was as follows:

One *dalgi* (section)	10 men
One *tawalli* (platoon)	10 *dalgi-ha* = 100 men
One *kundak* (regiment)	10 *tawalli* = 1,000
One *qita'* (brigade)	2 or more *kundaks*

Officers — cavalry and infantry

Dah bashi or *dalgi-mishar*	section commander
Yuz bashi or *tawalli-mishar*	platoon commander
Mang bashi, beg bashi, or *Kundak-mishar*	regiment commander
Amir-i lashkar	brigade commander
Sipah salar or *sardar-i sardaran*	commander-in-chief

Officers — artillery

Zamburakchi, shahanchi or *Shanhangchi*	artillery man or gunner
Shahanchi bashi or *jazailchi bashi*	artillery officer
Topchi bashi or *Mir-i Atesh*	chief artillery commander

(Singh, 361)

The irregular army consisted of three-fourths cavalry and one-forth infantry who were tribal levies. It included the feudal units who provided service during war in lieu of payment of land revenue; tribal levies provided by chiefs who were paid or held tax-free land in exchange for supplying a commensurate number of fighters; or tribal cavalry who was employed for the protection of the borders, collection of revenues, police duties, and similar tasks.

At the call of the king, the chiefs and notables holding land rallied with the number of troops required of each. Weapons were issued to them for the duration of war.

AHMADZAI. A section of the Sulaiman Khel division of the **Ghilzai** tribe. They are settled in a triangle" formed by a line drawn from **Kabul** to **Jalalabad** and **Gardez**. They are generally wealthy and often employed as traders, while some have held high positions in the Afghan government and have intermarried with the **Durranis**. Amir **Abdul Rahman** settled a number of Ahmadzai families in northern Afghanistan to weaken their power and have them serve as **Pashtun** colonists among the Turkic population. Only a small number of Ahmadzai is nomadic.

AIR BASES, UNITED STATES AND COALITION. The most important of Coalition bases is **Bagram** Air Base, built with Soviet assistance in the 1950s, north of **Kabul** and five miles west of **Charikar**.

Because of its proximity to Kabul, it was one of the first air bases occupied by British and American forces. It became the home of the U.S. Army's 10th Mountain Division and the 101st Airborne, as well as **Special Forces** units who participated in **Operation Anaconda**. American forces were strengthened by some 1,700 British Royal Marines, Canadian troops, and peacekeeping forces from Germany, The Netherlands, Finland, Austria, Turkey, and Denmark. Bagram has a 9,700-foot runway which accommodates all types of aircraft, including "Nightstalkers" and "Warthog" ground attack aircraft.

Next in importance is the **Kandahar** International Airport, built with American support and opened in 1962. It was one of the largest airports in Central Asia, but was bypassed by international travel as a result of long distance jet travel. American troops took command of the airport in December 2001 and the 15th and 26th U.S. Marine

Expeditionary Units established a base to intercept **Taliban** and **al-Qaeda** troops. A helicopter base was established in Pul-i Kandahar, about 20 miles west of Kandahar. Chinook transport helicopters and Apache and Cobra attack helicopters were used in March 2002 to launch sorties during Operation Anaconda. Near **Khost** an airfield serves as a major logistics and supply area for U.S. Special Forces and Coalition units fighting in eastern Afghanistan. This airfield has repeatedly come under enemy fire. A small contingent of American troops from the Army's 10th Mountain Division is based at the **Mazar-i Sharif** airfield. A French infantry company was deployed to provide area security.

Staging points outside Afghanistan were Dalbandin Air Base west of Quetta, Jacobabad, and Pasni in **Pakistan**. Under an agreement with Uzbekistan, U.S. transports and Special Forces were able to use a former Soviet air base at Karshi/Khanabad, and the French Air Force deployed 160 C-130 aircraft in Dushanbe, Tajikistan.

AIR FORCE, AFGHAN. The Afghan government took the first steps at creating an air force during the reign of King **Amanullah**. The importance of aerial warfare became apparent during the **third Anglo-Afghan war** when British planes bombed **Jalalabad**, the king's palace, and the ammunition factory at **Kabul**. Therefore, in 1921 Amanullah acquired a British fighter plane (which made a forced landing in Katawaz—the Afghans returned the pilot and kept the plane) and subsequently purchased a number of additional planes from **Britain** and the **Soviet Union**. By the end of the 1920s, Afghanistan's air force consisted of 22 machines (Bristol Fighters, D.H. 9s, Caprioni Scouts, and a Junkers Monoplane) that were operated by 25 officers, three of whom were Afghans, four Germans, and the rest Russians. The Soviet Union had donated a number of aircraft on condition that they be operated by Soviet nationals. Young Afghans were sent for training to the Soviet Union, Italy, India, and other countries to create a small cadre of pilots and aircraft mechanics. Amanullah used his aircraft with considerable effect during the **Khost Rebellion**, 1924–1925, and subsequent tribal revolts. But the conditions for maintaining an effective air force did not yet exist: Afghanistan depended on foreign supplies of spare parts and most of the king's aircraft were not in proper operating condition when he was deposed in the 1929 civil war.

During the reign of **Muhammad Nadir Shah** (1929–1933), the Russian personnel was gradually eliminated, and in the mid-1930s, **Zahir Shah**'s prime minister negotiated with Britain for the purchase of 24 aircraft and the training of 10 pilots, six officers, and 30 mechanics. When the British government wanted assurance that the Afghans would build up their air force from primarily British sources, negotiations came to a halt.

In the mid-1930s, landing strips existed in **Herat, Kandahar**, Kabul, and Jalalabad, but only Kabul had a ground organization and hangar accommodations for 16 aircraft. Aviation fuel had to be imported from India, and supplies never exceeded 10,000 gallons. To carry 15,000 gallons required more than 500 camels. Winds, excessive heat, and snow made flying conditions good only in October and November (HBAA, 1933). Because of the war in Europe, development of the air force was limited until the Soviet Union became the major factor in the creation of modern Afghan armed forces.

In the mid-1950s, Ariana Afghan Airlines was established with technical support provided by Pan American Airways, and the airports of Kabul and Kandahar were modernized for international flights. The Kandahar airport, built with American aid, became one of the military's regional headquarters after the Soviet intervention. By 1960 the country's air force included four helicopters and about 100 Soviet combat aircraft, and in 1979 some 140–170 fighters and 45–60 helicopters were organized into a tactical force of seven air regiments, including a strength of 7,000–8,000 men, which remained relatively intact throughout the 1980s.

During the civil war, the air force, like the army, broke into a number of sections, with General **Abdul Rashid Dostum** and the forces of President **Burhanuddin Rabbani** gaining a major part. But, again, a problem of servicing and the provision of spare parts prevented any of the warring parties from gaining aerial superiority.

The **Taliban** inherited what was left of the Afghan air force and the American intervention led to its destruction, except for a few helicopters. The **United States** now has control of Afghan airspace. It appears that the Pentagon and U.S. Air Force officers cannot agree whether the new air force should be equipped with "slightly-used" F-16s or with a cheaper turbo-prop trainer/attack aircraft, such as the Brasilian Super Tucano. The use of a "combat crop duster," built for spraying drug crops has also been suggested. The question remains as to who will pay for it. *See also* AIR BASES, UNITED STATES AND COALITION.

AK-47 (AVTOMAT KALASHNIKOV). Full or semiautomatic assault rifles of Soviet, Chinese, or Egyptian make that became the weapons of choice of the **mujahedin**. Initially, they were captured, bartered, or surrendered by deserters from the Afghan army, but the need for these weapons was great. To ensure "plausible deniability" of outside support, Soviet weapons from Egyptian stores were channeled to the mujahedin, and when foreign assistance had become an open secret, kalashnikovs of Chinese and other origins were brought in. The kalashnikov proved to be an effective weapon in ambushes of highway convoys and fortified posts. In 1994 the enormous numbers of assault weapons in Afghan hands reduced the price of an AK-47 to $100 in Kabul. *See also* ARMS BAZAARS, AFGHAN; KALASHNIKOV, MIKHAIL.

AKBAR, SARDAR MUHAMMAD (called Ghazi). The ambitious son of **Amir Dost Muhammad** (1826–1838 and 1842–1863) and "Hero of Jamrud," who defeated the **Sikh** army of Hari Singh in April 1837. He was a major figure in the defeat of the British in the **first Anglo-Afghan war**. Akbar was the premier of the Afghan chiefs with whom the British force of occupation sought to negotiate safe passage from **Kabul** to India (*see* CAPITULATION, TREATY OF). During negotiations with **Sir William Macnaghten**, he killed the British envoy "in a fit of passion." He saved the lives of British women and children as well as a number of officers whom he had taken into "protective" custody during the arduous retreat. Few others survived the massacre of the British expeditionary force of some 16,000 troops and camp followers (*see* DEATH MARCH). Akbar wanted to regain territory lost in the **Panjab**, but his father, Amir Dost Muhammad, who had been restored to the throne in 1842, favored a policy of accommodation with **Britain**. In 1845 Akbar rebelled, but he died at the age of 29 of poisoning before he could pose a serious challenge to his father. He is revered by Afghans and called **Ghazi** (Victor against Infidels). A residential area of Kabul and a major hospital have been named after him, Wazir Akbar Khan.

AKBARI, USTAD MUHAMMAD. A **Qizilbash** with the title Hujjat al-Islam. He was head of the **Shi'a Hizb-i Wahdat** (Unity Party) political committee who lost in a power struggle with **Abdul Ali Mazari** and joined **Burhanuddin Rabbani**'s **Jam'iat-i Islami.** Faced with the superior power of the **Taliban,** Akbari surrendered in November 1998 and made his peace with the new rulers until their demise in 2001. He subsequently negotiated for a return to the **Abdul Karim Khalili** faction of the party.

AKHTAR KHAN, LIEUTENANT GENERAL ABDUL RAHMAN. Director general of the **Pakistani** military's **Inter-Services Intelligence** (ISI) directorate from 1980 to 1987, who was said to have coordinated with William Casey, director of the CIA, the operations and supply network for the Afghan **mujahedin.** Brigadier **Mohammad Yousaf,** Akhtar's deputy and head of the Afghan Bureau, controlled the flow of thousands of tons of arms into the hands of the mujahedin and directed every aspect of military activities from training of Afghan guerrillas and logistics support to the planning of ambushes, assassinations, raids, and rocket attacks against the Soviet/Kabul forces. Akhtar was promoted to chairman of the Joint Chiefs of Staff Committee and replaced by General Hamid Gul when the mujahedin started carrying attacks into Soviet Central Asia. Akhtar perished in a plane crash on August 17, 1988, together with Pakistani President Zia-ul-Haq, American Ambassador Arnold Raphel, Brigadier General Herbert Wassom, the U.S. defense attaché in Islamabad, and eight Pakistani generals. American sources attributed the crash to engine failure, but most Pakistanis believe it was a result of sabotage, variously blaming the KGB, **WAD,** or CIA.

ALIJARIS (ELJARIS). An unpaid reserve of the Afghan army, recruited from the population. All Afghans are potential soldiers, and in case of emergency, **maliks** and chiefs throughout the country are required to levy a specific number of troops from their communities.

ALIM. See **ULAMA.**

ALI MASJID. Scene of a battle during the **first Anglo-Afghan war,** when Lieutenant Colonel Wade proceeded from Jamrud through the **Khaibar Pass** and captured the town on July 27, 1839. He encountered determined resistance from **Afridi** forces. With 12 British officers in his force of levies, he set up fortified perimeter camps and successfully picketed the heights to ensure success. His losses were 180 killed and wounded. A small British post remained at the village. In October 1839 Khaibar tribesmen who invested Ali Masjid were bought off with the promise of an annual subsidy. In April 1842 Ali Masjid was again in the hands of the Zakka Khel Afridis and had to be recaptured by General **George Pollock** at the cost of 135 killed and wounded. On November 21 (the **second Anglo-Afghan war**), British forces under **Sir Sam J. Browne** failed in an attack on Ali Masjid with a force of 7,800 troops with 26 guns. The town was held by 3,500 Afghan regulars and 600 **khasadars** with 24 guns. A failure of coordination prevented a concerted frontal attack with a turning movement from the northeast. A battery had to be withdrawn when its ammunition was exhausted. This had a bad effect on the infantry. One portion of the force attacked prematurely without the support of other units. British casualties were 22 killed and 34 wounded. At daybreak on November 22, the main force prepared for attack only to discover that the Afghan position had been evacuated during the night.

AL-QAEDA. *See* **QAEDA, AL-.**

AMANULLAH, KING (AMAN ALLAH, called Ghazi). King of Afghanistan, 1919–1929. Born in 1892, the son of Amir **Habibullah** and Sarwar Sultanah, the *Ulya Hazrat* (queen). When Amir Habibullah was assassinated in **Jalalabad** in February 1919, Amanullah Khan was governor of **Kabul** and in possession of the arsenal and the treasury. He was crowned in Kabul over the prior claims of his uncle Nasrullah, whom he denounced as a usurper and an accomplice in the murder of his father. King Amanullah (he assumed the title of king in 1926) was an ardent reformer and contemporary of like-minded rulers, Muhammad Reza in Iran and Kemal Atatürk in Turkey. He demanded a revision of the Anglo-Afghan agreements concluded by Amir **Abdul Rahman**, which left **Britain** in charge of Afghanistan's foreign relations in exchange for protection from unprovoked Russian aggression and a subsidy in money and military materiel (*see* FOREIGN RELATIONS). British reluctance to accept a change in the status quo led to Afghan armed attacks, culminating in the start of the **third Anglo-Afghan war** on May 3, 1919. **Britain** was war-weary and in no condition to wage war on the Indian frontier, and, after lengthy negotiations in Rawalpindi, Mussoorie, and Kabul, peace was restored, leaving Afghanistan free and independent from British control. (*See* ANGLO-AFGHAN TREATY, 1919; 1921.) King Amanullah became a national hero and turned his attention to reforming and modernizing his country. He established diplomatic and commercial relations with major European and Asian states, founded schools in which French, German, and English were the major languages of education, and promulgated a constitution that was to guarantee the personal freedom and equal rights of all Afghans.

He built a new capital, named Darulaman (Dar al-Aman—Abode of Peace), which included a monumental parliament and other government buildings as well as villas of prominent Afghans. Social reforms included a new dress code, which permitted women in Kabul to go unveiled and encouraged officials to wear Western dress. Modernization proved costly for Afghanistan and was resented by the traditional elements of Afghan society. The **Khost Rebellion**, a tribal revolt in 1924, was suppressed and Amanullah felt secure enough to travel to Europe in December 1927. Upon his return he faced increasing opposition, and, in 1928, an uprising of **Shinwari** tribesmen, followed by attacks of the Kohdamani and Kuhistani forces of **Habibullah Kalakani**, forced the reformer king into exile. After an unsuccessful attempt at regaining the throne, he crossed the Indian border on May 23, 1929, and settled in Italy and Switzerland until his death on April 26, 1960. He was buried in Jalalabad next to the tomb of Amir Habibullah.

AMBALA CONFERENCE. A meeting in March 1869 between **Amir Shir Ali** and Lord Mayo, the viceroy of India, in which the amir sought an alliance with **Britain**. Shir Ali had recaptured the **Kabul** throne and had consolidated his power to the extent that he felt secure to accept an invitation by Lord Mayo's predecessor to visit the viceroy at Ambala, a town about 200 miles north of Delhi. Shir Ali was alarmed by the fact that Russian influence had reached Afghanistan's northern boundaries when the Amirate of Buchara became a czarist protectorate. The Afghan ruler wanted a promise of British help in case of Russian aggression, support against domestic rivals, and British recognition of his dynasty and of his son, Abdullah Jan, as his immediate successor. Mayo assured the Afghan ruler of his government's sympathies, but refused to give any specific promises. As a sign of its friendship, the Indian government presented the amir with 600,000 rupees, 6,500 muskets, four 18-pounder siege guns, two 8-inch howitzers, and a mountain battery of six 3-pounder guns. But when an uninvited Russian mission under Major General **Stolietoff** managed to reached Kabul in the summer of 1878, a British army invaded Afghanistan on November 21, 1878. *See* SECOND ANGLO-AFGHAN WAR.

AMBUSH. A surprise attack used by Afghan forces with great success in their wars against foreign invaders. The Afghans knew the terrain, passes, valleys, and routes an invader or his supplies had to traverse. During the wars with British forces, isolated posts and convoys bringing supplies from India were the choice targets of ambushes. British and **Soviet** forces also resorted to this method but with relatively little success, because the Afghans usually were well informed of the enemy's movements by local villagers. McMichael (1991) quotes the **mujahedin** commander, Abdul Haq:

> In order to discourage the enemy, we simply ambush the ambushers. With reliable advance information about the time and place of the ambush we took position before the arrival of the enemy. We carried out five operations of this kind, and each time we killed 10 to 15 Russians, all the elite commandos whom the Russians were not very eager to lose, and our action produced its expected results.

AMIN, HAFIZULLAH. Born in 1929 in Paghman, Kabul Province. President of the **Democratic Republic of Afghanistan (DRA)** from September 1979 until his assassination on December 27, 1979. He was a member of the Kharoti (**Ghilzai Pashtun**) tribe, whose family came to Paghman in the 19th century. Educated in Afghanistan and the **United States**, where he was known as a Pashtun nationalist, he became a teacher and later principal of Ibn Sina and Teachers Training schools in Kabul. His conversion to Marxism is said to have occurred in 1964. He was elected to the 13th session of Parliament (1969) as a representative of Paghman. During the republican period (1973–1978), he successfully recruited followers in the army in competition with **Parchami** efforts. After the **Saur Revolt** he was appointed vice premier and minister of foreign affairs. In April 1979 he became prime minister and, after he ousted **Nur Muhammad Taraki**, he became president on September 16, 1979. He was at odds with **Alexander Puzanov**, the Soviet ambassador at Kabul, and successfully demanded his recall. Some observers called him the

Afghan "Tito" because of his independence and nationalistic inclinations. He was accused of responsibility for the assassination of thousands. Soviet special forces attacked him and his bodyguard in Darulaman, assassinating him on December 27, 1979. *See* APPENDIX 1.

AMIR. Commander, also nobleman, prince, ruler, chief (from A. *amara,* to command). Caliph Omar (634–644) first assumed the title Amir al-Mu'minin (Commander of the Believers). In Afghanistan the **Sadozai** rulers carried the title "king" (*shah*), but the **Muhammadzai** rulers from 1826 assumed the title "amir" until **Amanullah** Khan adopted the title of king in 1926. Among some **mujahedin** and **Islamist** groups, an amir is a commander with civil and military powers.

AMU DARIA (34-40' N, 59-1' E, DARYA). A river, called Oxus by the ancient Greeks, which forms for about 280 miles the boundary between the former **Soviet Union** and Afghanistan. Its easternmost sources are the Ab-e Wakhan and the Ab-i Pamir, which rise in the Little Pamir Mountains and run into the Ab-e Panj near the village of Qal'a-ye Panjeh. It is fed by the Kukcha, and further west, the **Kunduz** Rivers, at which point it is called the Amu Daria. It then flows in a northwesterly direction to run into the Aral Sea. It is navigable only in parts, although its length from the farthest source to the mouth of the Aral Sea extends some 1,500 miles. A bridge near Hairatan, completed in 1982, links the Afghan highway from **Mazar-i Sharif** with the rail terminal at Termez, now in Uzbekistan. Another bridge was constructed at Sherkhan/Qala Kutarma in Kunduz Province. The bridges became vital links for the supply of Soviet and Afghan forces in Afghanistan.

ANGLO-AFGHAN RELATIONS. When Afghanistan emerged as an independent state in 1747 **Great Britain** had already established a foothold in India. The **British East India Company** was the de facto ruler of Bengal and ready to expand the area under its control. **Ahmad Shah Durrani** defeated the powerful **Mahratta** confederation in the **Battle of Panipat,** north of Delhi, in 1761. When **Zaman Shah** (1793–1800), invited Lord Wellesley (1798–1805), governor general of the Company, to cooperate in the conquest of northern India, the British governor general enlisted Persia in containing Afghanistan. An attempt at forging an alliance with Afghanistan was the mission of the British envoy **Mountstuart Elphinstone** to the court of **Shah Shuja ul-Mulk** at Peshawar in 1808–1809. It was to establish "eternal friendship" between the two countries and called for joint action in case of Franco-Persian aggression. But Afghanistan lost in quick succession control of Kashmir, Sind, the Western Punjab, and Peshawar to the British ally **Ranjit Singh** (r. 1780–1839). Thus was born the British "forward policy" and Afghan strategy of resistance, resulting in three Anglo-Afghan wars. Britain was in search of the "scientific frontier," first at the Indus River, and then at the passes controlling access to India, if not at the **Hindukush** or the **Amu Daria**. By the end of the 19th century **Russia** had extended its influence to the Amu Daria and Britain had extended its control to the southern and eastern borders of Afghanistan. Failing the conquest of Afghanistan, Britain wanted to keep Afghanistan under its influence. One move to achieve this objective was the **first Anglo-Afghan war** (1838–1842) when Britain attempted to instal **Shah Shuja ul-Mulk** (r. 1803–1810 and 1839–1842) to the Afghan throne. The British disaster in this war, led to a period of "masterly inactivity," which was to leave Afghanistan to the Afghans. But the lessons of the disaster were ignored a generation later, when the Indian government attempted to depose Amir **Shir Ali** (r. 1863–1879) in the **second Anglo-Afghan war**. Although not a similar disaster as the first war, Britain was resigned to recognize Amir **Abdul Rahman** (r. 1880–1901) as the new ruler, in spite of the fact that he had entered Afghanistan with the assistance of **Russia**.

A new period of coexistence followed during which the **amir** permitted Britain the control of his foreign relations with other powers. In exchange the amir received a guarantee of protection from Russian aggression. The Afghan ruler regarded his agreement as a treaty between equals and did not permit Britain to gain a foothold in Afghanistan under the aegis of their common defense. Afghanistan's borders were defined with British assistance, including the **Durand Line**, and Abdul Rahman consolidated the power of the state in a number of domestic wars. Although Britain was not completely satisfied with her agreements with the Afghan rulers, both countries were at peace until the reign of King **Amanullah** (r. 1919–29), when this Afghan king won his independence from British hegemony in the **third Anglo-Afghan war**.

After that event, Afghanistan established relations with the major powers of the world, and Britain became just one of the players on the diplomatic scene. India was partitioned in 1947 and Pakistan became Afghanistan's neighbor and inheritor of the dispute for control over the independent tribal territory. During the Cold War period the **United States** had become a major power in Kabul until the Soviet intervention in support of the Marxist government. Only after the defeat of the **Taliban** regime, did British soldiers again enter Afghan territory. This time they come as members of an international coalition defending Afghanistan from Taliban and **al-Qaeda** guerrillas.

ANGLO-AFGHAN TREATY OF 1809. *See* **ELPHINSTONE, MOUNTSTUART.**

ANGLO-AFGHAN TREATY OF 1905. Renewal in form of a treaty of agreements signed between Amir **Abdul Rahman** and **Sir Lepel Griffin**, chief political officer in Afghanistan, in June and July 1880. At the death of Amir Abdul Rahman on October 3, 1901, the British Indian government insisted that the agreements with the amir were personal and therefore subject to renegotiation with his successor. The government of India sought modifications and concessions, including a more "liberal commercial policy" on the part of Afghanistan, delimitation of the Mohmand border (between Afghanistan and India), and noninterference by Afghanistan in the politics of the transborder (Indian) tribes. **Great Britain** exerted great pressure, stopping subsidy payments and prohibiting Afghan imports of arms, but Amir **Habibullah** did not yield. He invited **Louis W. Dane** of the Indian Foreign Department to **Kabul**, and, after three months of negotiations, the "Independent King of Afghanistan and its Dependencies" and Louis W. Dane, "Foreign Secretary of the Mighty Government of India," signed the treaty at Kabul on March 21, 1905. For Amir Habibullah this was a great victory: none of the British objectives was won, the arrears in subsidy were paid, and Britain affirmed that it would not interfere in the internal affairs of Afghanistan. This treaty remained in force until it was repudiated by Amir **Amanullah** in 1919.

ANGLO-AFGHAN TREATY OF 1919. Peace treaty between the British and the Afghan governments after the **third Anglo-Afghan war**. It was negotiated at Rawalpindi and signed on August 8, 1919, by A. H. Grant, foreign secretary of the government of India, and Ali Ahmad Khan, Afghan commissary for home affairs. The treaty made a return to the "old friendship" between the two states contingent on negotiations started after a six-month waiting period. In the meantime **Britain** would not permit Afghanistan to import arms and ammunition through India, the payment of a subsidy would be ended, and the arrears in payments would be confiscated. Finally, a British commission was to demarcate undefined portions of the **Khaibar**, and Afghanistan was to accept the Indo-Afghan frontier as marked. An annexure stated that "the said Treaty and this letter leave Afghanistan officially free and independent in its internal and external affairs." British hopes that a contrite **amir** would again conclude an exclusive alliance were soon seen to be unrealistic. Amir **Amanullah** sent a mission to the **Soviet Union**, Europe, and the **United States** and acted on his right to establish diplomatic relations with foreign powers. The **Pashtun** tribes on the Indian side of the frontier were made to believe that the treaty represented only a cease-fire, after which war was to be resumed if Britain did not agree to various Afghan demands. Indeed, it was only after a fruitless, three-month conference at **Mussoorie** (April 17–July 18, 1920) and the **Kabul** Conference (*see* treaty below) that normal neighborly relations between Britain and Afghanistan were established.

ANGLO-AFGHAN TREATY OF 1921. Also called "Treaty of **Kabul**" because **Henry R. C. Dobbs**, the British envoy, and Mahmud Tarzi, chief of the Afghan delegation, negotiated and signed it after arduous, 11-month negotiations. The treaty restored "friendly and commercial relations" between the two governments after the **third Anglo-Afghan war** as well as negotiations at the **Mussoorie Conference** and Rawalpindi. The negotiations proceeded in four phases: During the first session, January 20 to April 9, 1921, the Afghan **amir** unsuccessfully demanded territorial concessions, while **Britain** wanted the exclusion of **Russian** consular offices from southeastern Afghanistan. In the second phase, from April 9 to mid-July 1921, Britain asked Afghanistan to break the newly established diplomatic relations with Russia in exchange for a subsidy of four million rupees and weapons, as well as guarantees from unprovoked Russian aggression. During the third stage, from mid-July to September 18, when the British foreign office informed the Italian government that it was about to conclude an agreement that would "admit the superior and predominant political influence of Britain" in Afghanistan, the Afghans refused to accept an "alliance." An exclusive treaty was impossible after Afghanistan announced ratification of the Russo-

Afghan Treaty of 1921 (see RUSSIAN-AFGHAN RELATIONS). In the fourth and final stage of negotiations, from September 18 to December 8, 1921, the British mission twice made preparations to return to India, when finally an agreement was signed at Kabul on November 22, 1921. Ratifications were exchanged on February 6, 1922.

The treaty stipulated that both governments "mutually certify and respect each with regard to the other all rights of internal and external independence." Afghanistan reaffirmed its acceptance of the boundary west of the **Khaibar**, subject to minor "realignment." Legations were to be opened in London and Kabul, consulates established in various Indian and Afghan towns, and Afghanistan was permitted to import arms and munitions through India. No customs duties were to be charged for goods in transit to Afghanistan, and each party agreed to inform the other of major military operations in the frontier belt. Representatives of both states were to meet in the near future to discuss the conclusion of a trade convention, which was signed in June 1923.

ANGLO-AFGHAN WARS. See **FIRST ANGLO-AFGHAN WAR; SECOND ANGLO-AFGHAN WAR; THIRD ANGLO-AFGHAN WAR.**

ANGLO-RUSSIAN CONVENTION OF 1907. An agreement between **Great Britain** and **Russia** concluded on August 31, 1907, which was to "ensure perfect security on their respective frontiers in Central Asia and to maintain in these regions a solid and lasting peace." It divided Iran into spheres of influence between the two powers, permitted Russia to have direct relations of a nonpolitical nature with local Afghan officials in northern Afghanistan, and provided for equal access to "commercial opportunity." Tibet was to be under Chinese sovereignty, but the British were free to deal with Tibetans in commercial matters while Russian Buddhists could deal with the Dalai Lama on religious matters. Although Britain was to continue its treaty obligation of 1905 to protect Afghanistan from unprovoked Russian aggression, and Russia declared Afghanistan outside her sphere of influence, Amir **Habibullah** saw this agreement as an attempt to solve the "Afghanistan Question" over his head. Amir Habibullah was on a state visit to India in January 1907 when Britain and Russia negotiated the treaty, but he was not informed of the convention until September 10, 1907. He was shocked and felt betrayed by the British, and when he was requested to agree to the convention, he took a year with his reply, refusing to ratify the agreement. Russia never obtained the expected commercial and political benefits, and the Bolshevik government repudiated the convention in 1918 in an attempt to win the goodwill of its Asian neighbors. As far as Afghanistan was concerned, the convention was a "dead letter" from the beginning.

ARG or ARK. A citadel within a walled city, traditionally the residence of a ruler. After the **Bala Hisar** was destroyed by British forces in 1879, Amir **Abdul Rahman** built the new Arg, located in the center of **Kabul**. It took five years to build and housed in addition to the **amir** and his court the major government buildings. It was surrounded by a moat and a 50-foot wall. Later additions and modifications radically changed the original plan when modern buildings replaced the early residences. In the Salam Khana (Audience Hall) the affairs of government were conducted. The Del Kusha (Heart's Delight) Palace was added by Amir **Habibullah**, and the Gul Khana Palace was built to be the royal office of King **Amanullah**. After the coup by **Muhammad Daud** in July 1973, the president's office was established in the Arg. During the Khalqi period (1978–1979), **Nur Muhammad Taraki** moved in and the Arg was renamed the "House of the People" (Khana-yi Khalq). In December 1979 **Hafizullah Amin** left the Arg and established himself in the Tapa Taj Beg Palace in Darulaman, where he was assassinated by Soviet troops. After the capture of Kabul in April 1992, the Arg became the residence of the president of the **Afghan Interim Government**, **Burhanuddin Rabbani** and later **Hamid Karzai** resided in the Arg, as did ex-King **Muhammad Zaher**.

ARMS BAZAARS, AFGHAN. As a landlocked country, Afghanistan depended for its weapons' supply on foreign imports, smuggled and captured arms, and, to a limited extent, on local manufacture. Since most supplies had to enter Afghanistan by way of India, **Britain** had a monopoly on the sale of weapons and tried to control the supply and quality. Amir **Abdul Rahman** founded the *mashin-khana* factory, where guns and ammunition were produced. In addition, numerous workshops existed on the Afghan frontier, where guns of all types were manufactured. Because of a lack of electricity, machinery was operated by human or animal power. The tradition of arms manufacture and sales in specialized communities exists to this day. One major weapons bazaar exists in Darra on the Pakistani side of the border and is probably the largest open arms market in the world. In about 100 shops, one can buy anything from rifles to mortars, and the price of an AK-47 in 1980 was $1,500 which in 1987 was reduced to $750 (Yousaf 1992, 135) and, in 1994, to $100 in **Kabul**. The influx of captured Soviet weapons and arms supplied by the supporters of the **mujahedin** produced quite a glut on the market. Even **Stinger** missiles, supplied by the **United States** to the mujahedin, were sold to the highest bidder.

ARMY, AFGHAN. Afghanistan's army evolved from its traditional beginnings under **Ahmad Shah** (*see* AHMAD SHAH, MILITARY ADMINISTRATION) in a process of gradual modernization throughout the 19th and first half of the 20th centuries. First efforts at modernization began during the reigns of Amir **Dost Muhammad** (1826–1838 and 1842–1863), who mustered a standing army of 15,000 and 45 guns that was gradually increased. **Shir Ali** Khan (1863–1879), after visiting India in 1869, adopted Indian titles: *briget* (brigadier), *karnel* (colonel), *kaptan* (captain), *subedar*, *havildar*, and so forth. Both lacked the type of modern weapons being employed by Afghanistan's neighbors and the nucleus of a modern officers' corps. Officers were appointed on the basis of loyalty rather than skill, and any Afghan who could ride a horse or carry a gun was considered fit regardless of age. Military skills were passed on from father to son, one cannoneer of advanced age had to be carried along on a stretcher to perform his functions. Western military technology came to Afghanistan by means of prisoners of war or foreign mercenaries. One such person, **William Campbell**, alias Shir Muhammad Khan, became commander in chief of the Turkestan army.

In the 1830s the composition of the Afghan army was described as "Pathan, Hindus, Kuzzelbashes, and a few deserters from the Sikh army." Muslims from neighboring countries joined the Afghan forces, including Indian officers of the "Great Sepoy Mutiny" of 1857–58. The reorganized army included a cavalry force of about 15,000 men, divided into two divisions headed by Amir Dost Muhammad's sons. A specially trained infantry force of about 2,000 men was armed with large muskets, and an artillery branch disposed of 50 to 60 serviceable guns. European-type uniforms were first used (Gregorian, 76). Military pay was partially in cash and in kind, but usually in arrears. Recruitment was often by seizure of able-bodied men, a practice not exclusive to Afghanistan at the time. There also existed a militia of *jezailchis* (riflemen) and feudal irregular forces. A British military mission headed by Major H. B. Lumsden is said to have contributed advice about the modernization of the Afghan army. Amir **Shir Ali** continued the modernization process. He obtained a number of artillery pieces and some 5,000 Snider rifles in 1875, but the ensuing civil war in Afghanistan postponed major military reforms to the time of Amir **Abdul Rahman.**

The "Iron Amir" spent most of his subsidy from the British-Indian government on the purchase of arms, and he expanded the local production of weapons (*See also* INTRODUCTION, p. 12). The first attempt to create a modern officers' corps was made in 1904 when Amir **Habibullah** (r. 1901–1919) founded the Royal Military College. By 1910 it enrolled 80 cadets, mostly the sons of **Durrani** chiefs, who studied, in addition to Islamic topics, arithmetic, geometry, and military logistics and underwent rigorous physical training and drills. In 1907 a Turkish officer, Mahmud Sami, was put in charge of the college, marking the beginning of Turkish influence in the Afghan army.

King **Amanullah** (r. 1919–1929) neglected the army at the cost of his throne. He saw his as an "era of the pen—not of the sword" and devoted his resources to the modernization of his country. Turkish advisers were still prominent in the army, including **Jamal Pasha**, one of the triumvirate rulers of the Ottoman War government. Germans, the teachers of the Turks, were also employed as were members of various other nationalities. The nucleus of an **Afghan air force** was created in the 1920s, in which experts from the **Soviet Union** participated.

King Amanullah's army was about 50,000 strong, comprising an infantry of about 38,000 men divided into 78 battalions armed with Martini-Henri and Snider rifles; a cavalry of about 8,000 sabres divided into 21 units; and about 4,000 artillerymen employing some 260 breach-loading guns, mainly German Krupp 75mm and 7-pounders (O'Ballance, 55). An arsenal at **Kabul** held 15,000 small-bore rifles, 400,000 Martinis, and a few old machine guns. Heliography had still not replaced telegraph communications.

Nadir Khan, as commander in chief, established six army corps headquartered at Kabul (2), **Jalalabad**, Matun, **Herat**, and **Mazar-i Sharif. Kandahar** was added and all were headquarters of principal formations. In practice, many corps were severely undermanned.

Muhammad Nadir Shah took power with tribesmen and reconstituted the army in 1930. He faced many insurrections: 1) the

Koh Daman revolt (Nov. 29–June 30); 2) the **Shinwari** Rebellion (Feb. 1930); 3) the operations against **Ibrahim Beg** (Nov. 1930–Apr. 1931); 4) the **Ghilzai** threat (1931); 5) the Darre Khel revolt (Nov. 1932); and 6) the **Khost** disturbances.

Schools for cavalry, artillery, and infantry were established. German, Italian, and Turkish officers were employed. Pay was increased, and there were improvements in clothing and accommodation by 1933.

Under **Muhammad Zahir Shah**, a striking improvement occurred. In 1936 the army was about 60,000 strong. It played an important role in internal security, and although regularly paid and housed in better barracks, it was still inferior to British-Indian standards.

Peacetime organization included: Two corps Kabul; Southern Province three divisions; one division Household troops (Guards Division); one artillery division; and two independent mixed divisions. Total: 13 divisions and one artillery division (MR).

King Muhammad Zaher Shah (r. 1933–1973) realized that for domestic stability and defense against foreign aggression he needed a strong, modern army. His uncle, Shah Mahmud, minister of war and commander in chief of the army until 1946, embarked on a project of military reorganization. He purchased weapons from **Germany**, **Britain**, Italy, and Czechoslovakia as well as airplanes and tanks. He also created the first mechanized forces. Additional officers' schools were established in Maimana, Mazar-i Sharif, and those in Kabul and Herat were expanded. Afghan officers were sent abroad for additional training, and Turkish officers replaced European advisers at the advent of World War II. A combination of compulsory and voluntary enlistment increased the Afghan army from 70,000 men in 1934 to 80,000 in 1936. About 50 percent of Afghanistan's revenue of 150 million afghanis was devoted to military expenditures (Gregorian, 371).

After World War II, the Afghan army had reached its traditional size of about 90,000 men, but its weapons and equipment were largely obsolete. The Afghan prime minister, Shah Mahmud, envisaged a "small but well-trained internal security force," reducing the size of the army by half and expanding a central police force to 20,000 men (Bradsher 1983, 18). Formal requests for arms purchases from the **United States** were repeatedly rebuffed; therefore, in early 1955 Prime Minister **Muhammad Daud** turned to the Soviet Union for help. The **Pashtunistan** dispute with **Pakistan**, a member of the

Baghdad Pact and unofficial ally of the United States, was one of the reasons for the growing influence of the Soviet Union in Afghanistan's army. In July 1956 the Soviet Union granted a loan of $32.4 million in military assistance, which greatly helped to modernize the Afghan army. But Afghanistan became dependent on Soviet expertise and supplies, and some 3,725 Afghan military personnel went to the Soviet Union for training. On the eve of the Marxist coup in 1978, the Afghan army included all branches of infantry divisions, mechanized, paratroop, commando, and artillery brigades. Equipment included a sizable tank force and an air force of some 140–170 fighter planes and 45 to 60 helicopters. (*See* AIR FORCE, AFGHAN; INTRODUCTION p. 19). Following the Soviet intervention, a Status of Armed Forces Agreement was signed in April 1980, which was to legalize the presence of the **Limited Contingent of Soviet Forces in Afghanistan**. (*See* APPENDIX 3.)

During the 1980s the Afghan army fluctuated in size between 40–60,000 but disintegrated with the defeat of the Kabul regime, soldiers deserting or joining rivaling mujahedin groups. The **Taliban** regime saw a recrudescence, drawing primarily on **Pashtuns** and foreign volunteers, which enabled them to control most of Afghanistan. The American intervention in fall 2001 quickly brought local forces into the play to become the foot soldiers of the campaign. The Afghan army again broke into its ethnic parts, under the control of local leaders/ warlords, which left the Kabul government of **Hamid Karzai** unable to extend its control over the country. With American support a new Afghan National Army (ANA) was gradually created, which by early 2005 amounted to about 20,000 soldiers.

The American military started training ANA recruits, initially for 10 weeks of basic training, followed by two months of specialty training. A recruit makes $70 a month and a sergeant about $180, which is good pay in Afghanistan. Attempts are made to maintain an ethnic balance, and recruits are tested and evaluated to determine if they were junior enlisted, senior enlisted, or officer material. A new military academy is being created and a military justice code has been drafted.

The ANA began to see action in the provinces in December 2003, when it forced local warlords to disarm. In March 2004 the Kabul government sent two battalions to Herat when forces of **Muhammad Ismail Khan** clashed with a progovernment commander, and again in September, removing Ismail Khan from his control of Herat. At times high ranking military advisers were "embedded" into ANA battalions and American aerial support made the new army an increasingly powerful force. A Central Corps was established in Kabul and a command headquarters was established in Kandahar in September 2004. The ANA now consists of five corps, the first is the 201st based in Kabul which became fully staffed in May 2004, and four regional corps came on line in Kandahar, Gardez, Mazar-i Sharif, and Herat. A $63 million ANA base is being constructed near Herat with more than 100 buildings, including offices, barracks, a power plant, wastewater facility, hospital and sports field. An American sergeant is paying the troops, but this and many other tasks will soon be taken over by Afghan soldiers.

ARMY OF THE INDUS. The British-Indian army and **Shah Shuja**'s forces that invaded Afghanistan during the **first Anglo-Afghan war** totaled some 39,000 men. It was composed of three sources, the Bengal army, the Bombay army, and the army of Shah Shuja, most of whose men were transfers from the East India Company's troops. The Bengal army consisted of the British 16th Dragoons (Lancers), the 13th Foot (Light Infantry), one regiment of Bengal European infantry, two of Light Cavalry, two of Local Horse, and seven of Native Infantry. They were complemented with one troop of all-European horse artillery and two all-Indian companies of sappers and miners. From the Bombay army came the 4th Light Dragoons and the 4th and 17th Regiments of Foot (all from British service), one regiment of Light Cavalry and one of Local Horse, two troops of horse artillery, two companies of foot artillery (all European), four regiments of Native Infantry and one company of sappers and miners.

The British infantry, engineers, and heavy cavalry wore red coats; the Light Cavalry and artillery wore blue coats. The Indian sepoys in the infantry wore red uniforms, and the cavalry gray, whereas the irregular troops did not wear uniforms. Most were equipped with flintlock muskets (O'Ballance, 10).

Shah Shuja's forces included two regiments of cavalry, four regiments of infantry, and a troop of horse artillery. Two additional infantry regiments were recruited later. All together his forces comprised 6,000 men. Shah Shuja's son Timur commanded a force of 6,000 Sikhs and 4,000 of Shah Shuja's men who invaded Afghanistan from Peshawar.

Because of the lack of roads fit for wheeled traffic, the Army of the Indus depended on animal transport. Some 60,000 Indian and several thousand Afghan camels were employed, as well as hundreds of bullock carts and a number of baggage elephants. The invasion proceeded without great difficulty. The British forces reached the **Kandahar** area on April 14, 1839, and on April 25, Shah Shuja entered the city to popular acclaim. **Sir John Keane**, the commander in chief, departed from Kandahar on June 27, 1839, and moved against **Ghazni**, and on July 23, he succeeded in capturing the city after blowing up the **Kabul** Gate (*see* GHAZNI, CAPTURE OF). The British army took Kabul in the face of little opposition, and on August 7, Shah Shuja formally entered the city. In September the Bombay Division returned to India, and a month later parts of the Bengal Division left. Most of the remaining troops and camp followers did not survive the invasion. *See* ANGLO-AFGHAN WARS; DEATH MARCH.

ARMY RANKS. In the late 1920s, army ranks were as follows:

Wazir-i Harbiya	Minister of War
Arkan	General Officers
Sipah Salar	Commander in Chief
Na'eb Salar	General
Firqa Mishar	Divisional Commander
Amiran	
Ghund Mishar	Regimental Commander
Kandak Mishar	Divisional Commander
Zabitan	Junior Commissioned Officers
Katib-i Ghund	Regimental Head Clerk
Toli Mishar	Company or Squadron Commander
Katib-i Kandak	Battalion Head Clerk
Boluk Mishar	Plaroon or Troop Commander
Khurd Zabetan	
Sarparak Mishar	Sergeant Major
Katib-i Toli	Company Clerk
Parak Mishar	Sergeant
Salahandar	Rifleman
Dalgai Mishar	Corporal
Sepoy	Private

(HBAA, 1927)

ATA, MUHAMMAD USTAD (ATTA). A **Tajik**, member of the **Jami'at-i Islami** party and major rival of the **Usbek** General **Abdul Rashid Dostum**, after the defeat of the **Taliban** in northern Afghanistan. Together they captured **Mazar-i Sharif**, and although both are members of the **Northern Alliance**, they were vying for territory in northern **Kunduz** Province and have continuously clashed. Muhammad Ata was governor of **Balkh** in the **Hamid Karzai** government.

A-TEAM. The standard, 12-man teams that make up the U.S. Army Special Forces. It is also called Operational Detachment Alpha (ODA). *See also* SPECIAL FORCES A-TEAM.

AUCKLAND, LORD. Governor General of India (1837–1842), who in defiance of the Court of Directors of the **East India Company**, started the disastrous **first Anglo-Afghan war** to replace Amir **Dost Muhammad** with **Shah Shuja**.

He subsequently wrote to the court of directors that "the increase of Russian and Persian influence in Affghanistan, and the impression of the certain fall of **Herat** to the Persian army, have induced the Ameer Dost Mahomed Khan to avow and to insist upon pretensions for the cession to him, by Maharajah Runjeet Sing, of the Peshwur territory, and to take other steps which are tantamount to the rejection of the friendship and good offices of the British Government; and have in consequence led to the retirement of Captain **Alexander Burnes** from the territories of Cabool.

"The emergency of affairs may compel me to act without awaiting any intimation of your views upon the events which have recently occurred in Persia and Afghanistan" (Auckland to secret committee of the declaration of war).

Initially, it was decided to give a major role in the task of restoring **Shah Shuja** to the **Kabul** throne to **Ranjit Singh** and his army, but the Sikh ruler was not eager and Auckland subsequently felt that he could not be trusted to carry it out successfully. Therefore, the British **Army of the Indus** was to do the job. Early successes in the war led to his being created Earl of Auckland in 1839. Following the debacle, Auckland was denounced and recalled.

AVIATION IN AFGHANISTAN. Aviation in Afghanistan began in 1921 when King **Amanullah** acquired a British fighter plane. Additional planes were purchased or acquired as gifts from **Great**

Britain and the **Soviet Union**; the latter donated a number of aircraft on condition that they be operated and serviced by Soviet nationals. By the end of the 1920s Afghanistan's air force consisted of 22 machines (Bristol Fighters, D.H. 9s, Caprioni Scouts, and a Junker Monoplane) operated by some 25 officers, three of them Afghans, four Germans, and the rest Russians. Young Afghans were sent to Italy, the Soviet Union, India, and other countries for training as pilots and aircraft mechanics.

The air service was largely devoted to transporting the mail, foreign diplomats, and members of the Afghan government. In 1926 average flying times were: **Kabul** to **Kandahar**—three hours; Kabul to **Jalalabad**—50 minutes; Kabul to Termez (on the Soviet side of the Amu Daria)—two hours and 40 minutes; and Jalalabad to Kandahar—three and a half hours. The flight from Kabul to Moscow took five days, crossing the **Hindu Kush** at 5,000 meters.

Although half of the fleet was out of operation, control of the airspace proved important in suppressing the **Khost Rebellion** and other tribal revolts. After the ouster of King Amanullah, **Muhammad Nadir Shah** did not renew the Soviet concession, but Soviet planes continued at an irregular schedule to transport diplomatic personnel to the Soviet Union. In 1937 Lufthansa Airlines established regular air service from Berlin to Kabul, but this was discontinued with the outbreak of World War II. As a result of the division of Afghanistan into hostile territories, regional airlines came into existence to connect **Mazar-i Sharif**, Kandahar, and Jalalabad with neighboring countries. The **Taliban** regime maintained air service until a **United Nation**'s boycott reduced its links with the world. With the establishment of the Afghan **Interim Government** in December 2002, air service to foreign destinations was gradually restored. *See also* AIR FORCE, AFGHAN.

AYUB KHAN, MUHAMMAD (AYYUB). Son of Amir **Shir Ali** and full brother of **Yaqub Khan**. At the death of his father, Yaqub Khan was crowned king at **Kabul**, and Ayub took over the governorship of **Herat**. When he learned of the British occupation of Kabul, he incited the Afghan *sardars* to rise and expel the invaders. In June 1880 the ulama at Herat proclaimed him amir and he had coins struck in his name as a sign of his sovereignty. He then marched his army against **Kandahar** and on July 27, 1880, he met General **G. R. S.**

Burrows at **Maiwand** and virtually wiped out his forces. Ayub then proceeded to Kandahar and laid siege to the city, but General Roberts came to the rescue and he was forced to retreat to his base at Herat. He again moved on Kandahar in June 1881, at a time when Great Britain had recognized **Abdul Rahman** as amir of Kabul. The Iron Amir easily defeated Ayub's forces at Kandahar in September 1881 and at the same time dispatched his general, **Abdul Quddus** Khan, to capture the lightly garrisoned city of Herat. Being deprived of his base, Ayub was forced to flee to Iran, and after a number of years accepted asylum in India for himself and his retinue of 814 individuals.

- B -

BABA JAN, MAJOR GENERAL. A Khalqi and commander of the military academy in the **Nur Muhammad Taraki** government who also served as chief of the general staff of the Armed Forces, January 1980–January 1984. For a short time he was caretaker at the ministry of national defense. He was elected an alternate member of the **People's Democratic Party of Afghanistan** (PDPA) central committee and served as head of the Kabul military academy and as ambassador to Berlin (1985–1988). He was educated in military schools in **Kabul**, Turkey, and the USSR. He is a recipient of the "Order of the Golden Star." He was reportedly killed in Peshawar by **Taliban** supporters.

BABA JAN, LIEUTENANT GENERAL ABDUL WAHED. Major military commander of **Burhanuddin Rabbani**'s party after the fall of the Marxist regime in 1992. He defected with **Abdul Rashid Dostum** from the **Kabul** regime and thus contributed to the downfall of the **Najibullah** government. He was a member of the **Parcham** faction of the **People's Democratic Party of Afghanistan** (PDPA). In charge of Kabul security, he moved to Herat in April 2005.

BABA WALI KOTAL, BATTLE OF (31-40' N, 65-40' E). A village and pass, named after a holy man whose tomb is located about 3.5 miles northwest of **Kandahar**. It had been the scene of battles during the **first** and **second Anglo-Afghan war**s. On March 25, 1842, a portion of the Kandahar force under Colonel **George P. Wymer** met an Afghan contingent headed by Shahzada Saftar Jang and defeated the Afghans with only three killed and 39 wounded. Two months later, on May 29, 1842, Akhtar Khan's forces were attacked by

General **Sir William Nott** and driven with great loss through the pass and over the Arghandab River. In August 1880, after defeating General Burrows at the **Battle of Maiwand**, Sardar **Ayub Khan** stationed his forces at the pass and opened artillery fire on Kandahar. Then on September 1 General Roberts dispatched his Bombay Division and the 72nd Highlanders to capture the village of Pir Paimal and, after turning the right flank of the Afghans, threatened the Afghan position in the rear. The **ghazis** made a determined stand, but a charge of the 92nd Highlanders with support of the 2nd Gurkhas and 23rd Pioneers carried the position. The 3rd Sikhs carried the Afghan position by storm, and the British forces captured Ayub Khan's camp and artillery. British cavalry put 350 *jihadis* (holy warriors) to the sword and buried 600 Afghans and estimated another 600 dead carried off by the Afghans. According to **General Frederick Roberts**, British losses amounted to 40 killed and 228 wounded (Heathcote, 162).

BABUR, ZAHIR AL-DIN MUHAMMAD (1483–1530). Founder of the Moghul empire, the "greatest soldier of his age," and a talented writer and great poet (Sykes, 1940). He was a Barlas Turk who descended on his mother's side from Genghis Khan and on the male side from Tamerlane (Timur-i Lang). He was ousted from his native Ferghana, the Turkic lands north of the **Amu Daria**, and when he could not retake his homeland he settled in **Kabul** in 1504. Probing expeditions into India led to territorial conquests that became the foundation of the Moghul Empire. He loved Kabul and wrote fondly about the town and wanted to be buried in the Bagh-i Babur, a garden he had planted on the western slope of Sher Darwaza mountain. He died in Agra on December 26, 1530, and his body was transported to Kabul where his rather modest tomb is still located.

BACHA-I SAQQAU. *See* **HABIBULLAH KALAKANI.**

BADAKHSHAN (36-45' N, 72-0' E). A province in northeastern Afghanistan, comprising an area of 15,786 square miles and a population of about 484,000 (estimates vary up to 615,000). The province includes the **Wakhan** Corridor, a narrow valley which extends to the Chinese border and separates Tajikistan from the Indo-Pakistan subcontinent. The province is divided into five districts (*woluswali*) and seven subdistricts (*alaqadari*) with **Faizabad** as the administrative capital. The province is mountainous, with a number of high valleys and peaks reaching a height of 16,000 feet. It is rich in mineral resources including silver, copper, lead, precious stones, and virtually all the lapis lazuli mined in Afghanistan. Famed for its Marco Polo sheep, ibex, and snow leopards, Badakhshan was becoming an important hunting preserve for wealthy foreigners before the war in Afghanistan interrupted further development. The yak is still used in the Wakhan as a beast of burden. The population is **Tajik**, with **Uzbek** communities in the west and Wakhis and Qirghiz in the Wakhan Corridor (most of the latter have fled as a result of Soviet occupation).

Much of Badakhshan was ruled by autonomous khans until in 1850 **Dost Muhammad** took it under the direct control of the **Kabul** government. By the time of Amir **Abdul Rahman** (r. 1880–1901), it had become an integral part of the Afghan state. In 1893 a mission under **Sir Mortimer Durand** demarcated Afghanistan's northern border and allocated the Wakhan Corridor to Afghanistan. Amir Abdul Rahman was reluctant to accept this "arm that could easily be cut by an enemy" but agreed to accept the Wakhan as a buffer between the Russian and British empires when **Britain** offered to increase his subsidy by 650,000 Indian rupees for his cost of the administration and defense. During the civil war, following the fall of the Marxist regime, Badakhshan remained under the control of the **Jam'iat-i Islami** of **Burhanuddin Rabbani**.

BADGHIS (35-0' N, 63-45' E). Badghis is a province in northwestern Afghanistan that was part of **Herat** Province prior to 1964. The province has an area of 8,438 square miles and an estimated population of about 250,000. Major districts include Jowand, Ghormach, Qades, Murghab, Qal'a-i Nau, and Kushk-i Kohna. It borders on Turkmenistan (formerly the Soviet Union) in the north and Herat in the west. Badghis is a country of beautiful grassy hills but virtually without trees or even bushes in spite of an abundance of good water near the hills. The climate is, as in most parts of Afghanistan, cold in the winter and hot in the summer. Barley and wheat are the major crops, and pistachio nuts are harvested in considerable quantities. The area was densely populated until it was devastated by Mongol invaders (13th and 15th centuries) and again by the Safavids under Shah Abbas II (r. 1642–1666). Subsequently it was inhabited only by nomadic tribes because of the danger of Turkoman raids from the north. The present population includes **Pashtuns**, Jamshidis, **Hazaras**, and small communities of other ethnic groups.

BAGH, BATTLE OF. A village on the British side of the **Durand Line** and the scene of two battles during the **third Anglo-Afghan war**. It was occupied by Afghan troops on May 4, 1919, as a move to cut off the water supply to Landi Kotal. On May 8, British forces, including five battalions of infantry, two batteries of guns, a machine-gun company, a company of sappers, and two troops of lancers moved on Landi Kotal. Brigadier General **G. D. Crocker** ordered an attack to drive the Afghan forces from Bagh. The Afghans easily held their ground, and the British forces (the 1/15th **Sikhs** and the 1/11 Gurka Rifles) had to dig in to establish a defensive position. In the words of one historian, "The First Battle of Bagh, did little to convince the wavering tribes of the overwhelming might of the British" (Heathcote, 180). British airmen (and later, Soviet pilots elsewhere) suffered the unusual experience of being shot at by rifle fire from the crests of the flanking mountains. With considerable reinforcements the 1st Division, commanded by Major General **Fowler**, again attacked Bagh on May 11 with six battalions, covered by the fire of 18 pieces of artillery and 22 machine guns. He had another battalion covering his flank and three in reserve. Under the cover of darkness and after careful preparation, assault units moved up the steep foothills and, backed by covering fire, reached the Afghan *sangars* (stone barriers) and engaged the Afghans in hand-to-hand combat. Having protected their flanks, the British forces could advance and capture the village of Bagh. The British lost eight killed and 32 wounded and buried 65 Afghan soldiers. British estimates of Afghan casualties amounted to 100 killed and 300 wounded.

BAGH-I BALA. A garden in **Kabul**, near the present Intercontinental Hotel, where **Amir Abdul Rahman**'s palace is located. After his death, the garden and building were closed and fell into neglect. Because of its strategic location on top of a hill overlooking the city, it has become an important command post during wars. **Habibullah Kalakani** made it his base in the 1929 civil war, it was a government post during the Soviet occupation, and became a valued outpost during the civil war of the **mujahedin** groups.

BAGHLAN (36-11'N, 68-44'E). A province in northeastern Afghanistan with an area of 6,627 square miles and a population of about 486,000 (est. up to 630,000). Baghlan is also the name of the administrative capital of the province, with approximately 39,000 inhabitants. The province includes the northern slopes of the **Hindu Kush** range that are crossed by the Robatak, Barabi, Khawak, and **Salang** Passes. The northern part is largely agricultural, with irrigation from the Baghlan, Qara Batur, Chunghar, and Mar Khana Rivers. Sugar beets and cotton are the major crops, and pomegranates, grapes, and pistachio nuts are important items of export. Qaraqul sheep are raised in the northern part of the province. Sugar production, started in 1940 with Czech assistance, has become the most important industry. Coal is extracted in the Karkar valley near Pul-i Khumri. A silk industry was started in 1951. Not much is known about the effect of the war on the area.

BAGRAM (BEGRAM) (34-58' N, 69-17' E). Site of an ancient city with an abundance of Buddhist, Graeco-Roman, and Phoenician artifacts. According to some sources, it is the site of Alexandria ad Caucasum (Alexandria by the Caucasus, built by Alexander the Great in 330–329 B.C.), which flourished for centuries until it was destroyed by the hordes of Genghis Khan in the 13th century. The town is north of **Kabul** near the confluence of the **Panjshir** and Ghorband Rivers, about five miles west of **Charikar**. Bagram is now a small town, the center of the district of the same name in **Parwan** Province. It is the location of an air base built with Soviet assistance in the 1950s. On July 7, 1979, the first Soviet paratroop battalion deployed there, apparently in preparation for its occupation in December 1979, when one regiment of the 105th Guards Airborne Division landed. Bagram became a primary regional center for independent air regiments as a base for the protection of Kabul and the **Salang Pass**. Although well fortified, Bagram air base was frequently attacked. On June 3, 1985, **mujahedin** forces under Commander Abdul Karim led an attack in which he allegedly destroyed 60 to 70 aircraft and killed scores of Soviet soldiers. After the mujahedin capture of Kabul, Bagram became an important base of Rabbani's government until it was conquered by the **Taliban**. The fall of the Taliban regime let to British control of the base until the **United States** took over.

It has since become the primary American base in Afghanistan, covering an area of about 840 acres. It has a 10,000 foot long runway which can accommodate large cargo and bomber aircraft. Facilities include three large hangars, a control tower, and numerous support buildings. As many as 5,000 troops are stationed there. It occasionally comes under hostile fire, land mines have been found in the surrounding areas, and a large explosion occurred in 2004, which did not cost any American lives. There are recreation and fitness centers on the base, a post exchange (PX), and also a prison where suspects are detained for interrogation.

BALA HISAR. A citadel within a walled town usually on the crest of a mountain or hill, serving as the residence of an Afghan ruler or governor. The Bala Hisar of **Kabul** is a huge complex built southwest of the ancient wall on Sher Darwaza mountain. Until the 19th century its high stone walls surrounded a strong citadel that was the residence of the Kabul ruler and his court. **Babur** Shah and Timur-i Lang are said to have resided in it. High military and civilian officials were quartered within the outer walls. In the **first Anglo-Afghan war**, the British forces built their defenses around a rectangular cantonment in the valley below, instead of seeking the security of the Bala Hisar. This turned out to be a fatal mistake. The six-century-old fortress was destroyed on order of the British General **Frederick Roberts** after an explosion on October 16, 1879, in the arsenal killed a British officer and a number of soldiers of his Gurkha unit. The fortress lay in ruins until **Muhammad Nadir Shah** in the early 1930s started the process of reconstruction. It has served as a military college and garrison since 1939. On August 5, 1979, an army regiment at the Bala Hisar revolted against the **Khalqi** regime, and it took a four-hour battle in which MI-24 gunships and considerable heavy artillery were employed before the revolt was suppressed. Subsequently, the fortress was able to withstand **mujahedin** attacks and fell into their hands only with the capture of Kabul. In the present civil war the Bala Hisar of Kabul was occupied by the **Uzbek** forces of **Abdul Rashid Dostum**, who was in turn expelled by the forces of **Burhanuddin Rabbani**. Aerial warfare and modern weapons technology have made fortresses of this type obsolete.

BALKH (36–46' N, 66–54' E). A province in north-central Afghanistan with an area of about 4,633 square miles and a population of about 570,000 (1991 est. up to 717,000). The administrative capital of the province is **Mazar-i Sharif**, with about 103,000 inhabitants in 1978, and the location of a shrine Afghans believe to be the burial place of the Caliph Ali (d. 640). The town of Balkh, located on the Balkhab River about 14 miles west of Mazar-i Sharif, derives its name from the ancient city of Bactria amidst the ruins of which it is located. According to local tradition Balkh was founded by Balkh ibn Balakh ibn Saman ibn Salam ibn Ham ibn Nuh (Noah). Zoroastrian tradition holds that it was the birthplace of Zoroaster and was built by the Arian ruler Bakhdi (or Keiomarz?) who founded the Pishdadian dynasty. The city was captured by Alexander the Great (320s B.C.) and became the capital of the Greek satrapy of Bactria. In the second century B.C. Bactria was invaded by Turkic nomads who renamed the area Tukharestan. Subsequently the Kushans ruled over the area, followed by other dynasties. The ancestor of the famous Barmakid family of Abbasid wazirs (r. 781–803), Khalid ibn Barmak (priest), was a native of Balkh. Genghis Khan (r. 1206–1226) destroyed the city, but it was rebuilt during the Timurid period (15th century). In 1480 the tomb of the Caliph Ali was believed to have been discovered where Mazar-i Sharif is now located, and Balkh lost its significance. Because of its antiquity, the town is known as the "Mother of Cities."

BALUCH. One of Afghanistan's ethnic minorities located primarily in **Nimruz** and scattered in small numbers over **Helmand, Farah, Herat, Fariab, Jozjan, Kunduz,** and **Badakhshan** Provinces. Their numbers were estimated in the 1970s between 100,000 and 200,000. Virtually all are **Sunnis** and speakers of the Baluchi language (except for the **Dari**-speaking Qataghan Baluch). The Baluch are no longer organized into specific tribes and are largely sedentary; their "heartland" lies in the Baluchistan Provinces of Iran and **Pakistan,** where they are said to number about five million. Small numbers also exist in the Soviet Union. Since the mid-1970s some 2,500 Baluch guerrillas, fighting for autonomy in Pakistan, have found shelter in southern Afghanistan. The Brahui who speak a Dravidian language have now largely assimilated with the Baluch.

BAMIAN (BAMYAN, 34-50' N, 67-50' E). A province in central Afghanistan with an area of about 6,757 square miles and a population of about 285,000 (1991 est. up to 332,000) and a town of the same name that is the administrative center of the province. The town lies at an altitude of about 8,200 feet above sea level, about 205 miles by road north of **Kabul.** Bamian is part of the **Hazarajat,** the mountainous country of central Afghanistan, that is inhabited primarily by **Hazaras.** The province is famous for its two Buddha statues, respectively, 120 and 175 feet in height, dating from 507 and 551 A.D. respectively. The statues were hewn into solid rock and overlaid with stucco, and, although they suffered from the ravages of time and destruction by man, some of the stucco works and wall paintings were still preserved. The walls of the 300-feet high cliffs are honeycombed with caves that served as living quarters of Buddhist monks and are still inhabited today. The sculptures and paintings are an eclectic hybrid mixing Indian, Central Asian, Iranian, and classical European art styles and ideas. On February 26, 2001, Mulla **Muhammad Omar,** head of the **Taliban** regime, ordered the destruction of the statues, and, in spite of worldwide pleas for their preservation, demolition was started on March 1 and was completed within 10 days. According to some claims, Pakistani and Saudi nationals provided technical advice. In 2002 the **Hamid Karzai** government announced that the statues would be restored in tribute to Afghanistan's ancient culture.

BARNO, LIEUTENANT GENERAL DAVID. Commander of the 11,000-strong U.S. forces in Afghanistan (subsequently grown to 21,000) since November 27, 2003. His assignment marked a significant switch in strategy in American operations to provide reconstruction aid into insecure areas with the establishment of **provincial reconstruction teams** (PRT). These teams are to become peaceful islands and, in the words of Barno, make them "realize that's the death knell to terrorist organizations in that part of the country." To the 13 existing PRTs eight new ones were added and moderate elements of the old **Taliban** regime were to be brought back into the fold, if they "renounce violence, renounce terror, live as responsible members of the Afghan body politic." He obtained an M.A. degree from Georgetown University, is a graduate of the U.S. Army Command and General Staff College, and, as an Army Ranger, served in Grenada and Panama. He served in command and staff positions in many parts of the world, before being nominated to the rank of lieutenant general and assigned as commander of military operations in Afghanistan. He was succeeded by General **Karl Eikenberry** in May 2005.

BARRETT, GENERAL SIR ARTHUR (1857–1926). He commanded the North-West Frontier Force in the **third Anglo-Afghan war**. Previously he served in the **second Anglo-Afghan war** and participated at the **Battle of Kandahar**. In 1891 he took part in the second Miranzai expedition. He died on October 20, 1926.

BASMACHIS. An irregular force, called *basmachis* (T. bandits) by the Soviet government, that fought the Red Army in the mountains of Tajikistan and Ferghana in Central Asia from 1919 until the 1930s. Their leaders included Muhammad Amin Beg, **Ibrahim Beg**, and **Enver Pasha**, the Ottoman minister of war during the World War I.

King **Amanullah** supported their efforts for some time in the hope of ruling over a confederation of Central Asian states, but when continued support threatened relations with the Soviet Union, he abandoned that hope. During the Soviet occupation of Afghanistan, the Soviets called the **mujahedin** *basmachi* or *dushman* (D. enemy).

BEHESHTI, SAYYID ALI. President of the Revolutionary Council of the Islamic Union of Afghanistan (Shura-yi Inqelabi-yi Ittifaq-i Islami-yi Hazarajat), which until 1982 controlled large portions of the **Hazarajat**. He is a native of **Bamian** and was educated in Saudi Arabia and Iraq, where he was a contemporary of Ayatollah Khomeini. He opened a **madrasa** in Waras to spread his revivalist ideas among Hazaras and was speaker in the Takkia Khana at **Kabul** until the Marxist coup. In September 1979 he was elected president of the **shura** by a council of elders. He formed a traditional Islamic resistance group, commanded by Sayyid Muhammad Hasan "Jagran" (Major), with headquarters in Waras in **Ghor** Province, and became a major force in the Hazarajat until the Shura lost ground to the Islamist forces of **Nasr**. The Shura recruited its fighters from the Hazara peasantry, led by sayyids (*Sadat*), and had commanders in **Bamian, Ghor, Nimruz, Oruzgan,** and **Wardak** Provinces.

BIDDULPH, LIEUTENANT GENERAL SIR MICHAEL ANTHONY S. (1823–1904). Commanded the Quetta Field Force, the second division of the **Kandahar** Field Force, and the Thal-Chotiali Field Force from formation to their breakup during the **second Anglo-Afghan war**. He took part in the original advance on and occupation of Kandahar and Girishk. Born on July 10, 1823, at Cleeve Court, Somerset, he was commissioned second lieutenant in 1843. He served in Burma, the Crimean War, and was posted to India in 1861. In 1868 he left India and from 1889 to 1895 was groom-in-waiting to Queen Victoria. He died on July 23, 1904, in London.

BIN-I HISAR (BENI HISSAR). A village, at the foot of a spur of the same name, running down from the **Takht-i Shah**, which is of great strategic importance because it lies on the road to **Kabul** and commands a view of part of the city. **Sir Frederick Roberts** camped in this area on October 7, 1879, after the battle at **Charasia**. It was from the Bin-i Hisar spur that the 92nd Highlanders advanced on December 18, 1879, when the Takht-i Shah was carried. During the civil war for the capture of Kabul, the **Taliban** advanced to Bin-i Hisar, where they were able to bombard the Kabul airport and eventually capture the city.

BLOCKING TACTICS. An operation aimed at securing the advance of the main force by enveloping or encircling the enemy and threatening his rear and flanks. Called *killaband* by the Afghans, the method was perfected by **Ayub Khan** and was employed to pin down the British firing line, while the tribal contingents and cavalry moved around the British flanks and threatened the baggage train and logistic elements in the enemy's rear (Heathcote, 149). **Soviet** counterinsurgency tactics included the *blokirovka* enveloping formation, achieved by landing heliborne detachments in the rear and flanks of **mujahedin** forces to cut escape routes, and access to supply lines as well as to protect the advancement of heavy infantry or motorized convoys on the ground axis.

BLOWPIPE MISSILE. The **mujahedin** received British Blowpipe missiles in August 1986. The Blowpipe is an operator-guided missile, rather than heat-seeking, and therefore cannot be diverted by flares from the target. Brigadier **Muhammad Yusuf**, head of the Afghan Bureau of Pakistan's **Inter-Services Intelligence** (ISI), which supported the mujahedin effort, had a low opinion of the Blowpipe. He called it obsolescent and unable to take targets moving across the firer's front. The firer had to remain standing to aim, fire, and then guide the missile optically onto the target. Half of the missiles would not accept the command signal and would go astray. Yusuf claimed, "I do not recall a single confirmed kill by a Blowpipe" (1992, 88). It was the American-made **Stinger** which marked the turning point in the war of the mujahedin. **Soviet** aerial superiority was threatened with this escalation in weaponry.

BOMBERS. The **Soviet** forces employed the TU-16 Badger medium and SU-24 Fencer all-weather light bombers as well as the modern intermediate-range bomber in its counterinsurgency operations. High-altitude bombing was used in preparation for offensives against **mujahedin**-held bases or for shielding ground troops during engagements. This type of air war became especially important when mujahedin missiles made air transport and helicopter support difficult.

In the beginning of the **United States** intervention, American B-52 Stratofortresses were employed to bombard the major Afghan cities and **Taliban** bases. With a crew of five, the aircraft could deliver a load of 31,000 kg, consisting of bombs and cruise missiles. At a maximum speed of 1,046 km/h and a range of about 14,160 km these aircraft could take off in the United States or **Great Britain**, as well as from neighboring countries, until control of the **Bagram** airbase permitted them to operate within Afghanistan. Like the Soviet aircraft, the American B-52s were said to have lacked precision and therefore caused "friendly fire" civilian casualties. B-52s continued to be employed in local action but, once aerial control had been secured, Black Hawk and Chinook helicopters took over much of the action.

BONN CONFERENCE. A conference convened at the palatial Petersburg Hotel in Königswinter near Bonn from November 27 until December 5, 2001. It was held under the auspices of the **United Nations** to bring the Afghan representatives to agree on the formation of an **Interim Government** that was to prepare the way for creating a broad-based Afghan government.

Lakhdar Brahimi, the special UN envoy to Afghanistan, urged the assembled members "not to repeat the past mistakes . . . and choose compromise over conflict." The groups consisted of representatives of the **Northern Alliance**, which was in control of the capital **Kabul**, the Rome delegation of the ex-king's supporters, the Cyprus group of independent exiles, and the Peshawar group of **Sayyid Ahmad Gailani** supporters. German Foreign Minister Joschka Fischer stressed the importance of the meeting, saying: "They [groups] shouldered a historic responsibility to bring peace to Afghanistan after years of war." After arduous negotiations the representatives agreed to set up an Interim Government, headed by **Hamid Karzai**, in which the Northern Alliance secured the ministries of defense, interior, and foreign affairs. **Abdul Qadir**, a **Pashtun**, withdrew, protesting that Pashtuns were underrepresented in the new government.

The Bonn Agreement completed its task, selecting a **Transitional Government**, approved by a **Loya Jirga**, in which the Northern Alliance continued its dominant position.

BRAHIMI, LAKHDAR. Appointed on October 3, 2001, special representative for Afghanistan with authority for the humanitarian, human rights, and political endeavors of the **United Nations** in Afghanistan. He attended the **Bonn Conference** (November 27–December 5) where he succeeded in winning an agreement by four major groups for the establishment of a six-month **Interim Government**, which prepared the way for convening a **Loya Jirga** and establishment of a two-year **Transitional Government**. Brahimi served previously (July 1997 until October 1999) as special envoy to Afghanistan, but failed to bring the warring parties to agree to a peaceful solution. Great international pressure and the promise of considerable developmental aid made his second effort successful. Brahimi was born on January 1, 1934, and educated in Algeria and France. He served as ambassador to **Britain** and Egypt and was minister of foreign affairs of Algeria from 1991 to 1993. In addition to his activities in Afghanistan, Brahimi served as special representative of the United Nations in Haiti and South Africa. Brahimi was succeeded in Afghanistan by the Frenchman Jean Arnault on February 6, 2004.

BRITAIN. See **GREAT BRITAIN.**

BRITISH EAST INDIA COMPANY. See **EAST INDIA COMPANY, BRITISH.**

BROWNE, SIR SAMUEL J. (1824–1901). He commanded the 1st Division of the Peshawar Valley Field Force from its formation during the **second Anglo-Afghan war**. He was in charge of all troops in northern Afghanistan. He participated in the attack on **Ali Masjid**, forcing the **Khaibar**, and on the advance to Dakka, **Jalalabad**, and **Gandomak**. Born in India, he was gazetted as ensign and posted to 46th Bengal, 1848–1849, served in the Sikh War, and Indian Mutiny, 1857–1858. He died at Ryde, Isle of Wight. A military belt is named after him.

BRYDON, DR. WILLIAM (1811–1873). Assistant surgeon with Shah Shuja's contingent of Hindustani Infantry who was the sole survivor to reach **Jalalabad** on January 13, 1842, after the disastrous retreat that routed the British **Army of the Indus** and camp followers. Later, hostages and other survivors of the British expeditionary force of some 16,000 reached the safety of India. A painting by Elisabeth, Lady Butler, forcefully depicted the wounded physician on a dying pony at the gates of Jalalabad. This was a powerful reminder of the extraordinary loss to British prestige and fulfillment of a supposed prediction of **Akbar Khan** that he would annihilate the British army and leave only one man to tell. *See also* DEATH MARCH.

BURNES, ALEXANDER (1805–1841). A captain in the Indian army who was sent by **Lord Auckland**, governor general of the East India Company, to the court of Amir **Dost Muhammad** in September 1837 for the purpose of concluding an alliance with **Britain** and establishing peace between the Afghan ruler and **Ranjit Singh**, who had captured Kashmir and occupied Peshawar. Burnes was well received at **Kabul**, and it appeared that an agreement with the amir was possible; but in spite of Burnes's recommendations Lord Auckland was not willing to make any promises. He recommended that Dost Muhammad waive his claims on Peshawar and make peace with the **Sikh** ruler. The Afghan **amir**'s correspondence with **Russia** and the presence of a purported Russian emissary at Kabul, named **Vitkevich**, were India's reasons for starting the **first Anglo-Afghan war**. Burnes returned to Kabul with the invading forces to serve as deputy and presumed successor to **Sir William Macnaghten**, the envoy and minister of the British government at Kabul. A revolt in Kabul resulted in the assassination of Sir Alexander (he had been knighted shortly before) on November 2, 1841, and the British debacle in the war. *See* ANGLO-AFGHAN WARS.

BURROWS, BRIGADIER GENERAL G. R. S. Sent to oppose **Ayub Khan**'s army, General Burrows met the Afghan forces on July 27, 1880, near the village of **Maiwand** and was totally defeated. *See* MAIWAND, BATTLE OF.

- C -

CAMELS. The shaggy Bactrian breed of camel was the most important pack animal in Afghanistan. It is shorter and has stronger legs than the Indian camel. During the **second Anglo-Afghan war**, Indian camels starved, whereas the Afghan hill camel thrived. According to British military reports of 33,632 Sind and 55,979 **Panjab** camels, 66,000 were lost during the first phase of the war. Later, 39,000 out of 45,853 Panjabi camels were lost, making a total loss of 99,000 camels (MR, 1925). *See also* TRANSPORT, MILITARY.

CAMPBELL, WILLIAM (SHIR MUHAMMAD KHAN). A Scotsman, officer in the **East India Company** service, who fought in the army of **Ranjit Singh** and during the **second Anglo-Afghan war** in the service of **Shah Shuja**. He was wounded and captured by forces of **Dost Muhammad** and became a military adviser and an artillery instructor in the Afghan army. He eventually converted to Islam, assuming the name Shir Muhammad Khan, and rose to the rank of general and commander in chief of the Turkestan army at **Balkh**. As a youth, Amir **Abdul Rahman** learned his military sciences from

Campbell and succeeded him at his death in 1866 as commander in chief of the Turkestan army.

CAMP FOLLOWERS. Because of the caste system and the large number of servants English officers kept in India, the Indian army depended on a large number of camp followers "comprising the servants, suttlers, cantiniers, hostlers, water-carriers, snake-charmers, dancers, conjurers, and women." In February 1839, when a Bengal army of 15,000 men left Shikapoor for Afghanistan, it was accompanied by no fewer than 85,000 camp followers. The commander took with him six weeks' food for the entire 100,000, which quickly proved to be inadequate.

As for the perceived needs of British officers, a German visitor to India in the 1850s commented: "I saw a Captain of the Bengal army, on his way to the army of reserve at Ferozepore, with two large wagons drawn by oxen full of geese, fowls, pigeons, wine, sugar, coffee, tea, and numberless tin cases of delicacies, to say nothing of the goats, sheep, and the camels which carried his tents" (Cohen, 1971).

CAPITULATION, TREATY OF. On December 11, 1841, the British forces negotiated a surrender with Afghan chiefs, after it was clear that they were unable to defend themselves from increasing Afghan attacks.

The treaty was signed by **Eldred Pottinger**, the political agent at **Kabul**, Major General **William Elphinstone**, commander of the British forces in Afghanistan, and by Afghan notables, including **Muhammad Akbar Khan**. It demanded that the British troops speedily quit the territories of Afghanistan and march to India, and not return. Two *sardars* were to accompany the army to Afghanistan's border "so that no one should offer molestation on the road." Six English gentlemen were to remain "as our guests [and] shall be treated with courtesy." They would be permitted to leave when Amir **Dost Muhammad** returned. The British force at **Jalalabad** was to proceed to Peshawar before the Kabul army arrived, and the troops at **Kandahar** and other parts of Afghanistan were to depart. All property belonging to Sardar Dost Muhammad Khan was to be returned. If the Afghans needed assistance against a foreign invasion, the British government should help, and all detained Englishmen, including the sick and wounded at Kabul, would be permitted to leave. "All muskets and ordnance stores in the magazine shall, as a token of friendship, be made over to our agents."

Affixed to the treaty were the seals of 18 chiefs, including Muhammad Akbar Khan, son of Amir Dost Muhammad. (The text of the treaty differs to some extent from the version given by **Lady Florentina Sale** in her *Journal of the Disaster in Afghanistan*. This may be due to the fact that the treaty was amended several times before the final version was signed.) The treaty was never implemented because none of the parties trusted the other. **Sir William Macnaghten** was killed by Sardar Akbar Khan after he tried to make a deal with the *sardar*'s enemies, and the British refused to surrender all their weapons. The British army started its evacuation of Kabul on January 6, 1842, and was routed on its way to the border. (*See* DEATH MARCH; FIRST ANGLO-AFGHAN WAR. For the complete text of the treaty, see Sykes, 344–51.)

CAVAGNARI, SIR PIERRE LOUIS (1841–1879). A man of mixed British and French ancestry, described variously as having "great charm and ability" and being a man "of overbearing temper, consumed by the thirst for personal distinction." He was signatory for the British government of the **Treaty of Gandomak** (1879) with **Amir Yaqub Khan**. As commissioner of Peshawar, he crossed the Afghan border on September 21, 1878, with a small party to prepare the way for a British mission led by **Sir Neville Chamberlain** to **Kabul**. The party was stopped at **Ali Masjid** by the Afghan general, **Faiz Muhammad**, and the British government made this a casus belli. On November 21 an Indian army invaded Afghanistan. Cavagnari was appointed British envoy to the amir's court at Kabul after the conclusion of the **second Anglo-Afghan war**. He arrived in Kabul in July 1879, but on September 3, mutinous soldiers, joined by Kabuli citizens, attacked the British residence and killed Cavagnari and his staff. The British government feared a debacle similar to the **first Anglo-Afghan war** and extricated its forces from Afghanistan by recognizing **Abdul Rahman Khan** as the new amir. It was not until 1922 that a British envoy was again appointed to Kabul.

CAVAGNARI, SIR PIERRE LOUIS, RECEPTION OF. A Kabul telegram of July 26, 1879, reported that the "Embassy entered city this morning, and received a most brilliant reception. Four miles from city Sirdars Abdullah Khan, Herati, and Mullah Shah Mahomed, the foreign minister, with some cavalry and two elephants, met us. We proceeded on the elephants with a large escort of cavalry.... Large crowd assembled, and was most orderly and respectful." Cavagnari had an audience with the amir, and a news writer reported that "the general opinion in Kabul is that now that the British Envoy has arrived, the arrears of pay due to the troops will be paid; that compulsory enlistment will be discontinued; and that oppressive taxes on the peasantry and on the trading classes will be considerably reduced." But on August 3 it was reported that the **amir** contemplated a reduction of the allowance hitherto paid to the **Muhammadzai sardars**. Three days later it was reported that the "Herati troops move around town in a most disorderly manner, and creating some excitement amongst the rabble of the place." To appease them, two Herati regiments were paid, and two regiments were deprived of their ammunition. Eventually, all were paid and their ammunition was taken, but on September 3 the embassy was attacked and all members killed.

In a letter dated September 6, **Amir Yaqub** lamented to the British government: "Troops, city, and surrounding country have thrown off yoke of allegiance.... Workshop and magazines totally gutted: in fact, my kingdom is ruined. After God I look to the Government for aid and advice" (PP, Col.).

CHAMBERLAIN, SIR NEVILLE BOWLES (1820–1902). Commander in chief of the Madras army, selected by Lord Lytton for "his striking presence and address," to lead a mission to **Kabul** in September 1878. He was refused passage at **Ali Masjid** by the Afghan general **Faiz Muhammad**. This "insult" was taken as the casus belli for the British invasion of Afghanistan. Chamberlain served with General **Sir William Nott**'s force during the **first Anglo-Afghan war** at **Kandahar**, **Ghazni**, Kabul, and Istalif, and was wounded many times.

CHARASIA (CHARASIAB) (34-24' N, 69-9' E). A village about 10 miles south of **Kabul** that was the scene of a battle between **Sir Frederick Roberts**'s "Avenging Army" and Afghan forces under Nek Muhammad, son of Amir **Dost Muhammad** Khan. Roberts was marching on Kabul on October 6, 1879, when he found the range separating him from the Kabul valley occupied by Afghan troops. Parties of **Ghilzais** appeared on hills along both flanks of his camp.

One historian reported with some exaggeration that General Roberts's army was

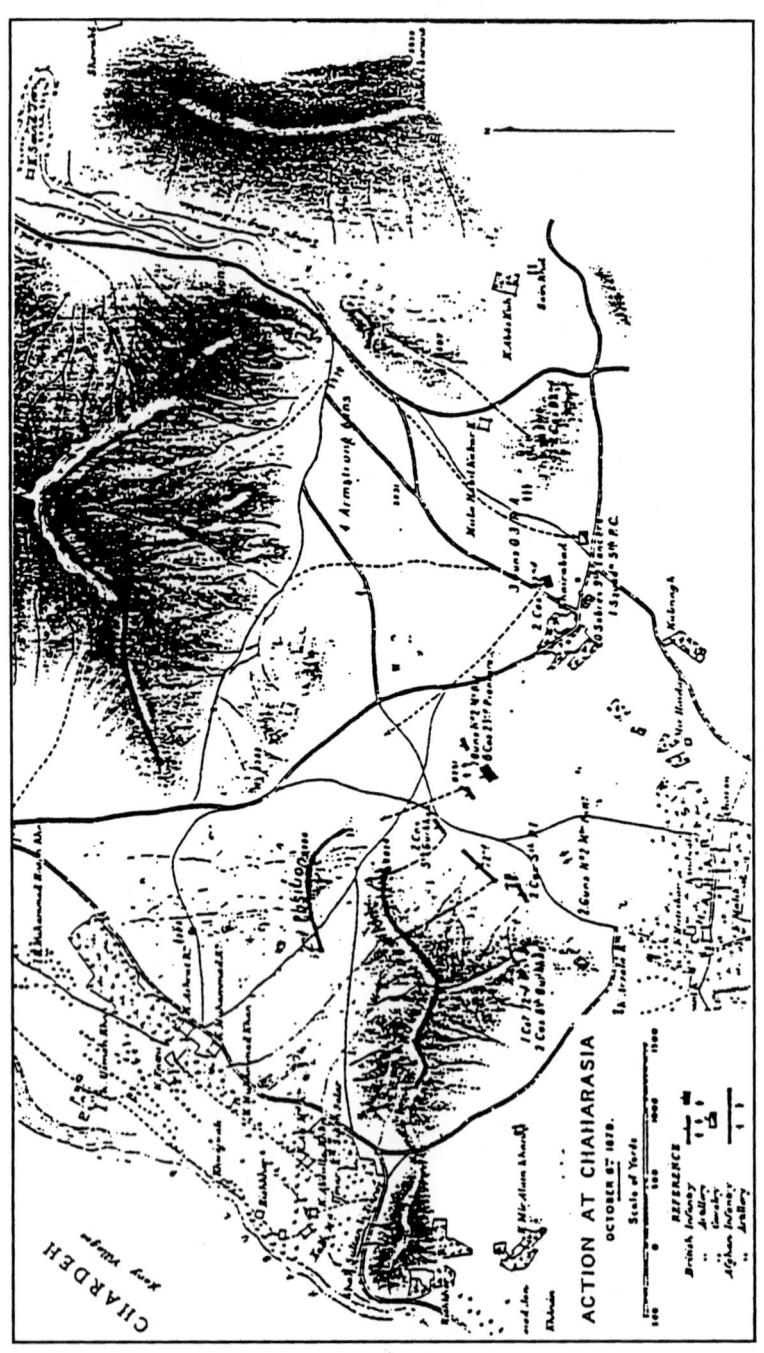

Plan 2. Action at Chaharasia (OA2)

a mere detachment marching against a nation of fighting men plentifully supplied with artillery, no longer shooting laboriously with jezails but carrying arms of precision equal or little inferior to those in the hands of our own soldiery. But the men, Europeans and Easterns, hillmen of Scotland and hillmen from Nepaul, strode along buoyant with confidence and with health, believing their leader in their discipline, in themselves.(Forbes, 192–93)

According to British estimates, no fewer than 13 regiments of the Afghan army, supported with large contingents of irregular fighting men, awaited the Britishers at the Sang-i Nawishta Pass. Roberts sent General Baker with 2,000 infantry and four guns to attack the Afghan right flank, and, following along the crest of the mountain, they were able to open the pass. Roberts was able to capture most of the Afghan artillery. British losses were 27 killed and 60 wounded, compared to Afghan losses estimated at about 300 killed. Roberts's forces then moved onto **Kabul** to take vengeance for the massacre of the British mission a month before.

CHARIKAR (35-1' N, 69-11' E). A town located at the mouth of the Ghorband about 40 miles north of **Kabul** in **Parwan** Province. The position of Charikar is of great importance because the roads over the **Hindu Kush** unite in its neighborhood. Charikar was a major British military outpost, manned by the 4th (Gurkha) Infantry. On November 13, 1841, with their water supply cut, some 200 men, still able to fight, tried to break through the besieging Kuhistani forces, but were wiped out. Only two British officers, including **Eldred Pottinger**, and a native managed to survive.

CHEMICAL WARFARE. According to one writer, the Soviet forces in Afghanistan employed "non-persistent agents," including harassing, incapacitating, blister, blood, and nerve agents, as well as napalm. The weapons were used sparingly in tactical operations, except during 1983 and 1986, when the primary motive seemed to be to use the battlefield as a testing ground (McMichael, 109). All the evidence is circumstantial and no confirmation has been obtained from Russian or other sources since the breakup of the **Soviet Union.**

CHRISTIE, JOHN (1806–1869). Raised for **Shah Shuja**'s army the First Irregular Cavalry, which became later known as Christie's Horse. He commanded his force during the occupation of **Kabul,**

1839–42 and participated in the occupation of **Kandahar** and fought at **Ghazni** and Kabul. He later joined Captain James Outram in the pursuit across the **Hindu Kush** of Amir **Dost Muhammad**. He received the "Order of the **Durrani**" for his services in Afghanistan and later became aide-de-camp to Queen Victoria.

CLARENDON-GORTCHAKOFF AGREEMENT. An agreement concluded in 1872–73 between **Great Britain** and **Russia** defining part of Afghanistan's northern frontier. The czar accepted the river Oxus (**Amu Daria**) down to Khwaja Salar as the northern boundary of Afghanistan, and pledged Russia to consider Afghanistan outside her sphere of influence. The Afghan **amir** was not consulted. *See* GRANVILLE-GORTCHAKOFF AGREEMENT.

CLIMATE AND WAR. Foreign invaders of Afghanistan encountered extremes in temperature, both seasonal and diurnal, hot wind storms and blizzards, and lack of precipitation during much of the year. During the march from **Kabul** to **Kandahar** in August 1880, British troops faced temperatures of 39 degrees Fahrenheit at dawn and 110 degrees Farenheit in the shade at noon. Temperatures in tents rose to 115 degrees. *Pakka wa Pustin* weather, as the Afghans call it. The *bad-i sad-o-bist ruza* (wind of 120 days) in the southwest of Afghanistan reaches a velocity of 110 miles per hour, and the *shamal* (northerly) raises clouds of dust and sand. Precipitation amounts to only about 11 inches of rain, and most of the irrigation of fields derives from the melting snow. The lack of water was often a serious problem for invaders. The passes of the **Hindu Kush** are snowbound in winter and, until completion of the **Salang Pass** in 1964, communications north from Kabul were not possible during the winter. For climatic reasons, invaders would choose spring or fall to stage their campaigns. Invading armies could be overtaken by the winter, as during the **first Anglo-Afghan war**, and the weather contributed to the disastrous defeat of the British **Army of the Indus**. *See also* GEOGRAPHY; LOGISTICS.

CLIMO, MAJOR GENERAL S. H. Commanded the Waziristan Force, consisting of the Bannu and Derajat areas, in the **third Anglo-Afghan war**.

CLOSE-BORDER POLICY. After the **third Anglo-Afghan war**, Waziristan on the North-West Frontier of India was in rebellion, and the Indian government vacillated between a "forward policy" and a "close-border policy." The secretary of state for India described the forward policy "in these days of acutest financial stringency" a mere counsel of perfection, and a close-border policy nothing more than leaving the tribesmen "free in their devils kitchen of mischief to brew incalculable trouble for us." But Sir Denys Bray, foreign secretary to the government of India, held, "In the domain of India's foreign politics I know of one fixed and immutable rule only. What India has, let India hold." Therefore, the Indian government decided against containment of the tribes and began to build roads into tribal territory to better pacify them (Maconachie, 1928). However, the frontier tribes have been able to maintain their autonomy to this day.

CONSTITUTIONAL DEVELOPMENT. Until the late 19th century Afghanistan was governed by a tribal aristocracy, first under the **Sadozai** and later under the **Barakzai** branch of the **Durranis**. Power was decentralized, and members of the royal clan ruled autonomously in the provinces, accepting the suzerainty of the king, or **amir**, in the capital. Although various administrative departments had already existed since the time of **Ahmad Shah**, the king headed all departments and made the influential officers share in the responsibilities of decisions. As his sign of sovereignty, his name was mentioned in the Friday sermon (*khutba*) and coins (silver and copper) were struck in his name.

The courts were in the hands of the clergy (**ulama**), but the death penalty had to be approved by the king or a governor. Ahmad Shah forbade the mutilation of limbs, and he drafted a code that was, however, never enacted. Little was changed until the time of Amir **Shir Ali**, who was the first Afghan ruler to establish an advisory council to serve as a consultative body. Amir **Abdul Rahman**, who increasingly centralized all powers in his hands, took the first steps to institutionalize a consultative body. He relied on advice from a council that was composed of three forces: the *sardars*, members of the royal clan; loyal tribal chiefs; and the ulama. The "Iron Amir" claimed all temporal and spiritual powers (*imarat* and *imamate*), and there existed no restraint on his arbitrary rule, except the obligation to conform his actions to the rules of Islamic law. Amir **Habibullah**, Abdul Rahman's son, continued the tradition of his father.

The first written document detailing the prerogatives of the ruler and the rights of the ruled was the Afghan constitution (*nizam-nama-yi tashkilat-i asasiya-yi Afghanistan*), promulgated by King **Aman-**

ullah in October 1923. It consisted of 73 articles that enumerated the rights and prerogatives of the king, presented a "bill of rights" of Afghan citizens, and outlined the duties of ministers and government officials. It authorized the establishment of an advisory committee and provincial councils, half of whose members were to be elected by the people, and established a supreme court (*divan-e ali*). Financial affairs and the activities of provincial departments were defined.

King Amanullah was the chief executive, commander in chief, and last court of appeals. He appointed the ministers and presided over cabinet meetings, unless he delegated this task to the prime minister. He was the "defender of the faith," had the sole right to issue currency and have his name invoked in the Friday sermons (*khutba*) during noon prayers. His power was absolute, but he established institutions that could have evolved into representative government and a constitutional monarchy. The constitution promised civil rights to all, abolished slavery, granted non-Muslims religious freedom (but missionary activity was forbidden), and declared the homes of citizens immune from forcible entry. A number of later statutory enactments (*nizam-nama*) further defined the powers and composition of Parliament, which was housed in a new building just completed in Darulaman. Social reforms, such as the emancipation of women and free compulsory education, were decreed. King Amanullah's constitution was never completely implemented, and his reforms were abandoned in a wave of reaction by a coalition of forces led by **Habibullah Kalakani**. Amir Habibullah (Kalakani) abrogated all constitutional reforms and attempted to rule in the tradition of Amir Abdul Rahman.

A new attempt at constitutional government was made in October 1931 by **Muhammad Nadir Shah** (1929–1933). His fundamental law (*usul-i asasi-yi daulat-i Afghanistan*) was similar to Amanullah's constitution. It included 16 sections with 110 articles, which outlined general principles and enumerated the rights of the king, the rights of the people, and the duties of a national council (*shura-yi milli*) and provincial advisory committees. Like his predecessor, Nadir Shah enjoyed emergency and veto powers. Non-Muslims had equal rights and were not required to pay a poll tax or be obligated to wear a distinctive type of dress. No legislation was to be contrary to Islamic law, but a distinction was made between civil and religious courts. Torture and confiscation of property were prohibited; publications, including newspapers, and free commercial activity were permitted. As a concession to the religious establishment, two members of the **Mujaddidi** family held the position of minister of justice until 1935. Members of the royal family held the important position of prime minister until 1963. A new, liberal era began with the promulgation of the 1964 constitution (October 1, 1964, *qanun-i asasi-yi Afghanistan*), which limited the participation of members of the royal family in government. Members of the royal family could serve in the foreign service, be advisers (*mushawer*), and hold low-level positions in government departments, but they could not hold the positions of prime minister, supreme court justice, and membership in Parliament. This was directed against Sardar **Muhammad Daud**, the king's cousin, a strong prime minister (1953–1963) whose **Pashtunistan** policy had been a disaster in foreign relations. While **Zahir Shah** (1933–1973) continued to hold supreme powers, he permitted an unprecedented degree of democratic government. His constitution, the result of a constitutional drafting committee, included a preamble and 11 titles, comprising 128 articles. Primogeniture was introduced with a provision that "the Throne shall pass to his [Zahir's] eldest son." Freedom of thought, possession of property, unarmed assembly, and education were guaranteed. Afghan citizens were given the right to a free press and to form political parties, subject to the provisions of certain ordinances, provided that no actions would be in violation of traditional norms and Islamic law. The king never ratified the provision on formation of political parties.

From the time of King Amanullah, constitutional development represents a process of modernization and the gradual introduction of concepts of the division of power and individual rights. It also brought into being a process whereby the symbols of democratic government were beginning to gain concrete reality. But socioeconomic factors prevented the rapid implementation of political reforms. Universal education, envisioned by the constitution, remained an aim rather than a reality, and Afghanistan has remained largely illiterate. The introduction of secular schools, in addition to the traditional mosque/**madrasa** system, produced two essentially hostile elites. Afghanistan is still predominantly agricultural, and a great division exists between the urban and rural populations. Sectarian and ethnic differences have prevented the forging of a heterogeneous population into a nation. When Sardar Muhammad Daud staged his coup in 1973, the experiment with democracy came to a halt.

Daud wanted a one-party government and "democracy based on social justice." His constitution (*qanun-i asasi-yi daulat-i jumhuri-yi Afghanistan*), promulgated on February 14, 1977, aimed at the "exercise of power" by the majority, the "farmers, workers, and enlightened people and the youth." In 13 chapters and 136 articles, the republican government presented its aspirations. It called for the "elimination of exploitation in all its forms," nationalized the mineral resources of the state, large industries, communications, banks, and "important food procurement establishments." Land reforms were to be carried out and cooperatives were to be encouraged. Women were to enjoy equal rights and obligations, and every Afghan 18 years or older was to have the right to vote. President Daud enjoyed absolute power: he could convene and dismiss the national assembly (milli jirgah), whose members were nominated by his party, and could veto any law. He felt he had to be strong to fight the evils of "hunger, ignorance, and disease," but his one-man rule proved to be fatal. His leftist supporters in the army did not permit Daud's shift to the right, and before he could eliminate them from positions of power, they staged the **Saur Revolt** of April 27, 1978.

The new regime wanted to establish a government of workers and peasants, with the **People's Democratic Party of Afghanistan** (PDPA) as a vanguard to implement its revolutionary objectives. Decrees demanded the emancipation of women, land reforms, and the introduction of far-reaching social changes. But the provisions of the "Fundamental Principles of the Democratic Republic of Afghanistan" could never be implemented. Armed resistance rose within a few months, which turned into a war of liberation after the **Soviet** intervention.

The government of Dr. **Najibullah** virtually eliminated the trappings of Marxist government in its Constitution of 1987, and the Afghan **Interim Government** of the seven **mujahedin** groups in Peshawar published the outlines of a constitution that favored the establishment of an Islamic state. The traditional groups, represented by **Sayyid Ahmad Gailani, Sebghatullah Mujaddidi**, and **Muhammad Nabi Muhammadi**, favored the establishment of a democratic Islamic government, not excluding the possibility of a constitutional monarchy. The Islamist groups, headed by **Gulbuddin Hekmatyar, Abdul Rasul Sayyaf, Yunus Khales**, and **Burhanuddin Rabbani**, as well as the newly formed **Taliban** movement, tended with some variations to favor an "Islamic state" on a more authoritarian model. They would limit the sphere of activity of women in public life and tend to limit manifestations of Westernization. The **Shi'a** groups appeared to favor a federated state in which the interests of the minorities are protected. The Shi'a community claimed to constitute a fifth of the Afghan population and wanted this to be reflected in parliamentary representation. As long as their claimed popular strength was not reflected in an Afghan Interim Government (AIG), they refused their participation. The war in Afghanistan politicized a large part of the hitherto quiescent population, and the prospects were for greater grassroots participation in the political life of Afghanistan.

A new beginning in a return to constitutional government was the establishment of a **Transitional Government** in June 2002, the drafting of a new constitution resembling the Constitution of 1964, and the presidential elections which **Hamid Karzai** won with some 55 percent of the vote. It is, however, too early to predict that a working government can be established and that the willingness for compromise exists to allow a measure of democracy.

CONTRACTORS/MERCENARIES. The State Department, the Central Intelligence Agency, the Defense Intelligence Agency—controlled by Defense Secretary Donald Rumsfeld—and other U.S. departments have begun to "outsource" many paramilitary tasks to private companies. One such company, MPRI, advertises itself as "a dynamic company with expanding requirements for top quality former military and law enforcement personnel, and DOD civilians." According to an article in the *Los Angeles Times* (September 20, 2004), MPRI has dozens of former generals and some 10,000 former soldiers in the field, including ex-members of the **Special Forces**. This "clandestine army" operates in many areas of the world, including Afghanistan. Some operate as soldiers, others as body guards—President **Hamid Karzai** has an American body guard. Others, again, were employed as prison guards or to provide protection for commercial interests. This contributes to a measure of confusion as authorities in the "host" countries do not know which of these soldiers of fortune operate as legitimate members of American agencies. A case in point is Jonathan 'Jack' K. Idema who maintained a private prison in Kabul in which he had kept eight Afghans who were tortured to extract confession about the activities of Afghan guerrillas. Idema claimed that he was hunting for terrorists with the knowledge of American agencies. But his claims were disputed by American sources and Idema and two of his colleagues were arrested on July 5, 2004, by

Afghan police, put on trial, and sentenced to eight and 10 years in jail. The sentence was halved in April 2005.

CONVENTION OF 1907. *See* **ANGLO-RUSSIAN CONVENTION.**

CONVOY OPERATIONS. Modern invaders of Afghanistan depended on supplies from beyond the borders of the country, and their lines of communication were always vulnerable to attack. Afghan guerrilla activities centered on harassing the enemies' lines of logistics. Until the **third Anglo-Afghan war**, British armies depended on pack animals to transport war materiel and supplies that could not be obtained locally. The caravans, or convoys, were slow and the animals subject to disease and the inhospitable climate. Almost 100,000 camels were lost during the **second Anglo-Afghan war**.

Soviet and **Kabul** government convoys, much more mobile and protected by aerial support, proved to be equally vulnerable. The **mujahedin** would block the movement of a highway-bound convoy by immobilizing some vehicles in a suitable location and destroying the trapped convoy before relief could arrive. The **Salang Pass**, located at an altitude of 13,350 feet, and the Soviet-built tunnel were frequent targets of attack. The vulnerability of the Salang Tunnel was clearly demonstrated in October 1982, when an explosion (or mujahedin action) in the tunnel was said to have caused the death of 1,000 people, including 700 Soviet troops. *See also* TRANSPORT, MILITARY.

CORRELATION OF FORCES. A doctrine with political, social, and ideological aspects that referred to the relative strength of socialism and capitalism as evaluated in Moscow. Its political aspect was seen in the "number of Communist countries in the world, their dynamism in international affairs, their prestige and self-confidence, as well as the strength and influence of Communists in other countries." The social aspect was manifested in "the **Soviet** view of class struggle and the influence that Marxist ideas have upon peoples throughout the world." The ideological aspect related to "the extent of revolutionary forces... leading to a Marxist system with a Leninist control imposed on it" (Bradsher, 1983, 128). The Soviet leadership felt that the correlation of forces had changed to the advantage of the socialist camp, and, although it downplayed its military aspect, it induced it to embark on such actions as the intervention in Afghanistan.

COTTON, SIR WILLOUGHBY (1783–1860). Described as a "roly-poly" old general who had served far too long in India and was slow and not very bright (Macrory, 98). He commanded the Bengal Division of the **Army of the Indus**, 1838–1839. On his way to Afghanistan, he was prevented from heading in the opposite direction to plunder the rumored wealth of Haiderabad. When he handed over command to General **William Elphinstone**, he told him, "You will have nothing to do here, all is peace" (ibid., 165). He served at **Ghazni** and left Afghanistan via **Kabul** in 1839.

COUNTERINSURGENCY. Conventional forces never quite succeeded in solving the problem of containing the Afghan tribes. The British leveled villages, destroyed crops, uprooted fruit trees, and, in 1916, constructed a 17-mile electric fence, which electrocuted 400 Mohmand tribesmen, but they could not prevent them from penetrating the administered territories (Nichols, 22).

The **Soviet Union** lacked a counterinsurgency doctrine to guide and organize its activities. Soviet forces were prepared for a conventional war with offensive operations for territorial gain, conducted by heavy armor that was supported by aerial and missile operations, as well as special units for defensive chemical warfare. Their force structure and tactical doctrine were not suited to military operations in Afghanistan. Eventually, adjustments were made permitting greater decentralization of command, the creation of small independent units to fight the **mujahedin** in inaccessible areas, night operations, and the employment of airborne, air assault/airmobile, designated reconnaissance flights, and special operations units, *Spetsnaz*. The latter were involved in much of the fighting and took the brunt of casualties. The Soviets were forced to fight a light infantry war in which the advantage of numbers and light weapons favored the mujahedin (McMichael).

The **United States** counterinsurgency struggle still going on in Afghanistan suffers from limitations similar to those of the Soviets. It aims at the destruction of the enemy and their bases, creating a situation where guerrilla forces do not move in a friendly environment, and engaging in civic action to win the support of the population.

The "Afghanistan model" of warfare, employing **Special Forces** teams, was successful in the war against the **Taliban/al-Qaeda** enemy. The teams, together with native ground forces, rapidly destroyed the bulk of the Taliban army. Special Forces teams pinpointed targets of enemy troops and fortified bunkers for aerial bombardment. Native forces then moved in to battle the enemy. It did not take long to disperse the enemy and to gain control of the land, although many places came under the control of warlords. Most of the non-Afghan soldiers were killed or captured, some escaped across the Afghan border into tribal territory, and most of the Taliban troops returned to their native areas. However, an insurgency rose quickly, engaging in a classical guerrilla war which attacked targets of opportunity. Most fighting occurred along the tribal border lands where a safe haven could be found in **Pakistan**. It was not feasible to move the civilian population into "fortified hamlets" as the British did in Malaysia. Aerial bombardments inevitably killed civilians which went counter to the effort of winning the support of the people.

Fortunately, nation building, a task not originally part of the American mission, has advanced. The newly elected government of President **Hamid Karzai** has been quite successful in extending its control over major regions. This is due in part to the growth of the **Afghan National Army** (ANA), a considerable expansion of the Afghan police force, and also, the creation of the multinational **Provincial Reconstruction Teams** (PTR) which cover more than half of the country and will soon cover the rest. The PTRs were originally criticized as wasteful by the Afghan minister of reconstruction as they cost at least $10 million each, and by members of humanitarian organizations, because they blur the line between military and humanitarian activities. But, apart from their tasks of building schools, roads, and trying to win the "hearts and minds" of the people, the PTRs were important as bases for collection of intelligence and support for the Kabul government.

The Afghan Army now participates in the fight against insurgency groups and the Pakistan government has begun to support the cause by trying to prevent its borderlands from serving as safe havens for the guerrillas. Afghanistan has a legitimate government, and it has few of the **Islamist** international fighters left. The Afghans helped to virtually wipe out their presence in the country, and attempts are under way to win remnants of the Taliban to recognize the authority of the Karzai government. **Osama bin Laden** is in hiding, the al-Qaeda organization is in a shambles, and it seems that the days of the few holdouts, notably **Gulbuddin Hekmatyar**, are numbered.

CROCKER, BRIGADIER GENERAL G. D. Described as "a gallant, but impetuous man," he commanded the 1st (Peshawar) Infantry Brigade during the **third Anglo-Afghan war**. He was unsuccessful in the first **Battle of Bagh** on May 9, 1919, when he underestimated the strength of the Afghan forces and employed an unduly large force for protective duties. He succeeded in the second battle with aerial support and fire from horse and mountain artillery and an ample amount of machine guns which enabled him to capture Dakka on May 17. However, because of **Muhammad Nadir** Khan's success on the Waziristan front, the attempt at advancing on **Jalalabad** had to be aborted.

- D -

DADULLAH, MULLA. A major **Taliban** commander in the besieged northern city of **Kunduz**, who allegedly played a leading role in the genocidal campaign against the **Hazara** people of central Afghanistan. He reportedly ordered the execution of the Red Cross worker, Ricardo Manguia, in March 2003.

DAISY CUTTER. Nickname of the BLU-82, the world's largest conventional bomb, used by the **United States** in Afghanistan as an antipersonnel weapon. It is a metal barrel filled with 5.600 kg explosive "slurry," dropped from a C-130 transport plane, parachuted and detonated just above the ground some 27 seconds after release. It was used in Vietnam to clear ground for helicopters with a lethal radius of from 300 to 900 feet. The bomb depends upon accurate positioning of the aircraft by either fixed ground radar or onboard navigation equipment and is detonated by a 38-inch fuze extender. The BLU-82 is employed as much for its psychological effect as for its antipersonnel effect.

DANE, SIR LOUIS WILLIAM (1856–1946). Foreign secretary to the government of India (1902–1908) and head of a British mission to **Kabul** (January 1, 1904–December 2, 1905) that negotiated the Treaty of 1905. *See* ANGLO-AFGHAN TREATY OF 1905; FOREIGN RELATIONS.

DARI. The name of the Farsi/Persian spoken in Afghanistan and with **Pashtu** one of the two "official" languages. The name derives from *darbar*, royal court, because it was the language of the Central Asian and Moghul Indian courts. Other etymologies suggested are *darra*, valley, or the language of Darius (522–486 B.C.), the Achaemenid emperor.

DAR UL-HARB (DAR AL-HARB). In Muslim constitutional law the world is divided into the *dar ul-Islam* (abode of Islam), land under Muslim rule, and the *dar ul-harb* (abode of war), potentially a land of war, **jihad** (holy war), which was to be brought under the domain of Islam. Some schools also recognize the *dar al-sulh* (abode of agreement), land not under Muslim rule, but in a tributary relationship with Islam. In 1920 the *hijrat* (emigration) movement arose in India, denouncing India, the *dar ul-harb*, and making it incumbent on Muslims to migrate to Afghanistan, the country of Islamic rule. The movement became known as the *khilafat* movement, and the emigrants were known as the *muhajerin*. King **Amanullah** encouraged the movement, hoping to gain skilled immigrants who might contribute to the development of Afghanistan, but his hopes were disappointed when most of the several thousand immigrants turned out to be poor and unskilled and depended on support from the Afghan government. After enthusiastic beginnings, the movement quickly dissolved.

DAR UL-ISLAM (DAR AL-ISLAM). The "abode of Islam," or a country in which the ordinances of Islam are established under the rule of a Muslim sovereign. The Shari'a, Islamic law, prevails in this area, leaving non-Muslims subject to their own religious and customary laws, but without the possibility of full citizenship. Hindus and Jews of Afghan citizenship enjoyed equal rights but at certain times had to pay a special poll tax and were exempt from military service. In 1920 the Indian *hijrat* (or *khilafat*) movement led to a mass emigration of Muslims from British India, the *dar ul-harb* (abode of war), to Afghanistan, the *dar ul-Islam*. After the **Taliban** established themselves in **Kabul**, they imposed a radical interpretation of Islam, extending Islamic law to also include non-Muslims and forcing Hindus to wear yellow identity tags. The hostile international reaction induced them to discontinue this practice.

DAR UL-ULUM HAQQANIAH. *See* **HAQQANIA.**

DARUNTA CAMP COMPLEX. One of the first targets of American bombing in October 2001 was a series of training camps in eastern Afghanistan. The Darunta Complex included the Al-Badr I base, the **Tora Bora** base, and the Abu Khabab camp in the **Jalalabad** area. Some of the cave complexes were first constructed by the U.S. Central Intelligence Agency for **mujahedin** fighters against the communist rulers of **Kabul**. The Tora Bora complex extended some 1,150 feet into a 13,000 feet mountain range and was capable of accommodating as many as 1,000 fighters. It was equipped with generators to provide electricity, featured an efficient ventilation system, and had offices, bedrooms, and communal rooms, as well as areas for storage of weapons. After extensive bombardment, American forces found computers, training manuals for weapons manufacture, and publications that identified desirable targets for terrorist attacks.

DAUD MUHAMMAD. *See* **MUHAMMAD DAUD.**

DEATH MARCH. After signing a treaty of virtual capitulation to Afghan chiefs in December 1841 (*see* CAPITULATION, TREATY OF), the British forces of occupation and camp followers, amounting to about 16,500 persons (690 British fighting men, 2,840 Indian infantry, 970 cavalry, and more than 12,000 camp followers—servants and merchants in charge of nonweapons logistics and a large number of women and children) embarked on a march toward the Indian border in which few survived. The retreat began on January 6, 1842, and only six miles were covered on the first day. The march quickly turned into a rout as traffic jams impeded crossing the **Logar** River and much of the baggage was abandoned. On the second day only five miles were covered to the well-fortified Khurd **Khaibar** Pass. A number of people froze to death, and **Amir Shah Shuja**'s cavalry escort deserted. On the next day the British rearguard was attacked. British officers tried unsuccessfully to separate their troops from the camp followers. **Ghilzai ghazis** attacked the retreating forces, killing some 500 troops and 2,500 camp followers. British women and children, as well as their husbands and a number of officers, were surrendered as hostages to **Sardar Muhammad Akbar** Khan and managed to survive. **Eldred Pottinger** claims that Akbar Khan treacherously shouted, "Spare them" in Persian and "Kill them" in **Pashtu** (George Pottinger, 1993, 163). On the fifth day a last stand was made at Jagdalak, by which time about 12,000 members of the retreating force had perished. Sardar Akbar Khan offered to pay 200,000 rupees to the Ghilzai chiefs if they would stop their attacks, but the Ghilzai were out for revenge. By the eighth day two British officers and seven or eight wounded men were taken prisoners, and only one man, Dr. **William Brydon**, managed to reach safety at **Jalalabad** (Dupree, 1967). This gave rise to the legend that Akbar Khan had predicted he would wipe out the British army and leave only one man to tell the tale.

DEFECTIONS, DESERTIONS, AND MUTINIES. Defections were common in the wars of the Afghan princes, as well as in wars of Afghan **ghazis** with British-supported Afghan troops. To avoid bloodshed and destruction, forces facing defeat deserted to the superior enemy. When **Sardar Ayub Khan** moved with his army against **Kandahar** in July 1880, the troops of the Wali, governor of Kandahar, deserted in a body to Ayub, taking with them their guns and ammunition. In the **third Anglo-Afghan war**, a large number of the Khaibar Rifles, a tribal militia of **Pashtuns** from the British side of the Durand Line, deserted, and the entire force had to be disbanded.

One year after the Soviet intervention in Afghanistan in December 1978, the size of the **Democratic Republic of Afghanistan** (DRA) army had dwindled from 100,000 men to about 50,000. Most of the loss was due to desertion. According to one source, the rate of defection from the DRA army was more than 10,000 per year (Amstutz). The defecting soldiers and officers frequently took with them their arms, including tanks and armored vehicles, trucks, assault rifles, and heavy artillery pieces. A large number of deserters with specialized military skills joined the forces of the **mujahedin**. One of the largest defections occurred on February 16, 1989, when three regiments amounting to nearly 10,000 men defected in **Takhar** and **Badakhshan** Provinces. Most of their weapons became part of Commander **Ahmad Shah Mas'ud**'s arsenal.

The summary execution by **Yunus Khalis**'s forces of some 37 deserters from the **Kabul** army in September 1982 may have been a reason for a reduced number of desertions thereafter. In the civil war for supremacy of the former mujahedin, commanders and leaders of parties frequently changed sides, regardless of ideological orientation.

As a result of the **United States** intervention, non-**Pashtun** ethnic groups, which had to yield to superior power, turned against the **Taliban**. One example is the **Hazara** leader **Muhammad Akbari**, who had recognized the Taliban regime. But even among the tribal Pashtuns there was resentment, while they did not necessarily reject some of the Islamist legislation of the theocratic regime, they did chafe under their dictatorial rule. When American money became available, they joined the war against the regime, extending little mercy to the foreign soldiers, but permitting most of their Pashtun brothers to fade away.

DEMOCRATIC REPUBLIC OF AFGHANISTAN (DRA). New name for the Peoples Democratic Republic of Afghanistan under President **Najibullah**. After the conquest of **Kabul** by the **mujahedin**, the designation Islamic Republic of Afghanistan (IRA) was adopted and the **Taliban** adopted the name Islamic Emirate of Afghanistan. *See also* PEOPLE'S DEMOCRATIC PARTY OF AFGHANISTAN.

DENNIE, WILLIAM HENRY (1785–1842). He commanded a brigade in 1838–1839 and led the storming party at **Ghazni** on July 23, 1839. He encountered an **Uzbek** force with **Amir Dost Muhammad** at **Bamian** on September 18, 1840, and dispersed it, but the amir managed to escape. He accompanied General **Robert Sale**'s forces from **Kabul** to **Jalalabad** in 1841. At the siege of Jalalabad he led a sortie and was fatally wounded on April 6, 1842.

DEOBAND. A town near Delhi, India, and the location of an Islamic university (*madrasa, dar al-ulum*) founded by Abdul Qasim Nanawtawi in 1867 (some sources credit Muhammad Subbed Essay). Deoband adopted Shah Waliullah (1703–1762) as its spiritual head and was greatly influenced by the teachings of Ibn Taymiyyah (1263–1328), which also inspired Abdul Wahhab (1703–1792) the founder of "**Wahhabism**" current in Saudi Arabia. The institution has traditionally supported pan-Islamic, anti-British, and **fundamentalist** causes and was opposed to the teachings of the modernist Muslim University of **Aligarh**. Graduates of Deoband established numerous **madrasas**, including some in the tribal belt bordering Afghanistan. They also found teaching positions in Afghanistan, where a madrasa of international reputation did not exist. Amir **Abdul Rahman** and King **Amanullah** at times forbade Deobandis from teaching in Afghanistan. **Muhammad Yunus Khales**, amir of the Islamist **Hizb-i Islami**, is a graduate of Deoband. It was reported that **Mulla Muhammad Omar** and **Osama bin Ladin** first met in Deobandi mosques in the **North-West Frontier Province** and Baluchistan and may have forged an alliance at that time. The largest of these institutions is the Dar al-Ulum al-**Haqqania**, the "Harvard" of the **Taliban** movement. The students of these schools, many of them orphans, were provided free education, food, shelter, and military training during the war against the communist government of Afghanistan in the 1980s. These students later became the core of the Taliban forces which ruled most of Afghanistan until their defeat in December 2001.

DIN MUHAMMAD, MUSHK-I ALAM (1790–1886). Considered a national hero by Afghans because of his implacable hostility to the British. He was a frontier **mulla** whose grandfather came from India and settled among the Andar **Ghilzai** near **Ghazni**. He studied with various **ulama** and was given the name *Mushk-i Alam* (Scent [or Musk] of the World), by one of his teachers because of his excellent mind. He was a militant mulla who opened a **madrasa** (school of higher Islamic studies) for the training of mullas and gained considerable influence among the Ghilzais. He received an allowance from Amir **Shir Ali** and preached **jihad** against the British during the **second Anglo-Afghan war**. When Amir **Abdul Rahman** tried to restrict his activity, he incited the Mangals and Ghilzais to rebellion. After his death in 1886, his son, Mulla Abdul Karim, led a Ghilzai uprising against Amir **Abdul Rahman**, which was suppressed only with great difficulty.

DOBBS, SIR HENRY (1871–1934). British envoy and chief of the British mission to **Kabul** that negotiated the **Anglo-Afghan Treaty of 1921** and established "neighborly" relations after the end of the **third Anglo-Afghan war**. Before that, he also headed the British contingent at the **Mussoorie Conference** (April 17–July 18, 1920), which failed to normalize Anglo-Afghan relations. He first came to Afghanistan in 1903, when as a political officer he directed a small British contingent whose task was to restore or repair boundary pillars at the Russo-Afghan border. He served as foreign secretary to the government of India (1919–1923). *See* FOREIGN RELATIONS.

DOST MUHAMMAD, AMIR (1826–1838 and 1842–1863). Afghan ruler, known as the "Great Amir," *Amir-i Kabir*, who was ousted by the British in the **first Anglo-Afghan war** but was able to regain the Afghan throne after four years in Indian exile. He was born in 1792 in **Kandahar**, the son of Painda Khan, who was killed by **Shah Zaman** when Dost Muhammad was only eight years old. He became acting governor of **Ghazni** and, after the death of Muhammad Azam in 1824, established himself as ruler of **Kabul**. He next defeated his rival, **Shah Shuja**, at Kandahar and gradually extended his control over the rest of Afghanistan. He defeated the **Sikhs** at the Battle of Jamrud (1837) and assumed the title *Amir al-Mu'minin* (Commander of the Faithful). The British-Indian government turned against him when Dost Muhammad made overtures to **Russia** and Persia and permitted a Russian agent to come to Kabul. Dost Muhammad wanted to regain territory captured by **Ranjit Singh** and was willing to ally himself with the British, but the British government decided to support the Sikh ruler and restore Shah Shuja to the Afghan throne. A British army invaded Afghanistan and destroyed Kabul on July 23, 1839. On November 2, 1840, after a few skirmishes, Dost Muhammad gave up; he surrendered to the British, who took him as a hostage to India.

However, the occupation of Afghanistan became increasingly tenuous as their lines of communication were disrupted and tribal forces slowly expelled garrisons from outlying areas. Eventually, the army in Kabul was forced to negotiate an ignominious retreat in which most of the British army was destroyed (*see* ANGLO-AFGHAN WARS; CAPITULATION, TREATY OF). Facing a situation of chaos in Afghanistan, the Indian government permitted Dost Muhammad to return and regain his throne. But it took him a number of years to consolidate his power: he took Kandahar in 1855 and **Herat** in 1863. Dost Muhammad died a few days after he entered Herat. Of his 27 sons, Muhammad Afzal and Muhammad Azim ruled for short periods, followed by **Shir Ali**.

DOSTUM, GENERAL ABDUL RASHID. Born in 1954 in Khwaja Dokoh, **Jozjan** Province, of an **Uzbek** family, he worked for the Oil and Gas Exploration Enterprise of Shiberghan and in 1980 went to the **Soviet Union** for training. He then joined the ministry of state security and became commander of Unit 374 in Jozjan. During the 1980s, he commanded the Jozjani "Dostum Militia" comprising some 20,000 regular and militia soldiers, most of them **Uzbeks**, and was entrusted with guarding Jozjan, **Fariab**, and Sar-i Pol Provinces for the **Kabul** government. He was awarded the distinction of "Hero of the Republic of Afghanistan" and was a member of the central council of the Watan (formerly **People's Democratic Party of Afghanistan**) party. He and a number of generals turned against President **Najibullah** and assisted the **mujahedin** in the conquest of Kabul. Dostum's followers are united in a party, called Junbish-i Milli-yi Islami, which controlled most of **Balkh**, Fariab, Jozjan, and **Samangan** Provinces until the **Taliban** conquest of the area. When President **Burhanuddin Rabbani** was unwilling to legitimize the position of Dostum by giving him a cabinet post, the latter joined forces with **Gulbuddin Hekmatyar**. In May 1996 Hekmatyar defected and joined the Rabbani government, but both were ejected, Dostum by his Uzbek rival General **Abdul Malik** and Hekmatyar by the Taliban.

Dostum returned in 2001 and supported the American air attacks on Taliban and al-**Qaeda** forces (in exchange for payment of $250,000 a month, *US News & World Report*, February 11, 2002). He was able to regain control of portions of north-central Afghanistan. He served as deputy minister of defense in the **Interim Government**, a position he no longer held in the **Transitional Government** of **Hamid Karzai** of December 2001. But on March 1, 2005, Karzai appointed Dostum chief of staff, and he resigned from his position as chief of Junbesh-i Milli in April. *See also* MAZAR-I SHARIF, FALL OF.

DURAND AGREEMENT. An agreement signed on November 12, 1893, at **Kabul** by **Sir Henry Mortimer Durand** and Amir **Abdul Rahman** that defined the boundary between Afghanistan and British India, subsequently called the "Durand Line." This boundary was drawn without regard to the ethnic composition of the population and severed a large portion of **Pashtu**-speaking Afghan from their brothers in Afghanistan. Amir Abdul Rahman accepted under "duress" a line running from "Chitral and Basophil Pass up to Peshawar, and thence up to Koh-i Malik Siyah in this way that Wakhan, Kafiristan, Asmar, Mohmand of Lalpura, and one portion of Waziristan" came under his rule. He renounced his claims for "the railway station of New Chaman, Chagai, the rest of Waziri, Biland Khel, Kurram, Afridi, Bajaur, Swat, Buner, Dir, Chilas and Chitral."

The Durand Line was never completely demarcated because of the hostility of the tribes, and the tribes on the Indian side of the border never came under the direct administration of the Indian, or subsequently **Pakistani**, governments. Abdul Rahman obtained an increase in subsidy of 6,000,000 rupees and a letter with the assurance that **Britain** would continue to protect Afghanistan from unprovoked **Russian** aggression, provided that the **amir** "followed unreservedly the advice of the British Government" in regard to his external relations. The Afghan government subsequently claimed that the agreement was forced on Afghanistan in the form of an ultimatum.

After the death of Amir Abdul Rahman, Britain insisted that the treaties with the late ruler were personal, rather than dynastic and therefore subject to renegotiation, but they excluded the Durand Agreement as not subject to this provision. Article 5 of the treaty of peace concluded at **Rawalpindi** on August 8, 1919, stated that "The Afghan Government accept the Indo-Afghan frontier accepted by the late Amir [**Habibullah**]," and the **Treaty of Kabul** carried a similar provision. When the state of Pakistan was created in 1947, the Afghan government demanded the right of the Pashtuns to decide whether they wanted an independent **Pashtunistan**, union with Afghanistan, or union with Pakistan. The Kabul government did not accept a plebiscite that allowed only a choice for union with Pakistan or India, and in 1979 the Afghan parliament repudiated the Durand Agreement. The Pashtunistan question has remained an issue between Afghanistan and Pakistan and has prevented the establishment of cordial relations between the two Muslim countries. The **Taliban**, dependent as they were on Pakistani support, never gave formal assurances that they recognized the Durand Line. In September 2003 the border issue flared up again, when Afghan sources claimed that the Durand Agreement was concluded for 100 years and should be renegotiated. *See also* FOREIGN RELATIONS.

DURAND, SIR MORTIMER (b. 1850). Foreign secretary to the government of India, sent to **Kabul** in September 1893 for the purpose of negotiating an agreement defining the Indo-Afghan boundary, subsequently called the Durand Line. (*See* DURAND AGREEMENT.) He served in the northwest provinces during 1829–1838 and was political secretary to **Sir Frederick Roberts** in Kabul in the campaign in 1879. He also served at **Charasia** and in the defense of **Sherpur**. He was British foreign secretary from 1884 to 1894.

DURRANI DYNASTY (1747-1973). The Durrani dynasty was founded in 1747 by **Ahmad Shah** "Durr-i Durran," who ruled Afghanistan until 1978. Ahmad Shah was a direct descendant of Sado, an Abdali chief at the court of the Savafid ruler Shah Abbas the Great (1588-1629). The Durrani are divided into the **Sadozai** branch (a section of the **Popalzai** tribe) and the **Muhammadzai** (a section of the Barakzai tribe). The succession from Ahmad Shah to **Muhammad Daud**, who established a republican government, is as follows:

Sadozai Dynasty 1747-1817

Ahmad Shah	1747-1773
Timur Shah (s.o. Ahmad)	1773-1793
Zaman Shah (s.o. Timur, deposed)	1793-1800
Mahmud Shah (br.o. Zaman, deposed)	1800-1803
Shah Shuja-ul-Mulk (br.o. Zaman, deposed)	1803-1809
Mahmud Shah (br.o. Zaman) (loses Kabul and Kandahar)	1809-1817

Ruling in Herat 1817-1863

Mahmud Shah (Sadozai, assassinated?)	1817-1829
Kamran (s.o. Mahmud, assassinated?)	1829-1841
Yar Muhammad	1841-1851
Said Muhammad Khan (s.o. Yar Muhd.)	1851-1855
Muhammad Yusuf Khan (Sadozai, deposed)	1855
Sirtap Isa Khan (Herati)	1855
Herat conquered by Persians	1856
Sultan Ahmad Khan (Jan) (nephew of Dost Muhammad)	1855-1863
Dost Muhammad Khan	1863

Ruling in Kabul 1817-1863

Muhammad Azim Khan	1817-1822
Habibullah Khan (s.o. Muhammad Azim) (deposed)	1822-1826
Dost Muhammad Khan (deposed) (uncle of Habibullah Khan)	1826-1839
Shah Shuja-ul-Mulk (Sadozai)	1839-1841
Zaman Khan (Barakzai)	1841-1842
Fath Jang (Sadozai Contender)	1842?
Dost Muhammad	1842-1863

Ruling in Kandahar 1817–1863

Pur Dil Khan	1817–1839
Shah Shuja-ul-Mulk (deposed)	1839–1841
Kohan Dil Khan (br.o. Pur Dil)	1842–1855
Dost Muhammad Khan	1855–1863

Ruling Afghanistan 1863–1978

Civil war and anarchy	1863–1868
Shir Ali Khan (br.o. Dost, deposed)	1863–1866
Muhammad Afzal Khan	1866–1867
Muhammad Azim Khan (br.o. M. Afzal) (deposed)	1867–1868
Shir Ali Khan	1868–1879
Yaqub Khan (s.o. Shir Ali, abdicated)	1879
Second Anglo-Afghan War	1879–1880
Abdur Rahman Khan (s.o. Muhd. Afzal)	1880–1901
Habibullah Khan (s.o. Abdur Rahman) (assassinated)	1901–1919
Amanullah Khan (s.o. Habibullah, deposed)	1919–1929
Inayatullah Khan (three days, abdicated)	1929
Habibullah Kalakani, Tajik (Jan. to Oct.) (Son of a Water Carrier)	1929
Nadir Shah (Musahiban family) (assassinated)	1929–1933
Zahir Shah (deposed)	1933–1973
Muhammad Daud (president) (assassinated)	1973–1978

DURRANI, LAND TENURE. Nadir Shah Afshar gave the Durranis the land of **Kandahar** as a military fief. The land had previously been held by a mixed peasantry population that paid taxes to the suzerain ruler since Safavid times. The land of Kandahar had been traditionally divided into *qulba* (plows), which designated the portion of irrigated land cultivated by one person, operating one ox and one plow, and which gave double space for sowing two *kharwar* of grain (one *kharwar*, literally a donkey load, amounted to 100 *man* [*maund*], the exact weight varied in different localities), one-half of which was cultivated each year while the other half remained fallow. Nadir Shah's agents ascertained the productivity of the land in various areas as a return of 25 *kharwar* for one *kharwar* of seed. Each *qulba* was assessed a land tax (*kharaj*) of 10 percent. As an innovation, every garden, tree, and vine was assessed one copper *pice*. About 3,000 double *qulba* were distributed to Durrani tribes in *tiyul* (fiefs), in exchange for providing 6,000 horsemen, one for each *qulba*.

DYER, BRIGADIER REGINALD EDWARD H. (1864–1927). In command of the "Thal Relief Force," during the **third Anglo-Afghan war**, to end General **Muhammad Nadir**'s siege of the strategically important town. His own 45th Infantry Brigade was strengthened with part of the 16th Division, which formed part of the Central Reserve. On May 30, 1919, he moved via Togh and Darmsamand and reached Thal on June 1. In the northwest he faced a few Afghan regulars with four guns and some 2,000 tribesmen. To the north and east, the tribes were waiting in the hills, not yet determined whether they should attack. On the hills south of the Kurram River was the Afghan main force. Dyer was able to disperse the tribes, and while making preparations for an attack on the main force, he was informed that King **Amanullah** had ordered a suspension of hostilities. When, on June 3, Dyer moved against the Afghan camp, he found it abandoned (Molesworth, 120). Dyer had won notoriety as commander at Amritsar, when he dispersed a political meeting, opening fire without warning, and in 10 minutes killed some 379 men and boys and wounded 1,500 in the "Amritsar Massacre." General **Charles Munro**, the commander-in-chief of India, relieved him of his command.

- E -

EAST INDIA COMPANY, BRITISH. The British East India Company was started in 1600 with a capital of £30,000 and a charter from Queen Elizabeth I for 15 years to have a monopoly of trade "together with limited authority to make laws and punish interlopers." The charter was periodically renewed, and by the middle of the 18th century the company was the de facto ruler of Bengal. Its Board of Control appointed a governor general as executive who governed the company until 1858, when the Crown ended the charter and appointed a **viceroy**, subject to the control of the London government. The company concluded treaties with local potentates and waged wars in its attempt to become the paramount power in India, and it bore the responsibility for the debacle of the **first Anglo-Afghan war**. Three presidencies in Bengal, Bombay, and Madras furnished the company's armies, which included both British and Indian branches of cavalry, artillery, and infantry. Vassals and mercenaries were also employed.

ECONOMIC WARFARE. Economic warfare, such as blockades, the destruction of villages, fields, orchards, water resources, and livestock, has been practiced by invaders since time immemorial. British forces resorted to it in fighting rebellious tribes, and **Soviet** forces employed it against areas supportive of the **mujahedin**. The orchards around towns and villages were excellent bases for ambush—they were often walled and surrounded by irrigation ditches, which made it difficult to bring in wheeled transport and necessitated hand-to-hand combat. Villages and trees were leveled to deprive the **ghazis** or mujahedin of shelter.

When the **Taliban** refused a **United Nations** ultimatum demanding an end to trafficking in illegal drugs, discrimination against women, and the surrender of **Osama bin Laden**, the UN Security Council adopted sanctions that imposed an embargo on arms sales and military assistance to the Taliban; withdrawal of foreign advisers from Afghan territory; the closure of Taliban overseas offices; a freezing of funds and assets belonging to Bin Laden and his associates; and a prohibition of the sale to the Taliban of heroin precursor chemicals. The sanctions came into force on January 19, 2000, but they had only limited effect. Afghanistan was awash in arms of all types, and smuggling could provide, in the short run, all the needs of the government. *See also* COUNTERINSURGENCY.

EIKENBERRY, MAJOR GENERAL KARL. General Eikenberry was appointed by President George W. Bush to be the commander of American forces in Afghanistan, replacing **Gen. David Barno**. Eikenberry served in Afghanistan before (9/2002–9/2003) as head of the U.S. military's office for military cooperation, charged with establishing the new **Afghan National Army**. Until spring 2005 the general was director of strategic planning for the U.S. Pacific Command in Hawaii, and he moved to Kabul on May 3, 2005. Eikenberry has M.A. degrees from Harvard and Stanford and a B.S. degree from the United States Military Academy. He was defense attaché at the American embassy in Beijing, China, from October 1997 to September 2000.

ELPHINSTONE, MOUNTSTUART (1779–1859). British envoy to the court of **Shah Shuja** in 1808–1809 who negotiated an alliance of "eternal friendship" with the Afghan ruler and called for joint action in case of Franco-Persian aggression. He left Delhi on October 13, 1808, with an escort of 400 Anglo-Indian troops and reached Peshawar on February 25, 1809, where he presented **Britain**'s proposals to the Afghan ruler. This was the first contact between a British official and an Afghan ruler. The Afghans wanted British assistance to put down the revolt by Shah Mahmud, but Elphinstone replied he would have to refer the matter to the governor general. The Afghans professed to be surprised as to the object of his mission, saying anything with which he was charged "could not have been entrusted to a chuprassy (simple foot soldier)." Elphinstone used the opportunity to learn as much as he could about the "Forbidden Kingdom" and later published a book on Afghanistan, *An Account of the Kingdom of Caubul* (1815), which is one of the first comprehensive accounts on Afghan society. He was rewarded for his services with the appointment as governor of Bombay. Elphinstone College in Bombay bears his name. Remarking on the proposed war, Elphinstone said:

> If you send 27,000 men up the Bolan Pass to Candahar (as we hear is intended), and can feed them, I have no doubt you will take Candahar and Caubul and set up Soojah [Shuja]; but for maintaining him in a poor, cold, strong, and remote country, among a turbulent people like the Afghans, I own it seems to me hopeless. (Macrory, 94–95)

ELPHINSTONE, MAJOR GENERAL WILLIAM (1782–1842). Commander of the British army in Afghanistan in 1841 and the person held responsible by British historians for the debacle in the **first Anglo-Afghan war**. General Elphinstone was 60 years old and infirm when he accepted the army command. (In the 19th century, old soldiers did not fade away.) Forbes (64) describes Elphinstone as

> wrecked in body and impaired in mind by physical ailments and infirmities, he had lost all faculty of energy, and such mind as remained to him was swayed by the opinion of the person with whom he had last spoken.

Elphinstone did not take "decisive" action when **Alexander Burnes**, the assistant to the British envoy at **Kabul**, was assassinated with members of his mission. He quartered his troops in the vulnerable cantonment, which was commanded from the nearby hills, instead of moving them to the protection of the **Bala Hisar** fortress. Surrounded by Afghan tribal armies, the British had to negotiate a retreat that turned into a rout in which most of the 16,000 troops and camp followers were massacred or died of the freezing cold weather. Elphinstone did not survive the disaster; on April 23, 1842, he died in captivity of exhaustion and various maladies. *See* AKBAR, SARDAR MUHAMMAD; ANGLO-AFGHAN WARS; CAPITULATION, TREATY OF; FOREIGN RELATIONS.

ENGLAND, SIR RICHARD (1793–1883). He commanded the Bombay Division in 1841. He was repulsed at Haikalzai on March 28, 1842, losing a quarter of his forces, who were killed or wounded, and was forced to withdraw to Quetta. Ordered to proceed to **Kandahar**, he joined General **William Nott** in Kandahar and in the victory over **Muhammad Akbar** Khan at the Khojak Pass.

ENJOINING THE GOOD AND FORBIDDING EVIL. One of the obligations of every Muslim, based on the Koran (22:41, *al-amr bi 'l-ma'ruf wa an'n-nahy 'an al-munkar*), which became institutionalized in offices like the muhtasib. In Afghanistan the police was responsible for law and order until the **Taliban** instituted the "religious police" to enforce attendance at prayers, moral behavior, and restrictions on women who were not permitted to participate in the economic life and venture abroad without the all-encompassing veil or without the company of a related male. Teams of Islamic guards would patrol the cities, especially **Kabul**, and beat citizens for minor infractions. The ministry also reintroduced such punishments as mutilation for theft and stoning for adultery. Since the establishment of the **Interim Government** of President **Hamid Karzai**, the police again resumed the enforcement of law and order, without the more radical innovations of the Taliban regime.

ENVELOPING TACTICS. A method of encirclement employed in ancient times as well as in more recent engagements. **Soviet** forces employed it in the rugged terrain of Afghanistan. McMichael describes it as follows:

> A special tactical formation split off from the main body and sent by a separate route to the rear or flank of the enemy in order to support the advance of the main body, or, to execute a separate mission which is complementary to the mission of the main body.

The method was used mainly as a **blocking tactic** to prevent the withdrawal of the **mujahedin** when faced with a direct assault. It was normally assigned to an airborne, air assault, or reconnaissance company (McMichael, p 68).

ENVER (ANWAR) PASHA. Minister of war and, with **Jamal Pasha** and Talat Pasha, member of the ruling triumvirate in the Ottoman war government (1913-1918). Sentenced to death in 1919, he fled in a German submarine to **Germany** after the war and then to the **Soviet Union.** He failed to gain Soviet support in replacing Kemal Atatürk as the head of the Turkish government and moved to Central Asia. He apparently intended to seek a safe haven in Afghanistan, where Jamal Pasha had already preceded him and was active as an adviser to King **Amanullah. Basmachi** counterrevolutionaries captured him, but he convinced them of his sympathies and became one of their leaders. He fought on their side against the Red Army until he was killed in a skirmish on August 4, 1922.

ETHNIC GROUPS. The Afghan population is heterogeneous with numerous ethnic groups, speaking various dialects or mutually unintelligible **languages**. The largest ethnic group is the **Pashtuns**, followed by the **Tajiks, Uzbeks,** and **Hazara**. Orywal (18, 1986) lists the following ethnic groups in Afghanistan:

Pashtun	Tajik	Uzbek
Hazara	Turkoman	Aimaq
Taimani	Tahiri	**Baluch**
Mauri	Brahui	Arab
Qirghiz	Moghol	Gujar
Qipchaq	Eshkashimi	Munjani
Rushani	Sanglichi	Shighnani
Vakhi	Farsiwan	Qarliq
Nuristani	Pashai	Firuzkuhi
Jamshidi	Timuri	Zuri
Maliki	Mishmast	Jat
Jalali	Ghorbat	Pikragh
Shadibaz	Vangavala	Qazaq
Qizilbash	Tatar	Parachi
Tirahi	Gavarbati	Ormuri
Jogi	Shaikh Muhammadi	Kutana

Jews (Yahudi)   **Sikh**   Hindu

Estimated population figures in millions (Groetzbach, 1990) are:

Pashtun	6
Tajik & Farsiwan	4.1
Uzbek	1.1
Hazara	1.0*
Aimaq	.8
Turkoman	.3
Baluch & Brahui	.17
Arab	.1
Nuristani	.09
Pashai	.08
Tatar	.06
Qizilbash	.06
Hindu & Sikh	.035
Qirghiz & Moghol	.11

* According to Hazara claims, they number as many as two million people in Afghanistan and another two million in Iran and Pakistan.

Virtually all the Jews left Afghanistan in the 1970s (of some 600 families, only one individual remained in **Kabul** in late 2005). The introduction of state-sponsored education dictated the use of **Dari** as the language of instruction. Dari has been the language of royal courts since **Ghaznavid** times and was widely used also by the Turkic rulers of Central Asia and the Moghuls of India.

Since the early 20th century Afghan governments have promoted **Pashtu** as the national language, but any attempts to replace Dari in education have failed. One of the first decrees (No. 4) issued by the Marxist government was to recognize and permit the use of Turkmani, Uzbeki, Baluchi, and Nuristani as "national languages" to ensure the "essential conditions for evolution of the literature, education, and publication in mother tongues of the tribes and nationalities resident in Afghanistan." It ordered the respective ministries to start broadcasting on radio and television and publishing newspapers in these languages. This was an adoption of the **Soviet** nationalities policy and was seen by some as an attempt to divide and rule. For information on major ethnic groups, see individual entries.

Caution on population statistics is in order: In the 1960s the government estimated the Afghan population at about 16 million and yearly added 2.6 percent to this number, until in the 1970s a demographic survey by a team from New York University conducted a sample census and arrived at a much lower figure (10,020,600). Hamidullah Amin and Gordon B. Schilz in their *A Geography of Afghanistan* (1976) give an agricultural population of 10,839,870 and 2,500,000 nomads for a total of 13,339,870. The government of **Hafizullah Amin** claimed a population of 15.5 million; Groetzbach's estimate (1990) agrees with this figure. Some contemporary writers claim the loss of life of some two million Afghans as a result of 23 years of war and accept a population in 2001 of about 26 million. To get realistic numbers we will have to await the results of the new national census commission.

EUROCORPS. The defense arm of the European Union, created in 1992, with five "framework" nations of Belgium, France, **Germany**, Luxembourg, and Spain, and headquarters in Strasbourg, France. Soldiers from Austria, Canada, Finland, Greece, Italy, the Netherlands, Poland, Turkey, and **Great Britain** also participate. It has developed its own rapid reaction corps and now provides the core of the **International Security Assistance Force** (ISAF VI) in **Kabul**. It is headed by Lieutenant General Jean-Louis Py and is "to assist the Afghan **Transitional Government** in providing a safe and secure environment within Kabul and its surrounding areas, which will assist in the reconstruction of a new Afghanistan." Although the Eurocorps cooperates with **NATO** and the **United States** forces in Afghanistan, it is an independent entity and serves as the nucleus of the European Union's army.

- F -

FAHIM, GENERAL MUHAMMAD QASIM. First vice president, marshal and commander of the **Afghan army** (essentially the Panjshiri forces), and minister of defense of Afghanistan. A friend and deputy of **Ahmad Shah Masud**, whom he succeeded after Masud's assassination on September 9, 2001. A **Tajik**, born about 1960 in the **Panjshir** Valley, he became the leader of the largest force of the **Northern Alliance**. After the conquest of **Kabul**, he served as minister of defense of the **Interim** and **Transitional**

governments. He took control of Kabul in contravention of the **Interim Agreement** and became the most powerful person in the country. When he decided to run for the presidential elections and refused to step down from his cabinet post, **Hamid Karzai** dismissed him as his running mate for the vice presidency. After the elections, Karzai replaced Fahim with General **Abdurrahim Wardak** and disarmed Divisions No. 2 and No. 6 which were under Fahim's command. Because of his title he enjoys certain privileges, such as a car with a five-star number plate, bodyguards and a surveillance system near his house, a salary, the right to attend official ceremonies, to sit in the front row at official ceremonies, and other privileges. He did not receive the customary land grant.

FAIZABAD (37-6' N, 70-34' E). Capital of **Badakhshan**, with about 12,000 inhabitants, the central commercial market of the province, situated on the Kokcha River at an altitude of 3,300 feet. Until the late 17th century the town was called Jauz Gun, or Jauzun, because of the abundance of nuts (*jauz*) in the area. The name of the town was changed to Faizabad (abode of divine bounty, blessing, and charity), when in 1691 Mir Yar Beg brought what was believed to be the Blessed Robe (*khirqa-yi mubarak*) of the Prophet Muhammad to the town. (**Ahmad Shah Durrani** later brought the *khirqa* to **Kandahar** where it still is today.) In 1821 Murad Beg, the ruler of **Kunduz**, destroyed the town, but a few years later it again reached a population of 8,000. Many **mosques** and historical shrines now exist in the area. In 1937 Faizabad became the terminal of a road, connected to the northern highway between **Baghlan** and Kunduz, which was later extended east toward the **Wakhan** Corridor. The natives speak a number of Badakhshi languages in addition to **Dari**.

FAIZAL, MULLA. The **Taliban**'s portly assistant defense minister, who wore an enormous black turban and green army jacket. Mullah Faizal had a ferocious reputation—when his forces captured **Mazar-i Sharif** from General **Abdul Rashid Dostum** in 1998, he reputedly presided over the massacre of at least 1,000 anti-Taliban fighters.

FAIZ MUHAMMAD, GENERAL. Governor of the Eastern Province who stopped the mission under **Neville Chamberlain** from entering Afghanistan on the eve of the **second Anglo-Afghan war**. **Louis Cavagnari** crossed the border on September 21, 1876, and met Faiz

Muhammad at **Ali Masjid**. He asked whether the Afghan governor would permit Chamberlain to pass and Faiz Muhammad said no, adding "You may take as kindness, and because I remember friendship, that I do not fire upon you for what you have already done" [Crossing the border without permission]. The British chose this "insult" as the casus belli for starting the Second Anglo-Afghan War.

Faiz Muhammad headed an army of 3,000 regular infantry, 600 levies, 200 cavalry, and 24 cannons and met General **Sam Browne** at the battle of Ali Masjid. Faiz Muhammad was forced to retreat and the British invaders marched on **Kabul** (Heathcote, 101).

FAQIR OF IPI, HAJI MIRZA ALI KHAN. A frontier **mulla** residing with the Waziri tribe on the Indian side of the **Durand Line**. He was an implacable foe of the British who incited the tribes to wage **jihad** against India. He collaborated with the Axis Powers during World War II and was in touch with their legations in **Kabul**. The Germans gave him the code name *Feuerfresser* (fire-eater) and supported his efforts by paying him a regular subsidy. The faqir's activities compelled **Britain** to keep large forces on the Frontier that could have been deployed elsewhere. At one time an army of 40,000 troops was searching for him; he always found shelter among the Waziris. After the creation of **Pakistan**, the faqir demanded independence for **Pashtunistan**; he was elected "president" of Pashtunistan by a tribal council and continued his fight against the new state. He received financial support from the Afghan government until his death in 1960.

FARAH (32-22' N, 62-7' E). A province in western Afghanistan with an area of 21,666 square miles; it is the second largest Afghan province, with a population of about 356,000 (estimates are as high as 404,000). The province is divided into the districts of Farah, Anardara, Bala Boluk, Purchaman, Bakwa, **Shindand**, Kala-i-Kah, Gulistan, Khak-i-Safid, and Farsi. The capital of the province is the town of Farah with about 18,800 inhabitants. The province is traversed by the Farah Rud, the Khash Rud, and the Harut Rud (rivers); major mountain ranges include the Khak-i-Safid, Siyah Kuh, Malmand, Kuh-i-Afghan, and the Reg-i-Rawan. The economy of the province depends primarily on agriculture and livestock breeding; barley, cotton, and wheat are the major crops, and livestock includes sheep,

Qaraqul sheep, goats, cattle, camels, and donkeys. An important junction in Indo-Persian trade in the 17th century, Farah was destroyed in 1837 and remained a small walled town until the early 20th century when a new town was gradually developed, with a population of about 6,000 in 1934. The town gradually declined when the new **Kandahar-Herat** Highway, completed in 1965, bypassed the town. In 1972 floods destroyed much of the town, and the provincial administration moved for two years to Farah Rud. The population is largely **Pashtun**, but **Tajik** and other ethnic communities are also represented in Farah.

FARIAB (36-0' N, 65-0' E). A province in north central Afghanistan with an area of 8,226 square miles and a population of about 547,000 (estimates are as high as 674,000). The province borders on Turkmenistan in the north, on **Badghis** Province in the south, and **Jozjan** in the east. The capital of the province is the town of **Maimana** with about 38,000 inhabitants. Fariab is famous for horse breeding and its *buzkashi* games (a kind of polo, using the carcass of a calf or sheep to carry to the opponent's goal). Melons, nuts, cereals, and cotton are the major agricultural products. Qaraqul sheep are bred for the export of skins, and carpet weaving is an important industry.

FATEH KHAN (FATH). Oldest son of Painda Khan (head of the **Muhammadzai** branch of the Barakzai tribe), born in 1777 in **Kandahar**. He was a skillful politician and soldier and helped Shah Mahmud (r. 1799–1803 and 1810–1818) gain the Afghan throne, capturing **Farah** and Kandahar, from the forces of **Zaman Shah**. He was given the position of grand wazir, established law and order, and conducted the government for Mahmud with great skill. When **Shah Shuja** (r. 1803–1810 and 1839) succeeded to the **Kabul** throne, Fateh Khan was again appointed grand wazir, but Fateh Khan remained loyal to Mahmud and helped to restore him to power. Fateh Khan consolidated Afghan control over Kashmir and established order in **Herat**. Kamran, son of Shah Mahmud, was jealous of Fateh Khan's increasing power and had him blinded and, in 1818, killed. The Barakzai chiefs revolted, and the ensuing conflict led to the overthrow of the Sadozai dynasty and the assumption of power by the Barakzai/Muhammadzai branch of the **Durranis**.

FATWA (FETWA). A formal legal opinion by a mufti, or canon lawyer, in answer to a question of a judge or private individual. Fatwas cover legal theory, theology, philosophy, and creeds, which are not included in fiqh (law books). Fatwas are informational and advisory and are generally not enforced by the state. In many Islamic countries countries a "grand mufti" advises a ruler on the constitutionality of laws.

FINN, ROBERT P. First American ambassador to Afghanistan in 20 years. He served as ambassador to Tajikistan before coming to **Kabul** in March 2002 and was succeeded by **Zalmay Khalilzad** in August 2003. Finn graduated from Princeton University and St. John's College and then embarked on a career in the foreign service and as a professor at Princeton University.

FIRST ANGLO-AFGHAN WAR (1838–1842). In the 19th century, European rivalry for commerce and empire quickly extended to the Middle East. In 1798 the Napoleonic invasion of Egypt temporarily established a French foothold in this strategic area, which **Britain** feared as an important step in a move against India. Russia moved into Central Asia and by the end of the 19th century the czar's influence extended to the **Amu Daria**. Britain was moving into the **Panjab** in search of a "scientific" frontier to make sure that her possessions in India were safe.

In **Kabul**, internecine warfare led to the ouster of **Shah Shuja**, the last of the **Sadozai** rulers, and **Dost Muhammad**, first of the **Muhammadzai** rulers, ascended the throne in 1826. He wanted an alliance with India and hoped to regain Peshawar, which had been lost in 1818 to the emerging **Sikh** nation under **Ranjit Singh**. **Lord Auckland**, the British governor general of India, chose an alliance with the Sikh ruler instead and decided to restore Shah Shuja to the Afghan throne. The presence of a purported **Russian** agent at Kabul (*see* VITKEVICH, CAPT. IVAN) and Dost Muhammad's hostility to the Sikh ruler were the reasons given for the declaration of war (*see* SIMLA MANIFESTO). In July 1838 a tripartite treaty was signed between Shah Shuja, Ranjit Singh, and Lord Auckland, and the **Army of the Indus** invaded Afghanistan. The invaders met with little resistance, **Ghazni** was captured on July 23 (*see* GHAZNI, CAPTURE OF), and **Kabul** was occupied on August 7. Shah Shuja was put on the Kabul throne, and Dost Muhammad was forced into

First Afghan War

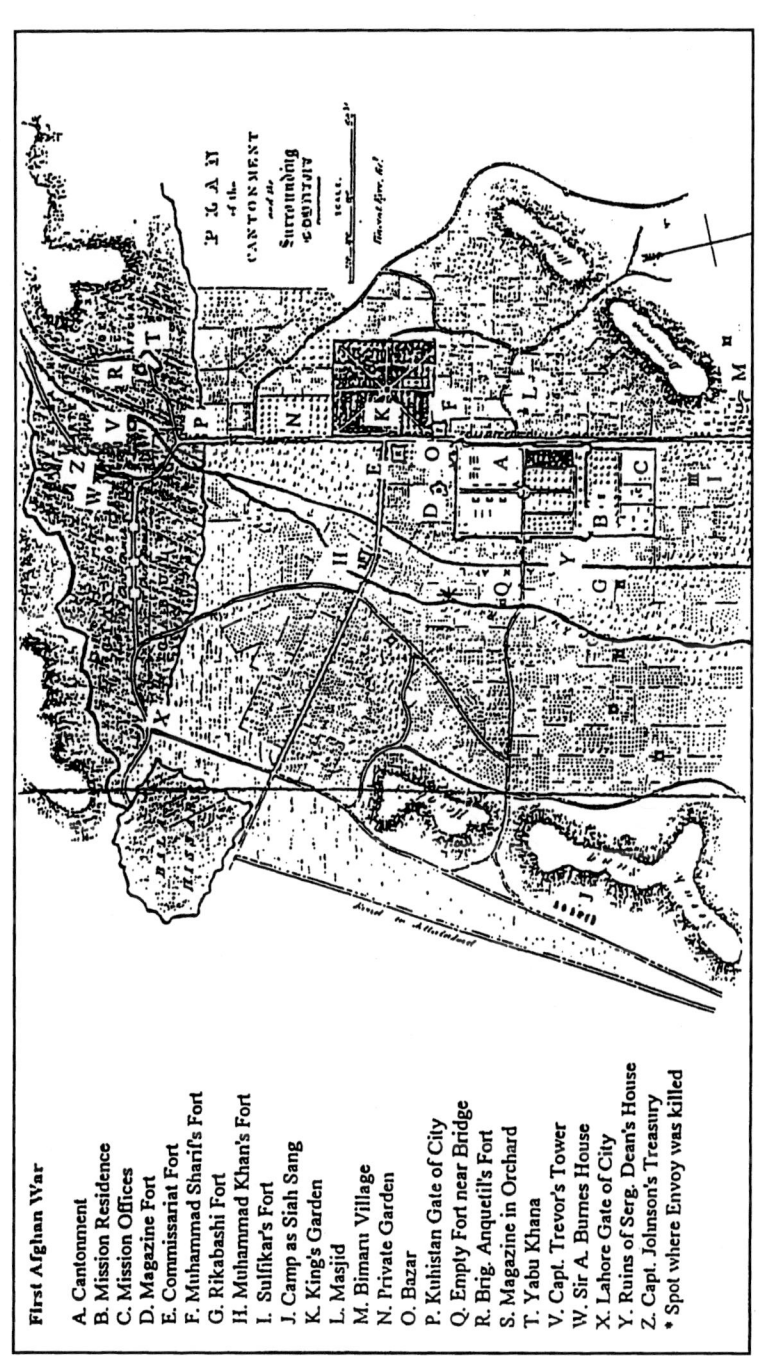

A. Cantonment
B. Mission Residence
C. Mission Offices
D. Magazine Fort
E. Commissariat Fort
F. Muhammad Sharif's Fort
G. Rikabashi Fort
H. Muhammad Khan's Fort
I. Sulfikar's Fort
J. Camp as Siah Sang
K. King's Garden
L. Masjid
M. Bimaru Village
N. Private Garden
O. Bazar
P. Kuhistan Gate of City
Q. Empty Fort near Bridge
R. Brig. Anquetil's Fort
S. Magazine in Orchard
T. Yabu Khana
V. Capt. Trevor's Tower
W. Sir A. Burnes House
X. Lahore Gate of City
Y. Ruins of Serg. Dean's House
Z. Capt. Johnson's Treasury
* Spot where Envoy was killed

Plan 3. Plan of the Cantonment (IOL, Eyre)

Indian exile. The major part of the British army left Kabul on September 18. But it was soon apparent that the Sadozai ruler needed British protection to maintain himself in power, and the army became a force of occupation. The families of British officers came to Kabul, and thousands of Indian camp followers engaged in the lucrative business of importing from India the necessities of colonial life.

But all was not well. On November 2, 1841, a Kabuli crowd stormed the British mission and killed its members, including its head. The Afghans captured some £17,000 from the treasury in an adjacent house and plundered the commissariat stores located in a number of forts outside the cantonment. **Muhammad Akbar**, a son of Dost Muhammad, together with a number of chiefs, now rallied his forces and increasingly threatened the occupiers. Major General **William Elphinstone** ordered the army to withdraw to the cantonment, which was commanded from nearby hills. He commanded seven regiments of horse and foot, with guns and sappers, English and Indian, and decided to recall General **Robert Sale** from **Gandomak** and **Sir William Nott** from **Kandahar**. But the roads were blocked by the onset of winter and by strong contingents of tribal *lashkars*, preventing a strengthening of the Kabul garrison. A raiding party sent out to silence Afghan guns was badly decimated and had to return, leaving their wounded behind. On December 11, 1841, the British were forced to negotiate a retreat that only few of the 16,000 troops and camp followers survived. (*See* CAPITULATION, TREATY OF; DEATH MARCH.) Britain felt it necessary to have its martial reputation restored, and in September 1842 General **George Pollock** wreaked vengeance on Kabul, laying torch to the covered bazaar and permitting plunder, which destroyed much of the rest of the city. The British forces left, and Amir Dost Muhammad returned in December 1842 to rule Afghanistan until he died a natural death 20 years later. The war cost Britain £20 million and some 15,000 lives of all ranks as well as camp followers.

Forces Employed. Army of the Indus—for action in Sind and Afghanistan:

A Bengal column, with 2,430 cavalry, 5,570 infantry, and 31 guns. A Bombay column, with 1,200 cavalry, 4,280 infantry, and 24 guns. Shah Shuja's contingent of Indian troops with British officers, with 950 cavalry, 5,000 infantry, and 12 guns.

The Shahzadah's (Prince Timur) contingent.

An army of observation furnished by Ranjit Singh.

In reserve at Ferozpur: A mixed Bengal division, 3,000 strong.

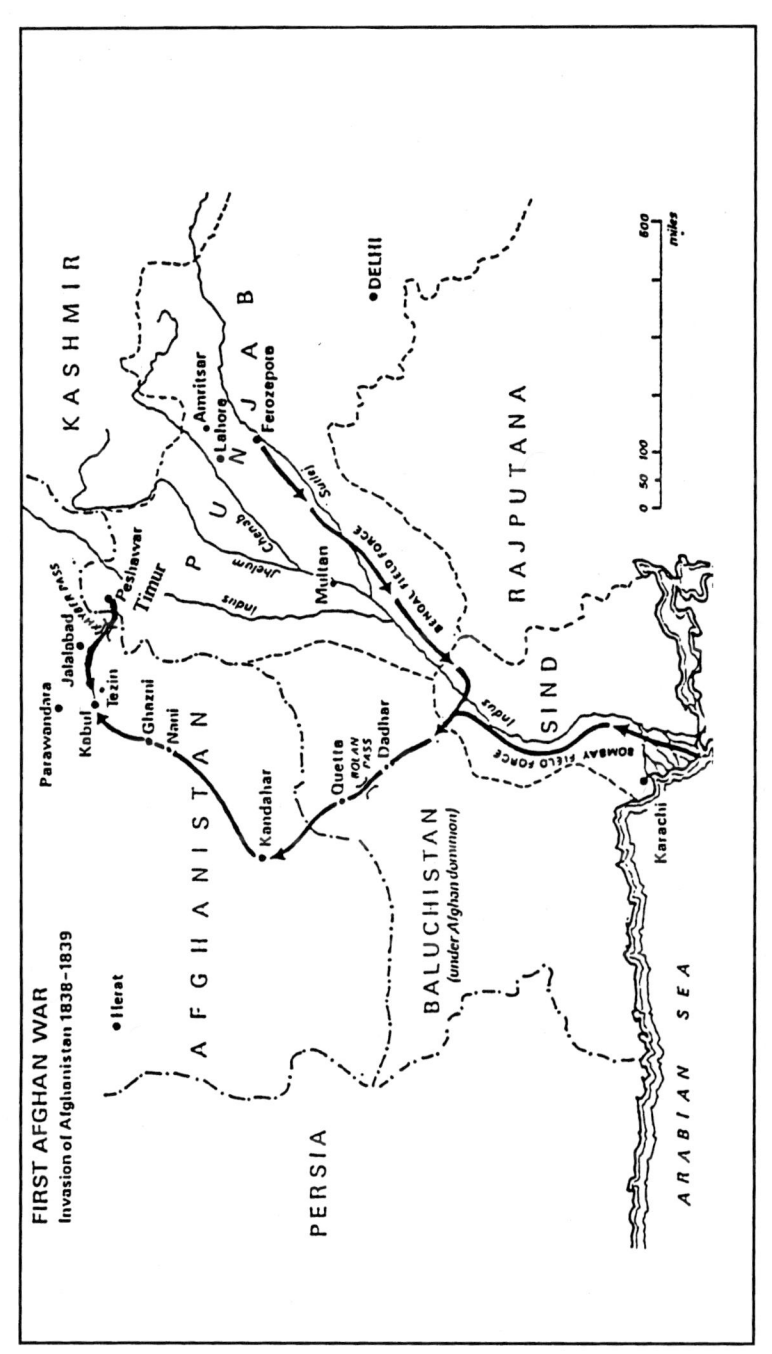

Plan 4. First Afghan War (adapted from Anglesey)

On the lines of communications: Karachi, 5,000 men. Base supply depot was at bridge of boats near Sukkur.

Concentration. The Bengal column, including 250 sappers and miners and 240 pioneers concentrated at Karnal at the end of October 1838; marched thence to Ferozpur, the point of assembly for the shah's contingent and Ranjit Singh's forces; left Ferozpur in early December and traversed the 38 marches to Rohri via Bahawalpur, by January 24, 1839.

The Bombay column, including 100 sappers and miners, landed near Karachi in December 1838, and marched up the right bank of the Indus. Shah Shuja's contingent marched ahead of the Bengal column and arrived at Shikarpur in January 1839.

All assembled at Shikarpur between February 16 and 20, 1839, and constituted what was named the "**Army of the Indus**," under the command of Lieutenant General Sir **John Keane**, commander in chief in Bombay. The regulars were armed with smootbore percussion muskets, the irregulars with flintlocks, both inferior in range to the matchlocks of the Afghans.

The transport consisted of about 60,000 Indian, and several thousand Afghan, camels, as well as a number of baggage elephants. Servants and camp followers raised the number of mouths to feed to about 100,000. Beyond Shikapur, no supply depots had been established; water was scarce and bad. Only the Bombay troops carried water bottles. The 150 miles of desert between Shikapur and the Bolan Pass caused severe losses among the followers, camels, and horses. Followers were put on half rations. The Bengal column reached Quetta by the end of March 1839, but supplies promised by the Khan of Kalat were not forthcoming. The distance from Quetta to **Kandahar**, 147 miles, took 20 days. Three days were needed to cross the Khojak Pass—guns and wagons had to be dragged up by hand and lowered by ropes down a precipitous western side. Afghan raiders harassed and looted the ammunition, baggage, and supply columns.

The British paid the chief of the Kakar tribe 1,000 pounds to win his support, which led to the flight of the Barakzai brothers and the governor of Kandahar. On April 25, 1839, Shah Shuja entered Kandahar, one day ahead of the leading portion of the Bengal column. Within the next two weeks the total British force at Kandahar numbered 8,800 men and 30,046 camp followers. The British forces had only three days of supplies. The Bengal column lost

20,000 camels and 350 horses. The excessive heat and low rations caused considerable sickness.

When on June 27 Sir John Keane left Kandahar for **Ghazni**, some 230 miles away, his troops were again on half rations.

Advance from Peshawar. During the invasion of southern Afghanistan the Shahzada's contingent was raised from **Pathan** tribesmen under Sikh domination. It included 1,000 cavalry, 3,500 infantry, and four guns. To this was added Ranjit Singh's contingent of Muslim Panjabi mercenaries, comprising 1,050 cavalry, 4,800 infantry, and 12 guns. They were strengthened by the addition of two Bengali infantry battalions and four *ghund* of the regular army. The forces reached Peshawar on March 20 and were placed under the command of Lieutenant Colonel Wade. He started from Jamrud on July 22, moved into the **Khaibar Pass**, and captured **Ali Masjid** on the 27th. By this time some of Amir Dost Muhammad's supporters began to desert him, and most of the **Qizilbash** deserted. The Army of the Indus entered Kabul on August 7, and Colonel Wade's forces reached the capital on September 3. Ranjit Singh's troops did not proceed beyond the Khaibar Pass (MR, 1924 and OASW).

FIRST ANGLO-AFGHAN WAR: CAUSES. During the siege of **Herat** in 1838, **Lord Auckland** determined to restore **Shah Shuja** to the throne of **Kabul**, in the hope of establishing a friendly power in Afghanistan, which was to form the first line of defense against the threatened advance of Russia on India. A tripartite treaty was concluded through English pressure, but neither Ranjit Singh nor Shah Shuja was happy. The former did not want to send his troops into Afghanistan, and the latter did not want to resign his claim on the **Panjab** and Sind. Lord Auckland informed the directors of the **East India Company** that

> the increase of Russian and Persian influence in Afghanistan, and the impression of the certain fall of Herat to the Persian army, have induced the Ameer Dost Mahomed Khan to avow and to insist upon pretensions for the cession to him, by Maharaja Runjeet Sing, of the Peshawur territory, and to take other steps which are tantamount to the rejection of the friendship and good offices of the British Government; and have in consequence led to the retirement of Captain Burnes from the territories of Cabool.

The Persian siege of Herat was ended, but Auckland was determined to make war. The resulting disaster was subsequently termed "Auckland's Folly."

FIRST ANGLO-AFGHAN WAR: COSTS. The cost of the war amounted to £20 million, 15,000 fighting men were killed or died of wounds and sickness, and tens of thousands of camp followers perished. Afghan casualties are not known.

FLARES. Flare-emitting devices air-dropped or fitted to aircraft to confuse the heat-seeking head of a missile. When the **mujahedin** acquired SA-7 missiles in 1983, the aerial superiority of **Soviet** forces was threatened and they began using various types of flares. To overcome these defensive measures, the mujahedin began to use British **Blowpipe missiles**, which had command-guided, rather than heat-seeking, systems. They did not prove to be very efficient, but **Stingers**, though heat-seeking, threatened Soviet control of the skies.

FORAGING. British military manuals suggested that foraging, to collect supplies for men and animals by cavalry alone, possible in other countries, was not advisable in Afghanistan. The generally difficult terrain gave the Afghans numerous opportunities for cutting off horsemen. They were not only impeded by the livestock and supplies they tried to carry off, but also by their own horses. (**Kandahar**, 1933, secret document.) *See also* LOGISTICS; SUPPLIES.

FOREIGN RELATIONS. Afghanistan's relations with her neighbors were always influenced by the fact that the territory inhabited by the Afghans was the "gateway" to the Indian subcontinent. The power that controlled the tribes and the passes leading south and east would not encounter any great physical obstacles in the conquest of the subcontinent and its fabulous riches. **Mahmud of Ghazni** (r. 988–1030), Tamerlane (Timur-i Lang, r. 1370–1405), and **Nadir Shah Afshar** (r. 1736–1747) crossed the Afghan passes for the propagation of Islam, glory, and booty. It is therefore not surprising that **Ahmad Shah Durrani** (r. 1747–1773), the founder of the state of Afghanistan, considered it his manifest destiny to create an empire that included a large portion of northern India. He invaded India nine times and defeated the powerful **Maratha** confederation at the **Battle of Panipat**, north of Delhi, in 1761. But by the turn of the century, the gradual northwest expansion of British influence resulted in a confrontation between **Britain** and Afghanistan that was to continue into the 20th century. *See* ANGLO-AFGHAN RELATIONS.

Afghanistan's foreign relations can be divided into seven major periods: first, the expansionist period, which lasted from 1747 to 1800; second, the period of foreign conflict, from 1800 to 1880, which involved Afghanistan in hostilities with Persia and the rising **Sikh** nation in the **Panjab** as well as with Britain and **Russia**; third, the period of defensive isolationism and "buffer-state" politics, initiated by Amir **Abdul Rahman** (r. 1880–1901) and continued by Amir **Habibullah** (r. 1901–1919) until his death; fourth, the period of defensive neutralism which opened Afghanistan to foreign influences and lasted until after World War II when Britain's departure from India ushered in a new, fifth, era of peaceful coexistence that, nevertheless, ended with the Marxist coup in 1978 and the **Soviet Intervention**. A sixth era began under the **Taliban**. When the Taliban conquered most of Afghanistan in the late 1990s, diplomatic relations were maintained only with **Pakistan**, Saudi Arabia, and the United Arab Emirates. The seventh period began with the American intervention in October 2001, but during this period there was little in the way of independent Afghan diplomacy.

During the expansionist period Afghan rulers conquered territories north of the **Hindu Kush** and east of the Indus River, but internecine fighting among the **Durrani** *sardars* (princes and chiefs) and the emergence of new players in the "**Great Game**" in Central Asia made the Afghan empire a short-lived enterprise. When in 1798 **Shah Zaman** invited the Marquess Wellesley, governor of Bengal (1798–1805), to join him in a campaign against the Maratha confederacy of northwestern India, Wellesley sought Persian assistance "to keep Zaman Shah in perpetual check." The period of foreign conflict saw the emergence of the Sikh nation under **Ranjit Singh** who wrested the Panjab from the Afghans. Britain feared the appearance of a French mission in Tehran in 1807 and considered the Russian territorial gains in the Caucasus a serious threat to India. Therefore, in 1808 the British governor general, Lord Minto, sent **Mountstuart Elphinstone** to Peshawar to conclude a treaty of friendship and common defense against Franco-Persian attacks. (*See* ANGLO-AFGHAN RELATIONS.) **Shah Shuja**, who had ascended the **Kabul** throne, agreed to prohibit Frenchmen from entering his realm in exchange for military support. This treaty as well as others concluded between Britain and Fath Ali Shah, the ruler of Persia, were "inoperative" almost as soon as they were ratified. Shah Shuja was ousted in 1810 and, after an interval of internecine fighting, the **Muhammadzai** branch of the **Durranis** replaced the **Sadozai** rulers. **Dost Muhammad**, a capable ruler, succeeded to the throne in 1826. He wanted British friendship but also wanted to regain Peshawar from Ranjit Singh, whose forces had conquered Multan in 1810, Kashmir in 1819, and Peshawar in 1823. But Lord **Auckland**, governor-general of the British **East India Company** (1836–1842), favored a forward policy; he concluded the **Tripartite Agreement** of July 1838 with Ranjit Singh and Shah Shuja to restore the shah to the Kabul throne. Dost Muhammad's negotiations with a purported Russian envoy and the amir's hostility to the Sikh ruler were the *casus belli*, and the **Simla Manifesto** of 1838, issued by the British-Indian government, constituted the declaration of war. The **Army of the Indus**, as it was proudly called, invaded Afghanistan in what came to be known as the **first Anglo-Afghan war**. Once installed on the Kabul throne, Shah Shuja was unable to consolidate his power even with British support. Afghan tribal forces attacked isolated outposts, and on November 2, 1841, the British Political Officer **Alexander Burnes** and his staff were assassinated. The British forces were compelled to negotiate an ignominious retreat that resulted in the virtual annihilation of the British-Indian forces *(see* CAPITULATION, TREATY OF; DEATH MARCH).

This extraordinary setback for Britain led to the restoration of Dost Muhammad (r. 1842–1863). Like Shah Shuja, he had been in Indian exile, and his return to Kabul began the rule of the **Muhammadzai** dynasty, a collateral branch of the **Sadozai**, which lasted until 1973. The British-Indian government resigned itself to a period of "masterly inactivity" which left Afghanistan to revert to civil war following the succession of Amir **Shir Ali** in 1863. But the search for a "scientific" frontier and the desire to fill a "power vacuum" in Afghanistan led to a return to a forward policy. **Baluchistan** came under British control in 1879, and the Indian government had to decide where its boundary with Afghanistan should be: the crest of the **Hindu Kush**, the **Amu Daria**, or the tribal belt of the northwestern frontier? Lacking any direct control over Afghanistan, Britain wanted envoys stationed at **Herat** and Kabul who could guard Indian interests in those vital areas. Amir Shir Ali was willing to forge an alliance with Britain, but he wanted protection from Russian aggression, a subsidy in weapons and funds, and British recognition of his son, Abdullah Jan, as his successor (*see* AMBALA CONFERENCE). When he could not obtain a clear commitment from Britain, he listened to the overtures of General **Constantin Kaufman**, the Russian governor general of Turkestan Province, and permitted a mission under Major-General **Stolietoff** to proceed to Kabul. The Russians gave the not quite ironclad promise "that if any foreign enemy attacks Afghanistan and the Amir is unable to drive him out. ... The Russian Government will repel the enemy either by means of advice or by such other means as it may seem proper."

The British government now insisted that the **amir** receive a mission, headed by General **Neville Chamberlain**. Shir Ali asked for a postponement of the mission, but it proceeded in spite of the wishes of the amir. When it was stopped at the Afghan frontier, Britain presented an ultimatum; on January 8, 1879, British troops occupied **Kandahar** in the start of the **second Anglo-Afghan war**. The promised Russian support was in the form of "advice," namely, that the amir should make his peace with the British. Shir Ali felt betrayed; he was forced to flee and died two months later near **Mazar-i Sharif**.

His son **Yaqub** Khan succeeded to the throne at the cost of ceding territory to British India in the **Treaty of Gandomak** and permitting Sir **P. Louis Cavagnari** to come to Kabul to head a permanent British mission. History repeated itself when Cavagnari and his staff were massacred in Kabul. General **Frederick Roberts**, son of Sir **Abraham Roberts**, the commander of Shah Shuja's forces during the First Anglo-Afghan War, occupied Kabul. In the meantime other contenders for the Kabul throne came to the fore. **Ayub Khan**, another son of Amir Shir Ali, wiped out General **G. R. S. Burrows**'s forces in the **Battle of Maiwand** (1880), and **Abdul Rahman** Khan, a grandson of Amir Dost Muhammad, entered Afghanistan after 12 years in Central Asian exile. To avoid disaster and to extricate their forces from Afghanistan, the British found it advisable to recognize Abdul Rahman as amir of "Kabul and its Dependencies." Amir Abdul Rahman (r. 1880–1901) was quick to eliminate all rivals to his power. He united the country, initiated domestic reforms, and formulated a foreign policy that served Afghanistan well until World War I. He fashioned a cautious alliance with Britain that obligated Britain to defend Afghanistan from unprovoked Russian aggression and strengthened his power with aid in money and arms. Abdul Rahman agreed to conduct his relations with foreign powers through the intermediary of the British government. Having protected himself from the danger in the north, the amir formulated a policy that was to prevent Britain from gaining influence within his domains under the aegis of their common defense. This policy rested on the following triad: militant assertion of independence, defensive isolationism, and a balancing of the pressures by the two imperialist neighbors.

The "Iron Amir" considered his agreement with Britain an alliance between equals in which the two partners contributed to their common defense. He permitted the establishment in Kabul of a British agency, headed by an Indian Muslim whose sphere of activity was strictly limited, but he refused to accept British military advisers and declined an offer of British help in extending the Indian rail system into Afghanistan. Although in 1893 he accepted under duress the **Durand** Line, which cut large portions of **Pashtun** territory from the Afghan state, he did not assist in the complete demarcation of the border and continued to lay claim to the free "unadministered" tribal belt, which he saw as a buffer between Afghanistan and India. When Britain made punitive expeditions into this area, the Afghan ruler supported the tribes with shipments of arms and granted fugitives from India shelter in his domains. Amir Abdul Rahman was on a state visit in India in 1885 when Russian troops moved into the Panjdeh oasis (*see* PANJDEH INCIDENT). The fact that Britain did not assist him against Russian aggression convinced him that he could only rely on himself.

Amir Habibullah (r. 1901–1919) continued the policy of his father. He resisted British demands for modifications of the agreements concluded with Amir Abdul Rahman and succeeded in 1905 in obtaining a treaty that confirmed all the existing provisions (*see* ANGLO-AFGHAN TREATY OF 1905). Two years later, Amir Habibullah visited India for talks with the governor general, Lord Minto, unaware of the fact that at the same time Russia and Britain had concluded the **Anglo-Russian Convention** of 1907. The amir never permitted Russia and Britain the commercial privileges expected under the Convention and made sure that his imperialist neighbors would not solve the "Afghanistan Question" at the cost of his independence. The situation was drastically changed during World War I when both the Central Powers and the Allies vied for the support of the Afghan ruler. The **Hentig-Niedermayer Expedition** (August 1915–May 1916) was able to conclude a treaty with the amir but Germany could not provide any tangible support in funds and weapons. Therefore Habibullah remained neutral, hoping to win rich rewards and complete independence from Britain; when these expectations were not realized he paid for the failure of his policy with his life. Amir Habibullah was assassinated on the night of February 19, 1919, at Kalla Gush in **Laghman** Province. **Amanullah** Khan ascended the throne over the rival claims of his uncle, **Nasrullah** Khan, and his brother, **Enayatullah** Khan.

King Amanullah (r. 1919–1929, he adopted the title of king in 1926) demanded a new treaty from British India that would recognize Afghanistan's absolute independence. When the Indian government was reluctant to comply, he started military action that resulted in the **third Anglo-Afghan war** of 1919. With India in semi-revolt and British forces demobilized after the European war, the British government did not find this an opportune time to wage war and agreed to a peace treaty at **Rawalpindi** (August 8, 1919, *see* ANGLO-AFGHAN TREATY OF 1919). It took another three months of negotiations at Mussoorie (**Mussoorie Conference**, April 17 to July 18, 1920) and almost one year of talks at Kabul, from January 1, 1921, to December 2, 1921, before normal, neighborly relations were established (*see* ANGLO-AFGHAN TREATY OF 1921). By that time Amanullah had established diplomatic relations with the Soviet Union, Turkey, Persia, and Italy and had modified Abdul Rahman's policy to end the isolation of his country. A contemporary of Reza Shah of Iran and Kemal Ataturk of the young Turkish republic, Amanullah initiated such drastic social reforms that he was ousted in a wave of reaction after a 10-year period of tenuous rule. Next followed the chaotic 10-month rule of a "lowly" **Tajik**, **Habibullah Kalakani** (January 18– November 3, 1929), called "The Son of a Water Carrier" (*Bacha-i Saqqau*) by his friends and "Amir Habib-ullah Ghazi, Servant of the Religion of the Messenger of God" (*Khadem-i Din Rasul Allah*), by his followers after his coronation.

The new dynasty of **Nadir Shah** (r. 1929–1933) and his son **Muhammad Zahir Shah** (r. 1933–1973) continued Afghanistan's traditional policy of foreign relations but now tried to enlist **Germany** as a "third power" in obtaining the technical and political support that the Afghan rulers did not dare to accept from their neighbors. Economic and cultural collaboration between Afghanistan and Germany was greatly expanded, and Germans were soon the largest European community in the country. But the deterioration of the political situation in Europe and the outbreak of World War II ended any possibility that the economic cooperation might evolve into political collaboration. Afghanistan remained neutral during the war.

The end of the war created an entirely new situation: the **Soviet Union**, although severely battered, acquired nuclear technology and emerged as a superpower, and Britain, in spite of her victory, was forced to relinquish her hold on India in 1947. During the short reign of King Amanullah, Afghanistan's border with the Soviet Union was open to commercial relations, and regular air service to Tashkent existed, but his successors maintained a closed-border policy. Keeping Afghanistan's border to the north closed was criticized in Moscow as inconsistent with friendly "neighborly" relations. Soviet demands for a "normalization" of relations could not be ignored, but it was hoped in Kabul that the **United States** would fill the vacuum left by the British and serve as a balancing force against the Soviet Union.

The United States formally recognized Afghanistan in August 1934 but did not have an accredited representative in Kabul until 1942, when it appeared possible that the German advance into the Caucasus might make it impossible to maintain a link to the Soviet Union through western Iran. In spite of Afghanistan's status as an independent state, Washington considered the country within the British sphere of influence and not very important in terms of international trade. With the onset of the Cold War during the Harry Truman administration and the policy of containment of communism under John Foster Dulles, secretary of state under President Dwight D. Eisenhower, the Afghan government might have entered into an alliance with the United States if it would have been given explicit guarantees of protection from Soviet attack.

The United States government had never been willing to give that kind of guarantee; a possible Soviet advance was to be stopped at the **Khaibar Pass**, not north of the **Hindu Kush**. The Baghdad Pact in 1955 (subsequently renamed in 1959 Central Treaty Organization, CENTO) united Turkey, Iraq, Iran, and **Pakistan** with Britain as the representative of the West and the United States as the sponsor and "paymaster." The alliance inherited the legacy of regional disputes between Middle Eastern neighbors and served to upset the balance of power.

A turning point occurred in December 1955, when Nikita Khrushchev and Nikolai Bulganin came to Kabul. The Soviets supported Afghanistan in the **Pashtunistan** dispute and offered massive aid, which the United States was unwilling to match. The government of Prime Minister **Muhammad Daud**, in spite of its misgivings, turned to the **Soviet Union** for the weapons it could not obtain from the West. The weapons arrived with Soviet advisers and experts, and thousands of Afghans went to the Soviet Union for military training. Graduates from Afghan institutes of higher education won fellowships to foreign universities, including those in the USSR, and there emerged a growing cadre of military officers, students, and technocrats with leftist and republican, if not pro-Russian, sympathies. When Sardar Muhammad Daud staged a coup against his cousin, the king, on July 17, 1973, he counted the Left (and **Parchamis**) among his supporters. Five years later a Marxist coup ended the "aristocratic" republic and established the **Democratic Republic of Afghanistan**. Its alliance with the Soviet Union and the subsequent war, which Soviet intervention in 1979 turned into a war of Afghan liberation, resulted in the eventual Soviet withdrawal in 1989 and a "simmering" civil war that was temporarily ended when the **Taliban** extended their control over much of the country. Under the Taliban, Afghanistan became a radical Islamic state which had increasingly bad relations with the West. It was, however, on good terms with **Pakistan**, whose **Inter-Services Intelligence** had been arming and training the **mujahedin**. The Taliban government gave shelter to **al-Qaeda** and permitted the establishment of bases for the training of Islamist revolutionaries elsewhere. Although they were internationalists and saw Afghanistan as the nucleus of a new Islamic empire, they were not willing to issue a declaration accepting the Durand Line as the Afghan border with Pakistan.

When in October 2001 American and Coalition forces defeated the Taliban government and dispersed their al-Qaeda allies, Interim and Transitional Governments were set up which proclaimed their intentions for maintaining good relations with all nations of the world. Nevertheless, relations with Pakistan were strained because remnants of the former regime had found shelter in the Pakistan tribal belt and conducted guerrilla activities against the new Afghan government. Conditions seemed to improve with the newly elected government of **Hamid Karzai**. The fact that foreign troops will remain in Afghanistan in the near future assures that there will not be any dramatic shifts in Afghan foreign relations. However, it can be assumed that the Afghan government will show its solidarity with the Islamic world, will support the forging of a just peace in the Arab-Israeli conflict, and will not, in the near term, revive the Pashtunistan issue.

FORWARD POLICY. *See* **FOREIGN RELATIONS.**

FOWLER, MAJ. GEN. General officer commanding the 1st (Peshawar) Division during the **third Anglo-Afghan war**. He directed the second, and successful, attack on **Bagh** on May 11, 1919.

FRANKS, GENERAL TOMMY. The commander-in-chief of the **United States** Central Command (CENTCOM) which has operational control in the Central Asia theater of war. A "plain-spoken artilleryman from Texas" who served in the army for 36 years, Franks retired in 2003. He had more than 150,000 troops under his command in Afghanistan and Iraq. During the Afghan war as combatant commander, he was based in Tampa, Florida. Franks is said to have antagonized Afghan commanders when he backed off from an Afghan embrace. According to Robert Moore, Franks inflated enemy casualties at **Tora Bora** to downplay the failure of conventional infantry operations (294). His education includes a B.A. degree in business administration from the University of Texas at Arlington in 1971 and an M.A. degree in public administration from Shippensburg University in Pennsylvania in 1985 (Robert Moore, 2003).

FUNDAMENTALISM. Fundamentalism was a term originally applied to a conservative Protestant movement in the **United States**. It has subsequently been applied to any major religion with tendencies like authoritarianism, messianic spirit, subordination of secular politics to religious beliefs, belief in the infallibility of holy scripture, charismatic leadership, and enforced moralism. During the **Taliban** regime a "religious police" enforced public conformance with the **Taliban Commandments**. The designation "fundamentalist" has been applied to puritanical Islamic revivalist movements such as those promoted by the 14th century Ibn Taymiya and since the 18th century by Muhammad ibn Abd al-Wahhab (1703–1792), Hassan al-Banna (1906–1949), Sayyid Abu'l A'la Mawdudi (1903–1979), Ayatollah

Ruhollah Khomayni (1900-1989), and Mulla **Muhammad Omar** of Afghanistan. *See also* ENJOINING THE GOOD AND FORBIDDING EVIL; ISLAMIST MOVEMENT.

- G -

GAILANI, SAYYID AHMAD (AFANDI SAHIB, GILANI). Descendant of the Muslim Pir Baba Abdul Qadir Gailani (1077–1166) and hereditary head of the Qaderia sufi fraternity. He succeeded to his position upon the death of his older brother, Sayyid Ali, in 1964. Born in 1932 in **Kabul**, the son of Sayyid Hasan Gailani, he was educated at Abu Hanifa College and the Faculty of Theology at Kabul University. He left Afghanistan after the **Saur Revolt** and founded the National Islamic Front (NIFA—**Mahaz-i Milli-yi Islami-yi Afghanistan**) in Peshawar. His movement was part of the seven-member alliance which in 1989 formed the "Afghan Interim Government." It is a liberal, nationalist, Islamic party and, according to its manifesto, advocates the protection of the national sovereignty and territorial integrity of Afghanistan as well as the establishment of an interim government that would draft a national and Islamic constitution with the separation of executive, legislative, and judicial powers. It demands an elected and free government, would guarantee such fundamental rights as free speech, freedom of movement, the protection of private property, and social justice, including medical care and education for all Afghans. NIFA denied the legitimacy of Professor **Burhanuddin Rabbani**'s tenure as president and called for the convening of a **Loya Jirga** to prepare for elections of a broad-based democratic government.

GANDOMAK (34-18' N, 70-2' E). A village on the Gandomak stream, a tributary of the Surkhab, about 29 miles southwest of **Jalalabad**. The area was the scene of a number of battles between British and Afghan forces, including the massacre of the last remnants of the British army in 1842. It was also the scene of a treaty that Major **Louis Cavagnari** and **Amir Yaqub Khan** concluded and signed on May 26, 1879. *See* GANDOMAK, TREATY OF.

GANDOMAK, TREATY OF. A treaty concluded between the British government and **Amir Yaqub Khan**, signed by the amir and Major

Plate 1. Amir Yaqub Signs Treaty of Gandomak

Louis Cavagnari on May 26, 1879, and ratified by Lord Lytton, viceroy of India on May 30, 1879.

The treaty was to establish "eternal peace and friendship" between the two countries upon conclusion of the **second Anglo-Afghan war** (Article 1). It provided amnesty for Afghan collaborators with the British occupation forces (Article 2) and obligated the amir to "conduct his relations with Foreign States, in accordance with the advice and wishes of the British Government." In exchange, Britain would support the amir "against any foreign aggression with money, arms, or troops" (Article 3). A British representative was to be stationed at Kabul "with a suitable escort in a place of residence appropriate to his rank and dignity," and an Afghan agent was to be at the court of the viceroy of India (Article 4). A separate commercial agreement was to be signed (Article 7), and a telegraph line from Kurram to Kabul was to be constructed (Article 8). The **Khaibar** and Michni Passes were to be controlled by Britain (Article 9), **Kandahar** and **Jalalabad** were to be "restored" to the **amir** with the exception of Kurram, Pishin, and Sibi, which were to be under British control but were not "considered as permanently severed from the limits of the Afghan kingdom." Afghan historians consider the treaty a sellout to Britain and a treasonable act by Amir Yaqub Khan.

GARDEZ (33-37'N, 69-7'E). Gardez is a town with about 20,000 inhabitants and a district in **Paktia** Province, located at an altitude of 7,620 feet. The town is inhabited largely by **Ghilzai Pashtuns** and some **Dari**-speakers. Most of the surrounding villages have been destroyed during the Afghan civil war. Gardez is a strategically important town because it controls the route north over the Altamur Pass (9,600 feet) to **Kabul**. It is an ancient town, with a strong citadel and fortress, which for a short time was the seat of the Kushanid rulers of Kabul. It was a center of Buddhist culture and, in the early Islamic period, a base of the Kharijite (*Khawarij*—The Seceders) sect of Islam. After the fall of the **Taliban** regime, American forces continued to be involved in fighting with purported Taliban/**Al-Qaeda** forces in the Gardez area.

GENEVA ACCORDS. The result of "proximity" talks between Afghanistan and **Pakistan** in Geneva, Switzerland, initiated on June 16, 1982, by **Diego Cordovez** under the auspices of the **United Nations** and concluded on April 14, 1988. The accords consisted of four documents and an annex: three between the Republic of Afghanistan and the Islamic Republic of Pakistan; one between the **Soviet Union** and the **United States**, promising to "refrain from any form of interference and intervention"; and an annex with a memorandum of understanding, assisting the United Nations in the implementation of the agreements. The United States and the Soviet Union were to be the guarantors of the accords. The talks aimed at ending the "external interference" in the war in Afghanistan with a view toward establishing peace. The accords resulted in the withdrawal of Soviet troops in mid-February 1989, but failed to end foreign interference or to bring the warring parties closer to peace. One reason for the failure was that the **mujahedin** were not a party to the accords, another was that Washington, and virtually everyone else, expected the Marxist government to disintegrate promptly. When the Soviets departed, they left a considerable amount of war materiel and promised to supply more under the Treaty of Friendship of December 1978 (*See* APPENDIX 2). The United States was obligated to cease military support of the mujahedin. The result was a haggling over "symmetry" and "negative symmetry" of arms supplies, not part of the formal agreements. Eventually, the Soviets and the United States informally agreed on "positive symmetry," that is to say, they reserved themselves the right to send arms in response to shipments by the other. The result was that both powers continued to support their "clients," and Pakistan continued to permit the passage of weapons through its territory. The war continued and the superpower guarantees of noninterference in the internal affairs of Afghanistan were ignored.

GEOGRAPHY. Afghanistan is a mountainous, land-locked state of about 245,000 square miles, which is approximately the area of Texas, and has a population of about 15.5 million in the 1970s (in 1991 estimated between 18 and 22 million).

The **climate** in Afghanistan varies in accordance with the particular geographic zone: subarctic conditions in the northeast and **Hindu Kush** mountains (with peaks at 14,000 to 17,000 feet), a semiarid steppe climate in low-lying areas, and mild, moist weather in the southeast bordering Pakistan. The estimated annual rainfall is between 11 and 15 inches with great variations—more on the southeastern slopes of mountains exposed to the monsoon rains and much less in the southwestern deserts.

About 83 percent of the *Wakhan-Pamir* area lies at an altitude above 10,000 feet and another 17 percent at an altitude of between 6,000 and 10,000 feet. Therefore, snow covers the mountains and most passes are seasonally closed. The yak and Bactrian **camel** are utilized in the transportation of men and goods.

A similar climate exists in the *Central Mountains,* including most of central and eastern **Hazarajat** and the Hindu Kush ranges, extending from the **Shibar Pass** through the **Koh-i Baba** in the west, which is crossed by the **Salang** Tunnel at an altitude of about 11,000 feet. A limited amount of agriculture exists in the valleys, and nomads seasonally graze their livestock in the foothills.

The *Eastern Mountains* include four major regions: **Kabul, Kohistan/Panjshir,** the Ghorband, and **Nuristan,** the latter being the most inaccessible. Snow exists at altitudes between 10,000 and 12,000 feet. Temperatures reach lows of one degree Fahrenheit, and winter lasts from December till March. Summer temperatures depend on altitude. In the southwest, stony deserts extend to the Iranian border, and the Registan, "Land of Sand," extends south of the **Helmand** River and eastward as far as Shorawak, forming a natural boundary with Pakistan. On the edges of the Registan the desert gradually changes into a hilly landscape of sand hills, thickly sprinkled with bushes and vegetation and grass after rains. **Baluch** and **Brahui** nomads seasonally graze their flock in this area. The major agricultural areas are confined to the valleys watered by the **Amu Daria** and the northern plains, the **Hari Rud/Murghab** system in the northwest, the Helmand/Arghandab system, and the Kabul River system. The melting snow feeds the dry riverbeds in spring and provides much of the water for irrigation (for specific rivers, see independent entries). About 12 percent of the land is arable, 46 percent meadows and pastures, 3 percent is forest and woodland, and 39 percent is desert and mountains.

The mountains, deserts, and the climate have been important factors in providing protection from foreign occupation. While it has been relatively easy to occupy the towns in the periphery, the terrain has favored guerrilla activity, which threatened lines of communications and facilitated the harassment of towns. Lack of potable water, endemic diseases, and extremes in temperature, both diurnal and seasonal, have exacted their toll on invaders. A well-equipped, loyal **Afghan Army** has been able to cope with these problems since the days of Amir **Abdul Rahman**. Once the new Afghan National

Army (ANA) has reached its projected strength of 70,000, Afghanistan should no longer require the support of foreign troops.

GERMAN-AFGHAN RELATIONS. German-Afghan relations date from the time of World War I when the **Hentig-Niedermayer Expedition** in August 1915 first established official contact with an Afghan ruler (the claim by one Afghan writer that a secret German mission was sent to the court of Amir **Shir Ali** cannot be substantiated on the basis of British or German archival sources). The first German known to reside in **Kabul** was Gottlieb Fleischer, an employee of Krupp Steelworks of Essen, Germany, who was contracted by Amir **Abdul Rahman** in 1898 to start manufacture of ammunitions and arms in the newly constructed factory (*mashin- khana*) at Kabul (he was killed in November 1904 near the border while traveling to India). Afghanistan existed in self-imposed isolation and the British-Indian government refused to permit passage to Afghanistan to other than their own nationals. It was not until World War I that Germans again appeared in Kabul. A number of Austrian and German prisoners of war, held in Russian Central Asia, escaped and made their way to Kabul, where they were "interned" but enjoyed freedom of movement and contributed their skills to various public works projects.

The first official contact was the Hentig-Niedermayer mission that included also Turkish and Indian members and was charged with establishing diplomatic relations between the Central Powers and Afghanistan. The Germans hoped that Amir **Habibullah** would heed the caliph's call to holy war and, together with the **Pashtun** Frontier tribes, attack India. The mission caused considerable anxiety in India, but although Amir Habibullah wanted to rid himself of British control, he was not to be drawn into a conflict whose outcome seemed at best dubious (*see* FOREIGN RELATIONS). Nevertheless, the mission was not a complete failure, as it forced **Britain** to maintain troops on its northwest frontier which could have been used in the European theater of war. Habibullah appeared to be willing to act but demanded assistance in funds and arms that only a victorious Germany could have provided. When it became apparent that no such victory was in sight, he informed Britain that he would remain neutral in the war in exchange for a financial reward and British recognition of Afghanistan's independence.

Germany rendered Afghanistan a potentially important service by insisting on **Russian** recognition of Afghan independence in Article VII of the Treaty of Brest-Litovsk (March 3, 1918), which ended Russian participation in World War I. German influence became solidly established during the reign of King **Amanullah** (r. 1919–1929). The "Reformer King" won the independence of his country in a short, undeclared war (*see* THIRD ANGLO-AFGHAN WAR) and quickly established relations with the major powers of the world.

In 1923 **Fritz Grobba**, the German minister plenipotentiary, joined the diplomatic representatives of the Soviet Union, Persia, Britain, Turkey, and Italy in Kabul, and it was soon clear that there existed a community of interest between Germany and Afghanistan. King Amanullah needed Western expertise for his modernization projects and felt that nationals from states, other than his powerful neighbors, should be engaged. The **United States** was reluctant to move into an area that it considered within the British sphere of influence; Italy was willing to assist, but the execution of an Italian who killed an Afghan policeman soured relations between the two countries. France was seen as a colonial power that had acquired large portions of the Ottoman Empire, whose ruling sultan/caliph Afghans recognized as the spiritual head of the Islamic world. Germany had been an ally of the Ottomans and offered Afghanistan industrial hardware and skilled technicians at competitive rates. A consortium of German enterprises formed the Deutsch-Afghanische Company (DACOM), which established an office in Kabul. In 1923 King Amanullah founded the German-language high school, Amani (called **Najat** under **Muhammad Nadir Shah**), in addition to French- and English-language secondary schools, and German influence was growing. By 1926 the German colony was second only to the Russians and soon became the largest of all groups.

Relations developed to the extent that major incidents that might have had a serious impact on German-Afghan relations were amicably resolved. In November 1926 a German national killed an Afghan nomad, and in June 1933 an Afghan student, and supporter of the deposed King Amanullah, shot Sardar Muhammad Aziz, a half-brother of Nadir Shah and his minister at Berlin. In September 1933, Muhammad Azim, a teacher at the German high school, wanted to provoke an international incident by shooting the British minister at Kabul (he killed an Englishman, an Afghan, and an Indian employee instead). The last two incidents were seen as the manifestation of a power struggle between the followers of King Amanullah and the new ruling family, and there existed some worries in Kabul that Germany was supporting the ex-king. These incidents had no lasting effect on German-Afghan relations.

In October 1936 the two countries agreed in a "confidential protocol" on the delivery of 15 million marks of war materiel on credit to be repaid in half with Afghan products. By that time Germany had become an important economic and political factor in Kabul, and the way seemed clear for even closer cooperation. In 1937 Lufthansa Airlines established regular service from Berlin to Kabul with the intention of eventually extending service to China. And in summer 1939, shortly before the outbreak of World War II, a German commercial delegation arrived in Kabul to expand German-Afghan trade; but the political situation precluded any desire of the Kabul government to tie itself even closer to Nazi Germany. German annexation of Austria in March 1938 and the annexation of Czechoslovakia a year later, and above all the conclusion of a nonaggression pact between Germany and the **Soviet Union** in August 1939, made it appear likely that Europe would be engulfed in war. Germany could no longer be a "third force" in Afghanistan's attempt to balance the influences of her powerful neighbors.

On the outbreak of World War II, **Zahir Shah** proclaimed Afghanistan's neutrality and was determined to stay out of the war. For Germany, Afghanistan's strategic location gained a priority over commercial considerations. The German foreign ministry and its political counterpart, the Aussenpolitische Amt, toyed with the idea of supporting a pro-Amanullah coup to establish a friendly government in Kabul. It sent Peter Kleist, a German diplomat, and Ghulam Siddiq Charkhi, a former Afghan ambassador and supporter of King Amanullah, to Moscow to query Vyacheslav Molotov, the Soviet foreign minister, as to whether the Soviets would support such a move. The Soviets were noncommittal, and nothing came of the project. When Germany invaded the Soviet Union in June 1941, Afghanistan's neighbors were allied for the second time since the **Anglo-Russian Convention** of 1907, and they were soon to take a common stand in Kabul: in separate diplomatic notes of October 9 and 11, 1941, the Soviet Union and Britain demanded the evacuation of all Axis nationals from Afghanistan. Prime Minister Muhammad Hashim was forced to comply, even though the Afghan government considered it an infringement of its sovereign rights. A **Loya Jirga**, national council, convened on November 5 and 6 and approved the decision after the Axis nationals had left for India and traveled under a promise of free passage to a neutral country. Axis diplomats were permitted to stay, and their contacts with Pashtun tribes on the Indian side of the border did not achieve any tangible results. In spite of sympathies for the enemy of Afghanistan's traditional enemies, there was no question of armed cooperation with Germany.

After its defeat in World War II, the German "phoenix" rose from its ashes again, and soon German expertise again found a ready demand in Kabul. Although Germany was unable for a while to deliver industrial products, her nationals would again be a major factor in Afghanistan's development projects. A dam and hydroelectric power station at Sarobi became one of the first major German projects after the war. American funds and German contractors built the new campus of **Kabul University**. German teachers served on the faculties of science and economics of Kabul University, and by the 1970s, German economic aid ranked third after Soviet and American assistance.

Najat School became a model institution, rivaling the French-supported Istiqlal Lycée, and the English-language schools in Kabul. The Deutsche Entwicklungsdienst (German Development Service), a volunteer organization, brought Germans with attractive skills to Afghanistan. The Goethe Institute for the promotion of German language and culture was opened in Kabul, and a consortium of German universities offered Afghans opportunities to study in Germany. East Germany, not recognized by the Afghans, eventually also appeared on the scene, vying with its Western "brothers" to win friends and influence people. West German influence lasted long after the Soviet intervention in Afghanistan, although East Germans gradually replaced Germans from the West. Because of Germany's long and fruitful association with Afghanistan, its nationals have enjoyed a good reputation in Kabul and may well continue to have an important cultural and economic role in Afghanistan. In July 1996, Norbert Holl, a German, replaced Mahmud Mestiri as special **United Nations** envoy to Afghanistan, to continue the futile task of bringing peace to Afghanistan.

After the fall of the **Taliban** government, Germany agreed to provide troops for the UN peacekeeping force, and its sponsorship of the **Bonn Agreement** was an important factor in establishing a new government for Afghanistan. On February 10, 2003, Germany and the Netherlands assumed command of the **International Security Force for Afghanistan** (ISFA) in Kabul. When NATO took over the peacekeeping task from ISFA, the first commander of NATO forces was the German Lieutenant-General **Götz Gliemeroth.**

GHAUSUDDIN KHAN, GENERAL. Commander of Afghan forces during the **Panjdeh Incident** in March 1885. He confronted Colonel Alikhanov, commander of the **Russian** forces, but was defeated by the superior power of the Russians. A British officer called him "a very superior Afghan. . . . He selected his position at Ak Teppe with a great deal of judgement. He . . . has shown much tact in his dealings with the Sarikhs [a Turkoman tribe], among whom he is as popular as an Afghan [**Pashtun**] can be." He is buried in Caliph Ali's Mausoleum in **Mazar-i Sharif.**

GHAZI. Originally the designation for Arab beduin raiders who would strike from their desert refuge, carrying raids (*ghazw*) for booty into enemy territory. (The European term *razzia* for a predatory raid or police raid is a corruption of *ghazw*.) After the advent of Islam, a ghazi was a holy warrior fighting against a non-Muslim enemy, synonymous with the term mujahed (pl. **mujahedin**) used by the Afghan resistance in the 1980s. During the Anglo-Afghan wars ghazis were irregular fighters who took vows to die in battle against the unbelievers and staged suicidal attacks against superior forces, for Paradise was assured to the martyr. They were often poorly armed, but their reckless bravery made them a dangerous enemy. A British military historian said:

> A true ghazi counts no odds too great to face, no danger too menacing to be braved; the certainty of death only adds to his exaltation. . . . If every Afghan were a ghazi . . . our defenses would have been carried, and enormous slaughter would have followed on both sides. (Hensman, 333–34)

The term became a title given to a victorious commander. **Mahmud of Ghazni, King Amanullah, Habibullah Kalakani, Muhammad Nadir Shah,** and others claimed this title.

GHAZNI (33-33' N, 68-26' E). The name of a province, population 646,000 (according to some estimates as high as 780,000), and a town in eastern Afghanistan. The town had about 32,000 inhabitants in 1978 (now estimated at 74,000) and is located at an elevation of some 7,000 feet on the road from **Kabul** to **Kandahar,** about 80 miles southeast of Kabul. The old town on the left bank of the river is walled and guarded by a citadel that was garrisoned by Afghan army units. Ghazni derives its fame from the fact that it was the capital of the Ghaznavid dynasty (977–1186). It is strategically located and was the scene of severe fighting between Afghan and British forces during the first two Afghan wars. A British garrison stationed in the town during the **first Anglo-Afghan war** was wiped out in December 1841. The population of the town is largely **Tajik** with some **Ghilzais, Durranis, Hazaras,** and a few Hindu shopkeepers.

GHAZNI, CAPTURE OF. In July 1839, during the first British invasion of Afghanistan, **Sir John Keane** marched his army from **Kandahar** against **Ghazni**, which he thought to be only weakly fortified. Having left his siege guns at Kandahar, he decided to take the town in a surprise attack by blowing up the Kabul Gate. A renegade Afghan had furnished the information that all gates had been bricked up, except for the Kabul Gate, which had been kept open in the expectation of reinforcements from Kabul. In the early hours of July 23, an explosion party, headed by three British officers, three sergeants, and 18 sappers, succeeded in carrying 300 pounds of gunpowder in 12 sandbags and, having positioned their artillery on both sides of the road leading to the Kabul Gate, successfully demolished it. An assault column of four European regiments commanded by General **Robert Sale** made good their entry into the city. The British found the citadel deserted by the Afghan commander Afzal Khan and took possession of it. Afghan losses were estimated at 600 killed, and the British forces counted 18 dead and 173 wounded (Heathcote, 41–42). On July 30 the British army moved against Kabul, leaving a garrison in command of the citadel. But Afghan forces returned and with the help of the inhabitants gained access to the town. The 27th Bengal Native Infantry was forced to retire to the citadel, where they held out until March 6, 1842, when lack of snow deprived them of their water supply. They then quartered themselves in town, where they were eventually forced to surrender. Most were killed or sold into slavery, but in September 1842 Major General **William Nott** advanced and reoccupied the town, liberating 327 sepoys (Indian soldiers) who had survived. General Nott gave orders to destroy the citadel to deprive Afghans of the stronghold.

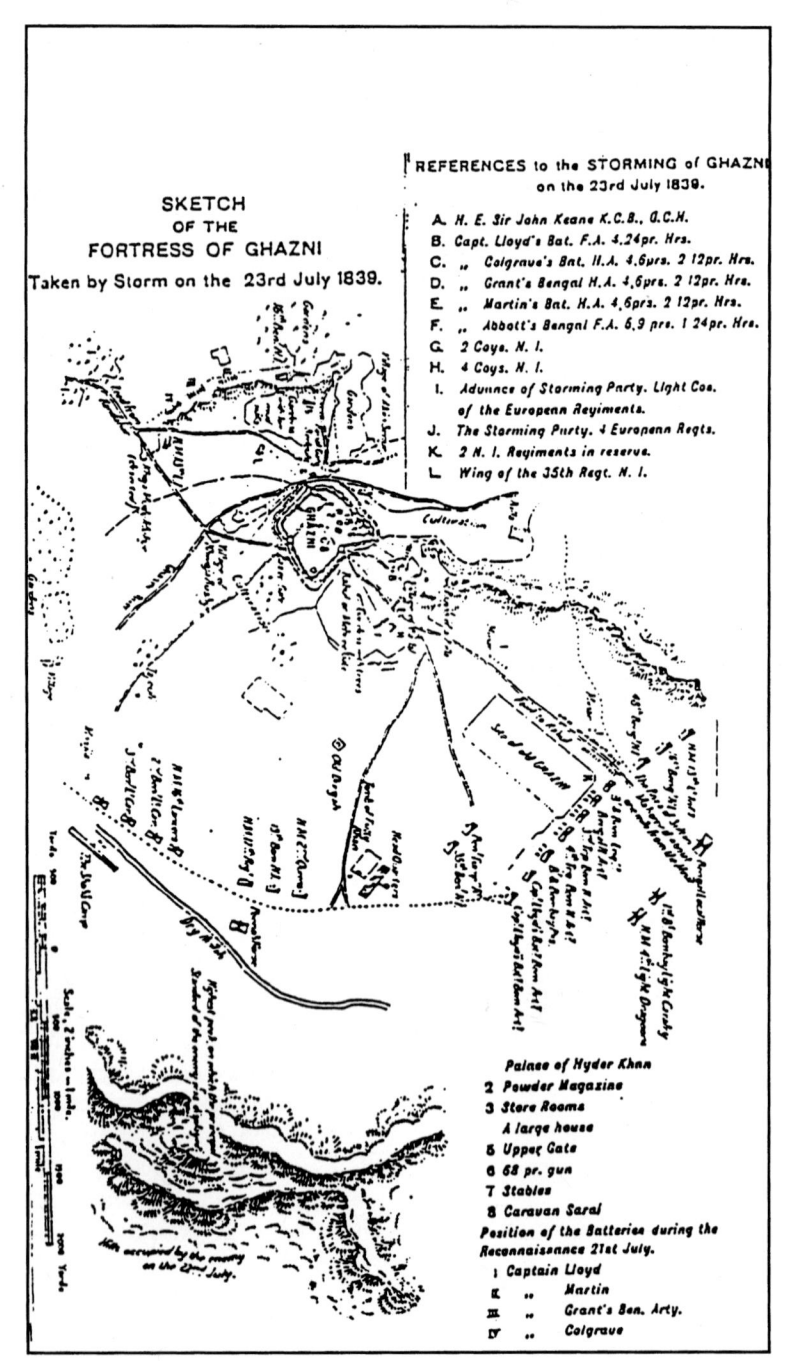

Plan 5. Fortress of Ghazni (IOL)

GHAZNIGAK, BATTLE OF. A town near Tashkurghan where a battle was fought on September 27, 1888, between the forces of Amir **Abdul Rahman**, headed by General Ghulam Haidar and Sardar Abdullah, against Ishaq Khan, a cousin of the **amir** and his governor of Afghan Turkestan. It was a bloody battle, lasting from early morning to late at night. Some of the amir's forces defected and

> galloped toward the hill where Mahomed Ishak was seated, to submit themselves to him. He, thinking . . . [they were] to take him prisoner, and that his army was defeated, fled away. Ishaq Khan fled to Russian Turkestan where he died shortly thereafter. (AR, 269)

GHILZAI. A major **Pashtu**-speaking tribe inhabiting an area roughly bounded by Kalat-i-Ghilzai in the south, the Gul Kuh range in the west, the Sulaiman range in the east, and the **Kabul** River on the north. The Ghilzai call themselves Ghaljai (pl. Ghalji) and count themselves the descendants of Ghalzoe, son of Shah Husain, said to have been a **Tajik** or Turk, and of Bibi Mato, who descended from Shaikh Baitan (the second son of Qais—progenitor of the Afghan nationality). The origin of the name Ghilzai comes from either *Ghal Zoe* (thief's son), *Khilji*, the Turkic word for swordsman, or the name of Khilji Turks who came into the area in the 10th century. From Ghalzoe the tribe divided into the Turan and Burhan Ibrahim branches.

The Sulaiman Khel are the most important of all, and the Ali Khel are the most important of the Burhan. In the 19th century they were said to number about 100,000 families, with 30,000 to 50,000 fighters. They were largely nomadic and called Powindas in India where they often traveled, making a living as merchant nomads.

The Hotaki Ghilzais achieved their fame in Afghan history as the liberators of **Kandahar** from **Safavid** control and as the leading tribe in the invasion of Iran and the destruction of the Persian Empire in 1722. **Mir Wais**, a descendant of Malakhi, a leading chief at **Kandahar**, was taken by the Safavid governor to Isfahan, but was later permitted to return. He raised a revolt against the Kandahar governor and ruled over the province for some years (1709–1715). His son Mahmud raised an army and invaded Persia, defeating the Safavid armies at the battle of **Gulnabad** in 1722. However, Mahmud was unable to hold on to his conquest. **Nadir Khan, Afshar**, founder of the short-lived Afsharite dynasty, reunited the Persian Empire and in turn invaded Afghan lands. After the death of Nadir Shah, the Ghilzai were weakened to such an extent that they could not prevent the emergence of the **Durrani** dynasty. The Ghilzai fought the British when they invaded Afghanistan and subsequently became the major rivals of the Durranis. They revolted repeatedly against Muhammadzai rule and were suppressed only with difficulty in 1801, 1883, 1886, and 1937. Urban Ghilzai have since intermarried with Muhammadzai. The Ghilzai were well represented in the Marxist leadership (**Nur Muhammad Taraki, Najibullah, Hafizullah Amin, Watanjar,** Layeq, Rafi'i, and many others) but also among the resistance (**Gulbuddin Hekmatyar** and **Abdul Rasul Sayyaf**), which prompted one expert to remark that for the first time power has passed from the Durrani to the Ghilzai. *See also* ABDUL KARIM.

GHOR (GHUR) (34-0'N, 65-0'E). A west-central province of Afghanistan with an area of 13,808 square miles and a population of about 341,000 (recent estimates are as high as 418,000) The capital of the province is the town of Chaghcharan with a population of about 106,000. The province is mountainous with some wheat and barley cultivation in the upper regions of the **Farah**, Hari Rud, and Murghab Valleys. Major mountain ranges include the Firuzkoh (Safidkoh), Siyahkoh, and Band-i Bayan. The population is primarily of Taimani (Chahar Aimaq) origin.

GILANI. *See* **GAILANI.**

GLIEMEROTH, LIEUTENANT-GENERAL GÖTZ. Commander of **NATO/ISAF** forces in Afghanistan. He took command on August 11, 2003, from Lieutenant-General Van Heyst, who headed the **International Security Force for Afghanistan** (ISAF) from February 10 till August 2003. It marked the **NATO** takeover of ISAF, bringing into Afghanistan a coalition of 31 countries. NATO is to operate under the ISFA banner and under an unchanged **United Nations** mandate. Major functions of the new command include building up and training Afghan security forces, such as the police force, the border police, and to a certain extent also the Afghan national army. Gliemeroth was born on October 21, 1943, in Göttingen, Germany. General Gliemeroth was commander of Joint Headquarters Center in Heidelberg, Germany, from March 21, 2001, until his move to **Kabul.**

GORTCHAKOFF, ALEXANDR MIKHAILOVICH K. *See* **GRANVILLE-GORTCHAKOFF AGREEMENT.**

GRANVILLE-GORTCHAKOFF AGREEMENT. An Anglo-Russian agreement based on assurances given in 1868–1869 and confirmed several times later in an exchange of letters between the foreign ministers, Lord George L. Granville and Prince Alexandr Mikhailovich K. Gortchakoff, which stipulated "**Badakhshan** with its dependent district of Wakhan from Sar-i-Kul on the east to the junction of the Kokcha River with the Oxus (or Panja) forming the northern boundary of this Afghan Province throughout its entire length." Further west, however, the border was not clearly defined, which eventually enabled **Russia** to annex **Panjdeh**. Russia agreed that Afghanistan was outside its sphere of influence and, except for the territorial changes of Shignan and Roshan and the Panjdeh oasis, the Afghan border has remained as it is today. The agreement is also known as the **Clarendon-Gortchakoff Agreement**.

GREAT BRITAIN. Great Britain shares with Afghanistan three centuries of relations which were, intermittently, hostile until the latter part of the 20th century (*see* ANGLO-AFGHAN RELATIONS). Until the middle of the 19th century, a governor general represented the **British East India Company**, followed after 1858 by a **viceroy** who headed the Indian government, subject to consultation with the India Office in London. In the early period communication was difficult, and the "man on the spot" could make history by provoking a conflict which led to war and the conquest of new territory. The approval of the London government could not be gotten in an emergency. Once a conflict had started, the prestige of the empire was at stake and London had to acquiesce after the fact. A case in point was **"Auckland's Folly"** that led to the disastrous **first Anglo-Afghan war**. Lionized at the beginning of the war, Auckland was forced to resign in disgrace.

The viceroy's sphere of control extended over the entire subcontinent and in the west included Egypt and the African coast where it rivaled the influence of the London government. British India was a rich continent, and it had to pay for its own wars and come to the rescue of London during the two European wars. For generations of Englishmen, India was the land of great opportunity. When, finally, Britain was forced to leave India, it was the end of a great empire. There was no longer a reason to hold on to British colonies and protectorates east of Suez because their acquisition was for the defense of India.

GREAT GAME. A term attributed to Rudyard Kipling describing the competition between **Russia** and **Great Britain** in the conquest of the territories lying between their colonial possessions. Russia sought access to the warm-water ports of the Persian Gulf, if not to the riches of India, and Britain wanted to prevent it. Afghanistan was a major player in this, desired by both as an ally. Afghan rulers realized that Russia needed to take Afghanistan to realize its objectives and therefore concluded a cautious alliance with Britain. Twice, during the 19th century, British armies invaded Afghanistan for the purpose of finding a "scientific frontier" on the crests of the **Hindu Kush** range or the **Amu Daria** (Oxus) River. When direct control failed, Britain resigned itself to concluding an alliance with the Afghan ruler and to support him against the eventuality of Russian aggression. When Britain left India in 1947, the "Great Game" seemed to be over, because the **United States** was unwilling to guarantee Afghanistan's territorial integrity from Soviet aggression. Therefore, the Soviet Union seemed to have won the game when, in 1978, it intervened militarily in support of the Marxist government of Afghanistan. As during previous invasions, the Afghan people eventually prevailed.

GRENADIER. Originally a soldier employed to throw handgrenades and subsequently the tallest and finest member of the elite company of every infantry battalion. The Grenadier Guards were the first regiment of foot guards in the British Household Brigade of Guards and were considered the finest corps in the army. It comprised 2,697 officers and men, was divided into three battalions, and was commanded by men of nobility, or distinguished landed gentry. Grenadiers as auxiliaries were employed during sieges for special tasks. British grenadiers served in the Anglo-Afghan wars, including the fateful **Battle of Maiwand.**

GRIFFIN, SIR LEPEL (1838–1908). Chief political officer at **Kabul** during the **second Anglo-Afghan war** whose negotiations with Sardar **Abdul Rahman** led to the recognition of the latter as **amir** of Afghanistan. At the death of Amir **Shir Ali** and the abdication of **Yaqub Khan**, Abdul Rahman entered Afghanistan with the intention of driving the British from his country.

Realizing its untenable position, the British government recognized Abdul Rahman to ensure an orderly withdrawal of its army to India. He supported education in India and the establishment of Punjab University. In 1885 he was one of the founders of the *Asian Quarterly Review.*

GROMOV, LIEUTENANT GENERAL BORIS V. Commander of the 40th Army, comprising the "**Limited Contingent of Soviet Forces in Afghanistan**," who spent three tours in Afghanistan. The 45-year-old general led a combined **Soviet/Afghan** force of some 10,000 troops from **Gardez** against **Khost**, temporarily lifting the siege of this strategic town in January 1988. It was the last major Soviet operation facing considerable **mujahedin** opposition and the type of action not originally considered his task. Gromov stated that Soviet forces were intended to establish garrisons, stabilize the situation, and refrain from significant combat operations, leaving **counterinsurgency** to the Afghan government forces (McMichael, 10). Eventually, only about 30 to 35 percent of Soviet forces were devoted to security and defense of fixed sites, and it was inevitable that defense also required counterinsurgency operations. McMichael quotes Gromov as saying, "The war in Afghanistan demonstrated a large rupture between theory and practice." But he felt it was unavoidable. Gromov was assigned the task of evacuating the last contingent of 450 armored vehicles and about 1,400 Soviet troops from Afghanistan. On February 14, 1989, he was the last Soviet soldier to cross the "Friendship Bridge" into Soviet territory. He announced to the assembled reporters, "We have fulfilled our international duty to the end" (O'Ballance, 196). He became minister of the interior in 1990 and commander of all Russian ground troops in 1992.

GUERRILLA WARFARE. Military operations conducted by combatants, mainly of the hit-and-run type, against a superior enemy. It was the typical warfare of the **ghazis** and **mujahedin** against British and **Soviet** forces. A temporary concentration of fighters go on the offensive and quickly disperse before countermeasures can be taken. **Counterinsurgency** measures, therefore, include the destruction of entire villages, crops, fruit trees, livestock, channels of irrigation (karez), etc., to deprive the guerrillas of their support. Although the Afghan ghazis, or mujahedin, fought under the banner of Islam, tribalism and nationalism, as well as sectarian allegiance, may in fact have been the dominant ideology. Unlike resistance movements in other parts of the world, the Afghans generally lacked a unified command. This was seen as a weakness by some, but turned out to be a factor of strength during the war; only when the war was won did the fragmentation of power contribute to an ongoing civil war for political control of the country. *See also* **AFGHANS, METHODS OF FIGHTING.**

GUL, MAJOR-GENERAL HAMID. Director general of **Inter-Services Intelligence** (ISI), 1987–1989, and ardent supporter of the **mujahedin** in their war against the communist regime. A **Pakistani Islamist** and supporter of radical causes, he strongly supported **Gulbuddin Hekmatyar** in preference to other mujahedin groups. A close aid to Pakistan President Zia ul-Haq, he tried to reconcile the rift between **Burhanuddin Rabbani** and Hekmatyar and, when this failed, he gave his support to the **Taliban**. Some called him the "Spiritual Father" of the Taliban movement.

He was responsible for urging the disastrous attack on **Jalalabad**, and blamed for the system of storing ammunition at the Ojhiri warehouse, resulting in the disastrous **Ojhiri Camp explosion.** He was forced into retirement in 1992. After the American intervention in Afghanistan, he became a major critic of the **United States**. In an interview he called for an alliance of communist and **Islamist** forces against the "global imperialist coalition." He acted as an adviser of the Islamist Mutaheda Majlis-i Amal (MMA) party and unsuccessfully ran for election on an Islamist ticket.

GULNABAD, BATTLE OF. An important victory of Afghan forces under Mahmud, son of the **Ghilzai** chief **Mir Wais**, which marked the end of the **Safavid** Empire of Iran. On March 8, 1722, Mahmud met and decisively defeated a superior Iranian army and then besieged Isfahan for six months before taking the capital of the empire. The Ghilzais proved to be better soldiers than empire-builders; they were forced to yield power to **Nadir Shah Afshar** and withdrew to their Afghan homeland, where they were superseded by the **Durranis** as the dominant tribe.

GUNSHIPS, AC-130. The AC-130 gunships went first into action in Afghanistan on October 16, 2001, when American aerial superiority was assured. The slow, low-flying, propeller-driven aircraft is a veritable fortress. It delivers a barrage of explosive fire against ground targets. Once a target is found the aircraft can use satellite data and its laser-target designation to concentrate fire on the target. Its fire power is such that it can devastate an area the size of a football field. The gunship is equipped with the following: a "Black Crow" radio signal sensor; a laser-target designator for painting targets so that laser-guided missiles can seek the reflected energy; twin 20mm vulcan cannons which fire 6,600 rounds per minute; 7.62mm "miniguns" which fire 3,000 rounds per minute; a 40mm Bofors cannon which can fire 100 rounds per minute; a Beacon-tracking radar; and two 105 howitzers. But the question remains: Was this type of sophisticated military technology cost-effective when there existed a minimum of major targets?

- H -

HABIBULLAH, AMIR (HABIB ALLAH, r. 1901–1919). **Amir** of Afghanistan who kept his state neutral in World War I, but wanted to end **Britain**'s quasi protectorate over his country. He was born in Samarkand on April 21, 1871, the son of Amir **Abdul Rahman** and an **Uzbek** lady from **Badakhshan**. He succeeded to the throne on October 3, 1901, and assumed the title *Seraj al-Millat wa'd-Din* (torch of the nation and religion). He increased the pay of the army, permitted exiles to return, including many *sardars* (nobles) and their families, released prisoners, and promised reforms.

The British government was not satisfied with some of the provisions of the agreements concluded with Amir Abdul Rahman, and therefore wanted to force certain changes before it recognized the new amir. London maintained that the agreements were with the *person* of the amir, not the state of Afghanistan, and therefore had to be renegotiated with his successor. In spite of severe pressures, Habibullah did not yield. In December 1904, he finally agreed to meet in **Kabul** with **Louis W. Dane**, foreign secretary of the government of India. The result was a complete victory for Habibullah. Britain was resigned to renew the agreements concluded with Amir Abdul Rahman in the form of a treaty (*see* ANGLO-AFGHAN TREATY OF 1905).

Amir Habibullah showed great interest in Western technology and embarked on a process of modernization. He imported automobiles and built roads, founded Habibia School in 1904, the first modern school in Afghanistan, and brought electricity to Kabul. In

January 1907 Amir Habibullah traveled to India and was cordially received by the viceroy, Lord Minto. A crisis in relations with British India occurred when Habibullah learned that Afghanistan's neighbors had concluded the **Anglo-Russian Convention of 1907**. This agreement divided Afghanistan (and Iran) into spheres of influence, with provisions for "equality of commercial opportunity" in Afghanistan for Russian and British traders and the appointment of commercial agents in Kabul. The amir was invited to ratify the agreement, but he refused and the convention was never implemented.

The outbreak of World War I posed another crisis in **foreign relations**: in spite of warnings not to do so from the viceroy of India, Amir Habibullah received a **German** mission at Kabul. He met with members of the **Hentig-Niedermayer Expedition** and initialed the draft of a secret treaty of friendship and military assistance with Germany to provide for the eventuality of an Allied defeat. Germany could not deliver, and Britain promised a handsome reward for Afghan neutrality; therefore, a realistic appraisal of the situation prompted the Afghan ruler to stay out of the war.

Britain showed itself miserly and, once the crisis was over, wanted to reestablish its exclusive control over Afghanistan. The "war party" at his court felt that the amir had failed to take advantage of a unique opportunity of winning independence from Britain and conspired to depose him. He was assassinated on February 20, 1919, while he was on a hunting trip at Kala Gosh in **Laghman**.

HABIBULLAH KALAKANI, AMIR. A **Tajik** of humble origins who was a leader of the anti reformist reaction that swept King **Amanullah** from power and placed him on the throne. He was known as *Bacha-i-Saqqao* (son of a water carrier), the occupation of his father, Aminullah, a Tajik from the village of Kalakan in the Kohdaman district (north of **Kabul**). With the support of a loose coalition of Kohistani forces, he took advantage of a tribal revolt to capture Kabul and have himself proclaimed amir. Following the custom of Afghan rulers, Habibullah adopted the title "Servant of the Religion of the Messenger of God" (*Khadem-i Din-i Rasulullah*) and set about to consolidate his power. Two factors militated against his royal aspirations: he was of Tajik, rather than the dominant, **Pashtun** ethnic background, and he was known as a brigand, albeit of a Robin Hood nature, as seen from the perspective of his Kohistani brothers.

Habibullah was a natural leader and had a charismatic personality, but his assumption of the throne was challenged from the beginning. A British officer reported from Peshawar that "Bacha-i Saqqao's accession has come as a profound shock to the tribes on both sides of the Durand Line." Even the **Shinwaris**, whose revolt had started the civil war, were not willing to submit to the new king. The fact that Habibullah had found some £750,000 at the conquest of the **Arg** (royal palace) permitted him to pay his troops and win some tribal support.

Forces loyal to King Amanullah were unable to recapture the throne, but **Muhammad Nadir** and his brothers succeeded. Shah Wali Khan, brother of Nadir and brother-in-law of King Amanullah, captured the Arg in October 1929, and Habibullah was forced to surrender. On November 1 Habibullah, his brother Hamidullah, and Sayyid Husain together, with nine leaders of their turbulent regime, were executed.

HAGENBECK, MAJOR GENERAL FRANKLIN L. "BUSTER." Army commander in charge of **Operation Anaconda** against an **al-Qaeda** force in the Takur Ghar range in eastern Afghanistan. General **Tommy Franks** called the operation "an unqualified and absolute success" while others called it "a big mistake." Hagenbeck later said "I view technology as an enabler, and we want more and more of it. But I don't think it is ever going to replace the soldier on the ground." Hagenbeck expected the enemy to flee, but they dug in on the high ground and an operation expected to last some 72 hours continued for 12 days of fierce fighting. Brendan O'Neill discusses the operation in *The Strange Battle of Shah-i Kot*. Born in Morocco of a U.S. Navy family, Hagenbeck is a graduate of the U.S. Military Academy at West Point and was commissioned in 1971 as an infantry officer. He was commanding general of the 10th Mountain Division (Light) at Fort Drum, New York.

HAMID GUL. *See* **GUL, HAMID.**

HAQANI, MAULAWI JALALUDDIN (JALAL AL-DIN HAQQANI). Minister of frontier affairs in the **Taliban** government in 1998 and minister of justice in the **Mujaddidi** government of 1992. He was deputy chief of Hizb-i Islami and joined **Muhammad Yunus Khales** after the break with **Gulbuddin Hekmatyar**'s faction in 1979. Born in 1930, a Jadran (Zadran) from **Paktia** Province, he was educated at a private **madrasa**. He was an important commander who controlled large areas of Urgun in Paktia Province. He and his brothers **Abdul Haq** and **Abdul Qadir** were leaders in the Jalalabad **Shura** that ruled **Nangarhar** Province until the capture of **Jalalabad** by the Taliban when they joined the new rulers. Haqani has since engaged in a guerrilla war against the **United States** forces and the **Hamid Karzai** government.

HAQQANIA, DAR AL-ULUM. Dubbed "University of Jihad," it is a **madrasa** in Akora Khattak, about 35 miles east of Peshawar, **Pakistan**, which trained many of the **Islamist** and **Taliban** leadership. Its graduates supported the war against the communist regime in Afghanistan and, on occasion, schools were closed to assist the Taliban in major campaigns. Some 2,500 students, aged from eight to 30 years, enjoy free tuition and board, and some 600 of the older students are enrolled in mufti (canon law) courses.(A World Bank study shows that the number of "jihadi" schools was greatly exaggerated). Most students are from **Pashtun** areas in Afghanistan and Pakistan, but there is also a sizable international student body. Maulana al-Haq, the principal of the madrasa, is also a head of the Jam'iat-i Ulama Islami, a Pakistani religiopolitical party. Notable alumni include Amir Khan Muttaki, minister of information and culture; Abdul Latif Mansur, minister of agriculture; Maulawi Ahmad Jan, minister of mines and industries; and Mulla Jalaluddin Haqqani, minister of frontier affairs in the former Taliban government. The government of President Pervez Musharraf was not able to force the school to abandon the martial aspect of education.

HARAKAT-I INQILAB-I ISLAMI. *See* **MUHAMMADI, MAULAWI MUHAMMAD NABI.**

HARAKAT-I ISLAMI. *See* **MUHSINI, AYATOLLAH MUHAMMAD ASEF.**

HASHT-NAFARI. A system of recruitment imposed on the frontier tribes by which they were to provide one able-bodied man out of eight (D. *hasht,* eight, nafar, persons). **Amir Abdul Rahman** introduced this system in 1896; similar to previous feudal levies, the notables and chiefs of tribes had to make the selection and provide the enlistee with all his needs. The tribes were willing to perform military service, but wanted to do so only during emergencies; therefore, there were occasional revolts, protesting the hasht-nafari recruitment during peacetime. Discontinued and, reintroduced in 1922, upon the advice of **Jamal Pasha**, the *hasht-nafari* system contributed to the growing opposition to **King Amanullah**.

HAZARAS and **HAZARAJAT**. The Hazarajat, heartland of the Hazara people, comprises **Ghor, Oruzgan, Bamian**, and portions of adjoining provinces. Hazara communities also exist in virtually all the major towns of Afghanistan. At the turn of the 20th century the Hazara were estimated at about 500,000 people, or some 120,000 families but their number has since increased to about 1.5 million. They are not tribally organized, but have been loosely identified under some seven or eight sections.

The Hazaras derive their name from the Persian *hazar,* meaning one thousand, which indicates that they may be the descendants of units of one thousand of the 13th-century Turco-Mongolian invaders who assimilated with local **Tajiks**. They speak a Persian dialect called *Hazaragi*, which also includes a number of eastern Turkic words and a few of Mongol origin. They are largely **Shi'as** of the Twelver (*ithna 'ashariya*), or *imami*, school, which is dominant in Iran, and may have been **Sunnis** until the **Safavids** converted them to **Shi'ism** in the 16th century.

Since the founding of Afghanistan in 1747, the **Sadozai** kings carried expeditions into the Hazarajat. The Besud, Foladi, and Bamian sections of the Hazarajat as well as the Turkman and Shaikh Ali Hazaras of the **Hindu Kush**, were taxpaying subjects of **Zaman Shah** (1773–1793). In 1842 Yar Muhammad, the de facto ruler of **Herat**, carried a campaign into Afghan Turkestan and transported a large number of Hazara families to the lower valley of the Hari Rud. During the reign of **Dost Muhammad** (1826–1848) much of the Hazarajat was under **Kabul** control, and Amir **Shir Ali** (1863–1879) brought additional sections under Afghan rule. In their struggle against Kabul the Jaghori Hazaras collaborated with **Britain** during the **second Anglo-Afghan war,** and in 1886 Hazaras supported the rebellious **Ghilzais** against the government of Amir **Abdul Rahman**. The "Iron Amir" finally subdued them in 1893, after a series of bloody wars (*see* HAZARA WARS).

The Hazarajat rose against the **Khalqi** regime in 1979 and, under the *shura* (Revolutionary Council of the Islamic Union of Afghanistan) of **Sayyid Ali Beheshti**, ruled the Hazara heartland until challenged by newly emerging Islamist movements. In the "battle for Kabul" the **Hizb-i Wahdat**, a coalition of largely Hazara groups, headed by **Abdul Ali Mazari** (killed in March 1995 while in **Taliban** custody), was one of the principal contenders for power. Ayatollah **Muhammad Asef Muhsini**, a **Pashtu**-speaking Hazara from **Kandahar** Province, headed a small independent group called *Harakat-i Islami*, but he resigned in February 2005.

HAZARA WARS. When in July 1880 **Britain** recognized Amir **Abdul Rahman** as "Amir of Kabul and its Dependencies," it was not certain what the "dependencies" would be. Britain had toyed with the idea of severing **Herat** and **Kandahar** from **Kabul** control, and **Russia** coveted Turkestan territory, finally annexing a section of northwestern Afghanistan in 1885 in the **Panjdeh Incident**. Afghanistan's boundaries were not clearly defined, and the "Iron Amir" found it necessary to extend his authority to every corner of his realm lest his powerful neighbors continue their **forward policies**. In a series of wars he eliminated rivals to his power and gained control of Kandahar, Herat, Afghan Turkestan, the Hazarajat, and **Kafiristan** (now Nuristan).

This extraordinary achievement of nation-building proved to be a calamity for the Hazara community. Amir Abdul Rahman stated his reasons for the war:

> The Hazara people had been for centuries past the terror of the rulers of Kabul, even the great Nadir who conquered Afghanistan, India, and Persia being unable to subdue the turbulent Hazaras; the Hazaras were always molesting travelers in the south, north, and western provinces of Afghanistan; they were always ready to join the first foreign aggressor who attacked Afghanistan. (AR, I, 276)

And, indeed, the Hazaras shared the inclination to raiding with other ethnic communities. As a religious minority, they were willing to collaborate with the enemies of the Kabul regime.

Initially, Amir Abdul Rahman embarked on a gradual process of reconquest. After three campaigns in 1881, 1882, and 1883, as well as attempts at peaceful penetration, the Shaikh Ali Hazaras northwest of **Bamian** were the first to be pacified in 1886. Shortly thereafter all Hazara tribes with the exception of those of Pas-i-Koh in **Oruzgan**

Province were forced to pay taxes on land and livestock. In 1890 Abdul Rahman appointed **Sardar Abdul Quddus** governor of Bamian and ordered him to win the submission of the Oruzgan Hazaras. The latter accepted a deal in which they were to retain their internal autonomy and pay no taxes for a number of years. When Abd al-Quddus again entered Hazara territory a year later with a 10,000-man force, he claimed to have met armed resistance and began to disarm Hazara communities and collected taxes from them. Thereupon the Sultan Muhammad Hazaras, headed by Mir Husain Beg, rose in rebellion and defeated the forces of Abd al-Quddus as well as a relief force sent by the amir under Faiz Muhammad. Their success encouraged other Hazara sections to join the general revolt, and the amir realized that the situation required a large-scale campaign to suppress the rebellion.

Amir Abdul Rahman felt that an all-out effort, including psychological warfare, was needed. The **amir** claimed that Iranian publications in the possession of Afghan **Shi'as** had insulted the **Sunni** caliphs as usurpers and urged the Shi'a community to rise against Sunni control. The amir's chief mufti (canon lawyer) issued a **fatwa** (legal opinion) declaring Shi'as infidels and proclaiming holy war on the Hazara. A council of Hazaras countered that instead of obeying a temporal ruler, they relied on their spiritual ruler, "the Master of the sword of Zulfikar" (Hazrat Ali, the Shi'a imam and fourth of the sunni caliphs).

In addition to regular forces, tribal levies were called up with great success as there was considerable promise of booty. Mullas accompanied the troops to keep passions high and incite them to heroic feats. **Pashtuns** flocked to the colors in considerable numbers, and, according to a British observer, "the Ghilzays ... showed more zeal than the **Durranis**." In spite of the holy-war fatwa, levies of Hazaras of the Dai Kundi, Behsud, and Jaghori sections were enlisted, but most of those who survived defected during the war.

In spring 1891 Amir Abdul Rahman ordered a concerted attack by Sardar Abd al-Quddus from Bamian, Shir Muhammad from Kabul, and Brigadier Zabardast from Herat that led to the occupation of Oruzgan. Hazara chiefs were brought to Kabul in an attempt to win their submission. But in spring 1892 the Hazara chiefs Muhammad Azim and Muhammad Husain, supported by their chief *mujtahid* (legal expert) Kazi Asghar, turned against Amir Abdul Rahman. Rebellion rose with new fury, and it was only when a concerted attack from Turkestan, Kabul, **Ghazni**, Herat, and Kandahar was renewed that the Hazara uprising was quelled. It was not until September 1893 that all Hazara sections were subdued. The amir had given the permission that "everybody would be allowed to go and help in the punishment of the rebels," and punishment was indeed severe. Forts were demolished and governors, judges and muftis were appointed in every district. About 16,000 Durrani and Ahmadzai Ghilzai tribesmen were ordered to settle in Oruzgan Province, and large numbers of Hazaras emigrated to Mashhad (Iran), and Quetta (India, now Pakistan) where they are still living today. In accordance with an old tradition, conquest by force (*'anwatan*) permitted the enslavement of prisoners, and thousands of Hazaras were taken to Kabul.

HEKMATYAR, GULBUDDIN. Amir of the Hizb-i Islami-yi Afghanistan (Islamic Party of Afghanistan), one of the seven **mujahedin** groups formed in Peshawar. His party is radical **Islamist** and fights for the establishment of an Islamic republic to be governed according to its interpretation of Islamic law. Born in 1947 in Imam Sahib, **Kunduz**, a **Ghilzai Pashtun**, Hekmatyar studied engineering at **Kabul** University for two years and became involved in campus politics. He became a member of the "Muslim Youth" movement in 1970 and was elected to its executive council (*shura*). He was imprisoned in Dehmazang jail in Kabul, from 1972 to 1973, and, after the Daud coup of 1973, fled to **Pakistan**. In 1975 he became leader of the Hizb-i Islami and began armed attacks from bases in Pakistan with clandestine support from the Zulfikar Ali Bhutto government. Isolated raids developed into modern guerrilla warfare after the **Saur Revolt** of April 1978. The party adopted from the Muslim Brotherhood such features as centralized command structure, secrecy of membership, organization in cells, infiltration of government and social institutions, and the concept of the party as an Islamist "vanguard" in Afghan society.

Being Islamist rather than nationalist, the party enjoyed considerable support from like-minded groups in Pakistan and the Gulf. His party received most of the armed support from the West and Gulf sources, and apparently was able to hoard a considerable amount of weapons, which served him well in the subsequent battle for Kabul. He surprised friends and foes alike when he allied himself with Lieutenant General **Shahnawaz Tanai**, a radical **Khalqi**, in a coup against the Kabul government of Dr. **Najibullah**. After the downfall of the Marxist regime, many of the Khalqi military officers joined

Hekmatyar's forces, as did General **Abdul Rashid Dostum**, a former **Parchami**, who controls large portions of northern Afghanistan. The Hizb-i Islami of Gulbuddin Hekmatyar and the Jam'iat-i Islami of **Burhanuddin Rabbani** were the major protagonists in the war for the conquest of Kabul until a new force, the **Taliban**, expelled Hekmatyar from his headquarters in **Charasia** and portions of Kabul. Hekmatyar fled to Sarobi, where his party had another base. In summer 1996, Hekmatyar made peace (or a temporary alliance?) with Rabbani and became his prime minister in Kabul. Expelled by the **Taliban**, Hekmatyar fled to Iran to return to Afghanistan in spring 2002 to continue his **jihad** against the American forces. He is rumored to be somewhere in the Pashtun tribal area. *See also* ISLAMIST MOVEMENT.

HELICOPTERS, SOVIET. Helicopters were first used in warfare during the **Soviet** intervention in Afghanistan. In 1980 the Afghan **air force** included about seven squadrons of 45–60 Soviet Mi-4s, Mi-8s, Mi-17s, and Mi-24s. This number rose within a year to almost 300. Helicopters were employed primarily for logistical support, reconnaissance, convoy security, evacuation, tactical lift, and fire support. They were utilized for such tasks as mine dispersal and **counterinsurgency** operations, where they proved to be extraordinarily effective and were greatly feared by the **mujahedin**. The Mi-24 Hind and the Mi-8 Hip were the "workhorses" of the rotary-wing force. Helicopters were less effective in ground-support operations in narrow valleys, where their mobility was greatly limited and where they were subject to fire from above for which they were not sufficiently protected. The rotary blades of the Mi-24s, with a span of almost 60 feet, were highly vulnerable to damage. When the mujahedin acquired surface-to-air missiles, their efficiency in providing tactical support was further reduced.

HELICOPTERS, UNITED STATES. Helicopters played an important role in the beginning stages of **Operation Enduring Freedom**. In early October 2001, bases for helicopter raids were established in Pasni on the Arabian Sea coast of **Pakistan**, where C-130 gunships and helicopters ferried **United States** Marines and **Special Forces Teams** into Afghanistan. At Dalbandin, Baluchistan, U.S. commandos and light infantry Rangers were stationed. In Jacobabad, on the road north to Quetta, helicopter equipment was kept and logistics and refueling personnel were stationed. In Termez, Uzbekistan, U.S. light infantry, specialized in mountain warfare, were ready to link up with Afghan militias. Three types of helicopters were employed: the Apache with a two-man crew and a speed of 186 mph, a range of 428 miles, and a ceiling of 10,200 feet. It was equipped with 'Hellfire' anti-armor missiles or anti-aircraft rockets. It was provided with laser/infrared systems to track and attack targets and was used primarily to escort troop transporters. The Black Hawk had a three-man crew, a speed of 170 mph, a range of 1,300 miles, and a ceiling of 9,375feet. It was equipped with 32 laser-guided 'Hellfire' anti-armor missiles, 7.62mm machine guns and mine dispensers, and able to resist most small-arms fire. It flies up to 11 soldiers into a battle zone and can lift light armored vehicles into place. The Chinook has a crew of two to four, a speed of 185 miles, a range of 700 miles, and a ceiling of 20,000 feet. It can transport 44 fully-equipped soldiers or 10 tons of cargo. The MH-47 version is adapted for U.S. Special Forces with night vision and navigation equipment.

HELIOGRAPHY. A method of signaling invented by the American Indians, called looking-glass signaling, and adopted by the British military in India prior to the introduction of telegraphic communication. A concave mirror is used to reflect the sunlight, or an artificial light, to signal in a prearranged code information to troops, covering as many as 40 mile distances in a direct line of sight. Heliography was to a certain extent the equivalent of Afghan drums (*dhol*), except that the latter were limited to simple signals. The Afghan term for the heliograph is *a'ina-i barqi*. Visual signaling, whether by flags, discs, lamps, or heliography, had the disadvantage that it could be used only within the line of vision and could be seen by the enemy, exposing the signaler to attack.

HELMAND (31-0' N, 64-0' E). A province in southwestern Afghanistan with a population of about 570,000 (1991 estimates are as high as 640,000) and an area of 23,058 square miles—the largest of Afghan provinces. The capital of the province (Girishk until 1957) is Lashkargah (Bost) with about 21,600 (1991 estimates as high as 69,000) inhabitants. The population is largely **Pashtun** with some **Hazara** in the north and **Baluch** in the south. The economy of the province is based primarily on agriculture: barley, cotton, wheat, and a great variety of fruit (during **Taliban** rule, and again after their fall, the province became a major producer of opium). Livestock raised include sheep, goats, cattle, camels, horses, and donkeys. The province is irrigated by the Helmand River, which also provides hydroelectric power. The river rises near the Unai Pass and with its five tributaries—the Kaj Rud, Tirin, Arghandab, Tarnak, and Arghastan—drains all of southwestern Afghanistan. After running in a southwestern direction as far as Khwaja Ali, the Helmand runs due west to Band-i-Kamal Khan and then north to the Lash Juwain hamuns. The river formed part of the border with Iran, and when it changed channels the Goldsmid boundary arbitration was again called into question.

HENTIG-NIEDERMAYER EXPEDITION. An expedition conceived in August 1914 by the **German** general staff for the purpose of "revolutionizing India, inducing Afghanistan to attack India, and securing Iran as a bridge from the Ottoman empire to Afghanistan." The leading members were Werner Otto von Hentig, a young German diplomat who had served in Iran, and Oskar von Niedermayer, a captain in the German army. They were accompanied by Kazim Bey, a Turkish officer, Maulawi Barakatullah and Mahendra Pratap, two Indian revolutionaries, and a number of **Afridi Pashtuns** who had been recruited from a prisoner of war camp. Hentig carried an unsigned letter purported to be from the German kaiser and a message from von Bethmann-Hollweg, the chancellor, for **Amir Habibullah**. He was to establish diplomatic relations and conclude a treaty of friendship or, if possible, an alliance, with Afghanistan. Niedermayer was to discuss matters of a military nature and the Indians were to appeal to Amir Habibullah for support in the fight against the British in India. Kazim Bey was to convey special messages from the sultan-caliph and the leaders of the Ottoman war government. Members of the expedition crossed Iran and entered Afghanistan in August 1915 and five weeks later reached **Kabul**.

Amir Habibullah was well aware of the power of **Britain** and, even though his heart and ultimate loyalty were with the Ottoman sultan-caliph, he was not willing to rush into a risky adventure. He initialed the draft of a treaty that was so extravagant in its demands that only a victorious Germany could have provided the financial and military support requested. The expedition disbanded in May 1916, and Hentig returned by way of the Wakhan Corridor to China and from there to the **United States** and Germany. Niedermayer went through Russian Central Asia to Iran and the Ottoman Empire. The expedition was the first diplomatic contact with Germany and marked the beginning of the end of Britain's monopoly over the conduct of

Afghan **foreign relations.**

HERAT (34-20' N, 62-12' E). Herat is a province in northwestern Afghanistan with an area of 16,107 square miles and a population of about 685,000 in 1979. The capital of the province is the city of Herat with about 140,000 inhabitants, and the third largest city in Afghanistan. Located at an altitude of 2,600 feet, the city is the major commercial center of western Afghanistan. The old town was surrounded by a wall built in 1885 and mostly destroyed in the 1950s. Herat is of great strategic importance and therefore has been the site of fortified towns since antiquity. It is an ancient city, first mentioned in the *Avesta* (the holy book of Zoroastrianism) as *Hairava*, which Afghan historians conjecture to be derived from Aria, or Ariana, the first "Afghan" kingdom flourishing around 1,500 B.C. The town was on the route of the Achaemenid armies of Cyrus and Darius and two centuries later of Alexander the Great, who in 330 B.C. built *Alexandria Ariorum* on the site of Herat. In the 11th century Herat became a famous urban center in Islamic **Khorasan** where scholars like Khwaja Abdullah Ansari and others flourished. In the 12th century, Turkomans destroyed the city numerous times, and a century later the hordes of Genghis Khan destroyed it, with only a handful of the population surviving a general massacre. In the 14th century **Timur-i-Lang**'s forces devastated the city. Rebuilt by Timur's son Shah Rukh, the city experienced a period of glory. Again in the early 16th century, Sultan Husain Mirza Baiqara made Herat "the most renowned center of literature, culture, and art in all Central and Western Asia."

In 1509 the city came under **Safavid** rule until, in about 1715, the Abdalis took control. In 1730 it was captured by **Nadir Shah Afshar** and in 1750 by **Ahmad Shah Durrani**. Next, Herat was ruled by various princes whose internecine fighting invited Persian attack. In 1834 and 1837 the Qajar ruler, Muhammad Shah, besieged the city, but the endurance of the Heratis and British intervention in the Persian Gulf forced him to give up after a nine-month-long effort. Nasiruddin Shah captured the city in 1856, but was forced to pull out when British troops attacked Bushire in 1857. Amir **Abdul Rahman** ended Herat's semi-independence. War in Afghanistan has led to considerable destruction. It began in March 1979 with a popular revolt against the **Kabul** government that was severely repressed. (*See* HERAT UPRISING.) Herat was regained for the Kabul government, but the **mujahedin** were able to control much of the country-

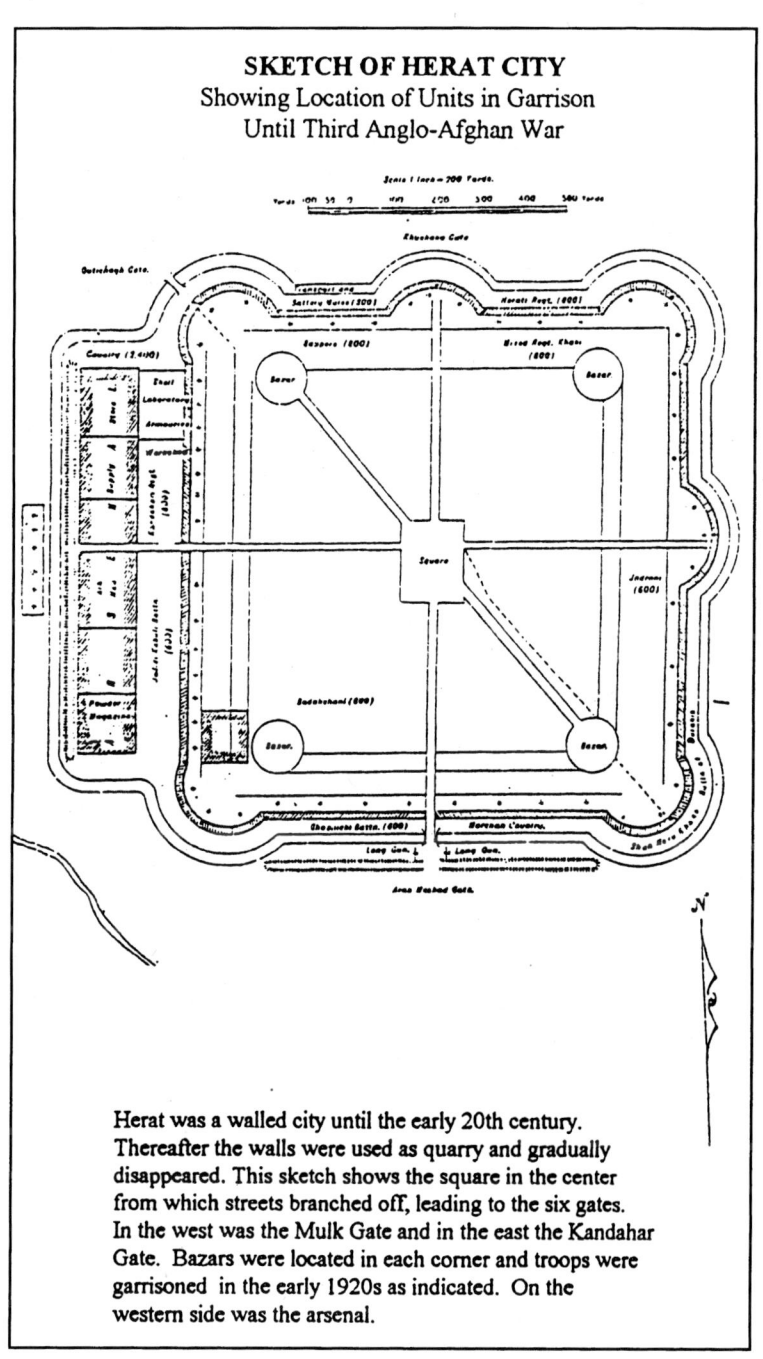

SKETCH OF HERAT CITY
Showing Location of Units in Garrison Until Third Anglo-Afghan War

Herat was a walled city until the early 20th century. Thereafter the walls were used as quarry and gradually disappeared. This sketch shows the square in the center from which streets branched off, leading to the six gates. In the west was the Mulk Gate and in the east the Kandahar Gate. Bazars were located in each corner and troops were garrisoned in the early 1920s as indicated. On the western side was the arsenal.

Plan 6. Sketch of Herat City (MR 1925)

side in spite of divisional offensive sweeps by Soviet/Kabul forces. In April 1988, some 3,000 government forces defected to the mujahedin when they were offered amnesty. After the fall of the **Najibullah** government, **Ismail Khan** became the paramount chief of Herat Province until he was dislodged in September 1995 by the newly emerging forces of the **Taliban**. Restored to power after the Taliban defeat, he ruled like an independent **amir** until he was finally deposed by the Kabul government in September 2004.

HERAT, SIEGE OF. Persia, encouraged by **Russia**, laid siege to **Herat** (1837–1838), but was unable to capture the city. A British officer, Major **Eldred Pottinger**, claimed an important role in the defense of the city. When **Britain** could not induce the shah to desist, Indian troops landed, on June 19, 1838, on the island of Kharak in the Persian Gulf. It was only then that Persia lifted the siege and withdrew in September 1838.

HERAT UPRISING. On March 21, 1979, demonstrators against the **Kabul** regime seized control of the city of **Herat** and liberated political prisoners. They proceeded to attack government officials and killed many of the Soviet advisers and their families, carrying the heads of some on pikes through the city of Herat. When the Marxist government sent troops to quell the uprising, the entire Afghan 17th Division mutinied and a powerful resistance organization was born, headed by Captain **Ismail Khan**. The Kabul government brought in air strikes, which eventually broke the resistance at the cost of some 5,000 deaths.

HINDU KUSH. The major mountain massif that originates in the southwestern corner of the Pamirs and with its extension, the Koh-i Baba, runs the entire length of central Afghanistan, constituting a formidable barrier to north-south communication. Its general elevation is between 14,500 and 17,000 feet, the highest peak Nowshak is at an altitude of some 24,000 feet (7,458 meters). Several passes leading across the massif lie at altitudes above 12,000 feet.

The name Hindu Kush is of uncertain origin and is not used generally by Afghans, who have local names for the range in their area. In the West the name has been interpreted as "Killer of Hindus"; but the name may be derived, according to some sources, from Hindu Kuh, marking the most northern extent of pre-Muslim Hindu control. The range is divided into three major sections: the eastern from the Pamirs to the Dorah Pass, the central from the Dorah to the Khawak Pass, and the western from the Khawak Pass to the termination of the range near the Shibar Pass. During the winter months, the mountain range seals off northern Afghanistan from the rest of the country, and the rugged terrain has allowed small populations to survive in remote, economically marginal valleys. Poor lines of communication fostered a measure of autonomy and extensive linguistic and cultural diversity. The construction of the **Salang** Tunnel and an all-weather road in 1964 have contributed to the strengthening of central control over the northern part of the country. In the 1980s the Salang Highway became an important artery for supplying the **Kabul** government with **Soviet** materiel and therefore was a frequent object of attacks by **mujahedin** forces, especially those of Commander **Ahmad Shah Mas'ud**. Frequently made impassable, the Salang Tunnel was repaired and in full operation in December 2003, after the destruction during the **Taliban** regime.

HIZB-I ISLAMI. *See* **HEKMATYAR, GULBUDDIN.**

HIZB-I ISLAMI (KHALES). *See* **KHALES, MUHAMMAD YUNUS.**

HIZB-I WAHDAT. A coalition of eight **Hazara Shi'a** parties led by **Abdul Ali Mazari** centered in the area of **Bamian** and **Wardak**. It forged an alliance with **Gulbuddin Hekmatyar**'s Hizb-i Islami in August 1993 and controlled parts of **Kabul** west of the Darulaman road and south of Sarak-i Say-i Aqrab, as well as parts of Kabul University and all of Kabul Polytechnic compound. Mazari prevailed in a power struggle with Muhammad Akbari, who was head of the Wahdat's political committee (Akbari was forced to flee and joined the forces of **Burhanuddin Rabbani**). In January 1995 Hizb-i Wahdat was fighting for turf with the Shi'a Harakat-i Islami of **Ayatollah Muhsini**. When Hekmatyar's forces were driven from Kabul in February 1995, Jam'iat captured the territory of the weakened Wahdat and Mazari joined, or surrendered to, the **Taliban** and was killed while in captivity on March 13, 1995. He was succeeded by Muhammad Karim Khalili. Another prominent leader is Haji **Muhammad Muhaqeq**.

HIZB-I WAHDAT, ORGANIZATION. Essentially a **Hazara** party, it is headed by **Abdul Karim Khalili** and organized into a seven-member Supreme Supervisory Council (shura-i 'ali nuzrat), and a six-member Central Committee (shura-i markazi), which is subdivided into departments for political, military, cultural, intelligence, and medical services, financial and public services, judiciary, public relations, archeology and heritage, and a women's committee. The Supreme Supervisory Council includes the religious scholars, the chairman Ayatollah Sadiqi Parwani, Ayatollah Qurban Ali **Muhammad Muhaqeq**, and Ayatollah Salihi Mudaris; two intellectuals, Sayyid Abbas Hakimi and Sayyid Ghulam Husain Musawi; and two technocrats, Sayyid Amin Sajjadi and Dr. Sultani. The 80-member Central Committee includes 10 women. It was headed by the secretary general, Abdul Karim Khalili, a vice president of the **Transitional Government** of President **Hamid Karzai** and Qurban Ali **Muhaqeq**, his planning minister, who resigned to run for president.

HUMVEE (HUMMER). The high mobile multipurpose wheeled vehicle developed by the **United States** military is a very rugged and long-lasting vehicle, used by the U.S. forces in Afghanistan (and Iraq). It is a jeep used for transport of soldiers, but an armored version under development is equipped with a laser beam, utilized to destroy land mines and cluster bombs from the battle field. Mounted on a turret, the laser is beamed at a target by a soldier sitting at a console, using a joy stick. When the beam strikes a mine, the heat burns off the explosive or detonates it. Some experts claim that it serves the military, but is not suitable for civilian use, because it will miss some mines and, while armies expect casualties, civilian farmers do not.

Humvees have been called "death wagons" in Iraq: they are soft-skinned and conceived as utility trucks, not as close combat vehicles. Welding steel plate for protection on the Humvee has caused the vehicles to roll over because of shifts in the center of gravity.

- I -

IBRAHIM BEG. An **Uzbek Basmachi** leader who fought the Bolshevik government in Central Asia, at times using Afghan territory as a safe haven. He visited **Kabul** in 1926 and was entertained as a state guest by **King Amanullah**, who was not averse to the idea of becoming ruler of a Central Asian confederation of Muslim states. In May 1929, Ibrahim Beg supported **Habibullah Kalakani** and fought King Amanullah's general, Ghulam Nabi Charkhi, taking a prominent part in the capture of **Mazar-i Sharif**. In 1930, after repeated representations by the **Soviet Union**, the government of **Muhammad Nadir Shah** took steps to prevent Ibrahim Beg from raiding across the border, with the consequence that he started raiding in Afghanistan as well. Therefore, he was finally driven from Afghan territory and captured by Soviet troops. Afghans call the battle between Afghan troops and Ibrahim Beg's supporters *Jang-i Laqay* (War of the Laqai, name of Ibrahim's Uzbek tribe). He was executed in April 1931.

INTERIM GOVERNMENT (INTERIM AUTHORITY). After the fall of the **Taliban** regime, representatives of four Afghan groups met in **Bonn**, Germany, to establish an Afghan interim authority. It was to rule for a period of six months, starting on December 22, 2001, and prepare the way for a **Loya Jirga**, which, in turn, was to elect a **Transitional Government**. This government was to have a tenure of two years, during which time it was to draft a constitution and prepare the country for elections. The talks began on November 27, 2001, and, after nine days of grueling discussion, the representatives selected **Hamid Karzai** as interim leader and the ex-king, **Zaher Shah**, to preside at the Loya Jirga. The four groups consisted of the Rome delegation of supporters of the king; the Cyprus representatives of notables in exile; the Peshawar delegation, composed largely of **Pashtuns** located in Peshawar, **Pakistan**; and the **Northern Alliance**. The latter gained the ministries of defense, foreign affairs, and interior (later given to a **Pashtun**). Haji Abdul Qadir walked out, protesting the fact that Pashtuns were underrepresented. To **Lakhdar Brahimi, United Nation** special envoy to Afghanistan, goes the credit for convincing the delegates to agree on a decision. Some 30 ministerial positions, including two women, were announced. The major loser was **Burhanuddin Rabbani**, who had already taken residence in the palace. To provide peace and stability in **Kabul**, the **International Security Assistance Force** for Afghanistan (ISAF), a multinational force, was set up. As scheduled, the Interim Government prepared the way for establishment of the Transitional Government. (For Interim Agreement *see* APPENDIX 6.)

INTERNATIONAL COALITION AGAINST "TERROR." A largely American-British force engaged in hunting down **Islamist** guerrilla forces in Afghanistan. As a result of the terrorist attack on the World Trade Center on September 11, 2001, the **United States** invaded Afghanistan and with the help of local militias was able to destroy the **Taliban** government and drive **al-Qaeda** forces from its bases. The campaign, dubbed **Operation Enduring Freedom**, at first involved only American troops which were quickly reinforced with British contingents. The United States appealed to the **North Atlantic Treaty Organization**, invoking Article 5 of its charter which says "an attack on one NATO nation is an attack on all," obligating the members to provide material assistance. The state department released a list of 37 countries providing some type of assistance, claiming that there are others who for "internal political reasons choose not to broadcast their participation." Most members of the coalition have given nonmilitary support; for example, **Pakistan** and Uzbekistan provided bases and overflight permission, Italy and France sent naval forces into the Arabian Sea and the Persian Gulf; Estonia, Norway, Jordan, and Denmark contributed de-mining units, and others supplied food, clothing, and medical aid for Afghanistan. The **International Security Assistance Force** (ISAF) for Afghanistan , operating under **United Nations** auspices, was not part of the coalition. It assumed the task of policing the capital, **Kabul**. It had leadership by rotation, but on August 11, 2003, was taken over by a NATO force under the German Lieutenant-General **Götz Gliemeroth** with a mandate to extend its activities to the provinces.

INTERNATIONAL SECURITY ASSISTANCE FORCE (ISAF). The **United Nations** Security Council authorized as part of the **Bonn Agreement** of December 2001, the establishment of a force of about 7,500 soldiers from some 22 states to assist the Afghan government in maintaining security in **Kabul** and surrounding areas. It was initially authorized for a period of six months but since extended. The force was under rotating command from individual countries and subsequently under **North Atlantic Treaty Organization** and the **Eurocorps** of the European Union.

ISAF I was headed by Major General McColl of the United Kingdom, December 22 until June 2002.
ISAF II was commanded by the Turkish Major General Hilmi Akim Zorlu from June 2002.
ISAF III was a German-Netherlands mission, headed by General Norbert van Heyst, from February 10 to August 11, 2003.
ISAF IV was started under NATO command, headed by Lieutenant General **Götz Gliemeroth** of Germany on August 11, 2003.
ISAF V NATO was commanded by the Canadian, Lieutenant General Rick Hillier, from August 2003 to August 2004.
ISAF VI was a NATO Rapid Reaction Corps, of the Eurocorps,

headed by the French Lieutenant General Jean-Louis Py. ISAF VII was commanded by the Turkish Lieutenant General Ethem Erdagi from February 13 to June 12, 2005, when Italy assumed command under Lieutenant General Mauro Del Vecchio.

ISAF's mission was to replace Afghan military personnel from the capital city, to assist the Afghan **Transitional Government** in maintaining security, and to provide a secure environment for the reconstruction of Afghanistan. ISAF was independent of the American Coalition and **Operation Enduring Freedom**, although the **United States** Central Command reserved to itself authority to guarantee that there are no conflicts in the activities of the two forces. Member states were to contribute personnel, equipment, and other resources at their own cost. In addition to securing the peace in the capital, ISAF has disposed of munitions and land mines and trained the first battalion of the new Afghan National Guard. It has been successful in providing a measure of security for the capital but did not agree to move beyond the capital until ISAF VI, for which the Eurocorps provided the core of troops. The **German** contingent is the largest with 1,480 soldiers as of September 2004. With only a few soldiers in each base and not yet sufficiently supplied with aerial support, ISAF would have difficulty in stopping widespread rioting or the attacks of a determined warlord. *See* APPENDIX 6.

INTER-SERVICES INTELLIGENCE, DIRECTORATE FOR (ISI). A Pakistani military intelligence organization, founded in 1948 by the British army officer Major General R. Cawthome, the then deputy chief of staff in the **Pakistan** army. Its function included collection of foreign and domestic intelligence. It is reported to have a total of 10,000 officers and staff members and has been dubbed "the invisible government." It was headed by General **A. R. Akhtar** from 1979 to 1987 and subsequently by General Hamid Gul and was heavily involved in the war against Soviet/**Kabul** government forces in Afghanistan. Brigadier **Muhammad Yusuf**, head of the Afghan Bureau of the ISI, claims credit for coordinating the logistics, recruitment, training, and assignment of missions, including raids into the **Soviet Union**. The ISI distributed the weapons and funds provided by friendly countries while the government of Pakistan maintained an increasingly "implausible deniability" of involvement in the war. Muhammad Yusuf detailed ISI activities in a book titled *The Bear Trap: Afghanistan's Untold Story*, edited by the military historian Mark Adkin. The ISI was heavily involved in supporting the **Taliban** regime, but since the **United States** intervention it has disbanded the Kashmir and Afghanistan units.

ISAF. *See* **INTERNATIONAL SECURITY ASSISTANCE FORCE.**

ISLAMABAD ACCORD. Signed by eight **mujahedin** leaders on March 7, 1993, in Islamabad, **Pakistan,** as an attempt to restore peace in the ongoing civil war. It provided for a government headed by President **Burhanuddin Rabbani** and Prime Minister **Gulbuddin Hekmatyar** for the subsequent 18 months. It called for formation of an election commission and a constitutional assembly for the drafting of a constitution. A defense council comprising two members of each party was to work on formation of a national army and establishment of security. Another committee was to supervise control of the monetary system. A cease-fire was to assure permanent cessation of hostilities. An annex enumerated the powers and duties of the president and prime minister. The agreement was reached with great pressure from Pakistan and Saudi Arabia and, like the **Peshawar Accord**, it did not succeed in bringing peace to Afghanistan. As before, Hekmatyar was the spoiler, and when he was finally invited to **Kabul** to assume his ministerial post, the newly emerging **Taliban** forces were able to capture the capital on September 27, 1996. A new attempt at forming a broad-based government started after the fall of the Taliban regime in December 2001. *See also* BONN CONFERENCE; INTERIM GOVERNMENT; TRANSITIONAL GOVERNMENT.

ISLAMIC ALLIANCE FOR THE LIBERATION OF AFGHANISTAN. A loose coalition founded on January 27, 1980, by five **mujahedin** groups with headquarters in **Pakistan.** The sixth group, **Gulbuddin Hekmatyar's** Hizb, did not participate because it was not given preeminent status. The alliance was formed for the purpose of gaining recognition as a government in exile and to secure support from the Islamic Foreign Ministers Conference, held in Islamabad in May 1980. The alliance disintegrated in December of the same year. In early 1981 the Pakistan government announced that it would henceforth recognize only six groups (later seven) and that all refugees in the country must register as members of one of these groups. Refugee aid as well as mujahedin support would be channeled through these groups. Thus in 1985 the alliance reconstituted itself under the label Islamic Unity of Afghan Mujahedin, with the moderates in the "Unity of Three" (**Sayyid Ahmad Gailani, Sebghatullah Mujaddidi,** and **Muhammad Nabi Muhammadi**) and the radicals organized in the "Unity of Seven," of whom only four (**Burhanuddin Rabbani,** Gulbuddin Hekmatyar, **Abdul Rasul Sayyaf,** and **Yunus Khales**) represented viable groups. While the moderates were reasonably united, the radicals were constantly at odds, especially the groups headed by Rabbani and Hekmatyar. In May 1983 the alliance elected Sayyaf chairman for a term of two years, but when, in 1985, he attempted to remain in this position, the members of the alliance objected.

Subsequently, a chairman of the alliance served on a rotational basis for three months. There was otherwise little coordination between the groups. Upon becoming spokesman in February 1988, Pir Sayyid Ahmad Gailani announced the formation of an Afghan Interim Government with Eng. Ahmad Shah as prime minister. Unity however, was not to be achieved. After the fall of the Marxist regime and the capture of **Kabul** in April 1992, an interim government was headed for two months by President Mujaddidi, who was followed by Burhanuddin Rabbani. Rabbani remained president of the Islamic Republic of Afghanistan in defiance of other major mujahedin groups and was embroiled in a struggle for control of the Afghan capital, which has led to considerable destruction of the city without the conflict being resolved. **Interim** and **Transitional governments** were established after the fall of the **Taliban** regime.

ISLAMIST MOVEMENT. The movement was born in large measure as a reaction to the process of Westernization in Afghanistan and the growth of secular, liberal ideologies among Afghan youth. The movement owes much of its organization and ideology to the influence of the **Muslim Brotherhood** of Egypt (Al-Ikhwan Al-Muslimin), and its adherents were therefore dubbed *Ikhwanis* by their opponents. The party originated in religious, intellectual circles in the late 1950s and had as its chief ideologues and mentors **Ghulam Muhammad Niazi, Burhanuddin Rabbani, Sayyid Musa Tawana,** and others who had studied at al-Azhar University in Egypt and taught at the faculty of theology of **Kabul** University. They soon attracted a circle of like-minded students, who organized themselves in 1970 in the **Muslim Youth** (Jawanan-i Muslimin) movement. At first they went through a process of ideological development when members studied the works of Islamic thinkers Hasan al-Banna' (1906–1949), the "Supreme Guide" of the Ikhwanis; Sayyid Qutb, executed in Cairo in 1966; and Abu'l Ala Maududi (died 1979), founder of the Pakistani **Jama'at-i Islami** and author of religiopolitical treatises.

The movement took a political turn during the premiership of Sardar **Muhammad Daud** (1953–1963) and the subsequent liberal period. Islamist students staged demonstrations, protesting government policies and such international issues as Zionism and the war in Vietnam. By 1970 Islamists won a majority in student elections, a fact that alarmed the Marxists and their supporters. In 1971 the movement began to formally organize at a meeting in **Kabul** at the house of Professor Rabbani. A leadership council was formed with Rabbani as the chairman, **Abdul Rasul Sayyaf** as deputy and Habiburrahman as secretary. Council members were assigned responsibility for financial, cultural, and political tasks. Some leaders, like Ghulam Muhammad Niazi, refrained from open participation, others, like **Gulbuddin Hekmatyar**, were jailed at the time. The organization selected the name **Jam'iat-i-Islami** (Islamic Society), but the student faction, operating quite openly, was known as the Jawanan Musulman (Muslim Youth) and popularly called Ikhwanis. Other Islamist individuals and circles, not affiliated with the Jam'iat were Minhajuddin Gahiz who in 1968 published his newspaper *Jarida Gahiz* (Dawn); Khuddam al-Qur'an (Servants of the Koran) founded by the Mujaddidi family; and the Jam'iat-i Ulama-i Muhammadi (Society of Muslim Ulama) founded by **Sebghatullah Mujaddidi**.

After the coup of Muhammad Daud (July 17, 1973), the movement was forced to go underground. Rabbani raised the question of armed struggle, and weapons were collected, but before any action could begin, the government police arrested many of the members, including Ghulam Muhammad Niazi. Rabbani and Hekmatyar fled to **Pakistan**, where they sought help from the Pakistan government and the Islamist Jama'at-i Islami. In 1975 Hekmatyar staged sporadic raids into Afghanistan, and when the attacks failed, the differences between Rabbani and Hekmatyar became public.

After the **Saur Revolt** of April 1978 an attempt at reconciliation was made. Each party nominated seven members to a 21-member reconciliation committee, including the mediators. The Jami'at members voted for Rabbani to be president of the party, and

Hekmatyar's party voted for Qazi Muhammad Amin as deputy president. The mediators voted for Maulawi Fayez who became the compromise president. But the Islamists were also divided on ethnic and ideological lines. The largely **Tajik** supporters of Rabbani favored preparation rather than precipitous armed activity. Hekmatyar aspired to leadership of the Islamists and advocated immediate struggle. In April 1978 **Maulawi Muhammad Nabi Muhammadi** was chosen as a compromise leader, but the movement broke up over the distribution of funds provided by foreign donors. Hekmatyar organized the **Hizb-i Islami**, and the traditionalist Muhammadi founded his own **Harakat-i Inqilab-i Islami** party. Rabbani worked with Mujaddidi and his **Jabha-yi Milli-yi Beraye Najat-i Afghanistan** (National Liberation Front), and continued to lead his own Jam'iat. **Muhammad Yunus Khales** formed his own **Hizb-i Islami** party in 1979.

The Islamists were puritanical moralists who perceived moral laxity, lack of respect for traditional values, and an infatuation with Western secular culture among Afghan youth, and were determined to impose the laws of Islam on the social and political life of the state. They were not **fundamentalist**, but reformist, and supported a political activism first seen in the great Pan-Islamist, Jamaluddin Afghani. They were critical of the fundamentalist views of the **ulama** and were themselves the object of criticism by the clergy. They went underground and organized in cells, were accused of resorting to political assassinations, and were themselves the objects of assassinations. They rejected aspects of both communism and democracy although they copied from both.

A new movement, the **Taliban**, emerged in November 1994 and within two years captured Kabul and eventually most of Afghanistan. They opposed the **mujahedin** groups and tried to establish their concept of an "Islamic State." Their radicalism and protection of **Osama bin Laden** led to **United States** intervention and the destruction of the Taliban regime.

ISMAIL KHAN. *See* **MUHAMMAD ISMAIL.**

ITTIHAD-I ISLAMI BARAYI AZADI-YI AFGHANISTAN. *See* **SAYYAF, ABDUL RASUL.**

- J -

JABHA-YI MILLI NAJAT-I AFGHANISTAN. *See* **MUJADDIDI, SEBGHATULLAH.**

JAGIR. A feudal, military fiefdom, such as granted by **Ahmad Shah Durrani** to chiefs of his tribe. It was an allotment of land that was tax free but required its holder to provide a number of troops and arms corresponding to the size of the *jagir* (also called *tiyul* and A. iqta'). Land was divided into divisions called *qulba* (plow), which designated the portion of irrigated land cultivated by one person, employing one ox and one plow. The area was divided into two sections for sowing two *kharwar* of grain (one *kharwar*, literally a donkey load, amounted to 100 *man*, up to 160 pounds). One section was cultivated each year while the other half remained fallow. About 3,000 double *qulba* were distributed to Durrani tribes in **Kandahar** for which they had to provide 6,000 horsemen for the **amir**'s army.

JALALABAD (36-46' N, 65-52' E). The capital of **Nangarhar Province** which had an estimated 54,000 inhabitants in the 1970s, reportedly increased in 1995, as a result of the influx of internal refugees, to about 200,000. The population is largely **Pashtun** of Khugiani, **Shinwari**, Tirahi (Tira'i), Mohmand, and **Ghilzai** tribal background, in addition to **Sikhs**, Hindus, and some **Tajiks** and Sayyids. It had the largest community of Sikh and Hindu merchants (about 4,000) of any Afghan city. Situated at an altitude of 1,950 feet in a fertile valley watered by the **Kabul** and **Kunar** Rivers some 90 miles east of Kabul, Jalalabad lies on the trade route to the Indo-Pakistani subcontinent. Invaders passed through the Jalalabad valley, including Alexander the Great (330 B.C.), Babur Shah (1504), and the British, who occupied the town in two Anglo-Afghan wars.

Babur Shah, the founder of the Moghul Empire of India, first planted beautiful gardens in the area, and in A.D. 1560 his grandson Jalaluddin Akbar founded the town, hence its name Jalalabad. In the 19th century it was a walled town with about 2,000 inhabitants, whose numbers increased during the winter to some 20,000. In March 1989 **mujahedin** forces attacked the city but were unable to take it. The city was occupied by mujahedin groups after the fall of the Kabul government until the rise of the **Taliban** movement. *See* JALALABAD, ATTACK ON.

JALALABAD, ATTACK ON. Soviet forces had left in February 1989 and **Kunar** was taken by the **mujahedin**. The time seemed ripe for the insurgents to progress from the stage of guerrilla to conventional warfare. **Jalalabad** seemed a suitable target for the first capture of a major Afghan city. It was located only about 37 miles from the **Pakistan** border and within easy access for reinforcement of men and munitions. If taken, the city could have served as the capital of the Afghan Interim Government (AIG) to be recognized and openly assisted by its foreign supporters. Hamid Gul, director of Pakistani **Inter Services Intelligence** (ISI), was heavily involved in various stages of the campaign. In March the mujahedin had gathered some 7,000 men in the area amid great publicity about their intended target. The men came primarily from **Gulbuddin Hekmatyar, Yunus Khales, Abdul Rasul Sayyaf,** and **Sayyid Ahmad Gailani**'s forces, although other groups also participated. The garrison was estimated at about 4,500, and the defenses were under the command of General Delawar, the Afghan chief of staff. Mine fields provided a secure perimeter and munitions had been collected in anticipation of the attack.

The mujahedin seemed to be well supplied with heavy artillery and surface-to-air missiles (SAM), including the dreaded **Stinger**, and began their attack on March 6, 1989, proclaiming an amnesty for enemy soldiers in the hope of achieving massive defections. They quickly captured Samarkhel, an important post in the defense of the city, and rocketed the airport to prevent supplies from being brought in. But the fighting quickly bogged down. The mujahedin fought only during the daylight hours and returned to rear bases for the night. Commanders did not always coordinate their actions, Hekmatyar being the major culprit, and they failed to maintain the blockade of the road from **Kabul**, which permitted convoys to supply the city. High-altitude bombing and close air support by MIG-21s, as well as SCUD missiles with 1,700 pounds of warheads, exacted a heavy toll on the mujahedin. In April the defenders were able to recapture the airport, and, after a 10-week-long siege, the Kabul government prevailed.

On May 10 foreign journalists were permitted to visit Jalalabad to see that the mujahedin had been defeated with heavy losses. One source claims that some 5,000 casualties resulted on all sides and most of the mujahedin casualties were caused by bombing and mines. On July 4 the Kabul government launched a surprise attack and consolidated its control of Samarkhel and the surrounding area, achieving a badly needed boost in morale for the **Afghan army** and permitting the Kabul regime to continue in power for another three years. It was only after the fall of Kabul in April 1992 that Jalalabad was taken by a council of mujahedin commanders.

JALALABAD, SIEGE OF. During the siege of the **Kabul** cantonment in the **first Anglo-Afghan war, Jalalabad** became an important base for British-Indian troops. **Sir Robert Sale**, the commanding general, was unable to come to the rescue of the Kabul forces; therefore, he decided to remain and took possession of the town on November 13, 1841. He worked on reinforcing the walls and fortifications, having only some 1,600 troops and six guns to defend a perimeter of about 2,200 yards. On November 15 an Afghan force, estimated by British officers at about 5,000 tribesmen, surrounded the town but was initially dispersed; however, the Afghans eventually captured the town, forcing the British brigade to withdraw into the citadel. On January 6, 1842, the Afghan commander demanded the British brigade to depart with honor to India in fulfillment of the Kabul **Capitulation Treaty**, but General Sale refused, not trusting the promise of safe conduct. On February 19, 1842, an earthquake destroyed the parapets, making a considerable breach in the ramparts, which had to be restored. Two days later, Sardar **Akbar Khan** attacked British foraging parties and established a rigorous blockade that lasted until April 7. Various sallies succeeded in capturing livestock for provisions, but the native troops were put on half rations and the camp followers on quarter rations. Starvation was averted when the British were able to capture a flock of 500 sheep and goats that had been grazing a little too close to the wall of the town. On April 7 General Sale sallied out with virtually all his forces and defeated Muhammad Akbar's army of some 6,000 men. According to British accounts, only 31 officers and men were killed and 131 wounded. On April 16 General **George Pollock** reached the city practically unmolested. Before the British departed, they destroyed the defenses of Jalalabad.

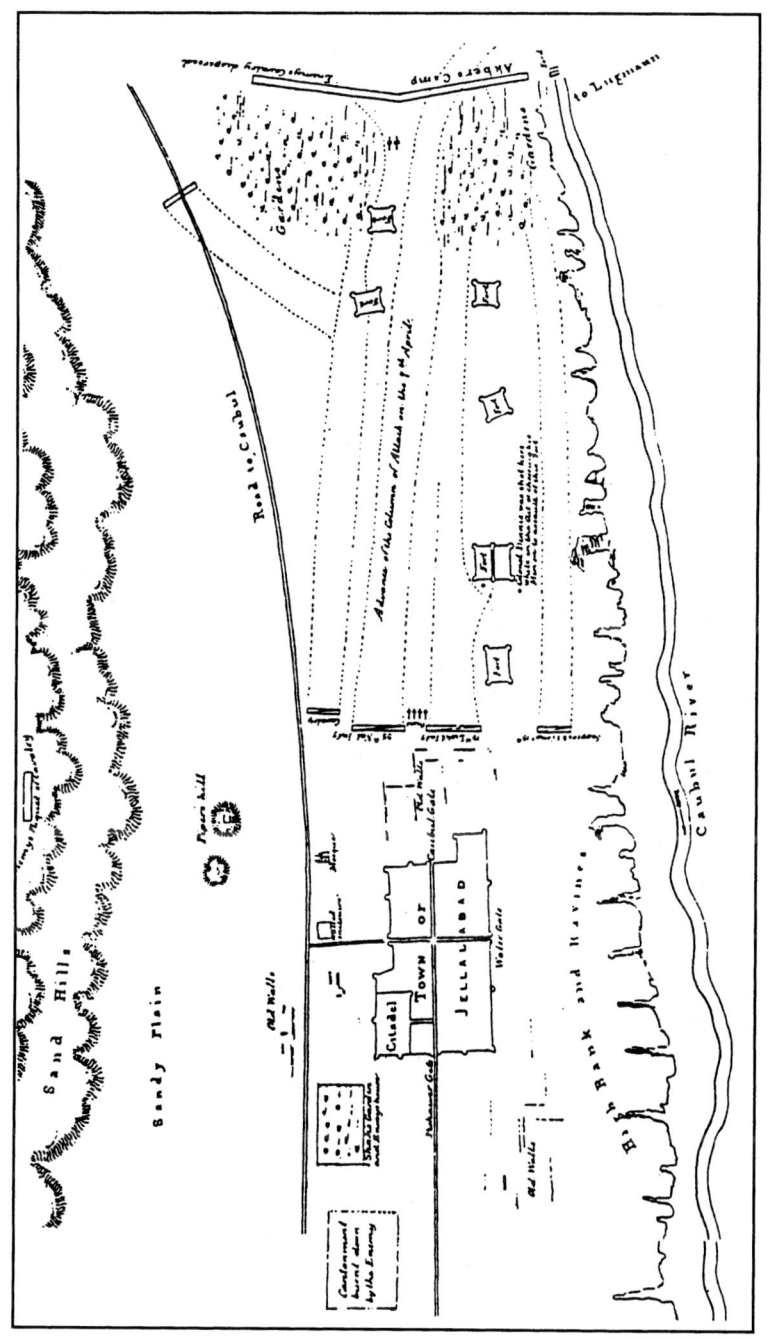

Plan 7. General Sale Defeats Akbar Khan's Forces, April 7, 1842 (adapted from Stocqueler)

JALALI, ALI AHMAD. Appointed minister of interior in January 2003, replacing Taj Muhammad Wardak and again in December 2004 in the **Hamid Karzai** government. The 62-year-old Jalali is charged with setting up a 40,000 man police force for Afghanistan. Jalali was a colonel in the **Afghan army** and a top military planner during the resistance to the **Soviet** forces in Afghanistan. He attended higher command and staff colleges in the **United States, Britain** and **Russia.** Prior to his return to Afghanistan, he served as chief of Afghanistan Services of the Voice of America. He is the author of a number of books on the Soviet military, a three-volume military history of Afghanistan, and, with Lester Grau, of *The Other Side of the Mountain: Mujahideen Tactics in the Soviet-Afghan War.*

JAMAL PASHA (JEMAL). Member of the Ottoman ruling triumvirate, serving as minister of the navy and governor of Syria during World War I. On October 27, 1920, he came with a small staff to Afghanistan to escape extradition for "war crimes." He took charge of the reorganization of the **Afghan army** and founded the "Qita Namuna," an elite force, comprising a battalion of infantry and a regiment of cavalry. He was responsible for reinstituting and expanding the hated *hasht nafari* recruitment system and other unpopular reforms. He left Afghanistan with some members of his staff in September 1921 and was assassinated by an Armenian near Tiflis on July 21, 1922.

JAM'IAT-I ISLAMI-YI AFGHANISTAN. *See* **RABBANI, BURHANUDDIN.**

JAMILURRAHMAN, MAULAWI HUSAIN (JAMIL AL-RAHMAN). Amir of the Jama'at-i Da'wa, an Islamic revivalist movement whose members call themselves *Salafis* and are popularly called "Wahhabis." He captured most of **Kunar** Province and proclaimed an "Islamic Amirate," which he ruled for a time to the exclusion of other **mujahedin** groups. Born in 1933 in the Pech district of Kunar Province of a Safi tribal family, he received a traditional education. In the early 1970s he became a member of **Jam'iat-i Islami** and took part in armed attacks against the government of President **Muhammad Daud.** After the **Saur Revolt** he joined the **Hizb-i Islami** of **Gulbuddin Hekmatyar** and until 1982 was his amir in Kunar Province. Eventually, he broke with Hekmatyar and ousted other mujahedin groups from his area. He issued decrees allowing only bearded men to enter his territory and prohibited the consumption of tobacco in all its forms. On April 20, 1991, an explosion at his Asadabad headquarters so decimated the ranks of his followers (including numerous Pakistanis and Arabs) that Hekmatyar's forces, supported by commanders of other groups, were able to capture Asadabad and expel most of the "Wahhabis" from Kunar Province. Muhammad Husain, alias **Jamilurrahman**, was assassinated by an Egyptian in Pakistan. One Maulawi Sami'ullah succeeded him as leader of the party.

JANAN, MULLA. Senior **Taliban** commander who was blamed for a rocket attack on an American military outpost in Deh Rawud, **Oruzgan** Province. He was captured by American forces and their Afghan allies in October (21?) 2003.

JAWAD, SAID TAYEB. Born about 1958 in Kandahar, the son of Mir Husain Shah (onetime dean of the faculty of literature, **Kabul** University). He was educated at Istiqlal Lycée and Kabul University with a degree in law and political science. In 1980 he left Afghanistan and studied law at the Westfälischen Wilhelms Universität in Münster, Germany. In 1986 he moved to New York to work for a Wall Street law firm, and in 1989 he moved to San Francisco where he graduated with an M.B.A. degree from Golden Gate University. He returned to Afghanistan in March 2002 and became President **Hamid Karzai**'s press secretary and in June Karzai's chief of staff. In October 2003 he was appointed Afghan ambassador to Washington and presented his credentials to Secretary of State Colin Powell on December 4, 2003. He is married to Shamim, who worked with an investment firm in San Francisco, and has one son, Iman. Jawad is fluent in English, German, French, Dari, and Pashtu.

JEZAIL. A long-barreled musket with a thin, curved butt that was the major Afghan firearm during the 19th century and can still be seen in the **arms bazaars** of the country. It was muzzle loaded and therefore required several minutes to prepare, but it is said to have had greater accuracy and could outrange the British muskets (Sir Charles Napier claimed the musket was, on balance, the better weapon, Macrory, 170). A *jezailchi* (rifleman) would carry several *jezail* on his horse and fire them in rapid succession, after which he would retire or join the enemy in hand-to-hand combat. It was the major Afghan firearm during the **Anglo-Afghan wars** and was eventually replaced by the breech loading Martini-Henry and other rifles of foreign and domestic manufacture.

JIHAD. Literally a "great effort," but generally "holy war," it is the obligation to fight against "unbelievers" until they accept Islam or submit to Islamic rule. Monotheists with a sacred book, like Christians and Jews, were not forced to convert and enjoyed the status of protected subjects (*dhimmis*). A Muslim who dies in jihad is a martyr, *shahid*, and is assured of Paradise. Technically, Muslims constitute one community, *umma*, and war between them is forbidden; therefore, an enemy is proclaimed sinful or apostate before he can be legally fought. During jihad, all tribal hostilities must temporarily stop. Muslim modernists quote a Koranic passage: "Fight in the Way of God against those who fight against you, but do not commit aggression...," maintaining that the obligation of jihad was binding only for the early Islamic period and that jihad also means fighting political and social wars and inwardly waging war against the carnal soul—a kind of moral imperative.

As of the downfall of the Marxist government in April 1992, the jihad ended and a civil war for political power between the **mujahedin** began. This was followed after the fall of the **Taliban** by a similar war against the foreign supporters of the previous regime.

JIRGA. A tribal council, which has legislative and juridical authority in the name of the tribal community. Although the Afghan government claims exclusive jurisdiction, it permits **Pashtun** tribes in the border areas to resolve internal disputes in their traditional manner. Jirgas can be composed of chiefs and notables or of adult male members of a tribe. A chief, or respected graybeard, leads the discussion, and votes are weighed according to the importance of the individual rather than being counted. The decision of a jirga is binding on all members of the tribe. Jirgas also resolve intra-tribal disputes, often with the mediation of a respected member of the **ulama** (clergy) or *pirs* (leaders of mystical orders).

In times of national emergency Afghan rulers have convened a **Loya Jirga** (Great Council), which includes representatives from all parts of the country. Its decisions thus become an expression of the "national will."

JOZJAN (JOWZJAN) (36-30' N, 66-0' E). A province in north-central Afghanistan with an area of 10,126 square miles and an estimated population of about 642,000. The administrative capital of the province is Shiberghan with some 19,000 (121,000 estimate in 1991) inhabitants. The province is rich in mineral resources; oil and natural gas have been discovered at Khwaja Gugirdak and Jarquduq, near Shiberghan, and reserves of natural gas have been estimated at 500 trillion cubic feet. A pipeline transporting natural gas to the **Soviet Union** was completed in 1968, and except for a limited amount of local use in the production of fertilizer, was delivered to the Soviet Union below the world market rates. One reason for this was, no doubt, the fact that the Soviet Union was the only feasible trading partner.

JOZJANIS. A militia composed largely of **Uzbeks** from **Jozjan** Province, numbering about 3,000—4,000 men in the 1980s, who served the **Kabul** government as a reliable and effective force in southern and western Afghanistan. It replaced the **Soviet** troops in **Kandahar**, where it protected the airport. After the fall of Kabul to the **mujahedin**, the Jozjanis seemed to have merged with the Uzbek forces of General **Abdul Rashid Dostum** and become one of the contenders for control of portions of Kabul. They first helped Jam'iat to capture Kabul and subsequently pulled out of the city at the insistence of **Gulbuddin Hekmatyar** in a deal with **Burhanuddin Rabbani**. Later, they joined Hekmatyar when Rabbani was unwilling to include Abdul Rashid Dostum in his government. The Jozjanis were feared as a fierce and unruly mercenary army and appear to be the defenders of Uzbek ethnic interests in present-day Afghanistan. They were part of General Dostum's army in north-central Afghanistan.

JUNBESH-I MILLI-YI ISLAMI. *See* **DOSTUM, GENERAL ABDUL RASHID.**

- K -

KABUL (34-31' N, 69-12' E). The capital and largest city in Afghanistan, situated at an altitude of almost 6,000 feet, and a province with an area of 1,822 square miles and a population of 1,372,000. In 1978 the city had some 500,000 inhabitants, but this number has, according to

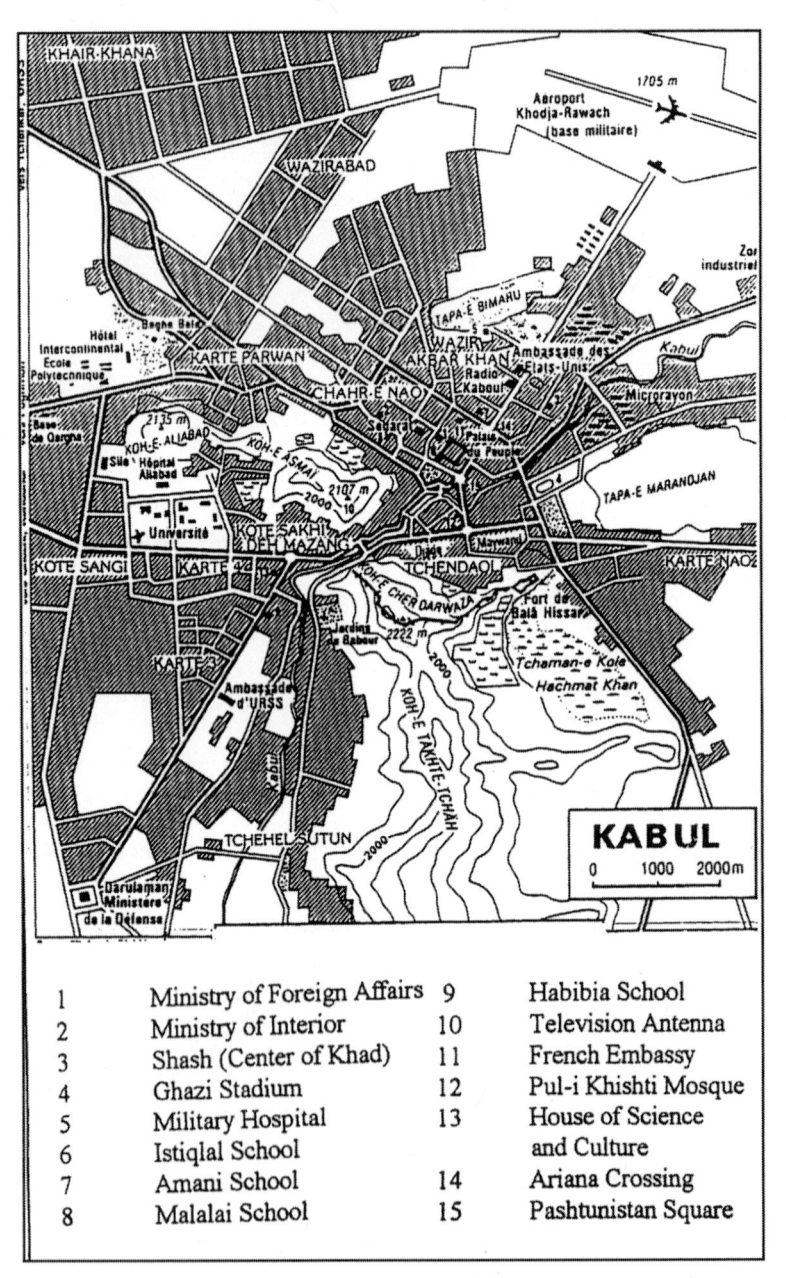

1	Ministry of Foreign Affairs	9	Habibia School
2	Ministry of Interior	10	Television Antenna
3	Shash (Center of Khad)	11	French Embassy
4	Ghazi Stadium	12	Pul-i Khishti Mosque
5	Military Hospital	13	House of Science
6	Istiqlal School		and Culture
7	Amani School	14	Ariana Crossing
8	Malalai School	15	Pashtunistan Square

Map 3. Kabul (Alain Marigo)

UN estimates, increased to about 1,500,000 as a result of the influx of refugees from war-ravaged areas. Kabul is strategically located in a valley surrounded by high mountains and at the crossroads of north-south and east-west trade routes. Therefore, it has been the site of towns since antiquity, called Kubha in the Rigveda (about 1500 B.C.) and Kabura by Ptolemy (second century A.D.). Muslim Arabs under Abdul Rahman Samurah captured Kabul in the middle of the seventh century A.D., but it took the Islamic invaders another 200 years before the Hindu rulers of Kabul were finally ousted. Kabul continued to be disputed, resulting in much destruction until Islam was definitely established under the Saffarids (ninth century A.D.). The city was part of the Ghaznavid Empire to suffer again from Genghis Khan's hordes (13th century A.D.). Kabul became the capital of a province of the Moghul Empire, whose founder, Babur Shah, is buried on the eastern slope of the Sher Darwaza Mountain. In 1775-1776 **Timur Shah** made Kabul his capital, and Afghan **amirs** ruled henceforth from that city. In the 19th century Kabul endured British occupation during the two Anglo-Afghan wars and suffered considerable destruction.

The city includes the old town, between the northern slope of the Sher Darwaza Mountain and Kabul River, and a new town (*Shahr-i nau*) begun in 1935. A large wall, 20 feet high and 12 feet thick, parts of which archaeologists believe to date from the fifth century A.D., still stands. It extends to the **Bala Hisar**, the citadel, an imposing fortress that was destroyed by the British in 1878 and rebuilt to serve as a garrison and military college in 1939. Afghan amirs resided in the Bala Hisar until Amir **Abdul Rahman** constructed the **Arg**, a walled palace, in the center of town. At the beginning of this century Amir **Habibullah** further modernized the town, providing electricity for the Arg and eventually for other parts of the town. In the 1920s the city had 60,000 inhabitants. King **Amanullah** constructed his own capital in Darulaman, about six miles from the center of town, with several government buildings and an imposing Parliament building. Members of the royal court and high government officials built their villas in the new capital, but after his fall from power, the center of government moved back into town.

The city grew rapidly after World War II with the addition of new quarters. Karta-yi Chahar (the Fourth District) was developed in 1942, followed by Khairkhana in the northwest, Nur Muhammad Shah Mina east of the old town, Nadir Shah Mina to the northeast, Wazir Akbar Khan east of Shahr-i Nau, and Khushhal Khan Mina.

In 1953 the Jada-yi Maiwand (Maiwand Street) was drawn through the old city, followed by paved avenues, villas, high-rise buildings, and prefabricated apartment complexes that replaced much of the old town. With assistance from the **Soviet Union**, the streets were paved and a grain silo and bakery were constructed.

A network of paved roads connects Kabul via the Salang Pass tunnel to the north, via the *Tang-i Gharu* (Gharu Gorge) to **Pakistan**, via **Kandahar** and **Herat** to Iran. Hydroelectric power stations in Sarobi (1957), Mahipar, and Naghlu (1966) provided electricity for the city. Soviet-style city planning and the construction of prefabricated apartment complexes have given parts of the town the appearance of a Soviet Central Asian town. Since the late 18th century, Kabul has been the seat of political power and is still the preeminent city in Afghanistan. Its population increased temporarily to almost two million as large numbers of the rural population fled to Kabul to escape the hardships of war. After the **mujahedin** conquest of Kabul in April 1992, large areas of the city were destroyed as a result of fighting between contending powers. The **Taliban** controlled Kabul and after their fall the city became an island of relative peace, protected by the **International Security Force** (ISAF) and the American armed forces. *See also* ANGLO-AFGHAN WARS; SHERPUR, SIEGE OF.

KABUL, TREATY OF. *See* **ANGLO-AFGHAN TREATY OF 1921.**

KAFIRISTAN (35-30' N, 70-45' E). "The Land of the Infidels" was an area in eastern Afghanistan that since 1906 has been called **Nuristan**, the "Land of Light," meaning the light of the Islamic religion that was brought into the area by conquest in 1896. The Kafirs, estimated at about 60,000 in the 1880s, had still preserved their traditional culture and religion, but spoke a number of related but mutually unintelligible languages. Only at the fringes of their territory had some converted to Islam when **Abdul Rahman** decided to integrate them into Afghanistan, although today all Nuristanis are Muslims. The Kafirs had a reputation as excellent fighters, and their mountainous, forested country had given them a refuge from their Islamic neighbors. When the **Durand Agreement** of 1893 included the larger part of Kafiristan within Afghan territory, Amir Abdul Rahman lost little time in taking control. *See also* KAFIR WAR.

KAFIR WAR. In his biography (AR 238–92) Amir **Abdul Rahman** gave the reasons for his action as necessitated by **Russian** penetration of the Pamir region and British control of eastern Kafiristan. If Kafiristan remained independent, the Russians (or British) might want to annex it, and, since **Panjshir, Laghman,** and **Jalalabad** once belonged to the Kafirs, the Russians "might persuade them to reclaim their old possessions." Furthermore, the warlike Kafirs would always pose a threat when the **amir** was engaged in fighting an enemy elsewhere. The Kafirs had continuously raided into Afghan provinces and had to be stopped once and for all.

The amir decided to start his campaign in the winter, when snow cover would prevent the Kafirs from seeking the safety of their mountain retreats. If the passes were open, the Kafirs could retreat into Russian territory and seek the support of that power. The war had to be short, before the neighboring powers could react and the Christian missionaries could make "unnecessary trouble."

In fall 1895 Abdul Rahman organized an army under Captain Muhammad Ali Khan, whose main force proceeded through **Panjshir** to Kulam; another force under General Ghulam Haidar Charkhi approached Kafiristan from the direction of Asmar and Chitral; and a third force under General Katal Khan approached the area from **Badakhshan.** A smaller, fourth force proceeded from **Laghman** under its governor, Faiz Muhammad Charkhi. Since all four bases were near the Afghan border, the movement of troops did not raise any suspicions of what was to come; suddenly in the winter of 1895 the four armies, supplemented by tribal levies, attacked simultaneously and conquered Kafiristan within 40 days. The Kafirs did not have a chance. Their weapons consisted primarily of spears, bows and arrows, and a few rifles, and their numbers, about 60,000, were no match against the amir's army which was divided into well-equipped artillery, cavalry, and infantry branches. Some Kafir prisoners were settled in Paghman, and after conversion to Islam a large number of their youth was trained for military service. Within a few years, all Kafirs were converted to Islam, and in 1906 **Amir Habibullah** changed the name of the country to Nuristan, the "Country Enlightened by the Light of Islam." This conquest greatly increased the reputation of the amir as the Islamic king of a unified and solidly Muslim state.

In commemoration of this victory, Abdul Rahman's general left behind the following inscription: "In the reign of Amir Abdul Rahman Ghazi, in 1896, the whole of Kafiristan, including Kullum, was conquered by him, and the inhabitants embraced the true and holy religion of Islam. [A Koranic inscription added:] Righteousness and virtue have come, and untruth has disappeared."

KALASHNIKOV, MIKHAIL T. Russian general and creator of the Kalashnikoff automatic rifle which is famous for its reliability in combat conditions. The name **AK-47** stands for the initials of Avtomat Kalashnikov and for the year of its selection in a statewide competition in 1947. It was first mass-produced in 1949 in Izhevsk, a town in the western Ural Mountains specializing in weapons production. General Kalashnikov celebrated his 85th birthday in Izhevsk in November 2004 and said he is going to write a book, because "books are now more important than weapons." The AK-47 and copies of it are now widely used all over the world. For all factions in the Afghan wars it became a weapon of choice. Kalashnikov was born on November 10, 1919, in Kurya Altay Territory.

KANDAHAR (QANDAHAR) (31-35' N, 64-45' E). A province in south-central Afghanistan with an area of 19,062 square miles and a population of 699,000, the second largest town in Afghanistan lying at an elevation of 3,050 feet and comprising an area of 15 square miles. In the late 1970s the city counted about 178,000 inhabitants. Its strategic location has made it a desirable spot for settlements since ancient times. It was the capital of Afghanistan from 1747 until 1775, when **Timur Shah** established his capital at **Kabul**. It is one of the major **Pashtun** cities and is inhabited mostly by **Durranis**, but also has a **Hazara** population and Afghans of other ethnic groups. The old, walled town, of which only traces remain, was built by Timur Shah. The mausoleum of **Ahmad Shah**, founder of modern Afghanistan, is one of the major architectural features, as is the mosque of the *Khirqa Sharif,* where the cloak of the Prophet Muhammad is believed to be kept under lock and key.

The city was part of the Achaemenid Empire of Darius I (521–485 B.C.). It was rebuilt by Alexander the Great in 329 B.C., hence the name Kandahar, a corruption of *Iskander*, the Eastern name for Alexander. Muslim Arabs conquered Kandahar in the seventh century. Thereafter, Kandahar formed part of various Islamic kingdoms.

In the 16th century the city was disputed between the rulers of the **Safavid** and Moghul empires until **Mir Wais**, a **Ghilzai** chief of

Kandahar, revolted against Safavid control and began the process that led to the establishment of Afghanistan in 1747. British forces occupied the city in two **Anglo-Afghan wars** and suffered one of their severest defeats nearby at the **Battle of Maiwand** (July 27, 1880), when Sardar **Muhammad Ayub** wiped out a British brigade under General **G. R. S. Burrows**. When **Russian** troops evacuated the city in spring 1989, Kandahar was controlled by a council of various parties, until the **Taliban** made it their "capital" in November 1994. After the **United States** intervention, Kandahar came again under Kabul control which was strengthened when the **Afghan Army** established a regional command headquarters in September 2004.

KANDAHAR, BATTLES OF. In the **Battles of Princes**, ex-king Shah Shuja marched in May 1834 from Shikarpur on the Indus River in present-day **Pakistan** and advanced on **Kandahar**. He defeated Kohandil Khan at the Khojak Pass and laid siege to Kandahar. It was a murderous engagement that seriously weakened both the defenders of the city and **Shah Shuja's** forces. The walled city was surrounded by large gardens, each enclosed in a wall and intersected by numerous irrigation channels, which greatly impeded the mobility of the cavalry, of which both forces were composed. Soldiers trapped in enclosures fought to the end, resulting in enormous casualties. On June 29 Shah Shuja led a sustained attack, but was eventually forced to retire when Amir **Dost Muhammad** came to the rescue of the besieged city. The butchery lasted for 54 days and is said to have cost the lives of about 16,000 men. **William Campbell**, alias Shir Muhammad Khan, was captured by Dost Muhammad's forces and entered the services of the amir.

During the **first Anglo-Afghan war**, the **Army of the Indus** took possession of the city on April 20, 1839, without any resistance. All was quiet, but in September 1841 Afghan **ghazis** cut the city's link with **Ghazni**, and by March 1842 tribal forces closed in on the city. General **Sir William Nott** conducted an aggressive defense, sending out raiding parties and defeating a force under Safdar Jang, a **Sadozai** chief, while the city was preparing its defenses. The gates were secured by piling grain sacks against them, and on March 10, the Afghan attack on the **Herat** Gate began. A British report said, "So reckless and daring were the assailants, that, notwithstanding the fearful havoc among them, eight or ten men actually forced their way by tearing down the burning fragments of the gate, and scrambling

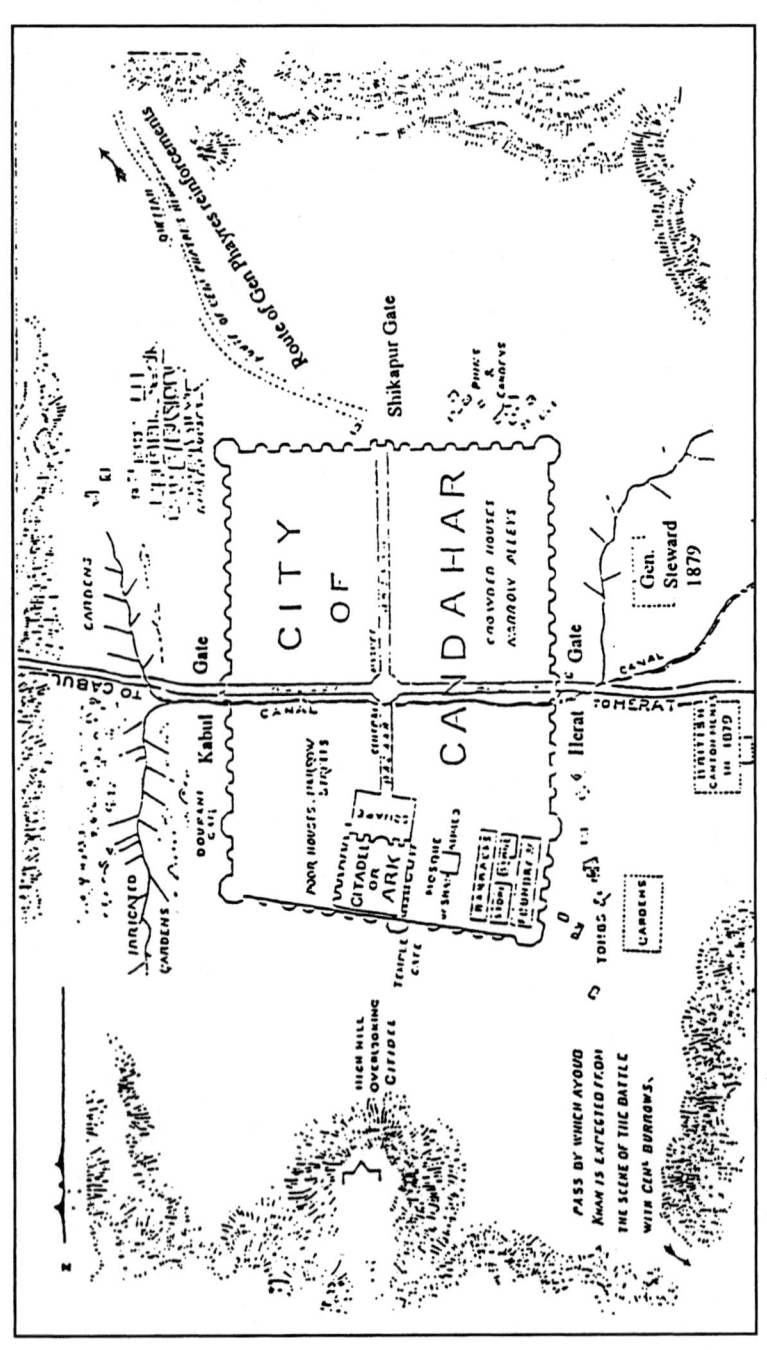

Plan 8. Kandahar (ILN 8/7/1880)

over the bags of grain. These were instantly shot. . . ." The British were able to bring in supplies and caused some disorder in the ranks of the Afghans. Another assault took place at the Shikarpur Gate, which also failed, and the Afghan forces suddenly retired in the early morning of March 10. On August 8, 1843, General **William Nott** evacuated the city and marched on **Kabul** prior to the British withdrawal from Afghanistan.

In the **second Anglo-Afghan war**, an advance force 6,000 strong under Sir **Michael Biddulph** moved from Quetta north and occupied Kandahar on January 8, 1879, without any opposition. The city was held by General **Donald Steward** and subsequently by General **J. M. Primrose** with a garrison of about 5,000 men. When after his victory at **Maiwand**, Ayub Khan advanced toward Kandahar, Primrose panicked. He gave orders to abandon the cantonment, where the troops had been stationed, and ordered a retreat into the city. All gates, except one was, closed and troops posted to defend some 6,000 yards of the city wall. Supplies coming from Quetta and the remnants of General **G. R. S. Burrows**'s brigade had difficulty entering the city through the one open gate. The British made feverish preparations for the defense: buildings outside the walls were razed, trees felled to provide a clear field of vision, and the **Pashtun** population of some 15,000 was expelled from the city. On August 8 the garrison had only two month's rations and 15 days of forage for their horses. On August 5 **Ayub Khan** reached the outskirts of the city and two days later the siege began. A sortie by Brigadier General Brooke, with a force of 300 cavalry, four companies of Royal Fusiliers, and eight companies of Bombay Infantry ended in heavy losses; 106 were killed, including Brooks, and 118 wounded. Having learned of the disaster at Maiwand, Sir **Frederick Roberts** left Kabul on August 8 and came to the relief of Kandahar by the end of the month. He met the forces of Ayub Khan at the Baba Wali Pass, and with an army of 3,800 British and 11,000 Indian troops as well as 36 guns, he was able to defeat Ayub Khan (*see* BABA WALI KOTAL, BATTLE OF). Abdul Rahman Khan occupied Kandahar, and on April 21, 1881, the British flag was hauled down, and six days later all British forces had left Afghan soil. Ayub Khan tried his fortune once more: he captured Kandahar in August 1881 but was decisively defeated on September 22 by Amir **Abdul Rahman**.

KAPISA (34-45' N, 69-30' E). A province created in 1964 with an area of 5,358 square miles and a 1991 population of about 400,000. Its capital, Mahmud Raqi, has an estimated population about 40,500. Kapisa Province was subsequently merged with **Parwan** Province. It is named after the ancient town of Kapisa, located at the present **Bagram**, which was said to have been founded by Alexander the Great (fourth century B.C.), and the summer capital of Kanishka, the ruler of the Kushanid Kingdom (second century A.D.). The city was destroyed in the eighth century.

The province is watered by the Nijrab, **Panjshir**, and Tagab Rivers. It is known for an abundance of mulberries and pomegranates. Major industries include the Gulbahar textile mills and cement production in Jabal-us-Siraj.

KARMAL, BABRAK. President and secretary-general of the **People's Democratic Party of Afghanistan** (PDPA) from January 1980 until May 1986, when Dr. **Najibullah** took over control of the Afghan government. He was born in 1929 in **Kabul**, the son of Major General Muhammad Husain (one-time governor of **Paktia** Province and purported to be a **Ghilzai Pashtun**). He adopted the pen name *Karmal* (friend of labor) in about 1954. A founding member of the PDPA, he was a student activist at Kabul University and known as a Communist. Jailed from 1953 to 1956, he then worked for the ministries of education and of planning. In 1965 and 1969 he was elected to Parliament as the representative for Kabul. He was a member of the central committee and subsequently secretary of the central committee of the PDPA. As a result of a dispute with **Nur Muhammad Taraki** over leadership of the party in 1965, the party divided and he led the **Parcham** faction until it reunited with the **Khalqis** in 1977. In 1978 he was imprisoned after the funeral of Mir Muhammad Akbar Khaibar, but liberated as a result of the **Saur Revolt**. He was then elected vicechairman of the revolutionary council and deputy prime minister of Afghanistan. In June 1978 the Khalqi regime purged the Parchami leadership, appointing Karmal Afghan ambassador to Czechoslovakia. In August 1978 he was accused of plotting against the Khalqi government and stripped of party membership and all his positions.

Restored to power with **Soviet** support, he succeeded **Hafizullah Amin** on December 27, 1979. Karmal was described as an idealist, rather than a revolutionary. He was an eloquent orator in Dari, an expert propagandist, and the best-known member of the Marxist leadership. He was unable to consolidate his position, and in 1986 he was replaced by Dr. Najibullah. He left Afghanistan for Moscow but returned to Kabul in June 1991. After the fall of the Marxist regime in April 1992, many **Parchamis** joined **Jam'iat-i Islami**. Babrak continued to reside in Microrayon, but eventually moved to **Mazar-i Sharif**, where his former comrade, **Abdul Rashid Dostum**, is the dominant political leader, and from there to Moscow. Karmal died in Moscow and is buried in Mazar-i Sharif.

KARZAI, HAMID (1957–). First elected president in Afghan history. He was sworn in for a five-year term on December 7, 2004, after an election on October 9, 2004, in which he won with a simple majority of more than four million votes. The inauguration ceremony was attended by some 150 dignitaries, including U.S. Vice President Dick Cheney and Secretary of Defense Donald Rumsfeld. This climaxed a career from fighter against the communist regime in **Kabul** to nomination as head of the **Interim** and president of the **Transitional Governments** after the fall of the **Taliban** regime. He was deputy foreign minister in the **mujahedin** cabinet of **Burhanuddin Rabbani**. A chief of the **Popalzai** tribe, he was asked to be permanent representative of the Taliban government at the **United Nations** in 1995, an assignment he did not accept. Following the **United States** intervention in Afghanistan, Karzai entered **Oruzgan** Province and started to organize **Pashtun** opposition to the Taliban government. Almost captured, he reorganized his forces and was instrumental in the defeat of the Taliban in southern Afghanistan. He originally supported the Taliban, but turned against them, accusing them of being supported by a foreign power and upholding a radical interpretation of Islam.

Ridiculed as "mayor of Kabul," Karzai played his cards well. He avoided confrontation with warlords at a time when he could not control them, and it was only when he chose his cabinet that he excluded his most powerful rivals. He ignored **Abdul Rashid Dostum**, coopted the "Amir of Herat" **Muhammad Ismail Khan**, appointing him minister of water and power, and removed Marshal **Muhammad Qasim Fahim** from his position as first vice president and minister of defense. **Yunus Qanuni**, who, with some 16 percent of the vote was a distant second in the presidential elections, was also not included in the new cabinet.

The debonair Karzai is fluent in **Dari**, Pashtu, English, French, Hindi, and Urdu; he dresses in the style of the urban Kabuli, rather than wearing the turban and tribal dress of the Pashtuns. He is an eloquent speaker and has been described as bookish, balding, with moderate views and favoring the rights of women. Born on December 24, 1957, his father Abdul Ahad Karzai, former president of the Afghan National Council, was assassinated by radicals in Quetta in 1999. Karzai was educated at Habibia School in Kabul and obtained B.A. and M.A. degrees in political science from universities in India.

KAUFMAN, GENERAL CONSTANTIN P. Conqueror of Samarkand in 1868 and Khiva in 1873, he became the first governor general of Russian Turkestan and subsequently aide-de-camp to the czar. He corresponded with Amir **Shir Ali** and his foreign minister and sent General **Stolietoff** to **Kabul** to conclude an alliance with **Russia**.

A treaty signed by the amir offered Russian support "either by means of advice or by such other means as it may consider proper." When **Britain** made war, Russia did not send any assistance, but advised Amir Shir Ali to make his peace with Britain. *See* FIRST ANGLO-AFGHAN WAR.

KEANE, LIEUTENANT GENERAL SIR JOHN (1781–1844). In 1838 he commanded the Bombay Division of the **Army of the Indus** during the **first Anglo-Afghan war.** Was given command of both the Bengal and Bombay columns advancing into Afghanistan via Quetta and **Kandahar**. He took **Ghazni** on July 23, 1839, and occupied Kandahar on August 7. He returned to India in October 1839.

KHAD, later **WAD.** *See* **AFGHAN SECURITY SERVICE.**

KHAIBAR PASS (KHYBER) (34-1'N, 71-10'E). A historic pass leading through a gorge and barren hills from the Afghan border to Peshawar, **Pakistan**. It starts at **Ali Masjid**, about 10 miles from Peshawar, narrows to about 200 yards, and reaches its highest point at 3,518 feet. The population inhabiting the pass is largely **Afridi**. Britain gained control of the pass in the Treaty of **Gandomak**, and this "Gateway to India" is now on the Pakistani side of the **Durand** Line. It was long considered impregnable, and many an invader of India preferred to pay for passage rather than try to enter by force. Akbar the Great, in 1587, was said to have lost 40,000 men in attempting to force the pass.

KHALES, MUHAMMAD YUNUS. Leader (**amir**) of the Hizb-i Islami, one of two groups with the same name headquartered in **Jalalabad**. He was born in 1919 in **Gandomak**, a Khugiani, and educated in Islamic law and theology. He is a radical **Islamist** and fervent anticommunist and in the 1960s contributed articles to the conservative *Gahis* newspaper. After the coup by **Muhammad Daud** in 1973 he was forced to flee to **Pakistan** because he had made many enemies among Daud's supporters. A member with **Gulbuddin Hekmatyar** of Hizb-i-Islami, he seceded and formed his own group with the same name, which fought the **Kabul** government in the Khugiani area. It is represented primarily in **Pashtun** regions, especially in **Nangarhar** and **Paktia** Provinces. His group enjoys some tribal support, especially among **Yunus Khales**'s own Khugiani and the Jadran tribes. Ideologically, the party of Khales differs little from the other Islamist groups, but, unlike Hekmatyar's group, favors cooperation with all **Sunni mujahedin** parties. Khales is opposed to universal suffrage, the emancipation of women, and has opposed **Shi'a** participation in the Afghan Interim Government (AIG). In May 1991 he resigned from his position as interior minister of the AIG. His base was in Jalalabad, where he had offered his services as Afghan president to succeed **Burhanuddin Rabbani**. In June 2005, Khales retired and his son took command of the Hizb-i Islami. *See also* ISLAMIST MOVEMENT.

KHALILI, ABDUL KARIM. Vice president in the **Transitional Government**. He succeeded **Abdul Ali Mazari** as head of the **Shi'a Hizb-i Wahdat** that controls the **Hazarajat**. He evicted his rivals Ustad **Muhammad Akbari** and **Muhammad Asef Muhsini** from **Bamian** in October 1995. Khalili was allied with **Abdul Rashid Dostum** against the government of President **Burhanuddin Rabbani**, but joined the latter to fight the **Taliban** movement. He was forced to flee to Iran in November 1998 and in November 2000 he submitted to the Taliban. He took advantage of the **United States** war against the Taliban and reestablished his control over much of the Hazarajat. He stepped down as head of Hizb-i Wahdat and became head of the Disarmament, Demobilisation, and Reintegration program.

KHALILZAD, ZALMAI. Appointed on December 31, 2001, as special envoy of the **United States** to Afghanistan and in 2003 as American ambassador to **Kabul**. Khalilzad served as special adviser to the state department between 1985 and 1989. He became undersecretary of defense for policy planning from 1991 till 1992, and moved to the

RAND Corporation during the Bill Clinton administration. He headed the George W. Bush-Dick Cheney transition team and advised incoming Defense Secretary Donald Rumsfeld. In May 2002 he was appointed assistant to President Bush and senior director of the National Security Council for the Persian Gulf and Southwest Asia. In anticipation of the war in Iraq, Khalilzad was appointed U.S. special envoy to the Iraqi opposition and on June 22, 2005, as ambassador to Baghdad. Khalilzad is an ethnic **Pashtun**, born in 1951 in **Mazar-i Sharif**. He graduated from Ghazi High School in 1968 and obtained B.A. and M.A. degrees from the American University in Beirut and a Ph.D. degree in 1979 from the University of Chicago.

KHALQ. See **PEOPLE'S DEMOCRATIC PARTY OF AFGHANISTAN.**

KHAN. Title of tribal chiefs, landed proprietors, and heads of communities. Feudal khans were given honorary military ranks in exchange for providing levies for the **Afghan army** in case of national emergency. The title was also used in designating the tribe of the ruling family, *khan khel*, and in positions like *khan-i ulum*, chief justice. Now khan is used like "mister" and placed after the name of a person.

KHAN, KHAN ABDUL GHAFFAR. Pashtun nationalist, acclaimed as the "Frontier Gandhi" because he advocated nonviolent means for gaining independence from **Britain** for the Frontier Afghans. He was born in 1890 in Utmanzai village in the **North-West Frontier Province** (NWFP) of India and educated in village schools and in high schools in Peshawar. He founded various organizations, including the Khuda-i Khidmatgaran (Servants of God), also called "Red Shirts," and attracted many followers in the NWFP and Afghanistan. He was imprisoned many times by the British, Indian, and **Pakistan** governments and was always an honored guest at **Kabul**, where the **Pashtunistan** issue was strongly supported. King **Amanullah** gave him the title *Fakhr-i Afghan* (Pride of the Afghans) and he lived intermittently in Kabul as guest of the royal, republican, and Marxist governments. He died in Peshawar in the late 1980s and is buried in **Jalalabad**. His funeral procession was attacked, resulting in many casualties.

KHASADAR. A tribal militia supplementing the regular **Afghan army**, usually under the direct command of provincial governors or district chiefs. They were employed in various duties, including collecting fines and as border guards. They were stationed throughout the country and only during campaigns did they come under the direct command of the army commanders. Many were recruited from Wazir and Mahsud tribes from the British side of the border, in spite of British protests.

KHATAK, KHUSHHAL KHAN (1613–1689). A celebrated warrior-poet and tribal chief of the Khatak tribe who called on the Afghans to fight the Moghuls then occupying their land. He admonished Afghans to forsake their anarchistic tendencies and unite to regain the strength and glory they once possessed. But he was pessimistic, saying, "The day the **Pashtuns** unite, old Khushhal will arise from the grave." Khushhal Khan was born near Peshawar, the son of Shahbaz Khan, a chief of the Khatak tribe. By appointment of the Moghul emperor, Shah Jehan, Khushhal succeeded his father in 1641; but Aurangzeb, Shah Jehan's successor, kept him a prisoner in the Gwaliar fortress in Delhi. After Khushhal was permitted to return to Peshawar, he incited the Pashtuns to revolt. His grave carries the inscription "I have taken up the sword to defend the pride of the Afghan, I am Khushhal Khattak, the honorable man of the age." The Khatak tribe of Khushhal Khan now lives in the areas of Kohat, Peshawar, and Mardan in the **North-West Frontier Province** of **Pakistan** and numbers between 100,000 and 160,000 people.

KHORASAN. "Land of the Rising Sun," the historical name of an area that included eastern Iran and Afghanistan and was the heartland of **Ahmad Shah**'s kingdom. A province in northeastern Iran still carries the name Khorasan.

KHOST (33-22' N, 69-52' E). A town (also called Matun) and district in **Paktia** Province, with a population of about 50,000 people. The area saw some of the fiercest fighting during the war against the Marxist government (*see* KHOST, FALL OF; ZHAWAR, BATTLE OF). The district is inhabited by Khostwals in the north and Waziris in the south, which impinges on Waziristan, a district in the **Pakistan** tribal area.

In addition to a limited amount of agriculture and livestock breeding, Khost supports a timber industry. It is one of few wooded areas in Afghanistan, and timber is smuggled to Pakistan where it fetches a good price. Because of the civil war, government prohibitions of timber exports to Pakistan were ignored, and deforestation is resulting in irreparable harm. The **Taliban** captured the area in September 1996 prior to their conquest of **Jalalabad** and **Kabul**. After the **United States** intervention, various tribal chiefs clashed over control of the area and the power of the government-appointed governor is still challenged.

KHOST, FALL OF. A town and district in **Paktia** Province, which had seen severe fighting because it was a major government base for cutting the line of **mujahedin** forces. The town was commonly called "Little Moscow" because many of the Marxist leaders were native to this area and therefore enjoyed the support of the population. Located only about 18 miles from the **Pakistan** border, the town was under siege since 1986 and had to be supplied mostly by air. The town was protected by a 3,000-man garrison, supported by militia units, and fortified with a mined perimeter that could not be easily breached. In March 1991 a unified mujahedin force, headed by a 23-member council in which **Jalaluddin Haqani** had a prominent role, began to close in on the town. The **Kabul** government may have had information of mujahedin plans and had reinforcements airlifted into the besieged town. High-ranking officers had arrived, among them Colonel General Muhammad Zahir Solamal, a deputy minister of defense. On March 13, a few days before the beginning of Ramadhan (the month of fasting), the mujahedin started with a three-day rocket barrage, followed by ground attacks from all sides, but it was not until March 30 that the airport was captured and a day later the garrison surrendered. Bad weather and surface-to-air missiles (SAM), including **Stingers**, did not permit close aerial support, but some 40 SCUD missiles were fired. It appears that the surrender was achieved largely as a result of negotiations, and the militia units are said to have changed sides in time to permit their escape. About 2,200 Kabul soldiers were taken, and 500 wounded were transported to receive medical assistance. About 300 were killed. Among the prisoners were Colonel General Solamal; Major General Ghulam Mustafa, chief of political affairs of the armed forces; Major General Muhammad Qasim, commander of artillery; Major Muhammad Azam, an air force commander; and Lieutenant General Shirin, commander of the Khost militia units.

For the mujahedin, this was a major morale booster; the Kabul government announced a "day of mourning" and accused the mujahedin of violating the "sanctity of Ramadhan." It blamed the defeat on Khalqi betrayal and claimed that Pakistani forces had participated in the assault. The relatively lenient treatment of the prisoners—some 2,000 (1,200 according to AFGHANews) families of Kabul supporters were permitted to find shelter in Pakistan—may be explained by the surrender and the fact that the battle was primarily between **Pashtuns** who did not want to incite tribal feuds. The town suffered from reprisal bombing and mujahedin plunder. The mujahedin obtained large quantities of arms and ammunition, including tanks, armored cars, helicopters, light and heavy guns. **Gulbuddin Hekmatyar's** forces were blamed for having snatched more than their "allotment." The number of mujahedin casualties was not given.

KHOST REBELLION. A rebellion led by the Mangal tribe that seriously threatened the rule of King **Amanullah**. The revolt started in March 1924 in response to the king's reforms. The Mangals under Abdullah Khan and Mulla-i-Lang (the Lame Mulla) were able to establish a base in Khost and were about to advance on **Kabul**. At the same time, Abdul Karim, son by a slave girl of ex-Amir **Yaqub Khan**, escaped from British-Indian exile and joined the rebels. In April 1924 the rebels were beaten but not yet defeated. Sulaiman Khel and Ali Khel tribes joined the revolt. In August King Amanullah dramatically proclaimed holy war against them. But it was not until January 1925 that the rebels were defeated. Abdullah Khan and Mulla- i-Lang were captured and executed together with 53 prisoners. The citizens of Kabul were treated to a victory parade, which carried the booty, followed by almost 2,000 prisoners, including women and children, organized according to tribal affiliation. The prisoners were, in the words of the German representative in Kabul, "wild men with sullen, taciturn faces who did not take the least notice of the amir." The revolt slowed down the **amir**'s process of reform until 1928, when King Amanullah again forced the process of Westernization.

KHURD KABUL PASS (34-23' N, 69-23' E). A pass about 20 miles east of **Kabul**, extending for a length of about six miles and only about 100 to 200 yards wide through which passes a road, crossing the Kabul River 23 times. On the third day of their **Death March** during the British retreat on January 8, 1842, **Ghilzai** forces blocked the pass and opened fire on the British troops and camp followers, causing panic of the "frightened mass, abandoning baggage, arms, ammunition, women and children, regardless of all but their lives" (GAZ 5). Some 3,000 soldiers and camp followers perished.

KUNAR (35-15' N, 71-0' E). A province in northeastern Afghanistan with an area of 3,742 square miles and a population of about 250,000 (1991 estimate 309,000), which is composed principally of **Nuristanis** in the north and west and **Pashtuns** in the south and east. The two ethnic groups have long been at odds because of infringement by the Pashtuns on Nuristani land. The province is traversed by the Kunar River which is fed by the Pech, Waigal, and Chitral streams and runs in a southwesterly direction into the **Kabul** River near **Jalalabad**. It provides irrigation for corn, rice, and wheat cultivation, largely on a subsistence level. Kunar and **Paktia** Provinces are the major forested areas in Afghanistan. Kunar borders on **Pakistan** in the east, **Nangarhar** Province in the south, **Laghman** in the west, and **Badakhshan** in the north. The administrative center of the province is Asadabad (near Chegha Sarai), which Afghans believe to be the birth place of Sayyid Jamaluddin Afghani. In the 1970s Kunar Province was absorbed into Nangarhar Province, with Asadabad (population about 40,000) the administrative center of the subprovince (loya woluswali), but in 1977 it was again designated a province. After the withdrawal of **Soviet** forces in 1988, the Kabul government created Nuristan Province from portions of Kunar and Laghman Provinces. The remainder of Kunar was once again consolidated into Nangarhar Province.

The **mujahedin** revolt began in 1978 in Kunar Province. Within a year government bases were captured. Virtually all mujahedin groups operated in the province, but in Asadabad the "Wahhabi Republic" (or Salafia, Islamic revival movement, also called ahl-i hadith, people of the traditions) headed by **Maulawi Jamilurrahman** and **Gulbuddin Hekmatyar**'s **Hizb** were the major contenders. Based on Saudi and Kuwaiti support, Jamilurrahman was able to win a large following, which adopted the alien Hanbali school as its religious authority. Radical **Islamist** volunteers from Pakistan and Arab countries provided both military and financial support to the Wahhabi forces. The Wahhabis were accused of killing their prisoners and enslaving women and have therefore come under criticism from other mujahedin groups. The Iraqi invasion of Kuwait led to a cut in funds and greatly limited the activities of Jamilurrahman's forces. In February 1991 he announced his cabinet and proclaimed his area an "Islamic Emirate."

Elections were held in the Kunar Valley in which the victory of the "Arabs" was disputed by Hekmatyar. Armed clashes between the Wahhabis and members of Hekmatyar's forces increased. After Hekmatyar made peace with the **Burhanuddin Rabbani** government in May 1996, one member of the Wahhabis was represented in Hekmatyar's cabinet of July 1996. But the independent enclave was ended when the **Taliban** captured Asadabad in September 1996.

KUNDUZ (QONDUZ) (36-45'N, 68-51'E). A province in northern Afghanistan with an area of 2,876 square miles and an estimated population of 575,000 (1991 est. 791,000). The province borders on Tajikistan in the north, **Takhar** Province in the east, **Baghlan** in the south, and **Samangan** in the west. The administrative capital of the state is the town of Kunduz, with about 53,000 (1991 est. 191,000) inhabitants. The Kunduz River, called Surkhab at its source in the Koh-i Baba range, meanders through Kunduz Province and runs in a northwesterly direction into the **Amu Daria**. Afghanistan's cotton industry began in Kunduz in the 1940s. An industrial complex, the Spin Zar Company, grew and ginned cotton and produced edible oil and soap. Sericulture was started at about the same time, and silk weavers produced colorful fabrics for local use and export. Uzbek garments, like the long-sleeved *japan* (caftans), soft-soled boots, and embroidered caps, constitute an important home industry. The population is largely Uzbek, but **Pashtuns** and Persian-speakers as well as other ethnic communities can also be found.

Germany maintains a **Provincial Reconstruction Team** (PRT) in Kunduz, operating under **North Atlantic Treaty Organization** (NATO) auspices.

- L -

LADEN, OSAMA BIN. Citizen of Saudi Arabia, born in Jeddah in 1957, the 17th son of Osama bin Muhammad bin Awad bin Ladin, a Yemeni construction tycoon and a Syrian mother. He graduated from King Abdul Aziz University in Jeddah in 1979 with a degree in economics and public administration and worked in the family business. In 1984 bin Laden moved to Peshawar to support the war against the communist government. He is said to have fought only at one battle, and his contribution was primarily as a fund-raiser. He is said to own the al-Hijrah Construction Company, an Islamic Bank, an import-export company, and an agricultural products firm. In 1989 he returned to Jiddah and worked in the family construction business, but in 1991 he was expelled from Saudi Arabia and moved to Afghanistan and a year later to Sudan. He protested the presence of American troops on Saudi soil and supported militant **Islamist** groups in addition to his own al-**Qaeda** organization, founded in 1988.

Forced to leave Sudan in May 1996, he went to Afghanistan where he established training camps for Islamist fighters to support the **Taliban** regime and Muslim fighters in Kashmir, Chechnya, Bosnia, and elsewhere. The **United States** government blamed him for the attacks on U.S. embassies in Kenya and Tanzania and demanded his extradition from Afghanistan. In retaliation, American cruise missiles bombarded the al-Shifa chemical plant in Sudan and three Islamist bases in Afghanistan. The refusal of the Taliban government to extradite bin Laden resulted in a **United Nations** boycott of Afghanistan, severely restricting Taliban movements. A U.S. "fact sheet," issued by the Office of Public Affairs of the American embassy in Islamabad, listed "criminal charges" against bin Laden including: repeatedly declaring war against the United States; being a terrorist and leader of the terrorist organization al-Qaeda; being responsible for the August 7, 1998, bombing of the U. S. embassies in Nairobi, Kenya, and Dar es-Salaam, Tanzania; and inciting in August 1996 Muslims to commence a "jihad against the Americans occupying the Land of the Two Holy Mosques" and ordering them to "expel the heretics from the Arabian Peninsula." In February 1998 a **fatwa** endorsed by bin Laden called on Muslims "to kill Americans—including civilians —anywhere in the world where they can be found."

When on September 11, 2001, suicide teams attacked the World Trade Center in New York and the Pentagon in Washington, D.C., the American government retaliated with war against al-Qaida and its Taliban protectors. On October 7, 2001, American forces began their attack, which quickly eliminated the Taliban regime, but bin Laden and Muhammad Omar managed to escape. Although dispersed in Afghanistan, reputed al-Qaeda remnants still carry out attacks. Some units are collaborating with Abu Musab al-Zarqawi in Iraq, where they are responsible for a number of suicide attacks.

All efforts to find bin Laden have so far failed. Is he hiding in a bunker in the tribal area, equipped with all his needs for a number of years? Or has he found shelter in one of the large Pakistani cities? A new effort has been made in the United States at the initiative of two Republican Party legislators. About $100,000 has been spent by an advertising agency on ads on Pakistani radio and in newspapers. And legislation has been passed, permitting President George W. Bush to increase the reward for the capture of Bin Laden to $50 million. To make the value of the reward comprehensible to potential informants, the legislators suggested that payments be made also in farm equipment and livestock, for people understand what a herd of cattle is worth.

LAGHMAN (35-0' N, 70-15' E). A province in eastern Afghanistan that comprises an area of 2,790 square miles and a population of about 387,000. Laghman borders on **Kapisa** in the west, **Badakhshan** in the north, **Kunar** in the east, **Nangarhar** in the south, and **Kabul** Province in the southwest. The administrative center is the village of Mehterlam. According to local legend, Laghman got its name from Lamech, father of Noah, whose ark is supposed to have landed on Kund Mountain, part of the **Kafiristan** mountain range. From Lamech the name changed to Lamakan and Laghman. Lamech was supposed to have taken the country from the **Kafirs** but was killed in the battle. **Sultan Mahmud of Ghazni,** inspired by a dream, went to Mehterlam and built a tomb over the presumed grave of Lamech. Originally occupied by Kafirs, the area was subsequently taken over by Jabbar Khel and Abu Bakar Khel **Ghilzais.**

LASHKAR. Afghan tribal armies, recruited during emergencies in support of the regular army. They fought under their own chiefs, often in competition with other *lashkar*s, and therefore not always cooperating in joint operations. The Sulaiman Khel **Ghilzais** were able to muster some 20,000 fighters and, the Afghan nomads, traveling yearly to India, could muster as many as 100,000 fighters. For a long time they were superior to the regular army, considered brave to the point of being reckless, but out for plunder and of limited staying power. They would be reluctant to operate far from their tribal areas. Feuds, temporarily ended to face a foreign invader, were quickly resumed. During the war of the 1980s, both the **Kabul** government and the **mujahedin** engaged tribal forces to protect their lines of supply. With the growth and modernization of the **Afghan army**, the *lashkar*s lost much of their importance.

LAWRENCE, COLONEL T. E. The Britisher of Lawrence of Arabia fame is suspected by many Afghans to have been a link in a conspiracy to topple King **Amanullah** from his throne. The Afghan government learned from reports in the *London Sunday Express* of September 13, 1928 that Lawrence was on the Afghan border on a "secret" mission. He was indeed there under the alias "Shaw." The Afghan paper *Aman-i Afghan* of December 12, 1928 commented that it was certain that the man who had "gathered the miserable Arabs in a revolt against the Turks" was up to mischief in Afghanistan. But the paper debunked his effectiveness on the Afghan Frontier, for, after all, "he is only an Englishman." The *London Daily News* of December 5, 1929, reported that Lawrence was in India, busily learning Pashtu and "inferred he intends to move into Afghanistan." Much of the non-British press was convinced that this was a conspiracy in support of **Habibullah Kalakani**. No sources have been found in British archives to support this conspiracy theory, and the British government denied all charges. After the British minister to **Kabul**, Sir Francis Humphrys, frantically appealed to London, Lawrence was finally sent back to **Britain**.

LIMITED CONTINGENT OF SOVIET FORCES IN AFGHANISTAN (LCSFA). Soviet term for its forces in Afghanistan, which included, according to McMichael (14), 85,000 ground troops, 25,000 support troops, and 10,000 air force troops. To this should be added some 30,000 soldiers and airmen who operated from Soviet territory. The ground units constituted the 40th Army Headquarters, five motorized rifle divisions, four to five separate motorized rifle brigades or regiments, three to four air assault or airmobile brigades, one to three brigades or special operations troops (**Spetsnaz**), one engineer regiment/brigade, and one army artillery brigade. About one-third of the force was concentrated in the **Kabul** area, and the rest was deployed in **Jalalabad, Kunduz/Mazar-i Sharif, Herat/Farah, Shindand,** and **Kandahar**. Smaller garrisons were stationed in other towns.

A Russian war manual, translated and edited by Lester W. Grau and Michael A. Gress, details the following numbers:

Year	Total Casualties	Officer Casualties
1979	up to 150	up to 15
1980	approx. 2800	approx. 320
1981	approx. 2400	approx. 300
1982	approx. 3650	approx. 400
1983	approx. 2800	approx. 350
1984	4400	up to 500
1985	approx. 3500	approx. 380
1986	approx. 2500	up to 300
1987	approx. 2300	up to 280
1988	approx. 1400	approx. 130
1989	up to 100	up to 15
Total	26000	2990

See also GROMOV, LT. GEN. BORIS V; LOGISTICS.

LINDH, JOHN WALKER. First American prosecuted for contributing his "service" to the **Taliban**. The then 20-year-old American was connected to the death of the Central Intelligence Agency officer who was killed in a Taliban uprising in the **Qala-i Jang** fortress. Eventually the government dropped nine of the charges and in a plea agreement Lindh was sentenced to 20 years in prison. A native of California, Lindh converted to Islam during high school and went to Yemen to study Arabic. He joined the **Pakistani** Harakat al-Mujahidin to fight against Indian forces in Kashmir, but then underwent military training at al-Faruq camp in Afghanistan to fight against the **Northern Alliance**. Lindh presents himself as a devout Muslim who wanted to "liberate" Indian-held Kashmir and help establish a "pure Islamic state" in Afghanistan. He claimed not to have been a terrorist, a member of **al-Qaeda**, or having foreknowledge of the attack on the World Trade Center in New York.

LOGAR (33-50' N, 69-0' E). A province south of **Kabul** with an area of 1,702 square miles and a population estimated in the late 1970s at 424,000 (in 1989 about 176,000 of this number were **refugees** in Pakistan). The province is bounded in the west by **Wardak** Province, in the north by Kabul, in the east by **Nangarhar**, in the south by **Paktia**, and in the southwest by **Ghazni** Province. The administrative center is the town of Pul-i-Alam, located about 35 miles south of Kabul. The population is largely **Pashtun** of the **Ahmadzai** tribe and some **Tajik** in the Khoshi area. In 1979, about 80 percent of the population were farmers, and the area was called the "granary of Kabul." Grapes, apples, and vegetables are the major cash crops. This is supplemented with animal husbandry and trading. Continuous war has caused considerable damage to the economy of the province.

LOGISTICS. The activities and methods connected with supplying an army with all its provisions, including facilities for storage, transport, and distribution, have always been a serious problem for an invader of Afghanistan. British forces included baggage trains, which limited the mobility of the army and were vulnerable to plunder during combat. **Rations**, officially designated, were seldom fully provided. Local resources were often inadequate and withheld and could be collected only by coercive measures.

The lack of water was always a serious problem, and many areas of Afghanistan would not support operations by large forces. The Dasht-i Margo and Registan, "The Country of Sand," in eastern and southern Afghanistan, were waterless deserts that long formed a natural barrier to an invader. In many operations water had to be carried along.

The amount of existing accommodation, usable for military purposes, was negligible, and troops had to be sheltered in tents at extremes in temperature. There were not enough facilities for the repair of equipment required by European armies. The **Soviet** forces had to undertake a building program to construct depots and storage facilities, repair or build roads, and expand or design new airfields. Fuel was scarce and had to be collected by foraging units or, during the 1980, imported from the Soviet Union.

Diseases took a toll of an invader's forces. Casualties from smallpox, malaria, dysentery, cholera, heatstroke, frostbite, pulmonary, and other diseases often exceeded those from combat. In the **second Anglo-Afghan war** five per thousand Europeans died of cholera. Medical facilities were inadequate, even during the Soviet intervention. About half of all Soviet conscripts were treated for dysentery, and about 20 percent were treated for skin infections.

The problems of logistics faced by the **United States** were quickly overcome. Unlike the Soviet Union, whose territory impinged on that of Afghanistan, the United States had to depend on bases in neighboring countries. But by December 2001 the American forces had captured air fields throughout the country. Provisions for the Coalition forces could be brought in and food drops were made to win the support of the local population.

Logistics is no longer a problem that the spending of money cannot solve. The **United Nations**, the **North Atlantic Treaty Organization**, and members of the Coalition are able to provide for their needs. Commissaries exist for the foreign community, and the public markets can provide the conveniences of life for those who can pay the price. *See also* CLIMATE AND WAR; TRANSPORT, MILITARY.

LOYA JIRGA. Great (or national) Council, it is the highest organ of state power that Afghan rulers convened to decide matters of national importance. **Ahmad Shah**'s assumption of the Afghan throne was legitimized by a Loya Jirga of tribal chiefs, as were the constitutions of King **Amanullah** (1923) and **Zahir Shah** (1964). When in October 1941 the Allies forced the Afghan government to expel all Axis nationals, the Loya Jirga reluctantly gave its approval, but insisted that they be given free passage through Allied territory. When Prime Minister **Muhammad Daud** in the 1950s decided to accept weapons from the **Soviet Union**, he also sought the approval of a Loya Jirga. The Marxist regime tried to legitimize its power with jirga approval, as did various **mujahedin** groups, with little success. One problem is that the Loya Jirga very often proved to be a rubber stamp for decisions decided by government; another, that it can be easily packed by supporters of one or another faction. President **Burhanuddin Rabbani** convened a *shura* (council) of "the people with power to loose and bind" (*ahl al-hall wa-al-'aqd*), trying to legitimize his position.

After the fall of the **Taliban** regime and the establishment of a **Transitional Government**, a Loya Jirga was convened to draft a constitution in **Kabul** on December 14, 2003. It consisted of 1,051 elected delegates, supplemented by about 550 appointed delegates who agreed on establishing an Islamic state, a presidential system of government, a two-house parliament, recognition of local languages in the areas of majority, equal rights for men and women, and appointment of the former king as lifetime "Father of the Nation." The jirga was too large to produce an effective decision-making body, the number of women representatives was smaller than desired, and intimidation and behind-the-scenes manipulations could not be prevented. Yet, the three-week jirga was able to set the stage for the establishment of a legitimate government for Afghanistan.

- M -

MACGREGOR, SIR CHARLES M. (1840–1887). Quartermaster general, commanded the First Division of the Peshawar Valley Field Force. During the second campaign in the **second Anglo-Afghan war**, he was chief of staff to **Sir Frederick Roberts**. He served with the **Kabul** Field Force and later commanded the Third Brigade of the Kabul-**Kandahar** Field Force, participated in the advance and occupation of Kabul, the relief of Kandahar, and the defense of **Sherpur**. Trousdale (7) says Sir Charles "lived an immoderate and increasingly intemperate life. He had driven others to death by the demands he had placed upon them . . . and now at 46 his constitution was completely broken." He was a simple soldier, a big bluff gruff man. He is remembered chiefly for compiling the *Gazetteer of Central Asia*, a work based on his wanderings and surveys in the area. He was born in 1840 in Agra, India, and died on February 5, 1887, in Cairo on his way to India.

MACNAGHTEN, SIR WILLIAM (1793–1841). British chief secretary to the Indian government, appointed envoy and minister to the court of **Shah Shuja**, after the occupation of **Kabul** on August 7, 1839, in the **first Anglo-Afghan war**. With the benefit of hindsight, historians gave him a good measure of the blame for the British debacle, which also cost Sir William his life. Soon after the invasion it became apparent that Shah Shuja would not be able to maintain himself on the throne without the protection of a British garrison. Therefore, Macnaghten was prepared for an indefinite occupation of Afghanistan. He became the power behind an insecure throne, paying subsidies to tribal chiefs and directing the affairs of the country to safeguard British imperial interests. Deceived by the apparent quiescence of the Afghan chiefs, he permitted the families of British officers to come to Kabul to join a colony of some 4,500 soldiers and 11,500 camp followers. All seemed well, and, as a reward for his services, Macnaghten was to receive the much coveted governorship of Bombay; **Alexander Burnes** was to succeed him in Kabul. But Afghan forces began to harass the British lines of communications and eventually a mob in Kabul attacked Burnes's residence and killed the members of the mission. Realizing the danger of his situation, Macnaghten concluded a treaty with the dominant tribal chiefs that provided for the withdrawal of the British army to India. But he had still not given up hope. Trying a divide-and-rule tactic, the envoy bribed some of the *sardars* after contracting with **Sardar Muhammad Akbar**, the ambitious son of Amir **Dost Muhammad**. When the latter discovered the duplicity, he killed Macnaghten in a "fit of rage." Only a few survived the retreat of the "**Army of the Indus**." *See* FOREIGN RELATIONS; SIMLA MANIFESTO.

MADRASA. A school of higher education in Islamic studies, usually attached to a principal **mosque**. In Afghanistan, as elsewhere in the Islamic world, education was the domain of the Islamic clergy. **Mullas** taught the basics, reading, and recitation of the Koran. The **ulama**, doctors of Islamic sciences, trained the judges (*qazis*), muftis, and other members of the religious establishment. In the 15th century, Timurid rulers established famous madrasas in **Herat**, some of which continued as major centers of education until the early 19th century; but invasions and civil wars led to a general decline of the educational system. After Amir **Abdul Rahman** ascended the throne in 1880, he founded the Royal Madrasa at **Kabul**, which became the foremost institution of its type. When Amir **Habibullah** founded **Habibia School** in 1904 as a secular school, he introduced a dual system of education that has continued to this day.

MAHAZ-I MILLI-YI AFGHANISTAN. *See* GAILANI, SAYYID AHMAD.

MAHMUD OF GHAZNI (998–1030). Son of Sebuktigin and creator of the Ghaznavid Empire that had its capital at **Ghazni**, southwest of **Kabul**, and controlled an empire extending from eastern Iran to the Indus River and from the **Amu Daria** to the Persian Gulf. Muslims see him as the epitome of the *ghazi* warrior, the "Breaker of Idols," as he called himself, and Hindus remember him as the plunderer of Hindustan. He lavished the treasures he had amassed in India on a court that was famous for its wealth and splendor and for being a center of intellectual life. The British historian Sir Percy Sykes called Mahmud "a great general who carefully thought out the plan of each campaign that he engaged in," who was not a fanatic, and "whose encouragement of literature and science and art was as remarkable as his genius for war and for government." Mahmud's tomb was spared Ghorid destruction and can still be seen in the outskirts of Ghazni.

MAIDAN (34-15'N, 68-0'E). A province in east-central Afghanistan that is now called **Wardak**.

MAIWAND, BATTLE OF. A battle on July 27, 1880, in which a force of 2,600 men under Brigadier General **G. R. S. Burrows** was totally defeated. At the end of the **second Anglo-Afghan war, Britain** had decided to dismember Afghanistan, severing **Kandahar** Province under Wali Shir Ali Khan, who was to be a vassal of Britain. **Sardar Abdul Rahman** was recognized as "Amir of **Kabul** and its Dependencies," but his cousin **Ayub** also had aspiration to the throne and had himself proclaimed **amir** at **Herat**. Kandahar was held by a garrison of some 4,700 British troops of all ranks to which were added the Afghan forces of the newly appointed "hereditary" ruler, Shir Ali Khan, when it was learned that Ayub Khan's army was moving south. Shir Ali felt he could not rely on his forces against Ayub and requested the assistance of a British brigade. General **J. M. Primrose**, the commander of Kandahar, dispatched Brigadier General Burrows with a brigade, about 2,300 strong, consisting of a troop of Horse Artillery, six companies of the 66th, two Bombay Native Infantry, and 500 Native Troopers.

At the approach of Ayub Khan, Shir Ali Khan's forces deserted en masse, taking most of their weapons with them. According to British estimates, Ayub Khan's regular forces numbered about 4,000 cavalry and between 4,000 and 5,000 infantry, as well as about 2,000 deserters and an unknown number of irregular **ghazis**. Burrows forces fell back to the vicinity of Kushk-i Nakhud, about 30 miles from Girishk and 40 miles from Kandahar, to block Ayub's approaches to these towns, but Ayub succeeded in moving his army around Burrows's forces, interposing himself between the British forces and Kandahar. The British brigade thereupon moved toward Maiwand in anticipation of Ayub's advance and to secure the provisions available at that village. On July 27, 1880, at about 10:00 a.m., the British brigade, replenished to 2,600 men, made contact with the Afghan forces, which had moved toward Maiwand on their left flank. At a ravine, the 66th Foot was on the right, its flank thrown back to prevent it from being turned. On the left were four companies of Jacob's Rifles (30th Native Infantry) and a company of sappers, while the center was held by the Horse Artillery and smooth-bore guns. The cavalry was in the rear to prevent the Afghans from encircling the British forces. The baggage was about 1,000 yards in the rear, only lightly guarded. In an artillery duel, lasting about two hours, the Afghans with 30 guns proved to be superior against the brigade's 12. By 2:00 p.m., the British cavalry had lost about 14 percent of its men and 149 horses (out of 460), and the Afghan horsemen had succeeded

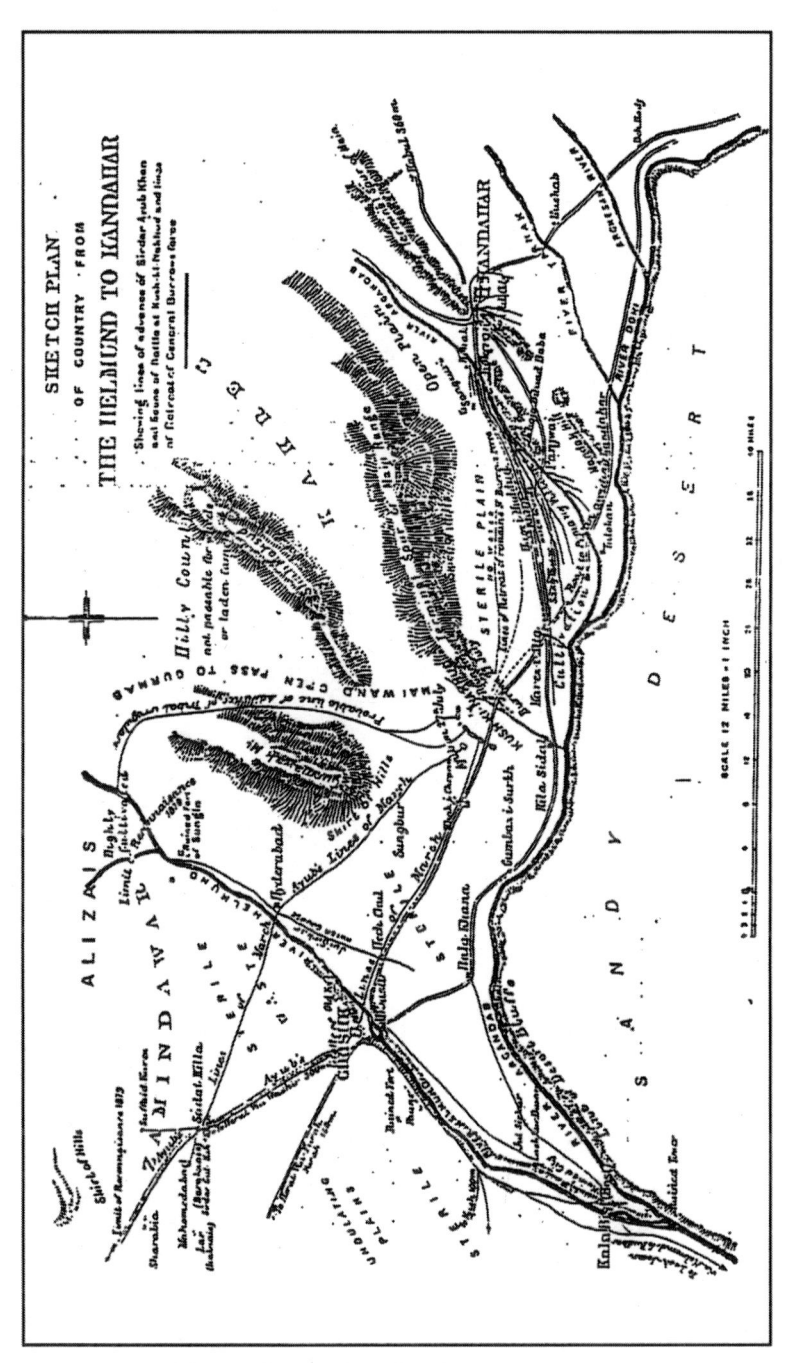

Plan 9. Sketch Plan of Helmand (ILN)

Plate 2. British Defeat at Maiwand (ILN)

in surrounding the brigade. Now swarms of ghazis went on the attack, quickly demoralizing the British troops. The 66th regiment was overwhelmed: "The slaughter of the sepoys was appalling—so utterly cowed were they that they scarcely attempted to defend themselves" (Forbes, 301). Afghan sharpshooters began to pick off British officers, who could be recognized by their helmets. A call for counterattack was ignored, and the British forces were in full flight, except for several attempts at a last stand, which no British eyewitness survived.

The British lost seven guns, 2,424 baggage animals and their loads, about 1,000 dead, and only 168 wounded survived. The rest fled to Kandahar, where many were ambushed on the way by Afghan villagers. British estimates of Afghan casualties were 1,250 regular troops and some 600 tribesmen (1,500 regulars and 3,000 tribesmen, according to Heathcote, 151). General Primrose, the commander of Kandahar, panicked and called for a British retreat inside the walls of the city, where they soon came under siege. *See* KANDAHAR, BATTLES OF. Legend has it that **Malalai**, a tribal maiden, used her veil as a banner to incite the Afghan forces to heroic deeds. The defeat at Maiwand was a factor in convincing the British occupation forces that Afghanistan could not be held at a tolerable cost.

MAIWAND, TELEGRAM FROM COLONEL ST. JOHN. Kandahar, to Foreign Department Simla, August 2, 1880. "Burrows marched from Kushk-i Nakhud on morning, 27th, having heard from me that Ayub's advanced guard had occupied Maiwand, about three miles from the latter place. Enemy's cavalry appeared advancing from direction of Haidrabad, their camp on Helmund ten miles above Girishk. Artillery and cavalry engaged them at 9 A.M., so shortly afterwards whole force of enemy appeared and formed line of battle—seven regiments, regulars in centre, three others in reserve; about 2,000 cavalry on right; 400 mounted men and 2,000 **ghazis** and irregular infantry on left; other cavalry and irregulars in reserve; five or six batteries of guns, including one of breechloaders, distributed at intervals. Estimated total force 12,000. Ground slightly undulating, enemy being best posted. Till one P.M., action confined to artillery fire, which so well sustained and directed by enemy that our superior quality armament failed to compensate for inferior number of guns. Formation being lost, infantry retreated slowly; and, in spite of gallant efforts of General **G. S. Burrows** to rally them, were cut off from cavalry and artillery. This was at 3 P.M., and followers and baggage were streaming away towards Kandahar. After severe fighting in enclosed ground, General Burrows succeeded in extricating infantry and brought them into line of retreat. Unfortunately no efforts would turn fugitives from main road, waterless at this season. Thus majority casualties appear to have occurred from thirst and exhaustion. Enemy's pursuit continued to ten miles from Kandahar, but was not vigorous. Cavalry, artillery, and a few infantry reached banks of Arghandab, 40 miles from scene of action, at 7 A.M.; many not having tasted water since previous morning.

"Nearly all ammunition lost, with 400 Martini, 700 Sniders, and 2 nine-pounder guns. Estimated loss, killed and missing,— 66th, 400; Grenadiers, 350; Jacob's Rifles, 350; Artillery, 40; Sappers, 21; Cavalry, 60. Officers killed, or missing,—Majors Blackwood, Osborne, Maclaine, Artillery; Henn, Engineers; Galbright, McMath, Garratt, Cullen, Roberts, Rayner, Honeywood, Barr, Chute, 66th; Owen, 3rd Cavalry; Hinde, Whitby, Grenadiers; Smith, Justice, Cole, Jacob's Rifles. Wounded,—Fowell, Artillery; Lynch, Preston, 66th; Anderson, Grant, Grenadiers; Iredell, Jacob's Rifles.

"Preparations being now made for siege. **Durani** inhabitants expelled. Provisions and ammunition plentiful. Wali was present during action, and is now with us, assisting actively. Of course, whole country will rise" (PP. L/P&S/20/MEMO/2).

MALALAI. A tribal maiden who contributed to the victory of **Ayub Khan** at the **Battle of Maiwand** against the forces of the British Brigadier-General **G. R. S. Burrows** on July 27, 1880. According to legend, she used her veil as a banner to incite the Afghan forces to heroic deeds. A girls school and a hospital are named after her.

MALIK. A "big man" or "petty chief" among the **Pashtuns** who possesses influence rather than power. He is a leader in war and an agent in dealings with representatives of the government. The term is synonymous with *arbab* in the west and *beg* and *mir* in the north of Afghanistan. In non-Pashtun areas, a malik is elected from among local landowners and acts as middleman in the collection of taxes and other services demanded by the central government.

MALLESON, MAJOR GENERAL WILFRID (1866–1946). Served as head of the army intelligence branch and accompanied the **Louis Dane** Mission to Afghanistan (1904–1905). He became chief censor of India, 1914. In 1918–1920 he headed the East Persian Cordon with headquarters in Meshed for the purpose of preventing Turkestan

Bolsheviks from sending armed assistance to Afghanistan during the **third Anglo-Afghan war**.

MANPOWER, AFGHAN ARMY 1936. According to an assessment of the Afghan army by the British-Indian general staff, Afghan manpower resources were as follows: Of a total population of 10 million, the maximum manpower was estimated at 1 million. There existed no arrangement for mobilizing the full manpower of the country, nor was there a reserve system or sufficient reserves of arms and clothing. Tribal levies can be raised only depending on a number of factors: whether the war was popular; in what area it was to be fought; tribal attachment to the existing regime; the amount of government power over tribe; funds available to buy their loyalty; the season of the year; and prospects of booty. Therefore, maximum regulars numbered 100,000 and tribal levies 300,000. Unless they can be fed, tribal forces will not remain more than a few days.

Recruitment. The best fighters are the tribes, but they won't furnish their quota. Therefore, the easiest supply comes from Hazaras, **Wardaks, Shinwaris, Tajiks,** Ahmadzais, and **Durranis,** as well as some **Afridis** from the British side of the border.

There were two systems of recruitment: *Hasht-nafari,* chosen by lot; and *Qaumi,* where a tribe has to provide a definite quota. Each village had to contribute fixed sums for the recruits' expenses. Service was for two years—recruits were often compelled to serve longer. Some extend their service. Soldiers were badly paid (in 1936 Rs. 24 ½ = Rs. 7 Indian) and had to pay for their rations. There were no pensions and discipline was only fair.

Officers. Were recruited from cadet college (Maktab-i Harbiya) and from the ranks. Courses lasted for three years, and separate classes existed for each arm. Promotion was slow, those with some education or from good families occasionally got commissions. Good and loyal service was sometimes rewarded by grant of a commission.

Administration. The nominal head was the king, but in fact, the minister of national defense, then Shah Mahmud, who was also commander in chief. The deputy (*muawin*) refers important matters to the minister.

Auxiliary Units and Semimilitary Forces:
Militia—Urgun Militia, of Wazirs, Mahsuds, and Kharots. Mostly from British side of border.
Armed Police (*Kotwali*), a gendarmerie. Under control of the ministry of interior. Units existed in every province. Used to

maintain public security. Mostly in big towns, posts along roads, and some at frontier.

Unarmed Police Ranks: Komandan, a Ghund Mishar; Sar Mamur, Chief Superintendent, a Kandak Mishar; Mamur, Superintendent, usually a Toli Mishar.

Khasadars, chiefly for road protection, wear Khaki uniform.

Tribal Levies. Response depended on: 1. degree of popularity of war, 2. whether **jihad** was called, 3. amount of money tribes can make for passage of army.

Tribal patriotism is local. A tribal *lashkar* will never stay for long in the field at full strength, as tribesmen will always be coming and going, particularly after a success when loot has to be taken home.

Special Bodyguard Troops. In **Kabul**, the Hazirbash — 300 men, recruited mostly from the southern province. Bodyguards of the royal family—resemble in dress the militias on the British side of border. They were under the command of the Guards Division.

Education. Cadet Colleges: 1. Maktab-i Ihzarieh, Preparatory School, 600 students, five-year course; 2. Maktab-i Rushdiyeh, Middle School, 280 students, three-year course, specialization begins; 3. Maktab-i Harbiya, 240 students, three-year course. All controlled by ministry of war. At 1. and 2. instructors are both civilian and military, education is general. Drill and physical training were taught and cadets wore military uniform. Kurs-i Ali, Advanced Course for Senior Officers, opened in 1935. It had 45 students and took three years. Chief instructor was a retired major of the German army. (Notes on the Afghan Army, 1936, General Staff, India L/MIL/17/14/18.)

MANUPUR, BATTLE OF. A battle on March 11, 1748, between an **Afghan army** of some 30,000 under **Ahmad Shah Durrani** and a Moghul army of some 60,000 and 140,000 camp followers under the command of Prince Ahmad, the heir apparent of the great Moghul emperor, Muhammad Shah. Ahmad Shah arrived near Lahore on January 8, before the Moghul army could reach the city. In a quick move Ahmad Shah crossed the Sutlij River and took possession of Sirhind Fort, where the Moghul baggage train was sheltered. The Moghul army camped at Sirhind and desultory fighting started on March 3. The Afghan army disposed of only one heavy gun, placed on a hill that overlooked the camp of the Indians, who had a greater arsenal of heavy artillery. By a lucky chance a cannon shot from the Afghan side killed Qammaruddin, the Moghul commander in chief. The Moghul army was hard pressed and its Rajput contingent deserted, when reinforcements saved the Moghul army from defeat. An explosion of ammunition stores caused heavy losses in the Afghan camp, and Ahmad Shah retreated, carrying his Sirhind treasure with him to Afghanistan. Prince Ahmad's father was in poor health; therefore, the Moghul prince decided to return to Delhi rather than give pursuit.

MARATHAS (MAHRATTAS). *See* **PANIPAT, BATTLE OF.**

MARATHA WEAPONS. The Marathas used old and new weapons. Stones were hurled from fortresses. At **Panipat**, bows and arrows were still used. Bows were of bamboo and steel. Crossbows were also employed. Cavalry used swords—mostly straight—daggers, spears, lances, and mace. Soldiers wore turbans, the officers, helmets and chain armor. Shields were fashioned of rhinoceros skin and steel, which "would easily turn a pistol ball." Cannons, pistols, revolvers as well as matchlocks—long barrel usually attached to the stock by leather strips. Guns were drawn by buffaloes.

MASHK-I ALAM. *See* **DIN MUHAMMAD.**

MAS'UD, AHMAD SHAH (MASSOUD). One of the most publicized **mujahedin** leaders from the **Panjshir** Valley of **Parwan** Province, north of **Kabul**. He withstood numerous **Soviet** invasions into his territory; but in 1983 he concluded a temporary truce with Soviet forces, which was described as a tactical measure since it did not prevent him from carrying out attacks elsewhere. (*See* APPENDIX 4.) He organized a supervisory council and is one of few commanders who sought to set up a civil administration, instill discipline in his troops, and use modern military principles of tactical warfare. He was a member of the Jam'iat-i Islami-yi Afghanistan, headed by Professor **Burhanuddin Rabbani**, which is largely of non-**Pashtun** background. After the withdrawal of the Soviet troops from Afghanistan, he was able to extend his territorial control, establishing his headquarters at Taluqan. His group was involved in bloody clashes with **Gulbuddin Hekmatyar**'s Hizb-i Islami, which resulted in considerable casualties to both sides. Because of his successes, Mas'ud is called "The Lion of Panjshir" by his admirers.

Born in 1956, he was educated at Istiqlal High School and the Military Academy, where he graduated in 1973. He was a member of the radical **Islamist Movement**. Mas'ud captured Kabul with the help of the **Uzbek** forces of General **Abdul Rashid Dostum**, but other groups, including the **Shi'a** Wahdat, carved out areas under their control and fighting continued over control of the city. Mas'ud was elected minister of defense, a post he relinquished in an attempt at compromise with the Hizb-i Islami of Gulbuddin Hekmatyar. Nevertheless, Mas'ud continued to control the armed wing of the Jam'iat-i Islami, and he gained control of the entire city of Kabul after defeating the other mujahedin groups. He was engaged in a struggle for survival against the **Taliban**, who captured Kabul in September 1996, and was assassinated in a suicide attack on September 9, 2001. Mas'ud was succeeded by **Muhammad Qasim Fahim**, who captured Kabul after the fall of the Taliban regime.

MAUDE, LIEUTENANT-GENERAL SIR FREDERICK F. (1821–1897). Commanded the 2nd Division Peshawar Valley Field Force of some 5,000 troops in the **second Anglo-Afghan war** from its formation until it was broken up on the conclusion of the first campaign. In December 1878, he commanded the first and second punitive expeditions against the **Afridis** in the Bazar Valley, causing great damage to the land, but little to the tribesmen who had withdrawn into the mountains.

MAZARI, ABDUL ALI. Chief of the radical Nasr (Victory) party, which succeeded in capturing most of the Hazarajat from traditional groups. In 1989 he joined the **Hizb-i Wahdat**, a coalition of seven **Shi'a** parties, and subsequently became its head. He collaborated with **Burhanuddin Rabbani**, but eventually allied himself with **Gulbuddin Hekmatyar**. A hard-liner, he was accused of having liquidated some of his opponents. He was himself killed in March 1995 in **Taliban** captivity, after he surrendered to this new force. He was buried in **Mazar-i Sharif**. He was born in 1948, the son of Haji Khodadad.

MAZAR-I SHARIF (36-42' N, 67-6' E). Capital of **Balkh** Province with an estimated population of 70,000 and at one time also the name of a province that included the present **Jozjan**, Balkh, and **Samangan** Provinces. Mazar-i Sharif, located about 13 miles east of Balkh village, is named "The Noble Tomb" because of a local claim that the Caliph Ali (r. 656–661) is buried in the city (Najaf in present Iraq is generally accepted as the burial place). According to that claim, Ali's body was placed on the back of a white camel that was permitted to wander about. It was decided to bury the **caliph** on the spot where the camel eventually halted. Two cupolas were constructed over the tomb by Sultan Ali Mirza in the early 15th century. Subsequently a great **mosque** and shrine were built in its location, and Mazar-i-Sharif became an important place of pilgrimage. As the town grew it eventually superseded Balkh in importance and became the capital of the province.

In the late 19th century the town had some 20,000 inhabitants, and by the 1930s it had become the major commercial center in northern Afghanistan. In the 1970s the new part of the town was built according to principles of modern town planning, with avenues intersecting at right angles and modern shops rather than the traditional **bazaar**. The town is an important commercial center famous for its Qaraqul skins, carpets, and melons and is developing into a major industrial town for fertilizer and textile production. Because of its proximity to the former Soviet border and its flat terrain, the area was easily defended from **mujahedin** attacks and became a stronghold of the Marxist regime. It lies about 270 miles northwest of **Kabul** on the paved road that connects the capital with northern Afghanistan. After the fall of the Marxist government in Kabul, General **Abdul Rashid Dostum** made Mazar-i Sharif his capital. He founded a university in Mazar which enrolled 6,000 students, about 35 percent women.

MAZAR-I SHARIF, FALL OF. The fall of Mazar-i Sharif precipitated the fall of President **Najibullah** and his **Kabul** government. It occurred in March 1992, not as a result of military conquest, but rather as the consequence of a power struggle within the Marxist leadership. Najibullah wanted to replace the **Tajik** general, Mumin, commander of the Hairatan garrison and guardian of the major weapons depot in the northern province, with the **Pashtun** general, Rasul. Mumin refused to go and allied himself with General **Abdul Rashid Dostum**, commander of the **Jozjani** militia, and Sayyid Mansur Nadiri, head of the Ismaili forces that control the area north of the Salang Pass. They cooperated with **Ahmad Shah Mas'ud** and assisted the latter in the capture of Kabul on April 25. Dostum then founded the National Islamic Movement (junbesh-i milli-yi Islami), with Nadiri and others and controlled the entire north-central area of Afghanistan until the **Taliban** conquest of the city. Mazar-i Sharif was taken by the **Northern Alliance** with American aerial support on November 9, 2001.

MCMAHON, ARTHUR HENRY (1862–1949). He accompanied the **Durand** Mission to **Kabul**, 1894, and was in charge of marking the boundary between Baluchistan and Afghanistan, 1897. He was in charge of Seistan Mission and British arbitrator for the Afghan-Persian boundary, 1903–1905, and served as the foreign secretary to the government of India, 1911–1914.

MCNEILL, LIEUTENANT GENERAL DAN K. Commanding general of **United States** and coalition forces in Afghanistan. He came to Afghanistan in May 2002 on a one-year tour of duty to be replaced by Major General **John R. Vines**. McNeill commanded 11,500 troops of whom 8,500 were American. He was a graduate with a B.S. degree from North Carolina State University in 1968 and from the U.S. Army War College in 1989. Before coming to Afghanistan he was Commander, XVIII Airborne Corps and Fort Bragg, North Carolina. When 48 people were killed and 117 injured in a bombing raid on a wedding party on July 1, 2002, McNeill visited Dehrawud to discuss the matter with local leaders and village elders. The Afghan government paid $18,500 in compensation to the victims: $200 for each killed person and $75 for each wounded and the U.S. provided tents and blankets to villagers in Dehrawud and Kakrakai in **Oruzgan** Province. McNeill claimed that U.S. planes had come under fire; Afghans say they fired rifles in celebration at the wedding. According to some sources, Afghan informers were feeding U.S. bombers wrong information. McNeill mediated between Gul Agha Sherzai, governor of **Kandahar**, and **Ismail Khan**, "**amir**" of **Herat**, to stop Herat from levying customs on Kandahar merchants (Robert Moore, 2003).

MILITIA. *See* **ARMY, AFGHAN.**

MINES. Mines, detonated by contact, magnetic, proximity, or electric command, were first used during the **Soviet** intervention in Afghanistan, where they were employed by all parties as a weapon of passive defense to protect bases and offensively to block lines of logistics. Villages suspected of harboring rebels were made uninhabitable by widespread sowing of mines. Antipersonnel mines, especially the PFM-1 "butterfly" mine, were most commonly dispensed by helicopters and scattered at random. The **mujahedin** eventually obtained various types of mines from foreign supporters, including plastic ones, which made detection difficult. The mujahedin mined roads in ambush operations, choosing places where an entire convoy could be blocked. According to McMichael, the Soviet forces planted literally millions, and the mujahedin thousands, of mines, which still pose a severe threat to life in Afghanistan many years after the end of the war.

MIR WAIS KHAN HOTAKI (1709–1715). A **Ghilzai Pashtun** and founder of the short-lived Hotaki dynasty (1709–1738). Leader of the Afghan tribal revolt against Persian domination that led to the foundation of modern Afghanistan. He was a Ghilzai chief who lived as a hostage at the court of the **Safavid** ruler in Isfahan while **Kandahar** was ruled by Gorgin Khan, a Georgian governor. Mir Wais got permission to go on a pilgrimage to Mecca, where he obtained **fatwa** (legal decision) authorizing revolt against the **Shi'a** domination of western Afghanistan (which is largely **Sunni**). Upon his return to Kandahar he used the fatwa to win the support of tribal chieftains and, in 1709, staged a successful revolt against Gorgin Khan's troops. Mir Wais and his Afghan forces defeated all attempts by the Safavid armies to recapture Kandahar and laid the basis for the Afghan invasion of Persia and the defeat of the Safavids at **Gulnabad** in 1722. *See also* HOTAKI.

MOHMAND. A powerful tribe of eastern **Pashtun** origin that migrated from the area north of **Kandahar** to the Peshawar area. Their territory was dissected by the **Durand Line** in 1893, but they continued to be a factor in the politics of both states. In the early 20th century they were estimated to comprise some 40,000 families and could raise 18,000 fighters. They supported Prince Kamran in the early 19th century and joined the **Shinwaris** in their revolt against King **Amanullah** in November 1928. In 1930 the Haji of Turangzai, a tribal **mulla**, led them against British forces on the frontier. The Mohmand area was always autonomous, and the British Indian, as well as later the **Pakistan** government, controlled the Mohmand Agency indirectly by means of an agent who acted as the representative of the government. In September 1935, they staged a major uprising against the British government. During the civil war in the 1980s, the Mohmands generally remained neutral.

MOSQUE (MASJID). The Islamic place of worship, where Muslims assemble for prayer, especially on Fridays when communal prayers are obligatory and the traditional sermon (*khutba*) is delivered.

Mosques vary in size from one-room buildings to monumental structures, but all mosques have a prayer niche (*mihrab*) that indicates the direction of the Ka'ba, the Islamic shrine in Mecca. Before prayer Muslims must perform a ceremonial washing, *wudhu'*, and enter the prayer room without their shoes. Prayer includes repeated bowings (*ruku'*) whereby one touches the ground with the forehead. Prayers are usually performed in unison with one person leading in prayer. Larger mosques have a pulpit, *minbar*, and minarets from which the "crier," *muezzin*, gives the call to prayer. Cathedral mosques usually have a large courtyard with fountains, high minarets, and buildings for schools and colleges (**madrasas**).

On special holidays Afghan kings attended prayers at the Idgah Mosque in **Kabul**, and high government officials attend prayers in provincial capitals. The Friday sermon is read in the name of the ruler and, therefore, has political significance. Until the government took over these functions, mosques were the main centers of education, public welfare, and social or political gatherings and even today their role is important. Mosques are supported by the state or local communities, as well as by pious endowments administered by the **ulama**. *See also* ISLAM; RELIGIOUS SCHOOLS.

MUHAMMAD DAUD, SARDAR (1909–1978). President of the Republic of Afghanistan from July 1973 until his assassination in April 1978 as a result of the **Saur Revolt**. Born in 1909 in **Kabul**, the son of Sardar Muhammad Aziz, and educated in Kabul and France, he embarked on a military career and was governor and general officer commanding the Eastern Province (1934), **Kandahar** (1935), and the Central Forces (1939–1947). He was stationed in Kabul and served as minister of defense in 1946. He was minister of the interior (1949–1950) and the prime minister (1953–1963). He encouraged social reforms and in 1959 permitted women to abandon the veil, thus contributing to their emancipation and participation in the public life of Afghanistan.

Muhammad Daud initiated two five-year plans (1956–1961 and 1962–1967) and a seven-year plan in 1976, and relied for military and developmental aid on the **Soviet Union**. He demanded the independence of **Pashtunistan**, the North-West Frontier Province of **Pakistan**, which led to repeated crises with Pakistan and ended with his forced resignation in 1963. Ten years later Muhammad Daud staged a coup against his cousin, King **Muhammad Zahir,** and in July 1973 proclaimed Afghanistan a republic. Whether he just wanted power or felt that the political liberalization during the democratic decade

(1963–1973) had failed to remedy the social and economic problems of Afghanistan is not clear. He relied on the support of leftists to consolidate his power, crushed the emerging **Islamist movement**, and in 1975 established his own "National Revolutionary Party" as an umbrella organization for all political movements. Thus he wanted to limit the power of the Left and create a left-of-center movement loyal to him. Toward the end of his rule Muhammad Daud attempted to purge his leftist supporters from positions of power and sought to reduce Soviet influence in Afghanistan. He sought financial support from Iran and the Arab Gulf states to enable him to repay Soviet loans and improve his relations with the West. He and members of his family were assassinated on April 27, 1978, as a result of the Saur Revolt, which brought Marxist parties to power in Kabul.

MUHAMMADI, MAULAWI MUHAMMAD NABI. Leader of the Harakat-i Inqilab-i Islami (Islamic Revolutionary Movement), a traditional Islamic **mujahedin** group headquartered in Pakistan. He was born in 1921 in **Logar**, the son of Haji Abdul Wahhab, and educated in **madrasas** (religious colleges) in Logar Province. In the 1950s he was one of the first members of the religious establishment who agitated against "Communist influence" in the Afghan educational system and was elected to Parliament in 1964 as a representative of Logar Province. After the Marxist coup, he fled to **Pakistan** and utilized a network of *maulawis* (graduates of madrasas) to organize armed resistance against **Kabul**. In the early 1980s his Harakat was the largest of mujahedin groups, but it lost members to the more radical Islamist parties of **Abdul Rasul Sayyaf** and **Burhanuddin Rabbani**. He has since joined **Gulbuddin Hekmatyar** against Rabbani. His party had primarily **Pashtun** support. In 1992 Muhammadi became vice president in Rabbani's government, but in March 1995 he recognized the **Taliban** movement, which many of his party joined. Muhammadi died on April 22, 2002, in Pakistan.

MUHAMMAD ISHAQ. Son of Amir Muhammad Azim Khan and cousin of Amir **Abdul Rahman** who in June 1888 had himself proclaimed **amir** and unsuccessfully fought Abdul Rahman for the throne. Born about 1851 of an Armenian mother, at age 18 he was in command of Abdul Rahman Khan's forces in Afghan Turkestan. He was defeated by Amir **Shir Ali** and lived with Abdul Rahman in exile at Samarkand. In 1879 he returned with Abdul Rahman Khan to Afghanistan. When the latter assumed the **Kabul** throne, he appointed Muhammad Ishaq governor of Turkestan, as the northern provinces were then called. Ishaq Khan was ambitious; he demanded autonomy amounting to virtual independence, subject to token allegiance to the Kabul throne. He next extended his control over **Herat** Province, and when Amir Abdul Rahman was ill in 1888, he proclaimed himself amir. The "Iron Amir" finally defeated him on September 29, 1888, at the **Battle of Gaznigak.**

MUHAMMAD ISMA'IL KHAN. Mujahedin commander affiliated with the Jam'iat-i Islami headquartered in **Herat.** He was the "**amir**" of Herat, **Badghis, Ghor,** and **Farah** Provinces and is said to have built a good military organization and was a good administrator. He was born in 1946 in **Shindand,** and after completing his elementary education in Shindand, he continued his education at **Kabul** Military School and the Military Academy. He was a second lieutenant in the 17th Division stationed in Herat when he defected and participated in the uprising of March 1979. When the uprising was suppressed, he fled to Iran and made his way to **Pakistan,** where he joined the forces of the mujahedin leader **Burhanuddin Rabbani.** In 1987 he was said to have received **Stinger** missiles, which helped him to secure control of much of Herat Province. He called himself "Amir" and seemed to have ambitions for autonomous rule, but was defeated by **Taliban** forces and forced to flee the country on September 5, 1995. Isma'il Khan was captured by General **Abdul Malik** and surrendered to Taliban forces in 1997. He managed to escape to Iran and, after the American intervention, resumed control of Herat Province until he was deposed by the **Hamid Karzai** government in September 11, 2004, but he was later appointed minister of water and power.

MUHAMMAD JAN, GENERAL. One of the ablest Afghan generals who outmaneuvered Generals Baker and Macpherson in December 1879 and defeated a force under General Massey. He captured **Takht-i Shah** and forced the British to retire to **Sherpur.** Muhammad Jan led the attack on Sherpur, but he was unable to overcome the British defenses.

MUHAMMAD NADIR SHAH. King of Afghanistan, 1929–1933. Born in 1883, the son of Sardar Muhammad Yusuf Khan, he embarked on a military career. Appointed a brigadier in 1906, he was promoted to lieutenant general (*naib salar*), for his services in suppressing the Mangal Revolt in December 1912. He was appointed general (*sipah salar*), in 1914. He and other members of the Afghan court had accompanied Amir **Habibullah** to **Jalalabad,** the winter capital, and when the **amir** was assassinated in his sleep, Nadir was arrested.

Amir **Amanullah** exonerated him of any involvement and sent him to command the troops in **Khost** Province. This threatened to cause a general uprising among the "British" Afghans and was one of the factors forcing **Britain** to accept Afghan independence. Amir Amanullah appointed him minister of war in 1919, in which post he served until 1924, when he was appointed Afghan minister in Paris. After the abdication of King Amanullah in January 1929, Nadir left France for India and established himself at the Afghan frontier. He collected tribal support, including Waziri tribal forces from the Indian side of the border, and, after initial setbacks, defeated **Habibullah Kalakani** and captured **Kabul** on October 13, 1929. Nadir Khan was proclaimed king two days later. He was assassinated in 1933 and succeeded by his son **Muhammad Zahir**.

MUHAMMAD OMAR. See **OMAR MUHAMMAD, MULLA.**

MUHAMMAD YUSUF (MOHAMMAD YOUSAF). Brigadier Muhamad Yusuf, head of the Afghan Bureau of the **Inter-Services Intelligence** of the **Pakistan** military from 1983 to 1987. He claims to have held a pivotal position in the war of the Afghan **mujahedin** against the Soviet and **Kabul** forces. In his book, *The Bear Trap: Afghanistan's Untold Story* (coauthored with Mark Adkin), this "commander-in-chief" of the mujahedin forces controlled the distribution of weapons bought with Central Intelligence Agency and Saudi Arabian funds from the **United States, Britain**, China, and Egypt. He organized the training of rebels and planned missions of sabotage, ambushes, and assassinations inside Afghanistan and the **Soviet Union**. He was succeeded in 1978 by General **Hamid Gul**, at a time when the Soviet government had decided to end its involvement in Afghanistan.

MUHAMMADZAI. The Muhammadzai (a branch of the Barakzai of the **Durrani** tribe) are the descendants of Sardar Painda Khan. They captured the **Kabul** throne in 1826 under Amir **Dost Muhammad** and continued in power (with the exception of the nine-month rule of **Habibullah Kalakani**) until the Marxist coup in 1978 deposed President **Muhammad Daud**. For Muhammadzai rulers, *see* DURRANI DYNASTY.

MUHAQEQ, AYATOLLAH MUHAMMMAD. Minister of planning and vice chairman in the **Transitional Government** of Hamid Karzai until he decided to run for election to the presidency on March 2, 2004. A **Hazara** military commander from **Parwan**, he fought the **Taliban** in central and northern Afghanistan. He is director general of the **Shi'a Hizb-i Wahdat**. He studied at Shi'a universities in Najaf, Iraq, and has become a "Source of Imitation" (*marja 'i taqlid*) for his followers. He was born in 1955 in Charkent, **Balkh**, the son of Haji Muhammad Sarwar who is originally from Balkh. He earned a B.A. degree in Islamic Studies. He served as chairman of the political committee of Hizb-e Wahdat-e Islami and administrator of the northern areas and became an important party member and a successful commander against the Taliban.

MUHSINI, AYATOLLAH MUHAMMAD ASEF. A **Hazara**, born in 1935 in **Kandahar** Province and educated at the **Shi'a** universities in Iraq. He is called ayatollah by his supporters. Upon his return to Afghanistan he founded a cultural organization called "Dawn of Knowledge" (sobh-i danesh), which became the nucleus of the rural-based **mujahedin** group, Harakat-i Islami-yi Afghanistan (Islamic Movement of Afghanistan). In 1980 he was elected chairman of the "Afghan Shi'a Alliance," a mujahedin umbrella group headquartered in Iran, but he subsequently left the alliance and moved to Quetta. His group once rivaled *Nasr* in importance and collaborated with *Nasr* in expelling the **Shura** of **Sayyid Ali Beheshti** from most of the **Hazarajat**. In June 1990 the Shi'a groups announced formation of a new organization, "The Unity Party" (**Hizb-i Wahdat**), but Muhsini presented a number of conditions for his joining the coalition. Some of his commanders joined the Hizb-i Wahdat. Muhsini is known as a moderate who did not receive support from Iran. Since the fall of the Marxist regime, his party has supported the government of President **Burhanuddin Rabbani**. He participated in the **Bonn Conference**, 2001, and the Loya Jirga of 2002.

MUJADDIDI, SEBGHATULLAH. Elected president in February 1989 of an Afghan Interim Government (AIG) made up of members of the seven-party alliance of **mujahedin** headquartered in Pakistan. He founded and still leads the National Liberation Front of Afghanistan (Jabha-yi Najat-i Milli-yi Afghanistan), which conducted armed attacks on **Soviet** and Afghan government forces since about 1980. Born in 1925 in **Kabul**, the son of Muhammad Masum, he was educated in Kabul and at al-Azhar University in Egypt, and subsequently taught Islamic studies at high schools and colleges in Kabul.

He publicly denounced "unbelievers" and Communists and was imprisoned (1959–1964) for involvement in a purported plot to assassinate the Soviet premier, Nikita Khrushchev. When he was freed, he traveled abroad for two years, and, upon his return, he founded the Jam'iat-i Ulama-yi Muhammadi (1972, Organization of Muslim Clergy). He was again politically active and participated in anti reformist demonstrations in Kabul in the 1970s and was forced to flee abroad in order to escape arrest. He was head of the Islamic Center in Copenhagen, Denmark (1974–1978), and, after the **Saur Revolt**, went to **Pakistan**, where he led the armed resistance of the National Liberation Front. His supporters are primarily **Pashtun** members of the Naqshbandi sufi order in **Paktia** and **Kandahar** Provinces.

In spite of his radical background, he was counted as a leader of the moderate groups which did not rule out the establishment of a constitutional monarchy. After the fall of the Marxist government in April 1992, Mujaddidi served as interim president for two months, in which capacity he amnestied his Communist opponents and promoted **Abdul Rashid Dostum** to the rank of general. In the subsequent power struggle in Kabul, Mujaddidi supported **Gulbuddin Hekmatyar** against **Burhanuddin Rabbani**, when the latter refused to step down at the end of his two-year appointment. After the **Taliban** captured Kabul in September 1996, Mujaddidi recognized their regime and ceased being politically active.

MUJAHEDIN (MUJAHEDUN). Fighters in a holy war **(jihad)**. Afghan resistance fighters adopted this designation to indicate that they were waging a lawful war against an "infidel" government. The mujahedin were organized in a tenuous alliance of seven **Sunni** groups stationed in Peshawar, including the moderate leaders **Muhammad Nabi Muhammadi, Sebghatullah Mujaddidi**, and **Sayyid Ahmad Gailani**, and the Islamist radicals **Burhanuddin Rabbani, Muhammad Yunus Khales, Gulbuddin Hekmatyar**, and **Abdul Rasul Sayyaf**. In 1989 these groups formed an Afghan Interim Government (AIG) with Sebghatullah Mujaddidi as the president. In 1989 a **Shi'a** alliance of eight groups (some of them small or inactive) in Iran united in an umbrella organization called **Hizb-i Wahdat** (Unity Party) that, however, refused to join the AIG of the Sunni groups because of what they considered insufficient representation. Refugees in **Pakistan** and commanders in the field were required to be affiliated with one of the seven groups if they wanted to receive outside assistance. The Pakistani government recognized only six (later seven) Sunni groups, preventing the proliferation of parties. The Pakistani military **Inter-Services Intelligence** (ISI) took an active part in planning and executing attacks and favored Islamist (rather than nationalist or moderate) groups, especially Gulbuddin Hekmatyar's Hizb-i Islami, with the supply of funds and war materiel.

Many of the commanders did not necessarily share the ideology of their leader and some switched "allegiance" when it helped in obtaining supplies. Mujahedin were also grouped according to regional, tribal, and ethnic origin; the Jam'iat of Rabbani, largely non-**Pashtun** in ethnic composition, was active in northeastern Afghanistan. The Jam'iat was in conflict with its ideological brother, the Hizb of Gulbuddin Hekmatyar. Ideological purity (never precisely defined) also suffered as a result of the "tactical alliance" in March 1990 between **Shahnawaz Tanai**, a **Khalqi** hard-liner, and Hekmatyar, one of the most radical Islamists. In the ever-changing constellation of forces, Hekmatyar made his peace with Rabbani in May 1996 and established himself in **Kabul** as prime minister. The **Taliban** ended the dream of the allies at Kabul, when they captured the city and conquered most of the country. After the fall of the Taliban, the major actors in the struggle for political power were General **Abdul Rashid Dostum**, a former Communist, in the north; the **Panjshiris** who occupied Kabul; "Amir" **Muhammad Isma'il Khan** in Herat; and the Hizb-i Wahdat, which controls most of the **Hazarajat**. The **Transitional Government**, headed by **Hamid Karzai**, is gradually extending its control over the provinces.

MULLA. A preacher and spiritual adviser as well as a teacher in elementary **mosque** schools. A mulla performs such religious activities as recitation of the *adhan* (call to prayer) in the ear of the newborn and presiding at marriage and burial ceremonies. He is paid for his services by donations from his parish and often needs to supplement his income by pursuing a trade or agricultural work. Mullas vary considerably in educational background, from the barely literate to those with some **madrasa** education.

Until the rise of the **Taliban**, they had never held political power on a national scale, but individual mullas exercised great influence on a grass-roots level. They mediate in tribal disputes (not being members of the tribe) and were active in mobilizing the masses against a foreign invader or an "infidel" ruler. Famous mullas include Mushk-i Alam (*see* DIN MUHAMMAD) who proclaimed **jihad** against the British in the **second Anglo-Afghan war** and subsequently led Mangal and **Ghilzai** forces against Amir **Abdul Rahman**, as well as Mulla-i Lang (the Lame Mullah) who led a tribal army against King **Amanullah** (*see* KHOST REBELLION). Amir Abdul Rahman first tried to keep mullas under state control by requiring tests for certification and made attempts at improving the quality of religious education in Afghanistan. Since the time of King Amanullah (1920s) the Afghan government established state-sponsored madrasas and in 1951 a faculty of theology affiliated with Al-Azhar University in Cairo, but the informal, private system of religious education has continued to exist to this day. *See also* ULAMA.

MUNRO, GENERAL SIR CHARLES. Commander-in-chief in India. He directed operations in the **third Anglo-Afghan war**.

MUSHK-I ALAM. *See* **DIN MUHAMMAD.**

MUSLIM BROTHERHOOD. The Society of Muslim Brethren (Jam'iat-i Ikhwan al-Muslimin), founded in 1929 in Isma'iliyya, Egypt by Hasan al-Banna (1906–1949). It was a religiopolitical organization that eventually spread to other parts of the Islamic world. Al-Banna, an ascetic and charismatic teacher, was the "Supreme Guide" (*murshid al-'amm*), who advocated social and economic reforms, expulsion of the British from Egypt, and establishment of an Islamic state. The movement is Pan-Islamic in outlook and aims at imposing Islamic law on all aspects of the social and political life of the Muslim nation (*umma*). As a political party it was never very successful, but it was able to mobilize considerable support among the masses of the lower urban and rural classes. The Ikhwan was accused of political assassinations, and Hasan al-Banna was himself assassinated in 1949 (reputedly by government agents). The Ikhwan was represented in the Egyptian Parliament, and other, more radical groups, have taken over the Islamist cause.

A number of founders of the **Islamist movement (Burhanuddin Rabbani, Abdul Rasul Sayyaf,** Ghulam Muhammad Niazi) in Afghanistan became members or sympathizers of the Ikhwanis while residing in Egypt for study and upon returning to Afghanistan contributed to the spread of the movement's ideology. They were the teachers of young radicals recruited from Afghan government schools who formed the nucleus of the **Islamist movement**.

MUSLIM YOUTH ORGANIZATION (SAZMAN-I JAWANAN-I MUSULMAN). An **Islamist movement** started in the late 1960s by theology students on the campus of **Kabul** University. It was advised by such teachers as Ghulam Muhammad Niazi who took no direct part in the organization. His namesake, but not a relative, Abdul Rahim Niazi was one of the first student leaders. The movement grew from only a few members in 1969 and spread to elementary and secondary schools in Kabul. It rose in reaction to leftist student agitation and eventually advocated violent action against them and the Afghan government. To prevent retaliation the movement organized into three layers of cells, each containing only a small number of members, who were promoted on the basis of ideological reliability and talent from the lower to the next higher circle (Edwards, 2002, 177). Destroyed as an effective force in 1975 by the regime of **Muhammad Daud** the survivors fled to **Pakistan** where they joined the **mujahedin** forces.

MUSSOORIE CONFERENCE. A conference held between April 17 and July 18, 1920, at Mussoorie, north of Delhi in India, which was to restore "friendly" relations between the governments of Afghanistan and British India after the **third Anglo-Afghan war**. It was a sequel to the peace treaty of Rawalpindi and pitted the Afghan foreign minister, Mahmud Tarzi, against the foreign secretary of the government of India, **Sir Henry Dobbs**, in a fruitless attempt to conclude a treaty of friendship between the two states. Lacking any agreement acceptable to the Afghans, a British aide-mémoire provided for some economic assistance but postponed the establishment of normal, "neighborly relations" for another conference at Kabul. *See also* ANGLO-AFGHAN TREATY OF 1919; 1921.

MUTAWAKKIL, WAKIL AHMAD. Senior political adviser and **Taliban** foreign minister from October 27, 1999, to October 2001, replacing Mulla Muhammad Hasan. In March 2001, during Mutawakkil's tenure, the ancient Buddha statues in **Bamian** were destroyed and the **United Nations** imposed sanctions, demanding the extradition of **Osama bin Laden**. He is said to have been a moderate, disagreeing with the protection of **al-Qaeda** and the presence of foreign fighters in Afghanistan. After the American intervention in October 2001, and the fall of the Taliban government, Mutawakkil surrendered to Afghan forces who handed him over to American custody. After he was released from **United States** custody at

Bagram in October 2003, he moved to **Kandahar**. Mutawakkil offered to negotiate peace between moderate Taliban and the **Hamid Karzai** government. He is a native of Kandahar and studied for a short period in a **Pakistan madrasa**. Mutawakkil decided to be a candidate in the parliamentary elections.

- N -

NADIR SHAH, AFSHAR. Ruler of Iran (1736–1747) and founder of the short-lived Afsharid dynasty (1736–1795). He was born in 1688 as Nadir Quli in northern **Khorasan**, the son of Imam Quli, a member of a clan affiliated with the Afshar tribe. He started life as a raider for booty and became one of the last great nomadic conquerors of Asia. He ended the **Ghilzai** dream of ruling an empire after Mahmud, son of **Mir Wais**, captured Isfahan in 1722. Nadir defeated the Afghans and drove them out of Iran. He attacked **Herat** and invaded India, where he defeated the Moghul army at Karnal, near Delhi, in 1739. Rather than fighting the Afghan tribes he enlisted them into his army, making Ahmad Khan Abdali (the subsequent **Ahmad Shah**, one of his military commanders. He moved the Abdali tribe from Herat to their original home in the **Kandahar** area and settled them on Ghilzai land. This led to the ascendancy of the Abdalis (**Durrani**) over the Ghilzais and contributed to the longstanding rivalry between these two **Pashtun** tribes. (Nadir Shah also settled Jewish and Armenian traders from Iran in Afghan towns to encourage trade with India.) Ruling over a heterogeneous population, he wanted to unite his subjects by proclaiming Shi'ism the fifth (Jafarite) orthodox school of **Sunni** Islam. The **Shi'a** clergy objected to this. Nadir became increasingly tyrannical and was eventually killed by his own tribesmen. Some of Nadir's **Qizilbash** soldiers settled in Afghanistan, where their descendants had successful careers in the army, government, the trades, and crafts. At the time of Nadir Shah's death, Ahmad Khan Abdali was able to fill the political vacuum and become the first Durrani ruler of Afghanistan.

NAJIBULLAH (NAJIB ALLAH). President of the Republic of Afghanistan and general secretary of the **People's Democratic Party of Afghanistan** (PDPA) from May 1986 to April 1992. Born in 1947 in **Kabul** of an **Ahmadzai** (**Ghilzai Pashtun**) family, he was educated at Habibia High School and Kabul University, graduating from the College of Medicine in 1975. He became a member of the **Parcham** faction of the PDPA in 1965 and was repeatedly arrested for his political activities. After the **Saur Revolt** he was appointed Afghan ambassador to Tehran (July–October 1978), in a move to get leading Parchamis out of the country, but was quickly dismissed with other Parchamis by the Taraki government, when they were accused of plotting a coup. He remained abroad and returned to Kabul with **Babrak Karmal** after the ouster of **Hafizullah Amin** in the final days of December 1979. He next held the position of general president of the **Afghan Security Service** (KHAD) (1980–1986) and in 1986 replaced Babrak Karmal as secretary general of the PDPA. He purged the central committee, brought in new members, and reorganized the government in 1988 and 1990. In March 1990 he successfully withstood a **Khalqi** coup, headed by **Shahnawaz Tanai**, his defense minister. He downplayed Marxist ideology and annulled most of the early "reforms." When he agreed to step down in April 1992, he was prevented from going into exile, as had been arranged with the **United Nations**. When the **Taliban** captured Kabul in September 1996, they took him from the UN compound, tortured and brutally killed him. He was married to a **Muhammadzai** woman.

NANGARHAR (34-45' N, 70-50' E). A province in eastern Afghanistan with an area of 7,195 square miles and a population of about 740,000 of which, in the 1980s, almost 400,000 were settled in **refugee** camps in Pakistan. The capital of the province is **Jalalabad**, with a peacetime population of about 56,000 (at times increased to 200,000). The population is largely **Pashtun** of the Khugiani, **Mohmand**, **Shinwari**, and Tirahi tribes, but other major ethnic groups are also represented in Jalalabad.

Local tradition associates the name, Nangarhar, with *nuh*—nine, and *nahar*—river, or, according to another version, with the Sanskrit *nau vihara*—meaning "nine monasteries." The Nangarhar area was a flourishing center of Buddhism until the fifth century A.D. Because of its mild climate, Jalalabad was the winter capital of Afghan kings after they were established in **Kabul**. The eastern part of the province is well irrigated, producing two or three crops a year. Wheat, corn, and some rice are the major crops, and Soviet-developed mechanized state farms produced olive and citrus fruits, much of which were formerly exported to the **Soviet Union**. Timber is cut on the upper slopes of the Safid Kuh and smuggled to Pakistan where it fetches a better price. The Darunta Dam on the Kabul River provides hydroelectric power and makes possible large irrigation projects.

In March 1989 a **mujahedin** assault on Jalalabad failed to dislodge the forces of the Kabul regime. This demonstrated the fact that the mujahedin were as yet unable to switch from **guerrilla warfare** to conventional war, which led to a lull in large-scale operations. After the capture of Jalalabad by the mujahedin, a council of mujahedin ruled Nangarhar for four years until the city was taken by the **Taliban** in September 1996. After the fall of the Taliban regime, the council (**Shura**) established itself again in Jalalabad, tacitly acknowledging the authority of the **Hamid Karzai** government.

NASR. A radical Islamist organization which is now part of the **Shi'a Hizb-i Wahdat**.

NATIONAL ISLAMIC FRONT OF AFGHANISTAN. *See* **MAHAZ-I MILLI-YI AFGHANISTAN**.

NATIONAL LIBERATION FRONT OF AFGHANISTAN. *See* **JABHA-YI MILLI NAJAT-I AFGHANISTAN**.

NATO. *See* **NORTH ATLANTIC TREATY ORGANIZATION**.

NEUMANN, RONALD E. Sworn in as ambassador to Afghanistan on July 26, 2005, to succeed **Zalmai Khalilzad** (who was appointed ambassador to Iraq). Born in 1944, the son of Robert G. Neumann who was ambassador to Afghanistan, 1966-1973, Ronald Neumann served as deputy chief of mission in Yemen, the United Arab Emirates; as ambassador to Algeria from 1994 to 1997; and chief of mission in Bahrain in 2001. He was appointed deputy assistant secretary in the Bureau of Near Eastern Affairs in 1997, and served as counselor for political-military affairs in Baghdad, Iraq.

NIEDERMAYER, OSKAR VON. A **German** officer from Bavaria and, in the years 1915–1916, coleader with **Werner Otto von Hentig** of an expedition to Afghanistan for the purpose of winning Amir **Habibullah**'s support for military action against British India during World War I. The expedition did not achieve its objectives (*see* HENTIG-NIEDERMAYER EXPEDITION). After the defeat of **Germany**, Niedermayer was in the **Soviet Union** under provisions of the secret Treaty of Rapallo of 1922, where he and other German military officers participated in the modernization of the Red Army. At the end of World War II Niedermayer was arrested by Soviet forces in eastern Europe and died in Moscow's Lubjanka prison in about 1945.

NIGHT LETTERS. Clandestine leaflets attacking Afghan rulers and government officials, which became a potent propaganda tool in the war of the **mujahedin** with the **Soviet/Kabul** forces. Night letters, protesting the secular policies of the Afghan government, were handwritten and copied and distributed by **Islamist** groups since the 1960s. President **Muhammad Daud** was the target of such leaflets, as were the Marxist and Soviet governments after 1978. Letters, written in **Dari** and **Pashtu**, called for resistance against government policies, urging Afghans not to "accept the orders of the infidels, wage **jihad** against them" (Bradsher,1983, 208). Soviet soldiers were addressed in Russian and told to resist the policies of their dictatorial regime. On February 21, 1980, one successful campaign summoned the citizens of Kabul to shout, "Allahu Akbar" (God is Great) from their rooftops. This was followed by rioting and a general strike, which was severely repressed. The letters were distributed at night, hence the name *shab-nama* (D. *shab,* night, *nama*, letter).

NIMRUZ (30-30' N, 62-00' E). A province in southwestern Afghanistan with an area of 20,980 square miles and a population of 112,000. The capital of the province is Zaranj, a small town built in the 1960s. The province was called Chakhansur until 1968 and is part of ancient Sistan. Although the second largest in area, it is the smallest province in population. The economy is based primarily on agriculture in the **Helmand** Valley and animal husbandry. **Baluch** nomads graze their herds in the deserts. A strong wind prevails for about 120 days a year and is harvested by countless windmills. Nimruz is watered by the Helmand, Khashrud, and **Farah** Rivers, which dissipate in the *hamuns* (salt lakes) east of Zaranj.

A multitude of *tepe*, mounds, indicating ancient settlements, and mud brick and baked brick ruins can be found throughout the province, testifying to a flourishing civilization before its destruction as a result of Mongol invasions.

NORTH ATLANTIC TREATY ORGANIZATION (NATO). Established in 1949 for the protection of western Europe and to contain **Soviet** expansion, NATO has found a new role in Afghanistan. As a result of the September 11, 2001, attacks against the **United States**, NATO allies for the first time invoked Article 5 of the Washington Treaty which states that an armed attack against one NATO member country will be considered an attack on all. NATO assumed command of the **International Security Assistance Force** (ISAF IV) in August 2003, headed by Lieutenant General **Götz Gliemeroth**, to set up and strengthen **Provincial Reconstruction Teams** (PRT) in Afghanistan. Originally based only in Kabul, NATO/ISAF troops moved to the major Afghan cities. As of September 2004 units of the Spanish Light Infantry Battalion were deployed in **Mazar-i Sharif** as a Quick Reaction Force (QRF), and an Italian battalion serves as an Operational Reserve in Theater, based in **Kabul**. PTR in **Faizabad**, **Kunduz**, and Pul-i Khumri are to be augmented, and air assets are provided by the Netherlands, **Britain**, Spain, Sweden, and the United States. Some of these aircraft are based outside Afghanistan in Bishkek, Kyrgyzstan, and Termez and Karshi Khanabad in Uzbekistan. Their function is to assist the Afghan government in maintaining security for the elections and facilitating the process of reconstruction in Afghanistan.

An agreement between NATO and the United States has been reached to merge their separate missions in Afghanistan, giving NATO command of an operation that for the first time will combine counterterrorism and peacekeeping activities. The merger will be accomplished by early 2006 and **Britain** will take over the command of the NATO force in Afghanistan.

Initially, reservations existed regarding the merger. The United States worried whether NATO "was up to the job." France feared that the force would become "an extension of Washington's own security interests." Germany does not want to engage in counterterrorism activities. Both countries wanted assurances that the United States would not leave after handing the job over to NATO. NATO has about 9,000 troops under arms and is expanding its activities to include nine PRTs, adding to the 13 maintained by the United States. Plans are under way to divide Afghanistan into four zones, with Germany commanding the north, Italy and Spain the west, Britain the south, and the United States the east.

NORTHERN ALLIANCE. A tenuous alliance of anti-**Taliban** forces founded in 1996–1997 that included the Itihad-i Islami of **Abdul Rasul Sayyaf**; the **Uzbek** Jumbesh-i Milli of **Abdul Rashid Dostum**; the Jam'iat-i Islami of **Burhanuddin Rabbani** (the nominal leader)

General **Isma'il Khan** in Herat, **Ahmad Shah Mas'ud** and the **Shi'a Hizb-i Wahdat** of **Karim Khalili**. The **Panjshiri** military arm of Jam'iat was able to capture **Kabul** and gain the most powerful ministerial positions in the **Interim Government** and **Transitional Government**. The forces of Dostum and **Ata Muhammad** of Jam'iat have frequently clashed over territory in northern Afghanistan.

As a result of the presidential elections in December 2004, the power of the Northern Alliance has been severely weakened. President **Hamid Karzai** formed a new cabinet which removed Marshal Muhammad Qasim Fahim from the position of minister of defense, ignored **Yunus Qanuni**, and Rabbani, gave Ismail Khan the portfolio of minister of water and power, coopted Dostum as commander in chief, and kept **Abdullah Abdullah** as minister of foreign affairs. The power of the Panjshiris, who controlled previous governments, was greatly reduced when they could muster only 47,750 voters.

NORTH-WEST FRONTIER PROVINCE (NWFP). The North-West Frontier Province of India (now **Pakistan**) is inhabited largely by **Pashtuns**, the same ethnic group that is politically dominant in Afghanistan. Because of the inaccessibility of the frontier area and the martial reputation of its people, the British and Pakistan governments found it preferable to rule the area indirectly, leaving it politically and culturally autonomous under their tribal chiefs. The province had been part of Afghanistan since 1747 but gradually came under British control as result of its **"forward policy."** In 1893 Sir **Mortimer Durand**, foreign secretary of the government of India, drew a boundary line, subsequently called the **Durand Line**, which bisected the Pashtun tribal area.

This was a decision Amir **Abdul Rahman** could not prevent. The 1893 agreement was reconfirmed in subsequent Anglo-Afghan treaties. When the state of Pakistan came into existence, the Afghan government wanted the Pashtuns of the NWFP to be given the choice of reunion with Afghanistan or independence in addition to the option of union with Pakistan or India. These choices were not given, and a minority of Pashtuns of the NWFP opted for union with Pakistan. The **Pashtunistan** Question subsequently had a deleterious effect on Afghan-Pakistani relations. In recent years Pashtun nationalists of the NWFP demand the right to call their province by its ethnic designation Pakhtunkhwa, "Land of the Pashtuns."

NOTT, GENERAL SIR WILLIAM (1782–1845). British general attached to the Bombay Force of General **John Keane** during the **first Anglo-Afghan war**. He defeated Afghan forces at **Kandahar** in 1839, but failed to come to the assistance of the **Kabul** garrison. He conducted an expedition against the **Ghilzai** in the spring of 1841 and successfully defended Kandahar from a **Durrani** attack. He left Kandahar in August 1842, evacuating Afghanistan by way of **Ghazni**, where he liberated some 327 British survivors captured when the city fell into Afghan hands. Nott returned to India via Kabul and **Jalalabad**. He was described as short-tempered but competent. *See also* GHAZNI, CAPTURE OF.

NURISTAN. *See* **KAFIRISTAN.**

- O -

OERLIKON AA GUN. The Oerlikon 20mm antiaircraft gun was one of the first antiaircraft weapons supplied to the **mujahedin**. It was used at the **Battle of Zhawar**, close to the **Pakistan** border, where it could be deployed without the need for long-distance transport. **Muhammad Yusuf** (Yousaf) described it as a "prestige weapon" that was not particularly effective. In fact, Yousaf claims that the Pakistani **Inter-Services Intelligence** (ISI) rejected the Central Intelligence Agency (CIA) gift as not suitable for Afghanistan. The gun was too heavy (1,200 pounds) and had a long, cumbersome barrel, which could not easily be transported on mules in the difficult terrain. The weapon was deployed in three sections that required 20 mules for transport. Its high rate of fire, 1,000 rounds a minute at the cost of $50 a bullet, required a considerable supply of ammunition. It was a weapon more suited for the defense of strong points than offensive operations because it impeded the mobility of the mujahedin. ISI objections were overruled and 40–50 guns were supplied (Yousaf, 87).

OJHIRI CAMP EXPLOSION. Ojhiri Camp was the **Inter-Services Intelligence** (ISI) command post for the war in Afghanistan. It comprised an area of 70–80 acres, located on the northern outskirts of Rawalpindi, about 8 miles from Islamabad. The camp included a training area, a psychological warfare unit, a **Stinger** training school, and mess halls for some 500 men. Most important, it contained the warehouses where 70 to 80 percent of all arms and ammunition for the **mujahedin** were held. On April 10, 1988, the entire stock was lost in a giant explosion. According to Yousaf (220), "Some 30,000 rockets, thousands of mortar bombs, millions of rounds of small-arms ammunition, countless antitank mines, recoilless rifle ammunition and Stinger missiles were sucked into the most devastating and spectacular fireworks display that Pakistan is ever likely to see." About 100 persons died, and more than 1,000 were wounded as people as far away as eight miles were hit by falling rockets. The depot was stocked to capacity with four months' supplies needed by the mujahedin for their spring offensive. The cause of the explosion was never examined in a public inquiry, and President Zia ul–Haq dismissed the government, which wanted to blame the ISI and the Pakistani army for this disaster. Conspiracy theorists saw it as a result of KGB or CIA sabotage, while others called it an accident. Fire was supposed to have started in a box of Egyptian rockets, which had not been diffused before shipping. A box was dropped, wounding several people, and the fire was permitted to burn for several minutes while the wounded were carried away. Ten minutes later, the entire depot went up and secondary explosions occurred for the following two days.

OMAR, MULLA MUHAMMAD. Supreme leader and founder of the **Taliban** movement in 1994 who ruled over much of Afghanistan until the start of the **United States** intervention in October 2001. Omar led his **madrasa** students in a spectacular campaign to capture **Kandahar** (1994), **Herat** (1995), **Kabul** (1996), and **Mazar-i Sharif** (1997) and finally to control most of the country (1998). The 44-year-old **mulla**, a **Pashtun**, born in **Oruzgan** Province (or Nodeh village near Kandahar) was a **mujahed** in the Hizb-i Islami of **Yunus Khalis** and rose to the rank of deputy chief commander. Of heavy build, he is an expert marksman and is reputed to have destroyed several tanks in battle with **Soviet** and Marxist forces. He was wounded several times and lost one eye. Omar is said to be of Hotaki **Ghilzai** background, he taught in a village madrasa in Sangsag (Sang Hisar) some 24 miles west of Kandahar but never finished his religious education; nevertheless, in April 1996 a **shura** of about 1,000 members of the **ulama** recognized him as *Amir al-Mu'minin*, (Commander of the Faithful). For this occasion, Omar wore what is believed to be the Cloak of the Prophet. He made Kandahar his center from where he directed the organization.

Mulla Omar wanted to establish a "true" Islamic state in Afghanistan and issued a number of **fatwas** to this effect. Men were to wear beards and native dress. He ordered the closing of girls' schools, and restricted women to their homes. He forbade photography of living creatures, music, TV, video cassettes, cockfights, kite flying, and made sportsmen wear pants from below the knee to the navel. Omar forbade women to walk in public without a male relative and initiated brutal punishment of enemies and "sinners," striking fear into those who did not accept his interpretation of Islam. He was also responsible for the destruction of the Buddha statues at **Bamian**. Mulla Omar had close relations with **Osama bin Laden**; some say he was dominated by the **al-Qaeda** leader. After the defeat of the Taliban regime, Omar fled and has not yet been captured. There is a bounty of 10 million dollars on his head. *See also* OPERATION ENDURING FREEDOM; TALIBAN GOVERNMENT.

OPERATION ANACONDA. A **United States** army attack on an **al-Qaeda** stronghold in the Shah-i Kot area, about 20 miles from **Gardez** which has been praised as "an unqualified and absolute success" by General **Tommy Franks** and a "big mistake" by others. Planned by Army Major General **Franklin Hagenbeck** as a 72-hour operation, the campaign lasted for 12 days and pitted a force of about 1,000 American troops, 1,000 Afghans, and a number of Coalition Special Forces teams against 500 to 1,000 of the enemy on the Takur Ghar range. Not unlike the **Soviet** experience in the 1980s, the American troops were pinned down and five of six Apache **helicopters** shot up and were made "nonmission capable" on the first day of fighting. Two helicopters crashed, resulting in the death of eight U.S. soldiers. The valley was narrow and the enemy was entrenched high on the slopes of the mountain. Fixed-wing aircraft had to fly at an altitude of 20,000 feet to avoid Soviet-made SA-7 surface-to-air missiles and, in spite of dropping about 6 million pounds of ordnance, the enemy fighters could not be dislodged from their bases and most of them seemed to have escaped. General Hagenbeck blamed the lack of adequate air support as aircraft had to be repositioned from Kuwait. Afghan allies claimed that the Americans failed to adapt to the enemy's guerrilla tactics and that they underestimated the tenacity of the al-Qaeda fighters. After the operation "fewer than 20 enemy bodies were found" (Brendan O'Neill, *The Strange Battle of Shah-i Kot*).

OPERATION ENDURING FREEDOM. As a result of the **terrorist** attacks in New York City and Washington, D.C., on September 11, 2001, and **Osama bin Laden**'s declaration of war on the **United States**, President George W. Bush announced strikes by the U.S. military "against **al-Qaeda** terrorist training camps and military installations of the **Taliban** regime." The objective was to destroy the al-Qaeda infrastructure in Afghanistan and capture its members and, secondarily, to replace the Taliban regime. The intervention began on October 7, 2001, when American and British aerial attacks quickly destroyed whatever existed of the Afghan communications system. For ground forces the allies employed fighters of the **Northern Alliance** and tribal groups from the **Pashtun** areas, who took advantage of the situation and extended their control over the country. The **Panjshiri** contingent of the Northern Alliance took **Kabul**, and **Burhanuddin Rabbani** established himself in the palace. Most of Afghanistan was quickly cleared of al-Qaeda and Taliban forces and an **Interim Government** and, subsequently, a **Transitional Government** was set up in which the Panjshiris continued to have dominant control. An international peace force, the **International Security Assistance Force** (ISAF), policed Kabul while American forces continued to hunt for leaders of the Taliban and al-Qaeda movement.

It has been estimated that the first three months of the war cost the United States $3.8 billion, and, while the Taliban regime was largely destroyed, warlords in the service of American campaigns were able to fill the political vacuum, establishing autonomous power bases in defiance of the Kabul government. At the time of writing, Osama bin Laden and **Muhammad Omar** have not been captured.

OPERATION ENDURING FREEDOM, THE CAMPAIGN. The American campaign against the **al-Qaeda** and **Taliban** regime began on October 7, 2001, with the launching of Tomahawk cruise missiles from ships and submarines in the Persian Gulf and Arabian Sea. Next, attack aircraft from the gulf and heavy bombers from Diego Garcia and Whiteman airbase in the **United States** continued their attacks: At 5:20 A.M. **Kabul** was first hit, with the palace, the TV tower, Radio Afghanistan, and the airports as targets. **Kandahar** was struck next to eliminate the airport radar facilities. Three training camps near **Jalalabad** were bombed, and oil depots in **Mazar-i Sharif** and **Herat** were destroyed. During the following days the same urban areas were repeatedly bombed, and by October 10 the United States claimed control of the airspace over Afghanistan. Bombardments intensified, on October 15 some 60 bombers carried out daytime raids, followed the next day by attacks on Kabul, Kandahar, Herat, and Mazar-i Sharif by 150 aircraft. On November 1, carpet bombing of Taliban positions began and between November 5 and 7, U.S. B52 bombers dropped cluster "**daisy cutter**" bombs on Taliban position. On the ground U.S. **Special Forces Teams**, supported by **Northern Alliance** troops, fought the retreating al-Qaeda/Taliban army. The U.S. allies captured Mazar-i Sharif by November 17 and Kandahar surrendered on December 6. **Tora Bora** was a mop-up campaign and by mid-December 2001 the war against the Taliban regime was ended. The new "Afghanistan Model" was deemed successful: the use of limited American ground forces resulted in a minimum of American casualties; some 3,000 of the enemy were killed and some 3,000 civilians became casualties of the war. Most of the Taliban/al-Qaeda leadership escaped and, lacking sufficient ground forces, local leaders/warlords filled the vacuum of power. The **Interim Government** of **Hamid Karzai** and the subsequent **Transitional Government** in Kabul could not extend their rule over the rest of the country. The result: a military success and a serious failure in the process of "nation building."

OPERATION ENDURING FREEDOM, THE FAILINGS. Carl Conetta offers an appraisal of the American campaign in a monograph titled *Strange Victory: A Critical Appraisal of Operation Enduring Freedom and the Afghanistan War.* He asks, What was the result of victory? and says, "Seldom has the gap been so great between the clarity of battlefield victory and the uncertainty of what it has wrought." He estimates the cost to the **United States** for the first three months of the war at $3.8 billion. Some 3,000 to 4,000 **Taliban** and foreign troops were killed and aerial bombardments resulted in the death of some 1,000 to 1,300 civilians. Stability and humanitarian goals were clearly subordinate. "The rush into a large and ambitious military operation precluded making adequate arrangements for the postwar political environment and humanitarian needs." It proved impossible to quickly assemble a Pashtun alternative as the **Northern Alliance** captured **Kabul** and controlled the new government. Conetta remarked that

> Enduring Freedom was also distinguished by the degree to which military expediency determined strategic choices—such as the

decision to unleash the Northern Alliance. This feature of decision-making in the war contributed to the preponderance of inadvertent and unplanned outcomes. . . . The United States engaged in a punitive expedition and a manhunt, not a nation-building exercise.

It relied on Afghan militias and the expenditure of 12,000 bombs and missiles, a mix which was wrong for the terminal phase of the war. Aerial bombardment proved too blunt an instrument for interdicting small numbers of enemy personnel because it increased the ratio of enemy to civilian casualties. Most of the Taliban leadership has survived the war.

This analysis dates from January 30, 2002; since that time an Afghan constitution has been approved, **NATO** has taken over the command of the **International Security Assistance Force** (ISAF), and elections were held in October 2004. However, local leaders/warlords still control most of the country and there is no guarantee that moderate forces will prevail in future elections.

OPERATION VALIANT STRIKE. An eight-day U.S. mission to search out enemy forces, weapons, and tactical intelligence and search villages for a "soft breach" that involved meeting with local elders to explain the American mission before conducting a sweep. On March 20, 2003, some 800 American troops, assisted by Romanian infantry and Afghan fighters, moved into the Sami Ghar area east of **Kandahar**. They were transported by Chinook and Black Hawk transport **helicopters** under escort from Apache helicopter gunships. A platoon of the 82nd Airborne 504th Parachute Infantry Regiment landed in the mountain range and began to search villages and cave complexes for **al-Qaeda** and **Taliban** fighters and weapons. A-10 Thunderbolt pilots of the 104th Expeditionary Fighter Squadron fired rockets, dropped bombs, and fired 30mm rounds during the offensive. The coalition forces failed to locate any **terrorists** but found three large weapons caches, capturing more than 170 rocket-propelled grenades, 180 land mines, 20 automatic rifles and machine guns, and tons of rockets, rifles, and launchers with a full range of accessories. A few individuals were taken into custody and one soldier, Sgt. Craig Pinkley, commented, "The difficult thing about missions like this is to know who is who." Lt. Col. Charlie Flynn, commander of the "White Devils," called the operation a great success.

OPIUM. *See* **POPPY CULTIVATION.**

ORUZGAN (URUZGAN) (33-15' N, 66-0' E). A province in central Afghanistan with an area of 11,169 square miles and about 483,000 inhabitants and also the name of a village and its surrounding district. The population is largely **Hazara** with some **Pashtuns** and other ethnic communities in the south. The administrative center of the province is Tirinkot with a population of about 50,000. The province is part of the **Hazarajat** and in the late 19th century was incorporated into **Kandahar** Province. In 1964 Oruzgan became a province and elected representatives to the Afghan parliament.

It is a mountainous area, easily accessible only from the south, through valleys at altitudes of 3,000 to 7,600 feet. It is traversed by the **Helmand** River and its tributaries. The province is largely agricultural with the cultivation of cereal grains a major activity. Major handicrafts include the production of woven carpets, called *gelim*.

OSAMA BIN LADEN *See* **LADEN, OSAMA BIN.**

OXUS. *See* **AMU DARIA.**

- P -

PAIWAR KOTAL, BATTLE OF. A battle for capture of a pass lying at an altitude of 8,531 feet astride one of the great lines of communication between India and Afghanistan. It lay on one of the routes of invasion during the **second Anglo-Afghan war** on December 2, 1878. General **Frederick Roberts** commanded a force of 5,500 men and 24 guns, which pushed forward in two columns. Lacking proper intelligence, Roberts ordered the left column to turn right of the supposed Afghan position to cut off the Afghan's access to the pass. But the Afghans were already in possession of the pass, forcing the left column to withdraw. The Afghan force, estimated by British officers at 3,500 regulars and a large number of tribal irregulars, was met by Brigadier Cobbe, who commanded the 8th (Queen's) and the 5th Panjab Infantry regiments, a cavalry regiment, and six guns. General Roberts directed the rest, consisting of the 29th Native Infantry, the 5th Gurkas, and a mountain battery—all under the command of Colonel Gordon; followed by a wing of the 72nd High-

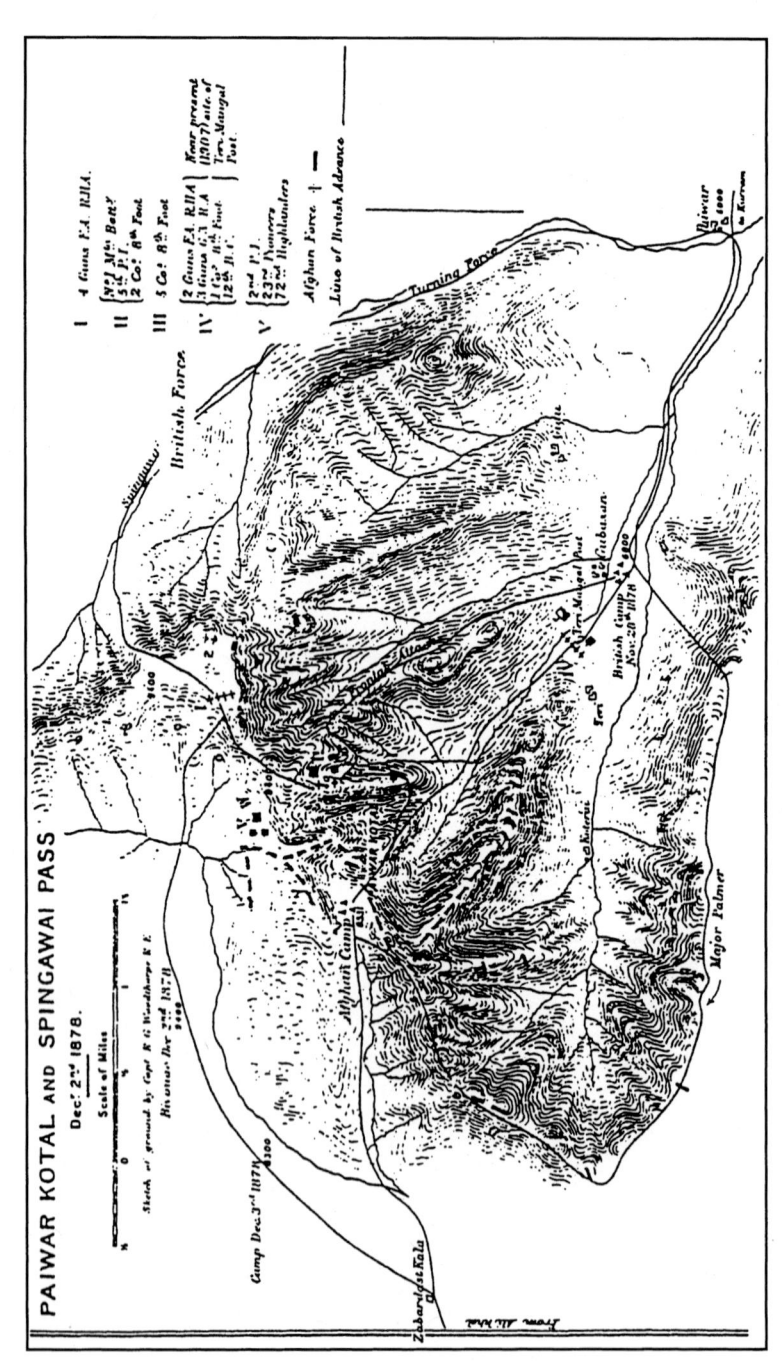

Plan 10. Paiwar Kotal (IOL)

landers, 2nd Panjab Infantry, and 23rd Pioneers with four guns on elephants under Brigadier Thelwall. The Gurkas and 72nd carried the first stockade, and the Afghan flank was turned and driven back. But the Afghans offered a resolute resistance and General Roberts decided to desist and make another turning movement, which brought the British forces to the rear of the Afghans. In a frontal attack Cobbe's infantry was able to move from ridge to ridge within 800 yards of the Afghans, placing the Afghans in a cross fire, which eventually forced them to abandon the pass. The British lost 21 killed and 72 wounded. The British estimated Afghan losses at about 500 killed and wounded.

PAKISTAN-AFGHAN RELATIONS. Relations between the two neighboring states have been marked by hostility since the founding of Pakistan in 1947. Afghanistan cast the only vote against admitting Pakistan to the **United Nations** on the grounds that the **Pashtuns** of the **North-West Frontier Province** had not had a fair plebiscite.

"Historical Afghanistan" at the time of **Ahmad Shah**, founder of the state of Afghanistan, included most of Pakistan territory up to the Indus River and south to the Arabian Sea. **Ranjit Singh** (1780–1839), of the ephemeral **Sikh** nation, deprived the Afghan ruler of his eastern provinces, and the British, in search a "scientific frontier" to defend their possessions in India, moved into tribal territory of the Afghan heartland. The **Durand Agreement** of 1893, signed under "duress" by Amir **Abdul Rahman**, divided Afghan tribal territory, leaving an autonomous area within British India. And when **Britain** finally agreed to relinquish her hold on India, the Afghan government demanded that the Afghans of the frontier belt be given the choice to opt for independence or union with Afghanistan, in addition to the choice of union with Pakistan or India. This was not granted. The British government replied that it held to the **Anglo-Afghan Treaty of 1921** by which the boundary was recognized by both states and asked Afghanistan to abstain from any act of intervention on the northwest frontier. Afghanistan began to agitate for creation of an independent **Pashtunistan** and Pakistan rejected all Afghan claims.

Armed conflict threatened in June 1949 when Pakistani planes bombed tribal territory as well as Moghalghai, a village within the boundaries of Afghanistan. In July 1949 the Afghan National Assembly repudiated the treaties with Britain regarding the tribal territory, and in May 1955 Afghanistan and Pakistan withdrew their diplomatic representatives.

The dispute gained an international dimension when the **Soviet Union** backed Afghanistan in the Pashtunistan dispute and the American-supported SEATO powers issued a statement declaring that "the region up to the Durand Line is Pakistan territory and within its treaty area." In August 1956 Prime Minister **Muhammad Daud** announced the conclusion of a military arms agreement with Czechoslovakia and the Soviet Union. Another break in diplomatic relations resulted in September 1961, which lasted until August 1963 when the two countries again exchanged ambassadors. In March of that year, Prime Minister Daud resigned and a new government was elected which concentrated its efforts on the development of the country. A pragmatic government wanted to improve relations with its neighbors and did not press the Pashtunistan issue, resulting in a period of relative calm.

When Muhammad Daud in July 1973 abolished the monarchy in a bloodless coup, Afghanistan's relations with Pakistan turned increasingly hostile. The Zulfikar Ali Bhutto government permitted members of the Afghan **Jami'at-i Islami** to stage raids into the **Panjshir** Valley, which marked the beginning of a **mujahedin** movement to fight the **Kabul** regime, after the Soviet intervention in Afghanistan. During the 1980s and 1990s Pakistan became the predominant power in Afghanistan. Pakistan was the conduit of funds and weapons and the haven of some 3 ½ million refugees who formed the reservoir of fighters against the Marxist regime. In 1981 Pakistan recognized six **Sunni** resistance organizations, and began to actively participate in the war effort. Brigadier Muhammad **Yousaf** (Yusuf), head of the Afghan Bureau of the **Inter-Services Intelligence** of the Pakistani armed forces, claimed a leading position in the war effort. Radical **Islamists** received preferential treatment in the supply of funds and weapons. Royalists, nationalists (like members of **Afghan Millat**), and **Shi'as** were neglected. Pakistan began to view Afghanistan as an area providing "strategic depth" in a confrontation with India. When the Marxist government was ousted, Pakistan supported the Islamist forces of **Gulbuddin Hekmatyar** in the struggle for power between the victorious mujahedin groups. The Islamists were seen as a pan-Islamist movement which was not expected to be concerned with the Pashtunistan question.

Eventually, the Pakistan government switched its support to the **Taliban** government, to which it provided financial aid. If it had not been for the fact that Afghanistan provided shelter to **Osama bin Laden**, the Taliban government might well have prevailed. The irony is that the Taliban regime did not prove to be a willing puppet of Pakistan. It gave shelter to **terrorist** groups who were wanted in Pakistan, pursued a radical **Islamist** policy that seemed to threaten to destabilize Pakistan society, and never issued a statement recognizing the Durand Line.

After the defeat of the Taliban government, the **Hamid Karzai** government expressed its willingness to maintain brotherly relations with Pakistan, but the fact that remnants of Taliban and **al-Qaeda** groups were still continuing guerrilla actions from the safety of the frontier areas has prevented the establishment of cordial neighborly relations.

PAKTIA (33-35'N, 69-35'E). A province in eastern Afghanistan comprising an area of almost 3,860 square miles and a population of about 550,000. The capital of the province is **Gardez**, with a pre-1978 population of about 10,000 (1991 est. 54,000). Until the early 1970s Paktia also included **Paktika** Province and southeastern parts of **Ghazni** Province. The province is largely mountainous, but well watered and cultivated and shares an almost 125 mile-long border with **Pakistan**. The population is largely **Ghilzai Pashtun**, but in the south and west are found Jadran and in the east Jaji, Mangal, Tani, and Waziri tribes.

The economy depends largely on agriculture with wheat, maize, barley, and rice being the principal crops. Land holdings are generally small, and animal husbandry and illegal timber cutting supplement agricultural activities.

Paktia was an area of strategic importance for the **mujahedin** because it has a common border with Pakistan and lies on the route to **Kabul**. There has been considerable fighting in the area because many of the **People's Democratic Party of Afghanistan (PDPA)** leadership were Ghilzais from Paktia, where the Kabul government enjoyed some support. A mujahedin offensive finally led to the capture of **Khost** on March 31, 1991. According to **United Nations** estimates a large portion of the population lived as **refugees** in Pakistan, more than from any other province. The area was controlled by various mujahedin groups until it was conquered by the **Taliban** in summer 1996. **United States** intervention, which led to the defeat of the Taliban regime in December 2001, established a base in the area for continued search-and-destroy missions of al-**Qaeda** and Taliban forces ensconced in parts of Paktia Province.

PAKTIKA (32-25' N, 68-45' E). Paktika Province was created during the tenure of President **Muhammad Daud** (r. 1973–1978) from the south-eastern districts of **Paktia** and **Ghazni** Provinces. It comprises an area of about 7,336 square miles and has an estimated population of about 245,000. The administrative center is Sharan with a population of about 40,000. The population is largely **Ghilzai** of the Sulaiman Khel, Kharoti, and Jadran tribes but also includes **Tajiks** and Waziri **Pashtuns**. About 31 percent of the population eventually settled as **refugees** in **Pakistan**.

Paktika suffered greatly from the war, and the destruction of the ancient system of irrigation in the Katawaz plain has greatly reduced the amount of cultivated land. Unrestricted cutting of timber has denuded formerly forested areas. From 1990 the province was in **mujahedin** control until captured by the **Taliban** in summer 1996 and held until their ouster in 2001.

PANIPAT, BATTLE OF. A battle on January 14, 1761, in which **Ahmad Shah Durrani** decisively defeated the **Maratha** tribal confederation near the town of Panipat some 50 miles north of Delhi. The Maratha Empire, founded in 1680 by Shivaji in the present Maharashtra Province, gradually grew in size and in a successful guerrilla war supplanted the Moghuls in a wide area of India. They were warriors and champions of Hinduism and became a serious threat to the Afghans when they occupied the **Panjab**.

Ahmad Shah was able to cross the Jumna River unopposed and took up a position near the Maratha army, commanded by Sadashiv Bhau. For two months the two armies engaged in skirmishes with varying success, but eventually the Afghan forces were able to block the Indians supply routes. Both armies were organized in the traditional left and right wings with large center divisions; the Afghans had the advantage in numbers, about 60,000 against 45,000 Indian troops. The Marathas were impeded with most of their camp followers, families, and supplies located in Panipat, which made it impossible for the Marathas to retreat quickly. Sadashiv Bhau therefore tried to negotiate, but when the Afghans refused to deal, he was forced into combat. The Afghans' pieces of artillery were lighter and more mobile than the heavy guns of the Marathas; nevertheless, in a desperate move, the Marathas almost succeeded in penetrating the Afghan center. But the Afghans were able to bring in reinforcements and envelop the Marathas from three sides. One squadron after another discharged their muskets, leaving the Indians little opportunity to regroup. Wishwas Rao, the nominal head of the Marathas, and Sadashiv were killed and the Marathas were routed. The battle ended the dreams of both the Marathas and the Afghans to become the rulers of India. Ahmad Shah's troops disliked the heat of the Indian plains and wanted to return home with their plunder, forcing the Afghan ruler to return.

PANJAB (PUNJAB). An area watered by five rivers (D. *panj,* five, *ab,* water), the Indus, Jhelum, Chenab, Rawi, and Sutlej in northern India. It is now divided into the western Panjab of **Pakistan** and the eastern Panjab of India. It is a rich and fertile area and has been the scene of numerous battles.

PANJDEH INCIDENT. A military encounter in 1885 in which a **Russian** force under General Alikhanov annexed the Panjdeh district north of **Herat** Province (now part of Turkmenistan). The military action pitted superior Russian troops against about 500 defending Afghan soldiers headed by the Afghan general **Ghausuddin Khan.** Afghan rulers claimed the area by virtue of the fact that the Turkomans of Panjdeh had been their occasional tributaries, but the Russians insisted that they were part of the Turkoman nation of Khiva and Merv, which Russia had annexed in 1881 and 1884.

An Anglo-Russian commission was to meet and resolve the dispute, but military action began on March 30, 1885, before Sir Peter Lumsden, a British Indian general, and his Russian counterpart arrived on the scene. Amir **Abdul Rahman** learned of the incident while he was on a state visit in Rawalpindi, India, and accepted the fait accompli at the urging of Lord Dufferin, the viceroy of India. The fact that **Britain** did not come to Afghanistan's defense, as she was obligated to do in case of unprovoked Russian aggression, confirmed the Afghan ruler in his belief that he could not rely on British promises of support.

PANJDEH, PRELIMINARIES TO WAR. When **Russia** extended its influence to Turkestan in 1884, the question arose whether the area of Panjdeh was part of Turkoman territory or part of the domain of the Afghan ruler. The Afghans had had governors there since 1860, and subsequently the area was under **Herat** control. Therefore, the governor of Herat appointed a governor over Panjdeh in April 1884 and sent Afghan troops to occupy the area. On June 16, 1884, Aminullah Khan, the new governor, accompanied General **Ghausud-**

din Khan with 1,000 levies, horse and foot, and 200 irregulars, with two guns. He had orders to construct a fort at Hauz–i Abdullah Khan, the northernmost point of Panjdeh. British reports stated, "The Sarik Turkomans were at this time hesitating as to 'which side they would incline,' and Russian emissaries, accompanied by Yulatan Sariks, were 'busily engaged in collecting information and tampering with the tribes.'"

Amir Abdul Rahman wanted British and Russian officers to meet with the Afghan agent on the spot to define the border. The British appointed Sir Peter Lumsden to find the "true limits of Afghan territory to which the agreement of 1872–73 applied." In a note of December 23, 1884, Lord **Granville** informed the Russian government that **Britain** did not agree with the Russian claim "that Pul–i Khatun and Panjdeh were outside the limits of Afghanistan."

After the Afghans occupied Ak Tapa and Sari Yazi in October 1884, the viceroy assured the **amir** that the British mission would do all in its power to "secure his just rights, and to lay down a frontier which might prevent future discussion."

The total forces at Panjdeh on March 11, 1885, included: four 9–pounder guns, four mountain 9–pounder guns. Artillery, 140 men; cavalry, 400 regular, 500 irregular; infantry, 1,000 regular, 400 irregular. The total equaled eight guns and 2,040 men.

General Komarof with 100 horsemen and a large quantity of provisions had come to Hazrat Imam. Colonel Alikhanof advanced with 100 Cossacks and Turkoman horsemen, with the intention of entering Panjdeh on November 22. Aminullah sent him a letter, saying that he would fight him if he proceeded further. The generals now hurled insults at each other.

Ali Khanoff sent a letter to General Ghausuddin, saying:

> Be it known to Ghaus–ud–din. I thought you were a wise man and were a General of an army, and I therefore wanted to come and see you. As you are such a bad man I do not want to see you, and I consider it a disgrace to meet you. But you must know that the order of our General is that, so long as the frontier dispute is not settled, your sowars should not come to this side of Arsh Doshan, nor will our sowars go beyond that place towards Panjdeh.

The reply:

From General Ghaus–ud–din Khan, **Ghazi**. Be it known to Ali Circasion [sic]. You write that, until the surveyors of the two Governments come, Arsh Doshan should be the frontier. You are mistaken. If God please, through the blessings of the Prophet, I will turn you out of Kara Bolan. All the servants who are in Panjdeh were glad to think that to–morrow they would be called Ghazis.

Russian forces: A regiment of infantry (4,000 men) and two regiments of Cossacks (800 men) left for Baku and the Afghan border. From Tiflis 20,000 troops had already left for same area (IOR: L/P&S/18/A58.d on March 27, 1885).

Captain Yate, a British officer at Panjdeh, reported on March 26, 1885, that Russian troops were "encamped in front of Ak–Tepe; a troop of about 100 Turkoman sowars came into Kizil–Tepe and advanced toward Pul–i–Khisti; the Afghan picket there warned them not to advance, and they at once retired."

PANJDEH, THE BATTLE. In another wire of March 29, Captain Yate stated: "Notwithstanding **Russian** assurances therein contained [between British and Russians], Russians are now drawn up in force almost within range of Afghan position, notwithstanding that Afghans have neither attacked nor advanced, and Panjdeh is perfectly quiet.... On Friday Colonel Alikhanoff with 300 horses, in spite of remonstrances, pushed through Afghan pickets with the intention of proceeding to Panjdeh around left flank of position, but was forced to return by superior Afghan force sent in pursuit. Simultaneously three companies of Russian infantry crossed the river and advanced around the right flank towards Panjdeh, but were anticipated, and retired before the Afghan force. Fighting is now imminent. Afghans cannot resist successfully. If defeated, road will be open to **Herat**."

In a telegram of April 1, it was reported that Captain Yate and all British officers at Panjdeh had left and "Russians attacked and defeated Afghans, and occupied Panjdeh on the 30th [March]. Afghans are said to have fought gallantly, and have lost heavily, two companies being killed to a man in entrenchments. Survivors retreated along Maruchak road. British officers, who were neutral, left, as Colonel Alikhanoff was reported to have urged Sariks to attack them, and have offered 1,000 krans a head."

On May 4, the Panjdeh question was solved. The secretary of state reported: "We propose to accept in principle this arrangement, which would leave to the Amir the three points, viz., Zulfikar, Gulran, and Meruchak.... The whole agreement to be ultimately embodied in a Convention between us and Russia" (L/P&S/18/A. 48–53/A).

PANJSHIR (34-38' N, 69-42' E). An administrative district in northern **Parwan** (now **Kapisa**) Province with an area of about 273 square miles and an agricultural population of about 30,000. The district is traversed by the Panjshir River, which rises on the southern slopes of the **Hindu Kush** in the vicinity of the Khawak Pass.

The population is largely **Tajik**, which has been converted to **Sunni** Islam since the 16th century. The area was often independent or autonomous, and, although the Panjshiris acknowledged the Afghan **amir** as their ruler, they rarely paid taxes to the **Kabul** government. It was only since the time of Amir **Abdul Rahman** that the Kabul government asserted its sovereignty over the area.

The Panjshir Valley is quite inaccessible; therefore, the **Soviet** and Kabul forces never succeeded in bringing it under full government control. Its location, impinging on the strategic **Salang** road, which connects Kabul with the northern provinces, made the Panjshir Valley an ideal base for **mujahedin** activity. **Ahmad Shah Mas'ud**, called "The Lion of Panjshir" by his admirers, was able to withstand numerous Soviet incursions and was not evicted from the valley, making him one of the most successful mujahedin commanders. President **Hamid Karzai** proclaimed Panjshir the 34th province of Afghanistan in April 2004.

PANJSHIR, SOVIET OFFENSIVE. Of about nine offensives, the seventh **Soviet** Panjshir offensive of April–May 1984 has been cited by military historians as the quintessential example of Soviet frustration in fighting a **counterinsurgency** war in this area. It began in response to **Ahmad Shah Mas'ud**'s refusal to renew his 1983 cease-fire with Soviet forces and involved some 10,000 Soviet and 5,000 Afghan troops (20,000 Soviet and 6,000 Afghans according to Isby, 1989, 32). According to Brigadier **Muhammad Yusuf** (Yousaf) (1992, 71–73), Mas'ud had learned of the planned offensive and organized the evacuation of hundreds of villages in the lower portion of the Panjshir Valley. He laid mines along the road up the valley, and in one successful ambush was able to destroy 70 fuel tankers and two important bridges. He then pulled back his forces before the start of aerial bombardment. Mountain ridges, rising to 19,000 feet, border the narrow valley and hindered proper approaches of the TU-16 (Badgers) and SU-24 (Fencer) bombers. The high-altitude bombing was often way off the mark, permitting the **mujahedin** to make spoiling attacks from the flanks. Heliborne units, landing in side valleys, executed blocking actions, but several landed too far from aerial support and were decimated by mujahedin forces. In eight days, the Soviets advanced about 40 miles up to the village of Khenj, and by May 7 Dasht–i Ravat was occupied. Afghan garrisons were established in the valley, and the Soviet/**Kabul** troops withdrew, permitting the mujahedin to move back into the valley by the end of June. Total Soviet casualties were said to have been about 500 and some 200 mujahedin were killed.

The Afghan garrisons found themselves isolated in hostile territory and eventually developed a modus vivendi in which they coexisted without causing much harm to each other. Mas'ud was soon free to again attack Soviet convoys on the **Salang** Highway, which provided much of the provisions for the survival of the Kabul government. Eventually, the mujahedin captured isolated posts when the garrisons surrendered or defected. Since the fall of the Kabul regime in April 1992, Panjshir has formed the heartland of Mas'ud's territory.

PAPUTIN, GENERAL LIEUTENANT VICTOR S. First deputy minister of internal affairs, said to have been in command of the **Soviet** special forces' attempt to capture, or assassinate, President **Hafizullah Amin**. Paputin and Colonel Bayerenov, a KGB officer, were killed in the mission. According to another version, Paputin committed suicide because of the failure of his mission to capture Amin alive.

PARCHAM. A weekly newspaper founded in March 1968 by the *Parcham* (Banner) faction of the **People's Democratic Party of Afghanistan (PDPA)**. It was published by Sulaiman Layeq and edited by him and Mir Akbar Khaibar, the faction's major ideologist. It carried articles in **Pashtu** and **Dari** and was openly critical of the Afghan government and was therefore closed in July 1969. One faction of the PDPA that supported **Babrak Karmal** in opposition to **Nur Muhammad Taraki** was subsequently named Parcham after this newspaper.

PARWAN (35-15' N, 69-30' E). A province located north of **Kabul** with an area of 2,282 square miles and a population of about 418,000. Parwan now includes the former province of **Kapisa** (created in 1964 and subsequently made a subprovince, *loya woluswali*). The capital of Parwan is **Charikar**, a town with 22,500 (1991 est. 120,000) inhabitants, located at the mouth of the Ghorband Valley about 49 miles north of Kabul. The province is of great strategic importance as it is crossed by the **Salang** Highway, which leads from Kabul north over the **Hindu Kush**.

PASHTUN (PAKHTUN, PATHAN). The Pashtuns have been the politically dominant group in Afghanistan, with a population estimated at from 6 to 7 million (in 1978) concentrated largely in the west, south, and east, but also scattered throughout Afghanistan. Another 7 million Pashtuns live in **Pakistan** across the **Durand** Line. Except for the Turis and a few groups in Pakistan, all Pashtuns are **Sunni** Muslims, and most were converted to Islam by the 10th century A.D. The Pashtuns are excellent soldiers, and many an invader of India chose to enlist them in his armies rather than force his way through their territory. Tribal society is organized along family, clan, and sectional lines. The tribe, *qabila*, is usually named after its ancestor and carries the suffix "zai," as in *Muhammadzai*, the "sons of Muhammad." Although the tribal system has undergone changes, traditionally, chiefs have to be successful leaders and exemplify Pashtun values. They are not absolute rulers of their fellow tribesmen. Each clan decides matters of its welfare by council, the **jirga**. Jirgas also arbitrate disputes between tribes.

The Pashtuns living in the inaccessible areas on both sides of the Durand Line adhere to their traditional code of behavior, the *Pashtunwali*, which guides the jirgas in resolving disputes. The principal pillars of this code are *nanawati* (mediation or protection); *badal* (retaliation); and *mailmastia* (hospitality). Urban Pashtuns still have a direct or emotional link to their tribes. The frontier Afghans are politically autonomous along the tribal belt on both sides of the Durand Line, but the rest have come increasingly under the control of the central governments.

PASHTUNISTAN. "Land of the **Pashtuns**" (or Afghans), the name given by Afghan nationalists to the **North-West Frontier Province** (NWFP) and parts of Baluchistan in present Pakistan. It was part of Afghanistan when the state was founded in 1747, but soon came under the control of the Sikh ruler **Ranjit Singh** and subsequently the British-Indian government.

Direct rule of the area was difficult because it is mountainous and difficult to access; therefore, the Pashtun tribes were allowed a considerable measure of autonomy. The British government cut the area from Afghanistan in 1893, drawing a border without regard to ethnic and cultural boundaries. Amir **Abdul Rahman** had scarcely consolidated his power and felt he had to accept "under duress" the Durand Line as his border (*see* DURAND AGREEMENT). In 1901, the British-Indian government created the North-West Frontier Province, but left the tribal lands outside of the directly administered areas. Five Tribal Agencies (Malakand, **Khaibar**, Kurram, North Waziristan, and South Waziristan) were set up with autonomous **khans** (chiefs), governed by tribal councils. A British agent protected the interests of the government. Tribesmen were engaged as militia to keep order in their own areas, and if a tribe conducted raids into the lowlands, punitive campaigns were organized.

In 1947, when India was to be divided on the basis of a plebiscite, the Afghan government and Pashtun nationalists demanded that the Pashtuns be given an option to vote, if not for union with Afghanistan, then for the creation of an independent "Pashtunistan." This option was not given, and, as a result of a boycott by members of the Frontier Congress, a Muslim Party allied with the Hindu Congress party, 68 percent of a low voter turnout agreed to union with Pakistan. Afghanistan protested the procedure and cast the only vote against a Pakistan's admission to the United Nations. Afghanistan's relations with Pakistan were subsequently plagued by the "Pashtunistan Question." The Afghan government supported the Pashtun nationalists, and Pakistan retaliated by closing the border at times and supporting guerrilla activities by Islamist forces against the government of President **Muhammad Daud**. Pashtun nationalists have protested the fact that the NWFP is the only province in Pakistan not named after its inhabitants, and they have unsuccessfully demanded the adoption of the name Pakhtunkhwa (P. for Pashtunistan). *See also* FOREIGN RELATIONS.

PEOPLE'S DEMOCRATIC PARTY OF AFGHANISTAN (PDPA). The Afghan Marxist party (after June 1990 called **Hizb-i Watan**, Fatherland party) was founded in 1965 and succeeded to power on April 27, 1978, in a coup, called the **Saur Revolt** (Revolution) (named after "Saur," the month of the revolt). The party was officially founded on January 1, 1965, at a meeting of 27 persons in **Nur Muhammad Taraki**'s house in Karte Char, **Kabul**. Taraki was chosen general secretary of the party and **Babrak Karmal** deputy secretary and secretary of a central committee whose membership consisted of Taraki, Karmal, Ghulam Dastagir Panjshiri, Dr. Saleh Muhammad Zirai, Shahrullah(?) Shahpar, Sultan Ali Keshtmand, and Taher Badakhshi. Alternate members were Dr. Shah Wali, Karim Misaq, Dr. Muhammad Taher, and Abdul Wahhab Safi. The party drafted a manifesto which stated that it was a workers' party. It declared Afghanistan a feudal society that should be transformed into a socialist state and announced its intention of obtaining power by democratic means.

From the beginning there was rivalry between the two leading personalities, Karmal being urbane and known from his activities on the campus of **Kabul** University and as a member of Parliament. He attracted followers among the Kabul intelligentsia, students, government officials, and some military officers of various ethnic backgrounds. Taraki, on the other hand, was more successful among the **Pashtuns**, military officers, and students and teachers at schools in which tribal Pashtuns predominated. The PDPA published a newspaper, *Khalq* (Masses), which first appeared on April 11, 1966. Only six issues were published until it was banned on the recommendation of Parliament for being "anti-Islamic" and opposed to the new constitution. By 1967 the party split into two entities, subsequently called **Khalq** and **Parcham**, after their respective newspapers. *Parcham* (Banner) was founded in 1968, published by Sulaiman Layeq and edited by him and Mir Akbar Khaibar. Having been successful in winning a parliamentary seat, Babrak Karmal was willing to cooperate with Afghan governments, while the Khalqis remained aloof. In 1977 the two factions reunited in a tenuous coalition with the help of Soviet and Indian Communist parties mediation.

The Saur Revolt was precipitated when the Parcham ideologue, Mir Akbar Khaibar, was assassinated, according to some sources, by *Khalqis* who resented his recruiting efforts in the army. The Marxists, however, accused the government of the deed, and the party followed up with a funeral procession that turned into a public demonstration by a crowd of about 15,000 against the **Muhammad Daud** government. The government reacted with arrests of the leadership, but three days later, on April 27, 1978, Marxist officers in the armed forces staged their successful coup. The Democratic Republic of Afghanistan (DRA) was proclaimed, and in early May the formation of a government was announced with Nur Muhammad Taraki as president and premier and Babrak Karmal as deputy premier. The majority of cabinet members were Khalqis. By July the Khalqis had purged members of the Parcham faction, including Babrak Karmal.

A number of decrees issued by the Khalq revolutionary council established Taraki as the "great leader" (No. 1), set up a government with Taraki as president of the revolutionary council and Karmal as vice president (No. 2), and abrogated the Daud constitution (No. 3). Subsequent decrees elevated the **Uzbeki**, Turkmani, Baluchi, and Nuristani languages to the status of "national languages," to be promoted in the Afghan media (No. 4), deprived members of the royal family of their citizenship (No. 5), canceled mortgages (No. 6), gave equal rights to women (No. 7), and ordered land reforms (No. 8). Former government officials and political opponents were arrested, and thousands were assassinated.

Khalqi supremacy did, however, not end strife in the PDPA. **Hafizullah Amin** had become vice premier and minister of foreign affairs, and on July 8, 1978, he was elected secretary of the secretariat of the central committee. By that time it became apparent that he was the dominant personality in the party. He became prime minister and minister of foreign affairs in April 1979, and president on September 16, 1979. Barely a month later, on October 9, Taraki was assassinated. A split occurred in the Khalqi faction between the "Red Khalqis" of Taraki and the "Black Khalqis" of Amin. A third faction, the followers of a Dr. Zarghun, already existed. They were called the **"Paktia** Khalqis." Increasing guerrilla activity of **mujahedin** forces prevented further strife in the Khalqi camp. Amin was said to have shown a tendency to develop into an "Afghan Tito" and demanded the recall of the Soviet ambassador, **Alexandr M. Puzanov**, who expected Amin to follow his bidding. Puzanov was reported to have been implicated in a plot to assassinate Amin.

Mass arrests and executions, blamed on the Taraki era, were not ended, as was apparent from a list published with about 12,000 names of killed or missing persons. Hafizullah Amin's intelligence service, KAM, replaced Taraki's AGSA, and new government and party positions were announced. About 5,000 Soviet advisers resided in Afghanistan when, on December 25, 1979, an airlift of Soviet troops began that eventually brought in some 115,000 troops. On December 27, a Parchami coup, with Soviet armed support, replaced Hafizullah Amin with Babrak Karmal.

Karmal announced a government that included the dreaded head of **Afghan Security Service** (AGSA, KAM), Asadullah Sarwari, as deputy premier and two other Khalqis, Sayyid Muhammad Gulabzoi as minister of interior, and Sherjan Mazduryar as minister of transport. KAM was purged and renamed KHAD, and the Parchami regime promised a new deal and an end to the excesses of the previous governments. Additional Soviet troops arrived in Afghanistan and established bases in various strategic locations. The government proclaimed a general amnesty and opened the doors of the feared Pul-i-Charkhi prison. Early Khalqi decrees of land reform (Nos. 6 and 8) and the emancipation of women (No. 7) were rescinded, and the tricolor replaced the red flag. But it was too late to overcome the "sins" of the past. The presence of Soviet forces in Afghanistan quickly transformed a civil war into a war of national liberation, and many of those freed from jail augmented the growing forces of the **mujahedin**.

Karmal's lack of success in destroying the mujahedin was the likely reason for his resignation (or ouster) on May 4, 1986, and his replacement by Dr. **Najibullah**, the one-time head of KHAD. Ideological evolution continued under Najibullah when the Kabul government initiated a policy of "national reconciliation" and changed the name of the PDPA to Hizb-i Watan (Fatherland Party). The early orthodoxy of adherence to Marxist-Leninism was gradually replaced by a general, socialist orientation and political liberalization, as the Parchamis attempted to survive in a national front coalition of "progressive" parties. Soviet troops withdrew from Afghanistan on February 15, 1989, but the party continued in power until President Najibullah announced his resignation in April 1992. After the mujahedin conquest of Kabul, the party ceased to exist, and many of its members joined opposing groups. In fall 1994, it was reported that members of the Communist Party met in the Microrayon quarter of Kabul and elected Mahmud Baryalai, half brother of Babrak Karmal, as its head. At the time of this writing, most of the Marxist leaders have found political exile abroad.

PESHAWAR ACCORD. An agreement concluded in April 1992 to form a transitional government after the fall of the Marxist government in Afghanistan. The 12-point program provided for a leadership council of 51 persons, headed by **Sebghatullah Mujaddidi** for a period of two months (1). **Burhanuddin Rabbani** was to be president of the Transitional State of Afghanistan for an additional four months (2), a period not to be extended even by a day (3). The prime minister and members of the cabinet to be appointed by the heads of the *tanzimat* (**mujahedin**) (4). The position of prime minister to go to the Hizb-i Islami (**Gulbuddin Hekmatyar**) (5). A deputy prime ministry and interior ministry are to go to Ittihad-i Islami (**Abdul Rasul Sayyaf**)

(6). A deputy prime ministry and the ministry of education to go to Hizb (**Yunus Khales**) (7). A deputy prime ministry and the ministry of foreign affairs to go to **Mahaz (Sayyid Ahmad Gailani)** (8). The ministry of defense to Jam'iat (Rabbani) (9), and the supreme court to Harakat-i Inqilab-i Islami (**Muhammad Nabi Muhammadi**) (10). The leadership council was to make appointments for the **Shi'a** and other parties (11), and the total process of interim government formation was to last for six month, after which a transitional government was to be established for a period of two years.

Hekmatyar opposed the appointment of **Ahmad Shah Mas'ud** as defense minister and the civil war between the various factions began, lasting until the **United States** intervention in October 2001.

PESHAWAR, TREATY OF (1855–1856). It opened diplomatic relations between **Britain** and Afghanistan. The treaty stipulated that "perpetual peace and friendship should be established between the two governments; that the British Government should respect the territories in possession of the **Amir**; that the Amir on his part should respect the territories of the British Government, and be the friend of its friends and the enemy of its enemies; and that the British should assist the Amir against his enemies, if they thought fit to do so" (MR, 28). Amir **Dost Muhammad** never knew whether the British "thought fit" to assist him against his enemies.

POLLOCK, GENERAL GEORGE (1786–1872). Commander of the "Army of Retribution" after the British debacle in the **first Anglo-Afghan war**. Pollock gathered an army of about 8,000 men composed of eight infantry regiments, three cavalry corps, a troop and two batteries of artillery, and a mountain train. He entered the **Khaibar Pass** on April 5, 1842, where he overcame an **Afridi** attack, and after additional encounters on the way, rescued **Jalalabad**, whose British garrison had nearly been starved to surrender. Marching on the route of the British retreat, Pollock's army saw the remnants of the **Army of the Indus**, the wheels of the gun carriages crushing the bones of their comrades. He defeated **Akbar Khan** in the **Battle of Tezin** and entered **Kabul** on September 16, 1842. He destroyed the fortification of the **Bala Hisar** and Kabul's magnificent bazaar and permitted his troops to plunder the city, which resulted in nearly total destruction. Many hundreds of Afghans were killed or executed (O'Ballance). In September he secured the release of the British hostages, after offering Saleh Muhammad, their guardian, a "reward" of 20,000 rupees and a pension of 12,000 rupees per year for life. Pollock's forces then moved against Istalif and **Charikar** and destroyed the towns, before evacuating Afghanistan on October 12, 1842.

POPPY CULTIVATION. There has always been some poppy cultivation in Afghanistan and opium was smuggled to China, India, and other destinations. During peace negotiations at the **Mussoorie Conference** (1920) the Afghan government asked for permission to export opium, hemp drugs, and ruble notes through India in bond and sealed packages, provided that it was not sent to "any destination to which the British Government are under obligation to prohibit or limit the dispatch" of these drugs. When this was no longer possible, some smuggling continued and in 1928 British sources reported the seizure of a consignment of cocaine and heroin in Paris. King **Amanullah** prohibited the consumption of drugs and there was not much of a market.

It was only as a result of the civil war of the 1990s that poppy began to be cultivated on a large scale. During the **Taliban** regime poppy cultivation in Afghanistan experienced a considerable increase, in spite of the fact that the use of opiates is forbidden in **Islam**. Unaware of the foreign political implications, the new rulers maintained that production was "only for export" and not local consumption. Only as a result of foreign pressure did the government realize that this was not an acceptable justification. The cultivation of poppies requires relatively little water and the raisin can be stored for long periods of time before it is processed into heroin. It is the ideal cash crop for impoverished farmers and the Taliban government derived a considerable income from its sale.

Poppy cultivation began to increase after the fall of the communist regime. By 1999 about 91,000 hectares were planted, which was reduced to about 8,000 hectares in 2001 when the Taliban regime, as a result of foreign pressure, forbade cultivation. After the American intervention, planting increased again and, by 2004, about 131,000 hectares were planted and Afghanistan became the world's largest opium poppy producer. According to the United Nations Office on Drugs and Crime (UNODC), cultivation has spread to all 34 provinces and the number of families involved has been estimated at 356,000. But only about $600 million was earned by the farmers out of a total of about U.S. $2.8 billion. There is irony in the fact that the mission of the Coalition forces was to hunt for terrorists to the exclusion of "nation building" or interdiction of the drug trade. In the meantime, the United States is very much engaged in nation building, but has not yet engaged in the task of fighting the drug problem. Haji Bashir Nurzai, the "Pablo Escobar" of heroin trafficking in Asia, was arrested in New York in late April 2005.

POTTINGER, MAJOR ELDRED (1811–1843). Sent to explore Central Asia, he came to **Kabul** disguised as a horse dealer. He reached **Herat** in 1837, and assisted in the defense of the city. **Lord Auckland** called him the "Hero of Herat," responsible for the successful defense of Herat during the second Persian siege of the city in 1837–1838. As a reward, he was appointed political officer to Kamran, the ruler of Herat. He was one of two Englishmen to survive the destruction of a British outpost at **Charikar** in November 1841, in which the 4th (Gurka) Infantry was wiped out. As the senior surviving officer at Kabul, he negotiated the **Treaty of Capitulation** with Afghan *sardars* in December 1841. And as a hostage of Sardar **Muhammad Akbar**, he was instrumental in negotiating a deal for the release of the hostages in exchange for a monetary reward to their guardian, Saleh Muhammad Khan. The seemingly indestructible Pottinger returned to India, where a court of inquiry in 1842–1843 accused him of drawing bills for 19 *lakhs* in favor of the Afghans and for signing a treaty without authorization. He was exonerated but did not get his back pay and was refused the award of a medal for his services. He died in Hong Kong of typhus.

PRIMROSE, LIEUTENANT-GENERAL JAMES M. (1819–1892). Commanded the Reserve Division, **Kandahar** Field Force in December 1878, and, in January 1879, he proceeded to Kandahar to take command of the 1st Division. During the second campaign, he commanded the Kandahar Field Force from March 1880 and the Kandahar force throughout the siege and at the Battle of Kandahar. *See* KANDAHAR, BATTLES OF.

PROVINCIAL RECONSTRUCTION TEAMS (PRT). Units of some 100 American and/or Allied troops, **Special Forces** units, and political advisers, operating since late 2002, engaged in building schools and roads, and trying to "win the hearts and minds of the Afghan people." At the same time they gather intelligence for the purpose of providing security and reconstruction, and to strengthen the central government.

Teams are located in **Kunduz**, where **Germans** operate under **North Atlantic Treaty Organization** (NATO) auspices; American and South Korean teams are in **Parwan**, New Zealand runs the **Bamian** PRT, and a British team is in **Mazar-i Sharif**. The **United States** also has teams in **Kandahar, Jalalabad, Gardez, Herat** Asadabad, **Parwan, Ghazni, Khost,** and **Zabul**. In September 2004 an all-German team began to be deployed in **Faizabad, Badakhshan** Province. They provided a measure of security during the presidential elections of October 2004, and are ready to do the same during the parliamentary elections. The American PRT include also civilian members from the U.S. State Department, the U.S. Agency for International Development, the U.S. Justice Department, and the U.S. Department of Agriculture.

The concept has been strongly opposed by a consortium of nongovernmental organizations (NGO), the Red Cross, and others, because it "blurs the lines between humanitarian workers and a combat military force." They also claim that the PRTs are not cost effective as operating costs amount to at least $10 million a year, building schools that are worth about $10,000 each. Nevertheless, they have been successful in curbing the power of the warlords. The allies divided Afghanistan into four zones, with Germany commanding the north, Italy and Spain the west, **Great Britain** the south, and the United States the east.

PROXIMITY TALKS. Negotiations under the auspices of the **United Nations** between Afghanistan and **Pakistan** leading to the withdrawal of Soviet forces from Afghanistan. *See* GENEVA ACCORDS.

PUZANOV, ALEXANDR. Soviet ambassador assigned to **Kabul** in 1972, the final year of **Muhammad Zahir Shah**, and an important figure during the republican and early Marxist periods. He was an active politician in Kabul and was therefore dubbed the "little czar." He was credited with helping to reunite the two factions of the **People's Democratic Party of Afghanistan** (PDPA) in 1977, and was quoted as saying that the **Saur Revolt** "came as a complete surprise to me." One expert describes him as "an alcoholic seventy-two-year-old castoff from Kremlin political struggles . . . [who] was trout fishing in the **Hindu Kush**" (Bradsher, 1983, 83) when the Saur Revolt occurred. He supported **Nur Muhammad Taraki** against **Hafizullah Amin** and was said to have lured Hafizullah Amin into an ambush. The "palace shoot-out" of September 14, 1979, misfired and

Amin demanded the recall of Puzanov; he left Kabul on November 19, 1979.

- Q -

QAEDA, AL- (The Base). A terrorist organization, founded by **Osama bin Laden**, Abu Ubayda al-Banshiri, and Muhammad Atif in 1988, for the purpose of "cleansing of the Muslim countries from corrupt and secular rulers, and fighting against the powers that threaten Muslim states and the holy places of Islam." Specifically, this meant achieving the withdrawal of **United States** troops from Saudi Arabia and winning independence for the Palestinian people (most American forces have since been withdrawn from Saudi Arabia). Al-Qaeda allied itself with **Islamist** forces in most parts of the Islamic world. It espouses a Hanbali interpretation of Islam, whose major protagonist is the 14-century jurist Ibn Taymiyya. The organization established its headquarters in Khartoum, Sudan, in 1992, and, in response to American threats, moved to Afghanistan in May 1996.

Al-Qaeda set up training camps in bases, established partly with American support in the war against the communist government, and, subsequently, provided considerable military assistance to the **Taliban** regime. Young Muslims from many parts of the Islamic world were trained in Afghanistan for military action in Kashmir, Chechnya, Bosnia, and other regions of conflict. The United States government holds al-Qaeda responsible for numerous attacks, including the August 7, 1998, bombings of its embassies in Kenya and Tanzania. In retaliation, President Bill Clinton ordered cruise missile attacks on Afghan terrorist training camps and the al-Shifa pharmaceutical plant in Sudan. Awards of $5 million each were offered for the capture or assassination of bin Laden and Muhammad Atif. The suicide attacks on the World Trade Center in New York and the Pentagon in Washington, on September 11, 2001, resulted in war and the destruction of the al-Qaeda network in Afghanistan. At the time of this writing, American military actions continue.

QAEDA, AL-, INTERNATIONAL. Once based in Sudan, then in Afghanistan, al-Qaeda is a worldwide organization whose aim is to establish a pan-Islamic caliphate under the banner of the "World Islamic Front for Jihad against the Jews and Crusaders." It is organized in cells with members and sympathizers in the Islamic world and elsewhere. It is led by **Osama bin Laden**, who rose to prominence when he called for the withdrawal of American troops from the territory of Saudi Arabia. Because of his hostility to the Saudi government he was deprived of his citizenship and started his search for a base elsewhere.

Al-Qaeda is only one of many similar groups, but, correctly or not, it has come to be blamed for terrorist actions in many countries, including Iraq where insurgents fight Coalition forces and their collaborators. Abu Musab Zarqawi is said to head the al-Qaeda wing in Iraq. Bounties on the heads of this and other organizations may eventually lead to their capture or killing, but this may not stop their activities. Al Qaeda has lost its base in Afghanistan but seems to have moved some of its operations to Iraq.

QAL'A. A citadel or fortification serving as the residence of a high government official. It is surrounded by a wall up to six meters high and two meters wide, with loopholed corner bastions and firing platforms on top of the wall. Quarters for troops are located along the interior of the walls, and a well, usually in the center of the yard, provides potable water of varying quality. The use of this type of fortification has become obsolete in modern military warfare, but it provides adequate protection from banditry and tribal conflicts. Therefore, tribal chiefs and local notables still reside in *Qal'a*s. *See also* SARAI.

QALA-I JANGI, BATTLE/MASSACRE. A revolt of some 600 **Taliban** fighters, held in the Qala-i Jang fortress west of **Mazar-i Sharif**, which only 86 "filthy and hungry prisoners" survived.

On November 24, 2001, some 300 Taliban soldiers who had surrendered in the battle for **Kunduz** were transported to the fortress. Only some of the prisoners were searched and some had concealed weapons which they used in suicide attacks on their jailers. One Central Intelligence Agency agent, Johnny (Mike) Spann, who interviewed prisoners, was killed, and another, "Dave," managed to escape. The prisoners were able to capture the armory and provide themselves with weapons and began a four-day battle which led to the decimation of the rebels.

American **Special Forces Teams** called in air strikes, pinpointing areas of Taliban concentrations with devastating effect. British SAS soldiers and **Abdul Rashid Dostum**'s troops stormed the parapets and picked off the rebels below. The survivors, including the American **John Walker Lindh**, were forced to surrender when the basements were flooded and burning oil poured upon them. "Hundreds of dead and dying" lay scattered over the field, some of them with their hands bound. Television crews from Reuters and the German ARD network filmed some of the action, which was subsequently shown on American television. *Time* correspondent Alex Perry gave a vivid description of the event.

QANUNI, YUNUS (QANOONI). Appointed interior minister in the **Transitional Government** but, because of overrepresentation of Panjshiris, made special adviser on security and minister of education. He was a member of the delegation to **Bonn** which elected an **Interim Government** in which he was at first appointed as interior minister. Qanuni resigned from his post in July 2004, when he unsuccessfully ran for presidential election in opposition to **Hamid Karzai**. He received the second highest number of votes with some 16 percent of the vote. Born in 1957 in the **Panjshir** Valley, he joined **Ahmad Shah Mas'ud** in the war against the Marxist regime and was wounded. He became "joint defense minister" in 1993 and retreated to the Panjshir Valley when the **Taliban** took **Kabul**. After the assassination of Mas'ud, on September 9, 2001, Qanuni became political head of the **Jami'at-i Islami** and formed a coalition to contest the parliamentary elections.

QIZILBASH. Meaning "Red Heads," who are named after the red pleats in their turbans. They were one of seven Turkic tribes who revered the **Safavid** ruler Ismail (1499–1524) as both a spiritual and a temporal ruler. The Persian ruler, **Nadir Shah Afshar**, stationed a rearguard (*chandawol*) of Qizilbash troops at **Kabul** during a campaign into India. They are **Shi'as**, and some 30,000 live in **Herat, Kandahar**, and Kabul. They performed a military function as a royal bodyguard until the 1860s, after which time they were employed in various functions in the administration of Afghanistan.

- R -

RABBANI, BURHANUDDIN (BURHAN AL-DIN, 1940–). Leader of the Jam'iat-i Islami-yi Afghanistan (Islamic Society of Afghanistan), the largely non-**Pashtun** group, and since 1993, president of the Islamic Republic of Afghanistan. He was born in **Faizabad, Badakhshan Province**, and educated in Islamic studies at **Kabul** University and Al-Azhar University, Cairo, where he received an M.A. degree in 1968. After returning to Afghanistan, he taught as a member of the Faculty of Theology at Kabul University. He became editor of

Majallat-i Shari'at (Journal of Islamic Law) in 1970 and was a leading member of the **Islamist Movement** since the late 1950s. He organized university students to oppose the secular trend in Afghanistan and to counteract the activities of leftist students on campus. The 15-member high council of the Jam'iat-i Islami selected him as its leader in 1971, and in 1974 he fled to **Pakistan**, where he sought the support of the Pakistan government and the Jama'at-i Islami, a radical Islamist party. In 1975, the Jam'iat carried out raids into Afghanistan, and the failure of the armed attacks revealed policy disagreements between Rabbani and **Gulbuddin Hekmatyar**. Thereupon Hekmatyar founded his Hizb-i Islami Party in 1976. Rabbani continued to lead the Jam'iat after the Saur Revolt. At the fall of the **Najibullah** regime, Rabbani's forces, under Commander **Ahmad Shah Mas'ud**, entered Kabul on April 25 and quickly expelled members of Gulbuddin Hekmatyar's forces from the presidential palace and the interior ministry. The **Uzbek** forces of General **Abdul Rashid Dostum** also cooperated with Jam'iat and other groups, including the **Shi'ite Hizb-i Wahdat**, who occupied portions of Kabul and began the struggle for power between the **mujahedin**. In March 1993, Rabbani succeeded **Sebghatullah Mujaddidi** as president of the Islamic Republic of Afghanistan, but he did not effectively control Kabul or the rest of Afghanistan. His refusal to step down after a two-year term resulted in considerable fighting and bombardment of Kabul, primarily by the forces of Hekmatyar. The **Taliban** finally expelled Rabbani from Kabul and attempts to reoccupy the presidency failed, after the **United States** intervention in October 2001. Rabbani now lives in Kabul, hoping to wield influence in the parliamentary elections.

RAIDS. Tribal raids for booty have been refined over the centuries and carried out in a distinct manner. The tribesmen are divided into three groups: the actual raiders, fit men who are well armed, active young men, and younger boys and old men. Ridgeway (26) describes the enterprise as follows:

> The first party proceed to the scene of operations, and there conceal themselves, waiting patiently for their opportunity for hours and even for days; the second and third parties meanwhile halt at certain prearranged places on the homeward route. Directly the raid has been committed, the raiders hurry off the cattle with all speed to the second party in reserve, and then disperse to find

their way home by unfrequented routes; meanwhile the second party, taking over the cattle and other spoil, hurry off to the third party, and so, by relays, the loot is rapidly borne away, far from the scene of the raid, in an incredibly short span of time.

Closer to home, the raiders protect the retreating parties. The raided party, if it guesses the origin of the raiders, will try to intercept them to recover their property. Since cattle cannot be moved very rapidly, they may have a chance at success. In warfare with Indian forces, the British have at times been able to snatch victory from defeat by intercepting the convoys with plunder.

RANJIT SINGH. King (1780–1839) of the newly founded **Sikh** nation, a religiopolitical entity, which in 1820 controlled most of the northern **Panjab**, Kashmir, and Peshawar. He captured Lahore from its Afghan garrison in 1798, compelling **Zaman Shah** to appoint the Sikh chief as governor of the Panjab. Ranjit Singh was described as of small stature and blind in his right eye, but quite fearless and a brilliant soldier. **Lord Auckland**, governor general of India, sided with the Sikh ruler and concluded an alliance with Ranjit Singh and **Shah Shuja** for the purpose of restoring the latter to the Afghan throne (*see* ANGLO-AFGHAN WARS; SIMLA MANIFESTO). Ranjit Singh, at that time "an old man in an advanced state of decrepitude," was wise enough not to send his army into Afghanistan and therefore did not share in the British disaster. Ranjit Singh died in 1839, and his empire was soon annexed by his former British allies. *See also* SUPPLIES, COLLECTION OF.

RAWALPINDI CONFERENCE. *See* **ANGLO-AFGHAN TREATY OF 1919.**

RAWLINSON, SIR HENRY C. (1810–1895). Political assistant to **Sir William Macnaghten** at **Kabul** and **Kandahar**. He participated in the Battle of Kandahar on May 29, 1842, and he retired with General **William Nott** to India via Kabul. He deciphered the fifth century B.C. Behistun inscriptions of Darius at Behistun near Kirmanshah in 1846. Subsequently he was a member of the viceroy's council of India, from 1858 to 1859 and 1868 to 1895, president, Royal Geographic Society 1871–1872 and 1874–1875, and president, London Oriental Congress, 1874.

REFUGEES. Decades of war in Afghanistan, severe drought, political insecurity, banditry, and hunger created the largest refugee problem in the world. Afghans fled in stages. A few thousand, mostly **Islamist** militants, fled to **Pakistan** after the **Muhammad Daud** coup of 1975. The numbers increased after the Marxist coup in April 1979, to turn into a flood during the Soviet intervention from 1980 to 1989 when about 3.5 million Afghans found shelter in Pakistan and some 2.5 million in Iran. Thousands found refuge in Europe, North America, Australia, and elsewhere. In Iran Afghans were dispersed throughout the country, working as day laborers and in other menial occupations. In Pakistan refugees were kept in camps, supported by the international community, and enlisted in the war against the communist regime. Each refugee family had to register with one of six (later seven) **mujahedin** parties to gain refugee status. Large camps provided the manpower for the war against the **Kabul** regime, where fighters could be rotated between periods of rest and armed activities. Afghan intellectuals, graduates of foreign univer-sities, and professional people found ready asylum in the West. The doors were wide open, as long as the war lasted against the communist regime. Things changed after the ouster of the Marxist regime in 1992 and the beginning of a period of civil war, which was as devastating as previous conflicts.

Although some 1.4 million refugees returned home in 1992, the emergence of the **Taliban** regime created a new refugee problems. By that time the international community was no longer as hospitable to the Afghans, and host countries began to refuse entry to most Afghans who were now considered "economic" rather than political refugees. At the end of 2001 there were still some 4.5 million Afghans living as refugees in various countries, most of them in Pakistan (2.2 million) and Iran (2.4 million). According to **United Nations** statistics, the **United States** intervention after September 11, 2001, produced a new wave of refugees: Russia 100,000; Central Asia 29,000; Europe 36,000; North America and Australia 17,000, and India 13,000. It is difficult to say how many internally displaced Afghans there are, but in 2002 alone some 230,000 of them were helped to return home. Support for refugees is still insufficient, "donor fatigue" and the change of focus to other areas of need have tended to keep this social problem unsolved. It can only be hoped that the establishment of the new government in 2004 will provide the security and prosperity to reintegrate all Afghans into their homeland.

RELIGIOUS SCHOOLS AND WAR. During the war against the communist regime in **Kabul**, **madrasas** and religious schools served as the recruiting grounds for **mujahedin**. The soldiers of **Maulawi Muhammad Nabi** were in the beginning a force of "maulawi," graduates of Afghan madrasas. In **Pakistan** the former military dictator, Zia-ul Haq, contributed to a considerable expansion of madrasas and religious schools. In 1947 there existed only 137 madrasas, which number had grown to some 20,000 religious schools by the end of the 20th century (according to a World Bank study, this number is greatly eccagerated). The public school system is inadequate to provide education for all, and religious schools offered free instruction, as well as meals and lodging. The **Islamist Deoband** madrasa trained teachers who fostered an extremist and sectarian interpretation of Islam and many schools included military training to win recruits for **holy war** in Afghanistan. Many of the **Taliban** soldiers came from such schools. Funds from supporters in Pakistan and abroad contributed to keep them in operation. During Taliban offensives, religious schools on the Pakistan frontier were closed to replenish the Taliban forces. Many of these recruits died or were captured after the fall of the Taliban regime, but radical Islamists are still threatening stability in Afghanistan.

Governments in many parts of the Islamic world have tried to control madrasas by appointing their shaikhs, paying a salary to **ulama**, requiring proper qualifications, and demanding a broadening of curricula to include secular subjects. But the majority of religious schools in the frontier areas are independent, supported by their local community, and headed by **mullas** who themselves often have only an elementary education.

RETALIATION, AMERICAN MISSILE ATTACK. On August 20, 1998, the **United States** fired cruise missiles at three training camps of **Osama bin Laden** who was held responsible for attacks on the American embassies in Kenya and Tanzania. Bin Laden had decided at the last moment not to visit the camps and therefore managed to escape unharmed. The camps concerned were the Harakat al-Jihad Islami of bin Laden and Jam'iat al-Mujahedin and Harakat al-Ansar where Pakistanis were trained for action in Kashmir. The three camps were totally destroyed, but one camp operated by Arabs "that also provided training into hijacking and exploding multistoried buildings" was not hit. About two dozen fighters were killed and many wounded, but casualties would have been much higher if many had not been commandeered to assist in the **Taliban** offensive at the time. One Pakistani intelligence source remarked "the most powerful army and the world's most dangerous terrorist organization have declared war against each other."

ROBERTS, GENERAL SIR ABRAHAM (1784–1873). Commander of **Shah Shuja**'s "**Army of the Indus**" in the **first Anglo-Afghan war** (1838–1842). He escaped the British debacle when he was recalled by **Lord Auckland**, governor general of India, who disliked Roberts's criticism of his policy. His son (below) was a British general in the **second Anglo-Afghan war**.

ROBERTS, GENERAL SIR FREDERICK S. (1832–1914). British general, the son of Sir Abraham (above), who commanded the Kurram Field Force in the **second Anglo-Afghan war** (1878–1880). He invaded Afghanistan through the Kurram Valley and reached **Kabul** on October 12, 1879, where he was the de facto ruler after the abdication of **Yaqub Khan**. He fought at **Paiwar Kotal** on December 2, 1878. After **Louis Cavagnari**'s assassination at Kabul, September 3, 1879, commanded the Kabul Field Force. He fought at **Charasia**, October 6, and received Amir Yaqub Khan's abdication and sent him to Indian exile, and engaged in operations around **Sherpur**, December 1879. After **Maiwand**, he marched from Kabul to **Kandahar** and defeated **Ayub Khan** at Kandahar, September 1. He was a legendary figure, called "Bobs" by his fellow generals and famous, or infamous, for ordering indiscriminate executions of Afghans. He arrested Yahya Khan, a nephew of Amir **Dost Muhammad**, for the purpose of looting his house. General **Charles MacGregor** said of him: "Bobs is a cruel blood-thirsty little brute, he has shot some 6 men already in cold blood. I have saved three men from his clutches already" (Trousdale, 1985). Although Sir Frederick was able to defeat Ayub Khan, the Indian government agreed to withdraw from Afghanistan in April 1881 to avoid a repetition of the disaster of the **first Anglo-Afghan war**. Sir Frederick died in 1914.

ROBERTS AND "RETRIBUTION." The *London Times* (February 18, 1879) reported that General **Frederick S. Roberts** had caused numerous villages to be looted and burned; that he ordered the cavalry to take no prisoners; that some 90 prisoners, tied together, were slaughtered. In response the general admitted that nine villages were looted and burned in retaliation for Mangal attacks after they

Plate 3. Execution of the Kotwal, Intelligence Officer of Kabul. Source: ILN

Plate 4. Execution of a Ghazi (PIN)

were warned not to do it. He called it an "act of retributive justice." He ordered Major J. C. Steward, who, with 40 sabres, charged some 400 men running out of a village, to take no prisoners—but he said he merely meant to disperse them. Only 30 to 40 were killed, but "a nought got added during its [official telegram] transmission" and the number appeared to be 300 to 400 killed. His force was too small; therefore, he felt justified in giving the order to kill. Admits that native officers tried to prevent the escape of prisoners and shot nine and wounded 13 mostly by bayonets. But he claimed that "every possible care was given to the wounded." Dated Camp Peiwar, April 1, 1879.

Roberts tried a number of Afghans before a military commission for participation in the attack on the British mission in **Kabul**. Four were executed "for dishonoring the bodies of the officers" in the embassy; four for possession of property belonging to the mission; six for being armed within five miles of the camp; four for attempting to free Afghan prisoners; and 69 for "inciting" people to rise, carrying arms, "traitorously firing and killing wounded soldiers."

ROKETI, MULLA SALAM. A colorful individual of **Abdul Rab Sayyaf**'s Ittihad-i Islami party who was robbed by Pakistanis of three **Stinger** missiles he wanted to sell. In retaliation, he took 10 Pakistani hostages, including the deputy commissioner of Ziarat and two Chinese engineers. He demanded that his brother be freed from a Pakistani prison and that the Stingers be returned, but he was eventually forced to give up his hostages when the **Pakistan** government threatened to close Sayyaf's offices in Pakistan.

RULERS OF AFGHANISTAN. *See* **DURRANI DYNASTY.**

RUSSIAN-AFGHAN RELATIONS. Formal diplomatic relations between Russia and Afghanistan began in June 1919, when the Soviet Union and Afghanistan announced their intention to establish legations in **Kabul** and Moscow. A cease-fire had just been declared in the **third Anglo-Afghan war** and King **Amanullah** wanted to demonstrate Afghanistan's independence by establishing diplomatic relations with European powers. A mission, headed by Muhammad Wali, proceeded to Tashkent and Moscow, where it was given a rousing welcome. N. N. Nariman, a spokesman of the foreign ministry, announced that "Russian imperialism, striving to enslave and degrade small nationalities, has gone, never to return." Muhammad Wali expressed the hope that "with the assistance of **Soviet**

Russia, we shall succeed in emancipating our Afghanistan and the rest of the East." He presented V. I. Lenin a letter from King Amanullah, which was received "with great pleasure." A Bolshevik diplomat, Michael K. Bravin (who subsequently defected and was killed by an Afghan), proceeded to Kabul to arrange for the arrival of a permanent representative, Z. Suritz, in January 1920. Suritz immediately set about negotiating the preliminaries for the Treaty of 1921, which recognized the "mutual independence" of both states and bound them not to "enter into any military or political agreement with a third State, which might prejudice one of the Contracting Parties."

The Soviet Union agreed to permit free and untaxed transit of Afghan goods and recognized the independence and freedom of Khiva and Bokhara "in accordance with the wishes of the people." It provided for Soviet technical and financial aid of one million rubles in gold or silver and promised a return of the "frontier districts which belonged to the latter [Afghanistan] in the last century," a reference to the area of **Panjdeh**. **Britain** had held a monopoly in the supply of arms and war materiel, which could only be shipped to Afghanistan by way of India; the treaty now opened a new avenue for materiel purchased in Europe. King Amanullah was able to crush the **Khost Rebellion** in summer 1924, with the assistance of several aircraft from the Soviet Union and a number of foreign pilots, including several Russians. In spite of the friendly rhetoric, differences existed between the two countries: King Amanullah wanted Khiva and Bukhara to be free from Soviet control, possibly associated with Afghanistan in a Central Asian confederation, but the "Young Khivan and Bukharan" revolted and opted for membership in the Soviet Union. The Soviet Union saw this as an expression of the "wishes of the people" and retained this czarist possession in Central Asia. A more serious crisis in Soviet-Afghan relations occurred in December 1925 when Soviet troops occupied the island of Darqad (also called Urta Tagai and Yangi Qal'a) on the **Amu Daria**. At the turn of the 20th century the course of the Amu Daria had changed from south of the island to north and, since the main stream was designated as the Afghan boundary, Kabul considered the island Afghan territory. After the Bolshevik Revolution, refugees from the Soviet Union settled on the island, including some **Basmachi** counterrevolutionaries, who made it a base for raids into Soviet Central Asia. The matter threatened to develop into an international conflict, but the Soviets apparently wanted good relations with King Amanullah and evacuated their troops on February 28, 1926. Moscow paid the promised subsidy only irregularly, and by the mid-1920s the Kabul government had expanded its diplomatic base to the extent that it did not need to maintain a special relationship with the Soviet Union.

During the 1929 civil war the Soviet Union had maintained its embassy in Kabul and immediately recognized the government of **Muhammad Nadir Shah**. The new king sent Muhammad Aziz, his half brother, as ambassador to Moscow, to indicate the importance of the post, but he was determined to end Soviet influence in Afghanistan. He renegotiated and signed (June 24, 1931) the treaty of 1921, with the inclusion of an article calling for the prohibition in both territories of activities that "might cause political or military injury" to the other. Nadir Shah was thinking of the followers of ex-King Amanullah who might attempt a return to power, and the Soviets were concerned about the Basmachi threat. A commercial treaty had to wait until 1936, and the Afghan government did not renew a Soviet airline concession and eventually dismissed all Soviet airline pilots and mechanics. The Afghan government turned increasingly to Germany for its technological and developmental needs, and a special relationship developed which greatly disturbed Moscow and was accepted in London only as the lesser of two evils. The outbreak of World War II and the temporary alliance between Germany and the Soviet Union resulted in fears in London and Kabul that the Soviets might support a pro-Amanullah coup. And, indeed, these worries were not unwarranted. The German foreign ministry considered **Muhammad Zahir Shah** pro-British and toyed with the idea of supporting a coup against the monarch. Count Schulenberg, the German ambassador in Moscow, queried Vyacheslav Molotov whether the Soviet Union would permit the transit of Afghan forces into northern Afghanistan. But Molotov was noncommittal, and the matter was dropped.

On June 22, 1941, Germany attacked the Soviet Union, and Moscow joined the Western alliance. The alliance of Britain and the Soviet Union caused considerable anxiety in Kabul because Afghan foreign policy had been based on the premise that its territorial security depended on the continued rivalry between its imperialist neighbors. Concerted Allied action was soon to follow: in October 1941, the Allies presented separate notes to the Afghan government demanding the expulsion of all Axis nationals. Kabul was forced to comply, and the Afghan king convened a **Loya Jirga**, Great Council, which gave retroactively its approval after the Axis nationals had left. The Afghan government insisted that they be given safe passage to a neutral country. From that time the Afghan government kept its northern border closed to nondiplomatic travelers, but trade continued between the two countries.

When India became independent in 1947 and the state of **Pakistan** was created, Afghanistan repudiated the treaties that accepted the **Durand** Line as the international boundary and demanded that the Afghans of the **North-West Frontier Province** (NWFP) be given the choice of independence. Afghanistan was the only country voting against the admission of Pakistan to the **United Nations**. The Cold War had begun, and the Dwight D. Eisenhower administration sought to contain Moscow's expansionism by sponsoring alliances with states bordering on the Soviet Union. Washington supported creation of the Baghdad Pact (later renamed CENTO), which united Britain, Turkey, Iraq, Iran, and Pakistan in a defensive alliance. This alliance guaranteed international borders but ignored irredentist and nationalist aspirations in the Middle East. As a result, relations between Afghanistan and Pakistan, a Western ally, turned increasingly hostile.

The Afghan government "normalized" its relations with the Soviet Union and in 1946 agreed to accept the *thalweg* (middle) of the **Amu Daria** as the international boundary. A telegraph link was established with Tashkent in 1947, and in 1950 Afghanistan signed a four-year trade agreement with the USSR. The Soviet government praised Afghanistan's "positive" neutrality and, when in December 1955 Nikita Khrushchev and Nikolai Bulganin came to Kabul, the stage was set for a major rapprochement. The two countries renewed the Treaty of 1931 for 10 years, the Soviet Union granting Afghanistan a $100 million loan at 2 percent interest for projects selected by a joint USSR-Afghan committee. The Afghan national airline started flights from Kabul to Tashkent in 1965, which were subsequently extended to Moscow and other European cities.

The Afghan government wanted to purchase arms from the **United States**, and when it was unable to obtain what it wanted, Prime Minister **Muhammad Daud** turned to the Soviet Union for help. In 1956 the first shipments of East Bloc weapons arrived and the Afghan armed forces began to be Soviet-equipped. Thousands of Soviet advisers came to Afghanistan, and thousands of Afghan technicians and military officers went to the Soviet Union for training. The result was a growing cadre of military officers, students, and technocrats with leftist, if not pro-Russian, sympathies. When Muhammad Daud staged a coup with leftist support on July 17, 1973, the stage was set for the **Saur Revolt** that brought a Marxist government to power. The new Kabul government accepted Soviet advisers in virtually all its civilian and government branches and concluded a series of treaties that made the Soviet Union the dominant influence in Afghanistan. On December 5, 1978, the **Nur Muhammad Taraki** regime concluded a treaty of friendship, similar to one the Soviet Union concluded with Vietnam, that also provided for military assistance and that became the basis for military intervention a year later. Resistance was growing against the Marxist regime, resulting in a civil war that turned into a war of liberation when Soviet troops tried to prop up a faltering regime. The war turned out to be costly to Afghanistan: **mujahedin** sources claim that as many as one million Afghans perished, whereas the Kabul government claimed that 243,900 soldiers and civilians were killed. After Soviet troops evacuated Afghanistan on February 14, 1989, Moscow announced it had suffered about 13,000 (according to later Soviet sources, 26,000) deaths and another 35,000 wounded. *See also* APPENDIXES 2 and 3; FOREIGN RELATIONS; LIMITED CONTINGENT OF SOVIET FORCES IN AFGHANISTAN.

RUTSKOI, ALEXANDR. One of the Russian **Afgantsy** who became vice president of Russia and head of the parliamentary opposition to President Boris Yeltsin in October 1993. He spent five months in Leforto prison in Moscow as a result of his challenge to Yeltsin. Rutskoi is leader of the conservative Great Power party. He served in Afghanistan in 1985–86 and again in 1988 and was a "Hero of the Soviet Union," having flown 428 combat missions and been shot down twice, once over Pakistan (Galeotti, 128). He became deputy commander of the 40th Army's air forces, and with other Afgantsy is an important figure of the political scene in Russia.

- S -

SADOZAI. *See* **DURRANI**.

SAFAVID DYNASTY (1501-1732). A dynasty named after Shaykh Safi al-Din (d. 1334), a **Sufi saint**, who established the Safavid order in Ardabil in northwestern Iran. A descendant of the **shaykh**, Shah Isma'il, founded the dynasty in 1501, unified the country, and established **Twelver Shi'ism** as the religion of the new state. He created a personal force, the **Kizilbash** (Red Heads), and a tribal force, the Shah Sevan (Friends of the Shah) as praetorian guards. His tribes venerated **Isma'il** and thought him invincible. It was only when the **Ottomans** defeated the shah in the battle of Chaldiran in 1514 that the ruler lost some of his charisma. But the Safavids retained some of the quasi-divine status. An Afghan army finally defeated the Safavids in the **battle of Gulnabad** in 1722.

SAFRONCHUK, VASILY S. Soviet economist and career diplomat who was in **Kabul** from May 25, 1979, to 1982. Officially, he was counselor-envoy of the USSR embassy, but unofficially he was an adviser to the Afghan foreign ministry. He unsuccessfully tried to prevent the rift between **Nur Muhammad Taraki** and **Hafizullah Amin** and was said to have recommended the establishment of a broad-based, national front government with the inclusion of non-communists. **Nur Ahmad Etemadi**, who was held in the **Pul-i Charkhi** prison at the time, was said to have been suggested for the position of prime minister. Hafizullah Amin refused, and Etemadi was executed in his prison cell (Cordovez and Harrison, 38). Safronchuk published two articles in *International Affairs* (Moscow, January and February 1991) in which he denied that he did more than advise Amin in matters relating to the **United Nations** and international relations. He characterized Amin as a "commonplace petty bourgeois and an extreme **Pashtu** nationalist."

SALANG PASS/TUNNEL (35-12' N, 69-13' E). A village and district in **Párwan** Province located near the Salang Pass at an altitude of 13,350 feet. It is a choke point to north-south traffic on the 300-mile-long Termez-Salang-Kabul Highway. The highway, and a 1.7-mile-long tunnel, located at an altitude of 11,000 feet, was built by Soviet experts and opened to general traffic in 1964. It was one of the routes of Soviet occupation in December 1978 and soon proved to be vulnerable to **mujahedin** attacks. In October 1984 an explosion in the tunnel was said to have led to the deaths of 1,000 people, including 700 Soviet troops. Commander **Ahmad Shah Mas'ud**, whose center of operations included the **Panjshir** Valley, staged numerous ambushes against the road, including one in March 1984, when he was reported to have destroyed 70 fuel tankers destined for **Kabul**. Repeated Soviet Panjshir campaigns could not secure safe passage through this vital link to Kabul.

Completely renovated by two Turkish construction companies under a World-Bank funded program, it became fully operational in mid December 2003. It has a capacity of between 1,500 and 2,000 vehicles per day and is the major channel of commerce and transit between the northern provinces and Kabul.

SALE, LADY FLORENTIA (1790-1853). Wife of Brigadier **Sir Robert Sale**, commander of the garrison at **Jalalabad** during the **first Anglo-Afghan war** (1838-1842). Lady Sale was a hostage with other British women and some of their officer husbands and thus escaped the general massacre of the British forces. She recorded her experience in a book *A Journal of the Disasters in Afghanistan, 1841-2*, which is an important source on the British misadventure.

SALE, GEN. SIR ROBERT HENRY (1782-1845). Controversial general, called "Fighting Bob" for his exploits in the Burmese War in 1823. When the **Army of the Indus** invaded Afghanistan during the **first Anglo-Afghan war**, Sale was in command of the First Brigade of the Infantry Division of the Bengal Column. He commanded an advanced brigade to **Kandahar**, April 1839; he was at Girishk, **Ghazni**, and **Kabul** and wintered in **Jalalabad**. He defeated **Amir Dost Muhammad** at **Parwan** Darra, November 2, 1840. He forced the **Khurd Kabul Pass** and reached Jalalabad on November 12, 1841. Unable to return as ordered by General **William Elphinstone**, he remained besieged in Jalalabad until April 7, 1842, when he sallied out of the city with almost his entire force of 1,430 men and six guns and defeated **Akbar Khan**. He was relieved by General **George Pollock**'s "Army of Retribution" and went to Kabul September 1842. A severe disciplinarian, he ordered hundreds of lashings for the least infringement by his soldiers. He returned to India in September 1842 and was made a Knight Commander of the Bath for the capture of Ghazni in spite of the fact that he "nearly muffed the whole operation" when he ordered the bugler to sound the retreat at the time a storming column had already effected a breach. He pursued Dost Muhammad into **Bamian**, but was repulsed by his forces and failed to come to Elphinstone's aid at Kabul. "He would have surrendered Jalalabad without firing a shot if Havelock and Broadfoot [two of his officers] had not intervened. His victory over Akbar outside Jalalabad was only achieved because his officers forced him to attack against his own judgement" (Pottinger/Macrory, 153). Many times wounded, Sale was killed in a battle with the **Sikhs** in 1845.

SAMANGAN (36-15'N, 67-40'E). A province in north-central Afghanistan with an area of 6,425 square miles and a population of

275,000 (1991 est. 337,000). The administrative center of the province is Aibak, with about 90,000 inhabitants, which abounds in important archaeological sites. The province is rich in mineral resources and is famous for its fruits, especially melons. The population is largely **Uzbek**, who breed horses for the famous Buzkashi games.

SARANDOY (TSARANDOY). The name of the Afghan Boy Scouts organization begun in 1932 and headed by the Afghan crown prince Muhammad Zahir (the subsequent king) and later by his son Ahmad Shah.

President **Muhammad Daud** organized a gendarmerie force called Sarandoy of some 20,000 men, which the **Khalqi** government continued and **Babrak Karmal** in 1981 reorganized into a defense force of six brigades, 20 battalions of 6,000 men, and various support units. The Sarandoy forces were stationed in major urban areas held by the **Kabul** government. The Sarandoy was under the direction of the ministry of interior and was a Khalqi stronghold under Colonel General Gulabzoy and his successors. It used to rival the power of the Parcham-dominated **Afghan Security Service** (KHAD) until the **Tanai** coup of March 1990. After the fall of the Marxist regime the organization disintegrated, its members joining competing **mujahedin** groups.

SAUR REVOLT (REVOLUTION). Marxist coup of April 27, 1978, named after the Afghan month (7 of Saur 1357), which initiated 11 years of rule by the **People's Democratic Party of Afghanistan.**

SAYYAF, ABDUL RASUL (ABD AL-RABB AL-RASUL). Leader of the Ittihad-i Islami Barayi Azadi-yi Afghanistan (Islamic Union for the Liberation of Afghanistan), a radical **Islamist movement** that aims at the establishment of an Islamic state in Afghanistan. He was born in 1946 in Paghman and was educated in Paghman, at Abu Hanifa Theological School, and at the Faculty of Theology at **Kabul** University. He went to Egypt and obtained an M.A. degree at Al-Azhar University. He was a member of the Islamist movement and in 1971 deputy of **Burhanuddin Rabbani**. In 1974, when he was about to leave for the **United States** for legal training, he was arrested at Kabul International Airport by intelligence officers and spent more than five years in prison. Freed by the **Parcham** regime in 1980, he went to Peshawar and joined the **mujahedin** as spokesman for the alliance. Elected for a period of two years (1980 to 1981), he wanted to continue in this position but was forced to step down. He then formed his own group, the Islamic Union for the Liberation of Afghanistan. He is an eloquent speaker in Arabic and has been able to receive financial support from Arabic Gulf states. He is ideologically close to the groups headed by **Gulbuddin Hekmatyar** and **Yunus Khales**, and had allied himself with Arab "Wahhabi" mujahedin groups. During the present civil war he had frequent clashes with the **Hizb-i Wahdat** and has allied himself with the Jam'iat of Rabbani. Driven from his base in Paghman, he fled with his forces to **Jalalabad**. Since the **United States** intervention in Afghanistan, Sayyaf teaches at the faculty of theology of Kabul University.

SAYYID-I KAYAN. Sayyid Shah Nasser Nadiri, commonly called Sayyid-i Kayan, is head of the Ismaili community in Afghanistan and leader of a force that has attempted to protect its community from **Soviet/Kabul** attacks and **mujahedin** penetration of their territory. In a series of tactical alliances, the Sayyid-i Kayan's forces were cooperating with General **Abdul Rashid Dostum** against **jam'iat-Islami** forces.

Sayyid Nadiri was born in 1933 in Darra-yi Kayan in **Baghlan** Province. He was elected to Parliament in 1965, and in 1968 he became vice president of the *wolesi jirga*. Six months after the republican coup of 1973, Sayyid Nadiri and his four brothers were imprisoned. Freed after two years, Sayyid Nadiri and his brothers were again jailed after the **Saur Revolt**. He was in Pol-i Charkhi prison until **Babrak Karmal** proclaimed an amnesty in 1980. Sayyid Shah Nasser Nadiri left Afghanistan in 1981 and now lives in England. His brother Sayyid Mansur is acting head of the community.

SCUD MISSILE. The SCUD-B is a tactical, guided, battlefield missile with a range of about 200 miles and a warhead of 2,000 pounds, which was introduced into Afghanistan in 1988 by the **Soviet Union** and employed for the protection of major cities. Although not very accurate and useful in fighting insurgency forces, the missiles were successfully employed in the siege of **Jalalabad** in February–November 1989. Several hundred were said to be still in possession of Afghan commanders, including one launching area in Darulaman, which was the prize possession of Harakat-i Islami of **Muhammad Asef Muhsini**, but was captured by **Gulbuddin Hekmatyar**'s forces in September 1994, and by the **Taliban** in 1995. With the departure of Soviet advisers, it is not clear whether any of the **mujahedin** groups were able to operate them.

SECOND ANGLO-AFGHAN WAR (1878–1879 [–81]). The "Signal Catastrophe" of the previous war inclined the British to pursue a policy of "masterly inactivity," which was to leave Afghanistan to the Afghans. But a generation later the advocates of a "forward policy" to counter Russian moves in Central Asia succeeded in being heard. Technology had considerably advanced since the **first Anglo-Afghan war** and British conquests had extended across the Indus River and approached the passes leading into Afghanistan. British-Indian telegraph lines and rail terminals had reached the borders of Afghanistan. The Indian forces, now wearing khaki uniforms, were equipped with breech-loading Martini-Henry and Snider rifles, which were faster to operate. The Afghan army still depended largely on the **jezail** and muzzle-loading rifles.

Amir **Shir Ali** (1863–1879), a son of Amir **Dost Muhammad**, had ascended the Afghan throne after eliminating a number of rivals. He gained British recognition in 1869 and was invited to meet Lord Mayo in Ambala, India. Shir Ali was worried about Russian advances in Central Asia and wanted British guarantees from Russian aggression and recognition of his son, Abdullah Jan, as crown prince and his successor; but the viceroy was not willing to make any such commitment and merely gave the Afghan king 600,000 rupees and a few pieces of artillery. Disappointed, Shir Ali was receptive when General **Constatin Kaufman**, the Russian governor general at Tashkent, made overtures, promising what Britain was not willing to give. General **Stolietoff** arrived uninvited in **Kabul** on July 22, 1878, with the charge to draft a treaty of alliance with the Afghan ruler. Lord Lytton was now alarmed and sent General **Neville Chamberlain** to lead a British military mission to Kabul. Arrangements had been made with the independent tribes on the frontier for the mission's escort of one thousand troops, but when the British reached the border, they were prevented from entering Afghan territory. In response to this "insult," the Indian government issued an ultimatum and dispatched an army under General **Frederick Roberts** that entered Kabul on July 24, 1879. Shir Ali fled north in the hope of receiving Russian support. No help was forthcoming, and the amir died of natural causes in **Mazar-i Sharif** on February 21, 1879.

Plate 5. Bala Hisar. Source: Burke

GENERAL ROSS'S DIVISION CROSSING THE LOGHUR RIVER ON ITS WAY TO MEET SIR DONALD STEWART. Plate 6. Source: ILN

Plate 7. Evacuation of Wounded. Source: ILN

Plate 8. Fort and Village of Mollah Abdul Guffoor, Captured and Destroyed by Brigadier-General Charles Gough (ILN)

Plate 9. Guns over the Khojak Pass (ILN)

Plate 10. Ghazis Fire from Sangar (PIN)

Britain recognized his son **Yaqub Khan** as the Afghan ruler (Abdullah Jan had preceded his father in death) at the cost of his signing the **Treaty of Gandomak** on May 26, 1879. **Louis Cavagnari** was established as British envoy at Kabul, and history repeated itself when on September 3, 1879, mutinous troops, whose pay was in arrears, stormed the British mission and assassinated the envoy and his staff. The incident encouraged attacks on British positions elsewhere, which grew, in spite of British attempts at pacification, culminating in the rout of General **G. R. S. Burrows** at the **Battle of Maiwand** on July 27, 1880. Fearing a repetition of the "Signal Catastrophe," the British-Indian government recognized **Abdul Rahman** as "amir of Kabul and its dependencies" and thus facilitated an orderly exit from Afghanistan.

For India, the war was an economic disaster, instead of the original estimate of £5 million it cost £19.5 million exclusive of 395,000 rupees paid to the amir, and an additional sum of 50,000 rupees per month for six months. The exchequer bore the share of £5,000,000, the Indian revenues paid the rest (OA 2, 723).

The greatest number of troops employed in Afghanistan at any one date was about 20,000, with 72 guns in the main theater and 50,000 men with 74 guns on the lines of communication (MR, 65). According to one source (Hanna, 1910), the British suffered 40,000 casualties, which, if correct, must include thousands of camp followers. Almost 99,000 camels perished, a loss that was long felt in the areas from which they had been requisitioned.

O'Ballance says, "The real winners of this war were the breech-loading Martini and Snider rifles, and the disciplined direction under which they were employed" (49).

SECOND ANGLO-AFGHAN WAR, OPERATIONS. The plan of campaign was an advance by three lines as follows:

Northern line—Peshawar forces under Lieutenant General **Sam Browne** with 10,000 combatants, 48 guns, and 10,000 followers with the objective of taking Dakka.

Central line—Kohat force under Major General F. Roberts with 6,500 combatants, 18 guns, and 6,500 followers with the objective of moving up the Kurram valley.

Southern line— Quetta force under Lieutenant General **Donald M. Steward** with 12,800 combatants, 78 guns, and 12,000 followers.

Reserves for the northern and central lines under Brigadier General **F. Maude** consisted of 5,000 troops; and for the southern line under Brigadier General **J. M. Primrose** 6,000 combatants. The entire British forces amounted to 40,300 combatants, 144 guns, and 29,300 followers.

The advance of the northern line was secured with the promise of payment of an annual allowance of 87,000 rupees to the **Khaibar** tribes to compensate them for the loss of a subsidy from the Afghan **amir**. Not all tribes accepted. The first operation began with an attack on November 21 on **Ali Masjid**. A force of 7,800 British troops with 26 guns faced an Afghan force of 3,500 Afghan regulars and 600 **khasadars** with 24 guns. After a vigorous resistance, Afghan forces abandoned the post. The British forces moved on and occupied **Jalalabad** on December 20 without any resistance. A minor expedition into the Bazar valley was of limited success as the Zakka Khel and other **Afridis** withdrew and continued to inflict losses when the British "punitive" force withdrew. A squadron of the 10th Husars trying to ford the **Kabul** River were swept down the stream and one officer and 46 men drowned.

The central line crossed the Afghan frontier at Thal on November 21 and advanced to the Kurram fort. After a failed attempt on an Afghan force near the **Paiwar Kotal**, General **Frederick Roberts** was able to turn the Afghan lines, and on December 2, 1878, he defeated the Afghans, who lost about 500 killed or wounded compared to 98 British casualties. Four days later Ali Khel was occupied, where the British forces remained until April 1879.

The southern line concentrated at Quetta early in November 1878, and crossing the Khojak and Gwazha passes the troops proceeded to Takhta-i Pul and entered **Kandahar** on January 8. On January 16, the 2nd Division, leaving a garrison at Kandahar, started for Girishk with 20 days of supplies, for British, and three days, for Indian, troops. Girishk was occupied from February 2 to February 22, but on the return British forces were harassed with some losses. Cholera took a heavy toll of the Kandahar force, claiming the lives of about 500 men.

On the northern line, the Peshawar Field Force established itself in **Nangarhar** Province. Supplies were collected locally and punitive expeditions were staged against hostile **Shinwari** tribes. Lacking sufficient transport to proceed to **Kabul**, the 1st Division established itself at **Gandomak** in April 1879. A month later **Yaqub Khan** succeeded **Amir Shir Ali** on the throne and signed the Treaty of Gandomak with Britain. This ended the first phase of the second

Anglo-Afghan war, and British forces withdrew from Afghanistan, except for a force at Kandahar.

Second phase, 1879–1881. As a result of the attack on the British mission in Kabul on September 3, 1879, and the assassination of its staff, the Indian government decided to take punitive measures. The plan of operation was as follows:

1. An invading column, called the "Kabul Field Force," was set up. It was headed by General Roberts and included one cavalry brigade (one British and two Indian regiments); two infantry brigades (two British and five Indian battalions); three batteries and two gatlings, one company of sappers and miners; altogether 6,600 fighting men, 18 guns, and 6,000 followers, to march from Kurram to Kabul.

2. Two mixed infantry brigades, 4,000 strong, to keep the line between Thal and Ali Khel open.

3. A force, 6,600 strong, to secure the **Khaibar-Jalalabad-Gandomak** line, with a movable column to establish communications onward to Kabul.

4. A strong reserve force between Peshawar and Rawalpindi.

5. A force of 9,000 strong to hold southern Afghanistan, dominate the Kandahar Province, occupy Kalat-i Ghilzai, and threaten **Ghazni**, with its communications to the Indus kept open by a brigade of Bombay troops.

Transport was again a serious problem for the invaders: only 2,000 mules, 750 camels, 650 bullocks, and 100 donkeys could be organized within a short time. Nevertheless, General Roberts was able to reach **Charasia** in October 1879, where he was able to prevail in a battle on October 6.

The Peshawar force consisted of one British and four Indian cavalry regiments, five British and 12 Indian battalions, seven companies of sappers and miners, three horse, one field, and two mountain batteries. The army consisted of 13,400 combatants. The forces left Landi Kotal and occupied Jalalabad on the 12th and Gandomak on the 24th of October and opened communications with General Roberts by December.

The Kandahar garrison, 4,726 strong, was dispatched on September 23, a column of all arms, 1,400 strong with 1,300 followers and a month's worth of supplies to proceed via Kalat-i Ghilzai toward Ghazni. Kalat-i Ghilzai was garrisoned and the troops returned to Kandahar.

In the meantime General Roberts established himself in Kabul and set up a court of retribution, which speedily executed a number of Afghans, including 49 men of the regiments that had attacked the British mission. Yaqub Khan abdicated on October 12, 1879, and General Roberts started a number of punitive expeditions. Not all was well for the British, as large numbers of Afghan forces, estimated by the British at about 100,000 (improbable), laid siege to General Roberts's forces at the Sherpur Cantonment (*see* SHERPUR, SIEGE OF). A victory by General Steward at **Ahmad Khel** on April 19, 1880, was followed by the disastrous **Battle of Maiwand** in which Ayyub Khan defeated General **G. R. S. Burrows** on July 27. To avoid the disaster of the first Afghan war, Britain recognized **Abdul Rahman Khan** as amir of Kabul and its Dependencies.

SECOND ANGLO-AFGHAN WAR, DECLARATION OF WAR. On November 21, 1878, Lord Lytton, the viceroy of India, issued a proclamation in which he recalled the British assistance given to **Amir Shir Ali** to consolidate his power and help in fixing the boundary with Russia. He complained,

> For all these gracious acts the Amir Shir Ali Khan has rendered no return. On the contrary, he has requited them with active ill-will and open discourtesy. . . . He has closed against free passage to British subjects and their commerce the roads between India and Afghanistan. He has maltreated British subjects, and permitted British traders to be plundered within his jurisdiction, giving them neither protection nor redress. [Having refused to receive a British mission and not answered communication] he has, nevertheless, received formally and entertained publicly at **Kabul** an Embassy from Russia. . . . The Amir has forcibly repulsed, at his outposts, an English Envoy of high rank.

He added ominously, "The Amir Shir Ali Khan, mistaking for weakness the long forbearance of the British Government, has thus deliberately incurred its just resentment. With the **sardars** and people of Afghanistan this Government has still no quarrel, and desires none. . . . Upon the Amir Shir Ali Khan alone rests the responsibility of having exchanged the friendship for the hostility of the Empress of India" (OF 2, 636–38).

SECOND ANGLO-AFGHAN WAR, PROCLAMATION BY SIR F. ROBERTS TO THE PEOPLE OF KABUL, October 12, 1879. "I warned against offering any resistance to the entry of the troops. . . . That warning has been disregarded. The force under my command has now reached **Kabul**, and occupied the **Bala Hisar**; but its advance has been pertinaciously opposed, and the inhabitants of the city have taken a conspicuous part in the opposition offered. They have therefore become rebels against His Highness the **Amir**, and have added to the guilt already incurred by abetting the murder of the British Envoy and of his companions . . . . It would be but a just and fitting reward for such misdeeds if the city of Kabul were now totally destroyed, and its very name blotted out. But the great British Government is ever desirous to temper justice with mercy . . . . and I now announce . . . . that the city will be spared. [But] such of the city buildings as now interfere with the proper military occupation of the Bala Hisar, and the safety and comfort of the British troops to be quartered in it, will be at once leveled with the ground. Further, a heavy fine, the amount of which will be notified hereafter, will be imposed on the inhabitants, to be paid according to their capabilities . . . . All persons convicted of bearing a part in it [assassination of British mission] will be dealt with according to their deserts. [City and surroundings placed under martial law] a military governor of Kabul will be appointed to administer justice and to punish with a strong hand all evil-doers. [Carrying of weapons of all types prohibited] any person found armed within these limits will be liable to the penalty of death. Property looted from British must be returned, anyone found with any articles from the British Embassy will be subject to the severest penalties. [Weapons seized by Afghan troops will be purchased.] A reward was to be given for the surrender of anyone who participated in the attack of the British Embassy (OF 2, 656)." The Kotwal, chief of police, of Kabul was hanged, and a good number of Afghans, who were not aware of the proclamation, were executed for carrying arms or being in possession of items belonging to the British mission.

SECOND AFGHAN WAR, REASONS FOR ENDING, An interesting source as to the reasons for ending the Second Afghan war is a memo by T. F. Wilson, July 10, 1880. It gave the "political and financial reasons why we should withdraw from Northern Afghanistan." It stated that for 18 months the government had carried on a war for the establishment of peace. Not a petty war, but one involving 50,000 men and more. "This has denuded India to a great extent of troops, and left our garrisons weak, especially in European soldiers." The majority of the viceroy's council had protested against the war, and he quotes **Sir Henry Durand**, "Peace in India is but an armed truce." Our Asiatic subjects see "that we have met with considerable difficulty and opposition, while the persistent drain on the country for transport animals, such as bullocks, asses, mules, ponies, and camels, has brought the matter home in a convincing manner to even remote parts of India by the detrimental effect which it has more or less exercised on agricultural industry." Members of the Native Army were away too long. He quotes the commander in chief, "The position is very serious; we have to face extended operations in Afghanistan, and a more or less prolonged occupation of the country. Our cavalry regiments on service, instead of being 500 strong, have only 378 effectives, and our infantry corps, instead of 800, have only 587 effectives. Constant marching and fighting, and harassing fatigues, and the vicissitudes of a climate severe and trying beyond measure for natives of India, have reduced our numbers and impaired the health of every Native regiment, while recruiting is at a standstill, the entire Bengal Army having obtained only 46 recruits during the month of January late. . . . Such is the picture of the Bengal Native Army in 1880, painted by its own chief. Even in the darkest days of the mutiny of 1857 no difficulty existed in raising new regiments. Stories of First War seem to discourage others. [We] underestimated cost of war at 14 million, add to this renewals required, pensions to Afghan collaborators—altogether no less than 20 million."

"It is now nine months since we occupied Cabool—after a resistance just sufficient to throw the Commander of the army off his guard . . . followed by the narrowest escape of his force from destruction; this last resulting in a scare which has never been entirely shaken off.

"In fact, the occupation of Cabool has been marked by three distinct epochs; the first that of heedless audacity and misguided unnecessary executions and severity; the second by surprise and defeat, followed by timidity, want of enterprise, and a general condonation of all offenses; and the third by aimless, costly, and weak attempts at diplomacy resulting in fruitless efforts to win over influential people to our interests.

"Since early in January last, our force at Cabool has not been less than from 8 to 9,000 . . . . yet it has never taken the initiative or ventured to do much more than hold the position of Sherpore . . . . fortifications continued to be piled on each other, the army being allowed to grow into a belief that it could only command the ground on which it stood behind its defenses.

"Seeing all this, and remembering how their foot soldiers captured our horse artillery guns, drove us into Sherpore, and plundered the city at their leisure under our eyes; is it to be wondered at that the Afghan nation continue elated and defiant?

"Kabul is 190 miles from Peshawar, 19 marches, but 15,000 men are barely sufficient to keep the line open.

"In short, our military position in Afghanistan is this. We have 11,500 men at Candahar, and on its line of communication with India; 20,000 at Cabool, or in its immediate vicinity; 15,000 holding the line through Jellalabad and the Khyber to Peshawar; and 8,500 locked up in the Kurram valley; or a total of 57,000 men in the field, yet we command little more than the ground on which we stand.

"The creation of 'the strong and friendly Government at Cabool,' and our determination 'to have an English Ambassador at the Dooranee Court,' are now but dreams of the past, from which English-men turn to the thought of, How can we best get our army back to India? How can we best disentangle ourselves from the false position we occupy?

"We have recently based our hopes on Abdool Raheeman as the best candidate for the vacant masnud . . . [but] we must not forget that he has for years past been in receipt of a liberal pension, and an honored guest in Russian dominions. This need not result in any gratitude to the Russians for whatever he may now say or promise, he will in the future act only according to his own views and belief . . . if we can come to some patched up arrangement with this man that will enable us to quit the country without absolute discredit. . . .

"Whenever we withdraw care must be taken to avoid all appearance of precipitancy . . . . the enemy should be prevented from following our troops. The last withdrawal awoke in India a belief that we had at last met with a nut we could not crack; and two legacies resulted—the long and severe struggle with the Punjab and the Mutiny.

"In every Native Court it will be said 'the Feringhees could not hold Cabool.'" He did, however, recommend to keep **Kandahar** and demand some border adjustments.

"In the present temper of Parliament, and the people of England . . . whether we leave the 'strong and friendly Government' behind us or anarchy . . . Government or no Government, Ameer or no Ameer, *coute qu'il coute*, we shall withdraw early in the autumn."

"Abdool Raheeman is playing with us. . . . Evidently he is not such a fool as to come to Cabool and accept the throne from us." And, indeed, the amir came with an army, possibly to make war with Britain, but he concluded an agreement which permitted the British forces to withdraw with a semblance of dignity.

SHAH-I KOT, BATTLE OF. On March 2, 2002, U.S. **Special Forces Teams**, the 101st Airborne, and soldiers of the Army's 10th Mountain Division supported by other allied troops and Afghan auxiliaries moved against a concentration of **al-Qaeda** and **Taliban** forces near the village of Shah-i Kot in **Paktia** Province. The objective was to destroy the last base of the enemy. About a week of aerial bombing had preceded the move and it was hoped to encircle the enemy with blocking positions. But no sooner had the choppers landed infantry troops than they were attacked from the mountain slopes by intensive small-arms, mortar, and rocket-propelled grenade fire. The blocking forces remained trapped for some 18 hours until they could be evacuated. Aerial support brought in fighter jets, bombers, AH-64 Apache helicopters and AC-130 gun ships. On March 4 two Chinook helicopters that brought in supplies were downed and at least seven U.S. soldiers were killed. They were the first U.S. aircraft brought down by hostile fire since the beginning of the Afghan war. A newly developed "thermobaric" bomb was used, which creates a huge cloud of solid fuel that ignites into a fireball to send a lethal shock wave deep into a cave complex without sealing a cave entrance with debris.

It was expected that the enemy would avoid confrontation with some 1,700 American and allied troops and 1,000 Afghan auxiliaries, but the enemy made a stand in a combat that lasted 12 days. Afghan units of the **Northern Alliance** were commanded by General Gul Haidar and a U.S.-trained Afghan force was led by General Zia Lodin; Saifur Rahman Mansur, a former **mujahedin** commander, who joined the Taliban and was deputy commander of the garrison at Kargha near **Kabul**, was lionized by the enemy as the "heroic fighter" against a superior American attack. The Pentagon estimated that about 800 rebels died at Shahi Kot and about 20 prisoners were taken. Afghan soldiers claim they found only about 100 bodies and believe that most of the enemy, Pakistanis and Arabs, escaped.

SHAH SHUJA-UL-MULK (r. 1803–1810 and 1839–1842). Born about 1792, the seventh son of **Timur Shah**, he became governor of Peshawar in 1801 during the reign of his full brother **Zaman Shah**. In 1803 he captured **Kabul**, imprisoned his brother Mahmud, and proclaimed himself king. He accepted a British mission in 1809 under **Mountstuart Elphinstone** and concluded a treaty of alliance, which states in Article 2:

> If the French and Persians in pursuance of their confederacy should advance towards the King of Cabool's country in a hostile manner, the British State, endeavoring heartily to repel them, shall hold themselves liable to afford the expenses necessary for the above-mentioned service to the extent of their ability.

This treaty was to prevent a Franco-Persian invasion of India that never occurred; but it did not protect the **amir** from attack by Persia alone. At that time Mountstuart Elphinstone described the Afghan ruler as "a handsome man . . . his address princely," and he marveled "how much he had of the manners of a gentleman, or how well he preserved his dignity, while he seemed only anxious to please" (Macrory, 32). Two years later Mahmud, who had managed to escape, captured Kabul and forced Shah Shuja to flee to Bukhara and later to India, where he remained as an exile for almost 30 years. En route to India he had to pass through the territory of the **Sikh** ruler **Ranjit Singh**, who took from him the Kuh-i-Nur, a prized diamond that is now part of the British crown jewels. The internecine fighting between the **Sadozai** princes brought **Dost Muhammad** to power and marked the end of the Sadozai dynasty. In 1839 **Britain** invaded Afghanistan and restored Shah Shuja to the throne in a campaign that became known as the **first Anglo-Afghan war**. At that time the amir was described as "elderly, stout, pompous and unheroic" (Macrory, 298). The Sadozai ruler was not able to govern without British protection; he remained ensconced in the protection of the **Bala Hisar** and was assassinated by a Barakzai sardar on April 25, 1842, only a few months after the British army was forced to a disastrous retreat.

SHELTON, BRIGADIER JOHN (d. 1844). Commander of the 44th Regiment during the **first Anglo-Afghan war** and second in command to General **William Elphinstone**. He had lost his right arm in a previous campaign and was said to have only two qualifications for the post: "long service in India and a good measure of physical bulldog courage" (Macrory, 164). He was an angry, morose, obstinate, and cantankerous man, and his contempt for his commanding officer was only exceeded by his violent dislike of his superiors. He refused to cooperate with General Elphinstone, and his defeat in an action on the Bimaru Hills contributed to breaking Elphinstone's spirit of resistance. He became one of the prisoners of **Akbar Khan** and thus survived the general massacre. After returning to India, he was court-martialed for issuing unauthorized orders to prepare for retreat, for showing open contempt for his senior officer, and for negotiating with Akbar Khan for forage to feed his own horse, but he was given only a reprimand (Pottinger, 1987, 205).

SHERPUR, SIEGE OF. General **Frederick Roberts**, who had become the de facto ruler of **Kabul** after the abdication of **Yaqub Khan** in October 1879, soon realized that his position in Kabul was in danger. He ordered the British troops to withdraw into the Sherpur cantonment from the **Bala Hisar**, where an explosion had resulted in British casualties, and from Kabul city, which was increasingly threatened by **ghazis**. The cantonment abutted on the Bemaru hills, the crests of which were strengthened with earthen breastwork. It had been originally built by Amir **Shir Ali** to station his newly created army, and was near the cantonment that sheltered the British army during the **first Anglo-Afghan war**. The cantonment was large enough to shelter all European and most native soldiers, as well as their horses, and transport animals and adequate supplies. Provisions were forcefully collected from nearby villages under the maxim "Soldiers must live, although villagers starve" (Forbes). Feverish repairs were made on the walls, and the army of some 6,500 men went into defensive positions. The Afghans were not long in starting their siege. General Roberts was asked by an emissary to forthwith leave the country and threatened, "We have a lakh of men;

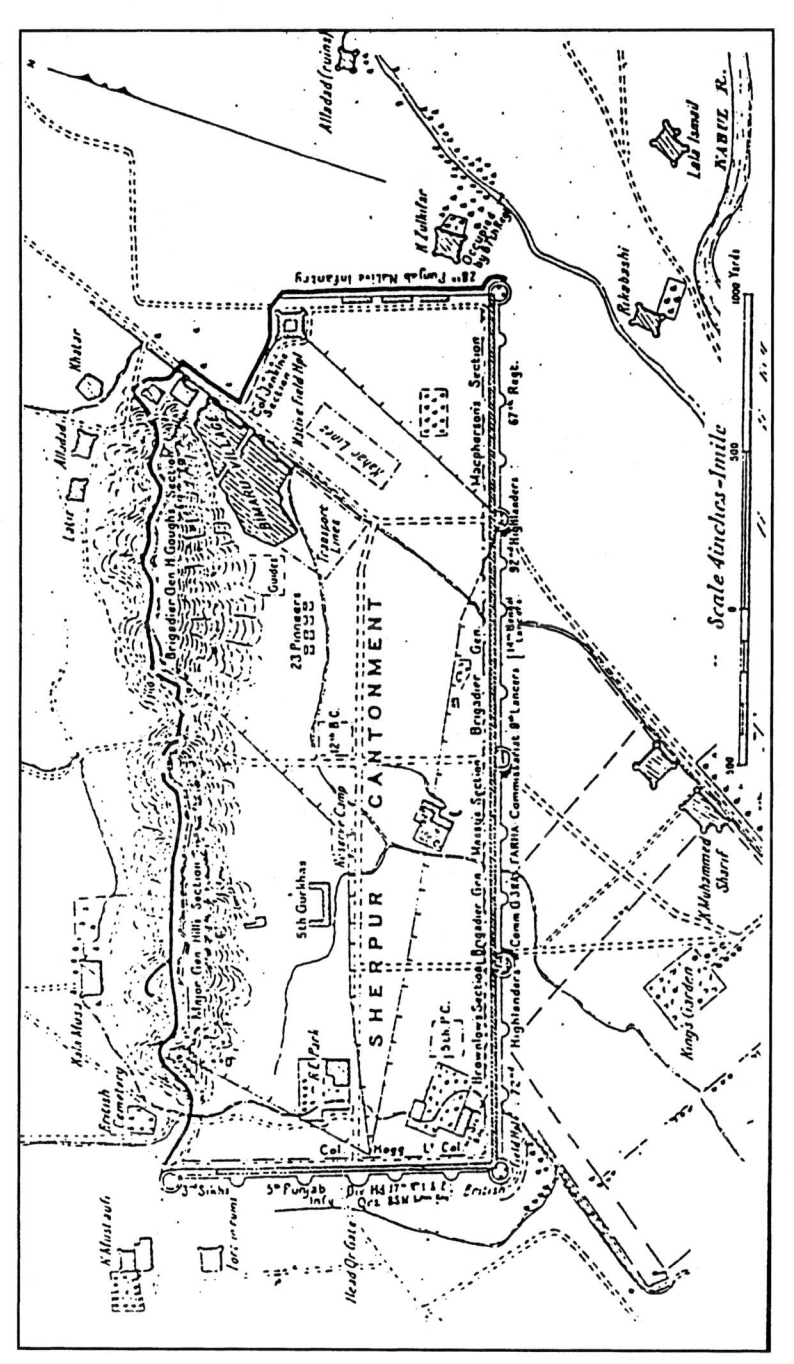

Plan 11. Sherpur Cantonment (MR)

They are like wolves eager to rush their prey. We cannot much longer control them" (Forbes, 257), and the Afghans were quick to attack: "From beyond Behmaroo and the eastern trenches and walls . . . . came a roar a roar of voices so loud and menacing that it seemed as if an army of fifty thousand strong was charging down on our thin line of men" (Forbes, 260). But the British were able to hold. They survived the winter and with reinforcements were able to execute a peaceful evacuation, after recognizing Sardar **Abdul Rahman** in July 1880 as **amir.**

SHI'A, SHI'ISM. A Muslim sect that derives its name from *shi'at Ali*, the party of Ali, and holds that leadership of the Islamic community should be by dynastic succession from Imam Ali (cousin and son-in-law of the Prophet Muhammad) and his descendants. Their view conflicts with the **Sunni** principle that Muhammad's successor, *khalifa* (**caliph**), should be elected. Shi'as divide into three major sects according to which of their imams is believed to be the "Expected One," who will return on judgment day: the fifth, seventh, or twelfth. In Afghanistan the small **Qizilbash** and Farsiwan communities, and most of the **Hazara** population, are "Twelver" (*Ithna'ashariyya*, or *imami*) Shi'as, the same sect that predominates in Iran. There are also small groups of Isma'ilis, or "Seveners," who live in northeastern Afghanistan.

The Twelvers believe their imam is infallible and that their theologians, the *mujtahids*, may legislate in the absence of the imam. In addition to Mecca and Medina, their holy places are Najaf and Karbala in Iraq, as well as Mashshad and Qum in Iran. They accept the practice of temporary marriages, *mut'a* (called *sigha* in **Dari**), and *taqqiya*, prudent denial of their religion if in danger of persecution. They believe in an esoteric interpretation of the Koran but like the Sunnis accept the Five Pillars of Islam with only minor exceptions. The Shi'as constitute about 15 percent of the Afghan population and, in addition to being a sectarian minority, they are also an ethnic minority. *See also* SHI'A MUJAHEDIN GROUPS.

SHI'A MUJAHEDIN GROUPS. The people of the **Hazarajat**, home to a large part of the Afghan **Shi'a** population, rebelled in February 1979 and by the end of the year had liberated their area from Marxist control. The Revolutionary Council of Islamic Unity of Afghanistan (Shura-yi Inqilab-i Ittifaq-i Islami-yi Afghanistan) established a government headed by **Sayyid Ali Beheshti** with its administrative center at Waras in **Bamian** Province. It set up offices, formed a defense force drafted from the local population, and collected taxes to defray the costs of running a state. Until about 1983, the **Shura** was the dominant movement; but radical **Islamist** parties emerged, which challenged the authority of the traditional Shura. The Sazman-i **Nasr** (Organization for Victory), headed by Mir Husain Sadeqi and the Pasdaran (Guardians), modeled after the Iranian Sepah-i Pasdaran and following the "line" of Ayatollah Khomeini, gained strength and conquered much of the Hazarajat from the Shura. Smaller groups controlling enclaves in the Hazarajat were the Ittihad-i Mujahedin-i Islami (Union of Islamic Fighters), led by Abdul Husain Maqsudi and the **Harakat-i Islami** (Islamic Movement) of **Muhammad Asef Muhsini**, headquartered in Quetta and subsequently allied with **Burhanuddin Rabbani** at **Kabul**. Numerous groups, like Ra'd (Thunder), headed by Shaikhzada Khaza'i, and Hizbullah (the Party of God) of Shaikh Ali Wusuki, and others, **Islamist** or Marxist, published their manifestos but never succeeded in winning popular support.

Unifying efforts were not successful. In 1987 they founded the Council of Islamic Alliance, which the Shura joined a year later. And during a meeting of commanders in Bamian on June 16, 1990, creation of the Party of Islamic Unity of Afghanistan (**Hizb-i Wahdat-i Islami-yi Afghanistan**) was announced. **Abdul Ali Mazari** was appointed its leader, followed by **Abdul Karim Khalili** after Mazari's assassination. **Ustad Muhammad Akbari**, who broke away from **Wahdat**, also joined the Rabbani government at Kabul. Major divisions exist between the traditional and Islamist groups and a multitude of notables and **khans**, *sayyid*s, and the new elite of Islamists who are competing for leadership. Wahdat issued a declaration supporting the independence of an indivisible Afghanistan, demanding freedom for all nationalities and sects, and seeking security and social justice for all. It supports women's rights, including the right to vote.

The spectacular victory of the **Taliban** in September 1996 and their capture of Kabul enabled them to extend their hegemony also into the Hazarajat. But the Hizb-i Wahdat was not defeated, as demonstrated by their quick recovery and reconquest of much of their heartland after the **United States** intervention in 2001.

SHINDAND (SABZAWAR) AIR BASE (33-18' N, 62-8' E). A town and district in **Farah** Province and the location of the largest operational air base of **Soviet** forces in Afghanistan. It was one of the objectives in a pincer move into Afghanistan on December 27, 1978, when the 357th Motorized Rifle Division advanced from Kushka to **Herat** and established its control at Shindand. The airfield was considerably expanded in 1980–1982 to become the largest Soviet air base in Afghanistan. It was the main base of Hind D helicopters, and the 5th Guards MRD, as well as some 45 fighter and fighter bombers, which operated from the relative safety of the base. It was located in flat territory and surrounded by a three-ringed security belt, covering an area of 40 kilometers. Although it was well protected, **mujahedin** claim to have destroyed some 22 aircraft, two helicopters, and 18 oil tankers in a spectacular case of sabotage on June 8, 1985. After the fall of the **Kabul** regime, Shindand became the major air base of **Muhammad Ismail Khan** until it was captured by the **Taliban** on September 2, 1995. Forces of the **Afghan National Army** and Coalition troops are now stationed there.

SHINWARI. The Shinwaris are **Pashtuns** who migrated in the 16th century into the area of **Nangarhar**. The tribe consists of four divisions: the Mandezai, Sangu Khel, Sipah, and Alisher Khel who can muster a fighting force of 12,000 men. The Alisher Khel, on the **Pakistani** side of the **Durand** Line, have a reputation as excellent soldiers.

In the early 11th century the Shinwaris accompanied **Mahmud of Ghazni** on his invasions of India. They fought the British in three **Anglo-Afghan wars** and in the late 19th century repeatedly rose against Amir **Abdul Rahman**. The Shinwaris were members of a coalition of tribal forces that caused the downfall of King **Amanullah**.

SHIR ALI, AMIR (1863–1879). One of Amir **Dost Muhammad**'s 27 sons who became **amir** of Afghanistan in 1862–1863, and spent much of his tenure to meet challenges from his brothers, who governed various provinces. By 1869 he had consolidated his power and traveled to Ambala, India, in response to an invitation from the viceroy, Lord Mayo. He was willing to form an alliance with India in exchange for British protection from Russian attacks, assistance in weapons and money, and recognition of the succession of his favorite son, Abdullah Jan. But the viceroy merely expressed his pleasure that the civil war among the princes had come to an end and, as a gesture of friendship, gave the Afghan ruler a present of 600,000 rupees and a few pieces of artillery.

Disappointed in his dealings with **Britain**, the amir decided to listen to Russian overtures. Russia sent General **Stolietoff** to **Kabul** on July 22, 1878, and the general promised what Britain was not willing to grant. Alarmed, the viceroy's government decided to send General **Neville Chamberlain** to Kabul, but he was not permitted to enter Afghanistan. Following an ultimatum, a British army invaded Afghanistan in a campaign known as the **second Anglo-Afghan war**. Shir Ali left his son **Yaqub Khan** in command at Kabul and went north to seek Russian support, but General **Constantin Kaufman**, the Russian governor general of Turkestan Province, merely advised Shir Ali to make peace with the British. Shir Ali died on February 21, 1879, in **Mazar-i Sharif**, and was succeeded in Kabul by his son Yaqub.

Shir Ali was the first to initiate modern reforms: he established an advisory council to assist in the administration of the state and created an army organized along European lines. He abolished the feudal system of tax farming, set up a postal system, and published the first Afghan newspaper, *Shams al-Nahar* (Sun of the Day).

SHURA. Council, a consultative body or parliament. Islamic political theory demands that rulers seek council, shura. Islamic modernists base their demands for a representative government on this principle. After the downfall of the Marxist government in **Kabul**, local **mujahedin** groups, remnants of the Afghan army, and even some Marxist groups have united in shuras to maintain local control in various areas of Afghanistan.

SHURA-I INQILAB-I ITTIFAQ. *See* **BEHESHTI.**

SHURA-I NAZAR- SHAMALI (SUPERVISORY COUNCIL OF THE NORTH). A party founded by **Ahmad Shah Mas'ud** which is part of the **Northern Allliance**. It is essentially a party of **Panjshiris**, headed in the **Hamid Karzai** government by **Muhammad Qasim Fahim**, vice president and minister of defense; **Abdullah Abdullah**, minister of foreign affairs; and **Yunus Qanuni**, minister of education and special adviser to the president on security affairs. Originally part of the **Jam'iat-i Islami** of **Burhanuddin Rabbani**, members of the Shura-i Nazar distanced themselves from Rabbani, whom Mas'ud blamed for responsibility in the civil war when he refused to step down at the end of his term.

SIKH, SIKHISM. A religiopolitical community that rose in the **Panjab**, India, in the 15th century, founding a state that reached its height under **Ranjit Singh** in the late 18th century. Sikhism began as a syncretist religion, combining Islamic and Hindu beliefs under Nanak, the first *guru* (sage). Subsequently, belief in 10 gurus and the Granth Sahib, their sacred book, constituted the creed of the Sikhs. In constant conflict with Indian and Afghan rulers, the Sikhs became increasingly militant and under Ranjit Singh captured Multan in 1818, Kashmir in 1819, and Peshawar in 1834.

The Sikh nation supported the British invasion of Afghanistan in the **first Anglo-Afghan war**, but after the death of Ranjit Singh, the British ended Sikh rule when it annexed the Panjab in the "Sikh wars" of 1845–1846 and 1848–1849. In the 1970s there were about 10,000 Sikhs in Afghanistan.

SIKHS, WEAPONS OF. In 1831 **Ranjit Singh** reorganized his army. He modernized his artillery, which was horse-driven (*aspi*); bullock-driven (*gavi*); elephant driven (*phili*); and camel-driven (*shutari*). He used European weapons: the matchlock—with a long barrel, attached to a wooden belt and wrapped with metal bands. Priming powder was loaded with muzzle-loading rods. The flintlock was introduced in India in the late sixteenth century, but replaced the matchlock only in the eighteenth, which "had self-contained ignition mechanism. A hammer striking the flint caused sparks which ignited priming powder." The *jezail* (swivel gun) was eight feet long, carrying iron balls; it was fixed on a pivot or wall. The carbine, "Blunderbuss," with a three-foot long barrel and trumpet-shaped mouth, was a cavalry weapon. Ranjit also used cannons, howitzers for siege, mortars, field guns, and siege guns. *Studies in Indian Weapons and Warfare* (Pant, 1970).

SIMLA MANIFESTO. A document issued by the governor general of India on October 1, 1838, which declared war on the Afghan **amir**, **Dost Muhammad**. It accused him of "a sudden and unprovoked attack" on its ally, **Ranjit Singh**, and announced **Britain's** intention of restoring to the Afghan throne **Shah Shuja** "whose popularity throughout Afghanistan had been proven to his Lordship [the governor general] by the strong and unanimous testimony of the best authorities" (Sykes, 339). The result was the **first Anglo-Afghan war** (1839–1842) and the British disaster in Afghanistan. *See also* FOREIGN RELATIONS.

SOVIET-AFGHAN RELATIONS. *See* **RUSSIAN-AFGHAN RELATIONS.**

SOVIET INTERVENTION/INVASION. The question as to the motive for Soviet intervention in Afghanistan was a matter of conjecture. Some saw it, as well as the Marxist coup in Afghanistan, as part of a master plan with the objective of gaining access to the resources and the warm-water ports of the Persian/Arabian Gulf. But recent revelations of politburo notes indicate that it was to be a temporary effort to rescue a faltering **Kabul** regime from defeat by rebel forces. Recent disclosures of minutes of politburo meetings in March 1979 indicate that requests by **Nur Muhammad Taraki** for direct military assistance were at first not granted. Yuri V. Andropov, chairman of the KGB, is quoted as having said, "We can suppress a revolution in Afghanistan only with the aid of our bayonets, but that is for us entirely inadmissible. . . . Thus our army if it enters Afghanistan will be an aggressor." Prime Minister Alexei N. Kosygin added, "We cannot introduce troops. . . . There would be huge minuses for us . . . and no pluses for us at all." In a meeting with Taraki in which Defense Minister Dimitri F. Ustinov also participated, the Soviets pointed out that Vietnam never demanded assistance of foreign troops. Taraki was told that he could expect considerable assistance, "You have working for you 500 generals and officers. If necessary we can send an additional number of party workers, as well as 150–200 officers," but, he was told, the introduction of Soviet forces would alarm the international community and would involve the Soviets in a conflict with the Afghan people and "a people does not forgive such things." By the end of 1979, these prescient words were forgotten or the situation had deteriorated to such a degree that the Kremlin agreed on intervention. Its legality was based on the Soviet-Afghan Treaty of Friendship and cooperation of December 5, 1978 (*see* APPENDIX 2), which stated in Article 4

> The high contracting parties . . . will hold consultations and, with the agreement of both parties, take appropriate measures with a few to ensuring the security, independence, and territorial integrity of the two countries.

The "temporary occupation" was legalized under a Status of Armed Forces Agreement signed in April 1980. The Kabul government claimed that the rebels were supported by foreign powers and that the

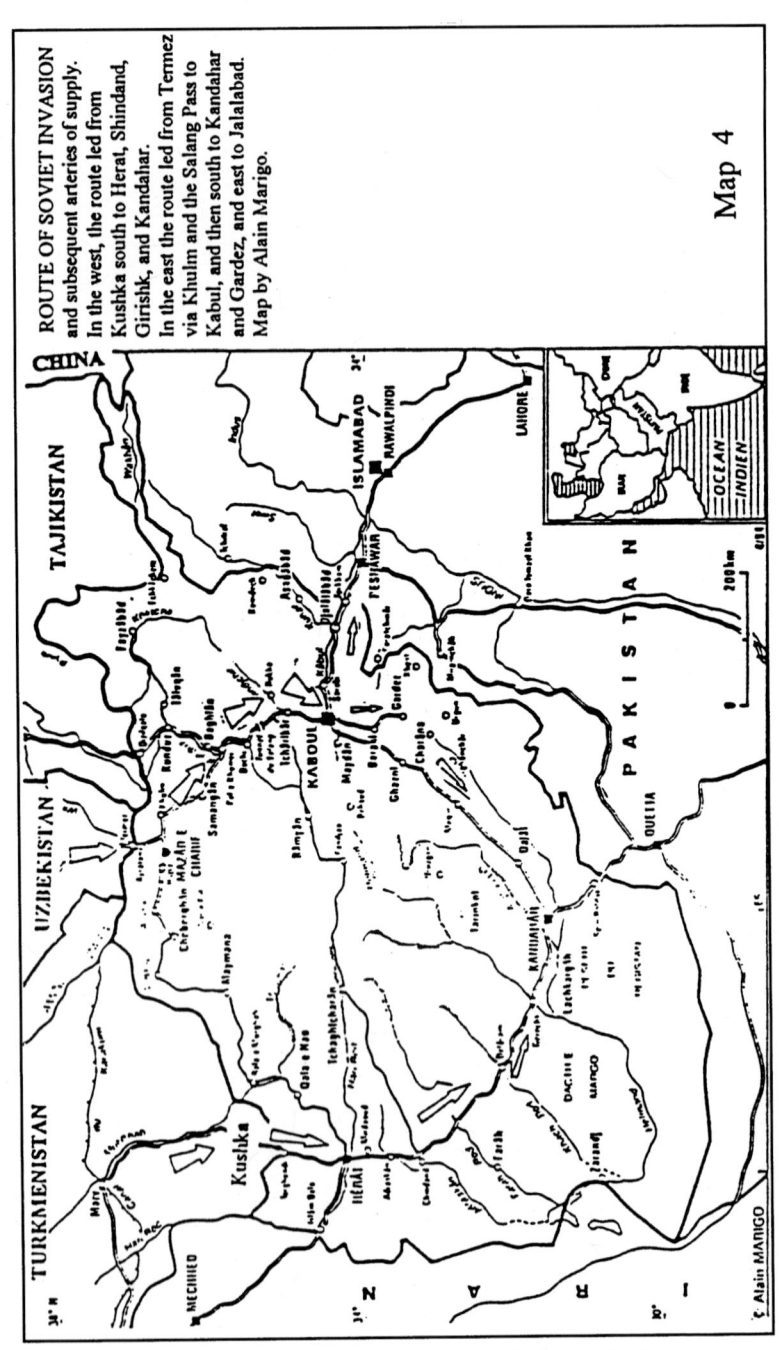

Map 4. Routes of Soviet Invasion (Alain Marigo)

Plate 11. Soviet "Stalin Organ." Source: Shah Bazgar

Plate 12. Burning Soviet Helicopter. Source: Mahaz

Plate 13. Mujahed Aiming a Stinger Missile. Source: S. Thiollier

Plate 14. Kabul Tank Force. Source: *Afghanistan Today*

Plate 15. Mujahedin Anti-Aircraft Unit. Source: E. De Pazzi

Plate 16. Mujahedin on a Mission. Source: T. Niquet

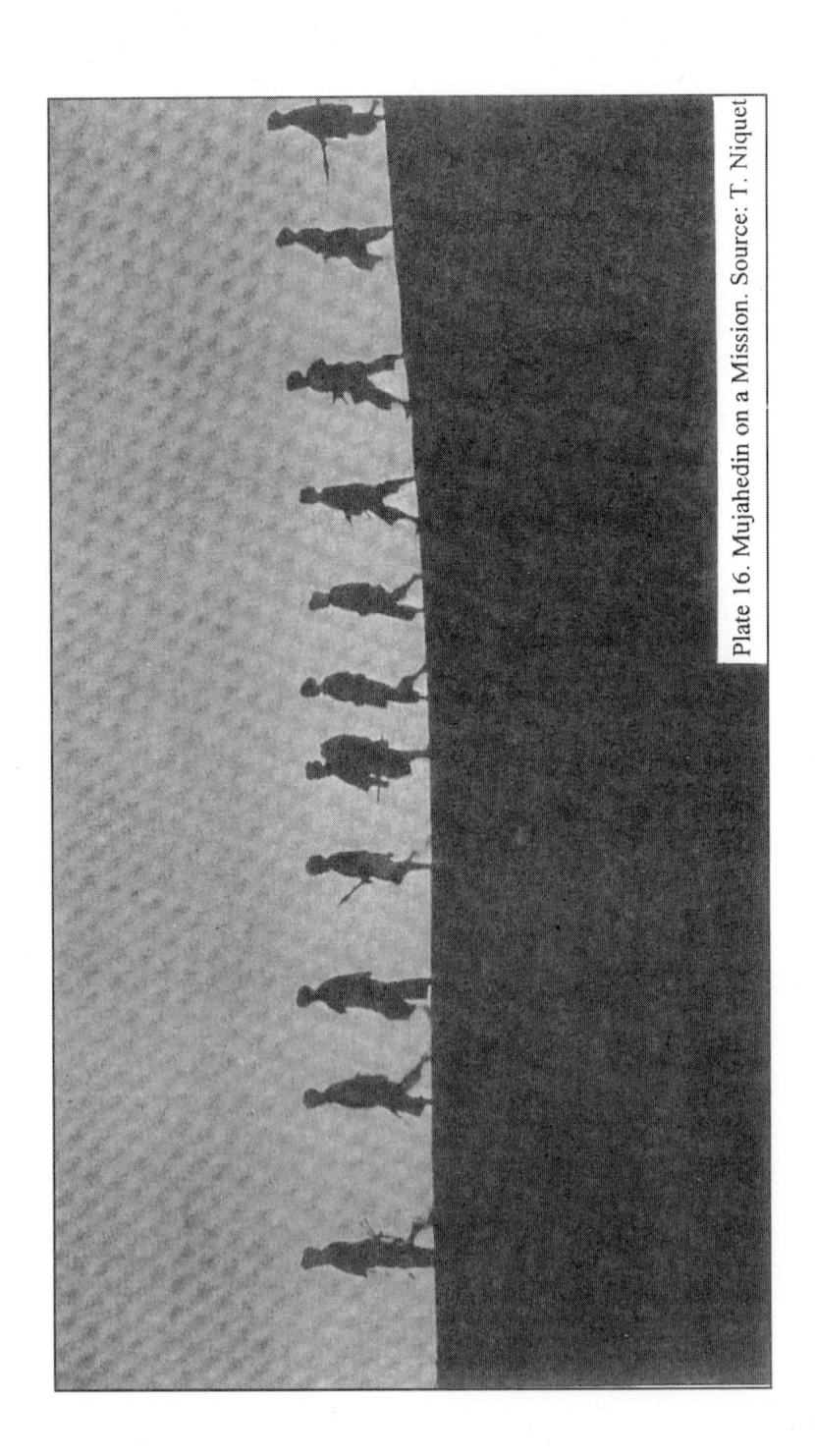

Plate 17. Destroyed Soviet Tank. Source: Jam'iat

Plate 18. Parade of Kabul Forces. Source: *Afghanistan Today*

Limited Contingent of Soviet Forces in Afghanistan (LCSFA) would withdraw at the end of foreign interference.

The reconnaissance for the intervention was said to have been carried out by General Ivan Pavlovski, a Soviet deputy defense minister who spent three months in Afghanistan prior to the invasion. The overall command was under Marshall Sergei Sokolov. By the time the Soviet 40th Army entered Afghanistan on December 27, 1979, two airborne assault brigades had already secured the **Bagram** air base, about 40 miles north of Kabul, and in 180 sorties of Antonov–12 and Antonov–22 transport aircraft, escorted by 100 combat aircraft, troops and munitions were brought in. The **Salang Pass**/Tunnel and the Kabul airport were secured by paratrooper and **Spetsnaz** units. Two motorized rifle divisions crossed the **Amu Daria** on pontoon bridges, and in a pincer movement the 357th proceeded from Kushka south to **Herat** and **Shindand**; the 360th "Nevel-Polovsk" moved from Termez to Salang and to Kabul and **Kandahar** (Isby, 1989, 23). (Urban [42] gives the route to Kandahar via Herat.) The Soviet forces were equipped for conventional war, including an SA–4 antiaircraft missile brigade and chemical warfare decontamination units. Within a week some 50,000 Soviet troops with some 350 tanks and 450 other armored vehicles had crossed the Amu Daria (O'Ballance, 89). The objective was to secure the key cities and links of communication. The Soviet armed forces were intended for the protection of major towns and lines of communication, leaving counterinsurgency tasks to the Afghan army, but they were inevitably drawn into search-and-destroy missions that cost 80 percent of Soviet casualties. *See also* AFGANTSY; REPORT ON INTERVENTION, APPENDIX 1; STATUS OF SOVIET FORCES, APPENDIX 3.

SOVIET INVASION COMMAND. The Soviet invasion team consisted of Marshal Sergei Sokolov in overall command; General Valentin Varennikov in command of operational planning; Colonel General Yurii Maximov and Colonel General Petr Lushev in charge of Turkestan and Central Asian military districts; Lieutenant General Tukharinov in operational command.

The commanders of the 40th Army included Lieutenant General Tukharinov until September 23, 1980; Lieutenant General B. I. Tkach until May 7, 1982; Lieutenant General V. F. Ermakov until November 4, 1983; Lieutenant General I. E. Generalov until April 19, 1985; Lieutenant General I. N. Rodionov until April 30, 1986; Lieutenant General V. P. Dubyninun until June 1, 1987; and Lieutenant General **B. V. Gromov** until end of war (Galeotti, 1995, 174-75).

SOVIET OPERATIONAL AND STRATEGIC LESSONS OF THE WAR. Mark Galeotti, in his excellent study of the **Afgantsy** and the effects of the war on the former Soviet Union, *Afghanistan: The Soviet Union's Last War,* declares that the real importance of the war in wider military thinking is fourfold:

1. It accelerated the rise of new commanders, a generation eager to make its presence felt in a time of change and with a different set of formative experience.
2. It uncovered problems and identified weaknesses within existing thinking.
3. It provided a new fund of combat experience at the very time when new-generation weapons, vehicles and communications systems were having their impact on Soviet doctrine.
4. It forced the Soviets to come to terms with low-intensity warfare at the very time when perestroika was sparking such unrest within the USSR itself (208). *See also* INTRODUCTION.

SOVIET OPERATIONS. Colonel **Ali Ahmad Jalali** (also Isby, 28) describes the inherent weakness of early Soviet military operations as follows: "Soviet troops, in the spring and summer of 1980, moved in heavy columns along the major roads. Closely supported by aircraft and helicopter gunships, these columns found comfort in technical superiority. Obsessed by massive firepower to support the advance, they fired to the front and flanks (sometimes at random) to suppress suspected **mujahedin** positions. The lack of troops patrols and the absence of tactical reconnaissance and security elements, especially on the ridges and high ground that so often dominate the roads, was exploited by the mujahedin, who on several occasions launched successful **ambushes**, despite being deployed where they could have been easily outflanked and routed. The inexperienced Soviet troops would not dismount and resort to close combat. Firepower could not produce results because it was not exploited at close quarters. The mujahedin, short of weapons, often defeated totally mechanized Soviet forces, unable to operate effectively in the rugged and close terrain where the guerrillas moved. In 1980, Soviet forces were unsupported by light infantry." In the following year, some modifications such as leap-frogged mechanized forces were only partially successful. The change to an "air war" was equally unsatisfactory, and **Spetsnaz** and other elite counterinsurgency forces supported by close air power were increasingly drawn into combat. When the mujahedin acquired surface-to-air missiles, including **Stingers** in 1986, the war entered a new stage that put Soviet forces on the defensive. *See also* INTRODUCTION, p. 25–26.

SOVIET UNION. *See* **RUSSIA.**

SPECIAL FORCES A-TEAM. What came to be called the "Afghanistan Model" of unconventional warfare consisted of 12 to 14 man special forces units who entered enemy territory to locate forces hostile to the **Taliban.** They had authority to pay, hire, and bribe their own intelligence sources, and develop agents and assets with links to the enemy. Their major task was to use laser markers to pin point enemy targets for precision bombing.

Each team consisted of

> a commander, usually a captain, and a warrant officer as the executive officer and second in command; sergeants, or gifted noncommissioned officers; two intelligence sergeants, two weapons sergeants, two medical specialists, two demolition sergeants, and two communications specialists. Each member was cross-trained in at least one more skill. Two Air Force sergeants, one a senior targeteer/observer and a targeteer/ observer. (Robert Moore, 18)

A 12-man A-Team 595 landed 50 miles south of **Mazar-i Sharif** with the mission to

> find and support Dostum, stay with him and help. Go with him wherever he goes—if he wants to take **Kabul**, go. If he wants to take over the country, that is fine too. If he starts mass executions on the way, call HQ and advise, maybe exfil if you can't reign him in.

The team had difficulty communicating, but eventually Russian served for rudimentary understanding. Some 316 Special Forces Teams and 110 CIA officers distributed about $70 million in direct cash outlays on the ground in Afghanistan (Woodward, 317).

There are said to be two types of special operations forces: the white special forces who are trained to develop sources and cultivate informants and the black special forces who are the door kickers and parachute artists, assigned to go after "high-value targets."

SPECIAL FORCES, EQUIPMENT. Soldiers carry a considerable amount of equipment on their bodies. Clipped on their helmets they carry night-vision goggles, powered by two AA batteries. A communications unit consists of radio, GPS location system, power supply for radio, and laser light for carbine. Ammunition includes six fragmentation grenades, spare M4 carbine magazines, and 9mm pistol magazines. The soldiers wear bullet-proof Kevlar vests and wear a Beretta 9mm pistol and combat knife. Supplies include emergency rations and a Camelback water carrier. Fighting with Afghan ground forces, the Special Forces soldier would point a red aiming dot on the target for devastating aerial attacks. The "Afghanistan model" of warfare was successful in quickly defeating the **Taliban/al-Qaeda** forces, but lacking American ground forces, Afghan warlords filled the vacuum and have as yet not yielded power to the Kabul government.

SPETSNAZ. Special Operations Forces (Spetsnaz) are an elite counterinsurgency force that, together with airborne, air assault/air mobile, and designated reconnaissance units, made up 10 to 20 percent of the Soviet forces deployed in Afghanistan. The elite force was created in 1941–1942 during World War II and in the 1960s expanded to battalion size. In December 1978, Spetsnaz forces were said to have been employed in securing airfields, communications centers, and other key points in Afghanistan prior to the invasion. They constituted the commando that was responsible for the assassination of **Hafizullah Amin**. Spetsnaz operated as raiders, sabotage teams, reconnaissance, and intelligence commandos. According to McMichael (108), they operated in disguises such as shepherds, nomads, and itinerant traders. It is not clear how effective they could have been, since they were primarily of Slavic background, blond and blue-eyed and not familiar with any Afghan languages. About nine battalions each with 250 men are said to have been active in Afghanistan. They were stationed at Asadabad, Baraki-Barak, **Ghazni**, Shahjoy (about midway between **Ghazni** and **Kandahar**), Lashkargah, **Farah**, **Kandahar**, and **Jalalabad**. Brigade headquarters were at Lashkargah and Jalalabad.

STEWARD, SIR DONALD (1824–1900). Field Marshal. Carried out several expeditions against tribes on the Afghan border, 1854–1855. Commanded Peshawar Division, 1886–1889. During **Second Anglo-Afghan War** he was in command of the Quetta army which took control of **Kandahar**, 1878–1880. He led the march on **Kabul** and there took command of the Northern Afghanistan Field Force, 1880. He dispatched General **Frederick S. Roberts** on his march from Kabul to Kandahar. He served as military member of the Viceroy's Executive Council and was appointed commander-in-chief of India, 1881–1885. MacGregor did not like Steward, calling him masterful and decided, but cynical. Steward died in 1900 in Algiers.

STINGER. An American infrared, heat-seeking missile, with a high-explosive warhead, capable of engaging low-altitude aircraft, including high-speed jets, which has been credited in dipping the tactical balance in favor of the **mujahedin**. Long sought by the resistance, the first missiles were fired in September 1986 and became an immediate success. According to General **Muhammad Yusuf** (Yousaf), head of the **Inter-Services Intelligence** (ISI), the American government trained **Pakistanis**, who then trained Afghans. The first missiles were delivered to commanders of **Gulbuddin Hekmatyar** and **Yunus Khales**, and possession of a Stinger soon became the ultimate status symbol. The American government agreed to deliver 250 grip stocks with 1,000 to 2,000 missiles per year (Yousaf, 1992, 182). The missiles had been deployed by American forces first in 1981, but had never been used in combat. According to Yousaf, the mujahedin achieved a hit rate of 70 percent to 75 percent (68 percent, according to Isby, 1989), much better than the rate of their Pakistani or American teachers. To reward success, mujahedin commanders were given two Stingers for each hit (Rubin, 1995, 196). As was to be expected, a **Spetsnaz** commando was able to capture a number of missiles in an ambush, and one commander, Mulla Malang, boasted of having sold four launchers for $1 million each with 16 missiles to Iran (Rubin, 336, n. 45). Overby (115) claims that of 1,150 Stingers originally sent, only 863 reached the mujahedin. China obtained several Stingers and was said to be copying them (*Nouvelles*, No. 63). In 1987 the Soviet/Kabul forces had 150 to 200 air losses, and the much-feared Hind D helicopter never recovered its tactical preeminence. Isby (114) quotes Commander **Ahmad Shah Mas'ud**, as saying, "There are only two things Afghans must have: the Koran and Stingers." *See also* ROKETI, MULLA SALAM.

STOLIETOFF, MAJOR GENERAL. Head of an uninvited Russian mission sent to the court of **Amir Shir Ali** by General **Constantin Kaufman** in 1878 to conclude an alliance against **Britain**. Stolietoff reached **Kabul** on July 22 at a time when General Kaufman was dispatching a force of 15,000 men to the upper reaches of the **Amu Daria**. Not being able to prevent the mission from reaching Kabul, the amir treated the Russian and his staff of six officers with courtesy. Stolietoff presented several "letters of friendship," in one of which Kaufman wrote:

> I have deputed my agent, Major-General Stolietoff, an officer high in the favour of the Emperor. He will inform you of all that is hidden in my mind. I hope that you will pay great attention to what he says, and believe him as you would myself. . . . The advantage of a close alliance with the Russian Government will be permanently evident.(Sykes, 97)

The draft of a treaty promised what Britain was not willing to offer: protection from foreign aggression and recognition of his son Abdullah Jan as heir apparent. Article 3 of the treaty stated:

> The Russian Government engages that if any foreign enemy attacks Afghanistan and the Amir is unable to drive him out, and asks for the assistance of the Russian Government, the Russian Government will repel the enemy either by means of advice or by such other means as it may consider proper. (Sykes, 107)

The fact that the type of Russian support was left to the discretion of the Russian government apparently did not occur to the amir. His refusal to permit a British mission under General **Sir Neville Chamberlain** to proceed to Kabul was taken as Lord Lytton's excuse for starting the **second Anglo-Afghan war**.

STRONGHOLD STRATEGY. Invaders of Afghanistan during the past two centuries never succeeded in pacifying the country; therefore, they had to rely on a stronghold strategy, holding large towns, key facilities, economic centers, and transportation links. Inevitably, these bases became the targets of guerrilla attacks, making it necessary to stage offensive sweeps that only provided temporary relief. Lines of logistics became vulnerable to attacks and the invaders became captives in their stronghold positions. Not much changed in this respect, even at a time when **Soviet/Kabul** forces held aerial superiority. Since the **United States** intervention, the **North Atlantic Treaty Organization** (NATO) and American Coalition allies have adopted the **International Security Assistance Forces** (ISAF). They are deployed throughout the country in major urban areas and help the Kabul government to regain control of the country.

SUNNI (SUNNITES). The major branch of two Islamic traditions (in distinction to the **Shi'a** branch), comprising about 80 percent of the Muslim population. Sunnis are called the "people of custom and community" (*ahl al-sunnah wa 'l-jama'a*) or "orthodox" Muslims. They recognize the first four **caliphs** as rightful successors to the Prophet Muhammad and accept the legitimacy of the Umayyad and 'Abbasid caliphates. They are divided into four schools of law, the Hanafi, Maliki, Shafi'i, and Hanbali schools, the Hanafi being the largest and the Hanbali school the most restricted in its interpretation of the Koran and the Sunnah. In Afghanistan the majority of Sunnis are of the Hanafi school.

SUPPLIES, COLLECTION OF. The British-Indian army depended on local supplies when it invaded Afghanistan, but the availability of supplies depended on a number of factors: When British prestige was high during a rapid campaign, there was little difficulty in purchasing supplies. But after a reverse on the battlefield, supplies immediately dried up. The British found that once established in the country, it was best to set up a free market where the natives could make a profit selling their goods. Another means was to requisition supplies but offer immediate payment. If the natives were unwilling to deliver supplies, requisitioning by force would be required. *The Handbook for the Indian Army* (66) suggests the use of "adequate force to seize state granaries, the inhabitants animals and stocks of grain, and the timber of their houses for fuel." It advised that

> strong mobile columns, of all arms, will be required for rounding up livestock, for the collection of supplies and for the removal of both to the collecting centre. . . . Foraging by Cavalry alone, possible in other countries, is seldom advisable in Afghanistan.

The overriding maxim was, "Soldiers must eat, even if villagers starve." *See also* FORAGING; LOGISTICS.

- T -

TAJIK. A name, generally applied to Farsi/**Dari** speakers whose number has been estimated at about four to five million people in 1978. The term comes from the Persian *tazi* (running) or *taj*, (crown?) meaning "Arab," but the Turks applied it to non-Turks and eventually only to Farsi-speakers. They are largely **Sunni** Muslims, except for the "mountain Tajiks" who are **Isma'ilis** (*see* **Shi'a**) and inhabit various areas of **Badakhshan** Province.

The Tajik are the ancient population of **Khorasan** and Sistan who were sedentary and made a living as traders. They were also located in northern Afghanistan and predominated in **Balkh** and Bukhara, until they moved south as a result of Timurid invasions. Now they are scattered all over the country, but are concentrated in communities in western, northern, and northeastern Afghanistan. They are mainly agricultural, except in the towns where many are artisans or engage in commercial activities. They have been engaged as clerks and predominate in the government administration. As a community, the Tajik are relatively better educated and more modernized. Conscious of a great cultural tradition, the elite of the Tajiks have been the "men of the pen," whereas the **Pashtuns** have been the "men of the sword" of Afghanistan.

TAKHAR (36-30' N, 69-30' E). A province in northeastern Afghanistan with an area of 6,770 square miles and a population estimated at 528,000 (1991 est. 545,000). Since 1963 the administrative center of the province has been Taloqan, a town of about 20,000 (1991 est. 170,000) inhabitants. Major agricultural products of the province include cotton, corn, and wheat; local industries include gold and silver mining and carpet production. Takhar provides two-thirds of the salt used in Afghanistan.

TAKHT-I SHAH. A mountain south of **Kabul**, with which the Sher Darwaza heights are connected by a narrow ridge, and the most commanding point in the immediate vicinity of Kabul. The Afghans under Muhammad Jan captured it on December 11, 1879, and in a seesaw battle fought off British troops under Brigadier General Baker. It was one of the battles in which General **F. Roberts** decided to abandon Kabul and retreat into the **Sherpur** cantonment. The situation looked like a repeat of the defeat of December 1841, and a British historian commented, "It must never be forgotten that at this time our people in Afghanistan held no more territory than the actual ground they stood upon and the terrain swept by their fire" (Forbes, 246). The British forces remained under siege in Sherpur during the winter and recognized Sardar **Abdul Rahman** in July 1880, before evacuating their forces from Afghanistan. *See also* SHERPUR, SIEGE OF.

TALIBAN. A movement of *"taliban,"* students, who attended religious schools (**madrasas**) in **Pakistan** and the Afghan tribal belt, and suddenly emerged as a politico-military force in Afghanistan. Headed by **Mulla Muhammad Omar**, a **Nurzai** from **Oruzgan**, and his deputy Maulawi Muhammad Hasan, the movement first came to public attention in November 1994 when it rescued a Pakistani truck convoy bound for Central Asia from **mujahedin** captors. The Taliban then captured the city of **Kandahar** and moved north against **Kabul**. On Monday, February 13, 1995 they captured Pul-i Alam and the next day Charasiab, the stronghold of the Hizb-i Islami leader **Gulbuddin Hekmatyar**. Hekmatyar was forced to flee to Sarobi, about 37 miles east of Kabul. In March 1995 the **Shi'a Hizb-i Wahdat** surrendered its enclave in Kabul to the Taliban, but its leader **Abdul Ali Mazari** was killed while in Taliban captivity. On September 3 the Taliban captured **Shindand,** an important airbase, and two days later the city of **Herat**. In September 1996 the Taliban renewed their offensive and captured **Jalalabad**, Sarobi, and by the end of the month they were installed as rulers in Kabul.

It came as a surprise to many that they were able to quickly defeat the supposedly battle-hardened mujahedin. Afghans were sick of war and the rule of warlords, and financial support from the Gulf and armed assistance from the Pakistani **Inter Services Intelligence (ISI)**, as well as foreign volunteers, made the difference. Often they conquered without a fight as ex-army officers and mujahedin commanders defected or were bribed to join the new force. The Taliban claimed not to be affiliated with any of the mujahedin groups and only desired to unite Afghanistan, end the power of the war lords, and create a "true" Islamic state. Their rule was ended only as a result of **United States** intervention in December 2001.

Taliban forces were dispersed and the majority of their soldiers returned to their villages. Only the leadership and those who are accused of atrocities, as well as a small group of radicals, are still ensconced in the border area. Some guerrilla activity continues, but it is not likely that they will be a major military force in the near future. Negotiations, denied by the Taliban, are under way to pardon those who are willing to accept the authority of the **Hamid Karzai** government. *See also* ENJOINING THE GOOD AND FORBIDDING EVIL.

TANAI, LIEUTENANT GENERAL SHAHNAWAZ. Member of the **Khalq** faction of the **People's Democratic Party of Afghanistan** (PDPA), chief of general staff since 1986, and minister of defense from 1988 to 1990. A **Pashtun** born in **Paktia** Province of the small Tani tribe. A captain major until the **Saur Revolt**, he was considered a rising star in the PDPA, when on March 6, 1990, Tanai and several Khalqi officers staged a coup against the **Najibullah** government from the **Bagram** air force base. They attacked the presidential palace and key government facilities in **Kabul**, but were unable to topple the government. Tanai and some of his closest supporters escaped from the Bagram air base in three military aircraft and a helicopter and landed in Parachinar, Pakistan. **Gulbuddin Hekmatyar**, leader of the **Islamist** and most radical of **mujahedin** groups, gave the coup his support. This alliance of hard-line Khalqis and radical Islamists caused considerable consternation in Afghanistan. Tanai and Hekmatyar were seen as determined to win power, regardless of ideological considerations. Najibullah's control of the air force and scrambling of the communications network enabled him to rout the rebels. On March 16 Tanai made his appearance in the Hekmatyar camp in **Logar** Province, claiming to continue the campaign against Najibullah but remaining a loyal member of the PDPA. After the fall of Najibullah in April 1992, many Khalqi officers also joined Hekmatyar's forces.

TARAKI, NUR MUHAMMAD. Leader of the **Khalq** faction of the **People's Democratic Party of Afghanistan** (PDPA) and, after the **Saur Revolt**, president and prime minister of the Democratic Republic of Afghanistan. In the 1950s he became known as an author and a journalist. He convened the "founding congress" of the PDPA on January 1, 1965, which was attended by 27 persons. Taraki was elected secretary general, and his rival **Babrak Karmal** became secretary of the central committee. After the Saur Revolt, Taraki was extolled as the "Great Leader," and a personality cult prepared the way to legitimize his rule as the "teacher and great guide." His life was cut short when he was executed on order of Hafizullah Amin on October 9, 1979.

TERRORISM. There seems to be no commonly agreed definition. President Ronald Reagan's "freedom fighters," who fought communism in Afghanistan, quickly became terrorists when they continued their **jihad** after the fall of the communist regime. One definition states:

> Criminal acts intended or calculated to provoke a state of terror in the general public, a group of persons or particular persons for political purposes are in any circumstances unjustifiable, whatever the considerations of a political, philosophical, ideological, racial, ethnic, religious or other nature that may be invoked to justify them. UN Resolution language (1999)

A more concise definition calls terrorism a

> deliberate use of violence against noncombatants for political ends. Perpetrators can be states, agents of states, or individuals or groups acting independently or in cells. [It] does not apply to all acts of politically inspired violence. (*The Oxford Dictionary of Islam*, ed. John Esposito)

In other words, the criterion of a terrorist act is violence against the civilian population. In practice much guerrilla activity also harmed noncombatants as did counterinsurgency measures by the state and its allies. In the war against communism in Afghanistan and the subsequent civil war, combatants did not respect the laws of war as defined by the Geneva Conventions.

As a result of the attacks of September 11, 2001, President George W. Bush issued a declaration of war (*see* APPENDIX 4), stating that the **United States** would carry out strikes against **al-Qaeda** terrorist training camps and military installations of the **Taliban** regime in Afghanistan. **Operation Enduring Freedom** began with aerial bombardments on October 7, 2001, and by the end of December the Taliban regime was destroyed. Far-reaching changes have been introduced in American society to forestall future terrorist attacks on the United States.

TEZIN, BATTLE OF (34-21' N, 69-35' E). Tezin is a collection of settlements in the valley of the same name, lying near a pass on the **Kabul-Jalalabad** road. It was strategically important and therefore the scene of a number of engagements during the **first Anglo-Afghan war**. Brigadier **Robert Sale**, retiring from Kabul to Jalalabad, was able to defeat a body of Afghans on October 22, 1841. During the **Death March** in January 1842, the remnants of the retreating force took shelter in the valley.

General **George Pollock**, advancing on Kabul in September 1842, encountered strong Afghan resistance at the pass. Sardar **Muhammad Akbar** had occupied the heights, and Pollock approached the mouth of the pass, where he left two guns, two squadrons of Her Majesty's 3rd Light Dragoons, and a party of the 1st Light Cavalry and of the 3rd Irregular Cavalry. An attempt by the Afghans to capture the baggage train was foiled by the Dragoons and Native Cavalry. British troops then mounted the heights, and the Afghans made the mistake of advancing to meet them, engaging in hand-to-hand combat. The Light Company of Her Majesty's 9th Foot, led by Captain Lushington, ascended the hills to the left of the pass and was able to dislodge the Afghans. "The slaughter was considerable, and the fight continued during a great part of the day, the enemy appearing resolved that the British should not ascent the Haft Kotal," but they succeeded, "giving three cheers when they reached the summit." A British historian described the capture of the heights, saying, "Broadfoot's bloodthirsty little Goorkas who, hillmen themselves from their birth, chased the Afghans from crag to crag." According to British estimates, General Pollock was opposed by some 15,000 men in the field, a large part cavalry, led by Sardar Muhammad Akbar and a number of other chiefs. Afghans lost their guns and three standards, and several hundred were killed, as compared to British claims of 32 killed and 130 wounded (40 killed and 91 wounded, according to MR).

THAL, SIEGE OF (1919). An action in the **third Anglo-Afghan war** that pitted General **Muhammad Nadir Khan**, the subsequent king of Afghanistan, against Major General Eustace and his garrison at the fort and village of Thal. Thal was of considerable importance for the control of the autonomous tribal belt in the **North-West Frontier Province** (NWFP) of India. It was where Waziristan, home of the Waziri tribes, impinged on the territories of the **Shi'a** Turis in the Kurram valley. It was an important staging area for an invasion of

Afghanistan. A small-scale railroad and metaled roads led from Bannu and Kohat to the village. Nadir Khan moved from **Khost** with an army of 3,000 regular and about 6,000 tribal forces equipped with two 10cm Krupp howitzers and seven 7.5cm Krupp mountain guns. As he advanced some 30 miles toward Thal, the British withdrew from their small posts, which were quickly occupied by Afghan regular troops. Members of the British-led Waziristan Militia began to desert and turned against their British officers. Nadir Khan established his headquarters at Yusuf Khel on the Kurram River, about three miles from Thal, and on May 27 began to invest the fort. His artillery caused considerable damage, and the infantry advanced and occupied Thal village. The British mountain guns were outranged by the Krupp howitzers, and even attacks by two R.A.F. aircraft were not able to silence the Afghan guns. On May 28–29 the Afghans captured a tower from which they were able to dominate the fort's water supply. On May 30 an all-day bombardment cause additional damage to the fort. The "British" tribes were watching the situation, ready to join the Afghans if the fortunes of war should turn against India. The British had planned to follow up on their territorial gains at Dakka with a move against **Jalalabad**, but the danger of a tribal rebellion on the Frontier led them to dispatch the "Thal Relief Force," headed by Brigadier General **R. E. H. Dyer**. After dispersing the tribal forces that threatened to block his advance, Dyer came to the rescue of the besieged fort. By May 30 he disposed of a force of 19,000 troops and 13 guns, as well as 22 "dummies," tree trunks covered with canvas to resemble guns. The next day Nadir Khan informed the British general that Amir **Amanullah** had ordered him to suspend hostilities because of the beginning of peace negotiations. On June 3 the armistice was signed and the Afghans withdrew. British casualties numbered 94, eight were killed, including one British officer and seven Indians, and four died later of wounds. The importance of the action at Thal was that it stopped British attempts to advance on Jalalabad, and fear of a general uprising of the tribes on the British side of the border made peace seem a preferable alternative to continuation of the war.

THIRD ANGLO-AFGHAN WAR (1919). A short war between Afghanistan and British Indian forces, which lasted from May 4 until the conclusion of a cease-fire on June 3, 1919. Amir **Amanullah** had ascended the throne in February 1919, after the assassination of his father, Amir **Habibullah**. He was an ardent nationalist and reformer

Plate 19. British Air Raid, 1919. Afghans soon learned to disperse at the approach of an aircraft and seek shelter. (ILN)

and was said to have been a member of the "war party" at the Afghan court, which favored an attack on India during World War I. Afghanistan had remained neutral in the "**holy war**" against **Britain**, and Amir Habibullah expected a generous financial reward and British recognition of Afghanistan's complete independence. But once the European conflict had ended, Britain showed no intention of freeing the country from its control.

Upon accession to power, Amir Amanullah demanded a treaty that would end Afghanistan's political dependence on Britain and establish normal, neighborly relations between the two states. Lord Chelmsford, the viceroy of India, however, suggested that no new treaty was required, despite the fact that previously India had held that the agreements with Afghan rulers were personal and therefore subject to renegotiation with each new ruler. He merely acknowledged Amanullah's election as amir "by the populace of **Kabul** and its surrounding," implying that he was not in complete control of his country. The subsidy given to previous Afghan rulers was halted, and when Amanullah sent his new envoy to India he was asked "what amir" he represented.

On the occasion of a royal darbar on April 13, 1919, Amanullah showed himself belligerent, announcing to an assembly of dignitaries:

> I have declared myself and my country entirely free, autonomous and independent both internally and externally. My country will hereafter be as independent a state as the other states and powers of the world are. No foreign power will be allowed to have a hair's breath of right to interfere internally and externally with the affairs of Afghanistan, and if any ever does I am ready to cut its throat with this sword. (Adamec, 1974, 47)

He turned to the British agent and said, "Oh Safir, have you understood what I have said?" The British agent replied, "Yes I have" (Adamec, 1967, 110). To emphasize his demands, Amanullah sent three of his generals to the border: Saleh Muhammad, the commander in chief, arrived at Dakka, the border town, on May 3; Abdul Quddus, the prime minister (*sadr-i a'zam*), moved to the area of **Qalat**-i Ghilzai on May 5; and a day later Muhammad Nader, the commander in chief (and subsequent king of Afghanistan), moved to **Khost** with a tribal *lashkar* (army) of several thousand men in addition to his regular forces.

On May 5 the government of India stopped demobilization of all combatant forces in India and began to recall all British officers.

India intended to confront the Afghans with an overwhelming force in the **Khaibar** to induce them to withdraw quietly.

Lieutenant General G. N. Molesworth described the Afghan regular forces as ill-trained, ill-paid, and probably under strength. The cavalry was little better than indifferent infantry mounted on equally indifferent ponies. Rifles varied from modern German, Turkish, and British types to obsolete Martinis and Sniders. Few infantry had bayonets. Artillery was pony-drawn, or pack, and included modern 10cm Krupp howitzers, 75mm Krupp mountain guns, and ancient 7-pounder weapons. There were a few, very old, four-barrel Gardiner machine guns. Ammunition was in short supply and the Kabul arsenal inadequate.

The British North-West Frontier Force consisted of two cavalry brigades (1st and 10th), two infantry divisions (1st and 2nd), and three frontier infantry brigades (Kohat, Bannu, and Derajat). Each division had 18-pounder field guns, R.F.A.; four 4.5in. howitzers, R.F.A.; and eight 2.75in. mountain guns, R.G.A. Each cavalry brigade had four 13-pounder guns, R.H.A. The available striking force in the Khaibar area had six cavalry regiments, 24 infantry battalions, 40 pieces of artillery, and 48 machine guns. The forces in the Peshawar area were needed for internal security.

The superiority of the British-Indian forces was to a certain extent matched by the power of the **Pashtun** tribal *lashkars* from both sides of the border. They were aggressive fighters and operated in an inaccessible terrain that was well known only to them. The Pashtun soldiers of the British Khaibar Rifles were not willing to fight their Afghan brothers, and, given the choice, 600 men out of 700 elected to be discharged, making it necessary for the British to disband the units (OF 3, 22–23).

Lord Chelmsford was warned by the London government, "You will not have forgotten [the] lessons of history, that we have not so much to fear from [the] Afghan regular Army as from the irregular tribesmen and their constant attacks on our isolated camps and lines of communications" (Adamec, 1967, 116).

Hostilities began on May 4, 1919, when Afghan troops cut the water supply to Landi Kotal on the Indian side of the border and Britain retaliated by closing the Khaibar Pass. (*See* BAGH, BATTLE OF.) The Afghans wanted to make a concerted effort involving the Frontier tribes and the people of Peshawar, but a Peshawar revolt was prevented when British forces cut the supplies of water, electricity, and food to the city. Saleh Muhammad's forces became prematurely engaged and had to give ground. It was primarily on the Waziristan front that the Afghans were able to break through the British defenses and lay siege to the British base at Thal. (*See* THAL, SIEGE OF.) The entire Northwest Frontier was in ferment, and Indian tribesmen were ready to rally to support the Afghans.

John Maffey, the chief political officer with the field force, indicated in a letter that the "threat to Thal has delayed the **Jalalabad** move, as the motor transport available does not admit of two simultaneous offensives." He also was afraid that British forces would have to push so far that there would be nobody to settle up with (Adamec, 1967, 118).

Therefore, the Indian government permitted the Afghan envoy in India to proceed to Kabul to persuade Amanullah to end his hostile activities. Amanullah agreed, and a cease-fire was concluded leading to peace and the establishment of normal neighborly relations after long and heated negotiations at **Rawalpindi, Mussoorie,** and Kabul. On the southern front British forces captured Spin Boldak, but could not follow up on their conquest, and no major campaign occurred on the northern, Chitral, front. British casualties included 236 killed (49 British ranks), 615 wounded (133 British ranks), as well as 566 deaths of cholera and 334 of other diseases and accidents. British "ration strength" reached 750,000 British and Indian troops, and the animals involved numbered 450,000 (Molesworth, vii). No figures are available on Afghan casualties. *See also* AFGHAN FOREIGN RELATIONS; ANGLO-AFGHAN TREATY, 1919; 1921; MUSSOORIE CONFERENCE.

THIRD ANGLO-AFGHAN WAR, AFTERMATH. Following the war, the autonomous tribes of the Frontier were in semi revolt, assuming that the cease-fire was only temporary and that the Afghan government would continue the war if King **Amanullah**'s demands were not met. **Afridis,** Wazirs, and Mahsuds continued their raiding of British positions, and the Indian government faced a slow process of reasserting its authority in the area. Sir Hamilton Grant recommended to the viceroy on October 9, 1919, the bombing of tribal villages without warning, reporting, "As the aftermath of the Afghan war we have an outbreak of raiding such perhaps as has never before discredited our administration." Dealers and shopkeepers were holding up their stock, and there was an imminent danger of bread riots and disturbances in the Peshawar area. The viceroy answered,

"I am up against a serious financial situation and an army which is tired of war." On December 13 he reported that the operation against the Afridis was so far successful,

> although I am sorry to say we have lost another aeroplane and the two airmen if alive are prisoners in the hands of the Afridis, I trust they will be given up unharmed.... The constant raiding by Afridi gangs into the Peshawar District is sorely discrediting our administration. It is astounding that such a state of affairs should be possible with the number of troops we have got in the Peshawar Valley and shows how very difficult it would be to make any military operation of trans-frontier areas really successful.

He felt that "the only real cure is the radical cure, namely, an Afridi war and the subjugation of the whole tribe, but this, unless we are forced to do it, would be a most formidable and undesirable undertaking."

On January 26, 1920, he reported on operations against the Mahsuds:

> The Mahsuds are putting up a good fight, and indeed the whole operations are very different from any I remember on the Frontier. The Mahsuds attack with extraordinary recklessness, and hand to hand fighting is quite common; but this is to our advantage, for it means very heavy casualties to them. These must tell in the end; and unless we suffer any serious reverses, I think the Mahsuds must chack up the sponge before very long. Force is expensive. It takes nearly a hundred thousand men with miles of mechanical transport, railway trains, camels, mule carts etc. to have about 18 battalions in the field, but such is modern war. (Hamilton Col. I.O. MSS Eur. D. 660)

The British eventually prevailed: some of the more militant members of the tribes withdrew into Afghanistan, and the rest made their peace with the British. Eventually, they intervened for their militant brothers, which enabled them to return to their homes.

THIRD ANGLO-AFGHAN WAR, BRITISH PLAN OF CAMPAIGN. The British military command stated the following objectives:

"1. To undertake an offensive with the main striking force against **Jalalabad** with the object of dividing the **Afridis** and Mohmands, and strike at any Afghan concentration within reach, and to thus induce the withdrawal, for the purpose of covering **Kabul**, of Afghan forces from our borders elsewhere.

"2. To maintain an active defense on other portions of our front.

"3. In the Tochi and Derajat areas, we are prepared to evacuate temporarily, should the necessity arise, those portions of country held by Frontier Militias between the Administrative and Political borders, the retention of which would possibly result in a series of sieges necessitating relief measures and consequent dissipation of transport."

The operations were directed by General **Sir Charles Munro**, the commander in chief in India. Army headquarters were at Simla, and the army was first organized into two forces: 1. The North-West Frontier Force, commanded by General Sir Arthur Barrett. 2. The Baluchistan force, which included the troops guarding the Nushki-Duzdap Railway and the L. and C. through east Persia to Meshed, commanded by Lieutenant General **R. Wapshare**. Further decentralization developed by formation of the "Waziristan Force" under the command of Major General **S. H. Climo**, consisting of the troops in the Bannu and Derajat area. The force comprising the East Persian Cordon under Major General **W. Malleson**, with headquarters in Meshed, was charged to intervene if Turkestan Bolsheviks were sending assistance to the Afghans.

The third Anglo-Afghan war differed from the previous wars in several respects. Before, the British made war when they were ready —this time the Afghans were the aggressors. Troops were engaged along the entire Afghan frontier from Chitral on the northeast to Seistan on the southwest, a distance of about 1,000 miles. Use by the British of the system of tribal militias failed, which necessitated their disbandment or serious reduction. The British realized that in a war with Afghanistan, they would always have the Afghan tribes on their side of the frontier turn against them.

THIRD ANGLO-AFGHAN WAR, LESSONS OF. Britain again learned the bitter lesson that her hold on the tribal territory on the northwest frontier of India was as tenuous as it had been in the past. The Frontier Militias had to be disbanded because they were unwilling to fight their Afghan brothers, and the entire tribal belt was preparing to obey the Afghan king's call to **jihad**. The British realized, "We must expect a portion, or all, of them to be hostile to us in the case of another war with Afghanistan." The extremes in temperature, lack of water and supplies, endemic disease, and the inhospitable nature of the territory proved to be serious problems in spite of the British advantage of superior weapons technology. The use of the Frontier Militias as a covering force behind which the Field Army was to concentrate proved a failure in the **Khaibar** and Waziristan. The lesson to be learned was that "irregular troops should not be left to meet the first onslaught of the invader." They should be replaced with strong, mobile columns of regular troops. The British employed a system of troop movements whereby "the 1st Division was replaced at Peshawar and Nowshera by the 2nd Division, which in turn was pushed forward when relieved by the 16th Division." This caused the staff and transport to become disorganized, and the Field Army disintegrated.

The tactical lesson of the value of pursuing a vigorous offensive was proven correct, because it kept the fence-sitting tribesmen out of the war; whereas inaction at Dakka and the Khaibar encouraged the tribesmen to join the Afghan forces. This was the first major use of aerial warfare and, although it had a great moral effect, there were limits to air power. Most of the British planes were obsolete, their climbing power was low, so that the tribesmen were able to shoot at them from the hilltops; but the bombing of Dakka, **Jalalabad**, and **Kabul** proved to have a great moral effect. In short-distance tactical reconnaissance, aircraft were of no value, because the tribesmen soon learned to break up into small groups and take cover at the sound of an approaching aircraft. The armored car possessed great fire power and was an invulnerable target. But its use was limited to patrolling roads, it was liable to engine trouble, and the heat in the turrets when closed became intolerable. Howitzers were employed with great effect, and machine guns were eminently suitable to the hilly terrain as they could be employed for direct overhead cover. Grenades were used to good effect, but many failed to explode or were thrown without the pin being removed. The British felt that permanent pickets proved to be preferable to temporary ones, although it deprived them of their mobility. The British felt a need for more effective training to "cultivate dash, and a desire to close with the enemy with the bayonet." Much more transport than in previous wars was needed because of the more extensive use of artillery and machine guns (OF, 1919 War).

For the Afghan side, the lesson was clear that great efforts were needed for improving the effectiveness of the Afghan army. New weapons, more intensive training, and a rationalization of logistics were only some of the needs. As in the past, the tribesmen proved to be better fighters, but lacked staying power, having provisions for only a few days. They were prone to plunder, which they wanted to carry to their villages. They operated best in their own tribal areas and were good in short aggressive attacks. Afghan offensives on the Waziristan front were largely due to tribal support. The tribes on the British side of the border were ready to join the war against India, but they could not be mobilized and equipped before the short war was ended.

THIRD ANGLO-AFGHAN WAR, PHASES OF OPERATION.
Phase 1. From May 6 to 25. Actions on the **Khaibar** front and attempted Afghan penetration through Mohmand country. Movements of British reserves to northern area and the formation of a further reserve by the creation of the 60th Brigade at Ambala, the 61st Brigade at Jubbulpore, the 62nd Brigade at Dhond, and the 63rd Brigade at Lucknow. During this period the border tribes were quiet.

Phase 2. From May 26 to June 2. Invasion of the central area by Nadir Khan and siege of Thal. Evacuation of militia posts in Waziristan and mutiny of the North and South Waziristan Militias. Diversion of British reserves to Kohat and Bannu. The armistice. During this period the border tribes were showing signs of hostility.

Phase 3. From June 3 to August 8. Cessation of hostilities on the part of the Afghan regulars, but general activity on the part of the Afghan border tribes (OF 3, 25).

THIRD ANGLO-AFGHAN WAR, PRESS REACTION. The British press complained about scandal and mismanagement in the war. One officer told the *Army and Navy Gazette* (September 16, 1919) of a case of mismanagement: 300 horses were sent in corrugated iron trucks. Instructions to thatch the roofs and spray them with water at stops were ignored. Simla said not necessary! The result was that 150 horses died on the journey and 75 more on arrival.

Under the heading "Afghan Frontier Scandal," *The Englishman* (September 13, 1919) reported that the army was not prepared. Transport was missing. "Airplanes available were all of an antiquated type, save the two Handley-Page machines, of which one flew once and the other not at all."

"British troops at Dakka for three weeks had no rations save bully beef, biscuits, tea and sugar." The troops never received more than half rations. Hospital conditions were a disgrace: "Cholera patients had to be put in tents at 115 degrees heat." "While Simla rewarded itself with a stream of foreign decorations...."

"Mesopotamia was bad, but Afghanistan is worse, because it shows that the lesson of the former debacle was not learnt."

TIMUR-I LANG (TAMERLANE r. 1370–1405). "The Lame Timur" founded the Timurid dynasty and wreaked destruction on the towns he conquered but made Samarkand into a city of splendor. He was a warrior, not an empire builder, and could not hold his extensive territorial conquests. Timur was a Turk, born at Kesh, near Samarkand, who claimed Mongol descent and began his career as a raider for booty. Claiming to wage **jihad**, holy war, he fought Muslim rulers in Russia and India and subdued the Ottomans at the Battle of Ankara in 1404. He was preparing a campaign against China when he died in 1405. His son Shahrukh chose **Herat** as his capital and made it an important cultural center. Under Husain Baiqara (r. 1468–1506), the last of the great Timurid rulers, Herat experienced a cultural renaissance, and artists, poets, and scholars enjoyed the sponsorship of the Timurid court. Architectural remains from the Timurid period include the Musalla (minarets) and the mausoleum of Gauhar Shad, the wife of Shahrukh. Timurid rule ended when the **Uzbek** Shaibanid dynasty took Herat in the early 16th century. While the government of Uzbekistan celebrates Timur as a national hero and great humanitarian, others remember him as a destroyer of civilizations no less than Genghis Khan.

TIMUR SHAH (r. 1773–1793). One of **Ahmad Shah**'s six surviving sons and governor of **Herat** at the time of the death of his father. He defeated his brother Sulaiman Mirza and quickly established himself as successor to the Afghan throne at **Kandahar**. To weaken the power of the **Durrani** chiefs, he moved his capital to **Kabul**, where he continued his father's policy of forging an alliance with the Barakzais, granting hereditary offices, and maintaining a strong army. He made alliances by marriage and further strengthened his power by creating an elite bodyguard of non-**Pashtun** soldiers. However, he was unable to create a centralized state. Afghan historians describe him as "humane and generous but . . . more a scholar than a soldier." He appointed his sons Zaman, Humayun, Mahmud, Abbas, and Kohandil as governors of Afghan provinces, and upon his death in 1793, they started an internecine struggle for power that eventually cost the **Sadozai** rulers their throne.

TODD, ELLIOT D'ARCY (1808–1845). A Bengal officer attached to the British legation with the Persian camp at **Herat** in 1838. He entered the besieged city in which **Eldred Pottinger**, another Englishman, was helping in the defense of the city. The negotiations of the two men did not have any effect on the siege. Deputed to make a treaty with Shah Kamran at Herat, he remained as a political agent, from 1839 to 1841. He was removed by **Lord Auckland** because of his independent actions. Todd was killed in 1845 at the battle of Firuzpur during the Sikh wars. A nine-pounder round shot hit him in the face and severed his head from his body.

TOMAHAWK CRUISE MISSILE. A long-range missile with a warhead of either 340 kg of high explosives or a cluster bomb containing 166 can-sized bomblets. It is programmed with the coordinates of the route, the height of the land over which it will fly and digital images of the target. Once over land, the missile scans the ground and compares radar altitude readings with the map stored in its computer. Links to global positioning satellites confirm its position and route. It flies at about 550 mph at extremely low altitudes to avoid enemy radar. As it nears the target, it switches on its video camera. By digitally comparing images to those stored in its memory it should be able to make final course adjustments. Each missile costs more than $1 million.

TORA BORA, BATTLE OF. A campaign to destroy al-**Qaeda** and **Taliban** forces and capture **Osama bin Laden** who controlled a complex of cave fortifications near the village of Tora, about 35 miles south of **Jalalabad**, near the **Pakistan** border. After the capture of **Kandahar** by **United States** and allied forces on December 11, 2001, U.S. Special Forces, supported by Hazrat Ali and Haji Zaman and their Pashai and Khugiani tribal contingents, moved east to trap the enemy ensconced in the Tora Bora mountain range. Pakistani forces sealed the border. U.S. ground soldiers operated as spotters for B-52 sorties coming in at 20-minute intervals. Allied tribal forces did much of the fighting. The enemy, estimated at 1,500 Arab and Chechnyan fighters, proved to be fierce opponents, holding out until December 16, when some 21 al-Qaeda fighters were taken prisoner, an unknown number were killed, and most managed to escape. Osama bin Laden was last seen in the final days of November 2001, when he made preparations to flee to the autonomous tribal area on the Pakistani side of the border. Although the American allies fought bravely, they may have permitted the enemy to escape.

TORA BORA, CAVE FORTIFICATIONS. Caves in many parts of Afghanistan served to shelter the **mujahedin** in their war against the communist forces. They stored weapons, food, and the necessities of life in these caves, some of which, near the **Pakistan** border, were excavated to hold as many as 1,000 fighters. One such complex of caves at **Tora Bora** was carved 1,150 feet into a 13,000ft. mountain and was said to have served as **Osama bin Laden**'s headquarters. Mountain streams generated hydroelectric power and a complex system of ventilation brought air into the caves. A main entrance leads through a 50-foot tunnel, wide enough to permit vehicles to enter. Staircases connect to offices, dormitories, and communal rooms. Weapons are stored in armories. The complex is not visible from the air, and exits are closed with steel doors or hidden behind mud walls. Some exits are booby-trapped. According to one report, American bombing closed the main entrance, but another bomb opened it again. If it had not been for the American intervention, no Afghan rival could have defeated the **Taliban** and their **al-Qaeda** allies.

TRANSITIONAL GOVERNMENT (TRANSITIONAL AUTHORITY). Established on June 20, 2002, for a two-year period as a result of an emergency **Loya Jirga** and selection of cabinet members by President **Hamid Karzai**. The **Panjshiris** retained the positions of defense and foreign affairs, but **Yunus Qanuni** lost control of the interior ministry, which was given to the 80-year-old **Pashtun**, Taj Muhammad Wardak (and subsequently to **Ali Ahmad Jalali**). Qanuni became special adviser to the president on security. **Muhammad Qasim Fahim** became first vice president and retained the position of defense minister. Powerful local commanders (warlords), including **Ismail Khan, Abdul Qadir** (later killed), **Abdul Rashid Dostum, Ata Muhammad,** and Gul Agha, formed the national defense commission. Hedayat Amin Arsala was replaced by Ashraf Ghani to head the finance ministry. Sima Samar, the former minister of women's affairs, was replaced by Mahbuba Hukukumal, but retained the position of human rights commissioner. It was clear that Karzai was under intense pressure to reserve positions for the major actors on the political scene. **Burhanuddin Rabbani**, the one-time president of Afghanistan, did not receive a portfolio but attention was paid to keep an ethnic and sectarian balance. It is not surprising that Karzai was unable to satisfy all contenders. For members of the Transitional Government, *see* CHRONOLOGY.

A dramatic change in the Afghan power relationship occurred as the result of presidential elections on October 9, 2004, in which Karzai was the winner with 55.4 percent of the vote. He formed his new cabinet, replacing the leaders of the powerful **Northern Alllliance**. Fahim, Qanuni, Muhaqeq, were out, Dostum ignored, and Ismail Khan, the only survivor, was coopted as minister of water and power. Karzai declared that he would not form a coalition government, even with Qanuni, who was a distant second in the election with 16.3 percent. This marked the end of the Transitional Government and the beginning of the first government chosen by the Afghan people.

TRANSPORT, MILITARY. Until the end of the World War II, motorized transport was limited to the major roads, leading from **Herat** to **Kandahar** and from there to **Kabul** or south to Quetta. A road connected the capital over the Lataband, about 20 miles east of Kabul, with **Jalalabad** and the Indo-Pakistani subcontinent. From Kabul to **Mazar-i Sharif** a tortuous road led over the **Salang** Pass, which was not passable in the winter. The **Hazarajat** in the center of the country was closed to motorized traffic. Until the 1930s only a few landing strips existed for small aircraft. Therefore, invaders of Afghanistan depended on large numbers of animal transport. Bullocks, donkeys, ponies, horses, and camels were the major animals used; elephants and mules were less frequently employed. Donkeys were excellent for transport work: they could easily move in the mountainous terrain and carry loads up to 160 pounds. The Afghan camel was superior to camels from India; it was sure-footed and hardy, could travel with ease over mountain tracks, and was used for long-distance travel. The British army lost 20,000 camels during the **first Anglo-Afghan war** and 100,000 during the second (*Handbook*, 1933) and had difficulty in providing replacements by hire or confiscation from the Afghans. British lines of communication remained vulnerable to Afghan attacks. Overby (167) quotes Amir **Abdul Rahman** as saying, "100,000 English soldiers require more transport animals than 1,000,000 Afghans, because they require so many kinds of provisions. . . . The Afghans are such a strong, healthy people that they can run over the mountains nearly as fast as horses, carrying their guns and food on their backs."

In the 1980s no more than 3,000 miles of hard-surface roads existed, and many of those were severely damaged as a result of the war. The **mujahedin** employed contractors who used their own pack animals to transport supplies into Afghanistan. As animals died, horses and mules were imported from Argentina, China, and Pakistan. Mules would carry mortars, machine guns, and other heavy equipment, as well as ammunition, close to the firing points. Initially, convoys of pack animals traveled by night, but during the latter stages of the war they traveled unhindered even during the day. However, in many areas close to the enemy, the mujahedin had to carry their heavy weapons over paths that did not permit the use of pack animals.

The **United States** faced no serious problems with transportation. It was, indeed, costly to ferry coalition troops and weapons into the country, but everything needed could be provided. As a priority, the Kabul-Kandahar highway was resurfaced, other strategic roads were repaired, and vehicles of various types could be employed to carry men and their arms to areas of conflict. In a country with a largely destroyed communications system, satellite phones made effective communication possible. *See also* LOGISTICS.

TREATIES. *See under individual treaties below*; ANGLO-AFGHAN WARS; FOREIGN RELATIONS.

TREATY OF KABUL. *See* **ANGLO-AFGHAN TREATY OF 1921.**

TREATY OF PESHAWAR, 1855. A treaty of friendship and alliance between Amir **Dost Muhammad** and the government of India, which stipulated "perpetual peace and friendship, that the British government should respect the territories in possession of the Amir, and the amir respect the territories of the British government. The Afghan ruler was to be the friend of **Britain**'s friends and enemy of her enemies, and that the British should assist the amir against his enemies."

TREATY OF SIMLA. *See* **TRIPARTITE AGREEMENT.**

TRIBES, PASHTUN. *See* **PASHTUNS, TRIBES.**

TRIPARTITE AGREEMENT. An agreement, also called Treaty of Simla, signed on July 16, 1838, among **Ranjit Singh**, ruler of the **Sikh** nation of the Panjab, **Shah Shuja**, the exiled king of Afghanistan, and the British government. It stipulated relations between the future Afghan ruler and Ranjit Singh and allied the three powers in an attempt to restore **Shah Shuja** and the **Sadozai** dynasty to the **Kabul** throne. Ranjit Singh was not required to commit his army and wisely left the task of invading Afghanistan to the British "**Army of the Indus.**" He was thus spared the British defeat in the first **Anglo-Afghan war.** See also AFGHAN FOREIGN RELATIONS; ANGLO-AFGHAN WARS; SIMLA MANIFESTO.

- U -

ULAMA. A collective term for the "doctors of Islamic sciences." They are graduates of **madrasas**, colleges of Islamic studies, or of private study with an *'alim* (pl. *ulama*, one who possesses the quality of *'ilm*, knowledge of the Islamic traditions, law, and theology). Commonly referred to as the Islamic clergy, they have been in the forefront of the struggle against non-Muslim invaders and, during the **Taliban** period, have become an important political factor.

UNITED NATIONS AND AFGHANISTAN. Afghanistan joined the United Nations in 1946 and soon benefitted from various types of assistance. It became a member of such organizations as the International Bank for Reconstruction and Development (IBRD), the International Development Association (IDA), the International Monetary Fund (IMF), the United Nations Development Program (UNDP), the World Health Organization (WHO), the Food and Agriculture Organization (FAO), the United Nations Educational, Scientific and Cultural Organization (UNESCO), and others. UN experts visited Afghanistan to assist in agricultural, industrial, rural and educational development. The UN sponsored malaria eradication and vaccination projects, and provided emergency food shipments and economic aid at various times.

Afghanistan opposed **Pakistan**'s admission to the United Nations because of the **Pashtunistan** problem (*see* PAKISTAN-AFGHAN RELATIONS). The country was honored when in 1966 **Abdul Rahman Pazhwak** was elected president of the Twenty-First Session of the General Assembly. Politically, the United Nations became involved in mediation of disputes during the Marxist period when the General Assembly voted with an overwhelming majority to urge the withdrawal of "foreign forces" from Afghanistan. Diego Cordovez, undersecretary-general for political affairs, initiated "proximity" talks between Afghanistan and Pakistan under the auspices of the United Nations, which, after six-years of grueling negotiations, resulted in the **Geneva Accords** of April 1988 and the withdrawal of Soviet forces from Afghanistan in 1989. During the civil war, following the fall of the Marxist regime in April 1992, United Nations representatives vainly tried to mediate between the various factions. **Lakhdar Brahimi**, a former Algerian foreign minister, and the German diplomat Norbert H. Holl unsuccessfully continued the effort to end the Afghan civil war. The UN was unable to save ex-President **Najibullah** from **Taliban** assassins after he had found shelter in the UN compound in **Kabul**. Eventually, the UN took an increasingly hostile stand against the Taliban regime for its support of international terrorism, trafficking in illegal drugs, discrimination against women, and for refusing to surrender **Osama bin Laden**. On November 19, 1999, the UN Security Council imposed sanctions that required an embargo of arms sales and military assistance to the Taliban; withdrawal of foreign military advisers from Taliban territory; closure of all Taliban overseas representative offices; closure of Ariana Afghan Airlines' overseas offices; a freeze on funds and assets belonging to bin Laden, his associates, and his **al-Qaida** organization; and a ban on the sale to the Taliban of heroin precursor chemicals. The sanctions came into force on January 19, 2000.

It was only as a result of American intervention and the destruction of the Taliban regime that Brahimi was able to bring the forces together to agree on an **Interim Government** established on December 22, 2001. This prepared the way for a **Transitional Government** under President **Hamid Karzai** and the election of Karzai on December 7, 2004, as president. The UN became heavily involved in "nation building" to help produce a democratic, Islamic government in Afghanistan. *See also* APPENDIX 6.

UNITED NATIONS' DISARMAMENT, DEMOBILIZATION, AND REINTEGRATION PROGRAM (DDR). The program began in October 2003 in Kunduz and was subsequently extended to other provinces. The UN Assistance Mission in Afghanistan (UNAMA) and the UN Development Program (UNDP), in cooperation with the Afghan ministry of defense, are supporting Afghanistan's New Beginnings Program (ANBP) which coordinates the DDR efforts in Afghanistan. Its task is to "honorably decomission" the Afghan military forces not yet integrated in the Afghan national army (ANA). By early May 2005 some 30,800 weapons were collected as well as about 9,000 heavy weapons. In 228 locations a total of 1,145,573 pieces of ammunition were found, but almost none for the popular AK-47. The country is, however, still awash with small arms and warlords and local chief have still-hidden arms caches.

Demobilized officers and soldiers will be helped to enter the ANA or return to civilian life. Most will be absorbed in the agricultural and small-business sectors. Some 850 unofficial militias, controlled by warlords, drug lords, or local strongmen, with more than 65,000 members have not been included in this program. On May 2, 2005, 30 Afghans were killed and more than 70 wounded when the secret arms dump of a local strongman exploded. An underground bunker in Bajgah, Baghlan Province, north of Kabul, belonging to one Jalal-i Bajgah, exploded and destroyed a great number of houses in the village. Jalal was not home at the time, but 22 members of his family were among those killed. Jalal's forces had been decommissioned, but his stock of ammunition had not yet been surrendered.

UNITED STATES-AFGHANISTAN RELATIONS. The United States was slow in establishing diplomatic relations with Afghanistan because of several factors. Afghanistan had achieved independence from **Great Britain** in the **third Anglo-Afghan war**, but Washington still considered the country within the British sphere of influence. Afghanistan was not attractive as a market for American industrial products nor as a source of vital raw materials. Americans knew little about the country; and whatever the U.S. government wanted to know it learned from the British, and they were not eager to have American competition in Afghanistan. Therefore, it is not surprising that Washington did not establish a legation at **Kabul**. The mission of Wali Muhammad, which visited European capitals for the purpose of establishing diplomatic relations, arrived in Washington in July 1921 with high hopes.

The Afghan government wanted to embark on a plan of development and modernization for which it needed the assistance of Western know-how. Both Britain and the **Soviet Union** were too close to permit a relationship of dependency. Kabul, therefore, hoped that the United States would become a "third power" that would balance the influences of Afghanistan's neighbors. Afghanistan offered incentives to American enterprises: In 1930–1931 an American firm sold 68 trucks for $121,000 to the Afghan government, but Britain made this an expensive deal, insisting that the trucks be transported on the Indian railroad rather than proceeding on their own power. In the same year the U.S. consul at Karachi came to Kabul, but when asked why the United States was not ready to establish diplomatic relations with Afghanistan, he could not give a satisfactory reply. The speaker of Parliament reproached him, saying "Americans had always said kind things about Afghanistan but, despite the fine opinion of the country, they refused to recognize a friendly state." In May 1935, W. H. Hornibrook arrived from Tehran to arrange for accreditation of U.S. diplomats stationed in India. The Afghans were ready to offer an oil concession to the United States. The Afghan foreign minister explained: "For obvious reasons we cannot give the concessions to the British and for the same reasons we cannot give it to the Russians.... We therefore look to your country to develop our oil resources." He added that this would require a permanent American legation in Kabul. An oil concession was signed and ratified with the Inland Oil Exploration Company in April 1937, but the company canceled the concession a year later "in view of the worsening of the international situation."

Finally, in 1942 the U.S. government established a permanent legation in Kabul because of geopolitical reasons. The **German** advance on Stalingrad threatened the Allied logistics link through western Iran. Eastern Iran or western Afghanistan were the only areas for an alternate route. An American presence in Kabul could help gain Afghan approval for construction of a railroad. Therefore, on June 6, 1942, Cornelius van Engert became the first resident minister. The German defeat at Stalingrad made it unnecessary to raise the question of a railroad project with Kabul.

In the post World War II era the United States provided aid for the wartorn and impoverished world, and Afghanistan received loans in 1950 and 1954 to finance its **Helmand** Valley electrification and irrigation projects. The American Morrison-Knudsen Construction Company undertook the ambitious task, which consumed a considerable amount of Afghanistan's hard currency reserves and did not live up to expectations. The beginning of the Cold War further complicated U.S.-Afghan relations.

The United States sought allies in its effort to contain Soviet expansionism and promised economic and military assistance to those states that were willing to join. The Afghan government was unable to obtain American guarantees of protection from Soviet aggression, but **Pakistan** did and became a member of the Baghdad Pact. The U.S. Department of State made the decision to defend the Indian subcontinent at the **Khaibar** rather than at Afghanistan's northern boundary. This was bound to exacerbate relations with Pakistan (*see* PASHTUNISTAN) and prompted the Afghan government to pursue a policy of "positive neutrality," which eventually led to dependence on the Soviet Union. The American government was willing to help, but Washington was not ready to match Soviet aid. Between 1950 and 1971 the total of American loans and grants amounted to about $286 million, as compared to $672 million from the Soviet Union. American policy was to foster cordial relations with Afghanistan, help expand its communications infrastructure, participate in certain sectors of education, and provide moral, but not military, support to strengthen Afghanistan's independence. In the late 1970s the U.S. Department of State downgraded the American embassy in Kabul to the category of missions of countries of least importance to the United States, and Afghanistan was tacitly left in the Soviet sphere of influence.

After the **Saur Revolt**, the United States recognized the Marxist government, but relations quickly deteriorated. The assassination of the American ambassador, Adolf Dubs, in February 1979, in a botched rescue attempt from kidnappers by Kabul police, further worsened relations. The Soviet military intervention in December 1979 resulted in vital American support for the **mujahedin**, forcing the Soviet government to withdraw its forces by February 1989. Fearing a general massacre in Kabul and the quick defeat of the Kabul government, the United States closed its embassy for "security reasons" in January 1989 and prevailed on others to do likewise. But the Marxist government continued to rule Kabul until 1992. As a result of the **Taliban** capture of Kabul in September 1996, the American government evaluated developments to determine whether conditions permitted the establishment of diplomatic relations, but in view of the Taliban's harsh regime, human rights violations, and toleration of continued poppy cultivation, decided against it. It was only after the fall of the Taliban regime that Washington resumed diplomatic relations and appointed Robert P. J. Finn as American ambassador to Kabul, who was succeeded by the Afghan-born **Zalmai Khalilzad** on November 29, 2003.

Although American objectives were to destroy the Taliban regime and its **al-Qaeda** supporters and arrest or kill its leadership, eventually the task of "nation building" could not be separated from the mission to strengthen the Kabul government. Considerable American and international aid was forthcoming, and repairs of the communications infrastructure, and demobilization of armed militias were showing results. Presidential elections, which legitimized **Hamid Karzai**'s government, permitted curbing the power of warlords. The establishment of **Provincial Reconstruction Teams**, with the participation of the **North Atlantic Treaty Organization**, allowed further consolidation of the Kabul government.

With the election of an Afghan parliament, the mandate of the **Bonn Conference** comes to an end. No status of forces agreement exists to regulate the presence of foreign troops in Afghanistan, but steps were taken in May 2005 to come to some kind of arrangement. In February 2005 the U.S. Senator John McCain visited Kabul and called for the establishment of "joint military permanent bases" in Afghanistan. On May 5 President Karzai convened an assembly of almost 1,000 notables, some members of the 2003 **Loya Jirga**, to discuss the establishment of a "strategic partnership" with the United States. On May 23, on the occasion of his visit to the United States, President Karzai signed an agreement with President George W. Bush which states "U.S. military forces operating in Afghanistan will continue to have access to Bagram Air Base and its facilities, and facilities at other locations as may be mutually determined and that the U.S. and Coalition forces are to continue to have the freedom of action required to conduct appropriate military operation based on consultations and pre-agreed procedures." The agreement, called by Karzai a "Memorandum of Understanding" and by President Bush a "Strategic Partnership," does not specify the duration of foreign troops in Afghanistan. It remains to be seen if the parliament will agree to the establishment of permanent American bases in Afghanistan. *See also* APPENDIX 6; FOREIGN RELATIONS; GERMAN-AFGHAN RELATIONS; RUSSIAN-AFGHAN RELATIONS.

UNITED STATES-AFGHANISTAN STRATEGIC PARTNERSHIP. With the presidential and parliamentary elections of 2004 and 2005, the mandate of the **Bonn Conference** has ended and Afghanistan has a legal government. But no status of forces agreement existed with

Plate 20. Army soldiers prepare a humvee to be sling-loaded by a Ch-47 Chinook helicopter in Bagram. (DoD / Sgt. Sandra Watkins Keough)

Plate 21. Member of Marine Security Forces fast ropes from an MH-60s Nighthawk. (DoD / Jim Jenkins)

Plate 22. U.S. Army soldier sets up defensive position with his M-249 Squad automatic weapon during a patrol in the Daychopan district of Zabul Province. (DoD / Staff Sgt. Joseph P. Collins Jr.)

Plate 23. U.S. Marines patrol through a dry creek bed in Khost Province. (DoD / Lance Cpl. Justin M. Mason)

Plate 24. Marines patrol on foot through downtown Sarobi, Kabul Province. (DoD / Lance Cpl. Justin M. Mason)

Plate 25. Member of Special Forces Group in an up-armed high mobility multi-wheel vehicle mans a turret-mounted 50-caliber machine gun. (DoD / Sgt. Joe Belcher)

Plate 26. New recruits of the Afghan National Army line up to receive their new uniforms and equipment. (DoD / Sgt. Kevin P. Bell)

Plate 27. Afghan Security Force members search an individual during training class at Asadabad, Kunar Province. (DoD / Sgt. Horace Murray)

the United States and Coalition forces, who came as conquerors, legalizing the presence of foreign troops in Afghanistan. Therefore, **Hamid Karzai** convened a meeting of almost 1,000 notables to agree to the creation of a "strategic partnership" with the United States. The vaguely-worded document permits the presence of foreign troops outside the jurisdiction of Afghanistan for an indefinite period of time and the establishment of American bases.

The document calls for cooperation for "Democracy and Governance, for Prosperity, and for Security." And it states:

> It is understood that in order to achieve the objectives contained therein, U.S. military forces operating in Afghanistan will continue to have access to Bagram Air Base and its facilities, and facilities at other locations as may be mutually determined and that the U.S. and Coalition forces are to continue to have the freedom of action required to conduct appropriate military operation based on consultations and pre-agreed procedures.

It further adds that

> as Afghan Government capabilities increase, Afghanistan will continue to cooperate against terrorism, to promote regional security, and combat the drug trade; the Afghan Government, over time, will move to assume Afghan security force sustainment costs.

Afghanistan will not have a veto over foreign military activity, nor will it hold prisoners taken by the Coalition forces. It is clear to see that this agreement, called a "Memorandum of Understanding" by Karzai, may become a source of trouble for him once parliament is established.

UNITED STATES INTERVENTION. In response to the suicide attacks on the World Trade Center and the Pentagon and the declaration of war by **Osama bin Laden,** President George W. Bush issued a declaration of war (*see* APPENDIX 5). Aerial bombardments started on October 7, 2001, and 10 days later the United States conducted the first ground combat operations.

The American military command devised what came to be known as the "Afghanistan Model" of warfare: Afghan ground troops supported by American **Special Forces A-Teams** who targeted aerial bombardments. One team was instructed to find and support Dostum, stay with him and help. Go with him wherever he goes—if he wants to take over Kabul, go. If he wants to take over the whole fucking country, that is fine too. If he starts mass executions on the way, call HQ and advise, maybe exfil if you can't reign him in. (Moore, *The Hunt for Bin Laden: Task Force Dagger*)

Some $70 million were spent to win the support of local leaders/warlords. Rules of engagement were agreed upon. Under the heading "Military Strategy," allies and local "assets" were told:

1. Instruct all tribal allies to ground and identify all their aircraft immediately.
2. Instruct the tribals to cease all significant military movement—basically to stand down and hold in place.
3. The future plan was to have the opposition forces drive to isolate enemy forces, but to wait before moving.
4. Instruct all assets throughout Afghanistan to begin sabotage operations immediately everywhere. This would include tossing hand grenades through **Taliban** offices, disrupting Taliban convoys, pinning down those moving Taliban supplies and ammunition, and generally making pests of themselves.
5. Informing all of them that paramilitary insertions would go forward in the south and be combined with more specific air strikes.
6. All would have to design no-strike zones—hospitals, schools.
7. All tribal factions and leaders should identify and locate primary targets.
8. Assets should identify possible escape routes out of Afghanistan for bin Laden and his al Qaeda leadership—and then try to set up reconnaissance of the routes for interdiction.
9. Be prepared to interrogate and exploit prisoners.
10. Assess humanitarian needs. (Woodward, *Bush at War*)

One question to resolve was who should occupy Kabul. During a meeting in the Oval Office, Vice President Dick Cheney suggested, "We should encourage the **Northern Alliance** to take **Kabul**." CIA Director George Tenet said, "We can't stop them from trying to take Kabul—the only issue is whether they can do it or not." (*Ibid.* 215) National Security Advisor Condolezza Rice wrongly stated: "You know, the Russians never took Kabul" (Ibid. 219). It was also decided not to support the king to head the government. Eventually, it was the **Panjshiris** of the Northern Alliance who took the capital and filled the most important ministries in the **Interim Government**. American and allied forces quickly eliminated the Taliban regime and dispersed its **al-Qaeda** supporters (*see* OPERATION ENDURING FREEDOM: THE CAMPAIGN). Subsequent actions were **Operation Valiant Strike** at Sami Ghar, east of **Kandahar**; the **Battle of Tora Bora**; **Operation Anaconda** in the **Shah-i Kot** area, about 30 kilometers from **Gardez**.

Some of these engagements were not unqualified successes (*see* OPERATION ENDURING FREEDOM, A CRITIQUE), neither **Muhammad Omar** nor Osama bin Laden were captured. The Pentagon held the mission to destroy the Taliban/al-Qaeda leadership and not to get involved in "nation building" or interdicting the narcotics trade. It was only with the establishment of **Provincial Reconstruction Teams** and the formation of the Afghan National Army (*see* ARMY, AFGHAN) that efforts were made to support the **Hamid Karzai** government in the provinces.

The United States maintains about 20,000 troops in Afghanistan, supported by a **North Atlantic Treaty Organization** force of about 9,000 soldiers, and a growing national Afghan army of 21,000. The American intervention in Afghanistan has resulted in breaking the power of the warlords, and negotiations are under way to transfer the American war effort to NATO. *See also* LT. GENERAL DAVID BARNO; DAISY CUTTER; GENERAL TOMMY FRANKS; MAJOR GENERAL FRANKLIN HAGENBECK; INTERNATIONAL COALITION AGAINST TERROR; INTERNATIONAL SECURITY ASSISTANCE FORCE; LT. GENERAL McNEILL.

URUZGAN. *See* **ORUZGAN.**

UZAMA. *See* **LADEN, OSAMA BIN.**

UZBEK (UZBAK). The largest Turkic-language group in Afghanistan, estimated to number about 1.3 million (in the 1970s). They inhabit northern Afghanistan from **Fariab** Province in the west to **Badakhshan** Province. The Uzbek trace their name to an eponymic ancestor or a major tribe that migrated from the area north of the Syr Daria to the area north of the Afghan border. In the 15th century the Uzbeks were clients of various Timurid princes but soon struck out independently and by the early 16th century had captured Bukhara, Samarkand, and Khiva. They expelled **Babur Shah** from Ferghana, were defeated by Shah Isma'il of Persia in 1510, and carved out a khanate in Transoxania. **Ahmad Shah Durrani** gave **Balkh** to Haji Khan Uzbek, to protect the border from raids, but after the latter's death the khanate became a source of dispute between the Afghans and the amir of Bukhara. In 1869 Amir **Shir Ali** placed the khanate under the administration of the governor of Balkh.

The Uzbeks are largely sedentary agriculturalists. The Marxist government tried to win their support and proclaimed Uzbeki a national language, permitting the use of the language in education, the press, and the broadcasting media. Some Uzbek groups served the Marxist government in **Kabul** as militia units in **Pashtun** areas, and General **Abdul Rashid Dostum** controlled six predominantly Uzbek provinces in north-central Afghanistan. After the fall of the **Taliban**, Dostum again established himself as the dominant warlord/leader in the Uzbek territories. The new constitution of 2003 recognized Uzbeki as a "national language" in areas where Uzbeks are a majority. *See also* JOZJANIS.

- V -

VICEROYS AND GOVERNOR GENERALS OF INDIA.

Governor General:
Hastings, Warren	1774–85
Cornwallis, Charles C.	1786–93
Wellesley, Richard Colley	1798–1805
Cornwallis, Charles C.	1805
Minto, Gilbert Elliot	1808–14
Marquis of Hastings	1813–23
Amherst of Arakan, William P.	1823–28
Bentinck, William Henry C.	1834–39
Auckland, George Eden	1836–42
Dalhousie, James Andrew	1848–56

And Viceroy:
Canning, Charles John	1858–62
Elgin and Kincardine	1862–63
Napier, R. off.	1863
Denison, W. off.	1863
Lawrence, John Laird Mair	1864–69

Mayo, Richard Southwell B.	1869–72
Strachey, John off.	1872
Lord Napier off.	1872
Northbrook, Thomas George B.	1872–76
Lytton, Edward Robert B.	1876–80
Ripon, George Frederick R.	1880–84
Dufferin and Ava, Frederick T.	1884–88
Lansdowne, Henry Charles K.	1888–93
Elgin and Kincardine, Victor	1894–99
Curzon, George Nathaniel	1899–1905
Baron Ampthill off.	1904
Curzon, G. N.	1904
Minto, Gilbert John Murray	1905–10
Hardinge of Penshurst	1910–16
Chelmsford, Frederic John	1916–21
Reading, Rufus Daniel I.	1921–26
Earl of Lytton actg.	1925
Baron Irwin	1926
Viscount Goschen actg.	1929
Willingdon, Earl of	1931
Sir G. F. Stanley actg.	1934
Linlithgow, Victor Alexander	1936–43
Baron Brabourne actg.	1938
Wavell, Viscount	1943
Sir John Colville actg.	1945
Mountbatten, Viscount	1947

(Incomplete list, IO)

VITKEVICH, CAPTAIN IVAN (VICKOVICH). A Russian agent, or adventurer, of Lithuanian descent who came to **Kabul** in December 1837 for the purpose of establishing commercial relations with Afghanistan. He carried a letter from Count Simonich, the Russian ambassador to Tehran, and an unsigned letter purported to be from the czar. **Alexander Burnes** was also at Kabul on a similar assignment for the British-Indian government. Consulted by the **amir**, Burnes told him to receive Vitkevich and inform the British of his objective. **Dost Muhammad** wanted to regain Peshawar from **Sikh** control, but Burnes told him that he must surrender all claims to Peshawar and make his peace with the Sikh ruler. Having gotten no help from the British, Amir Dost Muhammad negotiated with Vitkevich for Russian support. Vitkevich was later repudiated by the

Russian government and, upon his return to St. Petersburg, committed suicide. The mission aroused fears in **Britain** that Dost Muhammad would ally himself with **Russia**, and the decision was made to depose the Afghan ruler. *See also* ANGLO-AFGHAN WARS.

- W -

WADE, SIR CLAUDE M. (1794-1861). From 1823 to 1839 he served as political agent in Ludhiana, responsible for relations with Afghans in exile, **Shah Shuja-ul-Mulk**, and with **Ranjit Singh**. He led a column which forced the **Khaibar Pass** and marched on Kabul during the **first Anglo-Afghan war**.

WAHDAT. *See* **HIZB-I WAHDAT**.

WAKHAN (37-00' N, 73-00' E). The extreme northeastern district of **Badakhshan** Province, extending from Ishkashim in the west to the borders of China in the east and separating Tajikistan from the Indo-Pakistani subcontinent. The Anglo-Russian Boundary Commission awarded this area in 1895-1896 to Afghanistan to create a buffer between the two empires. Amir **Abdul Rahman** was reluctant to accept this gift, declaring he was not "going to stretch out a long arm along the **Hindu Kush** to have it shorn off." But eventually the **amir** accepted the award when the gift was sweetened with a special annual subsidy of 50,000 rupees. The Wakhan was inhabited by some 6,000 **Isma'ilis** (Wakhis) and fewer than 2,000 **Sunni Qirghiz**. The latter emigrated to Turkey as a result of the **Soviet intervention** in Afghanistan. The area was ruled by an independent *mir* (from A., **amir**, prince) until 1882 when it came under the administrative control of the governor of Badakhshan. The corridor consists of high valleys traversed by the Wakhan River, which flows into the Ab-i-Panj, as the upper **Amu Daria** is called there. The two-humped Bactrian camel and yak are the major beasts of burden. In the years before the **Saur Revolt** the Wakhan Corridor attracted hunters for Marco Polo sheep and alpinists who explored its peaks. The Qirghiz herders lived in a symbiotic relationship with the agricultural Wakhis.

WAPSHARE, LIEUTENANT GENERAL R. (1860–1932). Commanded Baluchistan force in the **third Anglo-Afghan war**. He attacked and captured Spin Boldak at the cost of 18 killed and 40 wounded. The British counted 170 bodies and captured 169 of the 600-man garrison.

WAR, THE CLASSICAL ISLAMIC CONCEPT OF. Modernists claim that war is unavoidable, not desired or sought after. They stress that Muslims should "fight in the path of Allah against those who fight against you, but do not transgress" (II, 190). The Koran says: "But if the enemy incline towards peace, do thou (also) incline towards peace, and trust in Allah." Martial **jihad**, means "fighting in the path of Allah by means of life, property, tongue and other than these." It is a general duty which suffices, if accomplished by a sufficient number, and does not involve every Muslim.

Lawful wars include: (1) the continuation of war after a cease-fire or expiration of a peace treaty, (2) a defensive measure if Muslim territory has been invaded, or if the enemy has behaved in an unbearable manner, (3) a sympathetic measure to help Muslims suppressed by a non-Muslim government, (4) an idealistic measure to uproot godlessness and spread the faith. The latter is advocated by **Islamists**, but repudiated by modernists, who claim that this was an injunction during the early period of Islam, when the small community was threatened.

A number of acts are forbidden, including: (1) unnecessarily cruel or tortuous ways of killing, (2) killing of noncombatants, (3) decapitation of prisoners, (4) mutilations of men and beasts, (5) treachery and perfidy, (6) destruction of harvests, (7) adultery with captive women, (8) killing enemy hostages, (9) killing of peasants when they do not fight, and so forth.

Muslim prisoners of war are to be ransomed (zakat, the arms tax, to be used for this purpose) and enemy prisoners can arrange to be ransomed.

When a non-Muslim fortress was besieged, the enemy was given three choices: convert to Islam and become a Muslim citizen with all civil rights; surrender and become a protected resident (*dhimmi*) in Muslim lands, or have one year to decide to leave the Islamic domain; fight to the end, and let Allah decide the outcome. In such case the defeated enemy can be enslaved.

In Afghanistan, all these injunctions have been observed and violated at times. A jihad against Muslims was often justified by claiming the enemy an apostate, infidel, and therefore subject to destruction. Non-Muslims were not involved in such disputes and generally left in peace. Muslim modernists feel that the interpretation of Islam by 10th-century jurists was valid for the early period of Islamic history and must be reinterpreted to adapt to 21st-century conditions. They point out that jihad also means inwardly waging war against the carnal soul—a kind of moral imperative. The latter is called "The Great Effort" (*jihad al-akbar*) and is more important as it strives to achieve man's personal perfection. The "martial jihad," on the other hand, is the "Small Effort" (*jihad al-asghar*).

WARDAK (34-15' N, 68-0' E). A province in east-central Afghanistan (formerly called **Maidan**) with an area of 3,745 square miles and a population of about 310,000 (1991 est. 363,000) of whom about 23,000 lived as **refugees** in **Pakistan**. The administrative center is the newly constructed town Maidanshahr with an estimated population of about 27,000 (replacing Kot-i Ashro), located a few miles west of the **Kabul-Kandahar** highway. The province is mountainous, crossed by the Kabul-Kandahar highway and the road west into the **Hazarajat** and northwest to **Bamian** Province. The inhabitants are **Ghilzai** and **Durrani Pashtuns** in the south and **Hazara** in the north and west. The province is 80 percent pasture land. About 60 percent of the farms comprise areas of less than five *jaribs* (one *jarib* = about 0.5 acre). The province suffered considerably during the 1980s and has seen large-scale destruction of the infrastructure built during the 1970s.

WARDAK, GENERAL ABDUL RAHIM (1945–). Minister of defense in the **Hamid Karzai** government of December 2004. He served as deputy minister of defense with Marshal **Muhammad Qasim Fahim** in the **Transitional Government**. Born in **Wardak** Province, he graduated from Habibia High School and the Afghan Military Academy. He received advanced military training by Soviet instructors in **Kabul** and, subsequently, at Lackland Airforce Base, Ft. Benning, Ft. Knox, Ft. Sill, and Ft. Leavenworth in the **United States** and at the Nasser Academy of the Egyptian War College. He served as instructor at the Afghan Military Academy and deputy director of foreign relations at the ministry of defense at Kabul. He was military attaché at the Afghan embassy in New Delhi and defected in 1978 and joined the resistance. He was chief of staff of the **National Islamic Front** and the moderate Alliance of **Sayyid Ahmad Gailani, Muhammad Nabi Muhammadi**, and **Sebghatullah Mujaddidi**. In 1992 he served as a member of the Kabul defense and security council at the fall of the Kabul government and became chief military adviser to the Afghan **Interim Government**. During the jihad he served in major operations, including **Khost, Kunar,** Kabul, **Nangarhar,** and was three times wounded in action. Wardak is the author of three books: *Fundamentals of War, Geopolitics,* and *Afghan Military History* as well as a number of articles in the *Military Review, Logistics Review, Military Academy Review,* and other journals.

WATANJAR, MUHAMMAD ASLAM. Held positions as minister of communications, interior, and, finally, defense in Prime Minister Fazil Haq Khaliqyar's government of May 1990. A member of the **Khalq** faction of the **People's Democratic Party of Afghanistan** (PDPA), he had a leading role in the coup of **Muhammad Daud** (1973) and the subsequent **Saur Revolt** (1978). In both events he rode the lead tank in the assault on the palace, and his tank was placed on a pedestal in the square facing the presidential palace in commemoration of the 1978 coup. In April 1978 he and General **Abdul Qadir** headed the Revolutionary Council, which formed the government until **Nur Muhammad Taraki** was installed as president. He fled abroad after the fall of the communist regime in April 1992 and died in November 2000.

WEAPONS BAZAAR. *See* **ARMS BAZAAR.**

WILSON, CHARLIE. Member of the U.S. House of Representatives, who "was known for his abiding fondness for hot tubs, women and Scotch whiskey" and was credited for having been a "major player" in the Afghan war. During the 1980s he "used his seat on a military appropriations committee to steer billions of dollars in secret funds to the Central Intelligence Agency to funnel arms to the mujahedin." George Crile describes Wilson's activities in a book titled *Charlie Wilson's War: The Extraordinary Story of the Largest Covert Operation in History.* It was the first time that the CIA operated with "Presidential Findings" that authorized it to mount operations to kill Soviet soldiers in Afghanistan (168). Crile comments:

> No insurgency had ever enjoyed such a range of support: a country (**Pakistan**) completely dedicated to providing it with sanctuary, training, and arms; a banker (Saudi Arabia) that provided hundreds of millions in funds with no strings attached; governments (Egypt and China) that served as arms suppliers; and the full backing of a superpower (the **United States** through the C.I.A.). All of that plus various kinds of support from different Muslim movements

and governments, as well as the intelligence services of England, France, Canada, Germany, Singapore, and other countries. (408)

WYMER, SIR GEORGE PETRE (1788–1868). He served under General **William Nott** at **Kandahar** during the **first Anglo-Afghan war** and relieved **Qalat**-i Ghilzai. He commanded the First Brigade of the Kandahar Force and participated in the capture of **Ghazni**. He was named aide-de-camp, 1842–1854.

- Y -

YAQUB KHAN, AMIR MUHAMMAD (r. February– October 1879). Born about 1849, the son of Amir **Shir Ali** and his governor of **Herat**. Yaqub Khan also coveted **Kandahar** and was greatly disturbed when in 1868 the **amir** gave his favorite son Abdullah Jan that post. In 1871 Yaqub Khan revolted and marched on **Kabul** but was forced to retreated to Herat. Amir Shir Ali forgave Yaqub Khan and reappointed him governor of Herat. Yaqub Khan came to Kabul under a promise of safe conduct, which the amir did not keep, holding him in confinement until December 1878, when British troops invaded Afghanistan. Amir Shir Ali fled to northern Afghanistan and appointed Yaqub his regent. The latter proclaimed himself amir in February 1879, after he learned of the sudden death of his father. Hoping to save his throne, Yaqub concluded the **Treaty of Gandomak** with **Britain** and accepted a mission under **Sir Louis Cavagnari** at Kabul. When the latter was assassinated during an insurrection of troops, the British took control of government powers and Yaqub was forced to abdicate in October 1879. He went to India and lived there until his death in 1923. *See also* ANGLO-AFGHAN WARS.

YAR MUHAMMAD, WAZIR. Wazir (prime minister) of Prince Kamran (r. 1829–1841) who ruled **Herat** as an independent principality. Yar Muhammad is said to have been an able but cruel man who eventually became the virtual ruler of Herat. He ably withstood Persian attempts to capture Herat and led the defenses in two sieges in 1833 and 1837–1838 in which the Russian general, Berovski, participated on the Persian side and **Eldred Pottinger** on the side of the defenders. Yar Muhammad had Prince Kamran assassinated in 1841 and embarked on an ambitious plan of conquest. He allied himself in marriage with **Akbar Khan**, son of Amir **Dost Muham-**

mad, and conquered the western **Uzbek** khanates of Afghan Turkestan. He died in 1851.

YAZDAN-BAKHSH, MIR. Born in 1790, the son of Mir Wali Beg, the chief of Behsud, **Hazarajat**. He expelled his older brother, Mir Muhammad Shah, who had become chief of Behsud after his father was assassinated by a minor chief. Mir Yazdan-Bakhsh consolidated his power to become the undisputed chief of the **Hazaras** (r. 1843–1863). Amir Dost Muhammad Khan called him to **Kabul** and had him imprisoned. He escaped and fled to **Bamian**, where he was assassinated.

YOUSAF, MOHAMMAD (YUSUF, MUHAMMAD). Brigadier Mohammad Yousaf, head of the Afghan Bureau of the **Inter-Services Intelligence** of the **Pakistan** military from 1983 to 1987. He claims to have held a pivotal position in the war of the Afghan **mujahedin** against the **Soviet** and **Kabul** forces. In his book, *The Bear Trap: Afghanistan's Untold Story* (coauthored with Mark Adkin), this "commander-in-chief" of the mujahedin forces controlled the distribution of weapons bought with Central Intelligence Agency (CIA) and Saudi Arabian funds from the **United States**, **Britain**, China, and Egypt. He organized the training of rebels and planned missions of sabotage, ambushes, and assassinations inside Afghanistan and the Soviet Union. He was succeeded in 1978 by General Hamid Gul, at a time when the Soviet government had decided to end its involvement in Afghanistan.

YUNUS KHALES. *See* **KHALES, MUHAMMAD YUNUS.**

YUSUFZAI. A **Pashtun** tribe, originally settled in Peshawar, which migrated to the **Helmand** Valley and the **Kabul** region in the fifth century A.D. and in the 16th century returned to the northeastern corner of the Peshawar Valley. They now inhabit the Pakistan districts of Peshawar, Mardan, and Swat. They divided into two great branches: the Yusufzai and the Mandanr. They are agriculturists and usually dress in white clothes and shave their heads, leaving "a pair of love locks" at their temples. They have been romanticized as the "Pashtuns of the Pashtuns" among whom the **Pashtunwali** is still a living code of behavior. **Khushhal Khan Khatak**, not himself a Yusufzai, extols their sense of honor, saying:

The nobles of the Afghans are the Yusufzai'is,
Hard in battlefield and hospitable at home,
All Pakhtuns possess the sense of honor (*nang*)
None, however, can vie with them.

- Z -

ZABUL (32-0' N, 67-15' E). A province in south-central Afghanistan with an area of 6,590 square miles and a population of 181,000 (1991 est. 221,000). The administrative center of the province is the town of **Qalat** (population about 20,000), located about 87 miles northeast of **Kandahar**. The province is arid with almost perpetual winds, and agriculture is limited to the valleys of the Tarnak and Arghastan Rivers and a few areas that are irrigated by means of underground channels (*kariz*). The province, however, abounds in almond trees, one of the major items of export. The Zabulis are noted as good horsemen and perform a game, called "tent pegging" (*naiza bazi*), in which they spear pegs planted in the ground. The population is largely **Pashtun** in the south and **Hazara** in the north.

ZAHIR SHAH, MUHAMMAD. King of Afghanistan, 1933–1973. Born on October 15, 1914, the only surviving son of **Muhammad Nadir Shah**, he was educated in **Kabul** and in France. He was proclaimed king on November 8, 1933, within a few hours after his father's assassination, and adopted the title *al- Mutawakkil Ala'llah, Pairaw-i Din-i Matin-i Islam* (Confident in God, Follower of the Firm Religion of Islam). During the early period of his reign (1933–1946), the young king reigned while his uncles Muhammad Hashim and Shah Mahmud Ghazi ruled, successively holding the powerful position of prime minister. His cousin **Muhammad Daud** succeeded as prime minister from 1953 until 1963, when Zahir Shah forced his resignation. In 1964 he promulgated a new constitution that excluded members of the royal family from certain government positions (*see* CONSTITUTIONAL DEVELOPMENT), provided for a bicameral parliament, free elections, a free press, and the formation of political parties. He ushered in a period of unprecedented political tolerance, which was marred only by the intransigence of parliamentary representatives who could not establish a working coalition. The law on political parties was never ratified by the king, but parties were tolerated, although not legally permitted, and numerous groups published their manifestos in privately published newspapers and periodicals. Members of Parliament were elected as independents and not members of a party, but Parliament was stymied by political infighting. Foreign aid from East and West kept flowing into the country, and Kabul experienced considerable growth. However, not all sectors of Afghan society benefitted from the economic development. Zahir Shah toured Afghanistan on several occasions and frequently traveled abroad. During one of his trips abroad, his cousin Muhammad Daud staged a coup and established a republican government with himself as president. Zahir Shah abdicated on August 24, 1973, and lived in Italy. After the defeat of the Taliban regime, Zahir Shah returned to Afghanistan and carried the honorific title "Father of the Nation." He has not been involved in politics but supported the establishment of a **Loya Jirga**, the creation of transitional governments, and new presidential and parliamentary elections.

ZAMAN SHAH (r. 1793–1800). Born in 1872, one of 23 sons of **Timur Shah**, and his successor to the throne in 1793. During most of his reign he was engaged in intermittent warfare with his brothers Mahmud and Humayun. He wanted to win the British for a concerted war against the **Maratha** confederacy in India. Instead, the British concluded an alliance with Persia to keep the Afghans out of India (*see* AFGHAN FOREIGN RELATIONS). Shah Zaman appointed **Ranjit Singh** governor of Lahore, in spite of the fact that he had previously revolted. He abolished the hereditary posts established by **Ahmad Shah Durrani** and carried out bloody executions that antagonized many Afghans. While he was in the **Panjab**, Mahmud captured the **Kabul** throne. Shah Zaman was blinded and imprisoned but eventually escaped and lived in Indian exile until his death in 1844.

ZHAWAR, BATTLE OF. Zhawar is a village in **Khost** Province, south of Parachinar and about six miles from the **Pakistan** border. It was the major base along the **mujahedin** supply route for attacks on the **Kabul** garrison at Khost. The importance of the base can be seen from the fact that about 60 percent of mujahedin supplies passed through Zhawar and Ali Khel (Yousaf, 1992, 164). The base, built by a Pakistani construction company, had large underground facilities — seven tunnels housed living and medical quarters as well as depots of weapons and other facilities. Generators provided electricity and permitted radio communication. The base was defended by commanders of **Yunus Khales, Gulbuddin Hekmatyar, Muhammad Nabi Muhammadi,** and **Sayyid Ahmad Gailani. Jalaluddin Haqqani** was one of the major commanders. Some 400 men provided close protection and administrative support, and some additional 10,000 mujahedin controlled positions between Zhawar and Ali Khel. Because of Zhawar's proximity to the Pakistan border, reinforcements could quickly be obtained. The mujahedin had antiaircraft protection, including British **Blowpipe** missiles, three Oerlikon guns, and shoulder-fired SA-7s. Antitank minefields, mortars, and other heavy artillery provided for a formidable defense. Destruction of the base and closure of the supply line had long been an object of the Kabul government, and in early 1986 it started a major offensive. Major General **Shahnawwaz Tanai,** who was a native of this area, was in tactical command, and Brigadier Abdul Ghafur led the **Soviet**/Afghan contingent. The Soviets deployed one air assault regiment of the 103rd Guards Airborne Assault Division, and the Afghan forces included units of the 7th and 8th Divisions in Kabul, the 12th Division of **Gardez**, and the 14th Division at **Ghazni** and Khost, numbering altogether about 12,000 men. After a slow and fiercely disputed advance, the Soviet/Kabul forces reached Zhawar on April 11, and during the coming week succeeded in isolating the base and destroying the underground structures with laser-guided bombs. A Soviet heliborne commando brigade, landing in an open area, was destroyed to a man. The mujahedin fired 13 Blowpipe missiles, without destroying an aircraft (Yousaf, 1992, 171); nevertheless, at the end of the battle, the mujahedin claimed to have downed 13 helicopters and aircraft. The Kabul government captured the base but withdrew shortly thereafter, and the mujahedin returned within 48 hours. The Kabul government claimed to have killed 2,000 and wounded 4,000, and the mujahedin claimed to have captured 100 Afghan soldiers and killed or wounded about 1,500. A mujahedin spokesman said only 300 mujahedin were killed. The Kabul campaign did not achieve its objective.

Appendix 1

Soviet Report on Intervention in Afghanistan in December 1979

After a coup d'état and the murder of the CC PDPA General Secretary and Chairman of the Revolutionary Council of Afghanistan N.M. Taraki, committed by Amin in September of this year, the situation in Afghanistan has been sharply exacerbated and taken on crisis proportions. H. Amin has established a regime of personal dictatorship in the country, effectively reducing the CC PDPA and the Revolutionary Council to the status of entirely nominal organs. The top leadership positions within the party and the state were filled with appointees bearing family ties or maintaining personal loyalties to H. Amin. Many members from the ranks of the CC PDPA, the Revolutionary Council and the Afghan government were expelled and arrested. Repression and physical annihilation were for the most part directed toward active participants in the April revolution, persons openly sympathetic to the U.S.S.R., those defending the Leninist norms of intra-party life. H. Amin deceived the party and the people with his announcements that the Soviet Union had supposedly approved of Taraki's expulsion from party and government. By direct order of H. Amin, fabricated rumors were deliberately spread throughout the DRA, smearing the Soviet Union and casting a shadow on the activities of Soviet personnel in Afghanistan, who had been restricted in their efforts to maintain contact with Afghan representatives.

At the same time, efforts were made to mend relations with America as a part of the "more balanced foreign policy strategy" adopted by H. Amin. H. Amin held a series of confidential meetings with the American charge d'affaires in Kabul. The DRA government began to create favorable conditions for the operation of the American cultural center; under H. Amin's directive, the DRA special services have ceased operations against the American embassy.

In this extremely difficult situation, which has threatened the gains of the April revolution and the interests of maintaining our national security, it has become necessary to render additional military assistance to Afghanistan, especially since such requests had been made by the previous administration in DRA. In accordance with the provisions of the Soviet-Afghan treaty of 1978, a decision has been made to send the necessary contingent of the Soviet Army to Afghanistan. Riding the wave of patriotic sentiments that have engaged fairly large numbers of the Afghan population in connection with the deployment of Soviet forces which was carried out in strict accordance with the provisions of the Soviet-Afghan treaty of 1978, the forces opposing H. Amin organized an armed operation which resulted in the overthrow of H. Amin's regime. This operation has received broad support from the working masses, the intelligentsia, significant sections of the Afghan army, and the state apparatus, all of which welcomed the formation of a new administration of the DRA and the PDPA. The new government and Revolutionary Council have been formed on a broad and representative basis, with the inclusion of representatives from former "Parcham" and "Khalq" factions, military representatives, and non-party members. In its program agenda announcements, the new leadership vowed to fight for the complete victory of the national-democratic, anti-feudalistic, anti-imperialistic revolution, and to defend Afghan independence and sovereignty.

[signed]

Yu. Andropov
A. Gromyko
D. Ustinov
B. Ponomarev

31 December 1979

Appendix 2

Treaty of Friendship, Good-Neighborliness, and Cooperation Between the Union of Soviet Socialist Republics and the Democratic Republic of Afghanistan

The Union of Soviet Socialist Republics and the Democratic Republic of Afghanistan, reaffirming their fidelity to the goals and principles of the Soviet-Afghan treaties of 1921 and 1931, which laid the bases for friendly and good-neighbor relations between the Soviet and Afghan peoples and are in their fundamental national interests, desiring to strengthen in every way friendship and all-round cooperation between the two countries, filled with determination to develop the social and economics achievements of the Soviet and Afghan peoples, to safeguard their security and independence, and resolutely to support the solidarity of all forces struggling for peace, national independence, democracy and social progress, expressing a firm determination to promote the consolidation of peace and security in Asia and the world over and to make a contribution to the development of relations among states and to the strengthening of fruitful and mutually advantageous cooperation in Asia, and attaching great importance to the further strengthening of the treaty basis of their relations, reaffirming their fidelity to the goals and principle of the UN Charter, have decided to conclude this Treaty of Friendship, Good-Neighborliness and Cooperation, and have agreed on the following:

Art.1.- The high contracting parties solemnly declare their determination to strengthen and deepen the indestructible friendship between the two countries and to develop all-round cooperation on the basis of equality, respect for national sovereignty, territorial integrity and noninterference in each other's internal affairs.

Art.2.- The high contracting parties will make efforts to strengthen and expand the mutually advantageous economics, scientific and technical cooperation between them. To this end, they will develop and deepen cooperation in the fields of industry, transportation, communications, agriculture, the use of natural resources, the development of the power industry and in other economic fields and provide assistance in the training of national cadres and in planning the development of the economy. The parties will expand trade on the basis of the principles of equality, mutual advantage and most-favored-nation treatment.

Art.3.- The high contracting parties will promote the development of cooperation and exchanges of experiences in the fields of science, culture, the arts, literature, education, public health, the press, radio, television, movies, tourism and sports and in other fields.

The parties will promote the expansion of cooperation between bodies of state power, public organizations, enterprises and cultural and scientific institutions with a view to more thorough familiarization with the life, labor, experiences and achievements of the two countries' people.

Art.4.- The high contracting parties, acting in a spirit of the traditions of friendship and good-neighborliness, as well as in the spirit of the UN Charter, will hold consultations and, with the agreement of both parties, take appropriate measures with a view to ensuring the security, independence and territorial integrity of the two countries.

In the interests of strengthening the defense capability of the high contracting parties, they will continue to develop cooperation in the military field on the basis of appropriate agreements concluded between them.

Art.5.- The Union of Soviet Socialist Republics respects the policy of nonalignment pursued by the Democratic Republic of Afghanistan, which is an important factor in the maintenance of international peace and security.

The Democratic Republic of Afghanistan respects the policy of peace pursued by the Union of Soviet Socialist Republics, which is aimed at strengthening friendship and cooperation with all countries and peoples.

Art.6.- Each of the high contracting parties solemnly declares that it will not enter into military or other alliance or take part in any grouping of states or in actions or measures directed against the other high contracting parties.

Art.7.- The high contracting parties will continue to make every effort to protect international peace and the security of peoples, to deepen the process of the easing of international tension, extend it to all parts of the world, including Asia, and embody it in concrete forms of mutually advantageous cooperation among states, and to settle disputed international questions by peaceful means.

The two parties will actively promote the cause of general and complete disarmament, including nuclear disarmament, under effective international control.

Art.8.- The high contracting parties will promote the development of cooperation among Asian states, the establishment of relations of peace, good-neighborliness and mutual confidence among them, and the creation of an effective security system in Asia based on the joint efforts of all the continent's states.

Art.9.- The high contracting parties will continue a consistent struggle against the schemes of the forces of aggression and for the final elimination of colonialism and racism in all their forms and manifestations.

The parties will cooperate with each other and with other peace-loving states in supporting the just struggle of peoples for their freedom, independence, sovereignty and social progress.

Art.10.- The high contracting parties will consult with each other on all important international questions affecting in the interests of the two countries.

Art.11.- The high contracting parties declare that their commitments under existing international treaties are not at variance with the provisions of this treaty, and they pledge not to conclude any international agreements incompatible with it.

Art.12.- Questions that may arise between the high contraction parties with respect to the interpretation or application of any provision of this treaty will be resolved bilaterally in a spirit of friendship, mutual understanding and respect.

Art.13.- This treaty will be in effect for 20 years from the day it enters into force. Unless one of the high contracting parties declares, no later than six months before the expiration of the above term, its desire to terminate the treaty, it will remain in force for the next five years and until such time as one of the high contracting parties, no later than six months before the expiration of the current five-year period, gives written notice of its intention to terminate the treaty.

Art.14.- If one of the high contracting parties, during the treaty's 20-year term, desires to terminate the treaty before this term expires, it shall, no later than six months before the date it specifies for termination of the treaty, give the other high contraction party written notice of its desire to terminate the treaty before its term expires, and it may consider the treaty terminated as of the date thus set.

Art.15.- This treaty is subjected to ratification and will enter into force on the day that instruments of ratification are exchanged, which shall take place in Kabul.

This treaty is drawn up in duplicate, in the Russian and Dari languages, both texts being equally authentic. Done in Moscow on December 5, 1978 - (signed) For the Union of Soviet Socialist Republics - L. BREZHNEV; for the Democratic Republic of Afghanistan - N. MOHAMMAD TARAKI. (Current Digest of the Soviet Press, Vol. XXX, No. 49, January 3, 1979)

Appendix 3
Status of Soviet Forces Protocol

Secret Protocol regarding the treaty* between the Government of the Union of Socialist Soviet Republics and the Government of the Democratic Republic of Afghanistan about the conditions for the temporary stationing of Soviet forces in the territory of the Democratic Republic of Afghanistan (DRA).

In agreement with the treaty between the Government of the Union of Socialist Soviet Republics and the Government of the Democratic Republic of Afghanistan about the conditions for the temporary stationing of Soviet troops on the territory of the Democratic Republic of Afghanistan from January 1980

the contracting parties agree to the following:

1. The temporary stationing of Soviet troops on the territory of the Democratic Republic of Afghanistan to a maximum number of 60,000 men.

The troops will consist of infantry, artillery, armor and other types of forces.

In addition an air force of up to 200 aircraft and helicopters will be stationed.

For the leadership of the troops appropriate cadres will be created.

In the cities of Kabul and Herat representatives of Soviet command headquarters will be stationed in charge of matters relating to the temporary stationing of Soviet Troops in Afghanistan.

2. Afghanistan provides according to Annex** by January 30, 1980, for, under Point 1 in this Protocol mentioned Soviet troops, the necessary and appropriate barracks and living quarters in towns and garrisons as well as service and other buildings, in addition to airports including exercise and training areas and other facilities on these airports.

Areas for troop training, maneuvers, and firing ranges, in preparation for combat will be used in cooperation with the National Forces of the DRA.

If necessary for improvement of facilities and for safeguarding campaign preparations in their areas of garrisons, Soviet forces are authorized to erect the required structures (Anlagen) which will become the property of the Soviet Union.

3. The Soviet forces, which are temporarily in the territory of the Democratic Republic of Afghanistan, have the right to communicate and link up with each other and with the command headquarters of Soviet troops on the territory of the Union of Socialist Soviet Republics and the Democratic Republic of Afghanistan, utilizing all means of communication, according to the regulations in force for the armed forces in the Union of Socialist Soviet Republics.

4. The Soviet air force is authorized to fly over the territory of the Democratic Republic of Afghanistan and conduct flights in preparation for combat as well as conduct air transport for Soviet troops and to commute between the territory of the Democratic Republic of Afghanistan and the Union of Socialist Soviet Republics. This according to the rules which the command headquarters of Soviet Forces and the command headquarters of the National Forces of the DRA have agreed to.

The employment of Soviet air defense forces, which are temporarily stationed on the territory of the Democratic Republic of Afghanistan, for use against foreign violators of the airspace of the Democratic Republic of Afghanistan will be carried out according to the special regulations which the command headquarters of the Soviet Forces and the command headquarters of the National Forces of the DRA have agreed to.

5. The movement of Soviet forces between training centers and their bases will be carried out according to the plans of the command headquarters of Soviet forces.

Areas for maneuvers with participation of one division and more will be determined after discussions between responsible authorities in matters concerning the temporary stationing of Soviet Forces in the Democratic Republic of Afghanistan. This will be determined according to Article 13 of Treaty between the Government of the USSR and the government of the DRA, regarding the conditions of the temporary stationing of Soviet Forces on the territory of the Democratic Republic of Afghanistan.

6. This Protocol becomes effective simultaneously with the Treaty between the Government of the USSR and the Government of the DRA regarding the conditions for the temporary stationing of Soviet Forces in the territory of the Democratic Republic of Afghanistan, signed on ... January 1980 in two copies and is an integral part of it. It will remain in force for the duration of treaty.

Concluded in the city of   On ... January 1980 in two copies, each in Russian and Dari, whereby both texts have equal validity.

For the Government	For the government
of the Union of Socialist	Democratic Republic of
Soviet Republics	Afghanistan

English translation from German by Adamec from *Sowietische Geheimdokumente zum Afghanistankrieg* (1978-1991), Pierre Allan and Paul Bucherer, et al.

Dokument 17: 17.12 P. 253.

* German text 17: 17.2.

** List of places and garrisons placed at the disposal of Soviet forces include Faizabad, Kabul, Bala Hisar, Kota-i Ashro (Maidan), Bagram, Charikar, Jabal us-Siraj, Doshi, Khyber, Pul-i Khumri, Baghlan, Murghab (Herat), Shindand, Deh-i Nau, and Adraskan.

Airports used jointly by Soviet and Afghan forces include Shindand, Kabul, Bagram, Kandahar, and Kunduz.

Appendix 4
Draft of Protocol for Cease-Fire

Concerning Conditions for Mutual Relations Between the Leadership of Soviet Forces in Afghanistan and the Armed Opposition of Panjshir (IOAP). Motivated by good intent and a desire to consolidate peace in Afghanistan, the contraction parties have signed to the present protocol, in accordance with which they assume the following obligations:

1: To fully halt military actions in the Southern Salang and in other regions adjacent to the Kabul-Hairatan route, including any firing from any sort of weaponry upon positions held by brigades and groups of the IOA, villages, sentry brigades and posts of Soviet and Afghan troops, the MGB (Border Guards) and Tsarandoi.

2: The armed detachments of Panjsher take upon themselves responsibility for safeguarding communications between Tadzhikan and Chaugani with the aim of preventing shelling, robbery and other actions against Soviet and Afghan troops.

3: The Soviet side undertakes to provide according to mutual agreement the necessary quantity of provisions, articles of immediate necessity and other material within the time agreed upon by the parties for the material maintenance of Panjsher and those regions belonging to the indicated portion of the route.

4: Detachments and groups of other parties will not be permitted to enter the region under discussion with the goal of firing upon Soviet and Afghan columns, carrying out terrorist acts, or sabotage of the pipe-line. Should attempts by armed members of such parties to carry out these acts occur, the Soviet side expresses it willingness to provide the armed detachments of Panjsher at their requests with artillery and aviation support.

5: To exchange information and exert cooperative efforts to seek out Soviet and Afghan citizens who have disappeared within the region under discussion.

6: In the case of the heightened tensions to conduct meetings with purpose of mutual consultations concerning the avoidance of renewed military actions in the interest of maintaining peace in the specified zone.

7: The effect of the present protocol extends throughout the territory stretching for 30 kilometers in both directions from the line of communication between Tadzhikan and Chaugani. Beyond these boundaries, Soviet troops and the armed forces of Panjsher have the right to conduct operations aimed at the liquidation of armed detachments and groups belonging to any parties which have not halted military action against contracting side.

8: The present protocol takes effect from the moment of signing. Source of Information: The Operations Group of the MO SSSR in Afghanistan, December 1988 (the document was visaed by Lieutenant- General B.V. Gromov, RA Minister of Defense, Shah Nawaz Tanai, and Ahmad Shah Massoud) (Shebarshin 177-214) Boris V. Gromov, former commander of the Soviet Fortieth Army, Afghanistan, Leonid Shebarhin, former Director, First Department KGB. IOA (Islamic Society of Afghanistan).

Appendix 5

American Declaration of War

Presidential Address to the Nation
The Treaty Room

1:00 P.M. EDT
THE PRESIDENT: Good afternoon. On my orders, the United States military has begun strikes against al Qaeda terrorist training camps and military installations of the Taliban regime in Afghanistan. These carefully targeted actions are designed to disrupt the use of Afghanistan as a terrorist base of operations, and to attack the military capability of the Taliban regime.

We are joined in this operation by our staunch friend, Great Britain. Other close friends, including Canada, Australia, Germany and France, have pledged forces as the operation unfolds. More than 40 countries in the Middle East, Africa, Europe and across Asia have granted air transit or landing rights. Many more have shared intelligence. We are supported by the collective will of the world.

More than two weeks ago, I gave Taliban leaders a series of clear and specific demands: Close terrorist training camps; hand over leaders of the al Qaeda network; and return all foreign nationals, including American citizens, unjustly detained in your country. None of these demands were met. And now the Taliban will pay a price. By destroying camps and disrupting communications, we will make it more difficult for the terror network to train new recruits and coordinate their evil plans.

Initially, the terrorists may burrow deeper into caves and other entrenched hiding places. Our military action is also designed to clear the way for sustained, comprehensive and relentless operations to drive them out and bring them to justice.

At the same time, the oppressed people of Afghanistan will know the generosity of America and our allies. As we strike military targets, we'll also drop food, medicine and supplies to the starving and suffering men and women and children of Afghanistan.

The United States of America is a friend to the Afghan people, and we are the friends of almost a billion worldwide who practice the Islamic faith. The United States of America is an enemy of those who aid terrorists and of the barbaric criminals who profane a great religion by committing murder in its name.

This military action is a part of our campaign against terrorism, another front in a war that has already been joined through diplomacy, intelligence, the freezing of financial assets and the arrests of known terrorists by law enforcement agents in 38 countries. Given the nature and reach of our enemies, we will win this conflict by the patient accumulation of successes, by meeting a series of challenges with determination and will and purpose.

Today we focus on Afghanistan, but the battle is broader. Every nation has a choice to make. In this conflict, there is no neutral ground. If any government sponsors the outlaws and killers of innocents, they have become outlaws and murderers, themselves. And they will take that lonely path at their own peril.

I'm speaking to you today from the Treaty Room of the White House, a place where American Presidents have worked for peace. We're a peaceful nation. Yet, as we have learned, so suddenly and so tragically, there can be no peace in a world of sudden terror. In the face of today's new threat, the only way to pursue peace is to pursue those who threaten it.

We did not ask for this mission, but we will fulfill it. The name of today's military operation is Enduring Freedom. We defend not only our precious freedoms, but also the freedom of people everywhere to live and raise their children free from fear.

I know many Americans feel fear today. And our government is taking strong precautions. All law enforcement and intelligence agencies are working aggressively around America, around the world and around the clock. At my request, many governors have activated the National Guard to strengthen airport security. We have called up Reserves to reinforce our military capability and strengthen the protection of our homeland.

In the months ahead, our patience will be one of our strengths—patience with the long waits that will result from tighter security; patience and understanding that it will take time to achieve our goals; patience in all the sacrifices that may come.

Today, those sacrifices are being made by members of our Armed Forces who now defend us so far from home, and by their proud and worried families. A Commander-in-Chief sends America's sons and daughters into a battle in a foreign land only after the greatest care and a lot of prayer. We ask a lot of those who wear our uniform. We ask them to leave their loved ones, to travel great distances, to risk injury, even to be prepared to make the ultimate sacrifice of their lives. They are dedicated, they are honorable; they represent the best of our country. And we are grateful.

To all the men and women in our military—every sailor, every soldier, every airman, every coast guardsman, every Marine—I say this: Your mission is defined; your objectives are clear; your goal is just. You have my full confidence, and you will have every tool you need to carry out your duty.

I recently received a touching letter that says a lot about the state of America in these difficult times—a letter from a 4th-grade girl, with a father in the military: "As much as I don't want my Dad to fight," she wrote, "I'm willing to give him to you."

This is a precious gift, the greatest she could give. This young girl knows what America is all about. Since September 11, an entire generation of young Americans has gained new understanding of the value of freedom, and its cost in duty and in sacrifice.

The battle is now joined on many fronts. We will not waver; we will not tire; we will not falter; and we will not fail. Peace and freedom will prevail.

Thank you. May God continue to bless America.

END 1:07 P.M, EDT October 7, 2001.

Appendix 6

Military Technical Agreement

Between the International Security Assistance Force (ISAF) and the Interim Administration of Afghanistan ('Interim Administration').

Preamble
Referring to the 'Agreement on Provisional Arrangements in Afghanistan pending the Re-establishment of Permanent Government Institutions,' signed in Bonn on 5 December 2001 ('Bonn Agreement'), The Interim Administration welcomes the provisions of United Nations Security Council Resolution (UNSCR) 1386.
The ISAF welcomes the Interim Administration's commitment in the Bonn Agreement to co-operate with the international community in the fight against terrorism, drugs and organised crime and to respect international law and maintain peaceful and friendly relations with neighbouring countries and the rest of the international community.

Article I: General Obligations

1. The Interim Administration understands and agrees that the Bonn Agreement requires a major contribution on its part and will make strenuous efforts to co-operate with the ISAF and with the international organisations and agencies which are assisting it.
2. Interim Administration understands and agrees the Mission of the ISAF is to assist it in the maintenance of the security in the area of responsibility as defined below at Article I paragraph 4(g).
3. The Interim Administration agrees to provide the ISAF with any information relevant to the security and safety of the ISAF mission, its personnel, equipment and locations.
4. For the purposes of this Military Technical Agreement, the following

expressions shall have the meaning described below:

    a. 'The Parties' are the Interim Administration and the ISAF.
    b. 'ISAF' includes all military personnel together with their aircraft, vehicles, armoured vehicles, stores, equipment, communications, ammunition, weapons and provisions as well as the civilian components of such forces, air and surface movement resources and their support services.
    c. The 'Interim Administration' is the organisation as detailed in the Bonn Agreement.
    d. 'Military Units' includes all Afghan factions, armed representatives or personnel with a military capability, to include all mujahidin, armed forces, and armed groups, other than the 'Police Force' defined at paragraph 4e. The definition of 'Military Units' in this context does not include the ISAF, Coalition Forces or other recognised national military forces.
    e. The Interim Administration 'Police Force' means individuals who have been formally appointed as Police by the Interim Administration, are recognisable, and carry official identification. The Police Force includes the national security police, the criminal police, the uniform police, the traffic police and the border police.
    f. 'Host Nation Support' (HNS) is the civil and military assistance rendered by the Interim Administration to the ISAF within Afghanistan.
    g. Area of Responsibility (AOR) is the area marked out on the map attached at Annex B (not included).
    h. 'Coalition Forces' are those national military elements of the U.S.-led international coalition prosecuting the 'War on Terrorism' within Afghanistan. The ISAF is not part of the 'Coalition Forces.'
    i. An 'Offensive Action' is any use of armed military force.
    j. Designated Barracks to be agreed between the parties and to be detailed at Annex C.

5. It is understood and agreed that once the ISAF is established, its membership may change.

Article II: Status of the International Security Assistance Force

1. The arrangements regarding the Status of the ISAF are at Annex A.

Article III: Provision of Security and Law and Order

1. The Interim Administration recognises that the provision of security and law and order is their responsibility. This will include maintenance and support of a recognised Police Force operating in accordance with internationally recognised standards and Afghanistan law and with respect for internationally recognised human rights and fundamental freedoms, and by taking other measures as appropriate.
2. The Interim Administration will ensure that all Afghan Military Units come under its command and control in accordance with the Bonn Agreement. The Interim Administration agrees it will return all Military Units based in Kabul into designated barracks detailed at Annex C as soon as possible. Such units will not leave those Barracks without the prior approval of the Interim Administration and notification to the ISAF Commander by the Chairman of the Interim Administration.
3. The Interim Administration will refrain from all Offensive Actions within the AOR.
4. A Joint Co-ordinating Body (JCB) will meet on a regular basis. The JCB will comprise of designated Interim Administration officials and senior ISAF representatives. The purpose of the JCB will be to discuss current and forthcoming issues and to resolve any disputes that may arise.

Article IV: Deployment of the ISAF

1. UNSCR 1386 authorises the establishment for six months of an international force to assist the Interim Administration in the maintenance of security in the AOR. The Interim Administration understands and agrees that the ISAF is the international force authorised by UNSCR 1386 and may be composed of ground, air and maritime units from the international community.
2. The Interim Administration understands and agrees that the ISAF Commander will have the authority, without interference or permission, to do all that the Commander judges necessary and proper, including the use of military force, to protect the ISAF and its Mission.
3. The Interim Administration understands and agrees the ISAF will have complete and unimpeded freedom of movement throughout the territory and airspace of Afghanistan. The ISAF will agree with the Interim Administration its use of any areas or facilities needed to carry out its responsibilities as required for its support, training and operations, with such advance notice as may be practicable.
4. In consultation with the Interim Administration, the ISAF Commander

is authorised to promulgate appropriate rules for the control and regulation of surface military traffic throughout the AOR.

5. The ISAF will have the right to utilise such means and services as required to ensure its full ability to communicate and will have the right to the unrestricted use of all of the electromagnetic spectrum, free of charge, for this purpose. In implementing this right, the ISAF will make every reasonable effort to co-ordinate with and take into account the needs and requirements of the Interim Administration.

Article V: Illustrative Tasks of the ISAF

1. The ISAF will undertake a range of tasks in Kabul and surrounding areas in support of its Mission. ISAF will make every reasonable effort to co-ordinate with and take into account the needs and requirements of the Interim Administration. Possible tasks, which may be undertaken jointly with Interim Administration Forces, will include protective patrolling.

2. By mutual agreement between the ISAF Commander and the Interim Administration the ISAF may:
   a. Assist the Interim Administration in developing future security structures.
   b. Assist the Interim Administration in reconstruction.
   c. Identify and arrange training and assistance tasks for future Afghan security forces.

3. The ISAF will liaise with such political, social and religious leaders as necessary to ensure that religious, ethnic and cultural sensitivities in Afghanistan are appropriately respected by the ISAF.

Article VI: Identification

1. ISAF personnel will wear uniforms and may carry arms if authorised by their orders. Police Force personnel, when on duty, will be visibly identified by uniform or other distinctive markings and may carry arms if authorised by the Interim Administration.

Article VII: Final Authority to Interpret

1. The ISAF Commander is the final authority regarding interpretation of this Military Technical Agreement.

Article VIII: Summary

1. The purposes of the obligations and responsibilities set out in this Arrangement are as follows:
   a. To provide the necessary support and technical arrangements for the ISAF to conduct its Mission.
   b. To outline the responsibilities of the Interim Administration in relation to the ISAF.

Article IX: Final Provisions

1. Certified copies of this Military Technical Agreement will be supplied in Dari and Pashto language versions. For the purposes of interpretation the English language version of this Military Technical Agreement is authoritative.

Article X: Entry Into Force

1. This agreement will enter into force upon signature by the Participants.

Signed: Yunus Qanuni	Gen. McColl
Minister of Interior	COMISAF
On behalf of Interim Administration	On behalf of International Security Assistance Force

Witnessed by BG DE Kratzer
for Lt. Gen. PT Mikolashek
Coalition Forces Land Component Commander

Annexes:
A. Arrangements Regarding the Status of the International Security Assistance Force.
B. Map of Area of Responsibility. Not provided.
C. Designated Barracks. Not provided

Annexes are not listed.

This agreement has been superceded by the **United States-Afghanistan Strategic Partnership.**

Appendix 7

English-Afghan Military Terms

Adjudant	rais-i arkan
Admiral	amir al-bahri
Advance	pishraft
Aide-de-Camp	yawar
Air Force	quwa-i hawai
Airplane, Fighter	taiyara-i muhariba
Airplane, Bomber	taiyara-i bambandaz
Airplane Reconnaissance	taiyara-i kashf
Air Raid	hujum-i hawai
Ambush	kamin, shabkhun zadan
Ammunition	jabbakhana
Antiaircraft	dafi-i taiyara (hawai)
Anti-Tank	dafi-i tank
Approach	taqarrub
Armor	zira
Artillery, Heavy	topchi sangin
Artillery, Mountain	topchi jabal
Assault Troups	Qashun-i hujumi
Ballistic Missile	roket-i balistik
Barbed Wire	sim-i khardar
Barracks	qishla, barak
Base	markaz
Battle	muhariba
Battle Field	maidan-i jang

Bayonet	barcha
Blockade	muhasara
Bomber	bam andaz
Bunker	penahgah
Camouflage	satro ikhfa
Cartridge	kartus
Cavalry	risala
Cease-Fire	atesh bas
Close Formation	halat-i tajammu
Combatant	muharib
Command	qumanda
Commando	quwa-i dharba
Conceal	tasatur kardan
Convoy	qatar, badraqah
Corps	qul-i urdu
Counterattack	hujum-i muqabila
Counteroffensive	hujum-i mutaqabil
Covering Fire	atesh-i himaya
Cross Fire	atesh-i miqrazi
Defeat	shikast
Deploy	inbisat
Depot	tahwil khana, dipo
Desert	firar kardan
Detachment	qit'a
Detonate	infilaq kardan
Disarm	khal-i salah kardan
Drill	ta'lim-i warziah
Dugout	mahalli mahfuz
Forage	azuqa-i asbha
Formation	tartib
Grenade, Hand	bam-i dasti
Guard	muhafiz
Guide	rahbar
Infantry	piyada
Intelligence	istikhbarat
Irregular	ghair nizami
Leader	sar afsar
Liaison Officer	mamur-i ertibat
Machine Gun	mashindar
Maneuver	manawr
Marksman	nishanchi

Martial Law	hukumat-i askari
Military	askari
Mobile	harakat
Mortar	men andaz
Night Operations	'amaliat-i shabana
Raid	hujum-i nagahani
Rank	qatar
Rearguard	dumdar
Reconnoiter	kashf kardan
Reinforce	taqwiyah kardan
Revolver	tufangcha
Rocket	raket
Round of Fire	marmi
Sapper	istihkam
Scout	kashshaf
Shell	gulla
Signals	isharat
Small Arms	asliha-i khafifa
Sniper	nishanchi mahir
Staff	arkan
Staging Area	markaz-i amaliat
Stronghold	sangar-i makam
Supply, Supplies	azraq wa ikmalat
Tank	tank
Telegraph	tiligiraf
Transmitter	mursila
Transport	naqliyat
Warlords	Jangsalaran
War of Attrition	jang-i farsayeshi

BIBLIOGRAPHY

The sources presented in the following sections are a representative selection of books and articles in English with also a few titles in French and German.

The reader who desires a comprehensive survey for older titles may refer to the bibliographies by Keith McLachlan and William Whittaker (1983) and the two-volume *Bibliographie der Afghanistan-Literatur* (1968 and 1969), which also lists sources in Dari and Pashtu. The existence of the Internet has made bibliographies dated, for anyone can now consult the Library of Congress catalog from a personal computer.

No reference works dealing specifically with Afghan military history from 1747 to the 1990s exist. Standard reference works such as *Brassey's Battles*, by John Laffin; *A Dictionary of Battles*, by David Eggenberger; and *The Encyclopedia of Military History: From 3,500 B.C. to the Present*, by Ernest R. Dupuy and Trevor N. Dupuy, are too large in scope to be useful for Afghan military history.

However, there are a good number of excellent sources examining various periods of Afghan military history, most of them produced by British authors for the period from 1747 to the early 20th century. They include official accounts of Anglo-Afghan wars, such as *The First Afghan War and Its Causes*, by Sir Henry M. Durand; *The Afghan Wars 1839–42 and 1878–80*, by A. Forbes; *History of the War in Afghanistan*, by Sir J. W. Kaye; *Signal Catastrophe: The Story of the Disastrous Retreat from Kabul, 1842*, by Patrick A. Macrory; *The First Afghan War, 1838–42*, by James A. Norris; and *Journal of the Disasters in Afghanistan, 1841–2*, by Lady F. Sale.

Major works on the second Anglo-Afghan war include *The Second Afghan War, 1878–80*, an abridged official account by F. G. Cardew; *Recollections of the Kabul Campaign, 1879 and 1880*, by Joshua Duke; *The Second Afghan War, 1878–79–80, Its Causes, Its Conduct, and Its Consequences*, by Henry B. Hanna; *The Afghan War of 1879–80*, by

Howard Hensman; *The Second Afghan War, 1878–80*, Official Account by the Indian Army Intelligence Branch; *Kurum, Kabul & Kandahar, Being a Brief Record of Impressions of Three Campaigns Under General Roberts*, by Charles G. Robertson; and finally *The Afghan Campaigns of 1878–80, Compiled from Official and Private Sources*, by Sydney Shadbolt. Numerous military officers published books on their exploits.

For the short, third Anglo-Afghan war, the reader will have to rely on *Afghanistan, 1919: An Account of Operations in the Third Afghan War*, by George N. Molesworth, and on the official account of *The Third Afghan War, 1919*, by the General Staff Branch of Army Headquarters in India.

An excellent account of all three Anglo-Afghan wars was produced by T. A. Heathcote, entitled *The Afghan Wars, 1839–1919*. The recent period, including the Soviet intervention in Afghanistan and the Afghan civil war, is discussed at great length by participants, journalists, world travelers, and others. A most important source for the Soviet involvement in Afghanistan is the *Sowietische Geheimdokumente zum Afghanistankrieg (1978–1991)* by Pierre Allan, Paul Bucherer, et al. It lists numerous Soviet archival documents in Russian and German. Another important German source is *Zwischen Bürokratie und Ideologie: Entscheidungsprozesse in Moskaus Afghanistankonflikt*, by Pierre Allan and Dieter Kläy. Major works dealing with the technical aspects of the war are *Russia's War in Afghanistan*, by David C. Isby, as well as several of his other publications; *The Stumbling Bear: Soviet Military Performance*, by Scott McMichael; *The Bear Trap: Afghanistan's Untold Story*, by Mohammad Yousaf and Mark Adkin; and *War in Afghanistan*, by Mark Urban. An excellent work that deals with the *Afgantsy* (Soviet veterans) and the political impact of the war on the Soviet Union is *Afghanistan: The Soviet Union's Last War* by Mark Galeotti.

Many other excellent works, too many to list here, will be found in this select bibliography dealing with the social, economic, and political aspects of the war. *Islam and Resistance in Afghanistan*, by Olivier Roy; *Afghanistan and the Soviet Union*, by Henry S. Bradsher; and *Afghanistan's Two Party Communism*, by Anthony Arnold have become classics. An excellent recent addition to the literature is Barnett R. Rubin's *The Fragmentation of Afghanistan*.

Important works on the Taliban and al-Qaeda include all publications by Olivier Roy, including his latest with Miriam Abu Zahab, titled *Islamist Networks: The Afghanistan-Pakistan Connection*. Rohan Gunaratna's *Inside Al Qaeda: Global Network of Terror* is a major contribution to the field. Ahmad Rashid's classic *The Taliban: Islam, Oil, and the New Great Game in Central Asia*, as well as his articles in the *Far Eastern Economic Review* are must reading.

On the United States intervention in Afghanistan, Anthony H. Cordesman is the military authority. George Crile's *Charlie Wilson's War: The Extraordinary Story of the Largest Covert Operation in History* deals with American support of the mujahedin in the war against the communist regime. Bob Woodward's *Bush at War* offers valuable insights into the policy-making process. An excellent work on the "secret history" of the CIA and its campaign against Islamic radicals is *Ghost Wars: The Secret History of the CIA, Afghanistan, and Bin Laden, from the Soviet Invasion to September 10, 2001*. Another recent publication is Schroen, Gary C. *First In: An Insider's Account of How the CIA Spearheaded the War on Terror in Afghanistan* New York: Presidio Press/Ballantine Books, 2005.

For general background, *The Historical Dictionary of Afghanistan* by this author is a handy reference source on Afghanistan, describing major events, important places, leading personalities—up to 2003—and significant aspects of culture, religion, and economy. His *Historical Dictionary of Islam*, also published under the title *The A to Z of Islam*, is a source on Islamic history, religion, philosophy, and political movements. John L. Esposito's publications on Islam and his latest book, *Unholy War: Terror in the Name of Islam*, investigates the religious aspects of unrest in the Islamic world.

CONTENTS

1.	References	369
2.	General	371
3.	War of Independence to First Afghan War	374
4.	Second Afghan War to 1901	377
5.	From 1901 to the Third Afghan War	381
6.	Soviet Intervention and Afghan Civil War	381
7.	Taliban and al-Qaeda	395
8.	United States Intervention	398

1. References

Adamec, Ludwig W. *Biographical Dictionary of Afghanistan.* Graz: Akademische Druck u. Verlagsanstalt (ADEVA) 1987.

———. *Historical Dictionary of Afghanistan.* 1st ed. 1991, 2nd ed. 1997, 3rd ed. Lanham, MD: Scarecrow Press, 2003.

———. *Historical and Political Gazetteer of Afghanistan.* 6 vols. Graz: ADEVA, 1972–1985.

———. *Historical and Political Who's Who of Afghanistan.* Graz: ADEVA, 1974.

Banks, Arthur. *A World Atlas of Military History, 1861–1945.* New York: Hippocrene Books, 1973.

Bellers, Jürgen, Thorsten Brenner, and Ines Gerke. *Handbuch der Aussenpolitik: Von Afghanistan bis Zypern.* Munich: R. Oldenbourg, 2001.

Black, J. L. *The Soviet Union and Afghanistan.* Institute of Soviet and East European Studies, Bibliography No. 2. Carleton University, 1983.

Bonarjee, Pitt D. *A Handbook of the Fighting Races of India.* Calcutta: Asian Publication Services, 1899.

Brereton, John M. *The Horse in War.* New York: Arco, 1976.

Burdett, Anita L. P. *Afghanistan: Intelligence Records, 1919–1973.* Slough: Archive Editions, 2002.

———. *Afghanistan Strategic Intelligence: British Records, 1919–1970.* London: Archives Editions, 2002.

Davis, Anthony. "The Afghan Army." *Jane's Intelligence Review* 5, no. 3 (March 1993).

Dupuy, R. Ernest, and Trevor N. Dupuy. *The [Jane's] Encyclopedia of Military History: From 3,500 B.C. to the Present.* London: Harper & Row, 1970 and 1986.

Eggenberger, David. *A Dictionary of Battles.* New York: Crowell, 1967.

Evans, Ann, Nick Manning, Yasin Osmani, Anne Tully, and Andrew Wilder. *A Guide to Government in Afghanistan.* Washington, DC: The World Bank, 2004.

Farrow, Edward S. *Farrow's Military Encyclopedia.* 3 vols. New York: The Author, 1885.

General Staff, India. *Military Report, Afghanistan.* Pt. 1, *History.* Simla: General Staff, 1940.

Harbottle, Thomas B. *Dictionary of Battles from the Earliest Date to the Present Time.* London: Gale Research Co., 1904.

Hayward, P. H. *Jane's Dictionary of Military Terms*. London: Macdonald, 1975.
Hogg, Oliver F. G. *Artillery: Its Origin, Heyday, and Decline*. Hamden, CT: Archon Books, 1970.
Intelligence Branch, Chief of Staff. *Frontier and Overseas Expeditions from India*. Vol. 3. Calcutta: Government of India Press, 1910.
Katz, David J. "Afghanistan Biographic Database Comprehensive List." Washington, DC: Department of State, 1989.
Keegan, John. *A History of Warfare*. London: Hutchinson, 1993.
Keegan, John, and Andrew Wheatcroft. *Who's Who in Military History*. London: Weidenfeld and Nicolson, 1976.
Knollys, William W. *A Handy Dictionary of Military Terms*. London, 1873.
Luttwak, Edward. *Dictionary of Modern War*. New York: Harper & Row, 1971.
Maguire, Thomas M. *A Summary of Modern Military History with Comments on the Leading Operations*. London: no pub., 1887.
Maksey, Kenneth. *The Penguin Encyclopedia of Weapons and Military Technology from Prehistory to the Present*. New York: Viking, 1993.
McLachlan, Keith, and William Whittaker. *A Bibliography of Afghanistan*. London: Menas Press, 1983.
Military Thought, 1937–1973. *Chronological, Author, and Title Index*. Washington, DC: Defense Intelligence College, 1981.
Nicolls, Sir Jasper. Commander-in-Chief, India. *Private Papers*. London: India Office Library.
Pant, G. N. *Studies in Indian Weapons and Warfare*. New Delhi: no pub., 1970.
Parkinson, Roger. *Encyclopedia of Modern War*. New York: Stein and Day, 1977.
Polmar, Norman et al. *Dictionary of Military Abbreviations*. Annapolis, MD: Naval Institute Press, 1994.
Ridgway, R. T. I. *The Pathans*. Calcutta: Government of India Press, 1910.
Saleem, Uzma. *Web Guide to Afghanistan*. Karachi: Church World Service Pakistan/Afghanistan, 2002.
Scott, Harriet Fast, and William F. Scott. *The Armed Forces of the USSR*. Boulder, CO: Westview Press, 1984.
Spaulding, Oliver L. et al. *Warfare: A Study of Military Methods from the Earliest Times*. Washington, DC: Infantry Journal Press, 1957.

U.S. Army Field Manual 100-2-3. *The Soviet Army: Troops, Organization and Equipment.* Washington, DC: U.S. Government Printing Office, 1984.

Wilhelm, Thomas. *A Military Dictionary and Gazetteer.* Philadelphia: L. R. Hamersly, 1881.

Wragg, David W. *Dictionary of Aviation.* Reading, UK: Osprey Publishing, 1974.

Yunas, S. Fida. *Afghanistan: Treaties, Agreements, Protocols, Contracts, etc. During the Period 1976-1990.* Peshawar: Area Studies Center, University of Peshawar, 2002.

2. General

Adamec, Ludwig W. *Afghanistan 1900–1923: A Diplomatic History.* Berkeley: University of California Press, 1967.

———. *Afghanistan's Foreign Affairs to the Mid-Twentieth Century: Relations with the USSR, Germany, and Britain.* Tucson: University of Arizona Press, 1974.

Ahady, Anwar-ul-Haq. "Afghanistan: State Breakdown." In *Revolutions of the Late Twentieth Century.* Edited by Jack A. Goldstone et al. Boulder, CO: Westview Press, 1991.

Al-Amri, Abdullah Sager. "The Doctrine of Jihad in Islam and Its Application in the Context of the Islamic Jihad Movement in Afghanistan, 1979–1988." Master's Thesis, University of Idaho, 1990.

Anglesey, Marquess of. *A History of the British Cavalry: 1816 – 1919.* London: Shoe String Press, 1973.

Argyll, George. *The Afghan Question from 1841 to 1878.* London: Strahan, 1879.

Baden-Powell, Sir Robert. *Memories of India: Recollections of Soldiering and Sport.* Philadelphia, PA: D. McKay, 1905.

Banuazizi, Ali, and Myron Weiner, eds. *The State, Religion and Ethnic Politics: Afghanistan, Iran and Pakistan.* Syracuse, NY: Syracuse University Press, 1986.

Barton, Sir William. *India's North-West Frontier.* London: J. Murray, 1939.

Bellew, Henry W. *Afghanistan and the Afghans.* London: Sampson Low Maiston, 1979.

Bonner, Arthur. *Among the Afghans.* Durham, NC: Duke University Press, 1987.

Caroe, Olaf K. *The Pathans, 550 B.C.–A.D. 1957*. London: Oxford University Press, 1958.
Cohen, Stephen P. *The Indian Army: Its Contribution to the Development of a Nation*. Berkeley: University of California Press, 1971.
Colton, T., and T. Gustafson, eds. *Soldiers and the Soviet State*. Princeton, NJ: Princeton University Press, 1990.
Cotton, Sydney J. *Nine Years on the North-West Frontier of India from 1854–63*. London: Bentley, 1868.
Delloy, Isabelle. *Women of Afghanistan*. Saint Paul, MN: Ruminator Books, 2003.
Dupree, Louis. *Afghanistan*. Princeton, NJ: Princeton University Press, 1973.
Elliot, James G. *The Frontier 1839–1947: The Story of the North-West Frontier of India*. London: Cassell, 1968.
Elphinstone, Mountstuart. *An Account of the Kingdom of Caubul, and Its Dependencies in Persia, Tartary, and India; Comprising a View of the Afghaun Nation, and a History of the Dooraunee Monarchy*. London, 1815; Graz: ADEVA, 1969.
Fraser-Tytler, W. K. *Afghanistan, A Study of Political Development in Central Asia*. London: Oxford University Press, 1958.
Galeotti, Mark. *The Age of Anxiety: Security and Politics in Soviet and Post-Soviet Russia*. London: Frank Cass, 1994.
Gaury, Gerald de, and H. V. F. Winstone. *The Road to Kabul*. London: Quartet Books, 1981.
Ghani, Ashraf. *Production and Domination: Afghanistan, 1747–1901*. NY: Columbia University Press, 1986.
Goddard, E. "The Indian Army; Company and Raj." *ASA* 63 (Oct. 1976).
Gregorian, Vartan. *The Emergence of Modern Afghanistan: Politics of Reform and Modernization, 1880–1946*. Stanford, CA: Stanford University Press, 1969.
Groetzbach, Erwin. *Afghanistan*. Darmstadt: Wissenschaftliche Buchgesellschaft, 1990.
Hamilton, Angus. *Afghanistan*. New York: Charles Scribner's Sons, 1906.
Kakar, Hasan. *Afghanistan: A Study in Internal Political Developments, 1880–1896*. Lahore: Punjab Educational Press, 1971.
———. *Government and Society in Afghanistan: The Reign of Amir Abd al-Rahman Khan*. Austin: Texas University Press, 1979.
Keppel, Arnold. *Gun-Running and the Indian North-West Frontier*. Quetta: Gosha-e-Adab, 1977.
Lala, Mohana. *Life of the Amir Dost Mohammed Khan of Kabul*. Karachi: Oxford University Press, 1846.

Lockhart, L. *The Fall of the Safavi Dynasty and the Afghan Occupation of Persia.* Cambridge: Cambridge University Press, 1958.

Martin, Denyse R. *The Postal History of the First Afghan War, 1838–1842.* London: Bath, 1964.

Marvin, Charles. *Reconnoitring Central Asia: Pioneering Adventure in the Region Lying between Russia and India.* London: Swan Sonnenschein, 1884.

Miller, Charles. *Khyber: The Story of an Imperial Migraine.* New York: Macmillan, 1977.

Morison, Frederick. *From Alexander Burnes to Frederick Roberts: A Survey of Imperial Frontier Policy.* London: no pub., 1936.

Nabi, Eden. *The Modernization of Inner Asia.* No pub. Date, 1991.

Nevill, Hugh L. *Campaigns on the North-West Frontier.* London, 1912. Reprint, Lahore: Sang-e Meel Publication, 1977.

Nichols, Robert. *The Frontier "Tribal" Areas, 1840–1990.* New York: Afghanistan Forum, 1995.

Nyrop, Richard F., and Donald Seekins, eds. *Afghanistan: A Country Study.* Washington, DC: American University Press, 1986.

Orywal, Erwin. *Die Ethnischen Gruppen Afghanistans.* Wiesbaden: Ludwig Reichert Verlag, 1986.

Poullada, Leon B. *Reform and Rebellion in Afghanistan, 1919–1929.* Ithaca, NY: Cornell University Press, 1973.

———. "Afghanistan and the United States: The Crucial Years." *Middle East Journal* 35 (1981).

Rasanayagam, Angelo. *Afghanistan, A Modern History: Monarchy, Despotism, or Democracy? The Problem of Governance in the Muslim Tradition.* London: I. B. Tauris, 2003.

Raverty, H. G. *Notes on Afghanistan and Baluchistan.* London, 1888. Reprint, Quetta: Gosha-e Adab, 1976.

Richards, D. S. *The Savage Frontier.* London: Macmillan, 1990.

Roberts, Jeffery J. *The Origins of Conflict in Afghanistan.* Westport, CT: Praeger, 2003.

Rodenbough, Theodore F. *Afghanistan and the Anglo-Russian Dispute: An Account of Russia's Advance toward India.* New York: G. P. Putnam, 1885.

Saikal, Amin. *Modern Afghanistan: A History of Struggle and Survival.* New York: I. B. Tauris, 2004.

Shahrani, M. Nazif. "State Building and Social Fragmentation in Afghanistan: An Historical Perspective." In *State, Religion and Ethnic Politics.* Edited by A. Banuazizi and M. Weiner. Syracuse, NY: Syracuse University Press, 1986.

Singh, Ganda. *Ahmad Shah Durrani*. Bombay: Asia Publishing, 1959.
Swinson, Arthur. *North-West Frontier: People and Events, 1839–1947*. New York: Praeger, 1967.
Sykes, Sir Percy. *A History of Afghanistan*. London: Macmillan, 1940.
Tarzi, Nanguyalai. *Les Relations Afghano-Russe*. Paris: Université de Paris, 1970.
Wylly, Col. Harold C. *From the Black Mountain to Waziristan, being an Account of the Border Countries and the More Turbulent of the Tribes Controlled by the North West Frontier Province, and of Our Military Relations with Them in the Past*. London: Macmillan, 1912.

3. War of Independence to First Afghan War

Abbott, Augustus. *The Afghan War, 1839–42: From the Journal and Correspondence of Major-General Augustus Abbott*. Edited by Charles Low. London: Richard Bentley, 1879.
Allan, J. "The Strategic Principles of Lord Lytton's Afghan Policy." *Journal of the Royal Central Asian Society* 24 (1937).
Allen, Isaac N. *Diary of a March Through Sinde and Afghanistan with the Troops under the Command of General Sir William Nott and Sermons Delivered on Various Occasions during the Campaign of 1842*. London: Hatchard, 1843.
Atkinson, James. *The Expedition into Afghanistan: Personal Narrative of the Campaign, 1839–40, Up to the Surrender of Dost Muhammad Khan*. London: W. H. Allen, 1842.
Bajwa, Fauja S. *The Military System of the Sikhs During the Period 1799–1849*. Delhi: Motilal Banarsidas, 1964.
Barr, William. *Journal of the March from Delhi to Caubul with the Mission of Sir C. M. Wade*. London: James Madden, 1844.
Barthrop, Michael. "The Sorties from Jellalabad 1842." *Journal of the Society for Army Historical Research* (JSAHR) 56 (summer 1976).
Buist, George. *Outline of the Operations in Scinde and Afghanistan*. Bombay: Times Office, 1843.
Colonial Society, East India Committee. *Report of the East India Committee of the Colonial Society on the Causes and Consequences of the Afghan War*. London: James Maynard, 1842.
Dennie, William H. *Personal Narrative of the Campaigns in Afghanistan*. Dublin: W. Curry, 1843. Compiled and arranged by William E. Steele.
Diver, Katherine H. M. *Kabul to Kandahar*. London: John Murray, 1935.
Diver, Maud. *The Hero of Herat*. London: John Murray, 1924.

———. *The Judgment of the Sword*. London: John Murray, 1913.

Dupree, Louis. "Afghan and British Military Tactics in the First Anglo-Afghan War (1838–1842)." *Army Quarterly and Defence Journal* (AQ) 107 (April 1977).

———. "The Retreat of the British Army from Kabul to Jalalabad in 1842: History and Folklore." *Journal of the Folklore Institute* (1967).

Dupree, Nancy H. "The Question of Jalalabad during the First Anglo-Afghan War." *Asian Affairs* 62 (Feb. and June 1975).

Durand, Sir Henry M. *The First Afghan War and Its Causes*. London: Longmans, Green, 1879.

Ewans, Martin. *Afghanistan: A New History*. London: Routledge Curzon, 2001.

Eyre, Vincent. *The Military Operations at Caubul*. London: W. H. Allen, 1843.

Fane, Henry E. *Five Years in India: Comprising a Narrative of Travels in the Presidency of Bengal, a Visit to the Court of Runjeet Sing, a Residence in the Himalayah Mountains, and Account of the Late Expedition to Kabul and Afghanistan*. London: Henry Colburn, 1842.

Forbes, A. *The Afghan Wars 1839–42 and 1878–80*. London: Seeley, 1892.

Gleig, G. R. *With Sale's Brigade in Afghanistan*. London: John Murray, 1846.

Greenwood, J. *Narrative of the Late Victorious Campaign in Afghanistan*. London: H. Colburn, 1844.

Havelock, Henry. *Narrative of the War in Afghanistan: In 1838–39*. 2 vols. London: Henry Colburn, 1840.

Heathcote, T. A. *The Afghan Wars, 1839–1919*. London: Osprey, 1980.

Holdsworth, T. W. E. *The Campaign of the Indus*. London: T. C. Saville, 1840.

Hough, William. *A History of British Military Exploits*. London: W. H. Allen, 1853.

———. *Narrative of the March and Operations of the Army of the Indus*. London: W. H. Allen, 1841.

Jacob, John. *Memoir of the First Campaign in the Hills North of Cutchee, under Major Billamore, in 1839–40, by One of His Surviving Subalterns*. London: no pub., 1852.

James, David. *Lord Roberts*. London: Hollis and Carter, 1954.

Kaye, Sir J. W. *History of the War in Afghanistan*. London: W. H. Allen, 1890.

———. *The Lives of Indian Officers*. London: A. Straham, 1867.

———. *Long Engagements: A Tale of the Afghan Rebellion*. London, 1846.

Kennedy, Richard H. *Narrative of the Campaign of the Army of the Indus, in Sind and Kabool in 1838–39*. 2 vols. London: Richard Bentley, 1840.

Lawrence, Sir George. *Reminiscences*. London: John Murray, 1875.

Low, C. R. *The Life of Sir George Pollock*. London: W. H. Allen, 1873.

———. *The Afghan War 1838–42: From the Journal and Correspondence of Major-General Augustus Abbott*. London: Richard Bentley, 1879.

Lunt, James. "The Illustrious Garrison." *History Today* 16 July 1966.

———. "Lady Sale in Kabul, 1842." *History Today* 9 October 1959.

Mackinnon, Daniel H. *Military Service and Adventures in the Far East: Including Sketches of the Campaigns Against the Afghans in 1839, and the Sikhs in 1845–6*. 2 vols. London: John Oliver, 1847.

Macrory, Patrick A. *The Fierce Pawns*. Philadelphia: J. B. Lippincott, 1966.

———. *Signal Catastrophe: The Story of the Disastrous Retreat from Kabul, 1842*. London: Hodder and Stoughton, 1966.

Malleson, George B. *Decisive Battles of India, 1746–1849*. London: W. H. Allen, 1883.

Melville, William H. *Remarks on the War in Afghanistan*. Edinburgh: no pub., 1842.

Neill, John M. B. *Recollections of Four Years' Service in the East with His Majesty's 40th Regiment: Comprising an Account of the Taking of Kurachee in Lower Scinde, in 1839; Operations of the Candahar Division of the Avenging Army of Afghanistan in 1841 and 1842; Under Major General Sir W. Nott*. London: R. Bentley, 1845.

Norris, James. A. *The First Afghan War, 1838–42*. London: Cambridge University Press, 1967.

O'Ballance, Edgar. *Afghan Wars 1839–1992*. London: Brassey's, 1993.

Outram, James. *Rough Notes of the Campaign in Sinde and Afghanistan*. London: J. M. Richardson, 1840.

Pearse, H. W. "First Forcing of the Khaibar Pass, 1838–39." *Journal of the Royal United Service Institution* (JRUSI) 41 (April 1897).

Pottinger, George. *The Afghan Connection*. Edinburgh: Scottish Academic Press, 1983.

———. *The Ten-Rupee Jezail: Figures in the First Afghan War 1838–1842*. Norwich: M. Russell, 1993.

Rawling, Gerald. "Afghan Disaster." *British History Illustrated* (BHI), 4 (September 1977).
Roberts, F. S. *Forty-One Years in India*. 2 vols. London: Richard Bentley, 1900.
Sale, Lady F. *Journal of the Disasters in Afghanistan, 1841–2*. London: John Murray, 1843.
Sale, Robert H. *The Defence of Jellalabad*. London: W. L. Walton, 1846.
Stocqueler, J. H. *Memorials of Afghanistan*. Calcutta, 1843. Reprint, Peshawar: Saeed Jan Qureshi, 1983.
Taylor, William. *Scenes and Adventures in Afghanistan*. London: Luzac, 1847.
Trotter, Lionel. *The Earl of Auckland*. Oxford: Clarendon Press, 1890.
Urquhart, David. *The Edinburgh Review and the Afghan War: Letters Reprinted from the Morning Herald*. London: Diplomatic Review Office, 1843.
Vigne, Godfrey T. *A Personal Narrative of a Visit to Ghuzni, Kabul, and Afghanistan, and of a Residence at the Court of Dost Muhammad: With Notices of Runjit Sing, Khiva, and the Russian Expedition*. London: Whitaker, 1843.
Waller, John H. *Beyond the Khyber Pass: The Road to British Disaster in the First Afghan War*. New York: Random House, 1990.

4. Second Afghan War to 1901

Adye, John. *Indian Frontier Policy: An Historical Sketch*. London: Elder, 1897.
———. *Sitana: A Mountain Campaign on the Borders of Afghanistan in 1863*. London: Richard Bentley, 1867.
Ali, Mohammad. "The Battle of Maiwand." *Afghanistan*, 2 October 1955, 26–38.
Anderson, J. H. *The Afghan War: 1878–1880*. London: no pub., 1905.
Ashe, Waller, ed. *Personal Records of the Kandahar Campaign, by Officers Engaged Therein*. London: David Bogue, 1881.
Bellew, Henry W. *Journal on a Political Mission to Afghanistan in 1857*. London: Smith Elder, 1862.
Brereton, John M. "Maiwand." *Blackwood's Magazine* (BLM), July 1976, 320.
———. "The Panjdeh Crisis, 1885." *History Today* 29 January 1979.

Brook, Henry F. *Private Journal of Henry Francis Brooke*. Dublin: no pub., 1881.
Brown, R. H. "Account of the Construction of Bridges Over the Kabul River, Near Jalalabad, During the Operations in Afghanistan, 1880," Ordnance Note No. 325. In United States, Ordnance Department, *Ordnance Notes*. 12 vols. Washington, DC, 1873–1884.
Bruce, G. *Retreat from Kabul*. London: Mayflower-Dell, 1967.
Cardew, F. G. *The Second Afghan War, 1878–80*. London: J. Murray, 1908. (abridged official account)
Colquhoun, James A. S. *With the Kurram Field Force, 1878–79*. London: W. H. Allen, 1881.
Combe, Boyce A. *Letters from B.A.C.: Afghanistan, 1878*. No pub.
Cotton, Sydney J. *Nine Years on the North-west Frontier of India from 1854–63*. London: no pub., 1868.
Davies, C. C. *The Problem of the North-West Frontier, 1890–1908*. London: Cambridge University Press, 1932.
Diver, Katherine H. M. *Kabul to Kandahar*. London: P. Davies, 1935.
Duke, Joshua. *Recollections of the Kabul Campaign, 1879 and 1880*. London: W. H. Allen, 1883.
Durand, Henry M. "Reminiscences of the Kabul Campaign, 1879–1880." *Blackwood's Magazine*, April and May 1917, 201.
Eastwick, William J. *Lord Lytton and the Afghan War*. London: R. J. Mitchell, 1879.
Elliott, William J. *Victoria Cross in Afghanistan, and the Frontiers of India During the Years 1877, 1878, 1879, and 1880*. London: Dean, 1882.
Gillham-Thomsett, Richard. *Kohat, Kuram, and Khost*. London: Remington, 1884.
Great Britain, War Office. *Military Operations in Afghanistan Commencing 7th June 1880*. Simla: Government of India Press, 1881.
Hambly, Sir E. "Russia's Approaches to Indian." *Journal of the Royal United Service Institution* 28 (1884).
Hamilton, Lillias. *A Vizier's Daughter: A Tale of the Hazara War*. Kabul: Shah Book, 2004.
Hanna, Henry B. *Lord Roberts in War*. London: Simpkin, 1895.
———. *The Second Afghan War, 1878–79–80: Its Causes, Its Conduct, and Its Consequences*. 3 vols. London: Constable, 1910.
———. "India's Scientific Frontier: Where Is It? What Is It?" *Indian Problems*. Westminster, Indian Problems, no. 2 (1895).
Haughton, J. C. *Chareekar and Service There*. London: Provost, 1879.

Hensman, Howard. *The Afghan War of 1879–80.* London: W. H. Allen, 1881.
Hills, John. *The Bombay Field Force 1880.* London: R. B. Johnson, 1900.
"Historic Reverse in Afghanistan: Maiwand, 1880." *Journal of the Royal United Service Institution* 78 (November 1933).
Hopkins, Adrian E. *Post Offices of the Second Afghan War, 1878–1881.* London: no pub.1965.
Hoskyns, C. "A Short Narrative of the Afghan Campaigns of 1879–80–81, from an Engineer's Point of View," Ordnance Note No. 219, September 22, 1882. In *Ordnance Notes.* Washington, DC: 1873-18-84.
India, Quartermaster-General's Department. *Photographs of Types of Native Arms; Views in Afghanistan, Taken During the War of 1879; Northwest Frontier of Hindustan, Burma, during the British Operations in That Country.* N.p., 1895.
Intelligence Branch, Army Headquarters, India. *The Second Afghan War, 1878–80.* (Abridged official account, compiled by S. P. Oliver.) London, 1908.
Kakar, Hasan K. *The Pacification of the Hazaras of Afghanistan.* New York: The Asia Society, 1973.
Khalfin, N. A. *Afghan War of 1879–80 and the Afghan Victory of Maiwand.* Moscow: Akademia Nauk, 1980.
Le Messurier, Augustus. *Kandahar in 1879: Being the Diary of Major Le Messurier.* Reprinted with corrections and additions from the *Royal Engineer's Journal.* London: W. H. Allen, 1880.
MacGregor, Charles M. *The Defense of India: A Strategic Study.* Simla: Government Central Branch Press, 1884.

———. *The Life and Opinions of Major-General Sir Charles Metcalfe MacGregor, K.C.B., C.S.I., C.I.E., Quartermaster-General in India.* Edited by Lady MacGregor. 2 vols. London: no pub., 1888.

———. *The Second Afghan War: Compiled and Collated by and Under the Orders of Major-Genl. Sir C. M. MacGregor, K.C.B., C.S.I., C.I.E., Quartermaster-General in India.* 6 pts. Simla: no pub. 1885.
Mackenzie, Colin. *Storms and Sunshine of a Soldier's Life.* London: no pub., 1884.
Male, Arthur. *Scenes Through the Battle Smoke.* London: Dean, 1890.
Malleson, George B. *History of Afghanistan from the Earliest Period to the Outbreak of the War of 1878.* London: W. H. Allen, 1879.
Martin, Denys R. *Further Postal History of the Second Afghan War, 1878–81. With Kandahar and Baluchistan, 1881–87; A Review in the Light of Contemporary Records.* London: Bath, 1961.

Maxwell, Leigh. *My God Maiwand! Operations of the South Afghanistan Field Force, 1878–80.* London: Cooper, 1979.

Mitford, Maj. R. C. W. *To Cabul with the Cavalry Brigade: A Narrative of Personal Experiences with the Force under General Sir F. S. Roberts, G.C.B.* London: W. H. Allen, 1881.

Northbrook, The Earl of. *A Brief Account of Recent Transactions in Afghanistan.* London: Private Printing, 1880.

Owen, Col. Edward. "The Maiwand Disaster and the Investment of Kandahar." *Army Quarterly and Defence Journal* 114, no. 2 (1984): 202–7.

Roberts, Frederick S. *Afghan War, 1879–80. Despatches of Lieutenant-General Sir Frederick Sleigh Roberts.* Lahore: no pub., 1880.

———. *Forty-One Years in India: From Subaltern to Commander-in-Chief.* London: Richard Bentley, 1897.

Robertson, Charles G. *Kurum, Kabul and Kandahar, Being a Brief Record of Impressions of Three Campaigns Under General Roberts.* Edinburgh: David Douglas, 1881.

Robson, Brian. *The Road to Kabul: The Second Afghan War, 1878 – 1881.* London: Arms and Armour, 1986.

———. "Maiwand, 27th July, 1880." *Journal of the Society for Army History Research* 51 (winter 1973).

Shadbolt, Sydney H. *The Afghan Campaigns of 1878–80, Compiled from Official and Private Sources.* 2 vols. London: Sampson Low Marston, 1882.

Sobolev, Leonid N. *Anglo-Afghan Struggle: Sketch of the War of 1879–80.* Translated by Walter Gowan. Calcutta: Government Printing Press, 1885.

Swinnerton, Charles. *The Afghan War: Gough's Action at Futtehabad, April 2, 1879.* London: W. H. Allen, 1880.

Thackeray, Edward T. *Reminiscences of the Indian Mutiny and Afghanistan.* London: Smith and Elder, 1916.

Thomsett, Richard. *Kohat, Kuram, and Khost: Or Experiences and Adventures in the Late Afghan War.* London: Remington, 1884.

Throusdale, William. *War in Afghanistan, 1879–80.* Detroit: Wayne State University Press, 1985.

Wynne, Maj. A. S. "Heliography and Army Signalling Generally." *Journal of the Royal United Service Institution* 24 (1880): 235–58.

Yapp, M. E. *British Strategies of British India.* London: Oxford University Press, 1980.

5. From 1901 to the Third Afghan War

Ali Mohammad. *Afghanistan, the War of Independence, 1919.* Kabul: Afghanistan Press, 1960.
Barrow, George. *The Life of General C. C. Monro.* No pub., 1931.
Cadell, P. *History of the Bombay Army.* London: Longmans, Green, 1938.
General Staff Branch, Army Headquarters, India. *The Third Afghan War 1919.* (official account) Calcutta: India Government Press, 1926.
Molesworth, George Noble. *Afghanistan, 1919: An Account of Operations in the Third Afghan War.* Bombay: Asia Publishing House, 1962.
Niedermayer, Oskar von. *Im Weltkrieg vor Indiens Toren.* Hamburg: Hanseatische Verlagsanstalt, 1936.
Taniguchi, Masaru. *The Soldier's Log: 10,000 Miles of Battle.* Translated by R. T. Fincher and Tashi Okada [Tokyo, 1940].

6. Soviet Intervention and the Afghan Civil War

"Afghan Militiamen Defect with Government Weapons." *Jane's Defence Weekly,* 9 January 1988.
"The Afghanistan Air War." *Warplane* 1, no. 1 (1985).
Ahady, Anwar-ul-Haq. "Afghanistan: State Breakdown." In *Revolutions of the Late Twentieth Century.* Edited by Jack A. Goldstone et al. Boulder, CO: Westview, 1991.
Akram, Assem. *Histoire de la Guerre d'Afghanistan.* Paris: Editions Balland, 1996.
Alexiev, Alexander. *Inside the Soviet Army in Afghanistan.* Santa Monica, CA: RAND Corporation, 1988.
———. *The United States and the War in Afghanistan.* Santa Monica, CA: RAND Corporation, 1988.
———. *The War in Afghanistan: Soviet Strategy and the State of the Resistance.* Santa Monica, CA: RAND Corporation, 1984.
Alexievich, Svetlana. *Zinky Boys: Soviet Voices from a Forgotten War.* London: Chatto and Windus, 1992.
Allan, Pierre, and Albert Stahel. "Tribal Guerrilla Warfare Against a Colonial Power." *Journal of Conflict Resolution* (Dec. 1983).
Allan, Pierre, and Paul Bucherer, et al. *Sowietische Geheimdokumente zum Afghanistankrieg (1978–1991).* Zürich: Hochschulverlag AG, 1995.
Allan, Pierre, and Dieter Kläy. *Zwischen Bürokratie und Ideologie: Entscheidungsprozesse in Moskaus Afghanistankonflikt.* Bern: Verlag Paul Haupt, 1999.

Amstutz, J. Bruce. *Afghanistan: The First Five Years of Soviet Occupation*. Washington, DC: National Defense University Press, 1986.

Anwar, Raja. *The Tragedy of Afghanistan: A First-Hand Account*. London: Verso, 1988.

Arnold, Anthony. *Afghanistan: The Soviet Invasion in Perspective*. Stanford, CA: Hoover Institution Press, 1985.

———. *Afghanistan's Two Party Communism: Parcham and Khalq*. Stanford, CA: Hoover Institution Press, 1981.

———. "The Ephemeral Elite: The Failure of Socialist Afghanistan." In *The State and Social Transformation in Afghanistan*. Edited by A. Banuazizi and M. Weiner. Syracuse, NY: Syracuse University Press, 1986.

———. *The Fateful Pebble: Afghanistan's Role in the Fall of the Soviet Empire*. Novato, CA: Presidio Press, 1993.

Ashrati, Abdul Ahad. "Soviet Influence on the Afghan Judiciary." In *A Decade of Sovietization*. Peshawar: Elmi, 1988.

Baumann, Robert. *Russian-Soviet Unconventional Wars*. Fort Leavenworth, KS: Combat Studies Institute Press, 1993.

Belitsky, S. "Authors of USSR's Afghan War Policy." Radio Liberty Report on the USSR, 28 April 1989.

Bennigsen, Alexandre. *The Soviet Union and Muslim Guerrilla Wars, 1920–1981: Lessons for Afghanistan*. Santa Monica, CA: RAND Corporation, 1981.

Bennigsen, Alexandre et al. *Afghanistan: Dix Ans Terribles, 1977–1987*. Paris: Internationale de la Résistance, 1988.

Bergmann, Ernest. *The Soviet Adventure in Afghanistan*. No pub., 1988.

Bernstein, Carl. "Arms for Afghanistan." *New Republic*, 18 July 1981.

Bertin, Giles. "Stingers Change the Face of War in Afghanistan." *Jane's Defence Weekly*, 10 October 1987.

Blank, Stephen. *Afghanistan and Beyond: Reflections*. Carlisle Barracks, PA: Strategic Studies Institute, U.S. Army War College, 1983.

———. "Imagining Afghanistan: Lessons of a 'Small' War." *Journal of Soviet Military Studies* 3, no. 3 (1990).

Bocharov, G. *Russian Roulette: Afghanistan through Russian Eyes*. New York: Amish Hamilton, 1990.

Bodansky, Yossef. "Afghanistan: The Soviet Air War." *Defense and Foreign Affairs*, September 1985.

———. "SAMs in Afghanistan: Assessing the Impact." *Jane's Defence Weekly*, 28 July 1987.

Bonner, T. D. *Soviet Strategy Then and Now*. No pub., 1991.

Bonosky, Phillip. *Washington's Secret War Against Afghanistan.* New York: International Publishers, 1985.

Borovik, Artem. *The Hidden War: A Russian Journalist's Account of the Soviet War in Afghanistan.* Boston: Atlantic Monthly Press, 1990.

Bradsher, Henry S. *Afghan Communism and Soviet Intervention.* Oxford: Oxford University Press, 1999.

———. *Afghanistan and the Soviet Union.* Durham, NC: Duke University Press, 1983.

———. "Stagnation and Change in Afghanistan." *Journal of South Asian and Middle Eastern Studies* (fall 1986).

Brigot, Andre, and Olivier Roy. *The War in Afghanistan.* New York: Harvester, 1988.

Broxup, J. M. "The Soviets in Afghanistan: The Anatomy of a Takeover." *Central Asian Survey.* 1983.

Bruce, James. "Afghan Rebels 'Downing More Soviet Helicopters.'" *Jane's Defence Weekly*, 15 November 1986.

Bucherer-Dietschi, Paul. *Afghanistan: Vom Königreich zur Sovietischen Invasion.* Liestal: no pub., 1985.

———. *Afghanistan, 1985/86: The Effects of Soviet Occupation and Warfare.* Washington, DC: Congressional Research Service, 1987.

Canfield, Robert L. "Afghanistan: The Trajectory of Internal Alignments." *Middle East Journal* 43 (1989).

———. "Islamic Coalitions in Bamyan: A Problem in Translating Afghan Political Culture." In *Revolutions and Rebellions in Afghanistan.* Edited by Shahrani and Canfield. Berkeley, CA: Institute of International Studies, 1984

"Caravans on Moonless Nights: How the CIA Supports and Supplies the Anti-Soviet Guerrillas." *Time*, 11 June 1984.

Cardoza, Anthony A. "Soviet Aviation in Afghanistan." *U.S. Naval Institute Proceedings*, February, 1987.

Carpenter, Ted Galen. "The Unintended Consequences of Afghanistan." *World Policy Journal* 5, 11, no. 1 (spring 1994).

Cassidy, Robert M. *Russia in Afghanistan and Chechnya: Military Strategic Culture.* Carlisle Barracks, PA: Strategic Studies Institute, U.S. Army War College, 2003.

Centlivres, Pierre et al. *Afghanistan: La Colonisation Impossible.* Paris: CEREDAF, 1984.

Chaliand, Gérard. *Guerrilla Strategies: An Historical Anthology from the Long March to Afghanistan.* Berkeley: University of California Press, 1982.

———. *Report from Afghanistan.* New York: Viking, 1982.

Cherkasov. "Afghan War: The Beginning." *Soviet Soldier*, May 1990.

Cockburn, Andrew. *The Threat: Inside the Soviet Military Machine*. New York: Random House, 1983.

Cogan, Charles. *Holy Blood: An Inside View of the Afghan War*. Westport, CT: Praeger, 1993.

———. "Partners in Time: The CIA and Afghanistan." *World Policy Journal* (summer 1993).

———. "Shawl of Lead: From Holy War to Civil War in Afghanistan." *Conflict* 10, no. 3 (1990).

Coldren, Leo O. "Afghanistan in 1984: The Fifth Year of the War." *Asian Survey*, February 1985.

———. "Afghanistan in 1985: The Sixth Year of the Afghan War." *Asian Survey*, February 1985.

Collins, Joseph. *The Soviet Invasion of Afghanistan: A Study of the Use of Force in Soviet Foreign Policy*. Lexington, MA: Lexington Books, 1986.

———. "The Soviet Invasions of Afghanistan: Methods, Motives and Ramifications." *Naval War College Review* (1980).

———. "Soviet Military Performance in Afghanistan." *Comparative Strategy* 4, no. 2 (1983).

Combined Arms Training Activity. *Light Infantry in Action*. Kansas: Fort Leavenworth, 1988.

Cordesman, Anthony H. *The Lessons of Afghanistan: War Fighting, Intelligence, and Force Transformation*. Washington, DC: The CSIS Press, 2002.

Cordesman, Anthony H., and A. R. Wagner. *The Lesson of Modern War*. Vol. 3. *The Afghan and Falkland Conflicts*. Boulder, CO: Westview Press, 1991.

Cordovez, Diego, and Selig S. Harrison. *Out of Afghanistan: The Inside Story of the Soviet Withdrawal*. Oxford: Oxford University Press, 1995.

Corwin, Phillip. *Doomed in Afghanistan: A UN Officer's Memoire of the Fall of Kabul and Najibullah's Failed Escape*. New Brunswick, NJ: Rutgers University Press, 2003.

Crisis and Conflict Analysis Team. *Report on Afghanistan*. Nos. 3, 4, 5, and 6. Islamabad, 1984.

Cronin, Richard. "Afghanistan After the Soviet Withdrawal: Contenders for Power." Washington, DC: Congressional Research Service, May 1989.

Dale, Tad. *Afghanistan and Gorbachev's Global Foreign Policy.* Santa Monica, CA: RAND Corporation, 1989.
Day, Arthur R. *Escalation and Intervention: Multilateral Security and Its Alternatives.* Boulder, CO: Westview Press, 1986.
Derleth, J. "The Soviets in Afghanistan: Can the Red Army Fight a Counter-insurgency War?" *Armed Forces and Society* 15, no. 1 (1988).
Dickson, Keith D. "The Basmachi and the Mujahedin: Soviet Responses to Insurgency Movements." *Military Review,* February 1985.
Dobbs, Michael. "Secret Memos Trace Kremlin's March to War." *Washington Post,* 15 November 1992.
Donnelly, C. "Afghanistan." Royal Military Academy Sandhurst SSRC Paper, 1981.
Dorn, Allen E. *Countering the Revolution: The Mujahedin Counterrevolution.* New York: Afghanistan Forum, 1989.
Dunbar, Charles. "Afghanistan in 1987: A Year of Decision." *Asian Survey,* February 1988.
——. "Afghanistan in 1986: The Balance Endures." *Asian Survey,* February 1987.
Dupree, Louis. "Red Flag over the Hindukush." Parts 2, 3, 4, 5, and 6. *American Universities Field Service Report.* New York: 1979–1980.
Edwardes, M. *Playing the Great Game: A Victorian Cold War.* London: Hamilton, 1975.
Edwards, David Busby. "The Evolution of Shi'i Political Dissent in Afghanistan." In *Shi'ism and Social Protest.* Edited by Juan Cole and Nikki Keddie. New Haven, CT: Yale University Press, 1986.
Eflein, Dennis. *A Case Study: Afghanistan—a Soviet Failure.* No pub., 1992.
Ellis, Deborah. *Women of the Afghan War.* Westport, CT: Praeger, 2000.
Emadi, Hafizullah. *State, Revolution, and Superpowers in Afghanistan.* New York: Praeger, 1990.
Eshaq, Mohammad. "Evolution of the Islamic Movement in Afghanistan." Pt. 1, "Islamists Felt Need for a Party to Defend Islam"; Pt. 2, "Daud's Hostile Attitude towards Islamists Led to Confrontation"; Pt. 3, "Panjshir Uprising of 1975"; Pt. 4, "Life in Exile from 1975 to 1978." *AfghaNews,* 1 and 15 January, 1 and 15 February 1989.
Evans, Richard. "The Battle for Paktia." *Far Eastern Economic Review.* 1991.
Farr, Grant M., and John G. Merriam. *Afghan Resistance: The Politics of Survival.* Boulder, CO: Westview Press, 1987.

Fullerton, John. *The Soviet Occupation of Afghanistan*. Hong Kong: Methuen, 1984.

Galeotti, Mark. *Afghanistan: The Soviet Union's Last War*. London: Frank Cass, 1995.

Gall, Sandy. *Afghanistan: Agony of a Nation*. London: The Bodley Head, 1988.

———. *Behind Russian Lines: An Afghan Journal*. London: Sidgwick and Jackson, 1983.

Galster, Stephen R. *Washington, Moscow and the Struggle for Kabul*. New York: Afghanistan Forum, 1990.

———. *A Chronology of Events Relating to International Aid to the Afghan Resistance*. Washington, DC: The National Security Archive, 1987.

Ghani, Ashraf. "Afghanistan: Islam and the Counterrevolutionary Movements." In John Esposito, *Islam in Asia*. New York: Oxford University Press, 1987.

Ghaus, Abdul Samad. *The Fall of Afghanistan*. Washington, DC: Pergamon-Brassey's, 1988.

Gibbs, David. "Does the USSR Have a Grand Strategy? Reinterpreting the Invasion of Afghanistan." *Journal of Peace Research* 24 no. 4. Oslo: Norwegian University Press, 1987.

———. "The Peasant as Counterrevolutionary: The Rural Origins of the Afghan Insurgency." In *Studies in Comparative International Development* 21, no.1. Brunswick, NJ: Transaction, 1986.

Gille, Etienne. "'Accession au Pouvoir des Communistes Prosovietiques." In *Colonisation Impossible*. Paris: CEREDAF, 1984.

Gille, Etienne, and Sylvie Heslot. *Lettres d'Afghanistan de Serge de Beaurecueil*. Paris: CEREDAF, n.d.

Girardet, Edward R. *Afghanistan: The Soviet War*. London: Croom Helm, 1985.

———. "Afghan Guerrilla Leader Holds His Own Against Soviet Offensive." *Christian Science Monitor*, 2 October 1984.

———. "Arming Afghan Guerrillas: Perils, Secrecy." *Christian Science Monitor*, 20 November 1984.

Goldman, Minton F. "Soviet Military Intervention in Afghanistan: Roots and Causes." *Polity* (spring 1984).

Goodwin, Jan. *Caught in the Crossfire*. New York: Dutton, 1987.

Grau, Lester W., and Michael A. Gress, trans. *The Soviet-Afghan War: How a Superpower Fought and Lost*. Lawrence, KS: Kansas University Press, 2002.

Gregory, David C. *Soviet Invasion of Afghanistan: Causes and Future Options*. Air War College, Air University, 1986.
Grevemeyer, Jan-Heeren. "Religion, Ethnizität und Nationalismus im Afghanischen Widerstand." *Leviathan* 1 (1985).
Grevemeyer, Jan-Heeren, and Tahera Maiwand. *Afghanistan: Presse und Widerstand*. Berlin: Verlag das Arabische Buch, 1988.
Gross, Natalie. "Soviet Press Review." *Jane's Soviet Intelligence Review*, July 1989.

———. "How Healthy Is the Soviet Soldier?" *Soviet Analyst*, 16 April 1986.

Gunston, John. "Afghans Plan USSR Terror Attacks." *Jane's Defence Weekly*, 31 March 1984.

———. "Soviets Using Su-25s in Attacks on Rebel Units." *Aviation Week & Space Technology*, 29 October 1984.

Gupta, Bhabani Sen. *Afghanistan Politics, Economics, and Society: Revolution, Resistance, and Intervention*. London: Frances Printer, 1986.
Hall, Jonnie H. "To Save the Pilot's Life: Soviet Air Rescue Service." *Air University Review*, May–June 1982.
Halliday, Fred. "Revolution in Afghanistan." *New Left Review* 112, 1978.

———. "War in Afghanistan." *New Left Review* 119, 1978.

———. "War and Revolution in Afghanistan." *New Left Review*, January–February 1980.

Hammond, Thomas. *Red Flag over Afghanistan: The Communist Coup, the Soviet Invasion, and the Consequences*. Boulder, CO: Westview Press, 1984.
Hansen, James H. "Afghanistan: The Soviet Experience." *Jane's Defence Review*, January 1984.
Haqqani, Hussain. "The Chinese Connection." *Far Eastern Economic Review*, 14 February 1985.
Harrison, Selig S. "Dateline Afghanistan: Exit Through Finland?" *Foreign Policy* (winter 1980–1981).

———. "Inside the Afghan Talks." *Foreign Policy*, no. 72 (fall 1988).

Hart, Douglas M. "Low Intensity Conflict in Afghanistan: The Soviet View." *Survival*, March–April 1982.
Hauner, Milan. *The Soviet War in Afghanistan: Patterns of Russian Imperialism*. Lanham, MD: University Press of America, 1991.
Hauner, Milan, and Robert Canfield. *Afghanistan and the Soviet Union*. Boulder, CO: Westview Press, 1989.

Heinamaa, Anna. *The Soldier's Story: Soviet Veterans Remember the Afghan War*. Berkeley: University of California Press, 1994.

"Helicopter Protection from IR Missiles." *Jane's Defence Weekly*, 5 October 1985.

Herda, D. J. *The Afghan Rebels: The War in Afghanistan*. New York: F. Watts, 1990.

Hilali, A. Z. *United States-Pakistan Relationship: The Soviet Invasion of Afghanistan*. Burlington, VT: Ashgate, 2005.

Holcomb, James F. "Recent Developments in Soviet Helicopter Operations." *Soviet Military Studies*, no. 3 (1989).

Holden, Constance. "Unequivocal Evidence of Soviet Toxin Use." *Science*, no. 216 (April 1982).

Holden, G. *Soviet Military Reform*. London: Pluto Press, 1991.

Huldt, Bo, and Erland Jansen, eds. *The Tragedy of Afghanistan: The Social, Cultural, and Political Impact of the Soviet Invasion*. London: Croom Helm, 1988.

Hussain, Syed Shabbir. *Afghanistan: Whose War?* Islamabad: World Affairs Publications, 1987.

Huxley, Tim. *The War in Afghanistan*. Canberra: Legislative Research Service, 1983.

Hyman, Anthony. *Afghanistan under Soviet Domination, 1964–81*. London: Macmillan, 1982.

———. "Politics and the Resistance." In *Afghans in Exile*. Conflict Studies, no. 202. London: Institute for the Study of Conflicts, 1987.

"Improvised Convoy Escort Vehicle." *Jane's Defence Review* 2, no. 2 (1982).

Information and Press Department, Ministry of Foreign Affairs. *The Undeclared War*. Kabul, 1984.

Isby, David C. *Russia's War in Afghanistan*. London: Osprey, 1986.

———. *The War in Afghanistan, 1979–1989: The Soviet Empire at High Tide*. Hong Kong, 1990.

———. *War in a Distant Country, Afghanistan: Invasion and Resistance*. London: Arms and Armour, 1989.

———. "Soviet Special Operations Forces in Afghanistan, 1979–1985." Report of Proceedings: Light Infantry Conference, Seattle, 1985.

———. "Soviet Tactics in the War in Afghanistan." *Jane's Defence Review* 4, no. 7 (1983).

———. *Weapons and Tactics of the Soviet Army*. London: Jane's Publishing Company, 1988.

Jalali, Col. Ali. "The Soviet Military Operation in Afghanistan and the Role of Light and Heavy Forces at Tactical and Operational Level." Report of Proceedings: Light Infantry Conference, Seattle, 1985.

———. Written presentation at a 26 April 2000 forum, "Can Anyone Win in Afghanistan? A Military Analysis," sponsored by the Central Asia-Caucasus Institute at Paul H. Nitze School of Advanced International Studies, Washington, DC.

Jalali, Ali, and Lester W. Grau. "Taliban—a Model for 'Islamicising' Central Asia?" *Cyber-Caravan*, 6 March 1999.

Jukes, Geoffery. "The Soviet Armed Forces and the Afghan War." Amin Seikal and William Maley, eds. *The Soviet Withdrawal from Afghanistan*. London: Cambridge University Press, 1989.

Kakar, Hasan Kawun. Afghanistan: *The Soviet Invasion and the Afghan Response*. Berkeley: University of California Press, 1995.

Kaplan, Robert D. *Soldiers of God: With the Mujahedin in Afghanistan*. Boston: Houghton Mifflin, 1990.

Karp, Aaron. "Blowpipes and Stingers in Afghanistan: One Year Later." *Armed Forces Journal International* (Sept. 1987).

Karp, Craig M. "The War in Afghanistan." *Foreign Affairs* (summer 1986).

Kemp, Ian. "Abdul Haq: Soviet Mistakes in Afghanistan." *Jane's Defence Weekly*, 5 March 1988.

Khalidi, Noor Ahmad. "Afghanistan: Demographic Consequences of War, 1978–1987." *Central Asian Survey* 10 (1991).

Khalilzad, Zalmay. "Moscow's Afghan War." *Problems of Communism*, January–February 1986.

———. "The Soviet Dilemma in Afghanistan." *Current History* (October 1985).

———. "Soviet-Occupied Afghanistan." *Problems of Communism* 29, June 1980.

Khan, Riaz Muhammad. *Untying the Afghan Knot: Negotiating Soviet Withdrawal*. Durham, NC: Duke University Press, 1991.

Klass, Rosanne T. *Afghanistan: The Great Game Revisited*. New York: Freedom House, 1987.

Konovalov, V. "Legacy of the Afghan War: Some Statistics." Radio Liberty Report on the USSR, 7 April 1989.

Koza, Catherine M. *Spoils of War: How International Assistance Can Influence Local Processes of Economic Change: The Case of Afghanistan*. Boston: M.I.T. Press, 1990.

"Kremlin Assails Its Afghan Role." *International Herald Tribune*, 24 October 1989.

Laber, Jeri, and Barnett Rubin. *A Nation Is Dying: Afghanistan under the Soviets, 1979–87*. Evanston, IL: Northwestern University Press, 1988.

Lajoie, Roland. *The 1979 Soviet Intervention in Afghanistan*. No pub. 1981.

Lohbeck, Kurt. *Jihad: Holy War*. Washington, DC: Mayday Press, 1984.

———. *Holy War, Unholy Victory*. Washington, DC: Regnery Gateway, 1993.

Mackenzie, Richard. "Afghan Rebels Never Say Die." *Insight*, 25 January 1988.

Magnus, Ralph H. *Afghanistan: Marx, Mullah and Mujahed*. Boulder, CO: Westview Press, 1985.

———. *Afghan Alternatives: Issues, Options and Policies*. New Brunswick, NJ: Transaction Books, 1985.

———. "The Military and Politics in Afghanistan: Before and After the Revolution." In *The Role of the Armed Forces in Contemporary Asian Society*. Edited by Edward A. Olsen and Stephen Jurika. Boulder, CO: Westview Press, 1985.

———. "Tribal Marxism: The Soviet Encounter with Afghanistan." *Conflict*, no pub., 1983.

Majrooh, Sayd Bahauddin, and Sayyid Muhammad Yusuf Elmi, eds. *The Sovietization of Afghanistan*. Peshawar: no pub., 1986.

Male, Beverly. *Revolutionary Afghanistan: A Reappraisal*. London: Croom Helm, 1982.

Malhuret, Claude. "Report from Afghanistan." *Foreign Affairs* (winter 1983–1984).

Marshall, William. *U.S. Policy Objectives in Aiding the Afghans*. No pub., 1991.

McDermott, David F. "The Invasion of Afghanistan." *Infantry*, January – February 1985.

McMichael, Scott. *The Stumbling Bear: Soviet Military Performance*. London: Brassey's, 1991.

Meschaninov, D. "A Powerful Blow by the Afghan Army: A Major Insurgent Base Destroyed." *Isvestiya*. November 26, 1986 (FBIS translation JPRS-UMA-87-006, Jan. 30, 1987).

Mills, Chris P. *A Strange War*. Gloucester: Sutton, 1988.

Moorcraft, Paul L. "Bloody Standoff in Afghanistan." *Military Review*, April 1985.

Morozov, Alexander. "Our Man in Kabul." *New Times*, Moscow, 24 September, 1 October, 14 October, and 21 October 1991.

Moser, Charles. *Combat on Communist Territory*. Washington, DC: Regnery Gateway, 1985.

Naby, Eden. "The Afghan Resistance Movement." In *Afghan Alternatives: Issues Options and Policies*. New Brunswick, NJ: Transaction, 1985.

Naqvi, M. B. "The Great Gamble." *The Herald*, Karachi, June 1988.

"New LAW Used in Afghanistan." *Jane's Defence Weekly*, 3 December 1988.

"New Mine Clearing Vehicle in Action." *Jane's Defence Weekly*, 16 January 1988.

"New Soviet Mine-Clearing Vehicle." *Jane's Defence Weekly*, 7 March 1987.

Newman, Joseph, Jr. "The Future of Northern Afghanistan." *Asian Survey* (July 1988).

Niesewand, Peter. "Guerrillas Train in Pakistan to Oust Afghan Government." *Washington Post*, 2 February 1979.

O'Ballance, Edgar. *Afghan Wars, 1839–1992*. London: Brassey's, 1993.

O'Brien, Michael C. "Political Legitimacy and the Soviet War in Afghanistan." Master's thesis, University of Virginia, 1989.

Operational and Strategic Lessons of the War in Afghanistan, 1979–90. Carlisle Barracks, PA: Strategic Studies Institute, U.S. Army War College. 1991.

Ottaway, David B. "Stingers Were Key Weapon in Afghan War, Army Finds." *Washington Post*, 5 July 1989.

———. "What Is 'Afghan Lesson' for Superpowers?" *Washington Post*, 12 February 1989.

Overby, Paul. *Holy Blood: The Afghan War from the Inside*. Westport, CT: Praeger, 1993.

Owen, Richard. "The Afghan Cloud on Andropov's Horizon." *Times* (London) 3 March 1983.

Owens, Daniel E. *Assessment of Politico-Military Lessons Learned from the Soviet Intervention in Afghanistan*. Maxwell Air Force Base, AL: U.S. Air Force Base, 1989.

Picolyer. "Caravans on Moonless Nights: How the CIA Supports and Supplies the Anti-Soviet Guerrillas." *Time*, 11 June 1984.

Pohly, Michael. *Krieg und Widerstand in Afghanistan*. Berlin: Das Arabische Buch, 1992.

Prokhanov, A. *A Tree in the Centre of Kabul*. Moscow: Progress, 1983.

Rees, David. *Afghanistan's Role in Soviet Strategy*. Conflict Studies, no. 118. London, 1980.

Reshtia, Sayed Qassem. *The Price of Liberty: The Tragedy of Afghanistan*. Rome: Bard Editore, 1984.

Richards, Martin. "Afghanistan: Stalemate or Climb Down." *The Army Quarterly and Defence Journal* (July 1983).

Ritch, John B. *Hidden War: The Struggle for Afghanistan*. Washington, DC: U.S. Government Publications Office, 1984.

Roberts, Jeffery J. *The Origins of Conflict in Afghanistan*. Westport, CT: Praeger, 2003.
Rogers, Tom. *The Soviet Withdrawal from Afghanistan: Analysis and Chronology*. Westport, CT: Greenwood Press, 1992.
———. "Refugees, Afghans in Exile: A Threat to Stability?" *Conflict Studies*, no. 202, London, 1987.
Roy, Olivier. *Afghanistan: From Holy War to Civil War*. Princeton, NJ: Princeton University Press, 1994.
———. *Islam and Resistance in Afghanistan*. Cambridge: Cambridge University Press, 1990.
———. *The Lessons of the Soviet-Afghan War*. London: International Institute for Strategic Studies, Adelphi Papers, no. 259, 1991.
———. "Le Facteur Massoud." *Afghanistan Information*, March 1992.
———. "War as a Factor of Entry into Politics." *Central Asian Survey* 8, no. 4 (1989).
Rubin, Barnett R. *The Fragmentation of Afghanistan: State Formation and Collapse in the International System*. New Haven, CT: Yale University Press, 1995.
———. "Afghanistan: The Next Round." *Orbis* 33 (spring 1989).
———. "The Fragmentation of Afghanistan." *Foreign Affairs* (winter 1989–1990).
Russo, Charles A. *Soviet Logistics in the Afghan War*. Carlisle Barracks, PA: Strategic Studies Institute, 1991.
Ryan, Nigel. *A Hitch or Two in Afghanistan: A Journey Behind Russian Lines*. London: Weidenfeld and Nicolson, 1983.
Safi, Major Nasrullah. "The Different Stages of Afghanistan's Jehad." *Quarterly Journal of the Writer's Union of Free Afghanistan* (January–March 1988).
Safronchuk, Vasily. "Afghanistan in the Taraki Period" and "Afghanistan in the Amin Period." *International Affairs* (Moscow, January–February 1991).
Saikal, Amin. *Regime Change in Afghan Foreign Intervention and the Politics of Legitimacy*. Boulder, CO: Westview Press, 1991.
Saikal, Amin, and William Maley. *The Soviet Withdrawal from Afghanistan*. Cambridge: Cambridge University Press, 1989.
Samimy, S. M. *Hintergründe der Sowjetischen Invasion in Afghanistan*. Bochum: Brockmeyer, 1981.
Sarin, Maj. Gen. Oleg, and Col. Lev Doretsky. *The Afghan Syndrome: The Soviet Union's Vietnam*. Novato, CA: Presidio Press, 1993.
Schultheis, Robert. *Night Letters: Inside Wartime Afghanistan*. New York: Orion Books, 1992.
Schwartzstein, Stuart J. D. "Chemical Warfare in Afghanistan: An Independent Assessment." *World Affairs* (winter 1982–1983).

Scott, Harriet F. "Rise of the Afghantsi." *Air Force Magazine* 76, no. 8 (1993).
Scott, Peter Dale. *Drugs, Oil, and War*. Lanham, MD: Rowman & Littlefield, 2003.
Shahrani, N. Nasif, and Robert L. Canfield, eds. *Revolutions and Rebellions in Afghanistan*. Berkeley: Institute of International Studies, University of California, 1984.
Shakaib, G. D. "Soviet Military Problems." *Quarterly of the Writer's Union of Free Afghanistan* (July–September 1987).
Shansab, Nasir. "The Struggle for Afghanistan." *Combat on Communist Territory*. Lake Bluff, IL: Regnery Gateway, 1985.
Shroder, John F. "Afghanistan Resources and Soviet Policy in Central and South Asia." In *Afghanistan and the Soviet Union: Collision and Transformation*. Edited by Milan Hauner and Robert L. Canfield. Boulder, CO: Westview Press, 1989.
Sikorski, Radek. *Dust of the Saints: A Journey to Herat in Time of War*. New York: Chatto and Windus, 1990.
———. *Moscow's Afghan War: Soviet Motives and Western Interests*. London: no pub., 1987.
Sliwinski, Marek. "The Decimation of Afghanistan." *Orbis* 33 (winter 1988–1989).
"Soviet Air Force in Afghanistan." *Jane's Defense Weekly*, 7 July 1984.
"Special Issue on Afghanistan." *World Affairs* (1982–1983).
"Special Report: Afghanistan." *Aviation Week & Space Technology*, 29 October 1984.
Stahel, A. A., and Paul Bucherer. *Afghanistan, 1985/86: Besetzung und Kriegsführung der UdSSR*. Liestal: Schweizerisches Afghanistan Archiv, 1986.
———. *Afghanistan: 5 Jahre und Kleinkrieg*. Frauenfeld: Huber, 1984.
———. "Afghanistan, 1984/85; Bezetzung und Widerstand." In *Allgemeine Schweizerische Militärzeitschrift* 12 (1985).
Steele, Jonathan. "Moscow's Kabul Campaign." *Middle East Report* (MERIP) (July–August 1986).
Storella, Mark C. *The Central Asia Analogy and the Soviet Union's War in Afghanistan*. New York: Afghanistan Forum, 1984.
Stork, Joe. "The CIA in Afghanistan." *MERIP* (July–August 1986).
Strand, Richard F. "The Evolution of Anti-Communist Resistance in Eastern Nuristan." In *Revolutions and Rebellions*. Edited by N. Shahrani and R. Canfield. Berkeley, CA: Institute of International Studies, 1984.

Suvorov, Viktor. *Spetsnaz*. Translated by David Floyd. London: Hamilton, 1987.

Tamarov, Vladislav. *Afghanistan: A Russian Soldier's Story*. Berkeley, CA: Ten Speed Press, 2001.

Taniwal, Hakim. "The Impact of Pashtunwali on Afghan Jihad." *Quarterly Journal of the Writers' Union of Free Afghanistan* (WUFA) 2 (January–March 1987).

Taniwal, Hakim, and Ahmad Yusuf Nuristani. "Pashtun Tribes and the Afghan Resistance." *WUFA* 2 (January–March 1987).

Tanner, Stephen. *Afghanistan: A Military History from Alexander the Great to the Fall of the Taliban*. New York: Da Capo Press, 2002.

Tawana, Sayyid Musa. "Glimpses into the Historical Background of the Islamic Movement in Afghanistan." Pts. 1–5. *AfghaNews*, 1 April 1989 and 1 June 1989.

Thorne, Ludmilla. *Soviet POW's in Afghanistan*. New York: Freedom House, 1987.

Todd, Ann H. *Hamid Karzai*. Philadelphia: Chelsea House Publishers, 2004.

Turbiville, Graham H. *Ambush! The Road War in Afghanistan*. Fort Leavenworth, KS: Combat Studies Institute Press, 1988.

———. *Soviet Combat Engineers in Afghanistan*. Washington, DC: National Defense University Press, 1989.

Umnov, Alexander. "Afghanistan: What Price Dogma?" *New Times*, no. 19, May 9–15.

Urban, Mark. *War in Afghanistan*. 2nd ed. New York: St. Martin's Press, 1990.

———. "The Limited Contingent of Soviet Forces in Afghanistan." *Jane's Defence Weekly*, 12 January 1985.

———. "A More Competent Afghan Army?" *Jane's Defence Weekly*, 23 November 1985.

———. "Soviet Army Turns Its Back on the War It Never Tried to Win." *Independent*, London, 14 February 1989.

U.S. State Department. *The Kidnapping and Death of Ambassador Adolph Dubs: Summary Report of an Investigation*. Washington, DC: U.S. Government Printing Office, 1980.

Vollmann, William T. *An Afghanistan Picture Show*. New York: Farrar, Straus & Giroux, 1992.

Wimbush, S. Enders, and Alex Alexiev. *Soviet Central Asian Soldiers in Afghanistan*. Santa Monica, CA: RAND Corporation, 1981.

Winchester, Mike. "Night Raiders on Russia's Border." *Soldier of Fortune*, September 1984.
Woodward, Bob. *Veil: The Secret Wars of the CIA*. New York: Simon & Schuster, 1987.
Yarushenko, A. "A Bright Hour: Even Today There Is a Place for Heroic Deeds." *Soviet Patriot*, 15 October 1986.
Yermakov, Oleg. *Afghan Tales*. London: M. Secker and Warburg, 1993.
Yousaf, Mohammad. *Silent Soldier: The Man Behind the Afghan Jehad*. Lahore: Jang Publishers, 1991.
Yousaf, Mohammad, and Mark Adkin. *The Bear Trap: Afghanistan's Untold Story*. Lahore: Jang Publishers, 1992.
Zaloga, Steven. *Armor of the Afghanistan War*. London: Arms and Armour Press, 1992.
———. *Red Hammer*. Presidio, 1995.

7. Taliban and al-Qaeda

Abu Khalil, Asad. *Bin Ladin, Islam, and America's New War on Terrorism*. New York: Seven Stories Press, 2002.
Abu Zahab, Mariam, and Olivier Roy. *Islamist Networks: The Afghanistan-Pakistan Connection*. New York: Columbia University Press, 2004.
Alexander, Yunah. *Usama bin Laden's al-Qaeda: Profile of a Terrorist Network*. Ardsley, NY: Transnational Publishers, 2001.
Anderson, Jon Lee. "Double Agents, Defectors, Disaffected Taliban, and a Motley Army Battle for Konduz." *New Yorker*, 10 December 2001.
Archer, Christon I. *World History of Warfare*. Lincoln: University of Nebraska Press, 2002.
Armstrong, Karen. *The Battle for God*. New York: Alfred A. Knopf, 2000.
Barth, Kelly. *The Rise and Fall of the Taliban*. San Diego: Greenhaven Press, 2005
Benjamin, Daniel, and Steven Simon. *The Age of Sacred Terror*. New York: Random House, 2002.
Bergen, Peter L. *Holy War, Inc.: Inside the Secret World of bin Ladin*. New York: The Free Press, 2001.
Bodansky, Yossef. *Bin Laden: The Man Who Declared War on Afghanistan*. Roseville, CA: Forum Press, 1999.
Brentjes, Burchard. *Taliban: A Shadow over Afghanistan*. Varanasi, India: Rishi Publication, 2000.
Brisard, Jean-Charles. *Forbidden Truth: U.S.-Taliban Secret Oil Diplomacy*. New York: Thunder's Mouth Press, 2002.

Burke, Jason. *Al-Qaeda: The True Story of Radical Islam*. London: I. B. Tauris, 2004.

Burns, John F., and Steve Levine. "How Afghanistan's Stern Rulers Took Power," *New York Times*, 31 December 1996.

Calabresi, Massimo. "The Bin Ladin Capture That Never Was." *Time*, 20 March 2000.

Chalk, Peter. "Bin Laden's Asian Network." *Jane's Intelligence Review*, 1 December 1998, p. 6.

Cody, Edward. "Taliban's 'Hide-and-Wait' Strategy Failed." *Washington Post*, 23 December 2001, p. 12.

Coll, Steve. *Ghost Wars: The Secret History of the CIA, Afghanistan, and bin Laden from the Soviet Invasion to September 10*. New York: Penguin Press, 2004.

Colton, Timothy J., and Thane Gustafson, eds. *Soldiers and the Soviet State: Civil-Military Relations from Brezhnev to Gorbachev*. Princeton, NJ: Princeton University Press, 1990.

Corbin, Jane. *Al-Qaeda: In Search of the Terror Network That Threatens the World*. New York: Thunder's Mouth Press, 2002.

Dorronsoro, Giles. *Pakistan and the Taliban: State Policy, Religious Networks and Political Connections*. Paris: Center for International Studies and Research, October 2000.

Dunn, Michael Collins. "Osama bin Laden: The Nature of the Challenge." *Middle East Policy*, October 1998, p. 23.

Edwards, David B. *Before Taliban: Genealogies of the Afghan Jihad*. Berkeley: University of California Press, 2002.

Erös, Reinhard. *Tee mit dem Teufel*. Hamburg: Hoffmann & Campe, 2002.

Esposito, John L. *Unholy War: Terror in the Name of Islam*. New York: Oxford University Press, 2002.

Gohari, M. J. *The Taliban: Ascent to Power*. Karachi: Oxford University Press, 2001.

Goldberg, Jeffrey. "Inside Jihad U: The Education of a Holy Warrior." *New York Times Magazine*, 25 June 2000.

Goodson, Larry P. *Afghanistan's Endless War: State Failure, Regional Politics, and the Rise of the Taliban*. Seattle: University of Washington Press, 2001.

Griffin, Michael. *Reaping the Whirlwind: The Taliban Movement in Afghanistan*. London: Pluto Press, 2001.

———. *The Taliban Movement in Afghanistan*. Sterling, VA: Pluto Press, 2001.

———. "Taliban's Grim Legacy: More Strife." *Los Angeles Times*, 23 December 2001.

Bibliography 397

Gunaratna, Rohan. *Inside Al Qaeda: Global Network of Terror.* New York: Columbia University Press, 2002.
Hoffman, Bruce. *Inside Terrorism.* New York: Columbia University Press, 1999.
Huggler, Justin. "Taliban Defectors Seek Power-Share in New Afghanistan." *The Independent* (London), 11 December 2001, p. 12.
Hussain, Zahid. "Top Taliban Defectors Set Up Splinter Group." *The Gazette* (Montreal), 4 December 2001, p. B12.
Jacquard, Roland. *In the Name of Osama bin Laden.* Durham, NC: Duke University Press, 2002.
Jalalzai, Musa Khan. *Holy Terror: Al-Qaeda, Taliban and Its Roots in Pakistan and Afghanistan.* Lahore: Dua Publications, 2002.
———. *Taliban and the Post-Taliban Afghanistan.* Lahore: Sang-e Meel Publications, 2003.
Jenkins, Brian M. *Countering Al-Qaeda.* Santa Monica, CA: RAND, 2002.
Labévière, Richard. *Dollars for Terror: The United States and Islam.* New York: Algora Publishing, 2000.
Lamb, David. "Taliban Tactics Sped Collapse, Analysts Say." *Toronto Star*, 27 December 2001, p. 8.
———. "Missteps Toppled Taliban, Analysts Say." *Los Angeles Times*, 27 December 2001, p. 3.
Mackey, Chris and Greg Miller. *The Interrogator's War: Inside the Secret War Against Al-Qaeda.* London: John Murray, 2004.
Maley, William. *Fundamentalism Reborn? Afghanistan and the Taliban.* New York: New York University Press, 1998.
Marsden, Peter. *The Taliban: War, Religion and the New Order in Afghanistan.* Karachi: Oxford University Press, 1998.
Moore, Molly, and Susan B. Glasser. "Disappearing with Hardly a Fight: Taliban Cedes Large Swath of Territory Much the Way It Took Control." *Washington Post*, 14 November 2001, p. 20.
Moore, Robert. *The Hunt for Bin Laden: Task Force Dagger.* New York: Random House, 2003.
Nojumi, Neamatullah. *The Rise of the Taliban in Afghanistan: Mass Mobilization, Civil War, and the Future of the Region.* New York: Palgrave, 2002.
Rashid, Ahmed. *The Taliban: Islam, Oil, and the New Great Game in Central Asia.* London: I. B. Tauris, 2000.
———. "Afghanistan: Epicentre of Terror." *Far Eastern Economic Review*, 11 May 2000, p. 16.

———. "The Taliban: Exporting Extremism." *Foreign Affairs* 78, no. 6 (November–December) 1999, 22–35.
Reeve, Simon. *The New Jackals: Ramsi Yusef, Osama bin Laden, and the Future of Terrorism.* Boston: Northeastern University Press, 1999.
Rubin, Michael, and Daniel Benjamin. "The Taliban and Terrorism: Report from Afghanistan." Washington Institute for Near East Policy *Special Policy Forum Report*, 6 April 2000.
Singh, Patwant. *The Sikhs.* New York: Knopf, 2000.
Smucker, Philip. *Al-Qaeda's Great Escape: The Military and the Media on Terror's Trail.* Washington, DC: Brasseys, 2004.
Tanner, Stephen. *Afghanistan: A Military History from Alexander the Great to the Fall of the Taliban.* New York: Da Capo Press, 2002.
Tomsen, Peter. "Response: A Chance for Peace in Afghanistan—the Taliban's Days Are Numbered," *Foreign Affairs* (January 2000).
Venter, Al. "Bin Laden's Tripartite Pact." *Jane's Intelligence Review*, 1 November 1998, p. 5.
Wastell, David, and Robert Fox. "Our Morale Was Getting Lower: We Couldn't Fight." *Sunday Telegraph* (London), 18 November 2001, p. 20.
Weaver, Mary Ann. "On Bin Ladin." *New Yorker*, January 2000.
Williams, Paul. *Al Qaeda: Brotherhood of Terror.* Parsippany, NJ: Alpha, 2002.
Yusufzai, Rahimullah. "Pakistani Taliban at Work." *The News*, 21 December 1998.

8. United States Intervention

Anonymous. *Imperial Hubris: Why the West Is Losing the War on Terror.* Washington, DC: Brassey's, 2004.
Arkin, William M. "Smart Bombs, Dumb Targeting?" *Bulletin of the Atomic Scientists* 56, nos. 46–53 (May–June 2000). Also available online at: http://search.epnet.com/direct.asp?an=3086677&db=mth
Baer, Robert. *See No Evil: The True Story of a Ground Soldier in the CIA'S War on Terrorism.* New York: The Free Press, 2002.
Barakat, Sultan. *Reconstructing War-Torn Societies: Afghanistan.* New York: Palgrave Macmillan, 2004.
Bently, Christopher S. "Afghanistan Joint and Coalition Fire Support in Operation Anaconda." Field Artillery, September–October 2002.
Biddle, Stephen. *Afghanistan and the Future of Warfare.* Carlisle Barracks, PA: Strategic Studies Institute, 2002.
Blohm, Craig E. *Weapons of War.* San Diego, CA: Lucent Books, 2004.

Borch, Fred L., and Paul S. Wilson. *International Law and War on Terror*. Newport, RI: Naval War College, 2003.

Briscoe, Charles A. *Weapons of Choice: U.S. Army Special Operations Forces in Afghanistan*. Fort Leavenworth, KS: Combat Studies Institute Press, 2003.

Budiansky, Stephen. "The Sky Has Its Limits: Why Bombs Defeat Armies More Effectively Than Cities." *Washington Post*, 16 December 2001, p. B3.

Carew, Tom. *Jihad: The SAS Secret War in Afghanistan*. Edinburgh: Mainstream, 2000.

Carney, John T. *No Room for Errors: The Covert Operation of America's Special Tactics*. New York: Ballantine Books, 2003.

Conetta, Carl. *Strange Victory: A Critical Appraisal of Operation Enduring Freedom and the Afghanistan War*. Project on Defense Alternatives Research Monograph no. 6, 30 January 2002.

———. *Operation Enduring Freedom: Why a Higher Rate of Civilian Bombing Casualties*. Project on Defense Alternatives Briefing Report no. 11, 18 January 2002.

Cordesman, Anthony H. *The Lessons of Afghanistan: War Fighting, Intelligence, and Force Transformation*. Washington, DC: CSIS Press, 2002.

———. *The War After the War: Strategic Lessons of Iraq and Afghanistan*. Washington, DC: CSIS Press, 2004.

Crile, George. *Charlie Wilson's War: The Extraordinary Story of the Largest Covert Operation in History*. New York: Atlantic Monthly Press, 2002.

Donini, Antonio, Norah Niland, and Karin Wermester. *Nation-Building Unraveled? Aid, Peace and Justice in Afghanistan*. Bloomfield, CT: Kumarian Press, 2004.

Dredel, Lou. *Operation Enduring Freedom*. Carrollton, TX: Squadron/Signal Publication, 2002.

Erwin, Sandra I. "Air Warfare Tactics Refined in Afghanistan." *National Defense* 86 (12–13 April 2002). Also available online at: http://www.nationaldefensemagazine.org/article.cfm?Id=755

———. "Costs for Operation Enduring Freedom: Up to $1b Per Month." *National Defense* 86 (15 December 2001). Also available online at: http://nationaldefense.ndia.org/article.cfm?Id=666

Fiscus, James W. *America's War in Afghanistan*. New York: Rosen Publishing Group, 2004.

Friedman, Norman. *Terrorism, Afghanistan, and America's New Way of War*. Annapolis, MD: Naval Institute Press, 2003.

Hamilton, John. *Operation Enduring Freedom.* Edina, MN: ABDO and Daughters, 2002.
Hanson, Victor Davis. *Between War and Peace: Lessons from Afghanistan and Iraq.* New York: Random House, 2004.
Hardcastle, Nate. *American Soldier: Stories of Special Forces from Iraq and Afghanistan.* New York: Thunder's Mouth Press, 2002.
Hersh, Seymour M. *Chain of Command: The Road from 9/11 to Abu Ghraib.* New York: Harper Collins, 2004.
Hirsh, Michael. *None Braver: U.S. Air Force Pararescuemen in the War on Terrorism.* New York: New American Library, 2003.
Jalalzai, Musa Khan. *The U.S. War on Terrorism in Afghanistan.* Lahore: Sang-e Meel Publication, 2003.
Knight, Charles, and Marcus Corbin. *The New Occupation: How Preventive War Is Wrecking the Military.* Project on Defense Alternatives, 4 January 2004.
Mackey, Chris. *The Interrogators: Inside the Secret War Against Al Qaeda.* New York: Little Brown, 2004.
Maley, William. *The Afghanistan Wars.* New York: Palgrave, 2002.
McElroy, Robert H. "Afghanistan: Fire Support for Operation Anaconda." *Field Artillery*, September–October 2002, p.5–9.
Miller, Raymond H. *The War in Afghanistan.* San Diego, CA: Lucent Books, 2004.
Misra, Amalendu. *Afghanistan: The Labyrinth of Violence.* Cambridge, UK: Malden Press, 2004.
Moore, Robin. *The Hunt for Bin Laden: Task Force Dagger.* New York: Random House, 2003.
Naylor, Sean D. *Not a Good Day to Die: The Untold Story of Operation Anaconda.* New York: Berkeley Books, 2005.
———. "Learning from Operation Anaconda." *Air Force Times* 29 July 2002.
Oliker, Olga. *Aid During Conflict: Interaction between Military and Civilian Assistance Providers in Afghanistan, September 2001–June 2002.* Santa Monica, CA: RAND, 2004.
Rogers, Paul. *A War of Terror: Afghanistan and After.* Sterling, VA: Pluto Press, 2004.
Schroen, Gary C. *First In: An Insider's Account of How the CIA Spearheaded the War on Terror in Afghanistan.* New York: Presidio Press/Ballantine Books, 2005.
Sperry, Paul E. *Crude Politics: How Bush's Oil Cronies Hijacked the War on Terrorism.* Nashville: WND Books, 2003.

Tripp, Robert S. *Lessons from Operation Enduring Freedom.* Santa Monica, CA: RAND Corporation 2004.

———. *Supporting Air and Space Expeditionary Forces: Lessons Learned from Operation Enduring Freedom.* Santa Monica, CA: RAND Corporation, 2004.

Vistica, Gregory L. "Military Split on How to Use Special Forces in Terror War." *Washington Post,* 5 January 2004.

Willis, Clint. *Boots on the Ground: Stories of American Soldiers from Iraq and Afghanistan.* New York: Thunder's Mouth Press, 2004.

Woodward, Bob. *Bush at War.* New York: Simon & Schuster, 2000.

———. *The Commanders.* New York: Simon & Schuster, 1991.

———. *Plan of Attack.* New York: Simon & Schuster, 2004.

———. *Veil: The Secret Wars of the CIA, 1981-1987.* New York: Simon & Schuster, 1987.

Yancey, Diane. *Life of an American Soldier in Afghanistan.* San Diego, CA: Lucent Books, 2004.

Zepezauer, Mark. *Boomerang: How Our Covert Wars Have Created Enemies Across the Middle East and Brought Terror to America.* Monroe, ME: Common Courage Press, 2003.

ABOUT THE AUTHOR

Ludwig W. Adamec (B.A., political science; M.A., journalism; Ph.D., Islamic and Middle East studies, UCLA) is a professor of Middle Eastern studies at the University of Arizona and director of its Near Eastern Center for ten years. Widely known as a leading authority on Afghanistan, he is the author of a number of reference works on Afghanistan and books on Afghan history, foreign policy, and international relations, including: *Afghanistan 1900-1923: A Diplomatic History*; *Afghanistan's Foreign Affairs to the Mid-Twentieth Century*; the six-volume *Historical and Political Gazetteer of Afghanistan*; *The Historical Dictionary of Islam*; and *The A to Z of Islam*.